'This fascinating volume is as much a contribution to royal legend as to the history of the war' *Daily Telegraph*

'Most – though by no means all – of the facts we know already: it is the angle from which they are viewed and the humour and intelligence of the observer which make these diaries both brilliantly entertaining and historically priceless' *Spectator*

'Lascelles' diary – now expertly edited by Duff Hart-Davis – offers fascinating and hitherto unseen glimpses of some of the most significant figures of our age … however, none emerges more engagingly than the diarist himself' *Sunday Telegraph*

'Sharply written diaries' *Spectator*

'An elegant and precise diary … a revealing glimpse into the drawing rooms of the great during the years of crisis and victory … Lascelles was an excellent judge of character and posterity has almost always proved him right' *Evening Standard*

'Offers genuine insights into the role of the King's adviser' *Independent*

'A great read, written with humour and elegance' *Belfast Telegraph*

Sir Alan Lascelles (always known as 'Tommy') was born in 1887, and educated at Marlborough and Trinity College, Oxford. As a member of the Bedfordshire Yeomanry, he fought in the First World War, winning a Military Cross, and in 1919 went out to India as ADC to the Governor of Bombay. At a round-up of wild elephants he met Joan Thesiger, daughter of the Viceroy, Lord Chelmsford; the couple were married in Delhi and, in due course, had a son and two daughters.

In December 1920, Tommy became Assistant Private Secretary to Edward, Prince of Wales, and served him until 1929, when he resigned, despairing of the Prince's character. From 1931 to 1935 he was Private Secretary to the Governor-General of Canada. He then returned to royal service, becoming Assistant Private Secretary to George V, Edward VIII and George VI, before being promoted to the position of Private Secretary to the King in 1943.

After the death of George VI in February 1952, he continued as Private Secretary to Queen Elizabeth for the first year of her reign.

Duff Hart-Davis has written or edited more than forty books, among them the earlier letters and diaries of Sir Alan Lascelles, *End of an Era* (1986) and *In Royal Service* (1989). His biographies include *Peter Fleming* and *Raoul Millais*, and his keen interest in natural history has resulted in *Monarchs of the Glen*, a history of deer-stalking in the Scottish Highlands, *Fauna Britannica*, a much-praised, illustrated encyclopedia, and *Audubon's Elephant*, a study of how the celebrated artist produced his master-work, *The Birds of America*.

Formerly Literary Editor and Assistant Editor of the *Sunday Telegraph*, he now lives in a 17th-century farmhouse on the Cotswold escarpment, whence, from 1986 until 2000, he contributed the weekly Country Matters column to the *Independent*.

King's Counsellor

ABDICATION AND WAR:
THE DIARIES OF SIR ALAN LASCELLES

edited by

DUFF HART-DAVIS

PHOENIX

A PHOENIX PAPERBACK

First published in Great Britain in 2006
by Weidenfeld & Nicolson
This paperback edition published in 2007
by Phoenix,
an imprint of Orion Books Ltd,
Orion House, 5 Upper St Martin's Lane,
London WC2H 9EA

An Hachette Livre UK company

1 3 5 7 9 10 8 6 4 2

A CIP catalogue record for this book
is available from the British Library.

ISBN 978-0-7538-2225-8

Typeset by Input Data Services Ltd, Frome

Printed and bound in Great Britain by Clays Ltd, St Ives plc

The Orion Publishing Group's policy is to use papers that
are natural, renewable and recyclable products and
made from wood grown in sustainable forests. The logging
and manufacturing processes are expected to conform to
the environmental regulations of the country of origin.

www.orionbooks.co.uk

Contents

List of Illustrations

The author and publishers thank the following for permission to reproduce
the illustrations in this book:

1 Private collection of the Lascelles family
2 Getty Images
3 Corbis
4 TopFoto
5 Illustrated London News

Biographical Sketch

1887   Born 11 April, son of Hon. Frederick Lascelles, younger brother of the 5th Earl of Harewood.

Christened Alan Frederick, but always known as Tommy.

His mother died when he was only four.

Education: Marlborough (which he hated, wishing he had gone to Eton) and Trinity College, Oxford.

Failed Foreign Office exam twice.

1914   Enlisted in Bedfordshire Yeomanry. Four years in France and Belgium. Wounded. Won MC. Many of his best friends killed.

1919   ADC to Sir George Lloyd, his brother-in-law, Governor of Bombay.

1920   Married Joan Thesiger, daughter of the Viceroy, Lord Chelmsford, in Delhi.

Family: John – died of cancer 1951.
          Lavinia, now Mrs David Hankinson
          Caroline, now Hon. Mrs David Erskine

1921   Assistant Private Secretary to Edward, Prince of Wales.

Travelled with him on tours of America, Canada and Africa.

1929   Resigned from the Prince's service, despairing of his character.

1931–5   Private Secretary to Governor-General of Canada.

1935   Assistant Private Secretary to King George V.

1936   Assistant Private Secretary to King Edward VIII.

1936–43   Assistant Private Secretary to King George VI.

1943–52   Private Secretary to King George VI.

1952–3   Private Secretary to Queen Elizabeth II.

1953   Retired. Lived in grace-and-favour house in Kensington Palace.
Chairman of the Historic Buildings Council; Director of the Midland Bank; Chairman of the Pilgrim Trust; President of the Literary Society.

1981   Died aged 94.

Introduction

For a man of such powerful intellect, Sir Alan Lascelles – always known as 'Tommy' – was curiously lacking in motivation. Throughout his long life he read voraciously, built up a commanding knowledge of English literature and history, never lost the Greek and Latin which he had learned in his youth, enjoyed a wide repertoire of music, and wrote with an elegance and precision that reflected his classical education. He would have loved to become an author, but never made any progress towards realising this ambition. Nor did he ever have any clear idea of what career he wanted to pursue.

Born in 1887 into an aristocratic family – his father Frederick was the younger brother of the 5th Earl of Harewood and his great-grandfather was the first Marquis of Clanricarde – he went to Marlborough and Oxford, where he obtained a disappointing Second in Greats (ancient history and philosophy). He then twice sat, and failed, the Foreign Office exam, tried without success for a job in journalism, and for a few months became, *faute de mieux,* a stockbroker. In April 1914 he set off on a tour of South America, intending to study the railways there, but his peregrinations were cut short by the outbreak of the First World War.

Returning to England post haste, he volunteered for the Bedfordshire Yeomanry – a cavalry regiment – and spent most of the war in France, waiting in reserve for a call to action while many of his closest friends were being killed. Nevertheless, he did in the end see action, was wounded and won a Military Cross. The trauma of those years never left him.

Not until the autumn of 1919 did fortune turn in his favour. Then Sir George Lloyd (later Lord Lloyd), who had married his sister Blanche and been appointed Governor of Bombay, took him to India as an ADC. In Mysore, during a round-up of wild elephants, Tommy met Joan Thesiger, daughter of the Viceroy, Lord Chelmsford (and a cousin of Winston Churchill), and the couple were married in Delhi on 16 March 1920.

Back in England that July, Tommy still had no permanent job in prospect, and for months he searched in vain for congenial employment. Then in November, when he was about to sign on as an apprentice in a printing firm, his friend Letty Elcho passed on an unofficial offer from Edward,

Prince of Wales, asking Tommy to join his office as an assistant private secretary, at a salary of £600 a year. The idea appealed to him at once. 'I have got a very deep admiration for the Prince,' he wrote, 'and I am convinced that the future of England is as much in his hands as in those of any individual.' After an initial meeting with Edward, he decided that 'he is the most attractive man I've ever met', and he started work at St James's Palace at the beginning of December 1920.

So began Tommy's career in royal service. For the next eight years he accompanied the Prince on all his travels – to America and Canada, to Canada again, and to Africa – but he gradually grew disillusioned: his admiration changed to despair, and in January 1929 he resigned, convinced that Edward was so self-absorbed and lacking in any sense of duty that he would never become fit to be King.

During 1929 and 1930 Tommy lived mostly at Sutton Waldron, his family home in Dorset, still hoping to make a living as a writer, possibly in the style of his friend John Gore, the author and journalist who for more than thirty years contributed a newsletter to *The Sphere* under the pen-name The Old Stager. Nothing came of his literary efforts, however, and in 1931 he again became a private secretary, this time to the newly appointed Governor-General of Canada, the Earl of Bessborough, for whom he worked until October 1935, taking his family to live with him in Ottawa. He clearly excelled at his job, for Bessborough's successor, Lord Tweedsmuir (the author John Buchan), wrote to him from Government House, Ottawa, on 6 December:

> You have left a mighty reputation here, and you are quoted as Roman lawyers quoted Justinian. Your 'Bible' makes our official path smooth. I need not tell you how grateful I shall be if you can ever find time to send me a line. Any criticism of my doings will be especially welcome.

Within a month of reaching England he received an invitation to return to royal service as Assistant Private Secretary to King George V. For a few days he havered: the King had been seriously ill, and Tommy was worried by the possibility that, if he died, he himself would be thrown back into close contact with the Prince of whom he had despaired. But, still being an ardent supporter of the monarchy, and immensely patriotic, at the age of forty-eight he agreed to rejoin the royal household as Assistant Private Secretary to the King. As he wrote to his sister Helen, 'It is no use going about the world singing "God Save the King" if one isn't prepared to assist the Deity when called upon.'

He was as good as his word and served the Royal Family with the utmost loyalty and integrity for a further seventeen years. In July 1943, when he succeeded Sir Alexander Hardinge as Principal Private Secretary to George VI, the war was at a critical stage, and, as he himself wrote later, 'the major preoccupations of the Sovereign and myself were (1) how to beat the Germans, and (2) how to retard the impending disintegration of the British Empire.' Sometimes, when he looked back, he seemed to regret that he had led such a cloistered and hothouse existence. Once, in retirement, he looked out of the window of his grace-and-favour house in Kensington Palace, and as he gazed down the drive said to his daughter Lavinia, 'If I had my life all over again, I would certainly not be a courtier.'

'What *would* you do, then?' she asked.

'I would breed horses,' he replied. 'Racehorses, or cart-horses: any sort of horses.'

In appearance Tommy was every inch the Private Secretary. He was six foot one tall, always elegantly thin, with dark hair parted in the middle of his scalp, neatly trimmed moustache and high-arched eyebrows that gave him a quizzical, almost challenging look. When on duty he was always soberly dressed, usually in a dark suit – but he took little heed of his shirts, and more than once the King told him off because his cuffs were frayed. He and Joan had three children: John, born in 1922, Lavinia (1923) and Caroline (1928). He gave all the children nicknames. John was 'Wool' because of his thick, curly hair. Lavinia was 'Charles', after a nanny had read her a story about a little boy with that name, and she responded by using it when talking or writing to her father. Caroline, for some reason now lost, was 'Mrs Mooch'. Tommy was an excellent father, and read aloud to the children whenever he could. When Lavinia showed promise in music, he would sit on the edge of her bed in the evenings and whistle passages from symphonies and operas, asking her to identify them. By the time she was ten or eleven, and a visiting opera company put on *Carmen* in Ottawa, she knew all the tunes by heart.

When the family returned from Canada in 1935, they lived for a while at Sutton Waldron. Meals there tended to be silent, for Tommy disapproved of chatter: between courses he would stand up and look out of the window, jingling the coins in his pocket. On the other hand, during holidays at Brancaster, on the Norfolk coast, he was full of jokes and conversation.

In 1937 a house on the corner of St James's Palace, overlooking the park, became available with his job. Once he had installed the family there, he first let Sutton, and then in 1939 sold it, evacuating Joan and the children first to Brancaster, and then to a rented house at Bepton, a village at the foot of the Sussex Downs. After returning to London for the summer of 1940, the family spent the winter with Tommy's sister, Daisy Balfour, at Holton Park near Oxford, and in 1941, after the death of his brother-in-law

George Lloyd, they stayed with his widow Blanche at Cloud's Hill, her home near Hitchin, in Hertfordshire. Throughout the war most of the accommodation in St James's Palace was occupied by the Red Cross, with only a top-floor apartment available to Tommy and his family, so he lived mainly in Buckingham Palace; but after the retirement of Sir Alec Hardinge in 1943 the family was based, to Joan's immense relief, at Winchester Tower, on the North Terrace of Windsor Castle, which the King made available to them. After the war they regained possession of the house in St James's Palace, and lived there until Tommy retired in 1953.

Tommy was, without doubt, an author *manqué*. He described himself as 'a confirmed diarist' – and so he was, even if his enthusiasm for keeping a record of events proved spasmodic. As schoolboy, undergraduate and young-man-about-town he kept voluminous journals, some of which had silver locks securing the covers and were inscribed at the front with the incantation: 'There are 29 distinct damnations – one sure if another fails – awaiting anyone who reads this book unbidden.'

In the 1920s and 1930s he allowed the habit to lapse – although he wrote long letters – but he suddenly started a diary again in June 1942, and from then until April 1946 made an entry almost every day. It is these three journals, extending in all to some 250,000 words, that form the main part of this book. They are written in ink, with astonishing precision and fluency – page after page grammatically perfect, with scarcely a word altered or crossed out. A scatter of later annotations reveals how often the author re-read his contemporary record.

Tommy enjoyed writing, knew he wrote well, and would have loved to see his words appear in print. Yet he never published anything except the odd pseudonymous contribution to *The Marlburian*, a few letters to newspapers, and one article on royal biographers in the *Sunday Times*. When he deliberately wrote for publication, he somehow lost the buoyant elasticity which normally made his style so attractive, and his prose became heavy as dough. Various other constraints inhibited him. One was his modesty, which made him doubt the value of anything he turned out. Another was his dislike of emotional display: even when his beloved sister Helen died of cancer, he allowed himself only the briefest threnody. But by far the strongest deterrent was his sense of duty.

He knew full well that it was his duty, as Private Secretary, to maintain absolute discretion about royal affairs, and while he was in office he did so scrupulously. After he had retired, however, he frequently returned to the possibility of publishing his wartime diaries, which he knew were in a different league from his earlier journals – enjoyable as those were – and of first-rate historical importance. He accepted that they should not be made public, for many years after the end of the period they covered – and yet he greatly hoped that one day they would appear.

In 1965 he explained the diaries' genesis in a letter to his successor in office, Sir Michael Adeane:[1]

All through the war period I was sadly lonely at Buckingham Palace, until you and Edward Ford[2] turned up. There was literally nobody to whom I could talk off the record. Eric Miéville[3] was a most competent Private Secretary, but no use as a friend, and off to White's Club the moment he had done his letters; Joey Legh[4] was an amusing brother-officer, but not always sound in his judgements; Bertie Clarendon,[5] kindest of men, was always asking for advice instead of giving it, and I had no elder statesman whom I could consult.

Very often I would come back to Buckingham Palace after dinner to find that great, dark, draughty house uninhabited save for a few housemaids and footmen. It was most depressing, and obviously long letters to Joan, in the country, would have been indiscreet at that time. I was a confirmed diarist ever since my private school, so, in 1942 I resumed the habit, and used it, night after night, as a safety valve. It was in no sense an official record, but just a time-filling record of a lonely and harassed individual. The idea that it, or even parts of it, might ever be published never entered my head.

The King knew I kept a diary, but he was too much of a gentleman to ask to see it. It would not have greatly embarrassed me if he had, for I never criticised him, or made any reference to his hopes and fears; to his financial affairs; to his religion; to his Ministers – save Dalton;[6] to his wife and daughters; to Politics, so far as he was pertinently involved in them; to his general likes and dislikes.

---

1   Michael Adeane (1910–84), grandson of 1st Baron Stamfordham, Equerry and Assistant Private Secretary to King George VI 1937–9 and 1945–52, Private Secretary to Queen Elizabeth II and Keeper of the Royal Archives 1953–72. He was knighted in 1955, and created 1st Baron (Life Peer) Adeane in 1972.
2   Edward Ford (1910–) had been tutor to Prince Farouk of Egypt 1936–7, was twice Mentioned in Despatches during his war service, and in 1946, at Tommy's instigation, joined the royal household as Assistant Private Secretary to King George VI. Knighted in 1957.
3   Sir Eric Miéville (1896–1971), Private Secretary to the Duke of York 1936, Assistant Private Secretary to King George VI 1937–45.
4   Lieut.-Col. the Hon. Sir Piers Legh (1890–1955), known as 'Joey', Equerry to King George VI 1936–46. His manner, relaxed to the point of lethargy, concealed many excellent qualities.
5   Herbert Villiers, 6th Earl of Clarendon (1877–1955), Lord Chamberlain of HM Household 1938–52.
6   Hugh Dalton (1887–1962), Labour politician, held many high offices and was Chancellor of the Exchequer 1945–7. Created Baron Dalton (Life Peer) 1960. The King could not bear him.

I can say with confidence that anybody reading the diaries in years to come will like and respect the King better than before. They are, in fact, the private, day-to-day ramblings of a hardened egotistical scribbler, in which my own family affairs and my amusements (e.g. fishing) play a large part. Somehow or other, I never thought of myself as a Private Secretary. It did not occur to me that I was the successor to Henry Ponsonby[1] or Arthur Bigge[2] – they seem to me landmarks in quite another world, creatures on a much higher plane than mine. So your very important point that any public revelations of my stuff might, in a sense, be selling the pass to my successors must most certainly be taken into account.

The only counter-point that strikes me at the moment is that the published memoirs of various holders of semi-confidential posts to past Sovereigns (e.g. Greville,[3] your cousin Mallet,[4] Lady Canning,[5] Fritz Ponsonby,[6] Lady Lyttelton[7]) have not seriously damaged the relationship, though I do not forget that Queen Victoria was as mad as a wet hen with Greville, and that when the King told me to consult Queen Mary about the publication of Henry Ponsonby's delightful letters to Lady P., she was indignant at the idea, and went so far as to say that no Private Secretary to the Sovereign ought ever to write to his wife at all.[8]

Our King and Queen, on the other hand, had no hesitation in giving Arthur Ponsonby permission to publish, and much enjoyed the book

---

1   Rt. Hon. Sir Henry Ponsonby (1825–95), Private Secretary to Queen Victoria 1870–87.
2   Rt. Hon. Arthur Bigge (1849–1931). Created 1st Baron Stamfordham 1911. Private Sec-
    retary to Queen Victoria 1895–1901, to the Prince of Wales 1901–10 and King George V
    1910–31.
3   Charles Greville (1794–1865) published several volumes of diaries, mainly political.
4   David Mallet (1705?–65), Under-Secretary to Frederick, Prince of Wales, 1742. Believed
    by some to have been the author of the ballad 'Rule Britannia'.
5   Charlotte Canning (1817–61), Lady-in-Waiting to Queen Victoria from 1842. When her
    husband, Lord Canning, was appointed Governor-General of India, she was caught up
    in the mutiny of 1857. A biography by Virginia Surtees included extensive extracts from
    her journals.
6   Sir Frederick Ponsonby (1867–1935), son of Sir Henry Ponsonby and known as 'Fritz',
    was Assistant Private Secretary to Queen Victoria 1894–1901, King Edward VII 1901–10,
    and King George V 1910–12. Keeper of the Privy Purse to George V 1914–35. Created 1st
    Baron Sysonby 1935.
7   Lady Sarah Spencer (1787–1870), later Lady Lyttelton (wife of 4th Baron Lyttelton),
    became Lady-in-Waiting to Queen Victoria in 1838, and later was governess to the royal
    children. *Correspondence of Sarah Spencer, Lady Lyttelton, 1787–1870*, was published in
    1912.
8   'Arthur Ponsonby (1871–1946), 1st Baron Ponsonby of Shulbrede, younger brother of
    Fritz, published their father's correspondence as *Henry Ponsonby, Queen Victoria's
    Private Secretary: His Life from His Letters* in 1942.

when it came out. So far as I know, the only nice things that have ever been written about that unfortunate and unattractive monarch James II are the many references to him in the diaries of Sam Pepys (certainly a confidential office-holder).[1]

It would not greatly distress me personally if I knew that all my diaries were going to be put in the fire as soon as I was dead. I've only kept them, with a number of quite interesting letters, because I believe that my four grandsons, to whom I am much attached, will find them amusing in future years, in that, whatever their demerits, they do give a vivid, light-hearted picture of an entirely extinct period.

That is a fair, if modest, appraisal. The journals throw fascinating light on King George VI, and on his relationship with his wartime Prime Minister, Winston Churchill. All the important visitors who came for an audience with the King – often five or six in a day – were received first by the Private Secretary, whose task it was to steady their nerves before they entered the royal presence. The diaries therefore also include snapshots of foreign potentates, leading statesmen, ambassadors, politicians, soldiers, bishops, editors and others (Peter of Yugoslavia, George of Greece, de Gaulle, Mountbatten, Montgomery, Eisenhower and Wavell.) If some of Tommy's attitudes now seem old-fashioned, it must be remembered that he was born well before the beginning of the twentieth century, and that in his heyday the British Empire was still flourishing.

Most of all, the diaries reveal the author's selfless devotion to duty. Historians have sometimes criticised Sir Alan Lascelles for being too rigid, and unsympathetic to individuals, in his interpretation of moral and con-stitutional issues; but his own record shows how faithfully he stuck to his task, which, as he saw it, was to sustain the Empire, the Dominions, the Monarchy and above all the King himself.

---

1   The diarist Samuel Pepys (1633–1703), who kept his journals in a form of shorthand, was, at various times, clerk of the King's ships, a clerk of the Privy Seal and surveyor-general of victualling for the Navy.

RETURN TO ROYAL SERVICE

On 13 November 1935 the King's Private Secretary, Lord Wigram,[1] sent Tommy a telegram from Buckingham Palace:

THANKS FOR YOUR LETTER THE KING AND QUEEN ARE DELIGHTED AND YOU WILL RECEIVE A WARM WELCOME

On the same day he wrote:

My Dear Tommy,

Thank you so much for your letter of the 11th instant, which I was so glad to receive last night on return from some days' shooting. I at once telephoned the good news to Sandringham, and I need hardly say how pleased the King and Queen are that you can join the Household Staff.

You will come in as Assistant Private Secretary to the King, and I understand that your consolidated pay will be £1,500 a year. If we can get a house for you, so much the better, but I cannot commit myself about this at present.

With all good wishes, and I am much looking forward to having you as a colleague.

Yours ever,
Wigram

On 14 November Alexander Hardinge,[2] Assistant Private Secretary to the King, wrote from Sandringham:

My Dear Tommy,

Just a line to say how very delighted I am that you will shortly become a colleague. I hope that the life will suit you – and I feel confident that it can be so arranged that you will have plenty of liberty – by which you, like me, set great store!

The King and Queen were extremely pleased when I went and told them,

---

1 Sir Clive Wigram (1873–1960), Assistant Private Secretary to King George V 1910–31, Private Secretary to the King 1931–6, had received a peerage in the Silver Jubilee honours of May 1935.
2 Alexander Hardinge (1894–1960), Assistant Private Secretary to King George V 1920–36, Private Secretary to King Edward VIII 1936, and to King George VI 1936–43. He was knighted in 1937, and succeeded his father as 2nd Baron Hardinge of Penshurst in 1944.

and I can assure you that everyone is delighted at the prospect of your coming.

Yours ever,
   Alec Hardinge

Confirming the appointment, Lord Cromer,[1] the Lord Chamberlain, wrote on 15 November:

Dear Tommy,
   This is just a line to let you know definitely that the King has approved the various Appointments to be made in the Royal Household in consequence of Fritz Ponsonby's death, your own included, and these will be published in the Press tomorrow, Saturday.
   As to the Uniform question, Hertslet[2] can give you the details, and I should imagine that the civil uniform you have been wearing in Canada can be adapted by changing the collar and cuffs to the red facings worn in the Household.
   If you have a Levée Dress Coat, I, personally, do not think you really need trouble about getting a Full Dress Coat, as you will hardly ever require this, and Assistant Private Secretaries do not, as a rule, get summoned for ceremonial duties, such as Courts and Levées. You probably already have white Knee Breeches in case you require them for a Court or State Ball, but it would be as well for me to have a talk with you before giving any orders to your tailor.

Yours very sincerely,
   Cromer.

Barely two months later, at 11.55 p.m. on the night of 20 January 1936, Tommy's worst fears were realised when George V died at Sandringham. In a letter to Eric Mackenzie, a former colleague in Ottawa, he wrote a memorable account of the aftermath:

26 January 1936   **Buckingham Palace**

My dear Eric,
   During his illness I never saw him at all; but went up to his room after

---

1   Rowland Baring, 2nd Earl of Cromer (1877–1953), Lord Chamberlain of the royal household 1922–38 and Permanent Lord-in-Waiting to King George VI 1938–52.
2   Austin Hertslet, the Chief Clerk.

his death, and though, like all our generation, I have seen all too many dead men, none has ever had a more peaceful face.

Next evening we took him over to the little Church at the end of the garden.[1] A dark and windy evening, with flurries of rain; there were not more than a dozen of us, including the Queen and the family: the coffin was on a little wheeled bier, flanked by a few towering Grenadiers from the King's Company; somebody had an electric torch, which was our only light; Forsyth, the King's piper, led us playing a lament I did not know.

As we came round the corner of the shrubbery that screens the Church, we saw the lych-gate brilliantly lit, with Fuller, the Sandringham rector, standing beneath it in his surplice and hood. There was nobody else in sight. The guardsmen, with scarcely a sound, slung the coffin on their shoulders and laid it before the altar; and there, after a very brief service, we left it, to be watched for thirty-six hours by the men of the Sandringham Estate. I daresay that when the tumult and shouting dies, that little ceremony will remain in my mind as the most impressive of all.

The departure from Sandringham was fine, too. After a short service the coffin was laid on a gun-carriage and we, with the King's white shooting-pony, walked behind it to Wolferton station on a perfect winter's morning. The road was lined with people, six and seven deep, all the way. At the top of the hill leading down to the station, a single cock pheasant rocketed across the road, very high, and immediately over the gun-carriage. All the way to London people were standing bare-headed by the track, on the roads and in the middle of the fields.

The Prince of Wales succeeded to the throne as Edward VIII, and Tommy found himself thrown back into the service of the man from whom he had parted company seven years earlier. But, as he himself wrote, 'junior members of the Household cannot walk out on a new King because they happen to have disapproved of the Prince of Wales.' So he did not resign again, but soldiered on through Edward's short reign and the protracted crisis of the Abdication in 1936.

He then settled down to work as Assistant Private Secretary to King George VI, and found his new employer far more congenial. 'Impressions of the King – good', he wrote to Joan from Sandringham at Christmas 1936:

Queen Mary is nursing a cough, and don't appear much. The other Queen is delightful, and the children are admirably brought up.

Selby,[2] our Minister in Vienna, writes that the Duke of Windsor vol-

---

1 In fact the church of St Mary Magdalene is just outside the grounds of the house.
2 Sir Walford Selby (1881–1965), Envoy Extraordinary and Minister Plenipotentiary in Vienna 1933–7.

unteered to go to the English church on Christmas Day and read the lesson. When I think of the hours we have all spent trying to get him to go to church in various parts of the British Empire, this makes me furious. And as for reading the lesson – ! There is no doubt that the family generally regard him as potty, but his eldest brother is very nice about him, and very anxious to do what he can to help.

Writing again on 4 January 1937, Tommy added:

HM took me for a long walk this afternoon. I really like him awfully, and he talks to me, and I to him, with a naturalness that was never there with the other man.

In February 1939 Tommy crossed the Atlantic to finalise plans for the State visit to Canada and America by King George VI and Queen Elizabeth, due to take place in May. For this, their first official tour abroad, the royal couple had received personal invitations from Mackenzie King, Prime Minister of Canada, and Franklin Delano Roosevelt, President of the United States. With the threat of war in Europe growing, it was clear that England might soon depend heavily on help from transatlantic partners, and the aim of the trip was to strengthen ties across the ocean.

On 18 February 1939 Tommy wrote to Joan from on board the Cunard White Star liner RMS Queen Mary *before she left Southampton:*

My Darling,

I feel like a film star or a crook – I'm not sure which, because they have given me a suite of unexampled luxury (but only one bed after all), with a parlour in which ten people could dine; and the latter because they smuggled me on board from the train with an Edgar Wallace technique, which would have thrilled John. It was most effective, however, and I reached my flat (which it really is) completely incog. I am lying low till the ship sails, which she is about to do. Billy Harlech[1] has just been in to see me, and as soon as we are under weigh, I shall take a walk and go and inspect the library.

Four days later he wrote again to report that he had been miserably seasick:

I have no doubt that the North Atlantic is the foulest and dreariest spectacle on this earth. It has been actively unpleasant this time, too; we have had a full gale in our teeth almost incessantly. I have spent most of the time in

---

1 William Ormsby-Gore (1885–1964) succeeded his father as 4th Baron Harlech 1938. Secretary of State for the Colonies 1936–8, High Commissioner for the UK in the Union of S. Africa 1941–4.

my cabin, and though I have never actually been sick, have felt continuously ill, and have practically subsisted on the excellent Glucose D. It is a depressing thought that I have got to cross this cursed ocean thrice more before mid-summer!

On 24 February the New York Herald Tribune, *misinterpreting his absence from the social scene on board the liner reported:*

Alan Frederick Lascelles, Under Secretary to King George VI, arrived incognito yesterday on the Cunard White Star liner *Queen Mary* to complete arrangements for the forthcoming visit of the King and Queen Elizabeth. The ship and line officials denied his presence on the ship, and many representatives of the *Queen Mary* appeared amazed that they had not known he was on board. He remained in his suite for meals, and emerged for his turn about deck only after dark.

He brought an attaché case and one Gladstone bag. Even the Customs officials here would not confirm his arrival until long after he had quit the West Fiftieth Street pier. He was granted the diplomatic courtesy of ranking diplomats of having his luggage stamped without examination.

Another newspaper got several of its facts right:

Mr Lascelles is quite informal, hates top hats, goes to the Eton and Harrow match with a pipe and bowler hat, has a great sense of humour and dresses like a cross between an untidy City man and an Oxford don. He is dark, of medium height, and wears a small black moustache. His friends call him Tommy, and all the newspapermen who know him in England like him immensely. Behind his very casual exterior he hides a brilliant brain.

Having made the necessary arrangements in Washington, Tommy went on to Government House, Ottawa, where he had worked from 1931 to 1935 as Private Secretary to the Governor-General, Lord Bessborough:[1]

To Joan
1 March 1939

Well, here we are, as old Bess[borough] used to say; but honestly, I can't feel sorry that it is only for a week. When I first walked up to the Cottage, and thought of Caroline, Toby and John[2] frisking down the steps to meet

---

1   Vere Brabazon Ponsonby (1880–1956) succeeded his father as 9th Earl of Bessborough 1920. Lawyer and MP, Gov.-Gen. of Canada 1931–5.
2   His son John and daughter Caroline, and Toby the family dog.

me, I had a tinge of regret; but otherwise, the Ottawa landscape, GM, and the old, familiar faces with their old, familiar conversational standards, make me thankful that I'm only a visitor.

During his brief visit he captivated the tough American journalists, as another newspaper report showed:

Captain A. F. Lascelles leaves the United States for England today having completed his discussions on the visit of the King and Queen. He has accomplished the more difficult part of his mission with complete success. The Washington reporters rank him next to Mr Anthony Eden[1] for clothes, and put him 'tops among Englishmen' for humour.

At the entrance to the State Department in Washington Captain Lascelles was waylaid by an army of press men and photographers. 'Are you related to Lord Harewood?' shouted a reporter.

'I am.'

'How?'

'Quite legitimately,' said Captain Lascelles quietly.

The answer, voted an excellent example of English humour, has gone the rounds of Washington.

My wisecrack [Tommy reported to Joan], in reply to the eternal question, 'Are you related to the Url of Hair-wood?', seems to have gone down well. I'm afraid poor Lascelles is going to have to fight a good many rearguard actions with the Press in the course of the next fortnight.

In the event, all the plans he made for the tour in May and June were thrown into chaos by the fact that the Empress of Australia, *in which the royal party sailed for Canada, was brought to a halt in mid-Atlantic by fog and ice:*

To Joan
14 May 1939

I think the fog began on Thursday – it came down like a blanket, as thick as I have ever seen; and for three days we sat motionless on the Atlantic (which was luckily placid as a pond), seeing nothing except for a brief half-hour after tea on Friday, when the curtain rolled back as if by magic, and revealed a handful of really formidable icebergs all round us. Then down it came again; but the glimpse was quite enough to prove to those who do

---

1 Robert Anthony Eden (1897–1977), Secretary of State for Foreign Affairs 1935–8, 1940–45 and 1951–5, Deputy PM 1951–5, PM Apr. 1955–Jan. 1957. Resigned over the Suez Crisis. Knighted 1954, created 1st Earl of Avon 1961.

not know the N. Atlantic that our captain's extreme caution was amply justified.

There have been brief intervals, by day and night, when, very gingerly, the ship could nose her way forward at the pace of a rowing-boat, with her siren, and those of the two escorting cruisers, roaring in a head-splitting symphony every two minutes. But they were negligible intervals, and during those three days I don't think we got more than forty miles nearer Quebec.

Meanwhile, with the time of our final arrival slipping more and more into the middle of next week, I was sending long code telegrams to Ottawa, suggesting successive reconstructions of our mangled programme, as one alternative position after another had to be abandoned.

[At last] the sea began to move a little, and the wind to stir a little, and by lunchtime we could see again, after three days of practical blindness. And when we did see, it was a remarkable sight – a wall of ice, looking like a continent, stretched across the horizon on both sides of us. There was a channel to the south-west, and down it we fled, followed by the two cruisers – the sun was out by now – and it was a lovely afternoon. After steaming hard for a few hours, we successfully rounded the southern promontory of what must have been a vast ice-field.

Our three fog-marooned days were really very curious. Michael [Adeane] said he got the feeling we had all been dead quite a long time. It *was* rather like that – a strange sensation of being suspended somewhere right outside the world, with no dimensions. Space was limited to the grey wall outside, and time was non-existent – we might have been there three days or three months.

The only experience that I have ever had at all like it was when, at Whitsun 1914, I was snowed up in the Andes, and spent two or three days in a derelict hotel, with a train-load of total strangers. But that was a gloomy episode, and here we were all, from Their Majesties downward, in hilarious spirits – at any rate till the last half-day, when we all, I think, were beginning to get a little apprehensive about ever seeing Canada at all.

As a matter of fact, it has done the King a power of good – it is the only really idle and irresponsible spell he has had since he acceded; there has been nothing for him to do, and Hitler has hardly been mentioned since we left England.

In Ottawa again, he was full of enthusiasm for the way things were going. On 21 May he wrote to Joan:

Government House, Ottawa

So far this tour is a roaring success – I've never seen such splendid crowds – not hysterical, extremely well behaved, and all roaring themselves hoarse,

with genuine feeling; and *millions* of them – we must have seen well over a
million people in Montreal alone. The crowd there in that big square
opposite Windsor Hotel was really unbelievable – better than outside Buckingham Palace on Coronation night. I think Their Majesties are really
pleased – everybody else is – and Mackenzie King[1] alternates between sobs
of emotion and grins of ecstasy. But he is behaving very well, and will give
no trouble now.

The Queen is looking radiantly beautiful, and has them all gasping like
goldfish – particularly the American Press-men. We had a most successful
garden party at Government House, and I could hardly get about, I was so
beset by old friends.

On 28 May he wrote from the royal train, which was then crossing British Columbia:

We have just finished Banff. Keeping our horde of Press followers sweet is
of course one of the major problems of the tour, but so far they are in good
humour, and last night, by a stroke of luck, the King and Queen, on their
way up to bed, bumped into a group of them outside the lift and had a
long, friendly chat with them, which has given immense pleasure, especially
to the Yanks. I wasn't there, but I'm told that one of the latter, who was
fairly tight, was considered to have been too familiar, and after Their
Majesties had gone, his American colleagues fell upon him like a pack of
wolves and abused him roundly for letting them down, 'when' (in the
words of Miss Dixie Tighe, the star of the lady correspondents of USA),
'we've all been trying like hell to behave like ladies and gentlemen.'

I hope people at home realise what a wow this adventure is being. It is
on a crescendo rather than a diminuendo. I hope Their Majesties will be
able to stand the strain for another seventeen days.

7 June 39   The Royal Train

The King, giggling in a most disarming fashion, knighted me in the train
tonight, as the train was approaching Buffalo. I think I can fairly claim to
be the first man to be dubbed in a train, and also the first Englishman to
be so treated by his Sovereign on American soil; so the episode has, at any
rate, some historic interest. The news of what happened to me had appeared
in Reuter telegrams half an hour before, so everybody on the train knew
all about it; and it was really very pleasant to find how glad they all seemed

---

1   William Lyon Mackenzie King (1874–1950), Liberal statesman, three times PM of Canada
    (1921–5, 1926–30, 1935–48).

about it, from the highest down to the faithful Percy and Robert, whose grinning faces have just appeared round my door. What pleased me most was the excitement of the Canadians, even those who appear to dislike such English survivals most.

The royal visitors scored another triumph in the United States, and the rapport which the King established with Roosevelt greatly increased the President's sympathy for Britain when war broke out that autumn. When Harry Hopkins came to England early in 1941 as Roosevelt's personal representative, he described the 1939 visit as an 'astounding success'.

WAR

With war imminent, Tommy rented a house for his family in Bepton, a village at the foot of the Sussex Downs. He himself lived where he worked, in Buckingham Palace. Joan was unhappy in the country, and Tommy had to write frequently in attempts to soothe her anxieties, always seeking to persuade her that she and the children were safer away from the capital.

1 September 1939   Buckingham Palace

My Darling,

   You are so good and calm and efficient that it is a comfort to hear your voice, and to know that you are seeing this thing in the right perspective. We are far luckier than so many thousands of others – I in a job that will probably give me better chances of seeing you than if I were on active service; you and the children in, to my mind, about the best place possible in England.

   Our immediate movements are still vague. At present (4.30) I understand that the King sleeps here, and I do the same, but I am prepared to move to Windsor at half an hour's notice. Many of the domestics etc. have already gone.

30 December 1939   Buckingham Palace

I want you to come back to London just as much as you do; I hate being separated from you, and I hate your being lonely at Bepton. Don't think I didn't realise that. We will arrange things somehow; but there are hard facts that have got to be faced, and though I've thought a lot about it lately, I can't yet see the perfect solution.

11 September 1940   Buckingham Palace

Our bomb was a delayed-action one, which fell up against the swimming pool in that excrescence just to the left of my office window – beyond the garden entrance from which the King and Queen always emerge for the Garden Party. It fell on Monday night, and went off at 1.30 a.m. on Tuesday; it blew the north end of the bath out, and smashed most of the windows all along the front, including those of all our offices, and Their Majesties' sitting room. So we are living rather hugger-mugger in the back rooms;

but I think all will be straight again tomorrow. Their Majesties were photographed among the ruins, and early this morning I conducted a party of about forty journalists round them.

2 October 1940   Buckingham Palace

Bombs don't upset me much, not because I am braver than other people, but because I happen to work, and sleep, in what is probably the safest place in London, and because the knowledge that it took two and a half years of the last war before anything hit me gives me a kind of unreasoning confidence.[1] But I just could not tolerate this existence if, every time I heard something fall out of the sky, I was wondering whether you were underneath it.

9 October 1940   Buckingham Palace

When I was in Pratt's on Monday, there was a crackle in the street like little boys letting off fireworks on Guy Fawkes' day, which proved to be the arrival of a bouquet of incendiary bombs. I had just sat down to a very good soft-roed herring, so stayed where I was; but E. Devonshire[2] (who is the proprietor of Pratt's), attended by his son Bill and H. Macmillan,[3] dashed up into St James's Street and spent an enjoyable quarter of an hour putting them out.

15 October 1940   Buckingham Palace

My poor old Travellers,[4] which has been a refuge to me for thirty years, was badly hit last night. The damage is not irreparable, but much of the top floor is burnt out, and the whole place is swimming in water, which may bring down some of the ceilings in the lower rooms.

We have escaped more lightly than the Carlton Club, which is a wreck.

---

1   In Nov. 1917, during a German attack near Cambrai, Tommy was hit in the right arm by a shell splinter and was temporarily invalided to England.
2   Edward, 10th Duke of Devonshire (1895–1950), owner of Chatsworth House, Derbyshire, Parliamentary Under-Secretary of State for India and Burma 1940–42, and for the Colonies 1943–5.
3   Harold Macmillan (1894–1986), diplomat and politician, Minister Resident at Allied Headquarters in NW Africa 1942–5. In 1954 and 1955 he was, consecutively, Minister of Defence, Foreign Secretary and Chancellor of the Exchequer, PM 1957–63. He married Lady Dorothy Cavendish, daughter of the 9th Duke of Devonshire, in 1920. Created 1st Earl of Stockton 1984.
4   Logically the name of the club should have an apostrophe at the end. Recourse to the archives shows that over the years the punctuation mark has come and gone – and Tommy did not use it.

It was full of members dining, but not a soul was hit. E. Devonshire's lovely house has had its top floor burnt out, but he told me he hoped to save all the furniture in the lower rooms. No. 10 Carlton House Terrace is much knocked about, and, thank God, the German Embassy. Whitehall has also suffered, and the kitchens at No. 10 Downing Street, but not, I gather, the house itself.

5 March 1941   Buckingham Palace

At dinner last night the Queen and I got on to the subject of the Harold Macmillans – I forget exactly how – and I said I had recently met their eldest son in Pratt's, and been much struck by his looks and his manners, in fact he was one of the nicest of his generation whom I had come across.[1] The Queen said, 'Well – *you* ought to know.' I didn't know what she meant, and asked, 'Why?' She said, 'Because your own boy is easily the best specimen of that generation that I have yet seen' – and she went on to talk of John in a way that made me blush. It pleased me, because it was obviously her genuine opinion, and a quite unnecessary tribute if she hadn't felt what she said.

7 March 1941   Glamis Castle

We reached here safely this evening after a tour of the Polish troops in this neighbourhood. They are a fine lot, and very warlike-looking, with expressive faces which generally wear a broad grin. They seem happy enough in Scotland, and most anxious to destroy Germans whenever and wherever they can get at them.

We lunched, in a large villa outside a sea-coast town, with Sikorski,[2] the Polish commander-in-chief, his wife and daughter, and a posse of their officers. Few of them can speak any language except Polish, which made conversation difficult; my pair knew nothing except their native tongue, so our intercourse was confined to bowings and gesticulations, like the sea cows in *The White Seal*.

During the spring of 1941 Joan moved from Bepton to Cloud's Hill, the Hertfordshire home of Tommy's sister Blanche Lloyd. Joan was no happier there

---

1 Maurice Macmillan (1921–84), later a Conservative MP, married The Hon. Katherine Ormsby-Gore (known as Kate) 1942.
2 General Władysław Sikorski (1881–1943), leader of the Polish government-in-exile, was killed in an air crash at Gibraltar in July 1943. The cause of the accident, attributed by some to sabotage, was hotly debated, and formed the theme of Rolf Hochhuth's controversial play *Soldiers* (1967).

than she had been in Sussex, and Tommy sympathised with her 'solitude and exasperation'.

2 September 1941   Windsor Castle

I wish I saw some solution of our problem, although it is not really an immediate one, because obviously you must stay quietly at Cloud's Hill till the end of the year at least. Even if we were offered a house here tomorrow, you couldn't attempt to move into it for several months; a move is the last thing you ought to undertake at present.

War is bound to bring unhappiness in some form to everybody; and I suppose that the only way to look at our separation is that it is our share of the unhappiness. With me, it is aggravated by all sorts of cross-currents. The hermit strain in me (from both sides of my family) gets stronger as the years go by; and I find the communal side of my profession more irksome every day. As you know, if I was free to choose, I should always plump for a resumption of our Sutton life, either at Sutton or elsewhere, and I really want nothing else from this world. That, of course, is unthinkable at present; not merely because I must obviously go on earning money for us all for a good many years yet, but also because, if hermitages are ever justified, they certainly aren't in war-time.

Worse still, the urge to escape, not from work altogether, but from this particular form of work, is often very strong. My great weakness is that I am not really interested in public affairs; I am always tempted to put down some State paper, which I ought to find absorbing, in order to go on reading a book like *Man and His Universe*, to talk to you on the telephone, or to listen to music. As the bulk of the work here is concerned with public affairs, that is a handicap! One which I ought to overcome, I know, but natural disabilities aren't easy to overcome as one gets older.

This makes all the sharper the point of the Damocles sword, which hangs continually over my head – the possibility of Alec Hardinge leaving and of my having to succeed him.[1] I have always disliked the idea, and should like it even less in wartime, though it would, of course, bring compensations as far as our domestic problem is concerned. It may never happen; on the other hand, the hair that holds the sword is perilously thin, and it would never surprise me to hear that it had snapped. If it did, it would be very wrong for me to think of going elsewhere, to do other

---

1 Damocles, a courtier of Dionysius the Elder, tyrant of Syracuse in the fourth century BC, was invited to a banquet by the ruler, but, on looking up, found that a sword was suspended above his head on a single horse-hair, positioned there to demonstrate how fragile were the privileges of wealth and power.

work, whether I was called upon to fill the chair or to install somebody else in it.

For the moment, I'm afraid, there is nothing to be done save to wait on events. As things are, I can't agitate for a house here; I'm not the head of a Department – and that has always been the qualification for having a house here; and, in theory at any rate, my work is evenly divided between here and Windsor and London – where I already have a house. And, though the intervals between my being able to get to you seem long enough, I have no real ground for complaint about leave. I get away a good deal more than anybody else doing Government work in London.

However, other people's troubles don't make one's own any easier, I know, and they certainly don't cure the loneliness which I continually feel, and which I know that you feel too. We can, in this and as in most other things nowadays, only sit and hope for a clearer sky. But it is a real consolation to me that, for these months of convalescence, boring though they must be for you, you should be in safety, in comparative comfort, and able to have at any rate one child with you, in a place where I can get at you so easily. That, at any rate, is something for which I am really thankful.

12 October 1941   Windsor

You said the other night that we ought to have something to take the place of going to church, and of formal religion in general. I have often thought the same thing – more in the past, perhaps, than just lately – but I have never found any solution to the problem. I envy people who can make 'religion' one of the foundations of their life, in the same way that I envy scientists or musicians; but I know now that I can no more hope to attain their way of thinking than I can hope to be a pianist or a physicist.

I've never been irreligious, and, whatever I may believe, I don't *dis*believe anything. But my own positive religious beliefs have long been so simple that there is really nothing to discuss about them. Christ said there are only two commandments, on which hang all the law and the prophets; the first being, roughly, one's duty towards God, the second one's duty towards his neighbour.

I have never been able to find any meaning in the first, except in relation to the second, and it would be humbug of me to pretend that I do. I don't in any sense deny the existence of God; but, from reading about the past and thinking about the present, I have never been able to find the slightest evidence of his having directly revealed himself to man or of his having given any direct evidence that he concerns himself, in any manner that we can possibly comprehend, with man's affairs on this earth.

My attitude, in fact, is that of the man who said 'Lord, I believe; help thou mine unbelief'. Further than that I can't honestly go; and, as a consequence, theology must be to me a book as completely sealed as is the study of any possible life after death.

The second commandment, to my mind, is the only one that matters in our present life; and I believe that if one does his best to keep that, he automatically fulfils the first; in fact, that we can only reach God through each other, and are not really meant to try to do so in any other way: the vast majority of us, anyhow – I don't exclude the possibility of there being a very few rare humans – Christ, Buddha and maybe others of whom we've never heard – who have superhuman qualities which enable them to get in touch with a superhuman order of life.

My religion is really summed up in the last three verses of that wonderful 'sounding brass and tinkling cymbal' chapter in Corinthians. I cannot see what St Paul meant by them, if he didn't mean what I do.

So, you see, there isn't really very much I can discuss, even with you. Still less with other people – especially the children; for my creed is obviously destructive of much of the accepted 'religion', and I think it is a crime to do anything tending to destroy the beliefs of others. What right has one to do so? They may be right and I may be utterly wrong – there is no yardstick of accuracy in such things, and verbal argument only leads to each mis-understanding the other's point of view. It is as hopeless as trying to argue about colour or sound.

Moreover, I feel very strongly that every man's religion is a matter for himself alone, and for nobody else; what were we given minds, and indi-viduality, for, unless to think out such things for ourselves? It is awfully difficult, too, to argue on metaphysical subjects without seeming cynical and flippant, and giving the impression that one is trying to shock, or be clever. Even you, you know, who ought to know better, are apt to accuse me of trying to 'lecture' you – a thing I have never attempted to do in my life, on any subject – when all I want to do is to get my own thoughts into some sort of coherent form, so that they may be intelligible, and possibly some use to you. Do remember that I am not good at putting my own point of view about anything; I can only do it by groping through a tangle of words, which, even if they sound didactic, are really a confession of inferiority and never an attempt to assert superiority – which is the attitude of the lecturer.

As to going to church – I gave up going regularly because I found, as a matter of experience, that, so far from doing me good, it did me harm; that it made me more materialistic, spiritually and mentally, and often physically uncomfortable. I now go to church for three reasons – One, if I have to go professionally; two, for aesthetic satisfaction – i.e., if it is a pleasant village church, or if the music is likely to be good; three, if you, or anybody else whom I like, should ask me to go with them. All those are essentially *human* reasons, and not because I think God is more likely to be found inside a church than out.

I gave up saying my prayers night and morning because I suddenly realised that it had become pure formalism, which I hate, and that I was constantly 'praying' – meditating, petitioning, confessing my short-comings, call it what you will – at other times throughout the day, when my praying was far more genuine than when I was just getting into or out of my bed.

The last time there was talk about a 'National Service of Prayer' I remem-ber saying to John Gore[1] (who characteristically used my remarks in his next weekly article) that my personal feeling was that the whole idea was an insult both to us and to God; to us, because there is only one possible prayer for these times, consisting of three words, 'God save England', and that every decent Englishman already said them in his heart every day and every hour (I must have repeated them, often aloud and in the street, thousands of times in the last two years); and to God, because the impli-cation is that he is susceptible to mass-production prayer and, like a German or an American, liable to be more impressed by mere figures, and, so to speak, the smell of burnt offerings from the altars of St Paul's Cathedral or Westminster Abbey. That seems to me a savage and Jehovaistic conception.

Nevertheless, had the King asked my advice as to whether the service should be held or not, I should unhesitatingly have said 'Yes', because I know that such services do bring comfort and strength to millions of people, and I wish with all my heart that they did to me too. But there again, my advice would have been based on purely *human* reasons, and not because I believe for one moment that God is any more likely to help us win the war because we all collect together at a given place on one day and ask him to in chorus.

Well – there are my religious views. I am always ready to discuss them, or yours, with you, when we are alone, *provided* that you will get into your head once and for all that whatever I may say, and in whatever tone of voice I say it, I am never trying to be 'superior' or to score off you in argument. It is, honestly, the fear that you may think that which has often muzzled me in the past; that, and also, as I said the other night, the feeling that you

---

1 1885–1983. Journalist and biographer. One of the author's oldest friends, and lifelong correspondent.

and I are so much part of each other that there is really no necessity for us to argue about anything.

At this point I re-read what I have written. I hope you won't think any of it priggish. Words are very difficult tools to handle. But there's one other point I must make. I've said, in effect, 'All we've got to think about in this life is our duty towards our neighbour – nothing else signifies, or can be made to signify.' Put like that, it sounds a drab creed, as if one could get nothing out of life save by 'good works', and being a professional Good Samaritan. I don't mean that; to me, the word 'neighbour' has the widest possible meaning, embracing everything in this world worth loving – human, animal, vegetable and inanimate. By 'neighbour' I mean all the good things in and on the human world. I include in my duty towards my neighbour, for instance, gardening; writing a good book; appreciating music, or the song of a thrush, or the bones of a landscape; making, or laughing at, a good joke – every activity, in fact, that goes to swell the sum total of human happiness – and animal happiness, too. And it is through the door of such happiness, I maintain, that one gets far more frequent glimpses of God than by trying to gate-crash his presence with the clumsy tools of man-made 'religion'. Conversely, an unkindness to a human or a dog is, to me, far worse blasphemy than a string of the most profane oaths ever invented.

John came up this afternoon, very smart and soldierly and contented with his lot. We walked through Eton, whose High Street was like Lord's in the interval – we were accosted at every step: the John Childs; Matt Ridley in a car with his two sons, who told me that Gwladys had been knocked down by a lorry and broken her leg – did you know this? Gerald Lascelles; and a dozen young friends, in and out of uniform. Timmy Forbes-Adam has got into Pop. We walked through the playing-fields, looking very mellow and autumnal, and back here to tea in the Equerry's room, where John was thrilled by the racing reminiscences of old Charles Moore,[1] who had come over to see HM about Turf matters.

I must go and dress. Good night, my darling. T.

---

1 Charles Moore (1880–1965), manager of the King's thoroughbred stud 1937–63.

1942

On 2 June 1942 Tommy suddenly resumed his old habit of writing a diary. He may have been prompted by Joan, who, during the Blitz of 1940, had urged him to keep a record, or even just to make notes. 'Do think about this, as it would be an occupation for those evenings in the dug-out, and you might never have the same amount of time on your hands again.'

Tuesday 2 June   Buckingham Palace

The noise made by the workmen excavating a vast new air-raid shelter in the north-east corner of the Palace, immediately outside my present room, has driven me across the passage into the little den (Room 379) which I had to occupy so long last year, when blitz and blast from various bombs had shattered my windows – since repaired with the admirable cellophane material that necessity has invented to take the place of glass. However, what I lose in amenity, I gain in quiet, for this room, looking on to the corner of the grand entrance in the quadrangle, is undisturbed save by the passage of some visitor's motor-car beneath its windows.

Today is the first this year that can be compared to a summer's day – it is, indeed, a perfect one; coming as it does with a spell of good news, it makes one wonder if the almost unalleviated sombreness and anxiety of the past two and a half years may not be beginning to lift. In the Travellers, at luncheon, I drew a smile on to the care-lined face of Charles Portal[1] by telling him of the scurvy treatment of Harris[2] by the *Evening Standard*, which last night reproduced a very unflattering photograph of him, and printed underneath, 'Is this the face that launched 1,000 ships?' But C.P.'s smile was due more to the success of our second raid into Germany with a force of over 1,000 bombers – Essen last night, and Cologne on Saturday.

On Saturday evening, towards midnight, I stood in the garden at Cloud's Hill[3] and listened to the great bombers streaming overhead like a well-

---

1   Marshal of the RAF Sir Charles Portal (1893–1971), generally known as 'Peter', Chief of the Air Staff 1940–45. Created 1st Viscount Portal of Hungerford 1945.
2   Marshal of the RAF Sir Arthur ('Bomber') Harris, Bt. (1892–1984), C-in-C Bomber Command, 1942–5. A controversial figure, considered by some to be too ruthless in flattening German cities.
3   His sister Blanche Lloyd's home in Hertfordshire. Her husband George, 1st Baron Lloyd of Dolobran (1879–1941), had become Secretary of State for the Colonies in 1940, but had died early the following year. In 1919 Tommy had gone out to India as his ADC when he was Governor of Bombay.

regulated flush of pheasants; and thought 'not without relish', in Winston's classic phrase, of the difference from fourteen months ago. Then, as we listened to that sinister drone of the wings of the Angel of Death over England, we said, 'Here they come.' Now, it is 'There they go'.

I dined with Helen and Eric Maclagan,[1] who told me what seems to be authentic news from the Red Cross in Geneva that their boy Gerald (the pilot of one of our Lancasters which did not return from the raid on Warnemünde three weeks ago) is a prisoner of war. This is a great relief. Mrs Belloc Lowndes[2] was at dinner, sister of Hilaire Belloc,[3] who gets a well-deserved CH [Companion of Honour] in the imminent list of the Birthday Honours. She gave me a lift home in her taxi, and I played billiards with Piers Legh, Master of the Household, and reminded him that the first Sir Piers Legh had his head cut off by his Sovereign (Henry IV).

Wednesday 3 June

Dined with Claud Hamilton[4] at the Turf Club off fried whiting, cold apple tart and bottled beer, and then sat in the garden at Buckingham Palace, reading a young American journalist's[5] *Last Train from Berlin*, which gives an encouraging analysis of German morale and the effect on it of the first six months of the Russian campaign. Today my daughter Lavinia joined the WRNS.[6] H. Belloc has refused the CH. I wonder why. [*Later note:* He didn't like Winston Churchill.]

Thursday 4 June

Kathleen Rutland[7] and her youngest son, Roger Manners, up from Eton,

---

1 Helen, the oldest of Tommy's four sisters and the one to whom he was closest, was married to Sir Eric Maclagan (1879–1951), Director of the Victoria & Albert Museum 1924–45. After the death of their mother, when he was not quite four, Helen became his surrogate parent. In their youth he called her 'Whelk' or 'Mollusc', among other endearments, and continued to address her thus in letters all her life.
2 Marie Adelaide Belloc (d. 1947), prolific author, widow of Frederic Lowndes, editor of *The Times* (d. 1940).
3 Hilaire Belloc (1870–1953), versatile author, now remembered chiefly for his *Cautionary Tales* and *A Bad Child's Book of Beasts*.
4 Capt. Lord Claud Hamilton (1889–1975), Comptroller and Treasurer in Queen Mary's household 1936–53.
5 Howard K. Smith.
6 The Women's Royal Naval Service, commonly known as the 'Wrens', which came into being in 1939.
7 1894–1989. Widow of the 9th Duke of Rutland. Formerly Kathleen Tennant, and known as 'Kakoo', she had been a friend of Tommy's for thirty years.

lunched with me. Took Joan Bright,[1] now one of the main springs of the War Cabinet Secretariat, to see *Watch on the Rhine* – a fine play, finely acted.[2] What an improvement on the old system is the wartime plan of starting a play at 6.30 p.m., and having a light meal after it. I hope we never revert to the old plan of a hurried dinner at 7.30, for an 8.30 play, for which one usually arrived late. On the other hand, the present arrangement must be a strain on the poor performers, if they have already had a matinée at 2.30.

Friday 5 June

Lunched at Travellers with Emrys-Evans,[3] Parliamentary Under-Secretary at the Dominions Office. Rather a solemn chap, but intelligent, and the right type for an MP. He fears that peace may come upon us unawares and unprepared; I agree – I've always thought it would come like a thief in the night, or as a half-dead tree falls with startling suddenness, when one is cutting it down. I said I hoped we should have a long and elastic armistice, and not attempt to formulate rigid peace-terms (especially as regards frontiers and forms of government) until we knew where we were, and what type of medicine our moribund civilisation needed. He said, 'Yes, but we ought instantly to form a "western bloc" of the sea-going nations – ourselves, Dutch, Belgians, Scandinavians and perhaps Portuguese – as a bridgehead, so to speak, for future peace-making.' There is a good deal to be said for this.

Dined at the Royal Automobile Club with old Dick Molyneux[4] – Perrier Jouet '28, which was delicious; one rarely gets stood champagne nowadays. Afterwards, in the cool of the evening, we sat by the lake in Buckingham Palace garden, gossiping of Courts, royal pictures (about which Dick has encyclopaedic knowledge) and whether royal control of ministerial activities, in the manner of Queen Victoria, will ever be possible again. We both thought not.

Lavinia rang up from Hampstead to say that she was quite happy as a Wren, but very hot from being made to do violent PT. Joan Bright told me last night that Winston had caused consternation in Whitehall by reading

---

1   Joan Bright (1910–) supervised the top-secret Intelligence Centre run by General 'Pug' Ismay. Among her many admirers was Field-Marshal Wavell, who wrote her long letters from his various wartime posts. Her memoir *The Inner Circle* (1971) described how she organised domestic arrangements for the British delegations at the international conferences at Tehran, Yalta and Potsdam. In 1949 she married Col. Philip Astley (1896–1958), a cousin of Wavell's deceased son-in-law Simon Astley.
2   By the American playwright Lillian Hellman (1905–84).
3   Paul Emrys-Evans (1894–1967), MP for South Derbyshire 1931–45.
4   Maj. the Hon. Sir Richard Molyneux (1873–1954), former Extra Equerry to Queen Mary.

out verbatim in the House of Commons passages from Auchinleck's[1] secret despatch from Libya, thereby hazarding the security of our most intimate cipher.

Saturday 6 June

A telegram from Lisbon gives an amusing story of General Giraud's[2] recent escape from Germany – that he let himself down from the window of his prison by a rope made from the string with which his parcels from France had been tied up; a motor (arranged from France) was waiting for him and put him in the next train for Switzerland. The Germans raised a hue and cry, and orders went out that all the men over six feet whom the police might encounter were to be examined. When they searched Giraud's train, he, being a fluent German scholar, started an earnest conversation with a German general in his compartment, and when the police came along and saw him thus engaged, they did not dare to interrupt. Giraud is still a mystery man, but I feel sure we shall hear a lot more of him. The *Daily Mail* recently had an amusing clerihew on him:

> I used to think General Giraud
> Was something of a hero.
>
> Now he's gone to Vichy,
> It all looks a bit fishy.

Tuesday 9 June

Malcolm Bullock, MP,[3] dined with me at the Travellers. He tells me that his father-in-law, old Derby, is pretty shaky nowadays. The majority of the Knights of the Garter are moribund, and it is very difficult to think of even one suitable *remplaçant* – let alone half a dozen, which we might be faced

---

1 Gen. (later Field-Marshal) Sir Claude Auchinleck (1884–1981) was then C-in-C British Forces in the Middle East.
2 A distinguished French soldier, Gen. Henri Giraud (1879–1949) excelled at evasion: he escaped from German captivity once in the First World War and once in the Second. In 1942 he gave his support to Marshal Pétain, but switched his allegiance to the American C-in-C Gen. Eisenhower, and later formed a Committee for National Liberation with Gen. de Gaulle.
3 Capt. Sir Malcolm Bullock (1890–1966), MP for the Waterloo Division of Lancashire (1923–50), was active in Anglo-French affairs. He married Victoria, daughter of the 17th Earl of Derby, in 1919.

with any day. The only obvious candidate, Zetland,[1] is getting one in the Birthday Honours list this week; and Augustus John[2] at last gets his OM [Order of Merit], which his farmyard morals have delayed unduly.

Thursday 11 June

The King and Queen went off to spend two days in Cambridgeshire, to include the Oaks and the Derby at Newmarket. I have been arranging this tour; one of the difficulties nowadays is to find suitable places in which the royal train can 'tie up' at night – an adjacent tunnel, or deep cutting, is essential, to give proper protection from the air; and such features are rare in the East Anglian landscape.[3]

Friday 12 June

Lunched with Eny Strutt[4] at the Lansdowne Club. We listened to the 'commentary' on the Oaks (won by the King's filly Sun Chariot) on the wireless. Time was when I would go miles to a racecourse; but now I would rather watch a race by radio, so to speak, and so escape the crowds and all the business of getting there and back.

Saturday 13 June

Went up to Lord's, where I haven't been since the war began, and saw some rather somnolent cricket – Cambridge versus a congeries of local clubs. Lord's looked much as usual – turf excellent, and no signs of any damage through enemy action. The only thing I missed was the Father Time weathercock on top of the new grandstand, which has probably been put into store.[5]

The King and Queen returned after tea, and I found him bearing his Derby disappointment reasonably well. He had won three classics this year, and his filly will very likely win the Leger, so he has not much to complain of.[6]

---

1 The 2nd Marquis of Zetland (1876–1961) had been Governor of Bengal 1917–22, and Secretary of State for India 1935–40.
2 Augustus John (1878–1961), artist celebrated for his bohemian way of life.
3 There was a suitable tunnel at Newmarket.
4 A close friend of the Lascelles family, Baroness Irene de Brienen (1883–1974), m. (2nd) Vice-Adm. the Hon. Arthur Strutt (1878–1973).
5 In fact Father Time had been dragged from his vantage-point by the trailing cable of a barrage balloon. Between thirty and forty bombs had fallen on the ground during 1940, causing considerable damage.
6 In the Derby the King's much-fancied colt Big Game had faded, and finished fifth.

Wrote to Joe Airlie[1] to congratulate him on the Thistle bestowed on him at the King's birthday, and told him that, with the Thistle in front and the key behind, he ought to be practically impregnable, but that he must not forget the Maginot Line.[2]

Sunday 14 June

There was a curious little ceremony outside Buckingham Palace after luncheon – at which the King and Queen had entertained such Heads of Allied States as could be mustered: Peter of Yugoslavia[3] (a very unimpressive little sovereign) and his mother: Haakon[4] of Norway, and Olaf: Bernhard of Netherlands[5] (his mother-in-law is in USA): Beneš[6] of Czechoslovakia: and the Polish President,[7] whose name I shall never learn to spell. The occasion – the saluting of the flags of the United Nations – was rather planted on us by the Americans, who can, of course, organise such affairs with plenty of advanced publicity, and without risk of interruption from hostile aircraft. We cannot, and consequently it was rather a hole-and-corner affair, which evoked little enthusiasm from the five or six hundred casual onlookers whom the sound of bands had collected round the Victoria memorial. I doubt if they had any idea what it was all about. Winston, who insisted on wearing all his medals on his frock-coat, looked rather bilious – I believe he had just heard that we had been driven out of 'Knightsbridge' in the Libyan battle, which is certainly gloomy news.

---

1 12th Earl of Airlie (1893–1968), Lord Chamberlain to the Queen 1937–52.
2 In full-dress uniform the Lords Chamberlain wear keys on their backsides. The Maginot Line was a chain of fortifications built at immense cost in the 1930s to protect France's eastern flank against attack; but when the German armies invaded in 1940, they easily outflanked it.
3 King Peter II (1923–70), the last monarch of Yugoslavia, fled to England in June 1941 as a refugee from Hitler, and set up his government in London. King George VI was his 'Koum', or Godfather, and so felt an obligation to look after him. Peter remained in exile throughout the war, moving to Cairo in October 1943, and returned to London to marry Princess Alexandra of Greece in March 1944 (see page 208). He never regained his throne, but settled in America.
4 King Haakon VII of Norway (1872–1957) rejected Hitler's demands for surrender in 1940 and came to England, returning to his own country at the end of the war. He married Maud, youngest daughter of King Edward VII, and their only son Olaf was born in 1903.
5 Prince Bernhard of the Netherlands (1911–2004), consort of Queen Juliana, became a pilot and flew with the Allied forces during the war.
6 Edvard Beneš (1884–1948), President of Czechoslovakia 1935–8, established the Czech National Committee in London 1940, returned to Czechoslovakia in Apr. 1945, and was again President, until he resigned in June 1948.
7 No wonder the name eluded Tommy: it was Władysław Raczkłewicz, who had set up a government-in-exile in London in June 1940.

Tuesday 16 June

Up to London [from Windsor] with the King, 10 a.m. The Prime Minister lunched with him, as he does practically every Tuesday, and was reported by the Equerry to be in good spirits. I can't think why, as the position in Libya seems to me to be very anxious, and the running of the Malta convoys not exactly successful, though we inflicted some damage on the Italian fleet. On returning to Windsor, I defeated Delia Peel[1] at croquet, which astonished me, as, when we last played, two years ago, she ran rings round me. This was a house-warming, so to speak, for the new bowling green-croquet lawn, which I have induced them to have levelled, just below the steps leading from the terrace to the golf links. The frost played mischief with the levelling operations last winter, and the turf is still poor, but the surface is a vast improvement on the Himalayan features of the old lawn.

Edward Halifax[2] in his last weekly political summary from Washington says that the Roosevelt[3] government have made up their minds to four postulates for the post-war period: 1. A long armistice, of possibly several years, before a final settlement is made. 2. Establishment of an international police force. 3. Abolition of Colonial Empires. 4. Equal access to the world's raw materials for all democracies.

I've always thought (1) essential – peace-making in a hurry was proved disastrous at Versailles. Harold Nicolson[4] urged a long armistice very convincingly in an excellent little pamphlet which he published earlier in this war. Nor have I any quarrel with (2) and (4), though I would make it a rider of (4) that the world's petrol supplies should be rigidly controlled by (2). (3), if it were published in this country, would raise a lot of dust. Apart from whether we should like it or not, I doubt if it is practicable. Granted that our administration of our colonial dependencies has been very far from perfect – especially in the last quarter of a century – somebody has got to look after them. Many of them are palpably unfit to administer themselves for many generations yet.

---

1 Lady Delia Peel (1889–1981), daughter of the 6th Earl Spencer, and widow of Col. the Hon. Sir Sidney Peel (1870–1938), under whom Tommy served in the Bedfordshire Yeomanry during the First World War. Lady-in-Waiting to Queen Elizabeth 1939–50.

2 Edward Wood, 1st Earl of Halifax (1881–1959), British Ambassador in Washington 1941–6, had been a member of the Baldwin, Chamberlain and Churchill governments, and Foreign Secretary 1938–40.

3 Franklin Delano Roosevelt (1882–1945), Democratic politician, first became President of the US in 1932. He was re-elected for a second term in 1936, for a third in 1941 and for a fourth in 1945. It was largely his advocacy that brought America into the war against Germany.

4 Politician, diplomatist and author, Sir Harold Nicolson (1886–1968) was National Labour MP for W. Leicester 1935–45. He married Vita Sackville-West in 1913, and was a lifelong friend of Tommy's.

Bad news about G. Maclagan. The Air Ministry have news that all in his aeroplane were killed. Yet, from what Helen told me on the telephone, it appears that the list of names which they have (I don't know from what source) does not include Gerald's; why did the Red Cross in Geneva report him individually as a prisoner? It is conceivable that, while the others baled out and possibly were killed, he may have succeeded in somehow bringing the machine to land. But I fear it is a poor chance.[1]

Sunday 21 June

Another perfect day, quite hot, and only clouded by the sudden and shocking news of the fall of Tobruk,[2] after an assault which cannot have lasted more than twenty-four hours. I fear we shall lose many troops and much equipment. Joan and I finished carting and stacking the hay at 11 p.m. I also got a lot of timber in during the day; and found my precious gold safety-pin, which I had dropped among the beeches a month ago.

Tuesday 23 June

At 10 p.m. we left Euston for our visit to Ulster – the King and Queen, Cynthia Spencer,[3] Piers Legh and I. The Home Secretary, Herbert Morrison,[4] came too, as Minister-in-Attendance. A man of mediocre quality, I should say. The Home Secretary ought to be a possible, though not necessarily a probable, Prime Minister, but in no circumstances could one conceive of this man adequately leading a British government. But he was first-rate in the London County Council, I believe, and is not a bad Home Secretary – though they say that he is intoxicated by his powers as official head of the police in this country. He is quite agreeable, and P. Legh and I sat talking to him till nearly midnight.

The new 'royal saloons', air-conditioned, were used by Their Majesties;

---

1   Gerald's death was soon confirmed.
2   In January 1941 the port of Tobruk, on the coast of Libya, with its strategically placed harbour, had been captured by British forces, and over the next eighteen months the garrison held out against numerous Axis attempts to regain it. But on 20 June 1942 it fell to a mass attack by forces under the German general Erwin Rommel.
3   Wife of 7th Earl Spencer, Lady of the Bedchamber to Queen Elizabeth the Queen Mother 1937–72.
4   Herbert Morrison (1888–1965), Labour politician, was Home Secretary and Minister of Home Security 1940–45, and a member of the War Cabinet 1942–5. Created 1st Baron Morrison of Lambeth 1959. Tommy later modified his strictures with an added note: 'He made a remarkably good speech at Hackney yesterday, all the same.'

the LMS railway has built them, and Harold Hartley,[1] whose especial care their construction has been, was at Euston in a fever of apprehension lest they should be found faulty in any detail.

Wednesday 24 June

Midsummer Day. We left our train just north of Stranraer, at 8 a.m. – 6 a.m. by the sun,[2] of course – and transferred to a lighter one, an operation made necessary by the fact that the newly-built line down to Cairn Ryan pier is not to be trusted. Embarked in the cruiser *Phoebe*, and breakfasted on board. Reached Belfast at noon; Abercorn[3] on the quay with Andrews,[4] the Prime Minister of Northern Ireland, and all his Cabinet, with a posse of municipal, military and naval swells. Visited Short & Harland's aeroplane works, where they build Stirlings, and lunched with Andrews at Stormont. Then through the Houses of Parliament, conducted by Bangor,[5] the Speaker of the Senate, and Henry Mulholland,[6] ditto of the House of Commons, and on to Harland & Wolff's ship-building yards.

Here there was a really remarkable demonstration of loyal enthusiasm, which I have never seen surpassed in my twenty years' experience. We were mobbed by a boisterous but thoroughly good-mannered crowd, who swept the Home Secretary and his Ulster opposite number, Sir Dawson Bates,[7] into some eddy from which they did not appear for an hour or more. Considering that strict secrecy had necessarily been observed about the visit till that morning, the streets were remarkably crowded, and always deafeningly vociferous.

Got to Hillsborough, the Abercorns' Government House, about 6.30 p.m. and found that the boxes, flown over from Buckingham Palace, contained mercifully little for me. It is a pleasant, solid house, and the Duke has put a lot of nice shrubs in the garden. Good cook, despite war rations, and

1 Brig.-Gen. Sir Harold Hartley (1878–1972), Chairman, Railway Air Services, 1934–45, had been Director of Research for the London, Midland and Scottish Railway since 1930. The royal carriages on the train were equipped with telephones, electric heaters and air-conditioning, and positioned between the men's accommodation at one end and the women's at the other.
2 Under the system of double summer time, clocks were advanced two hours during the summer months.
3 James Hamilton, 3rd Duke of Abercorn (1869–1953), Governor of N. Ireland 1922–45.
4 Rt. Hon. J. M. Andrews (1871–1956), PM of N. Ireland 1940–43.
5 Maxwell Ward, 6th Viscount Bangor (1868–1950), Speaker of the Senate of N. Ireland 1930–50.
6 Rt. Hon. Sir Henry Mulholland (1888–1971), Speaker of the House of Commons of N. Ireland 1929–45.
7 Rt. Hon. Sir Dawson Bates (1876–1949), Home Secretary for N. Ireland, 1921–43.

Veuve Clicquot for dinner, when I was between Andrews and D. Bates, charming old gents, both of them, but inelastic as granite. There will be no changes in Ulster's attitude to the South so long as that generation is in power.

Thursday 25 June

Off at 10 a.m. to visit the American troops in the Ballykinler area. An interesting day. Their equipment is superb, and though the men are not as physically hard as they might be, they are a good type, and the senior officers were charming and intelligent. I took a special liking to General Ward, from Colorado, who was next to me at luncheon. The Yanks are wonderfully good showmen; each item in the programme was explained by a young officer with a loudspeaker – obviously a trained radio commentator – who never hesitated for the *mot juste* – even if the military demonstration under review wasn't always proceeding exactly according to plan. Their field-engineering tools, hospital equipment, filters, cookers etc. seemed to me particularly good; and they had a remarkable little portable wireless sending and receiving set, which they call a 'walkie-talkie'.

Friday 26 June

The King inspected the two British divisions (59th and 61st) now in these parts. Good stuff, I thought, but, watching these boys march past their sovereign is always a sadness to me in these days – *morituri te salutant*.[1] We lunched with the RAF at Nutt's Corner, close to the east shore of Lough Neagh, and finished the day at Larne, where a number of British and American sailors had been collected, and at 6 p.m. embarked in *Bicester*, one of the new 'Hunt' class destroyers. Lovely crossing, and we were safe in the Royal train above Cairn Ryan by 8.30. I conceived a great affection for the old Abercorns. The King delighted them by giving the Victorian Medal to Mr Birt, a great character who has been their butler for twenty-seven years.

Saturday 27 June

A local petrol-controller has sent me coupons for eight gallons for the thirteen weeks beginning July 1st. This means that Joan ought to be able to make two trips per week into Hitchin (four miles) and back; better than I

---

1 'Those about to die salute you': salutation of Roman gladiators entering the arena.

expected. Blanche Lloyd is anxious to get a pony and cart, but they are hard to come by, and very expensive. We tried one out when I was last at Cloud's Hill, but the pony, though a good one, was too hard-mouthed to be driven safely by a woman. The owner (a Luton policeman) asked £78 for the outfit – a thirteen-hand pony, ancient governess cart, and ditto harness.

Sunday 28 June   Windsor

Interesting Foreign Office paper setting out the Government's ideas for dealing with 'war criminals'. We are committed to action of some kind, but they rightly wish to avoid any repetition of the foolish 'Hang the Kaiser' campaign after the last war, and want to treat all the guilty leaders by *political* (not judicial) procedure – as we did Napoleon; the lesser miscreants, whose activities are more or less local, to be handed over to, and tried by, the peoples whom they have wronged – Poles, Czechs, Belgians etc. There will not be much doubt about the verdict, but first catch your hare.

John, F. Legh and I played bowls after dinner, and induced the King to join us, he and John defeating F.L. and me – I cannot recollect a more perfect summer evening than it was.

Monday 29 June

Had a long talk with the King before dinner on the subject of his broadcast-addresses and the position of the Throne generally. He talked sound sense. The occasion was a note by some well-wisher (I suspect from internal evidence that it is the work of Lady Ampthill[1]) which Queen Mary has sent him. The writer claims that people are beginning to think (or are being subtly propaganded to think) that the King himself is losing faith in the institution of Monarchy, and feels that, now we are so closely allied with two republics, we shall soon have to adapt our constitution to their pattern. I think this is moonshine – there is no evidence for it. If people thought that, they would soon lose faith in the King himself, and nobody who follows him as closely as I do when he goes about could detect any sign of that.

I do not delude myself that the British Monarchy will be immortal, any more than any other human institution is; but at the moment I believe it rests on foundations as durable as it has ever had. Anyway, if the foundations are in process of disintegration, the process will not be arrested by turgid royal broadcasts, which is what the writer of this note advocates.

He (or she) prophesies dire things, on the analogies of the revolutions

---

1   Lady Margaret Ampthill (1874–1957), widow of 2nd Baron Ampthill (d. 1935). Lady-in-Waiting to Queen Mary.

in Russia and Spain, which I've always thought were false. The causes of those revolutions (oppression by priests or aristocrats, corrupt government, economic stringency) are not present in this country; we are not Latins or Slavs – our national characteristics and background are as different from theirs as chalk from cheese; and for centuries we have been a free people, detesting violence and not having hysteria. It is only slaves who go in for bloody revolutions. And to assume (as it is fashionable to do in certain circles) that because the war has made us bed-fellows of USA and Russia, we must necessarily adopt their political habits after the war, is as illogical as to prophesy that we shall all become baseball fans, or go dancing about in long boots. *Plus ça change* etc.

How like the post-French revolution period it is, when everybody foretold a wave of *sans-culottes*-ism, with aristocrats dangling from the lampposts all down St James's Street. What happened? We pinched various ideas from the French crucible, poured them into the British moulds, and then claimed them as our own. The same will happen again. Our 'levelling' process will doubtless follow a steeper gradient after this upheaval; but I don't believe it will ever become a precipice.

I sat up till 2 a.m. writing, at HM's behest, an answer to the note on these lines.

Wednesday 1 July

Wardlaw-Milne[1] solemnly proposed in the House of Commons this afternoon that Henry, Duke of Gloucester,[2] should be appointed Commander-in-Chief of the British Army! The Labour members put this astonishing proposal in its true perspective by shouting, 'That's put the lid on it! Let's divide.' But what an *ass* W-M must be, and in what a fog of unreality his mind must be. I've known Prince Henry, on and off, for twenty years; an excellent creature, and a genuinely keen soldier. But, in the opinion of those best qualified to know, the post of second-in-command of a regiment is the very highest to which his capabilities would justly entitle him. The Mother of Parliaments is sometimes made to appear very ridiculous.

Thursday 2 July

Augustus John, the painter, came to receive the OM from his Sovereign. I

---

1 Sir John Wardlaw-Milne (d. 1967) was Unionist MP for the Kidderminster Division of Worcestershire 1922–45.
2 Prince Henry, Duke of Gloucester (1900–74), third son of King George V and Queen Mary.

did not see him, but trust it was one of his sober days. Not long ago I asked Ainslie, the Steward here, why a certain footman had been dismissed. 'He took to drink, Sir,' he said. 'On one occasion, I even suspected him of being fuddled in the Presence.'

Met Joan, and Caroline, at the Curzon Club, which she has just joined. Old Margot Asquith[1] was sitting, hunched and witch-like, in the hall; I hadn't seen her for some years. I went on to lunch with Gladys Wyndham[2] and Lady Violet Astor,[3] whose husband owns *The Times*, in the former's flat. We canvassed that much-discussed topic, whether Edward Halifax has or has not been a success as our Ambassador in Washington. The balance of the evidence goes to show that he has not, but I have met several people lately from USA who maintain the contrary. Anyway, he has had a tough job, and P. Lothian[4] must have been a particularly difficult man to follow. But the fact is that Edward is altogether too fine-minded a creature for public life in these days, and the legend that his 'saintliness' is humbug (compare his nickname, Lord Holy Fox) had preceded him to America; moreover, he is tarred with the Munich brush. I believe Angus McDonnell[5] has been invaluable to him as a sort of courtier-jester-impresario; A. could always play on any collection of Canadians or Americans as if they were fiddles.

A story is going round that, on one occasion, E. Halifax suddenly found himself confronted by an assembly of about forty mayors. 'What shall I say to them?' he asked Angus. 'I've never seen so many mayors in my life.'

'Quite easy,' said Angus. 'Just whinny like a stallion.'

Tuesday 7 July

To my dentist, K. Campbell. Now that the majority of my teeth are his rather than mine, such visits have few of their former terrors – an advantage of *senectus* [old age] which I think escaped Cicero's notice.

In the Travellers, Evelyn Baring,[6] one of the many converts to Trollope

---

1 Countess of Oxford and Asquith (1864–1945), formerly Margot Tennant, widow of the PM, H. H. Asquith, 1st Earl (1852–1928).
2 Wife of Edward Scawen Wyndham (1883–1967), who succeeded his brother as 5th Baron Leconfield in 1963.
3 Lady Violet Elliot (d. 1965), married John Jacob Astor, chief proprietor of *The Times* 1922–66.
4 Philip Henry Kerr, 11th Marquess of Lothian (1882–1940), had died in only his second year as British Ambassador in Washington 1939–40.
5 Col. the Hon. Angus McDonnell (1881–1966), son of the 7th Earl of Antrim, was Attaché to the British Embassy in Washington.
6 Evelyn Baring (1903–73), Governor of S. Rhodesia 1942–4, High Commissioner for UK in S. Africa 1944–51, Governor and C-in-C, Kenya, during the Mau Mau emergency 1952–9. Created 1st Baron Howick of Glendale 1960.

in recent years, asked me to lend him *The Eustace Diamonds*. Lizzie Eustace is the best vamp since Becky Sharp, and I often wonder at what period in his bearded, bourgeois life old T. acquired such a clear vision of that particular type of female. Mrs Carbuncle is a great character, too.

Joan and I dined with the Devonshires[1] at the Mayfair Hotel, where they've established themselves since their lovely house in Canton Gardens (the nicest house in London) was blitzed in 1940. There: P. J. Grigg,[2] Secretary of State for War, and wife, and Waterson, High Commissioner For South Africa, and wife.[3] We dined off soup, roast mutton (a luxury in these days) and strawberry mess, drinking cider. What a contrast to a Devonshire House dinner party thirty years ago. But ours was, to my mind, the better party. The talk was largely anecdotal, but amusing. Grigg, whom I like particularly, is excellent company, and she, an ex-school marm, not so formidable as she appears at first sight.

Wednesday 8 July

Joan, Dinah Colquhoun[4] and I went to see the new film *The Young Mr Pitt*, which I found strangely moving, partly from the constant parallels with our present situation, and partly because I know all those late XVIII century people so well. It's a good film, well acted, and, I should say, reasonably accurate historically; of course, Donat[5] is not Pitt, and Morley[6] is not Charley Fox – who could be? But they give a reasonable approximation of the manner in which both of them would have reacted to the various situations portrayed.

There are too many cheering or hooting mobs (now we do our cheering or hooting in the columns of the Press rather than in the streets) [*1968 note*: Times have changed.] and too much concession to the 'love-interest' centring round Eleanor Eden. But the House of Commons scenes are admirable, as is the struggle of William Pitt against rapidly deteriorating health. But when will film-producers break away from the ridiculous con-

---

1 Edward, 10th Duke of Devonshire (1895–1950), and his wife, formerly Lady Mary Cecil.
2 Rt. Hon. Sir Percy James Grigg (1890–1964), Secretary of State for War 1942–5, had married Gertrude Hough in 1919.
3 Hon. Sidney Waterson (1896–1976), High Commissioner for the Union of S. Africa in UK, 1939–42. In 1924 he had married Hilda Markus.
4 Formerly Dinah Tennant, much admired by Tommy in his youth, married Sir Iain Colquhoun 1915.
5 Robert Donat (1905–58), stage and film actor, best known for creating the role of Richard Hannay in the first film version of John Buchan's *The Thirty-nine Steps*, directed by Alfred Hitchcock.
6 Robert Morley, actor and author (1908–92).

vention that when two foreigners are talking to each other they must do so in broken English? It is absurd, e.g., to make Talleyrand and Napoleon chatter together in the Tuileries like a couple of organ-grinders. If a British audience can't follow them in their native French, let them talk plain English.

The film has been criticised as making Pitt too genial & human; he was probably a good deal less approachable and humorous than Donat represents him, but though his contemporaries clearly thought him a starched, shy man by their own standards, one can't assume that he hadn't got a softer side. After all, a number of them called him Billy – presumably to his face as well as behind his back – and there is evidence somewhere of his being surprised playing bears with his nephews and nieces.

The Foreign Office print of Hughe Knatchbull-Hugessen's[1] telegram reporting the death of the Turkish premier says, 'He died of a burst (group undecipherable).' This sounds a dreadful end.

Saturday 11 July   Windsor

Walk with the King before luncheon. Long cipher telegram from Athlone,[2] who refuses to take on his staff in Ottawa the wretched young Duke of Connaught, whom his regiment (Greys) have had to get rid of, as he is wholly incompetent. I can't think what is to be done with him.[3]

Lovely evening. Bowls with Francis Legh after dinner. The Russian battle grows ever fiercer, & Egypt has flared up again, on our initiative, it appears.

Monday 13 July

Walked with the King before luncheon; warm work, as he likes to go even faster than I do, and I was grateful for the occasional pauses to inspect the hay along the river bank, or to encourage the Corgi dog, Crackers, to hunt for mice – which, incidentally, he always lets go if they are ever foolish enough to be caught.

We talked of the question of whether or no the Queen should register with her 'age-group', which was apparently called up yesterday. I said I could think of two good reasons against her doing so. 1. If the coronation-ceremony has any significance, it surely is that the King and Queen dedicate

---

1 Sir Hughe Knatchbull-Hugessen (1886–1971) was Ambassador to Turkey, 1939–44.
2 Alexander Cambridge (1874–1957), son of the Duke of Teck, married Princess Alice of Albany 1904. Created first and last Earl of Athlone 1917. Personal ADC to King George VI 1919–52, and Gov.-Gen. Union of S. Africa 1923–31 and Canada 1940–46.
3 Alastair Windsor, 2nd Duke of Connaught and Strathearn (1914–43).

themselves permanently to the service of the country. It is superfluous and undignified that the Queen Consort should have to fill in a buff form, whenever women in general are called on for some special duty towards the body politic. 2. So far from bringing home to the female population at large the importance of registering, it would, I believe, have exactly the contrary effect. No sane person imagines that, whether she has gone through the form of registration or no, the Queen will ever be under statutory compulsion to perform some specific job – e.g., work in a munitions factory. Consequently, the act of registration on her part will only appear purely formal to everybody, and even farcical to many. The tendency will be to assume, quite wrongly, that when other ladies of high degree register, it don't mean business in their case; their sisters, lower in the social scale, would say, 'Of course, *she* won't be called up. She's only done it as a matter of form – like the Queen' etc.

Wednesday 15 July   At Cloud's Hill

St Swithin. No rain. Got in the last of the hay. Letter from Arnold Bax,[1] the new Master of the King's Musick, asking if an honour can be given to Barbirolli,[2] the conductor, who, Bax declares, is British born and bred. Sent him the usual explanation – that the King initiates no honours save VO [Victorian Order] and OM – and advised him to write to No. 10.

After tea, we (Joan, Caroline and I) lay out in the garden and listened to a good Bach-Handel concert radioed from Albert Hall.[3] One of the minor curses of war is that one's tobacco is always dry, it being no longer packed in air-tight tins. I am trying to correct this by keeping slices of raw potato in my tobacco-box.

Thursday, 23 July

Willoughby Norrie,[4] just home from commanding the 30th Corps in Egypt, came to see Dermot Kavanagh[5] last night, and give him an account of the

1   Sir Arnold Bax (1883–1953), Master of the King's Musick, 1942–52.
2   Sir John Barbirolli (1899–1970), Permanent Conductor of the Hallé Orchestra, was of Italian and French parentage. He was knighted in 1949, and became a Companion of Honour in 1969.
3   Tommy's delight in classical music owed nothing to his father, whom he recorded as saying: 'Wagner? I can make as good music as Wagner by slamming my bedroom door.'
4   Lieut.-Gen. Willoughby Norrie (1893–1977), Governor of the State of S. Australia 1944–52, Gov.-Gen. New Zealand, 1952–7. Created 1st Baron Norrie 1957.
5   Col. Sir Dermot McMorrough Kavanagh (1890–1958), Equerry to King George VI 1937–41, Crown Equerry 1941–55.

recent fighting. He said Auchinleck was a great man, but singularly inept at picking his subordinates. Italian morale is now as low as possible, and is beginning to infect the Germans.

Behind us in the King's box [at a concert in the Albert Hall] was an agreeable young Canadian RA captain, whom we took to dine with us at the Hyde Park Hotel. He is (on his own account) working out the possibilities of getting supplies to Russia by sleigh, over the ice from Alaska, and asked me where he could get hold of books treating of ice conditions in those parts. I could only suggest the London Library, and when I got home, wrote a note to Vincent Massey[1] asking him to fix it up.

Friday 24 July

On July 1 there was a short poem in *Punch*, which I liked, over the signature 'C. O'R.' I meant to copy it out, but nowadays all the magazines are whisked away so quickly, for hospitals etc., that I missed it. So I wrote to E. V. Knox,[2] the editor of *Punch*, who is a fellow-member of the Literary Society,[3] and asked for a copy, which he sent me yesterday. This is it:

> I see nothing clearly;
> Nothing at all, nothing at all,
> But one fixed star:
> England's star merely.
> By it I stand or fall,
> Loving her dearly.[4]

Well, that is exactly how I feel about it all, though I suppose that, with the exception of some thirty or forty High Esoterics – the War Cabinet and its immediate minions – I get as much illumination on the drear fog of war as anybody in this country. Yet I am befogged, all right; and my faith in the star has never wavered.

Lunched with Joan and Caroline, whose insatiable passion for music had taken her to the Albert Hall all the morning, to hear the rehearsal of this

---

1   Rt. Hon. Vincent Massey (1887–1967), High Commissioner for Canada in UK, 1935–46.
2   Edmund George Valpy Knox (1881–1971), known as 'Evoe', editor of *Punch* 1932–49.
3   The dining club founded in 1807, to which Tommy had been elected in 1937 (along with T. S. Eliot, Peter Fleming and Lord Dawson of Penn), and of which he became president in 1955.
4   *Later note:* 'Knox said that C. O'R. was Connal O'Riordan – incidentally a strong Sinn Feiner – and that he would be much pleased if I wrote and told him that I liked his poem. So I did.'

evening's Prom. She has some friend who plays the 'cello in the London Philharmonic orchestra.

Saturday 25 July

Heard from Millard, the farmer at Sutton Waldron, that old White, who was our gardener there for about thirty years, is dead. He must have been all of ninety years old; a fine and faithful servant he was, and an unrivalled gardener. When I sold Sutton, I retained the cottage in which White was living; Millard now wants to buy it.

Sunday 26 July   Windsor

Bishop of Norwich[1] (Herbert, lately translated from Blackburn) preached in St George's Hall. Quite good, but he spun his web round St Matthew's call from the seat of custom, and I always think incidents such as that, and the conversion of St Paul, are unsatisfactory themes for us moderns. All of us, at any rate when we were younger, have hoped in vain for some such instant enlightenment – for an angel to come and tell us what it is all about; but we have long learnt that the way of revelation is a long and featureless road, uphill, and with no sudden glimpses of what lies beyond the ridge of our ignorance.

Old Sir John Hanbury-Williams,[2] last of the Edwardian beaux – I always thought him the best-dressed and most distinguished-looking man in London – and his daughter came to luncheon. They live in the Henry III Tower. Walked the Bishop down to Eton, he to see his son, I to take a walk with Tuppy Headlam,[3] lately returned to pedagogy from the fastness in the Welsh mountains to which he retired when he gave up his house at Eton, and where, by all accounts, he was supremely miserable.

Monday 27 July

Among the King's letters this morning was one from a Miss Katharine Parr,[4] who is described in *Who's Who* as 'sole organiser of the Crusade for

---

1 Rt. Rev. Percy Herbert (1885–1968), Clerk of the Closet to King George VI 1942–52, Bishop of Norwich 1942–59.
2 Maj.-Gen. Sir John Hanbury-Williams (1859–1946) was Extra Equerry to the King 1934–46.
3 Geoffrey Wycliffe Headlam (1879–1947), celebrated House Master at Eton 1920–35. A lifelong bachelor, he retired to a rented house in North Wales, but returned to the school to teach history during the war.
4 Olive Katharine Parr (1874–1955), author of many books about Devon, also styled herself

Chastity, which numbers among its members some of the most distinguished civilians, clergy and officers in the Empire'.

Tuesday, 28 July

I met Lady Astor,[1] who had been to see the Queen, in the passage this
morning, and walked her to the Privy Purse door. In all my official
dealings with her I have always found her quite exasperating; but when
I meet her off-stage, her friendliness and obvious kindness of heart
always melt me. She said, 'Don't you think the *Observer* is much better
now? And weren't we right to get rid of Garvin?[2] He had gone right over
to Beaverbrook,[3] you know.' I didn't know, and was interested to hear
this explanation of Garvin's dismissal from his editorial chair, which
caused a considerable flutter in the journalistic world at the time.

I went to a terrific luncheon party, given by the Bessboroughs[4] for
General and Mrs de Gaulle[5] at the Savoy – the first of such pre-war
entertainments that I've attended for a long time. Every time I see de G,
I feel more certain that the Free French, or the Fighting F., or what F.
you will, will never hitch their wagon to his uninspiring star.[6] We bought
a pig in a poke there. What he ought to be doing is commanding an
Armoured Division in Egypt. Mme de Gaulle is a shy little mouse, quite
pretty.

We had a brief air-raid alarm about 3 a.m., which woke me up. There
was some shooting, but I believe no bomb fell nearer than Harrow. Our
guns have got some kind of new projectile which makes a noise just like
the descent of a bouquet of incendiaries. There were about seventy German
planes over altogether, of which we definitely destroyed eight – say eleven
per cent, though doubtless a few more were 'probables'.

'Foundress of the Crusade of White Knights and Ladies'.

1 Nancy, Viscountess Astor (1879–1964), American-born widow of 2nd Viscount Astor
   (1879–1952). Social reformer; first woman MP to sit in what she called 'the Imperial
   Parliament', otherwise the House of Commons, as Unionist MP for Plymouth Sutton
   Division 1919–45.
2 J. L. Garvin (d. 1947), idiosyncratic editor of the *Observer* 1908–42.
3 Maxwell Aitken (1879–1964), mischievous newspaper proprietor and politician, was
   created 1st Baron Beaverbrook in 1917. A confidant of Winston Churchill, 'the Beaver'
   was detested by Tommy, largely because of his meddling in the Abdication crisis.
4 Vere Ponsonby, 9th Earl of Bessborough (1880–1956) and his wife Roberte. Tommy had
   been Private Secretary to Bessborough when he was Gov.-Gen. of Canada 1931–5.
5 Gen. Charles de Gaulle (1890–1970) had escaped from occupied France in 1940, and in
   England established himself as leader of the Free French, inciting his countrymen to
   continue the struggle against the Nazis.
6 In a later note Tommy added: 'But they did.'

The King had an investiture – a big one, at which Miers,[1] of the famous submarine *Torbay*, got his VC, and a number of his crew other awards of varying degree.

Thursday 6 August

Back to London with the King. Angus McDonnell came in to see me, full of praise for E. Halifax, whose stock, he says, has risen steadily all over USA lately. As Arthur Penn[2] and I were walking round the garden in the gloaming this evening, the Queen hailed us from the terrace, and told me to ask Joan to Windsor for the weekend, so that she might get a final glimpse of John: a kindly thought.

Friday 7 August

Nancy Astor has been scarified by the *Daily Herald*, and the Labour Party generally, because, in some recent speech, she said that it was all nonsense to gush over the Russians on the ground that they are fighting our battles; they are fighting for themselves, and nobody else, etc. I remember making the same sort of protest in my diary some twenty-eight years ago, apropos the slush that was then being talked about our having entered the war to protect 'gallant little Belgium', when it was patent that we were fighting primarily for our own existence. But one don't say that sort of thing out loud, certainly not if one is an MP. Truth, as Kipling says, is a naked lady.[3]

Saturday 8 August   Windsor

I met Joan at the Southern Railway station just before luncheon; we drove up in a royal brougham – the first time we had ever travelled together in such a vehicle. Luncheon enlivened by the presence of three or four wasps, which always excite the Royal Family; but later, in the afternoon, a more serious attack from the air occurred, when a stray German plane dropped

---

1   Rear-Adm. Sir Anthony Miers, VC, CB, KBE, DSO and Bar (1906–85), known as 'Crap' Miers, was a pugnacious disciplinarian, who, when his sailors committed misdemeanours, gave them the option of three rounds in the ring with him in lieu of regular punishment – an offer which most declined. He won the VC for his action on 4 Mar. 1942, when he took his submarine *Torbay* into Corfu harbour at night, following an enemy convoy, and in a dawn strike sank two supply ships. The *Torbay* then endured seventeen hours of attack from sea and air, surviving forty depth-charges before escaping.
2   Sir Arthur Penn (1886–1960), Acting Private Secretary to Queen Elizabeth 1940–46.
3   In his *Many Inventions*.

five bombs in Slough. We knew nothing of it till it was all over, as we were all in the Waterloo Chamber, seeing a bad film, and for some reason the castle siren was not sounded. End of double-summertime, alas – I love the long, light evenings – though the putting-back of the clocks gives us an extra hour in bed.

Sunday 9 August

The Government of India have arrested Gandhi,[1] Nehru,[2] Miss Slade etc. – the only possible move after Congress had approved the 'Quit India' resolution. The Viceroy's Council, Governors etc. seem to be unanimously against deportation, which the War Cabinet favoured. Gandhi, of course, will go on hunger strike again, and probably die; but though there will inevitably be a certain amount of rioting, I don't believe that the majority of Indians want us to clear out and leave them to the Japanese. And, as Leo Amery[3] pointed out, in quite a good broadcast this evening, about two-thirds of the Viceroy's Council are now Indians.

Tuesday 11 August   Balmoral

Reached Ballater 9.20 a.m. after an uneventful journey. Crazy old Aberdeen[4] was at the station as Lord Lieutenant; he gets madder each year; and Bulgy Thorne,[5] GOC Scottish Command. The Lovat Scouts constitute the castle guard this year. There has been heavy rain for the last two days, and the river is high and dirty.

Wednesday 12 August

Heavy showers throughout the day. River still rising. Walked with Delia.

Thursday 13 August

Arthur Penn and Jack Eldon[6] have arrived. Fine day, and river started to

---

1   Mohandas Karamchand Gandhi (1869–1948), barrister and inveterate political agitator, campaigned for the withdrawal of British from India, and was frequently imprisoned for civil disobedience.
2   Shri Jawaharlal Nehru (1889–1964), leading politician, PM of India 1947–64.
3   Rt. Hon. Leopold Amery (1873–1955), journalist, author and politician, Secretary of State for India and for Burma, 1940–45. It was he who told Neville Chamberlain, 'In the name of God, go.'
4   George Gordon, 2nd Marquis of Aberdeen (1879–1965).
5   Gen. Sir Andrew Thorne (1885–1970), C-in-C Scottish Command 1941–5.
6   John Scott, 4th Earl of Eldon (1899–1976), Lord-in-Waiting to King George VI 1937–52.

fall. I hooked, and lost, a good fish at the tail of the Boat Pool. He took my fly (Thunder & Lightning No. 5 greased line) in slack water at the end of the cast (which I hate) – a spectacular head-and-tail rise, and after jigging about in the stream for some time, he ran straight over to the far bank, taking out all my line and a lot of the backing. He then jumped twice, close in to the shore, having run upstream, and got a big belly in my line which, in the strong water, I could not remedy. With the second jump he shook the fly out of his mouth; he was over 20 lbs, and looked fairly clean.

The troubles following Gandhi's arrest seem to be subsiding, and Linlithgow,[1] the Viceroy, is pleased with the way things are going. But our convoy to Malta has been an expensive business, and only about one-third of it will reach the Maltese. Alec Hardinge gives me a summary of the news each day on the 'scrambler' telephone; it is a remarkable invention, and said to be perfectly secure.

Friday 14 August

The King started grouse-driving in earnest – hitherto they have only been walking, in the afternoons. They left 9.30 a.m. and didn't reappear till 5.30, the ladies having gone out to luncheon. I was clear of work by 11.30, and got Hall, of the Life Guards (second-in-command of the armoured car detachment which follows us about nowadays), to run me down to Birkhall. I lent him one of my rods, and fished the lower water myself. At this height of water the wading is very laborious, and even dangerous, as the river-bed is a mass of unfriendly boulders, with deep holes in between. Neither of us moved a fish all day. (Before the war, I used to shoot regularly when on duty at Sandringham and Balmoral. But I gave it up in 1939, for I found I couldn't cope with secretarial duties if I spent the day out shooting.)

Reading *Sir Richard Burton's Wife*, which the Queen lent me. My father met Richard Burton[2] in some country house once, and used to say that, in the smoking room after dinner, he invariably drank a whole bottle of whisky to his own cheek, and went to bed none the worse. It is a most entertaining book, written with a pleasant, and slightly cynical, detachment, by a young woman called Jean Burton, a great-niece, I believe, of R.B.

---

1 Victor Hope, 2nd Marquess of Linlithgow (1887–1952), was Viceroy and Gov.-Gen. of India, 1936–43.
2 Sir Richard Burton (1821–90), flamboyant traveller and explorer, especially in Africa and Arabia. He spoke twenty-five languages and translated (among other works) *Arabian Nights*, *The Kama Sutra* and *The Perfumed Garden*.

Sunday 16 August

Church at Crathie. Mrs Ronald Greville[1] came over to tea; she has been a consistent mischief-maker for twenty-five years, but I don't think she will make much more now. She is restricted to a wheeled chair, which I had to propel into the dining-room – no light task, made no easier by the fact that when we had got half-way, the Queen's dog Crackers was abysmally sick immediately in front of us.

Tuesday 18 August

Left Balmoral p.m. to relieve Alec Hardinge in London. The Ministry of War Transport, who control such things nowadays, had accorded me a sleeper from Aberdeen. I have got very fond of Balmoral, and regret only having had a week there. I am now engaged in collecting fifteen suitable books for the King to give the stalkers and keepers etc.

Wednesday 19 August

Reached King's Cross 9.15 a.m. instead of 7.30, two de-railed goods wagons having held up the train somewhere near Newcastle. Buckingham Palace in a nasty state of *déshabille*. No hot water in any of the bathrooms except the Queen's, which I have perforce to use.

   Dined with the Halifaxes at the Dorchester. They have had to postpone their return to Washington, and Dorothy, Victor Cazalet[2] (the only other guest) and I united in advising Edward to wait a bit longer, to see the PM after his return. Edward said, and I expect he's right, that it was essential that whatever 'conference' there may be after the war should be held in Washington rather than in London.

Thursday 20 August

The usual stream of boxes all day, as always when one is alone here. The results of [the raid on] Dieppe, as far as the air was concerned, were satisfactory, for we accounted for a gratifying number of Focke-Wulfs,

---

1   Since the death of her husband in 1908, the Hon. Mrs Ronald Greville (Dame Margaret Helen Anderson) had held court as a tirelessly intriguing London hostess. Tommy's prediction was accurate enough: she died on 15 Sept.
2   Lieut.-Col. Victor Cazalet (1896–1943), MP for Chippenham from 1924, was four times amateur squash champion. He served as political liaison officer to the Polish General Władysław Sikorski, and was killed in the air crash at Gibraltar in which the general died in July 1943.

though at considerable cost. On the ground, we don't seem to have achieved much, and the casualties among the Canadians are said to be very heavy.[1]

Every morning one of the staff-officers from the Cabinet War Room brings us the daily Report. One of these used to be a decent little man called Attenborough – a solicitor in civil life. Not long ago he disclosed to a lady friend, a Mrs Ridpath, the name of the ship in which her son – or brother – was being conveyed to another theatre of war, and its destination. This came to the ears of MI [Military Intelligence], who traced the leakage to Attenborough, and had him arrested and tried by court martial.

Hearing that he was languishing in Chelsea Barracks, still under arrest, I went this afternoon to see the poor little man, and give him such comfort as I could. He made no bones about his lapse – he had, indeed, pleaded guilty at his trial. It was, he said, scrupulously fair, and his only complaint was that seventeen days had gone by, and still he didn't know his fate. When I got back, the first box which I opened contained his court martial papers, submitted by the Secretary of State for HM's approval. He is dismissed the service; a severe sentence, but I suppose that as he was in a particularly responsible post, they had to make an example of him. So there he is, poor chap – one more victim of a tattling woman, and a warning to all of us. I am very sorry for him.

Victor Cazalet last night held forth a good deal about future strategy, 'second' fronts etc.: *doxa*, not *episteme*[2] – he clearly *knew* nothing; while Edward and I, who knew too much, sat silent. That is one of the paradoxes of war. But my impression of V.C. is that it is *doxa* all the way with him – and damned little else.

Friday 21 August

On leaving the Albert Hall [after a concert], we turned into the Park opposite the Albert Memorial, along with some fifty or sixty other citizens, when an excited park-keeper appeared from nowhere, and, shouting, 'Closing time – you can't come in here,' shut and locked the gates behind us. We naturally assumed that the gates at the other end would still be open, so walked on, to find them shut. So there we were, like so many foolish virgins, locked out, or locked in, for the night, the park-keeper having vanished into the fast-gathering darkness.

Fortunately the Germans had blown a hole in the railings at some period

---

1 In a largely abortive commando raid on the German coastal defences, the Canadian contingent, in spite of showing great gallantry, lost over 3,300 men killed, wounded or captured out of a force of 5,000.
2 'Opinion, not knowledge'.

of the Blitz, and it had been only sketchily repaired with barbed wire. Through this, at some peril to our clothes, we eventually crept into Kensington Gore and liberty. It was one of the most glaring instances of inconsiderate bumbledom that I have ever come across, and I came home determined to write to Wyndham Portal,[1] now First Commissioner of Works, and report the keeper. But when I took up my pen, I felt that this is no time in which to bother ministers with petty annoyances; so I laid it down again, and went to bed.

Saturday 22 August

Winston, in a telegram summing up the present state and temper of 8th Army in the Western Desert, describes General Corbett[2] as 'a very small agreeable man of no personality and little experience'. Tacitus could not do it better, nor Pope more devastatingly.

Much triangular telephoning to Balmoral and Dickie Mountbatten[3] regarding the King's future movements, and dates for a visit to Dickie's 'Combined Ops' circus on the west coast of Scotland.

Sunday 23 August

What I always disliked about war is the passion which soldiers have for doing things in the middle of the night. This morning the War Office had me out of bed at 3 a.m. to ask if the King would approve the announcement tomorrow of Maitland Wilson's[4] appointment as GOC Iran/Iraq command. I said he would (which I trust is true) and returned to my bed.

I went to see Helen [Maclagan], in a nursing home in Collingham Gardens.[5] On the whole, she looked better than I had been led to expect; but she has aged markedly, and her voice is sadly weak. We talked for three-quarters of an hour; I took her Miss Somerville's *The Big House at Inver* to read, and a posy of somewhat overblown roses, which, by leave of the King, I had gathered from the garden here.

---

1   1885–1949. Minister of Works and Planning, and First Commissioner of Works and Public Buildings 1942–4. Created 1st Viscount Portal of Laverstoke 1945.
2   Lieut.-Gen. Thomas Corbett (1888–1981), a corps commander, Middle East, 1942.
3   Adm. of the Fleet Lord Louis Mountbatten (1900–79). In 1942 he was Chief of Combined Operations, in 1943 he became the Supreme Allied Commander in SE Asia, and in 1947 he was appointed Viceroy of India and created 1st Earl Mountbatten of Burma. Assassinated by the IRA 27 Aug. 1979.
4   Gen. Sir Henry Maitland Wilson (1881–1964), known as 'Jumbo' from his size, C-in-C Middle East 1943, then Supreme Commander in the Mediterranean 1944. Head of Joint Staff Mission in Washington 1945–7. Created 1st Baron Wilson 1946.
5   Helen was suffering from cancer.

Monday 24 August

I went to my bootmaker for the first time since the war began, Joan having told me that it was wise to be well shod before all the good leather disappears. She said five coupons per pair of shoes would be necessary; but when, having ordered two pairs, I laid down ten coupons, the man said he must have fourteen, the ration being five for a woman but seven for a man. A monstrous discrimination between the sexes; I know many women whose feet need more leather to cover them than mine do.

I sent the King's home-coming message to Winston round to No. 10, but when 7 o'clock came, and no news of his arrival, I began to get anxious. His elimination would be such an overwhelming disaster that one is prone to imagine the worst when he is *en voyage*. However, I went round to the Travellers for dinner, and was talking to J.[1] after it when Bevir[2] telephoned from No. 10 that the PM had landed safely at some aerodrome or other at 9 p.m. I relayed the good news to Balmoral and to Alec Hardinge, and went home greatly relieved.

Tuesday 25 August

Dined with Tim Nugent[3] at White's, which is about the only club that preserves an outward semblance of cheerfulness (perhaps because they have a bar in the middle of the hall), and, when I got back to Buckingham Palace, heard that the Duke of Kent had been killed, with John Lowther,[4] his Private Secretary, through the aeroplane (a Sunderland) which was taking him to Iceland, crashing into a mountain somewhere north of Wick. There were sixteen people in the aeroplane, all of whom are said to be killed. Archie Sinclair[5] had already communicated the news direct to the King at Balmoral, but I had a lot of telephoning to do, and did not get to bed till nearly 1 a.m.

I have known the Duke of Kent, on and off, for twenty years, but never

---

1 Hon. Sir Jasper Ridley (1887–1951), barrister and banker, chairman of Coutts and (later) of National Provincial Bank. Married Countess Nathalie Benckendorff, daughter of the Russian Ambassador in London, 1919. One of Tommy's oldest friends.

2 Anthony Bevir (1895–1977), Private Secretary to Neville Chamberlain (1940), to Winston Churchill (1940–45), to Clement Attlee (1945–51), to Winston Churchill (1951–5) and to Anthony Eden (1955–6). Knighted 1952.

3 Terence Nugent, always known as 'Tim' (1889–1973), Lieut.-Col. Comptroller, Lord Chamberlain's Dept, 1936–60, and Extra Equerry to King George VI, 1937–52. Knighted 1945; created 1st Baron Nugent 1960.

4 John Lowther (1910–42), heir of 1st Viscount Ullswater.

5 Archibald Sinclair (1890–1970), Secretary of State for Air 1940–45. Created 1st Viscount Thurso 1952.

saw much of him continuously, save during the trip to Canada in 1927, when he came with the Prince of Wales. He was the only one of his family who made any pretensions to be cultured and well-read – and the only one who wrote an educated hand. He had, for most people, great social charm, and, since the [start of the] war, had done good work – notably in his very valuable tour of Canada last year. But – though I may be unjust – I never saw him without thinking of Reuben – unstable as water, thou shalt not excel.[1] Even when he was at his best, the air of the 'spoilt child' never quite deserted him. However, these impressions date from some years ago, and those who have been associated with him more recently have often told me that he had greatly improved. He adored his children; and was fond of music.

I deplore John Lowther's loss; he was a highly intelligent and altogether delightful boy – heir of old Ullswater, to whom he would have been a worthy successor. He leaves a son, less than a ten-year-old, I think.

Wednesday 26 August

A bad, exhausting day – much telephoning about funeral arrangements, and telegrams of condolence by the hundred. Weather unwholesomely monsoon-ish, and Russian news depressing. The young Duke of Connaught[2] came to see me about his forthcoming journey to Canada. He is quite a nice boy, but looks a bit raffish.

Thursday 27 August

The King and Queen returned from Balmoral. PM to luncheon. I caught a distant glimpse of him, and thought he looked jaunty. Telegrams all day. Joan dined with me at the Ritz, and we went to see the new Disney film, *Bambi*. The Russians announce that they have been attacking north-west of Moscow, apparently with some success.

Saturday 29 August

Alone at Buckingham Palace. The Duke of Kent was buried at Windsor. His death, to judge from the letters and telegrams, has greatly stirred the

---

1 Jacob's prophecy for his eldest son: 'Reuben, thou art my first-born ... Unstable as water, thou shalt not excel' Genesis 49:3–4.
2 1914–43. Son of the Duchess of Fife (Queen Victoria's granddaughter) and Prince Arthur of Connaught. Lieut. in the Royal Scots Greys, officially killed on active service, but in fact died of hypothermia when he fell out of a window, drunk, at Government House, in Ottawa.

public imagination all over the world. Even de Valera[1] sent a message of sympathy, and the Duke of Windsor one signed 'David' – the first *personal* communication that he has sent to his brother for some years. He asked that he might be represented at the funeral, and, by the King's direction, I got Lionel Halsey[2] to do this.

Dined at the Travellers with Willy Percy[3] and Frank Balfour,[4] and, as usual, got into a fierce argument with Willy, the most contumacious (but always agreeable) conversationalist that I know. His Fundamentalist faith always astonishes me. He believes, for example, that the Jewish problem in Palestine has been settled once and for all by some text in Isaiah, in which Jehovah is reported as giving an undertaking to restore them there some day or other. That is a road down which I cannot follow him any appreciable distance.

Monday 31 August

Their Majesties returned from Windsor, and at 7 p.m. we left for Scotland. The Germans have attacked in Egypt. I have rarely felt so tired.

Tuesday 1 September   Balmoral

Arrived Ballater 9.20 a.m. Eldons still here, and Delia Peel. River on the low side. Fished p.m. and rose a fish (small Thunder & Lightning) in the Boat Pool. Came in early, as I felt v. idle. The King told me that Rommel[5] is no longer commanding in North Africa, but was withdrawn some time ago, annoyed, it is said, at the meagreness of the supplies reaching him. The Gloucesters arrived before dinner.

Wednesday 2 September

After luncheon, walked down to the Clachan Tarn, at the head of the Abergeldy water, which is one of the few pools here that can be fished from the bank. Fished it all down with a small Thunder & Lightning, without

---

1   Eamon de Valera (1882–1975), Taoiseach (Head of Govt) of Ireland 1937–48, President of Ireland 1959–73.
2   Adm. Sir Lionel Halsey (1872–1949), Comptroller to the Prince of Wales 1920–36.
3   Col. Lord William Percy (1882–1953), second son of the 7th Duke of Northumberland.
4   Lieut.-Col. Francis Balfour (1884–1965), retired political officer, worked at the Ministry of Food 1939–51.
5   Field-Marshal Erwin Rommel (1891–1944). One of Hitler's most successful commanders, he scored spectacular successes in N. Africa before being defeated at the Battle of El Alamein in the autumn of 1942.

moving anything. Then put on a small Silver Doctor, and at 5 p.m. (incidentally, the sun was shining right down the river at the time) hooked and killed a nice little fish of $8\frac{3}{4}$ lbs. Walked home, $2\frac{1}{2}$ miles, feeling much better, and got the Lovat Scouts, whose headquarters is at Abergeldy, to bring the fish up in one of their vehicles.

Thursday 3 September

I have a heavy cold in the head, and dined on my own – not that I felt ill, but I have a horror of spreading cold-germs about any house in which I may be. As a matter of fact, I hardly ever do have a cold since I started annual inoculations (which I am due to have next month).

At 6.30 p.m. we all went to the service in Crathie Church, held in connection with the National Day of Prayer ordained to commemorate the beginning of a fourth year of war. I suppose these occasions are a comfort to a great number of people; the King continually gets letters from all over the country urging him to have another one. But the idea behind them seems to me inconsistent with any enlightened system of theology. Zeus, in Homer, and Jahweh, in the Old Testament, were thought to be susceptible to the concentrated smell of large quantities of burnt offerings – i.e., com-munal worship on a big scale. But to me it seems an insult to any civilised Deity to imagine that he is affected, one way or the other, by mass-production prayers, decreed by Government – which is all these 'national days' really are. Moreover, it is an insult to all of us also; every decent man has 'prayed' many times on each day and night during the last three years, of his own initiative and without any stimulus from the temporal powers. I prefer to think that such prayers, however brief and humble, are more likely to touch the heart of the Immanent Will than any herd dem-onstration. But I am confessedly an ochlophile[1] in all matters pertaining to man's relations with God. In which I am, to some extent, supported by the authority of St Chrysostom (who admits 'two or three' to be a representative gathering). I watched the congregation during this particular service. Most of them, it seemed to me, were much more occupied in observing the royal party than in their own devotions. But I daresay they went home feeling the better for it, which is the great thing.

The poor old Grand Duchess Xenia,[2] a pathetic but dignified figure (sister of the late Tsar), came and sat with Their Majesties in church. They

---

1   The Greek *ochlos* meant a throng of people, or the populace.
2   Grand Duchess Xenia Alexandrovna (1875–1960), sister of Tsar Nicholas II, had escaped, with other members of the Russian royal family, to Britain in 1919 aboard HMS *Marl-borough*, which rescued many Romanovs at Yalta on the Black Sea.

have installed her in Craigowan (normally the Private Secretary's house here) for the duration of the war. I wonder if, in her heart of hearts, she would be glad or sorry to hear that the Germans had taken Stalingrad – as they so nearly have.

Sunday 6 September

Four of the Lovats' officers came to dinner, and we were made to play charades till midnight.

Monday 7 September

On re-reading the last sentence, I am conscious of its inadequacy. How annoyed I should be if, in the memoirs of Lord Hervey or of Fanny Burney, I came upon a bald announcement of George II or III acting charades with their families, and no further elaboration of the theme; how lacking in imagination I should think them for not giving posterity a more detailed account of so interesting an episode in court life. But the plain fact is that our charades last night, as doubtless those of either George might have been, were very ordinary, and indeed rather dull. Without vanity, I can say that my own impersonation of a St Bernard dog was the only histrionic feature of any real merit; incidentally, it strained my vocal cords so severely that I could hardly speak next morning.

To begin with, a team comprising the King and Queen, Eldons and P. Legh acted 'sequin'; the second syllable, presenting the famous quins of Canada, was a noisy but creditable piece of acting, though my own guess was that it represented the parrot house at the zoo. Then the audience – the two Princesses, Delia Peel, three Lovats and myself – took the stage and did 'parson'. It was in the first scene, an Alpine pass, that I was cast for the dog, with a cylinder which holds the ice for the drinks slung precariously round my neck as a brandy keg. In the final scene, our entry into the vestry, to the strains of Mendelssohn's Wedding March (rendered vocally) was effective. They were, in fact, very like the usual after-dinner charades in a country house, only rather worse.

Friday 11 September

On Wednesday the Lord Chamberlain (Clarendon) and the Vice Chamberlain of the Household (Boulton[1]) came all the way up from London to

---

1 Sir William Whytehead Boulton (1873–1949), Vice-Chamberlain of HM Household 1942–4.

present addresses of condolence on the death of the Duke of Kent from their respective Houses of Parliament. The King was aghast when I first told him of this project; but I pointed out to him that if it was the wish of both Houses that it should be done, and if they set so much store by their ancient privilege of having their Addresses put into the Sovereign's own hands, it would be a pity for the Sovereign to discourage them.

So up they came, and of course they missed their connection at Aberdeen; and as the grouse must be shot whatever may or may not befall, the King went out shooting, and arrangements were made to bring the two Chamberlains straight from Ballater station to the spot selected for luncheon. This was Corndavon lodge, and as nice a place in which to lunch as you could find in the British Isles. I went out with the Queen and Princesses, and though the actual meal was to be eaten out of doors – it was one of our few agreeable days – I made preparations for the ceremony to take place in the empty dining-room of the lodge. But the King, when he came down off the hill, would have none of this, but sat down in the heather, took their documents off the two plenipotentiaries as if they were game cards, and signed his own replies thereto on his knee, with everybody else unpacking the luncheon baskets and distributing plates and mutton pies all round him. I think this was wrong.

Luncheon over, the Chamberlains returned to Ballater and thence to London, stopping for three-quarters of an hour at Balmoral, where I collected for them a hamper to stay their stomachs at dinner time (there are rarely, if ever, dining cars on the night trains now) and showed them the Castle.

Saturday 12 September

At 1.35 I listened on the wireless to the account of the St Leger, duly won by the King's filly Sun Chariot, who must be a smasher. Five minutes after the race was over, a flag was hoisted by the Lovats on Abergeldy Castle – a prearranged signal to convey to the shooters on the hill that Sun Chariot had won. The only flag which could be produced was the Faroese one – the regiment has recently returned from the Faroe Islands – but that served the purpose as well as any other.

Joan sent me a letter from Lavinia announcing that she is 'unofficially' engaged to Tom Ruck-Keene, Lt. RN. I've only met him once, at Cloud's Hill, and thought him a particularly nice boy. Exactly what interpretation that generation puts on the word 'unofficial' in this connection, I don't know. I suppose it corresponds, more or less, to what used to be called 'walking out'. But I hope it means they are prepared to take things calmly, and give time a chance to prove, or disprove, their assumption that they are made for each other. Lavinia is only just nineteen.

Sunday 13 September

Church a.m., and Grand Duchess Xenia to luncheon, after which the King and Joey left for Dunrobin, where HM is to see the scene of the Duke of Kent's crash, and thank some of the locals who did good work in recovering the bodies. From such accounts as I have seen of the accident, it seems pretty clear that it was not safe flying weather, and that they ought never to have started.

Monday 14 September

Left Ballater 11 a.m. in the royal train, for Inverness, where I joined forces with Cameron of Lochiel[1] (the Lord Lieutenant) and Ian Grant,[2] the GOC District; and subsequently with the King and Joey, who arrived by motor from Dunrobin. We then drove out to Fort George and inspected the joint depot of Cameron Highlanders, Seaforths and ATS. The fort, built in 1747, is a good, solid monument to General Wade.[3] We left Inverness by train 6.45 p.m. Reading C. S. Lewis's *Problem of Pain*, which Joan sent me recently.

Tuesday 15 September

Reached Euston 9.45 a.m., and a stormy morning cleared up into a perfect autumn day. Mrs Ronnie Greville is dead of an apoplexy. ὡς ἀπόλοιτο καὶ ἄλλος.[4]

Friday 18 September   Cloud's Hill

Carting potatoes, of which we have a fine crop, I was continually struck by the resemblance which the average large potato bears to General de Gaulle, though the potato is, of course, the more malleable of the two.

---

1   Col. Sir Donald Cameron of Lochiel (1876–1951), Lord Lieut. and Governor of Inverness-shire 1939–51.
2   Maj.-Gen. Ian Grant (1891–1955), ADC to the King 1944.
3   Gen. (later Field-Marshal) George Wade (1673–1748) was sent in 1724 to the Scottish Highlands, where he built military roads, which survive to this day.
4   'ὡς ἀπόλοιτο καὶ ἄλλος ὅτις τοιαυτά γε ῥέζοι.' 'So may perish anyone else who does such a deed' Homer, *The Odyssey*, I, 47. The goddess Athene on the death of Aegisthus, who murdered Agamemnon, King of Mycenae, on his return from the siege of Troy, but was himself slain by Agamemnon's son Orestes.

Wednesday 23 September

We had a very happy week at Cloud's Hill, busy all day, and scarcely left the garden. I count myself lucky in having been born with the temperament, if not the skill, of a jobbing gardener. Among other things, we bedded-out four of the seven *Piptanthus nepalensis*, which we started to grow from seed, brought home by me from the bush at Windsor about a year ago. They are now nearly four feet high, and extremely handsome.

Back to London this morning, and think the news, taken all round, is better than it has been for a long time. The prolonged resistance of Stalingrad, whether it should ultimately fall or not, is decidedly a bull point. Our tank-state in Egypt has taken a very favourable turn since I went away. Alexander[1] can now dispose of a substantial number of the new Shermans, of which all our experts have great hopes.[2] But the best item of all is the fate of our last convoy to Russia. When I left, on the 16th, it had only just begun its perilous voyage, and had already lost twelve ships out of forty. It seemed inevitable that at least as many more must be sunk before it reached safety, and the extravagant claims which the Germans have been making led me to fear the worst. But not at all – twenty-seven ships got to port unscathed, and we destroyed a considerable number of German dive-bombers, and possibly as many as ten submarines. This is a very fine performance, and the lies which the Germans have told about it are a hopeful symptom.

The Queen has been laid up at Balmoral with what sounds like a sharp attack of 'flu. The King returned there tonight for a few days. He was to have started at 7 p.m., but an aeroplane – one of ours – crashed on to the main line near Tring this afternoon, and they could not get the track clear till 9 p.m.

Lord Bath[3] dined opposite me in the Travellers tonight – the youngest-looking octogenarian I ever saw. But I am annoyed with his daughter, Mary Nunburnholme, who, for the second time in a few months, has written to ask me if I can send out by official channels a letter to her revolting husband in the Middle East. The first time, I wangled it through Miles Lampson,[4] in Cairo, but I won't do it again, and have told her so.[5]

---

1 Field-Marshal Harold Alexander (1891–1969), Irish Guardsman of legendary courage (DSO, MC, seven Mentions in Despatches), C-in-C Middle East 1942–3, C-in-C Allied Armies in Italy 1943–4, Supreme Allied Commander Mediterranean Theatre 1944–5, Gov.-Gen. Canada 1946–52. Created 1st Earl Alexander of Tunis 1952.
2 The new American tank, capable of 26 mph, was equipped with a 75–mm gun firing explosive shells. The British Army used the Sherman at El Alamein in 1942, and by 1943 it was the mainstay of Allied operations in Africa and Europe.
3 Thomas Henry Thynne, 5th Marquess of Bath (1862–1946).
4 Miles Lampson (1880–1964), British Ambassador to Egypt and High Commissioner for the Sudan 1936–46. Created 1st Baron Killearn 1948.

Thursday 24 September

In the street met Eddie Devonshire, who, with Harry Harewood, is urging the King to become Grand Master of the Freemasons in this country. There has always been an unwritten law, I believe, that the Sovereign ought not to be a Mason – obviously his Roman Catholic subjects wouldn't like it – but I daresay it might do good on balance. I know very little about Masonic matters.

Friday 25 September

Walter Buccleuch's[1] name was recently suggested as Colonel of the newly-formed Lowland Regiment, which wears the Buccleuch tartan. On the face of it this seemed a very doubtful proposition. W.B. was at one time decidedly *lié* with Hess, if not with Hitler himself, and made no secret, before the war, of his pro-Nazi sympathies. They led, in fact, to his replacement by Hamilton[2] in the office of Lord Steward. But Iain Colquhoun[3] says that, in Scotland, the man-in-the-street knows nothing of these heresies, which Buccleuch has now recanted. He has become extremely military, and is a candidate for the chairmanship of the Scottish Territorial Association. In fact, Iain clearly thought that the lost sheep ought to be welcomed back into any convenient fold.

Sent the Queen a copy of *Epitaph for a Spy*, one of Eric Ambler's[4] excellent thrillers. I don't know who he is, but I remember thinking *The Mask of Dimitrios* a first-class book of its kind. John Weir,[5] their homoeopathic doctor, has gone up to Balmoral to settle when she can safely be moved south.

---

5 Mary Thynne (1903–74) had married Charles Wilson, 3rd Baron Nunburnholme, in 1927. The couple were divorced in 1947, when Mary married Tommy's colleague Ulick Alexander. Nunburnholme was wounded at Alamein and discharged from the Army in 1943.

1 Walter John Montagu-Douglas-Scott (1894–1973) succeeded his father as 8th Duke of Buccleuch and 10th Duke of Queensberry 1935, Unionist MP for Roxburgh and Selkirk 1923–35. He was at one stage widely suspected of being a Nazi sympathiser.

2 Douglas Douglas-Hamilton (1903–73) succeeded his father as 14th Duke of Hamilton 1940. Lord Steward of HM Household 1940–64. It was he whom Hitler's Deputy, Rudolf Hess, tried to contact when he flew to Scotland on an abortive peace mission in May 1941.

3 Sir Iain Colquhoun 7th Bt. (1887–1948), Lord Lieutenant of Dumbartonshire.

4 1909–98. Prolific author who between 1936 and 1940 wrote four other classic thrillers: *The Dark Frontier* (1936), *Uncommon Danger* (1937), *Cause for Alarm* (1938) and *Journey into Fear* (1940).

5 Sir John Weir (1879–1971) had been official physician to George VI since 1937, and in 1944 was elected first president of the British Faculty of Homoeopathy. The King was a firm believer in homoeopathic medicine, and counted Weir a close friend.

Saturday 26 September

We bombed Oslo yesterday, the target being the Gestapo headquarters, which one of our Mosquitoes claims to have hit; anyhow, according to Stockholm reports, we disturbed Quisling[1] at a big meeting, and drove him underground. Quisling has achieved the rare distinction of putting his name in the dictionaries of the world.

Sunday 27 September

Interesting telegram from Lisbon saying that Laval,[2] with a bullet still in the neighbourhood of his heart, is not the man he was, and inclined to despair, realising that he will never get any good out of the Germans. The chief German agent in France now is apparently Achrenbach, of whom I know nothing; Abctz is a mere cipher. Russian reports more reassuring. Joe Stalin has, it seems, come to the conclusion that it wouldn't be a bad thing to revive the Russian church, for he has sent the Metropolitan of Kiev to our embassy to suggest an exchange of visits between the Orthodox Church and the Church of England!

Monday 28 September

The King returned from Balmoral this morning, having left the Queen convalescent, though she won't be able to come south for another fortnight.

Billy Bishop,[3] the Canadian Air Marshal VC, dined with me at Pratt's, where were also A. P. Herbert[4] and Randolph Churchill,[5] whose appearance has greatly improved. After dinner, I brought Billy back to Buckingham Palace, and sent him in to talk to the King, which he did for one and a half hours. A bit of a scoundrel, Billy, but I am fond of him; and there is no

---

1 Maj. Vidkun Quisling (1887–1945), the Norwegian officer who collaborated with the Nazis. His name became synonymous with 'traitor', and after the war he was executed for treason.
2 Pierre Laval (1883–1945), extreme right-wing PM of France during the 1930s, became one of the leading French collaborators with the Nazis during the war, and survived an assassination attempt when shot at during a military ceremony at Versailles. He was executed for crimes against the State on 15 Oct. 1945.
3 Air Marshal William Bishop (1894–1956), VC, DSO and Bar, outstanding Canadian air ace in First World War. Director Royal Canadian Air Force 1939–45.
4 Alan Patrick Herbert (1890–1971), barrister, MP and humorous writer, was knighted in 1945.
5 Hon. Randolph Spencer Churchill (1911–68), son of Winston Churchill, journalist, author and Conservative MP.

doubt but that, in the last war, he was the supreme master of air fighting, on our side at any rate. Sam Hoare,[1] home on leave from Madrid, lunched with the King. Being an ambassador (and, I am bound to say, a devilish good one) has improved him. He impresses one as being much steadier in his nerves, and the stream of staccato 'Yes, yes ... Really, really', which used to characterise his talk, is less noticeable. Sam is very clever; but I have always felt that he is a bit *kibdelos* (spurious, base, deceitful).

Tuesday 29 September

The Prime Minister, at his weekly luncheon with the King, told him that he contemplated sending Stafford Cripps[2] to outer darkness. Displacing him would have caused a furore a few months ago; now, I don't think it will raise more than sporadic clamour – and none in House of Commons, which will presumably be led by Eden. Cripps's stock has slumped steeply, and it is now generally held that he did more harm than good in India. When he went to see Gandhi, he ostentatiously put off his shoes in the verandah – a foolish and unnecessary gesture, either insincere or undignified, which cost him the goodwill of many in India, white and brown. Winston had not heard of the incident; but I think it is true – the King has had it from two sources – from the Viceroy via Duke of Gloucester; and from the Jam Saheb of Nawanagar,[3] who was in here recently.

Wednesday 30 September

Clark Kerr[4] reports a very frank conversation with Wendell Wilkie,[5] lately in Moscow, when the latter opened his heart about the extreme dislike of the British which he had found, he said, at every point of his journey from

---

1 Samuel Hoare (1880–1959), Ambassador to Spain on Special Mission 1940–44. Created 1st Viscount Templewood 1944.
2 Rt. Hon. Sir Stafford Cripps (1889–1952). An austere, teetotal vegetarian, the younger son of 1st Baron Parmoor. Barrister and Labour politician. British Ambassador to Russia 1940–42, Minister of Aircraft Production 1942–5, President of the Board of Trade 1945. In March 1942 he was sent to India to negotiate with the Indian National Congress on defensive measures.
3 Maharaja Jam Saheb of Nawanagar (1895–1966), nephew of the great cricketer Ranjitsinhji, represented India on the War Cabinet 1942.
4 Sir Archibald Clark Kerr (1882–1951), British Ambassador to Russia 1942–6, established a good relationship with Stalin. Created 1st Baron Inverchapel 1946.
5 Wendell L. Wilkie (1892–1944), US lawyer and Republican politician, ran against Roosevelt in the 1940 presidential election, and although defeated won more than 22,000,000 votes – the most ever received by a Republican to that date. He then became a strong supporter of Roosevelt's war policies.

Washington to Russia – especially in Cairo. Himself, he said, he was a whole-hearted believer in the necessity of Anglo-American cooperation for the future of the world; but, if he found anti-British feeling overwhelmingly strong in USA, he would be unable to 'play with us', and he would not hesitate to say so. This is serious, for W.W. is very likely to be the next President – a recent Washington report said that F.D.R. had practically adopted him as his political heir; a very curious turn in American politics, that.

I am afraid his impressions are only too well grounded; we *have* made ourselves profoundly unpopular all the world over in the course of the last quarter-century. This is largely due, I believe, to the fact that we have been sending an inferior type of Englishman (and woman) to represent us, politically and commercially, overseas. But W.W., I was glad to notice, made it clear that his remarks did not apply to these islands; and here, if we only take it, we have a great chance of making the Americans understand, and like, us. The letters which the American troops over here write home will have more effect on public opinion in USA than all the laboured propaganda which the Foreign Office and Ministry of Information may evolve. So far, I believe, that part of the battle is not going too badly; it is an all-important one – the whole future of civilisation may hang on it.

Thursday 1 October

An interesting estimate of German casualties, based on the figures of the State Insurance companies, to which we have somehow obtained access; it tallies remarkably nearly with the War Office figures, got through their various intelligence channels. For the period 1-1-42 to 1-7-42: killed in action, 218,193; died of wounds, 80,977; of illness, 128,118; from accidents, 9,846; through suicide, 10,000. Total dead: 447,142. To this add a total of 555,527 wholly unfit for further service, and you get a gross total of dead loss to the Wehrmacht of 1,002,669. The same total *for the whole war*, up to and including above period, is put at 3,463,523. If these figures are correct, one can safely estimate that a further million, at least, will be put out of action during the last half of this year; so that by 1-1-43 fully 4,500,000 will have 'gone west', so far as further active participation in the war is concerned. These figures do not include naval casualties, nor air nor civilian ones; nor the partially unfit. On the whole, I find them distinctly encouraging. The number of suicides is remarkable. CIGS, in his comments, says they are probably due to fear of the Gestapo, rather than to loss of military morale.

Monday 5 October   **At Appleton**[1]

Today came here, where the King has been since last Friday. It is an ugly villa, built for, and inhabited by, Queen Maud of Norway, but not uncomfortable, though our quarters are cramped. The Duke of Gloucester and Michael Bowes-Lyon[2] are here. Today, in perfect weather, they shot 350 brace of partridges on the Flitcham beat.

I was so annoyed by the illogical and irrelevant attacks on William Temple[3] which have been appearing in *The Times* lately that I wrote a letter and sent it to Robin Barrington-Ward[4] (now Editor). He told me that he agreed with every word of it, and published it today. I had signed it with the initials 'CMS', which have been my literary alias ever since I started contributing to the *Malburian*, forty years ago; but the printer's devil changed it to 'CM 5' – perhaps as well, as I wrote from the Travellers, and some irate member whose initials are CMS might have lodged an indignant protest. I don't defend the *matter* of William Temple's speech; whether what he said about banking is sense or nonsense, I don't profess to know; what I do defend is his right, both as an Archbishop and as a citizen, to speak his mind on matters social or economic, if he feels so inclined.

Monday 12 October

A great storm is raging over the action of the Germans in chaining our prisoners of war, as a reprisal for the binding of their prisoners of war whom we took in recent commando raids, and our counter-reprisals. The trouble seems to have arisen through the Canadian commandos having issued orders on their own that prisoners taken during the raids were to be tied up, which they did without reference to our military authorities, and in ignorance, presumably, of the Geneva Convention. In this they were probably wrong; but even so, the temporary roping of prisoners, taken in the heat of battle, is a very different thing from putting manacles on prisoners in a prisoner of war camp.

---

1   The house on the Sandringham estate in Norfolk used by the Royal Family during the war, while Sandringham House itself was closed. It had been given by Edward VII to his daughter, Queen Maud of Norway.
2   Hon. Michael Bowes-Lyon (1893–1953), brother of the Queen.
3   Most Rev. and Rt. Hon. William Temple (1881–1944), Archbishop of York 1929–42, Archbishop of Canterbury 1942–4.
4   Robert Barrington-Ward (1891–1948), editor of *The Times* 1941–8.

Tuesday 13 October

Lampson, in Cairo, reports an interesting talk he had with Standley,[1] the American Ambassador to Moscow, who is on his way home. Smuts[2] was also present. Standley said that the Russians were not unduly perturbed by the Stalingrad situation, and that oil convoys are going up the Volga uninterruptedly. Stalin wants a lot of lorries, aluminium and wheat, of which there is a vast surplus in Canada; if he can get these, he is prepared to let us off, in part at any rate, our promises to supply tanks and aeroplanes. The second-front agitation, in Standley's opinion, is largely being kept alive as a bargaining counter, to put pressure on us to provide other things.

Thursday 15 October

I moved today back into my own room, 385. They have at last finished the immense catacomb (the air-raid shelter) which they have been building all these months, and have covered the top with grass; whether for appearance sake, or to deceive the Germans, I don't know. Joan and I went down to Collingham Gardens to see Helen, who is as ill as she can be.

Monday 19 October

Dora Maclagan [Eric Maclagan's sister] telephoned to say that Helen, who is evidently sinking, was not conscious today.

Our daylight raid on the Creusot works seems to have been a masterpiece of accurate coordination – and of accurate bombing, too. I have just read the Air Ministry's summary of the results of our raids over a period of six weeks. In most instances, especially at Düsseldorf and Duisburg, they seem devastating. The photographs make these great cities look like burnt-out wasp combs. One cannot wish things otherwise, but such successes bring no sense of victory. Yet I suppose the carnage of Blenheim or Trafalgar, or of any of the great victories of the past, was relatively no less shocking – save that it was limited in its effects, whereas the effects, actual and prospective, of this kind of warfare on European civilisation generally cannot be foreseen. The cannonballs of the old battles killed and maimed a few thousands of men; but they made no impression (other than political) on

---

1 William H. Standley, US Ambassador in Moscow.
2 Field-Marshal the Hon. Jan Christian Smuts, OM, CH (1870–1950), S. African soldier, lawyer and statesman, was PM of the Union of S. Africa 1939–48, and GOC Union Defence Forces in the Field 1940–49.

the course of the world's immediate development; these 4,000-lb bombs may make a radical and permanent one.

Helen died this evening, between 7 and 8 p.m. so quietly that the exact moment of her death could not be determined. She was sixty-three nine days ago. Her heart was broken by Gerald's death, and I do not think she had any great wish to go on living. She was a very remarkable woman – of great wisdom, courage and humour; which are the three major virtues.

Wednesday 21 October

Mrs Roosevelt[1] was to have arrived this evening, but she is weather-bound in Newfoundland, so all our plans have to be re-modelled. I have been arranging for the King and Queen to take her down to the City, to see the blitzed areas, etc., with a visit to St Paul's en route, and had some trouble with the Guildhall people, who claimed that the Lord Mayor and his minions have a prescriptive right to meet them on the steps of the cathedral. We resisted this, but they were stubborn, until I harangued the City Remembrancer (Bowker[2] – not a bad chap) on the telephone, and pointed out to him that for Mrs Roosevelt's visit to begin with a piece of mediaeval ceremony, interesting perhaps but unsuited to the exigencies of war, would be unfortunate, when the main object of her coming to this country is to take home to the USA an impression that we are devoting ourselves exclusively to the defeat of Hitler. Moreover, neither she nor the score of American Pressmen and photographers who will be present could be expected to understand why it should be necessary for the Lord Mayor and his posse to be in attendance whenever the Sovereign wants to take a distinguished visitor to see what is to them, and indeed to most of us, the national church of the United Kingdom.

When I told the Dean that he would be allowed to do the honours of his cathedral without molestation from the civic authorities, he was delighted, and told me that they had, in point of fact, no right whatever to appear on the steps, which are ecclesiastical, not municipal, territory.

Smuts addressed both Houses of Parliament this evening, and I listened to a recording of his speech on the wireless after dinner. He began somewhat platitudinously, but warmed up and produced some fine passages later on. His style is simple and incisive, without any attempt at elaborate oratory, and he conveys an impression of the great wisdom that he undoubtedly has. He got a remarkable demonstration, and was suitably thanked by

---

1   Eleanor Roosevelt (1884–1962), wife of the US President.
2   Sir Leslie Bowker (1887–1965), City Remembrancer 1933–53.

Winston. It is curious to think that only forty years ago he was our bitter and active enemy.

Thursday 22 October

Mrs Roosevelt is still fog-bound at Foyne, in Limerick; I got so bemused by constant telephoning about this that I have twice referred to her as 'egg-bound'. I got Sir Charles Wilson,[1] Winston's doctor, to lunch with me at the Travellers. He was interesting about the PM's air trips, and made my hair stand on end by his account of how nearly they have ended in disaster on more than one occasion. There will, I hope, be no more of them for the time being; but the trouble is that Winston himself thoroughly enjoys them, and there isn't a soul in the Cabinet, or anywhere else, who will undertake to dissuade him from any project on which he has made up his mind.

Wilson said that Winston took no interest whatever in post-war problems, or indeed in any problem other than the winning of the war; his mentality is that of a man with a gun looking for a mad dog, solely concerned with the shooting of the dog, and not with the fate of those whom it may have bitten. Well, feeling as I do about the dog, I am not sorry that he should be so single-minded in its pursuit, otherwise we might not get it shot at all – or not until the whole world is hydrophobic. But it is disturbing that there should, so far as one can see, be nobody capable of handling post-war problems with anything approaching the vision and drive which Winston has devoted to those of the war itself.

A great deal of good stuff has been written on such topics; but where is the man who is going to implement it? Textbooks on strategy are no use unless there is a general capable of seizing the right moment, and the right means, of putting their teaching into practice. I can't see any such general on, or even below, our present political horizon. I am a great believer in the ram caught by the horns in a thicket; but at the moment, even Abraham would find him hard to discover.

Of Stalin, Wilson said that he was an extremely astute peasant, with all a peasant's engrained suspicion of everybody with whom he may come in contact.

John, who has been promoted lieutenant, writes to me that two young lance corporals in the Grenadiers, wishing to play a practical joke on a

---

1 Charles McMoran Wilson (1882–1977), physician to the King and to Winston Churchill, was created 1st Baron Moran of Manton in 1943. Author of *The Anatomy of Courage* (1945), a much-praised study of bravery, and of *Winston Churchill: the Struggle for Survival* (1966), published little more than a year after its subject's death, and widely vilified for its exposure of the Prime Minister's frailties.

friend, connected the electric light flex with the handle of the door. When the man came in, the shock killed him stone dead; so now the lance corporals are faced with trial for manslaughter. As my father would have said, they will know better next time.

Friday 23 October

As a rule, I cannot abide the trite little obituary notes which individuals contribute to *The Times* about their dead friends; but today's issue has such an admirable one about Helen that I have cut it out and pasted it into this book. Save that it makes no mention of her transcendent sense of humour, it is a perfect tribute to her.[1]

Mrs Roosevelt materialised at last, arriving 4.30 p.m. at Paddington, where the King and Queen met her, and her sole attendant, Miss Malvina Thompson. There was a notable dinner party for her at Buckingham Palace – Winston and Mrs Churchill, old Smuts and his son Jacobus, Elliott Roosevelt and the Louis Mountbattens.[2] I went in afterwards, to see the naval film *In Which We Serve*, recently produced by Noël Coward,[3] with D. Mountbatten[4] as his expert adviser. There are some admirable scenes in it, many of them intolerably moving; but I thought the tempo too rapid all through, and the abrupt changes of scene confusing. Noël Coward is unexpectedly good as the captain of the ship whose story the film tells, and his touch is sure; but, as on the stage, he speaks much too fast. To a sailor, I expect it is enthralling, for I believe it shows a sailor's life in wartime with entire accuracy; and it will do a lot of good to landsmen, who even now don't know what the Royal Navy has done for them, and is still doing for them, day and night.

My view of it was somewhat interrupted, for Winston was like a cat on hot bricks, waiting for the news of the start of Alexander's offensive in Egypt. This, as a matter of fact, had begun at 8 p.m. our time, and I had to go out in the middle to get the news by telephone from No. 10. After a brief interval, nothing would content Winston but to go to the telephone himself. His conversation evidently pleased him, for he walked back along the passage singing 'Roll out the barrel' with gusto, but with little evidence of

---

1   The obituary, anonymous in the newspaper, was written by Dame Una Pope-Hennessy. It described Helen as 'dependable, warm-hearted, generous ... stalwart, positive and often blunt, she inspired one with the conviction of complete faithfulness in things great and small'.
2   Mountbatten had married the Hon. Edwina Ashley (1901–60) in 1922.
3   Actor, playwright and composer (1899–1973). Made his first stage appearance aged eleven. Knighted 1970.
4   Mountbatten's nickname was Dickie.

musical talent. This astonished the posse of footmen through which we had to pass. I wondered what their Victorian predecessors would have thought, had they heard Dizzy, or Mr G., singing 'Knocked 'em in the Old Kent Road' in similar circumstances. I can't remember when I was last in the same room as old Smuts, but it must have been twenty years ago, and I could see no change in his appearance.

Saturday 24 October

We took Mrs Roosevelt on a tour of the City and East End this afternoon, beginning with half an hour in St Paul's. The swells were taken in charge by the good Dean, Matthews,[1] while I secured Cockin,[2] once in the sixth form at Marlborough with me and now a Canon, to conduct Miss Thompson and myself. In the crypt I saw for the first time in my life the incredible vehicle built to carry the Duke of Wellington's coffin. Built of solid bronze, it weighs God knows how many tons, and though drawn by twenty-four horses, it stuck so often on the way to St Paul's that it was three hours late getting there. It is a monstrous affair, and Cockin agreed with me when I said it ought certainly to be melted down as scrap. Nelson's tomb is, of course, bricked up as a precautionary measure.

Thence we went on to the ARP control room for the City, in Moorgate; drove through the blitzed areas of Stepney, of the Commercial Road – no longer such a scene of devastation as it must have been before the grass sprang up to cover the debris, but still a shocking sight; went over the huge underground shelter at the junction of Commercial and Whitechapel Roads – a grim, evil-smelling place, like the Catacombs; Miss T. said to me nervously, 'I hope somebody knows the way out', and it certainly gave one an unpleasant, claustrophobic feeling. Then to the Guildhall; they have got a roof on it now, and it looks comparatively normal, but the library and other rooms at the back are still an appalling mess. The last time I saw it was for the luncheon in June 1939, when the King spoke on his return from America.

We finished up with tea at the Mansion House, with old Laurie,[3] the Lord Mayor; Montagu Norman,[4] the Governor of the Bank of England, was there, and I reminded him how his brother Ronnie, when asked thirty years ago to recommend a safe mentor, under whom I could start my career

---

1 Very Rev. Walter Robert Matthews (1881–1973), Dean of St Paul's 1934–67.
2 Rt. Rev. Frederic Cockin (1888–1969), Canon of St Paul's 1938–44.
3 Lieut.-Col. Sir John Laurie (1872–1954), Lord Mayor of London 1941–2.
4 Montagu Collet Norman (1871–1950), Governor of the Bank of England 1920–44. Created 1st Baron Norman of St Clere 1944.

in the City, had selected G. L. Bevan, who within a few years got seven years' penal servitude for fraud. Old Montagu Norman always intrigues me, with his Mephistophelian beard and air of mystery. I am not at all sure that his reign as the uncrowned king of our national and international finance has not been an unqualified disaster. But I have never been able to understand such matters sufficiently to form a definite opinion of my own.

I dined at Buckingham Palace that night; Ernie Bevin,[1] Minister of Labour, and Woolton,[2] Minister of Food, were the only outside guests. I told the latter that I hold him a very fortunate man, for he is the only man in the Government at whom I have never heard anybody express the wish to throw a brick. He, or his ministry – and I think the man himself probably deserves most of the credit – have done a wonderful job in keeping these islands safe not merely from actual starvation but even from really short commons. Ernie Bevin, enjoying himself in every pore of his gross body, got on like a house on fire with Mrs Roosevelt, who, I believe, thoroughly enjoyed her day.

After dinner he smashed to fragments one of the King's pet brandy goblets by pinching it to see how strong it was. When the goblet exploded like a shell, the King merely said, 'Now you'll want some more brandy.' To which Ernie replied, 'Thank you, Sir, I think I will.' Two great gentlemen. Incidentally, the King invited him to squeeze the thing.

Alec Hardinge said he believes Bevin to be an honest man; I prefer to reserve judgement for the present.[3]

Sunday 25 October

No detailed news from Egypt, save that we secured practically all our first objectives. Eighth Army tank strength at the start of the battle was over 1,200. Smuts, the other evening, prophesied success, but said we should have a tough job in the initial phase, and suffer heavy casualties. Meanwhile, we are sending bombers to Genoa and Milan day and night.

Mrs Roosevelt, who now passes under the wing of the American Embassy, left Buckingham Palace 10.20, and I then drove down to Windsor with Miss

---

1 Rt. Hon. Ernest Bevin (1881–1951), Labour MP, started life as a farm labourer. For many years he was Secretary of the TGWU. Successful Minister of Labour and National Service 1940–45, and effective, tough Secretary of State for Foreign Affairs 1945–51.

2 Frederick James Marquis (1883–1964) was created 1st Baron Woolton of Liverpool in 1939. As Minister of Food 1940–43, he was blamed by members of the public for shortages caused by wartime rationing. The Woolton Pie, a meatless confection whose charms he promoted, attracted particular obloquy. He was created 1st Earl of Woolton in 1956.

3 In 1956 Tommy added a footnote: 'Ernie Bevin, whom later I came to know well, was indubitably an honest man, and a great Foreign Secretary. I was very fond of him.'

Crawford,[1] the King and Queen, who went to the Guards' Chapel with the Princesses, following later. I like Mrs Roosevelt; she looks like a she-camel, and is tough; but I like her, and see dignity, and even greatness, in her.

Wavell[2] has had two good articles on genius in generalship in *The Times*. I cut them out and sent them to John. Wavell writes admirably – terse, and with a Tacitean touch. He puts tactics ahead of strategy, and won't concede a first class to either Napoleon or Alexander (the Great, not GOC Middle East), with which I agree. Napoleon was a consistently lucky man; and Alexander inherited a perfectly trained and equipped Panzer army, so to speak, with which to fight people who were forty years behind the times. So no wonder he always over-ran them, just as the Germans over-ran the Poles. Caesar he qualifies as not much more than a 'sepoy general'; a bold statement, but perhaps not far wrong. Marlborough and Belisarius are his first choices, with Wellington, Hannibal and Scipio not far behind.

Down to Eton after luncheon, and sat in Luxmoore's garden with Tuppy Headlam, talking about what we used to call at Oxford 'God, freedom and immortality'. He agrees with me that pure theology is a science devoid of content, and so a fruitless study for humans.

Tuesday 27 October

In the Travellers at lunchtime I picked up Eric Linklater's little book *The Raft*,[3] and liked it so much that I bought two copies on the way home; one for myself, and the other I sent to Miss Malvina Thompson, telling her she will learn from it a lot about this country of ours, and maybe something about her own.

My cousin, Freddy Dalrymple-Hamilton,[4] now a Rear-Admiral, dined with me at Pratt's. He has been commanding our naval forces in Iceland, and has just come home to take on the job of Naval Secretary at the

1 Marion Crawford (1909–1987), governess to the Princesses Elizabeth and Margaret from 1932, always known as 'Crawfie'. She married a fellow Scot, Maj. George Buthlay. Egged on by him and by the American Beatrice Gould, editor of the *Ladies' Home Journal*, she published her memoirs, *The Little Princesses*, in 1950, thereby incurring powerful royal displeasure.
2 Gen. Sir Archibald Wavell (1883–1950), famous for his extreme taciturnity, was C-in-C, India, 1941–3, during which time he was also ADC General to the King. In 1943 he was promoted Field-Marshal and from 1943 to 1947 he was Viceroy and Gov.-Gen. of India. *Other Men's Flowers*, his anthology of verse compiled from poems he knew by heart, was published in 1944, to great acclaim. Created 1st Earl Wavell 1947.
3 *The Raft, and Socrates Asks Why: Two Conversations*, a discussion of Britain's international political future.
4 Adm. Sir Fredrick Dalrymple-Hamilton (1890–1974) was Naval Secretary to the First Lord of the Admiralty 1942–4, and second-in-command of the Home Fleet, 1944–5.

Admiralty, which suits me well, the N.S. being our channel of communication for all matters naval. The last time I saw him, he was Captain
of the Royal Naval College at Dartmouth, when the King and Queen went
there in July 1939. Since then he has commanded *Rodney*, and played an
active part in the sinking of the *Bismarck*.[1]

Wednesday 28 October

Joan and I to see *Henry IV Part I* at the little Westminster Theatre off
Buckingham Palace Road; what a play it is – not a dull line in it. Atkins[2] was
an A1 Falstaff – not too noisy and sack-sodden, and unfailingly humorous. It
was a good, all-round cast, but a moderate house, including Duff[3] and
Diana Cooper. Duff has got to look very paunchy and bloated.

I looked up the dates for the play last night. The action is obviously in
1403 – battle of Shrewsbury. At that time, in point of fact, Henry IV
was only thirty-seven, Hal fifteen, and John of Lancaster not more than
fourteen. If Falstaff were, as he suggests, about fifty-six, then in Part II
(death of Henry IV 1413), he would have been getting on for seventy. But
you can't act Part 1 with the King other than middle-aged, or with Hal and
Hotspur much less than twenty. Another inaccuracy of Shakespeare's is
that Edmund Mortimer was Hotspur's father-in-law, not brother-in-law.
But these are mere pedantries, which affect the greatness of the play not at
all.

Thursday 29 October

To Windsor p.m. At tea, Gerald Kelly,[4] Henry Game[5] (the Lord Chamberlain's reader of plays) and I were talking of Henry Wilson.[6] I told them
of my last personal encounter with him, shortly before he was murdered. I

---

1 The largest and most modern of German battleships was sunk on 27 May 1941 by ships
  and aircraft of the Royal Navy after an epic pursuit over 1,750 miles, lasting nearly five
  days.
2 Robert Atkins (1886–1972), actor and producer, had managed and produced the plays
  in the Open Air Theatre, Regent's Park, since 1933.
3 Duff Cooper (1890–1954), Minister of Information 1940–41, Chancellor of Duchy of
  Lancaster 1941–3, Ambassador to France 1944–7, had married Lady Diana Manners in
  1919. Created 1st Viscount Norwich 1952.
4 Sir Gerald Kelly (1879–1972), artist and art historian. President of the Royal Academy
  1949.
5 Henry Game (d. 1966), Examiner of Plays in the Lord Chamberlain's Office, 1936–52.
6 Field-Marshal Sir Henry Wilson (1864–1922), CIGS from 1918, was murdered by two
  members of the IRA on 22 June 1922.

was leaving the Travellers with Aubrey Herbert,[1] when the Field-Marshal joined us as we walked down Pall Mall. He and Aubrey started a discussion on Ireland, then the burning topic of the day. Aubrey said that the man in the street would not stand for something or other – I forget what. 'My dear Aubrey,' said Henry Wilson, 'the man in the street knows no more about Ireland than does this little citizen here,' and to illustrate his point seized a small, inoffensive man who was hurrying past us, shook him once or twice and dropped him in the gutter.

John Gore was probably the last person to speak to Henry Wilson. They passed the time of day on the steps of the Travellers. H.W. got into a taxi, and ten minutes later was shot down in the door of his house in Eaton Square. His wife did infinite harm to his memory by prematurely publishing his disjointed diaries, without getting anybody wiser than herself to edit them, and without reflecting that they were not the type of diary which a man wants read by anybody at all, let alone the public.

Sunday 1 November   **Windsor**

The Egyptian battle goes on steadily, and, I pray, surely; the reports from Alexander are laconic, but quite satisfactory as far as they go.

Yesterday the Germans tried a small, concentrated raid (the first such for months) on Canterbury, just before dusk. They sent thirty machines, and according to Air Ministry reports our fighters destroyed six and damaged five: AA destroyed three, damaged one; balloons destroyed one – i.e., less than fifty per cent got home scatheless. These figures should deter them from making a habit of such raids; and Canterbury is only about a dozen miles from the coast.

Have re-read R. L. Stevenson's *Wrecker*; a good book, but he don't sustain the interest. I had forgotten that the scene of adventure is Midway Island, which has figured so much in the Pacific war; and that the foppish naval lieutenant was called J. Lascelles Sebright. I wonder what made R.L.S. pitch on that combination of names; my great-great-uncle (I think) was the Rt. Hon. William Sebright Lascelles, but I can't imagine how R.L.S. ever heard of the old boy, unless he chanced on his name in some book of reference.

A few days ago I went into my house at St James's Palace and noticed that my faithful old grandfather clock, which has stood at 1.32 ever since we evacuated ourselves two years ago, has moved on, of its own volition, to 1.44. It is locked, and nobody can have wound it up or tampered with it,

---

1 Aubrey Herbert (1880–1923), second son of the 4th Earl of Carnarvon, father of Evelyn Waugh's second wife Laura.

so one can only infer that it is getting ready to welcome us home. *Prosit omen!*

I wrote this evening to Arthur Ponsonby, to congratulate him on the collection of his father's letters (Sir Henry Ponsonby, so long Private Secretary to Queen Victoria) which appeared recently under his expert editorship. I was concerned with the genesis of this book, having been called on to 'vet' the proofs, which A.P. rightly sent for the King's approval last spring. Neither Alec Hardinge nor I found anything to object to, but there was some opposition in the Royal Family, headed by Queen Mary, who thought that it was too soon to give the world such intimate details of Queen Victoria's life as the book inevitably contains.

Possibly it might have been better, in normal circumstances, to wait until the few remaining relations of Queen Victoria who knew her well are dead – e.g., Princess Beatrice (who I think is gaga, anyway), Princess Alice,[1] and Queen Mary herself. On the other hand, Arthur Ponsonby himself is no chicken, and his wish to see these papers, which are of considerable historical value and a great tribute to his father, properly launched under his own auspices, is quite understandable. Moreover, Henry P. has been dead nearly fifty years, and, generally speaking, half a century is quite long enough for private papers to lose any sting that they might have for contemporaries.

But, apart from the question of a time-limit, Queen Mary, I believe, took the line that they ought never to be published at all – indeed, that they ought never to have been *written*, and that a private secretary has no business to mention his work in his letters to his wife. That attitude is typical of the ostrich technique which this family so often adopts. Here you have an authoritative and definitive picture of a great sovereign, drawn by one of the most loyal and faithful servants a sovereign ever had, who literally dedicated his life to her service, and probably shortened it thereby. The picture is frank, and at times, no doubt, reveals defects in its subject; but it is essentially true, and just, and if greatness can't stand the searchlight of truth and justice, then it is but smallness.

As a matter of fact, H.P.'s picture of Q.V. don't detract one whit from her greatness; in the judgement of sensible people, the reputation of celebrities of her unquestioned calibre is, if anything, enhanced by the knowledge that they were not immune from ordinary human shortcomings – witness the wholesome revulsion from the 'pedestal' school of biographers, who, by sedulously concealing the weaknesses of their subjects, made their very

---

1   1883–1981. Granddaughter of Queen Victoria, married Alexander Cambridge, the first and last Earl of Athlone, brother of Queen Mary. She wrote a volume of memoirs, *For My Grandchildren.*

strengths seem unreal. Moreover, there is the 'anti-pedestal' school to reckon with – the sensation-mongering, 'black-washing' biographers. Plenty of them may yet try their hands on Queen Victoria; but the ground is largely cut from beneath their feet, when the world has already been given such a frank and unimpeachable account of her, by one who really knew to a millimetre both her good habits and her bad.

Take only one instance: unsavoury legends have sprouted, toadstool-like, on the curious obsession which Queen Victoria had for John Brown.[1] They can sprout no more; H.P. makes frequent allusions to John Brown, which make it quite clear that he was a drunkard and a nuisance, and that Queen Victoria carried her fondness for him to the point of foolishness; but equally clear that that is the whole story, of any more sinister side of which, had it existed, H.P.'s letters would certainly have shown some trace.

I feel strongly that nothing written by private secretaries should be published within a considerable time after their principals' deaths – its length varies in proportion to the importance of the principals in the historical perspective, and to the longevity of their immediate relations and descendants. It would distress me, for instance, if I thought that any allusion to the present King made in this book would be made public prematurely. But if Queen Mary's dictum were taken literally, if those 'behind the scenes' were never to put pen to paper, history would lose some of its most informative documents, and literature some of its treasures. Pepys, St Simon, Lord Hervey and Charles Greville, just to mention a few, would all have to be scrapped.

Nor is it fair to argue that the reputations of the defunct great always suffer from such confidential records; on the contrary, they are often enhanced – e.g., James II in Pepys's diaries. In my own letters to Joan during the years that I served the Prince of Wales, there is, so far as I recollect (I've never seen them since I posted them) a good deal of criticism; but there is also much that shows him in a better light than he might appear to some hostile biographer writing long after he is dead. Equally, there may be in them evidence to confound anybody who tries to sling mud at other members of his family for their attitude towards the Abdication. I don't see how history can arrive at the truth if contemporaries are not allowed to write it.

Tuesday 3 November   **Buckingham Palace**

In a brief telegram to Roosevelt this morning Winston implied that we

---

1 Queen Victoria's favourite Highland retainer was rumoured to have been her lover.

were in sight of great things in Egypt. Pray God he may be right. Joan came to London and lunched with me at the Ritz, where I was waylaid by Lady Astor, who wants the Queen to write an article for some American magazine – *Home Life*, I think. Americans can't realise the peculiar, indeed unique, position of a King and Queen in this country. It is nothing to do with pomposity, or precedent; but there are, in the British conception of sovereignty, certain things which those who exercise it just cannot do; in the same way that the Pope just couldn't go to a race-meeting, or the President to a bawdy house.

I had, reluctantly, to give an audience to Lady Leconfield[1] this afternoon; she is as mad as a march hare; but E. Miéville, whom I had suborned to burst in on us after twenty minutes, with news of an entirely imaginary meeting waiting my presence, did his job to perfection. But for that, I believe she would be here still. Her trouble, so far as I could make out from her really insensate monologue, is the Bruntisfield divorce, about which I know little and care less.[2]

Sunday 8 November

The balloon went up in North and North-West Africa, and the Americans made, apparently successfully, their various projected landings. I first heard of this operation, under its code-name 'Torch', some six months ago, and

---

1   Beatrice (d. 1956), who was later certified insane, wife of the 3rd Baron Leconfield (1872–1952).
2   Lady Bruntisfield, formerly Dorothy Rawson, was Lady Leconfield's sister. She and her husband, Victor Warrender, 1st Baron Bruntisfield (1899–1993), were divorced in 1945. Later, in a letter to Lady Delia Peel, Tommy enlarged on the incident:

> I recollect clearly my telephone at Buckingham Palace ringing one morning, and there was Calamity Kate [Kate Seymour, a lady-in-waiting] in a terrible stew. 'What *am* I to do?' she said. 'I've told Lady Leconfield she can come and see me, and you know, she's dreadfully old now. What *can* I say to her?' (Lady Leconfield had, at that time, just been surprised walking down the stairs at Claridge's without any clothes on at all – not C.K.'s way of going on.)
>
> 'Well,' said I (Don Quixote), 'you can tell the footman to show her into my room.' And that's what happened.
>
> She walked in, carrying an enormous empty trug, sat down in my armchair and lit a cigar. It was quite clear she was as mad as forty hatters, so there was I, wondering what I could say to the footman when he came in and found me all alone with a stark naked peeress. She wanted me to get the King to do two things: (a) To legitimise the Wyndhams, who are, genealogically, all bastards, and (b) to stop Warrender from divorcing her sister Dolly, who was carrying on no-how with quite a few Polish officers. She went into great detail about both these requests, but I did eventually convince her that the King had no more power to grant either of them than his predecessor, King Knut, had to stop the tide coming in.

have carried the secret uneasily in my bosom ever since – a difficult burden, when one has heard so much foolish talk about 'second fronts' going on around one.

Tuesday 10 November

The more I hear and read about 'Torch', the more I admire the staff work which has made it possible. It was a stupendous undertaking, executed, I should say, as efficiently and forcefully as any military operation in history. Winston, in his speech, gave the credit for its original conception to Roosevelt; but I believe it belongs more truly to himself.[1]

The effect of the past week's events on one's own state of mind is inexpressible; before it, one needed a bearing rein to keep his head up; now, a martingale to keep it down. What chance has a diarist in these days? The world canvas is so vast, the details on it so crowded, that detached comment is impossible.

Wednesday 11 November

The King opened Parliament and had Smuts to luncheon, leaving in the evening to visit British and American airfields. Thick fog, but the difference from the old-time pea-souper, due to the small amount of coal now being burned, is very marked. I went to see *The Importance of Being Earnest*. A star cast (Gielgud,[2] Edith Evans etc.), but I was only moderately amused. Too much wit and too little humour; and some of the wit is downright silly. The characterisation is poor, also – Lady Bracknell, Canon Chasuble and Miss Prism are just 'comic characters', lay figures whose bones rattle audibly under their smart trappings.

The fog was so thick when I came out of the theatre (the Phoenix, right down the Charing Cross Road) that all traffic had ceased, and I had to foot it to Pratt's, with only a moribund electric torch; I was rather proud of getting there without a single mistake. The policeman at Buckingham Palace, when I asked him if the King had got to Euston all right, said, 'Oh yes, but we had to take him there by hand' – which I suppose means that a policeman had to amble along on each side of the car.

---

1 This contention was strongly supported by Pug Ismay in his memoirs of 1960 (p. 281).
2 John Gielgud, actor and author (1904–2000). This was his production of *The Importance*, and with Edith Evans (d. 1976) playing Lady Bracknell it was considered definitive for a generation. She was created a Dame, 1946, and he was knighted 1953.

Saturday 14 November   Windsor

D. Kavanagh told me that Smuts, when he took him to see the King the other day, said, 'We can never trust the French, for they can never forget that they were masters of Europe for 200 years.' That is a very profound remark; and so perhaps is Winston's summing-up of Darlan – 'He's a bloody swine.'[1]

Sunday 15 November

This morning church bells throughout the country, dumb since June 1940, were bidden to ring again in honour of our victory. It was certainly heartening to hear them, and I doubt if there is much to be gained by reimposing the ban on them. Whether they could ever serve a good purpose by ringing an alarm if the Germans land in this country is questionable. While I was at Holton,[2] in the winter of 1940, there was a false alarm, and the local bell started to toll in the middle of the night. Most of the Home Guard, who should have rushed to their action stations, took not the slightest notice, and, when rebuked for their apathy, said, Yes, they had heard the bell, but had thought it was a funeral.

This alarm was started, I believe, by some junior officer on the staff of the Southern Command who, being possessed of the gift of mimicry, thought fit to exercise it by ringing up some colleague and telling him, in the voice of the GOC, that the Germans were upon us. This was taken seriously, the code-word (Cromwell) announcing such an event was sent to all stations, and the result (so far as it affected me) was that at about 1 a.m. Melville Balfour,[3] minus his false teeth, poked his head round my bedroom door and announced, 'They've landed'. We then spent several hours shivering over the telephone in the smoking-room, and did not get back to bed till some sort of an 'all clear' message arrived about dawn. The young gentleman responsible for all this (improbably named Shufflebotham) was, I am glad to say, subsequently tried by court martial, but escaped with nothing worse than a severe reprimand.

Delia Peel and I rendezvoused with Bear Warre, son of the former Head Master of Eton, who is staying in Eton, and took him over the Curfew Tower, an interesting corner of the Castle which I had never before seen. The clock, built by one Davis in Charles II's time, is a remarkable bit of

---

1   Adm. Jean François Darlan (1881–1942) allied himself with Pétain after the fall of France in 1942 and sided with the Germans. Assassinated at Algiers, 24 Dec. 1942.
2   Holton Park, near Wheatley, the Balfours' home in Oxfordshire.
3   Tommy's brother-in-law, married to his sister Daisy.

work, and the oak beams, which for more than 600 years have defied all kinds of marauding insects – even spiders shun them – are extraordinary. Old Sutch, the belfry-keeper, who is an intelligent guide, said he believed they were impregnated with some solution of which the secret is lost, but of which the basis was probably honey. Then to the organ loft in St George's. After the service Harris[1] played us the Bach B-minor toccata and fugue, and a César Franck chorale. Looking down on the choirboys during the anthem, I reflected that they were probably thinking of whether there would be buns for tea and similar mundane matters, and were quite unconscious that, for those of us up aloft, they were the authors of a volume of sound of transcendent beauty.

Perhaps we too, as we go about our earthly business, are also, though we never know it, the threads in a texture of beauty.

Monday 16 November

John writes that he was graded 'Distinguished' on passing out at the Southern Command Weapons Training School at Woolacombe Bay, where he has been for the last six weeks. They pressed him to remain as an instructor, but he rightly preferred to return to his battalion, where they have put him in charge of the snipers.

Tuesday 17 November

The Americans have won a considerable naval victory over the Japs in the Solomon Islands – not a Trafalgar, no doubt, but certainly a Quiberon Bay or Cape St Vincent. Yet, at a crowded luncheon to which Joan and I went, I never heard it mentioned. This is not apathy; I think it is because we do so much intensive thinking and talking about the war after the various BBC bulletins and after reading our newspapers that we put it from us when we see our friends.

[At the buffet lunch, for a wedding] somebody once said that a Buckingham Palace garden party was like the day of Resurrection, one saw so many people whom one had long thought of as dead. There is something of the same atmosphere about these rare wartime social functions; but they are, perhaps, more like going through a cupboard full of clothes that one has put away for a period; and, alas, the ravages of time and the moths are often only too apparent. There is also the constant dread of asking after

---

1 William Harris (1883–1973), organist of St George's Chapel Windsor 1933–61, President of the Royal College of Organists, 1946–8. Knighted 1954.

somebody's son, husband or brother, who, for all one knows, may have been killed months ago.

Still, this particular gathering was an agreeable one, though more representative of our generation than that of the bride and bridegroom. Old Margot Asquith was there, sitting unusually quiet in a corner; Lady Salisbury,[1] Eddie Marsh,[2] the Roger Fulfords,[3] Walter de la Mare,[4] etc. I fell in early with Lady Desborough[5] (who can't be far off eighty, and looks little different from what she did thirty years ago); she had written me that morning one of her highly confidential notes, asking me in effect if I thought Lady Leconfield (a friend of hers) was potty, or not potty. I had no hesitation in saying – with due reserve and circumlocution – that I certainly thought she was.

Thursday 19 November

Returned to London this evening from a two-days tour of Liverpool and Manchester – King and Queen, Patricia Hambleden,[6] D. Kavanagh and myself. Lancashire, as usual, mustered remarkably large and enthusiastic crowds; a million people, young and old, must have seen Their Majesties in the course of the two days. At Liverpool we went to Headquarters Western Approaches, where Percy Noble[7] (who is succeeding Andrew Cunningham[8] as head of our naval mission in USA) was on the point of handing over to Max Horton.[9] It was interesting to see the brains of our anti-U-Boat campaign in the Atlantic, though, as usual, I didn't understand more than half

---

1 Wife of the 4th Marquess of Salisbury (1861–1947), formerly Lady Cicely Alice Gore, daughter of the 5th Earl of Arran. Before the Trinity Ball of 1909 Tommy had sat next to her 'and loved her', describing her as a 'delightful chaperone'.
2 Sir Edward Marsh (1872–1953), classical scholar, civil servant and author. Private secretary, at various times, to H. H. Asquith, Winston Churchill, the Duke of Devonshire, J. H. Thomas and Malcolm MacDonald.
3 Roger Fulford (1902–83), royal biographer, married Sibell Lyttelton 1937. Knighted 1980.
4 Walter de la Mare, OM (1873–1956), poet and author.
5 Ethel (Ettie) Fane (1868–1952), wife of the 1st Baron Desborough (1855–1945) and mother of Julian Grenfell, author of the celebrated poem 'Into Battle', who died of wounds in May 1915. Tommy had known the family since he was an undergraduate.
6 Lady Patricia Hambleden (1904–94), wife of 3rd Viscount Hambleden, Lady-in-Waiting to Queen Elizabeth.
7 Adm. Sir Percy Noble (1880–1955), C-in-C Western Approaches 1941–2, Head of British Naval Delegation in Washington 1942–4, First and Principal Naval ADC to the King 1943–5.
8 Adm. of the Fleet Sir Andrew Cunningham (1883–1963), OM, First Sea Lord and Chief of Naval Staff 1943–6. Created 1st Viscount Cunningham of Hyndhope 1946.
9 Adm. Sir Max Horton (1883–1951), Flag Officer Submarines 1940–42, C-in-C Western Approaches 1942–5.

what I was told. I liked the new regional commissioner up there – Hartley Shawcross,[1] a rising young lawyer, just forty, who seemed to me highly efficient under a nonchalant exterior. They all like him in those parts, and told me that he is a first-class speaker.

Monday 23 November

To Cloud's Hill for luncheon on Friday. A lovely weekend, still and sunny, with the beech trees all burnished. I did some valuable digging, and with John's help finished off the dead limb of the oak tree in front of the house, which had defeated Cecil Liddell[2] and me a fortnight ago.

The Russians seem to have attacked successfully north-west of, and behind, Stalingrad. Cabinet changes, more or less as foreshadowed to me by the King some weeks ago: S. Cripps leaves the War Cabinet and takes aircraft production, *vice* Llewellin,[3] who goes to USA; A. Eden remains at Foreign Office, but will lead House of Commons; Bobbety Cranborne[4] takes Lord Privy Seal, and Oliver Stanley[5] goes to Colonial Office.

Leo Amery's[6] son – another knave, of criminal tendencies – is interned in Germany. Last week the Germans announced that he would speak on the Berlin radio. L.A. listened to the broadcast, and declares that the voice was certainly *not* that of his son.

Tuesday 24 November

The Dean of Westminster (de Labilliere[7]) lunched with me at the Travellers.

---

1 Hartley Shawcross (1902–2003), barrister and MP, Chief Prosecutor for the UK at the International Military Tribunal at Nuremberg (1946), Attorney-General 1945–51. Knighted 1945, created 1st Baron Shawcross of Friston 1959. The gloomy title of his autobiography, *Life Sentence* (1995), reflected an existence more troubled than Tommy suspected.
2 Tommy's cousin, who worked in Intelligence.
3 John Jestyn Llewellin (1893–1957), Minister Resident in Washington for Supply 1942–3, Minister for Food 1943–45. Created 1st Baron Llewellin of Upton 1945.
4 Robert Cecil, Rt. Hon. Viscount Cranborne (1893–1972), Secretary of State for the Colonies 1942, Lord Privy Seal 1942–3 and 1951–2, Secretary of State for Dominion Affairs 1940–42. Leader of the House of Lords 1942–5. Succeeded father as 5th Marquis of Salisbury 1947.
5 Rt. Hon. Oliver Stanley (1896–1950), politician, Secretary of State for the Colonies 1942–5.
6 His son John, known as Jack, became a fascist, broadcast enemy propaganda from Italy, and was hanged for treason in December 1945.
7 Rt. Rev. Paul Fulcrand Delacour de Labilliere (1879–1946), Dean of Westminster 1938–46, gave his recreation as 'Silence'. His great-nephew, Gen. Sir Peter de la Billière (who spells his name thus), commanded the British forces in the Gulf War of 1990–1.

I like him, and have always admired him for his unruffled fortitude the day after the Germans blew his beautiful deanery and all his possessions into dust and ashes during one of the worst Blitz-nights.

Thursday 26 November

A great Thanksgiving Day tea-party at Buckingham Palace this afternoon, to which some 200 American officers of all grades were bidden, with our Chiefs of Staff and such ladies as wartime London can produce. They were a nice lot, easy to entertain, and seemed to enjoy themselves thoroughly. The party was an unqualified success and may do a lot of good. The American officers were a very agreeable and well-behaved lot. With my past experience of transatlantic cocktail parties, I was struck by the quiet of this one; usually there is such a din of staccato voices that one can't hear himself speak. I believe the explanation is that the company at most such affairs to which English people usually go consists largely of folk from the north-eastern seaboard of America, where that deafening pitch of voice peculiar to New England, New Jersey and Ontario predominates. A great many of the officers serving in the US forces come from the West or Middle West – from Oklahoma, Ohio and Colorado, states quite unknown to us – where the native way of speaking is much more like our own. One young officer, enjoying a whisky and soda, was heard to say, 'I never get Scotch at the White House. I like this king-racket.'

Friday 27 November   Windsor

Tonight came the news that the Germans had occupied Toulon, and that the entire French fleet had scuttled itself. The bottom of Toulon harbour is probably the best place for it, in the long run, and this will finally sabotage the German pretence of 'cooperation' with France; nor will they ever dare now to arm any portion of the French army, while the French ships in Dakar and Alexandria will now probably be willing to take an active part on our side.

Began Arthur Bryant's[1] *Years of Endurance*, which promises to be a good book. In his preface he makes the point that it was, in part, his outlook *as a historian* that enabled Winston to rally the country after the fall of France: 'He knew that the lonely and desolate place in which his country stood was one in which she had stood before.'

---

1 Sir Arthur Bryant (1899–1985), historian. His series of books covering the period of the Second World War included *Unfinished Victory* (1940), *The Years of Endurance* (1942), *The Turn of the Tide* (1957) and *Triumph in the West* (1959). Knighted 1954.

Saturday 28 November

Walked down to Eton after luncheon with the P. Leghs, hoping to find a few friends [at the traditional St Andrew's Day celebrations]. As usual on such occasions, the first three people I met were the three biggest bores in England – John Christie,[1] O. Chadwyck-Healey[2] and Stephen Trevor.

Wednesday 2 December

Clark Kerr, our present Ambassador in Moscow, came to see the King. He said that, as regards geography, Russian communiqués were generally accurate, though he was not prepared to vouch for the reliability of their figures, of prisoners, captured guns and tanks etc.; but that when the snows had melted last spring, vast quantities of dead Germans had undoubtedly been revealed. I don't think the Russians ever tell him, or any other Foreign Mission, much about the details of the war.

Thursday 3 December

In the House of Commons yesterday 'Mr Eden commended as an epitome of good sense Mr Sumner Welles's[3] warning against an attempt from purely idealistic motives *to try to impose American standards on all peoples*, and he believed that that represented the great bulk of American opinion.' Well, that's exactly what the Foreign Office and the Ministry of Information are continually doing to us, with their recurrent requests for the Queen to pander to American journalists by giving interviews, answering questionnaires etc. They don't seem able to realise that, as long as there is a Monarchy in this country, it must conform to *British* standards, and cannot sacrifice them in order to 'promote good relations' (which is often only a euphemism for 'curry favour') with other nations who have quite other standards.

I am not the least pompous, or courtier-ish, about the Monarchy; on the contrary, I take perhaps too pragmatical a view of it. But I am convinced that, in any human society, people who fill offices of this kind ought to abide by the rules of conduct expected of them by those who put them there – and pay them. Exalted labourers, no less than humble ones, must be worthy of their hire; in the case of the British Royal Family, there are

---

1 John Christie (1882–1962), a former Trinity man, founder of the Glyndebourne opera.
2 Oliver Chadwyck-Healey (1886–1960), barrister and publisher, had also been at Trinity with Tommy.
3 Sumner Welles (1892–1961), US diplomat, Under-Secretary of State 1937–43, adviser to the President throughout the war.

certain things which the nation expects them to do, and certain things which it expects them *not* to do – e.g. not to marry a certain type of woman, as was shown with crystal clearness in 1936.

This is not because they are 'royal'; it is because their job-in-life has certain definite obligations. The Roman Catholic church would never tolerate a Pope who went habitually to Monte Carlo, nor the House of Commons a Speaker who came to the House in knickerbockers and a flannel shirt, because Popes and Speakers are not *meant* to do that sort of thing. And the British public do not think that the members of its Royal Family – certainly not the Queen Consort – are meant to publicise themselves in the Press, *à la* Mrs Roosevelt. The same idea was expressed by H. J. Massingham[1] in a phrase that has always stuck in my head, though it must be thirty years since I read it, in some article of his: 'The British people have no use for the chatty, handy type of monarch.' I believe that to be profoundly true; and, incidentally, it explains why Edward VIII, who thought chatty handiness was the beginning and end of kingship, would never have made a good King; or explains it in part – there were a variety of other equally cogent reasons.

I have been moved to write all this because a certain Mrs Gould[2] of USA, proprietress of the *Ladies' Home Journal*, which has an admittedly wide circulation in America, is making herself a great nuisance to me just now. She came over here more or less under the capacious wing of Mrs Roosevelt, and seems to have got a stranglehold on Richard Law,[3] now Parliamentary Secretary at the Foreign Office, and on that very foolish fellow Ronnie Tree, ditto at the Ministry of Information. Mrs G, after flagrantly gate-crashing Windsor Castle while Mrs Roosevelt was having her farewell tea with Their Majesties – a disgraceful episode, which let Delia Peel and me in for a very unpleasant quarter of an hour – wanted the Queen to answer (for publication in the *Ladies' Home Journal*) a long and elaborate questionnaire about the position of women all over the world, involving every sort of political, racial and religious issue. This was finally turned down, in a letter which I had to draft, and which I fondly hoped would dispose of the woman. Not at all.

I got yesterday a long letter from R. Law, enclosing the typescript of a wholly imaginary conversation between the Queen and Mrs R., and

---

1 Harold John Massingham (1888–1952), author of many books, especially about the British countryside.
2 Beatrice Blackmar Gould and her husband Bruce (both 1898–1981) were joint editors of the *Ladies' Home Journal*.
3 Richard Law (1901–80), journalist and MP, Parliamentary Under-Secretary of State at the Foreign Office 1941–3, Minister of State 1943–5, Minister of Education 1945. Created 1st Baron Coleraine of Haltemprice 1954.

recommending that Mrs Gould be given permission to publish it. The conversation is innocuous, and consists largely of pious sentiments about women's work, most of which the Queen has already expressed, and expressed better, in her own broadcasts. What prejudices me against it is that it is such a palpable *fake*. No sensible American, or Englishman, is going to believe that it is a genuine record of an actual talk between the two ladies. USA will, therefore, not be taken in by it, and UK will dislike their Queen being involved in such an obvious bit of machine-made propaganda. Consequently, it will do more harm than good – which is the first test I always apply to the multifarious requests involving Their Majesties which continually confront me.

Ever since I first went to USA in 1924, I have done what I could to better relations between this country and those who live on the other side of the Atlantic. This object was, in fact, one of the reasons which led me to transplant myself and my family to Canada for five years. But, the older I grow, the more certain I become that these relations are only harmed by artificial, patent-medicine propaganda; intelligent homoeopathy is the only system – continual and repeated doses of *individual* contacts, plus the familiarisation of each side with the cultural influences of the other, and intelligent interpretation of the political and social problems of both. The aphorism that 'Anglo-American relations will be all right so long as nobody tries to improve them' is perhaps too sweeping; but I prefer it to the principle that they will be improved by the use of the largest and most blatant advertisement hoardings which the Press and the radio provide.

Tuesday 8 December

The solution of the problem [of choosing a new Viceroy] was to prolong Linlithgow's term of office for six months – i.e., till October 1943. I suppose it is the best plan. Opinions as to L.'s merits as a Viceroy differ widely; the majority vote him a non-success. From what little I know of him, I should not say he is a great man; he is a curious mixture – pompous and sententious one moment, and the next indulging in the crudest schoolboy humour. An example of the latter is a stupid, vulgar Xmas card which he has just sent the King (who was disgusted with it), and which, if circulated throughout India as it doubtless will be, for it is obviously the official card of the Viceroy and Vicereine, will do serious mischief.

The Queen sent for me after luncheon and asked me to give Mrs Gould her quietus; so I waited on the lady in her room at the Ritz and talked to her for fifty minutes, during which I trust I convinced her that, though the Queen is brimming with sympathy for her objects, she (the Q.) had good reasons for deciding that Mrs G.'s proposed scheme is not the best method of furthering them. She's not a bad sort of woman *au fond*, though suffering from a rush of moral uplift to the head; and is probably quite sincere in her mission to make the women of the UK and USA understand each other better. But, as Kipling says, once a journalist, always and for ever a journalist. That is her trouble; she could never quite forget, it seemed to me, what a wonderful scoop for the *Ladies' Home Journal* this precious interview of hers would be. However, we parted the best of friends – outwardly, at any rate.

Wednesday 9 December

The King and Queen went off to Glasgow this evening, where she is due to launch *Implacable*, one of the new aircraft carriers. Rumour that Rommel has abandoned his El Agheila position and retired in the direction of Tunis; also that he is at sixes and sevens with the German High Command on the whole question of their North African strategy, he wanting to get right out while he can, and they ordering him to stay on at all costs. The campaign, whatever its ultimate issue, must anyhow be as great a drain on German resources as the Peninsular was on Napoleon's.

Friday 11 December

Lit. Soc. luncheon. Old Ian Hamilton,[1] rising ninety, asked me if I could explain to him why, when he dined with Queen Victoria at Osborne, some fifty years ago, the butler had filled each guest's glass with champagne poured simultaneously from a bottle held in each hand – like a French waiter pouring out *café-au-lait*. I couldn't; nor could the King enlighten me when I put the problem to him as we drove down to Windsor in the afternoon.

There are two other antiquarian riddles which I want to solve: One, when the Privy Council gave up writing 'Let the Messenger hasten' on their envelopes. Two, the claim of the Rev. Coppinger Hill, who writes to say that Henry VIII, in 1513, granted his ancestor and his descendants the right, *in perpetuo* of wearing their hats in the presence of their Sovereign.

The King is disturbed in his mind just now because Winston has foolishly thought fit to bring up again the question of the Duchess of Windsor becoming an HRH – which, God knows, is not going to make the world a better or a worse place, whichever way it be answered; and also because, in

---

1   Gen. Sir Ian Hamilton (1853–1947), GCB, DSO, took part in the Afghan War (1878–80), the Nile expedition (1884–5) and the Burmese expedition (1886–7), as well as in campaigns in Chitral, Tirah and S. Africa. He was CoS to Lord Kitchener 1901–2.

his last letter to Winston, Roosevelt begins 'My Dear Winston', and refers to O. Lyttelton[1] as 'Oliver', *tout court*. Well, I can't see that that matters much, either.

This afternoon the final performance of the Windsor pantomime, performed by the two Princesses and a posse of local school children, was given in St George's Hall. It was *The Sleeping Beauty*, and I felt rather apprehensive that I should myself qualify for the title-role. But I enjoyed it immensely; it was an admirable show, largely through the genius of Mr Tanner, the schoolmaster, who must be a first-class producer, and who, I believe, wrote most of the book. Some of the scenes would have done credit to Drury Lane, and the whole thing went with a slickness and confidence that amazed me. John, on his way to rejoin his battalion at Warminster, turned up and came to see it with me.

Alec Hardinge is away at Crichel, and I've had a busy day, with a spate of boxes. Eighth Army report that Rommel has withdrawn the bulk of his forces (said now to number 50,000) from El Agheila to a place called Buerat, on the west curve of the Gulf of Sirte. This will put another troublesome lap on to our lines of communication through Libya; on the other hand, the nearer Rommel gets to Tunis, the less food he is likely to find.

Sunday 13 December

In church this morning we sang 'Jesus shall reign'. The line 'The prisoner leaps to lose his chains' seemed to me tempting providence, when we are waiting to hear whether the Germans will or will not respond to our gesture of 'unshackling'. On the other hand, there was appropriateness in

'Let every creature rise and bring
Peculiar honours to our King',

for it is the couplet which always comes into my head when grappling with the letters and telegrams on the King's birthday (tomorrow), some of which are always very peculiar indeed.

Lady Castlerosse is dead, and, incidentally, they are holding an inquest on her. I never saw the lady, but Ulick Alexander (who is a gossip) told me the following. When Valentine Castlerosse[2] achieved his success as a journalist, he was making so much money that Beaverbrook feared he

---

1 Oliver Lyttelton (1893–1972), President of the Board of Trade 1941–2, Minister of Production and Member of the War Cabinet 1942–5, Secretary of State for the Colonies 1951–4. Created 1st Viscount Chandos 1954.
2 Valentine Browne, Viscount Castlerosse, 6th Earl of Kenmare (1891–1943), a bibulous crony of Beaverbrook's, had married Doris Delavigne in 1928 and divorced her in 1938.

would retire, and his services be lost to the *Sunday Express*. So he engineered a marriage between C. and the lady, who was a notorious international gold-digger, of most expensive habits, in the hope that she would spend so much of C's money that he would be obliged to stick to journalism. The medicine worked all right, until C. could stand her no longer, and separated from her; whereupon Beaverbrook, not to be outdone, brought them together again – temporarily, at any rate, for they have been divorced now for some years. A pretty story; what people do say about each other.

Monday 14 December

The King's birthday, and I have now (8 p.m.) grappled with over 150 telegrams, and have just told the telegraph-clerks (no doubt to their satisfaction) that I don't intend to grapple with any more tonight.

Tuesday 15 December

To London early. Investiture. After luncheon I went to see R. Law at the Foreign Office, and explained to him the reasons behind the Queen's refusal of Mrs Gould's request. I told him that, in weighing the merits of any request put to Their Majesties, one always had to take account of three factors: (1) Their *personal* reaction to it, as human beings; (2) Whether granting the request was consistent with the general rules of the game of Monarchy in the abstract; (3) Whether the amount of good which granting the request might do would outweigh the harm done by any infringement of those rules, which must admittedly be elastic up to a point. I reminded him, too, that the King and Queen looked to the Foreign Office to be a bulwark against, rather than an endorser of, obviously impracticable requests put forward by foreigners, however well disposed. He was quite understanding, and I think somewhat contrite, knowing that he had allowed his head to be ruled by his heart. He told me that Mrs G had returned to the USA in quite a good frame of mind, with her enthusiasm for this country undiminished.

In the current *Fortnightly* Harold Laski[1] has an article, inspired by Ponsonby's book, on 'The King's Secretary'. Alec Hardinge, discussing it with me tonight, said it appalled him when people wrote portentously about the amount of mischief which a King's secretary could do if found wanting in a time of crisis. Apropos the 1931 episode, which Laski instances as an example of the Crown's role in times of political stress, he told me that

---

1   Harold J. Laski (1893–1950), professor of political science in the University of London 1926–50, author of legal studies.

Wigram had very little to do with King George V's famous return from Scotland to London, and that the whole thing was inspired by Ramsay MacDonald.[1] Laski questions whether the King is ever justified in stepping down from the pedestal of absolute impartiality, even to save the constitution – i.e., he must always abide by the advice of his Ministers or, presumably, abdicate.

Thursday 17 December

Darlan has made several speeches, the substance of which ought to reassure even the most suspicious; but he has contrived to give himself such a bad name that most people persist in thinking that hanging is too good for him.

Monday 21 December

The Director of Army Education (now Burgon Bickersteth[2]) is producing a series of pamphlets for the instruction of the troops during the winter months, of which the first two numbers, sent me by B.B., are quite excellent. The series is called 'The British Way and Purpose', and gives synopses of the machinery of government, parliamentary and local, the social services, law, education etc., with an introduction, 'What is at Stake', giving the reasons why we are at war. They are written very simply and lucidly, and reading them has improved my own sadly deficient education in public affairs.

Tuesday 22 December

There is a tiresome *scompiglio*, as Greville would say, going on here over the question of where the lady clerks are to get their luncheon when the King and Queen are away, and the establishment is on board-wages. It is no direct concern of mine, but, as usual, those whose it is come to me in rotation and advance unanswerable arguments against whatever solution the other parties may have proposed. This wastes much of my time, and of my temper. It sounds, and is, a very trivial matter, except to the unfortunate females, for whom, in wartime conditions, it isn't easy to find an adequate meal in this neighbourhood.

---

1 On Friday 21 Aug., 1931, King George V left London by train for his annual holiday at Sandringham, but returned the next night in an attempt to solve the country's acute financial and political crisis. The PM, Ramsay MacDonald (1866–1937), offered to resign, but the King's intervention helped persuade him to stay on and form a National Govt.
2 John Burgon Bickersteth (1888–1979), Director of Army Education 1940–42.

Monday 28 December

The feature of the Xmas news was the assassination of Darlan in Algiers, by a boy of twenty, a Frenchman with an Italian mother, whose name is variously reported in today's telegrams as Fernand Bonnier de La Chapelle and as Bonny Chapelier. Nothing has yet been revealed as to his motives (he was shot yesterday) save that he is supposed to have had strong anti-Vichy prejudices. Whatever the causes, the effects of his action will certainly resolve what threatened to develop into a very unpleasant situation. All seems to be quiet in Algiers, and, as I hoped would happen, Giraud has been nominated as Darlan's successor. Meanwhile, operations in Tunisia are largely held up by mud, Rommel continues his retreat, and the Russians their southward advance. Altogether, it was a far brighter Xmas than we have had for many years.

The King delivered his broadcast extremely well, with only one slight hesitation, over the word 'cannot'. On the whole it sounded quite reasonably good stuff, and the confidence and emphasis with which it was delivered seem to have impressed people.

At Cloud's Hill, which I left early today, we read aloud an appreciable amount of the first volume of that great book, H. A. L. Fisher's *History of Europe*.[1] Writing it undoubtedly hastened his death, and it has always been a source of satisfaction to me that I was partly instrumental in getting him an OM before he died. I went to see him at intervals, over a period of years, and always admired his clear, ascetic brain.

Dined with C. Liddell at the Travellers. He told me of the conversations, overheard and recorded by us, between von Thema, the Prussian general recently captured in Libya and now in this country, and his room-mate. They habitually refer to Hitler as '*der Teppichbeisser*' [the carpet-biter], so apparently the legend of his carpet-biting paroxysms is well-founded. They inveigh against his constant interference with the dispositions of the German Higher Command – especially at Dunkirk, where, but for Hitler's contrary orders, they could have concentrated enough artillery to make our embarkation impossible. Altogether, they seem to be profoundly discontented with the *Partei* and with the Führer.

---

1   Herbert Albert Laurens Fisher (1865–1940), politician and historian. His three-volume *History of Europe* was first published in 1925.

1943

Friday 1 January

The New Year Honours List is so long that, with newspapers as limited in space as they are now, it has been thought necessary to publish it in two parts. The first appeared today. One of the new peers is Charles Wilson [Lord Moran], who held all lords in abhorrence when I knew him in the last war.

Monday 4 January

Arthur Penn gave me to read an account of the arrival in Algiers, and subsequent adventures, of the battalion of Grenadiers now out there, written by young Nigel Nicolson,[1] Harold's second boy; an admirably-written, vivid document, inspired by all the enthusiasms proper to a sub-altern entering on his first campaign. Particularly good was his description of the grand parade, on Austerlitz day, when Giraud – 'a king of a man' – got all the applause, and Darlan, fussing round like a provincial mayor, got none.

In Pratt's this evening, where was A. P. Herbert, indescribably grubby as usual, and still in command of some small vessel patrolling ·the lower reaches of the Thames; and Mouse Fielden,[2] still doing the very interesting job of running the aeroplanes which drop people behind the lines on the Continent, and pick them up again after an interval. He said that the bombing of the American Flying Fortresses was very accurate, but the number of German fighters that they claim to have bagged much exag-gerated. They are like the City gents who all shoot simultaneously at the same pheasant, and if it falls to earth, all claim it as the captive of their own bow and spear.

It is significant that, when two or three are gathered together, the talk now is not whether or when we shall beat the Germans, but how we shall dispose of them when they are beaten.

Writing to John today for his twenty-first birthday next Monday, I was struck by a strange coincidence. I spent my twenty-first birthday – or part of it – at Lulworth, where I have never been since; John Gore had been

---

1 1917–2004 MP, author and editor, published the official history of the Grenadier Guards in WWII.
2 Air Vice-Marshal Sir Edward Fielden (1903–86), Capt. King George VI's Flight 1936–52, and the Queen's Flight 1952–62.

doing a reading party there, and on 10 April I rode over from Sutton on our brown pony, and the following day (my birthday) we both went back to Sutton. Now, thirty-five years later, my son will spend *his* twenty-first birthday at the same place, where he has never been before.

Thursday 7 January

I was elected a little while ago to the Beefsteak club – an unwarranted extravagance on my part, but, leading this sort of life, I get so sick of seeing only the same people at the Travellers or Pratt's that I must have a change. Went there for luncheon for the first time today. It is run on much the same lines as Pratt's – a single room, with one long table; it is an unwritten law of the club that you take the first vacant chair, and talk to your neighbours.

Monday 18 January

General Bertie Lawrence[1] is dead – a great and good man. I always thought of him and his wife, my cousin Isabel Mills, as the ideal couple for a Governor-Generalship. Yesterday Lloyd George[2] celebrated his eightieth birthday, on which the King sent him a congratulatory telegram; a wicked old man, but we owe him as great a debt for his courageous leadership in 1916–18 as we do Winston for his conduct of the present war.

There was an air-raid on the London area in the early part of last night – only a small force of raiders, of which seven have so far been reported as destroyed. A live AA shell fell, and exploded, in the flower beds outside our offices at Buckingham Palace, but it don't appear to have done any damage.

Tuesday 26 January

We have entered Tripoli, and the Russians have had spectacular success at Voronezh and in the Caucasus; Leningrad has been relieved, and the Germans have spoken publicly and to their own people of 'the defeats sustained by our armies'.

John Gore wrote to me a few days ago, quoting an account, given him by an anonymous friend, of a conversation with Winston:

I said, with truth, that the war had destroyed the last fragment of my

---

1   Gen. the Hon. Sir Herbert Lawrence (1861–1943), veteran of many campaigns, including the Boer War, the Dardanelles, Egypt and France during WWI.
2   David Lloyd George (1863–1945), Liberal politician, PM and First Lord of the Treasury 1916–22. Created 1st Earl Lloyd George of Dwyfor 1945.

brain. He said that his, on the contrary, had never been so good; that he made better speeches than ever before and with less preparation, and that his memory was a miracle.

I asked if he didn't find anxiety very tiring? He said, 'I am never anxious.' He then began a close analysis of his own character – 'I am arrogant, but not conceited' – and was so entranced by it that he missed his indispensable after-luncheon snooze.

Re-reading some of this diary tonight, I was appalled to find how completely I had already forgotten some of the happenings, and people, mentioned in it only a few months ago. Unlike Winston, I find that the war has had a sad effect on *my* memory; and the war – or *anno domini* – makes me prone to strange absences of mind. Not long ago I had to write a letter to old Lady Ailsa,[1] who had sent the King some rubbishy pamphlets. I dictated the letter, which was brought to me, as usual, with the beginning and the end blank, to be filled in by me. This I thought I had done; but my secretary subsequently brought it back to me and pointed out that I had begun 'My Dear Lady' and ended 'Yours sincerely, Ailsa'.

Wednesday 27 January

A communiqué about the Casablanca conference was released last night, and it excludes practically all other news from today's newspapers. Of its results, only two important facts have been made public – F.D.R.'s 'unconditional surrender' pronouncement, and the fact that de Gaulle and Giraud were brought together there, and made to rub noses. But I gather that, behind the closed doors, all went well. The newspapermen are delighted by the discovery that Casablanca means White House. It will, no doubt, prove to be one of the most momentous of all such conferences since that of Lucca.[2]

Thursday 28 January

Mima Harlech,[3] writing from South Africa on 28 December, says of Smuts: 'Our Prime Minister returned absolutely delighted with his visit, and tremendously impressed both by the organisation of everything, and even

---

1 Isabella (b. 1891), widow of the 3rd Marquis of Ailsa.
2 When Caesar, Pompey and Crassus renewed their triumvirate in 56 BC.
3 1891–1980. Wife of William Ormsby Gore, 4th Baron Harlech, High Commissioner in the Union of S. Africa 1941–4. She was formerly Lady Beatrice Cecil, daughter of the 4th Marquess of Salisbury.

more by the people all over the country. He does give one a greater feeling of security and poise than almost anyone I've ever met.'

The Bishop of Mashonaland said to her that, greatly as he admired Smuts, he considered him a very callous man – 'He is passionately interested in the battle between Good and Evil, but not at all in how many people are killed.' In other words, he takes a sternly objective view of the war, as, I should say, every successful statesman must of any human problem. But I don't think that necessarily implies callousness; a general may be greatly moved, as a man, by the length of his casualty list – as Wellington was after Waterloo – even though he don't allow his emotion to affect his judgement, as a soldier, regarding the pros and cons of any military action.

Monday 1 February

Winston has achieved his meeting at Adana with the Turks and seems well pleased with them and with the results of their conversations. He has now gone to Cyprus to see his regiment, 4th Hussars, and should be back in Cairo tonight. Alec Hardinge having gone to Crichel, sick, and Eric Miéville still laid up after his recent operation for varicose veins, I am single-handed, and fully occupied.

Tuesday 2 February

Lunched Beefsteak – Duff Cooper, A. P. Herbert, C. B. Cochran[1] etc. I had never met Cochran, the famous theatrical producer, before; a quiet, distinguished-looking man, with great charm of manner. [*Later note:* He invariably drank an Imperial pint of champagne at 11 a.m., every day. That, of course, is the right time to drink it.]

Wednesday 3 February

Tedder,[2] Air Chief Marshal, came this evening to get knighted, and receive his GCB [Grand Cross of the Bath]. I had a brief talk with him and took a great liking to him. He is obviously a man of outstanding personality, and every airman will tell one that he is one of the brightest stars in that

---

1 Sir Charles Blake Cochran (1872–1951), theatrical manager, impresario and producer. Among his achievements he included 'Introduced roller skating in France, Germany and Belgium'.
2 Marshal of the RAF Arthur William Tedder (1890–1967), AOC-in-C RAF Middle East 1941–3, Deputy Supreme Commander under General Eisenhower 1943–5. Created 1st Baron Tedder of Glenguin 1946.

particular firmament. He is about to take over supreme command of the air in North Africa, an appointment which everybody welcomes. He brought with him a son and daughter, whom I showed what there is to see in this war-battered palace while he was with the King. Lady Tedder, poor thing, was recently killed in an air crash in Egypt.

Old Sir W. Holdsworth,[1] author of the monumental *History of English Law*, also came in, to get his OM. He began his magnum opus in 1901, published Vol. XII in 1928, and has still, he told me, got two or three volumes more to finish. Winston has reached Tripoli safely, and goes on to Algiers and then Gibraltar tomorrow.

Ken Stuart, Chief of the Canadian General Staff, told me a good story of Montgomery.[2] One of his staff asked another why he had issued a certain order. 'Because,' said the other, 'the Lord God Almighty told me to.' Monty, who had entered the room unseen, laid his hand on his shoulder and said, 'That's right, my boy; that is how I like my officers to speak of me.'

Friday 5 February   **Windsor**

Mack sent in an admirable day-to-day account of the Casablanca meeting, so far as it concerned de Gaulle and Giraud, with some intimate notes on the principal actors in the now somewhat sordid tragedy of France. De Gaulle, by refusing to go out there when he was told to, arrived three days too late, and, when he had got there, seems to have behaved with intolerable petulance and vanity.

It is the same story with all these Frenchmen – as soon as you try to negotiate with them, they waste half the morning vituperating other Frenchmen, much as de Valera prefaces every conversation with a lengthy tirade against Oliver Cromwell. So far as I can judge, Casablanca has brought us not a whit nearer the solution of the French problem.

Linlithgow telegraphs that Gandhi has now definitely announced his intention to put himself on a diet of 'fruit juice and water'. They have been arguing for weeks about what to do with G. if he goes on hunger-strike; at the last meeting of the Viceroy's Council, Firoz Khan Noon[3] made what has always seemed to me the only sensible suggestion – viz., to say to

---

1 Sir William Holdsworth (1871–1944), professor of law. He never completed his great work.
2 Gen. (later Field-Marshal) Sir Bernard Montgomery (1887–1976), Commander of 8th Army in the great victory of El Alamein in Oct. and Nov. 1942, C-in-C British and Allied Armies in N. France 1944, Commander 21st Army Group 1944–5. Created 1st Viscount Montgomery of Alamein 1946.
3 1893–1970. Barrister, Defence Member of Viceroy's Executive Council, India, 1942–5. Indian Representative British War Cabinet 1944–5, PM of Pakistan 1957–8.

Gandhi, as soon as he starts fasting, 'All right – we will have no truck with political blackmail of that sort. You leave prison, and if you die outside of it, that is your concern. But as soon as you have done your fast, you will come back.' That is, of course, only a variant of the cat-and-mouse tactics adopted with the suffragettes in 1912; but, if it is a clumsy manoeuvre, it was efficacious then, and, in Gandhi's case, what other alternative is there to either releasing him unconditionally, or letting him die in gaol – either horn of which dilemma we must avoid at all costs?

We came down here after luncheon, and immediately on arrival I dashed out to the saddler's in Eton to get my braces mended – a matter of great urgency now, when one can't buy new ones anywhere.

Winston, who had taken Tripoli and Algiers in his transcontinental stride homewards, is flying back from A. tonight. No. 10 have just (11 p.m.) assured us that the Mediterranean weather is perfect, and that the Air Ministry are quite happy about conditions nearer home; but the glass has been falling all day, and the wind, if not howling, is moaning dolefully, so one cannot but feel rather anxious.

Saturday 6 February

My apprehensions were groundless, as the PM never started after all. His Liberator developed slight engine trouble, so he is taking another day at Algiers – possibly, in his own phrase, not without relish.

Sunday 7 February

Winston arrived safely at Lytham about 10 a.m., and talked to the King on the telephone after luncheon. Busy all day, but went up to the organ loft for evensong in St George's. Harris played Bach's Passacaglia as a voluntary. The wind has got round to the north-east, which always makes Windsor like an ice-house.

Wednesday 10 February   Buckingham Palace

There is a refreshing element of flippancy in the telegrams which F.D.R. and Winston exchange; in his last one, the former says (referring to the de Gaulle–Giraud relationship) 'How are things between your bride and bridegroom, and is the crockery flying about? I hope the marriage has been consummated.' There was a good telegram from Alexander, too: 'On 18 August you instructed me to expel the enemy, with all his impedimenta, from Egypt, Libya, Cyrenaica, and Tripolitana. This has now been accomplished, and I await your further orders.'

His further orders, which Winston is to announce in the House of Commons tomorrow, will be to range himself under Eisenhower[1] as Deputy C-in-C of the Allied army, while Tedder takes supreme command of the air. All who know him agree that 'Ike' Eisenhower is a thoroughly honest and capable soldier. C. Portal, to whom I sat next at luncheon today, was loud in his praises.

Friday 12 February

E. Miéville, his leg looking like that of a horse that has got into barbed-wire, has returned to duty; and A. Hardinge, though still far from well, is back at St James's Palace and able to deal with the boxes. So I went down to Cloud's Hill, where I found Joan a bit better [after a hysterectomy and a severe attack of sciatica], but still suffering a lot; she has, fortunately, got an admirable large solid nurse, a Lincolnshire woman called Brocklesby. John is here too, on ten days' sick leave after his influenza.

Gandhi has started his fast, on the prospect of which an unending series of telegrams have been passing between the Viceroy and the Secretary of State. Linlithgow wanted to leave G. to starve, or not, as he felt disposed; but neither his Council nor his Governor would support him in that – probably rightly.

Wednesday 17 February

The King has decided (on the advice of the Government, of course) to offer Stalingrad a Sword of Honour, and Alec Hardinge and I spent some time today editing the usual somewhat cumbrous Foreign Office draft for a message to Kalinin,[2] making the offer. Originally, Eden suggested to the King that he should give the George Cross; but he wouldn't have that, saying he had given the GC to Malta, and wasn't going to do ditto for any place outside the British Empire. Then the idea was mooted that it should be the Military Cross, either surrounded with brilliants, or enclosed in a silver casket; but various authorities, including Clark Kerr, decided that this would not appeal to the Russians. Finally, somebody hit on the Sword of Honour, which seems to me a good solution.

---

1 Gen. Dwight D. Eisenhower, known as Ike (1890–1969), C-in-C Allied Forces N. Africa 1942–4, Supreme Commander Allied Expeditionary Force in W. Europe 1944–5, President of USA 1953–61.
2 Mikhail Ivanovich Kalinin (1875–1946), Chairman of the Presidium of the USSR Supreme Soviet 1937–46. Although titular Head of State, he was always under the control of Stalin.

Today I saw the first considered estimate of the length of the war, which Winston has committed to an official paper. Some group engaged in highly expensive research work asked for guidance, before expanding their plant, as to the possible duration of hostilities. It was referred to the PM, the substance of whose reply is that 'the war against Hitler may be reasonably expected to be over before the end of 1944, while that against Japan may last from eighteen months to two years longer'.

Dined with the Melville Balfours, where was Colin, their boy, looking very smart as a naval cadet; and young Charles Wiggin,[1] just returned from his training as an airman in Canada, under the wonderfully successful Empire Air Training scheme. The extent of Canada's war-effort, generally, grows more and more impressive; her financial help seems to me amazingly generous; and even his opponents admit that Billy King is proving a remarkably good and staunch-hearted war Prime Minister.

Stalin has sent a rather grouchy telegram to Winston saying, in effect, 'Your plans for 1943 are all very fine, but why can't you get on with them sooner?' I suppose nothing will ever make the Russians, essentially land-animals, realise that conducting a campaign – or rather a series of campaigns – across miles of salt water presents certain problems which don't arise in continental warfare.

Stanley Baldwin[2] came in to see the King yesterday; the old man is lame, and deaf, and shrunken, but looked a better colour than when I saw him last – which was when I breakfasted with him at the Dorchester nearly a year ago. Winston had suddenly bidden him to luncheon, tête-à-tête, at No. 10, and had kept him talking most of the afternoon, and been most friendly to him.

This was a generous act on W.'s part, for, politically, he hasn't had a good word for S.B. for a long time; and it is an object-lesson to those who refuse to admit any good in him. S.B.'s later years, indeed, have been a striking example of the evil that men do living after them, and the good being interred with their political bones. He is also an example of that common phenomenon in history, a statesman being ruined by one or two of his own chance utterances, for his reputation was entirely destroyed by his unlucky 'Safety First' slogan, and his pronouncement about the Fulham by-election; as Asquith was destroyed by 'Wait and see', Haldane by 'Germany is my spiritual home', or Wellington (for a period) by his declaration that the House of Commons was in no need of reform. The mob is always ready to convert such *obiter dicta* (often torn from their context and given a far

---

1   1922–77. Later a diplomat, Ambassador to Spain 1974–7. Knighted 1976.
2   Rt. Hon. Stanley Baldwin (1867–1947) was three times PM (1923–4, 1924–9 and 1935–7). He was created 1st Earl Baldwin of Bewdley in 1937.

wider meaning than the speaker ever meant them to have) into stones with which to pelt the great.

Friday 19 February

Eric Maclagan disputed my claim that the origin of 'love' in tennis is '*l'oeuf*' – i.e., a round O. We agreed to refer it to the New English Dictionary, and I find that it shirks the issue, mentioning the use of 'love' in various ball-games, but giving no special etymology for that connotation of the word; nor does Brewer's *Handbook*. I don't know what my authority for the theory is, but have always believed it. One of the books of reference which I consulted gives the origin of 'tennis' as '*tenez*' meaning 'take it'. Eric also denied that the Queen in chess is so called because she was originally the 'Vizier', which, in Norman circles, became corrupted into '*Vierge*'. But no one contested my derivation of 'Check mate' from the Arabic for 'The King is dead', which is something like '*Shah ek maté*'.

Saturday 20 February

The annual report of Trin. Coll. Oxon contains an appreciation of Blakiston,[1] who became President of the college in my second year, 1907, and died last July. It tells the story of how, reading a sermon from his own somewhat illegible manuscript, he began a sentence with the words 'The frivolous of course reply', and then, realising that this was not quite what he had written, corrected them to 'The followers of Christ rely'.

Blakiston, universally known as 'Blinks', was a man of singularly unimpressive exterior, and his apparently desiccated and sarcastic manner made him unpopular in his early years. Lionel Smith, son of the then Master of Balliol, observing him scurrying, beetle-like, down the Broad, once remarked, 'There goes Blinks, looking like something that somebody has forgotten to tread on (*cf.* Whistler, on ?Frank Harris – or Wilde? or George Moore? 'There he goes, looking like a hiccough coming out of a third-rate brasserie'). But his long and devoted service to Trinity, and his success as Vice-Chancellor, established him as a notable figure in the University; moreover, he mellowed with time (as many vinegary bachelors do) and became quite likeable. Incidentally, I have never met anybody with a more exact knowledge of the pedigrees of everybody in England.

Dear Bob Raper,[2] our historic Bursar at Trinity, used to take a delight in teasing him. In Common Room, after dinner, he could, at intervals, and

---

1 Rev. Herbert Blakiston (1862–1942), President of Trinity College, Oxford, 1907–38.
2 Robert William Raper (1842–1915), an early champion of conservation.

when a sufficiency of distinguished guests was present, tell the story of some night-alarm on board a ship in which he had been travelling; its climax was always, 'And all the ladies rushed up on deck in their pyjamas, which, as *you* know, Blakiston' – here came a pause until all eyes were fixed on the unhappy Blinks, blushing in virginal modesty at the end of the table – 'they wear next their skin.'

I once wrote a clerihew on Raper and his unspeakable old terrier, Finn:

> Yellow-bellied Finn
> Is the embodiment of Original Sin.
> Or, to put it terser,
> He resembles the Bursar.

With a pendant:

> The Reverend Mr Blakiston
> Said, 'Mr Raper is the slackest don
> I have ever seen.'
> But he quite forgot Mr Green.

Green, commonly called 'Creeper Green', was an old, old man with a white beard, very like the traditional portraits of the Deity; so far as I know, he never did anything for the college except eat and sleep in it. On riotous nights, when bonfires were blazing and the young men of Trinity flushed with wine, the cry would go up, 'Let's go and look at Creeper Green in bed'; and we would all burst into the poor old gentleman's chamber, comment dispassionately on whether he kept his beard inside or outside the sheets, and leave him to his broken slumbers. So far as I recollect, he never made any protest against these outrages. Perhaps he rather enjoyed them. He can have had few pleasures.

Monday 22 February

Drove back to London after breakfast with old Johnny Weir, the homoeopath, who had been inspecting the Queen. I've known him now for over twenty years, and at one time allowed him to dose me with some of his curious little powders. I like him as a man; as a healer of the sick, how much of him is Aesculapius'[1] and how much Quack, I have never been able to determine.

---

1 In Greek mythology Asklepios (Romanised as Aesculapius) was the god of medicine and healing, said to be the son of Apollo, and able to raise people from the dead.

Tuesday 23 February

It has fallen to me to provide a suitable sword of honour for the King to give to Stalingrad. I have asked Wellington[1] (a young chap, whom I've never met) if he can lend us any suitable models from the store that I am sure the Iron Duke must have accumulated, and got Eric Maclagan to look round for a craftsman who could make it, and a designer who could produce an original design if we can't find an old one that will do. The King wants it set with rubies; but as the tax-payer will have to foot the bill, I hope carbuncles or garnets will suffice.

The King is always asking me whom he can make Lord Chamberlain, when the present inept old donkey [Clarendon] retires. Looking through the peerage reveals nobody who could, or would be willing, to do the job; but I told him today that he might do worse than get Roger Lumley,[2] when he comes home from governing Bombay. His uncle, Scarbrough, whose heir he is, is rising eighty-six, and can't last much longer.

Thursday 25 February

I went to the National Gallery to hear Sir W. Beveridge[3] open an exhibition of designs for post-war housing, organised by the Royal Institution of British Architects. Bev., who resembles nothing so much as a gargoyle thatched with white hair, spoke well. He made one good point: in Victorian days our houses had had large nurseries, no bathrooms and no garages; in our day they had bathrooms and garages, but no nurseries worth speaking of; in future, they must have all three.

Kenneth Clark[4] wound up with a neat speech in which he said that the architecture of the Middle Ages had been inspired by man's faith in God, that of the Renaissance by their faith in the majesty of the human intellect, while that of the coming age would necessarily have a more utilitarian

1 Henry Wellesley (1912–43) had succeeded his father as 6th Duke of Wellington in 1941.
2 Lawrence Roger Lumley (1896–1969), Governor of Bombay 1937–43, did become Lord Chamberlain, but not until 1952. He succeeded his uncle as 11th Earl of Scarbrough in 1945.
3 Sir William Beveridge (1879–1963), economist and political scientist. The Beveridge Report of 1942, recommending widespread changes and improvements in the provision of social insurance, retirement pensions, unemployment and disability benefits, as well as proposing the creation of a national health service, aroused world-wide interest and led to heated debates in both Houses of Parliament. Created 1st Baron Beveridge of Tuggal 1946.
4 1903–83. Art historian, youngest Director of the National Gallery 1934–45, Surveyor of the King's Pictures 1934–44. He and his wife Elizabeth were frequently guests of King George VI and Queen Elizabeth. Created Baron Clark (Life Peer) 1969.

motive, and we must therefore be prepared for some sacrifice of aesthetic considerations. Dined at Buckingham Palace with the King and Joey Legh in the '44 room.

Tuesday 2 March

In the Travellers tonight I fell in, and dined, with Jack Maffey,[1] our High Commissioner in Dublin. I wanted to hear from him something about conditions over there, and de Valera's frame of mind. He derided the idea that the Germans have, or have had at any time during the war, secret facilities for their U-boats on the Irish coast. His chief worry now is trying to get de Valera to shut his eyes to the release from internment of any of our aviators who have to make a forced landing within his borders. He (Dev.) is quite good about those who come down in a non-operational machine, but sticks his toes in – and one can hardly blame him – when it has obviously been engaged on combatant duties. There are, therefore, about thirty of our RAF men now in confinement there.

We sent 350-odd bombers to Berlin last night, and seem to have given it a real dusting. Yesterday afternoon I called on the Sinclairs in the flat which they have on top of the Air Ministry building in Downing Street. Marigold S. said that the only time that the Maiskys[2] ever showed any appreciation of the work of the RAF was when we bombed Berlin. The last time it happened, Madame Maisky thanked Archie Sinclair effusively, implying that at last we had really done something directly helpful to Russia. I think the Russians must be parochially-minded, for they seem unable to grasp the extent of our war-effort in the air and on the sea – especially the latter.

John Colville,[3] who is due to fly to Bombay any day, came to say goodbye to me. He had just been doing the same by the PM, who, he said, was in capital form. 'What you must take to India,' said Winston, 'is lots of good English guts' – and then, remembering that he was talking to a staunch Scotsman, corrected himself. 'Of course, I mean British guts.'

This evening I took Delia Peel to the St James's Theatre to see Turgenev's admirable comedy *A Month in the Country*; a perfect example of what a

---

1 John Loader Maffey (1877–1969), diplomat and administrator, Gov.-Gen. of the Sudan 1926–33, Permanent Under-Secretary of State for the Colonies 1933–7, UK representative to Eire 1939–49. Created 1st Baron Rugby 1947.
2 Ivan Mikhailovich Maisky (1884–1975), Soviet Ambassador in Britain 1932–43. In 1922 he married Agnes Alexandrovna Skippin.
3 John Colville (1894–1954), Governor of Bombay 1943–8, acted as Viceroy and Gov.-Gen. of India in 1945, 1946 and 1947. Created 1st Baron Clydesmuir 1947.

comedy of manners should be, and well acted.[1] The sirens went, and our guns became noisy, half-way through the third act. Nobody on the stage or off it took any notice, but when it was over I made Delia come straight back to Buckingham Palace, where we each had a bowl of bread and milk in the new shelter, now a model of spacious and luxurious calm, with every convenience ancient or modern. Now that our barrage is so heavy, I think it foolish for anybody, especially women, to stay abroad a moment longer than is necessary when there is a raid on, let alone go and sit in some crowded restaurant. As a matter of fact, the raid was a mild affair, and petered out by 11 p.m.; it was obviously a propaganda affair, staged by the Germans to enable them to say that they had retaliated instantly for our attack on Berlin – where, according to Reuter, they have been without gas, electricity or water for some days.

Thursday 4 March

There was a horrible incident, not directly due to enemy action, in Bethnal Green last night. A long queue of people were lined up at the mouth of a shelter, reached by a narrow and tortuous staircase. Half-way down was a landing, on which somebody tripped and fell. There was no way of stopping the relentless, though quite orderly, pressure of the human stream coming down the stairs; in the dim light others stumbled over the person on the ground, and in a few minutes the landing became a shambles, from which were eventually extricated 178 corpses, all suffocated, and about sixty injured.

There is nothing more terrifying than the dead weight of a moving crowd in a confined space. After the Coronation [in 1937] we had to leave the Abbey down long tunnels of canvas, which became packed with people anxious to get home. At the exit it was raining hard, and there was a breakdown in the arrangement for getting cars; those who had arrived there not unnaturally halted, but those behind, knowing nothing of what was happening at the other end, pressed on inexorably. We were soon jammed like sardines; the atmosphere got thicker and thicker, and various ladies in my immediate neighbourhood began to show signs of fainting. At last I drew my tailor-made sword – we were all, of course, in full uniform – and slashed an impromptu door in the canvas wall, through which Joan and I escaped over the wet grass to an adjacent doorway – in which, incidentally, we had to wait till nearly 7 p.m. before we could get a lift home. [*Later note:* This exploit delighted the King, who used continually to twit me with it in after years.]

---

1   In this adaptation of Turgenev's play, adapted and directed by Emlyn Williams, Michael Redgrave played Rakitin.

Friday 5 March

Godfrey Thomas[1] sent over to me today the proofs of *The Times*'s 'cold-storage' obituary-notice prepared against the death of the Duke of Windsor. The writer, R. Shaw,[2] invited Godfrey's comments, and he in turn invited mine.

I read it with mixed feelings. For some years after I joined his staff, in 1920, I had a great affection and admiration for the Prince of Wales; in the following eight years I saw him day in and day out; I saw him sober, and often as near drunk as doesn't matter; I travelled twice across Canada with him; I camped and tramped with him through Central Africa; in fact, I probably knew him as well as any man did. But, by 1927, my idol had feet, and more than feet, of clay.

Before the end of our Canadian trip that year, I felt in such despair about him that I sought a secret colloquy with Stanley Baldwin (then Prime Minister, and one of our party) one evening at Government House, Ottawa, and, in his little sitting-room at the end of the passage on the first floor (which I have never since been able to enter without a reminiscent qualm) told him directly that, in my considered opinion, the Heir Apparent, in his unbridled pursuit of Wine and Women, and of whatever selfish whim occupied him at the moment, was going rapidly to the devil, and unless he mended his ways, would soon become no fit wearer of the British Crown.

I expected to get my head bitten off but he heard me to the end, and after a pause, said he agreed with every word I had said. I went on, 'You know, sometimes when I sit in York House waiting to get the result of some point-to-point in which he is riding, I can't help thinking that the best thing that could happen to him, and to the country, would be for him to break his neck.'

'God forgive me,' said S.B. 'I have often thought the same.' Then he undertook to talk straightly to the Prince at an early opportunity; but he never did, until October 1936 – too late, too late.

Before the end of the Canadian tour I was strongly inclined to leave his service; one cannot loyally serve a man whom one has come to regard as both vulgar and selfish – certainly not a Prince. But for domestic reasons, I put it off. Then came the 1928 trip to Kenya and Uganda, which was the last straw on my camel's back. It was finally broken by his incredibly callous behaviour when we got the news of his father's grave illness.

I remember sitting, one hot night, when our train was halted in Dodoma

---

1   Rt. Hon. Sir Godfrey Thomas, Bt. (1889–1968), Private Secretary to the Prince of Wales 1919–36.
2   Capt. Richard Shaw (1885–1946) had been an Irish specialist on *The Times*.

station, deciphering, with the help of dear Denys Finch-Hatton,[1] the last and most urgent of several cables from Baldwin begging him (the Prince) to come home at once. The Prince came in as we finished it, and I read it to him. 'I don't believe a word of it,' he said. 'It's just some election-dodge of old Baldwin's. It doesn't mean a thing.' Then, for the first and only time in our association, I lost my temper with him. 'Sir,' I said, 'the King of England is dying; if that means nothing to you, it means a great deal to me.'

He looked at me, went out without a word, and spent the remainder of the evening in the successful seduction of a Mrs Barnes, wife of the local commissioner. He told me so himself, next morning.

When, about the middle of December, we got home after a voyage that has become historic, the King was still very ill; indeed, when S.B. met us at Folkestone, he told us that HM might not live through the night. So it was no time for private affairs, and, at the end of the month, my own father died and I had a bad attack of influenza. But, before January 1929 was out, life was outwardly normal again, and one evening I sent the Prince up a note saying that I wished to resign. The following morning he sent G. Trotter,[2] still in high favour at that time, to argue with me, but I refused to discuss it with G.

That evening or the next, the Prince himself sent for me. The resultant interview was the most exhausting experience I've ever had. I did not consider myself any longer in his service, and, when he asked me why I wanted to leave, I paced his room for the best part of an hour, telling him, as I might have told a younger brother, what I thought of him and his whole scheme of life, and foretelling, with an accuracy that might have surprised me at the time, that he would lose the Throne of England.

He heard me with scarcely an interruption, and when we parted, said, 'Well, goodnight, Tommy, and thank you for the talk. I suppose the fact of the matter is that I'm quite the wrong sort of person to be Prince of Wales' – which was so pathetically true that it almost melted me.

Next morning he sent me a message to say that he accepted my resignation and would like to give me a motor-car, as proof that we parted friends; which I in turn accepted, in the spirit in which it was offered! So I, an inverted Falstaff, retired into the wilderness at the age of 42 (less my wages of £1,000 a year), and left Prince Hal to work out his own damnation. I have never had any doubt in my own mind that, by doing so, I served him

1 Hon. Denys Finch-Hatton (1887–1931), second son of 13th Earl of Winchilsea, pilot, big-game hunter and adventurer in E. Africa, lover of the author Karen Blixen, was killed in an air crash.

2 Col. Gerald Trotter (1871–1945), Gentleman Usher to King George V 1919–36, Groom-in-Waiting and Assistant Comptroller to Edward Prince of Wales 1921–36.

better than I could have by staying acquiescently on the staff.

He bore me no malice whatever; while I was in Canada from March 1931 to October 1935, when I was Secretary to the Governor-General, he twice sent me messages to say that he would be glad to take me back whenever I wanted to come; when I returned to England, he sent for me and talked away as if nothing had happened. Eventually, of course, by a strange turn of the wheel I did find myself in his service once more.

In October 1935, immediately on my arrival from Canada, Clive Wigram, then Private Secretary to King George V, approached me with a view to my becoming one of the King's private secretaries. I refused; I felt that I had already spent too much of my life in palaces and Government Houses, and pointed out that I should be in a queer position if the King were to die and the Prince of Wales to succeed.

Clive, always an indifferent seer, assured me that I need have no anxiety on that score. 'The old King,' he said, 'was never better in his life than he is now. He's good for another seven years at least.' So I yielded; within six weeks of my taking up the appointment, George V was dead and Edward VIII was King.

Looking back, I don't believe I could have done anything but what I did – namely to wait upon events. At such a time, junior members of the Household cannot walk out on a new King because they happen to have disapproved of the Prince of Wales; moreover, I had to think of my colleagues – for months we were all working at high pressure, with all the business of a new reign.

Several people, including Harry Harewood,[1] who should have known better, assured me that there was an excellent chance that the history of Prince Hal would repeat itself, and that we might look forward to a better and wiser monarch than Henry V ever was. I had been out of England for five years, and during that time had heard little of the Prince of Wales, and less of Mrs Simpson[2] and her immediate predecessors; so I believed – or half-believed – them.

The nightmare of 1936 has become, perhaps mercifully, a rather blurred memory in my mind. But it very soon became apparent that the philo-

---

1 Tommy's cousin Henry Lascelles, 6th Earl of Harewood (1882–1947). In 1922 he had married Princess Mary, the Princess Royal. When Tommy became engaged, in 1920, Harry gave him £30,000 (probably worth £1 million in the values of 2006), remarking, 'I am afraid all is poverty in these days – but it ought to provide biscuits and margarine if not bread and butter.'

2 The American Bessie Wallis Warfield (1896–1986) had married Lieut. Earl W. Spencer, US Navy, in 1916, and had been divorced from him in 1927. In 1928 she married Ernest A. Simpson, an American-born British subject, formerly in shipping, from whom she was divorced in 1936.

sophers of the Prince Hal school were wishful thinkers; that the leopard, so far from having changed his spots, was daily acquiring more sinister ones from the leopardess; and as early as February 1936, I remember Joey Legh warning me – and he was perfectly right – that plans were already afoot to liquidate Simpson (matrimonially speaking), and to set the Crown upon the leopardess's head. Simpson, who was nothing worse than a nincompoop, I believe – I have never met him – was aware of this plot, and for some reason best known to himself had thought fit to communicate the details of it privily to the Lord Mayor of London, of all people – an uneasy secret which the good man was naturally unable to keep to himself.[1]

My impression is that the Prince of Wales was caught napping by his father's death; like Clive Wigram, he expected the old man to last several years more, and he had, in all probability, already made up his mind to renounce his claim to the throne, and to marry Mrs S. I know that, long before this, he had confided to several American friends of his that he could never face being King; King George VI has told me that his brother, at the time of the Abdication crisis, said to him, 'It was never in my scheme of things to be King of England'; and to me, on board the *Nahlin*,[2] apropos the projected sale of his Canadian ranch, he said, 'You know, Tommy, I always planned to keep it as a place that I could retire to'; and when I said, 'You mean for a holiday, Sir?', he replied, 'No, I mean for good.' [*In 1966 the author added a footnote:* 'Ulick Alexander[3] told me recently that when he was staying at Sandringham in the early 1930s, King George V took him for a walk, in the course of which he said, 'My eldest son will never succeed me. He will abdicate.']

The comparatively sudden death of King George V upset any such plans. But I believe that even then, he would have clung to them (he always hated changing any scheme that he had evolved himself) but for the provisions of his father's will. The will was read, to the assembled family, in the hall at Sandringham. I, of course, was not present; but, coming out of my office, I ran into him striding down the passage with a face blacker than any thunderstorm. He went straight to his room, and for a long time was glued to the telephone.

Under the will, each of his brothers was left a very large sum – about

---

1   George Broadbridge (1869–1952), Lord Mayor of London 1936–7, was a staunch Freemason, as was Simpson. Knighted in 1937, created 1st Baron Broadbridge 1945.
2   The yacht on which the royal party, including Edward VIII and Mrs Simpson, sailed along the Dalmatian coast in the summer of 1936. Writing to Sir George Allen, the Duke of Windsor's solicitor, in 1956, Tommy confirmed the '*ipsissima verba* spoken to me in the Hellenic sunlight of the *Nahlin* cabin'.
3   Rt. Hon. Sir Ulick Alexander (1889–1973) was Keeper of the Privy Purse 1936–52 and Treasurer to the King 1941–52.

three-quarters of a million in cash; he was left nothing, and was precluded from converting anything (such as the stamp collection, the racehorses, etc.) into ready money. It was, doubtless, a well-intentioned will; but, as such wills often do, it provoked incalculable disaster; it was, in fact, directly responsible for the first voluntary abdication of an English King. Money, and the things that money buys, were the principal desiderata in Mrs Simpson's philosophy, if not in his, and, when they found that they had, so to speak, been left the Crown without the Cash, I am convinced that they agreed, in that interminable telephone conversation, to renounce their plans for a joint existence as private individuals, and to see what they could make out of the Kingship, with the subsidiary prospect of the Queenship for her later on.

The events of the next ten months bear out this supposition; for, throughout them, he devoted two hours to schemes, great and small, by which he could produce money, to every one that he devoted to the business of the State. Indeed, his passion for 'economy' became something very near to mania, despite the fact that his private fortune, amassed under Revelstoke's[1] able direction while he was Prince of Wales, already amounted to nearly a million – which sum he took with him, of course, when he finally left the country; it was substantially increased by the very considerable sums which his brother paid him for his life interest in the Sandringham and Balmoral estates, so that, by the time he married, having no encumbrances, no overhead charges and no taxes to pay, he was one of the richest men in Europe – if not the richest.

When, in December, the storm broke, he went one evening to see his mother at Marlborough House; she asked him to reflect on the effect his purposed action would have on his family, on the Throne, and on the British Empire. His only answer, I have been told on the best authority, was, 'Can't you understand that nothing matters – nothing – except her happiness and mine?' That was the motto which, for some years past, had supplanted 'Ich Dien' – and that was essentially the underlying principle of his brief reign.

It led to bewildering, and often ludicrous, situations. I shall never forget seeing Clive Wigram coming down the King's staircase at Buckingham Palace exclaiming at the top of his never well modulated voice (he was much given to soliloquy – a dangerous habit in secretaries), 'He's mad – he's mad. We shall have to lock him up.' The same thought, if we did not express it quite so openly, was in the minds of many of us during those sombre months.

---

1   John Baring, 2nd Baron Revelstoke (1863–1929), succeeded his father in 1897. A director of the Bank of England, and a partner in Baring Bros, he was Receiver-General of the

Ulick Alexander has told me that, in the May of that year, he at last induced the King, Edward VIII, to go round his immense kitchen garden and glasshouses at Windsor. The particular pride of the old Scottish gardener was the peach-house, at that time a mass of blossom, promising a record crop of peaches. The King passed no comment till his tour of inspection was ended; he then turned to the gardener, and told him to cut all the blossom on the following day, and to send it to Mrs Simpson and to one or two other ladies, to embellish their drawing-rooms in London. Caligula[1] himself can never have done anything more wanton.

Many people have asked me, 'Could nobody have averted the ultimate catastrophe of the Abdication?' My answer has always been, and always will be, 'Nobody.' Given his character, and hers, given the circumstances of their relationship, the climax was as inevitable as that of a Greek tragedy. He had, in my opinion and in my experience, no comprehension of the ordinary axioms of rational, or ethical, behaviour; fundamental ideas of duty, dignity and self-sacrifice had no meaning for him, and so isolated was he in the world of his own desires that I do not think he ever felt affection – absolute, objective affection – for any living being, not excluding the members of his own family.

The only possible exception was Prince George;[2] and he (the Prince of Wales) knew his brother's weaknesses far too well ever to seek his advice. If he ever looked like making a friend, he never succeeded in keeping him for any length of time; and the very devoted service given him by certain members of the staff, he appreciated so little that he could only reward them with rank ingratitude. Consequently, when he came to the parting of the ways, he stood there tragically and pitifully alone. It was an isolation of his own making: and the responsibility for it is entirely his own. Had he so chosen, he could have gathered round him the finest company of friends that England could produce. Thus, there was no hope of his finding the right answer to his problem in his own heart; he had himself destroyed the possibility of others finding it for him.

Mention of the *Times* obituary notice led me further afield than I had intended. What I really set out to do, was to put down my own comments on it. As I explained to Godfrey Thomas, my view is that, though, taking it by and large, Shaw [author of the notice] has done an extremely difficult job remarkably well, and with fairness, tact and delicacy, yet no article of this kind designed for publication immediately after the Duke of Windsor's

---

Duchy of Cornwall 1908–29.
1 Roman emperor (AD 12–41) notorious for his excesses.
2 Prince George, Duke of Kent (1902–42), younger brother of Edward VIII and George VI, killed in an air crash in Scotland (see page 50).

death can ever be wholly satisfactory, for it can't bring out what I regard as the key to his baffling character – one of the saddest instances in all history of 'lilies that fester smell far worse than weeds' – namely, that for some hereditary or physiological reason his normal mental development stopped dead when he reached adolescence. I don't mean his physical development, for, in body, he might have been a sculptor's model; but his mental, moral and aesthetic development, which, broadly-speaking, remained that of a boy of seventeen.

There was one curious outward symptom of this; I saw him constantly at all hours of the day and night, yet I never observed on his face the faintest indication of the bristles which normally appear, even in men as fair as he was, when one has passed many hours without shaving. (Frederick Smith, for many years his valet, told me that HRH never shaved in the morning at all, but only in the evening when dressing up for dinner.) Years ago I mentioned this peculiarity to Dawson of Penn,[1] who said at once that it was a common phenomenon in cases of arrested development.

If this theory is true, it would account for many of his vagaries of conduct, and for his often childish outlook on life – though I hasten to add that that outlook was often bewilderingly characterised by a shrewdness, a power of penetration, which hardened men of the world might envy. It would certainly account for the fact that, as I have already said, it was quite useless to expect him to appreciate any general rules of behaviour; his only yardstick in measuring the advisability or non-advisability of any particular action was, 'Can I get away with it?' – an attitude typical of boyhood. As a matter of fact, he usually *did* 'get away with it'; his one conspicuous failure to do so was, however, enormously expensive, for it cost him his Throne.

But, though any reader of history is well aware that his family, for many generations, has produced more than its fair share of eccentrics, any speculation on these lines – and admittedly it is only speculation – could not be appropriate in an obituary in *The Times*. All I suggested in this direction was that the allusion to his 'immaturity' in his early manhood might be amplified so as to indicate that that immaturity persisted into middle age.

I asked also that, in the paragraph about his education, some reference should be made to the astounding ignorance of English literature, common to three of the four Royal brothers, on which I've already commented in this book. The complete lack of any sort of acquaintance with English literature has always astonished me in the Royal brothers – with the excep-

---

1   Bertrand Dawson (1864–1945), physician to King Edward VII, George V, Edward VIII and George VI. Created 1st Baron Dawson of Penn 1920, and 1st Viscount Dawson 1936.

tion of the Duke of Kent. I can't think what old Hansell,[1] their tutor, used to teach them. Only a minority of the boys of the English upper classes could *quote* Gray's *Elegy*, no doubt; but practically all of them have been confronted with it at some time or another during their education, and know what it looks like. [*In another entry Tommy recorded:* 'Logue,[2] the King's voice expert, was with him today, and gave him Gray's *Elegy* to read as an exercise. The King had never seen the poem before.'] I recollect the Prince of Wales, years ago, coming back from a weekend at Panshanger and saying to me, 'Look at this extraordinary little book which Lady Desborough[3] says I ought to read. Have you ever heard of it?' The extraordinary little book was *Jane Eyre*.

Then there is the famous story of his having luncheon with Thomas Hardy[4] and his wife at Max Gate during a tour of the Duchy of Cornwall property in Dorset. Conversation flagged, and to reanimate it the Prince of Wales said brightly, 'Now you can settle this, Mr Hardy. I was having an argument with my Mama the other day. She said you had once written a book called *Tess of the d'Urbervilles*, and I said I was sure it was by somebody else.' Thomas Hardy, like the perfect gentleman he was, replied without batting an eyelid, 'Yes, Sir, that was the name of one of my earlier novels.' Walter Peacock,[5] who was present at the luncheon party, told me that story; and Max Beerbohm[6] wrote a sonnet about it.

---

1 Henry Hansell (1863–1935), tutor to the Prince of Wales and his brothers.
2 Lionel Logue (1880–1953), the Australian speech therapist who worked with King George VI to overcome his stammer.
3 Panshanger in Hertfordshire, the former home of the Earl and Countess Cowper, was left to the Earl's niece, Lady Desborough, when the Countess died in 1913.
4 The novelist (1840–1928) and his wife lived at Max Gate, a gloomy house near Dorchester, designed by Hardy himself. *Tess of the d'Urbervilles* was first published in 1891.
5 Sir Walter Peacock (1871–1956), author, was Treasurer to Edward Prince of Wales 1910–15.
6 Sir Henry Maximilian Beerbohm (1872–1956), caricaturist, essayist and critic. The poem was as follows:

> Lift latch, step in, you're welcome, Sir,
>   Although to see you I'm unglad
> And your face is tinged with a deathly shyness,
>   Bleaching what pink it may have had.
> Step in, step in, Your Royal Highness.
>
> No, Sir, the weather is not good
>   And the farmers are casting crabbed looks
> At tilth and pasture's dearth of spryness.
>   Yes, Sir, I have written several books.
> A little more chicken, Your Royal Highness?
>
> Lift latch, step out, your car is here
>   To bear you away from this antient vale.
> We are each of us changed by our brief strange nighness,

[The Prince's ignorance of literature] is by no means irrelevant to any picture of him, for a good deal of his nervous restlessness and consequent lack of balance may have been due to his complete inability to find a safety-valve in a book (even a shilling shocker), as ordinary men do when they are over-wrought or over-tired. Reading meant no more to him than does music to the tone-deaf.

Shaw, in his introductory summary of the Prince's life, tactfully introduces Mrs Simpson by saying, 'He fell deeply in love with a woman who had had two husbands.' That misses the main point; what shocked public opinion throughout the British Empire was that she had two husbands *still living*. Moreover, the implication is that he, a lonely bachelor, 'fell deeply in love' for the first time in his life with the soul-mate for whom he had long been waiting.

That is the romantic view which many people were inclined to take at the time of the Abdication (Americans, in particular, tried to represent it as an Abelard and Héloïse affair) and which sentimental biographers will doubtless take in the future. It is moonshine. From the time when, in 1918, he fell in love with Mrs Dudley Ward[1] (fell, God knows, as deeply as any poor lovesick young man can fall), he was never out of the thrall of one female after another; there was always a *grande affaire* and, coincidentally, as I know to my cost, an unbroken series of *petites affaires*, contracted and consummated in whatever highways and byways of the Empire he was traversing at the moment; for example, the above-mentioned Mrs Barnes of Tanganyika.

So, to represent him as King Cophetua[2] seeking to raise a long-sought beggar-maid to share his solitary throne, is not only a flat perversion of the facts of his life, but an injustice to the other actors in the Abdication tragedy – the present King, Queen Mary, Stanley Baldwin, Cosmo Lang[3] – who knew all too well how materially his whole existence had already been made to conform to what H. G. Wells[4] calls 'the urgency of sex', and that

---

Though each of us lives to tell the tale.
Farewell, farewell, Your Royal Highness.

Elsewhere Tommy recorded: 'When someone said to Clive Wigram that Thomas Hardy ought to get the OM, C.W. is traditionally supposed to have said, "What – that fellow who sells fishing tackle in Pall Mall? What's he done to deserve it?"'

1 Mrs Freda Dudley Ward became the Prince's mistress in 1918, and their relationship lasted until 1934.
2 Imaginary African king who, having spurned all other women, fell in love with Zenelophon, a beggar-maid whom he saw from his window.
3 Most Rev. and Rt. Hon. Cosmo Lang (1864–1945), Archbishop of Canterbury 1928–42, was created 1st Baron Lang of Lambeth 1942.
4 Herbert George Wells (1866–1946), prolific author, was well acquainted with 'the urgency

Mrs S. was no isolated phenomenon, but merely the current figure in an arithmetical progression that had been robustly maintained for nearly twenty years.

I shall, in all probability, be dead before the *Times* article is printed; but I hope sincerely that it will embody the modest emendation that I have made to it in this regard.

I have re-read all that I have written about him, probably the most spectacular, the most discussed personality with whom I shall ever be in intimate association. I can say with honesty that I have set down nothing in malice; indeed, knowing all that I do, I am like Warren Hastings, amazed at my own moderation.[1] Nor is there any reason why anything I write of him should be malicious. Though I wasted the best years of my life in the service of the Prince of Wales, towards him personally I feel no bitterness, for, in all the time of our association, he never said an unkind word to me. If I am in any way inclined to judge him harshly, it is solely because he did great wrong to England, and to himself.

To return from this excursion: the King and I this morning inspected the Iron Duke's collection of presentation swords, and a shoddy lot they are. There is not one among them that could give any inspiration to the four artists now engaged in preparing original drawings for the Stalingrad sword.

In the absence of the Dean, the sermon today was preached by the Rev. Kingston, Chaplain at Victoria Barracks. He had an agreeable adventure in Libya, in Auchinleck's day. With three or four others he was taken prisoner by a German armoured car. The German officer in charge, who spoke perfect English, remarked, 'Well, the war is over so far as you are concerned,' and bundled him into the front of the vehicle, which took its place at the end of a string of others. Kingston, pretending to grope for a dropped cigarette case, contrived to turn off the petrol; the car, after a few hundred yards of gradually retarded progress, naturally spluttered, fell astern and finally came to a standstill. After a good deal of fruitless tinkering with the carburettor, etc., by the unsuspecting Germans, three other armoured vehicles hove in sight. They were hailed peremptorily by the officer, but unfortunately for him proved to be full of British sappers, armed to the teeth, who promptly made prisoners of him and his crew. 'And now,' said Kingston, 'the war is over so far as *you* are concerned.' It must have been a very satisfactory moment.

---

of sex'. Among his numerous affairs was an explosive liaison with the writer Rebecca West.

1   In fact it was Lord Clive (1725–74 – 'Clive of India'), replying to a question during Parliamentary cross-examination, who said, 'By God, Mr Chairman, at this moment I stand astonished at my own moderation.'

At luncheon yesterday, Madame de Bellaigue, the Princesses' French governess, having heard how Delia Peel and I were surprised at the theatre by the recent air-raid, turned to me and said, 'I hear you were caught with Lady Delia the other night.' I could not but deny this serious reflection on a blameless friendship, and made her blush most becomingly.

Monday 8 March

The night was made hideous by something going wrong with the Castle siren (there was a brief air-raid alert), so that it screamed continuously in E-flat for about quarter of an hour. Cynthia Spencer, who is staying here, said that on being woken by the loud-speakers (another noisy feature of our ARP system), she was convinced that Clive Wigram had got into her bedroom. Actually, only two German aeroplanes penetrated into our area, so it was a great ado about nothing.

Sunday 21 March

This day twenty-five years ago Ludendorff[1] started his great, and last, offensive. I had reached headquarters 9th Cavalry Brigade the evening before, having been in England, wounded, since the battle of Cambrai. So good was our intelligence that, when I arrived, they said, 'The balloon goes up at 4 a.m. tomorrow morning' – and sure enough it did, to the accompaniment of as noisy a barrage as was ever heard. During the week that followed I had exactly eleven hours' sleep. So, as I stood in my train [back to London from Cloud's Hill], I was glad I was not standing where I was a quarter of a century before.

Monday 22 March

The King returned from a four-day visit to the Home Fleet at Scapa [Flow]. Dined with the Roger Fulfords in their little house in Wilton Street; the only other guest was Harcourt Johnstone,[2] MP, widely known as 'Crinks', now secretary to the Department of Overseas Trade. Now that he is middle-aged, he has lost the aggressive brilliance which characterised him when he was a clever young politician with a great future, and is proportionately more agreeable.

---

1 Erich von Ludendorff (1865–1938), German commander in WWI. In March 1918, peace made with Bolshevik Russia enabled him to withdraw large numbers of troops from the Eastern Front and deploy them against the British and French on the Western Front.
2 Rt. Hon. Harcourt Johnstone (1895–1945), Liberal MP.

R.F. is good company and a sound man of letters in his own period – Regency and Victoria – as shown by his editorship of Greville. But he has a tinge of affectation which is occasionally tiresome, and, on looking him up in *Who's Who*, I was shocked to find that he is one of those who indulge in facetious entries under the heading 'Recreations'. He gives his as 'Golf, talking about the Royal Family, and reading about Victorian clergymen'. That sort of thing is either preciousness or showing-off, but whichever it is, it is offensive.

Tuesday 23 March

Winston today resumed his weekly luncheons with the King, for the first time since his illness. His broadcast on Sunday evening has had an excellent Press. It was a notable, and adroit, exposition of his attitude towards post-war problems in general, and the Beveridge report in particular, and it was timely, for there has been a lot of sniping at him, chiefly by party politicians, on account of his reputed indifference to such things. It was a great stroke of luck that he was prevented by illness from participating in the Beveridge debate in the House of Commons, and so was able to deliver, *ex cathedra*, this calm and considered statement of his views, and to remind the world at large that he himself has taken an active part in the evolution of 'social security' for more than thirty years.

A more puzzling oration was Hitler's brief speech in Berlin, which has intrigued everybody by its colourlessness, and by the flat monotony of its utterance, so unlike Hitler's usual style. At the Beefsteak yesterday old Mottistone,[1] who claimed to have had two long talks with him some years ago ('claimed' because M. is a dreadful liar), said he was prepared to go into the witness-box and swear that it was not Hitler's voice. The mystery was deepened by the German announcer, after mentioning Hitler and Goering by name, referring to Keitel, Milch and Dönitz as the 'Commanders-in-Chief of the three fighting services, thereby implying that H. and G. are no longer the executive heads of the Wehrmacht and Luftwaffe respectively. But I believe they have since explained this away as a *lapsus linguae*.

Walton Butterworth,[2] late of the American Embassy here, and now *en poste* at Lisbon, lunched with me. He is lucky to be alive, for, when he last returned from USA in the Clipper, the machine was suddenly hit

---

1 Maj.-Gen. John Seely (1868–1947). Created 1st Baron Mottistone 1933. Soldier, Liberal politician and author.
2 Hon. Walton Butterworth (1903–75), US diplomat, American Minister, London, 1953–5.

and filled with water. W.B., with two ribs broken from being thrown against the table where he was sitting, only managed to clamber out through a window in the nick of time. He then had to swim about in the river Tagus for the best part of an hour, during which he succeeded in rescuing one woman from the submerged plane, in which six or seven other people were killed.

Dined with Bernard Paget,[1] C-in-C Home Forces, at his headquarters in a large block of flats, Latimer Court, in Kensington. He is very incensed at the inclusion of 'psychiatrists' on the boards who examine young officers seeking permanent commissions, and who subject these boys to a string of impertinent Freudian questions, and reject them if their answers are unsatisfactory. His own son had lately been through this ordeal, so he should know. The idea (borrowed from the Germans, who have now discarded it) is one of the many delusions of Ronald Adam,[2] now Adjutant General, who seems to have got himself thoroughly disliked by all ranks in the Army, from the King (who explodes at the mere mention of his name) downwards.

Wednesday 24 March

Went in the evening to a cocktail party given by Oscar Solbert,[3] now attached to the American Embassy as military attaché to Biddle,[4] their Ambassador to the Allied Governments in London. O.S., who is an adventurer but not a bad chap altogether, was here as military attaché shortly after the last war. When I went to USA with the Prince of Wales for his famous visit to Long Island in 1924, Solbert, then one of President Coolidge's aides, was accredited to our party. He is the only man who has ever offered me a direct bribe. We were riding through the woods of Syosset one morning when he told me that if I would write a series of anonymous articles on the private life of the Prince, for some American Press syndicate, a new Lincoln motor-car would be delivered free at the door of my house in London. I burst out laughing, which he did not take at all amiss, and merely changed the subject, just as if I had rejected the offer of a cigarette.

---

1 Gen. Sir Bernard Paget (1887–1961), C-in-C Home Forces 1941–3, C-in-C Middle East Force, ADC General (Extra) to the King 1944–6. He had married Winifred Paget in 1918.
2 Gen. Sir Ronald Forbes Adam, 2nd Bt. (1885–1982), Adj.-Gen. to the Forces 1941–6.
3 Maj. Oscar Solbert, US Army, acted as ADC to the Prince of Wales during his tour of America.
4 Maj.-Gen. Anthony J. Drexel Biddle (1896–1961), US Ambassador to the Govts of Poland, Belgium, the Netherlands, Norway, Greece, Yugoslavia and Czechoslovakia 1939–44.

Thursday 25 March

Everybody went to Windsor for a small dance that has been got up for the Princesses; but I, to my great comfort, was provided with a cast-iron excuse for non-attendance, in that I had to see a Regional Commissioner very early next morning, and so remained, officially, in London. Actually, I took the opportunity to dine and sleep at Cloud's Hill, where I found Joan definitely better and having had no pain to speak of for four days. Birds in great voice after the recent rain, for which the garden looks much better.

Friday 26 March

In the Travellers saw young Jock Colville,[1] just back from eighteen months' training for the RAF in South Africa. He rightly threw up his post as one of the Prime Minister's private secretaries to become an airman, and inadvertently became something of a *cause célèbre*. After he had been about a year with the Air Force, his local commanding officer reported that his intellectual attainments were too low to warrant his being given a commission. As Winston regards him as the best and brightest of his young men, he was enraged at this insult to his own judgement, and is reported to have flourished the report in Archie Sinclair's face, with words that shook the Air Ministry to its foundations. Anyhow, Jock is now a pilot officer, and talks of running for Parliament as Conservative candidate for Marylebone.

I warmly encouraged him in this project, in particular because I should dearly like to see that horrible fellow Cunningham-Reid[2] thrown out, and in general because it seems to me of paramount importance that young men of Jock's type should take part in public affairs, national or local, and not rush into the City, as they all did after the last war. But public life must be made more attractive to them financially, for they must also marry and beget huge families.

I asked Jock how he found the PM, after his period of absence. He thought his mind as vigorous, his heart as staunch as ever, but thought his physical appearance showed signs of wear and tear; and what else can be expected after four years of war, which have added about fourteen to the ages of even those who haven't had a hundredth part of Winston's anxieties?

---

1   John Colville (1915–87), known as 'Jock', was Private Secretary to Neville Chamberlain, Winston Churchill, Clement Attlee and Princess Elizabeth. In the autumn of 1941 he volunteered for the RAF and trained as a fighter pilot, but was summoned back to work for Churchill again in 1943. His Downing Street diaries, *The Fringes of Power*, were published to great acclaim in 1985, and reappeared in an expanded form in 2004. He was knighted in 1974.
2   Capt. Alec Cunningham-Reid (d. 1977) was MP for St Marylebone 1932–45.

Down to Windsor after luncheon, and, walking up from the Southern Railway station, came on the whole Royal Family basking in the sun under the terrace wall. They were obviously sleepy, and complained of sore feet, but seemed to have enjoyed their party, which I believe lasted till past 4 a.m. Windsor just beginning to wear its spring face, when it always looks its best.

Saturday 27 March

I have sat late, wrestling with a draft for a message from the King to the RAF on the twenty-fifth anniversary of its formation (April 1). These messages are very difficult, and I have tried to write too many in the last twenty years. In this case, there is so much that one would like to say – and so few words, suitable in a royal speech, in which one can say it.

Sunday 28 March

Kirk,[1] Bishop of Oxford and sometime fellow of Trin. Coll. Oxon, arrived last night, and preached today, quite interestingly. At luncheon he told us that the curator of the scientific museum at Oxford had, at the beginning of the war, buried in some secret cache of his own a valuable collection of early scientific instruments, some of them on loan. He then died, and left no clue as to their whereabouts, so nobody has the faintest idea where to start looking for them.

   The Dean last night was inveighing against the Ponsonby book, and said it was incredible that Henry Ponsonby should never, in all his letters to his wife, have dilated on Queen Victoria's merits. This seems to me to show a curious ignorance of human nature; intelligent courtiers don't gush about the Royal Family in their intimate correspondence,[2] especially when writing to somebody who knows them just as well as they do themselves, as Lady Ponsonby certainly did.

Wednesday 31 March

Eric Maclagan came in this morning, and we agreed that the best plan with regard to this infernal sword for Stalingrad was to make Gleadowe[3] produce

---

1   Rt. Rev. Kenneth Escott Kirk (1886–1954), Bishop of Oxford 1937–54.
2   *Henry Ponsonby, Queen Victoria's Private Secretary: His Life from His Letters.* Tommy later added a note: 'Nor in their diaries'.
3   Reginald Gleadowe (1888–1944), civil servant, head of Honours and Awards Branch, Admiralty, designer of the sword.

a revised version of one of the three alternative sketches that he submitted.

At Grillions[1] tonight there was one bad moment after dinner; we had been felicitating E. Devonshire on the birth of his first grandchild, and A. P. Herbert asked Lord Trenchard[2] how many grandchildren he had. When T. replied 'None', A. P. H. twitted him about it rather persistently. Poor old T. sat silent; probably no one in the room save myself knew why, and that his nice boy, Hugh, reported seriously wounded and missing, is almost certainly lying dead in front of the Mareth line.[3]

At the Buckingham Palace party I was introduced to Miss Eleanor Rathbone,[4] MP, who distinguished herself by making a slashing attack, in the best eighteenth-century manner, on Aneurin Bevan[5] in the House of Commons last week, after he had been baiting the PM. I believe she is normally both prosy and inaudible, but on this occasion she administered the perfect rebuke, to the satisfaction of the whole House. E. Devonshire told me that the late Speaker, Fitzroy,[6] had a habit of talking to himself, quite audibly to those sitting near the Chair; he particularly disliked Miss Rathbone, for some reason, and when she tried to catch his eye, used to mutter, 'Damned old hermaphrodite – thinks I'm going to call her, but I shan't'; and he very rarely did.

The King sent for me this evening to witness his will.

Thursday 1 April

Busy all morning writing a riposte to Sydney Carroll,[7] the journalist, who has sent us, via Louis Greig,[8] a long letter urging that more publicity be given to the doings of the King and Queen, and that it should be put in the hands of a professional 'Public Relations Officer'.

---

1   The dining club founded in 1812, and still extant, which took its name from the Grillions Hotel, where members used to meet.
2   Marshal of the RAF Hugh Montague Trenchard (1873–1956), GOC Royal Flying Corps 1915–17, Principal Air ADC to the King 1921–5, Commissioner Metropolitan Police 1931–5. Created Baron Trenchard 1930 and 1st Viscount Trenchard of Wolfeton 1936. One of his two sons and both his stepsons were killed in action.
3   His death was announced a few days later.
4   D. 1946. Author, Independent MP for the Combined English Universities 1929–46.
5   Son of a Welsh miner, Aneurin Bevan (1897–1960) went to work in the mines at thirteen, but became a formidable Labour politician, Minister of Health 1945–51.
6   Capt. the Rt. Hon. Edward Algernon Fitzroy (1869–1943), Speaker of the House of Commons 1928–43.
7   1877–1958. Australian-born journalist, managing editor of the *Daily Sketch* and *Sunday Graphic*.
8   Group Capt. Sir Louis Greig (1880–1953), Extra Gentleman Usher to King George VI 1937–52, Personal Air Secretary to Sir Archibald Sinclair 1940–46. In his youth he played rugby for Scotland, became a doctor, joined the Royal Marines and then the RAF.

John, who is spending nine days' leave at Cloud's Hill, came up, and we went to see *Arsenic and Old Lace* at the Strand; a very funny play, though a bit macabre at times.[1] We supped at the Savoy, whence he went on to a party at the 400 Club, and I to bed.

Tuesday 6 April

Their Majesties, with Cynthia Spencer, H. Campbell and myself, left in the evening for the north. At dinner the King told us he had just had a message from Winston telling him that the 8th Army had made a considerable advance and taken 6,000 prisoners.

Wednesday 7 April

Newcastle in the morning, in a tearing gale, which blew my hat off during a parade of Civil Defence workers and deposited it among the band – an incident which will long live in the royal memory. We lunched in a launch going down the Tyne, and visited sundry shipyards etc. in South Shields p.m. A tiring day.

Thursday 8 April

After an agreeably quiet night in the train, which 'tied up' at Featherstone (just south of Haltwhistle), we went to more shipyards, in Sunderland. They are doing very good work there, and I was encouraged by several of the magnates, who have recently been in USA, telling me that the almost fabulous figures of their tonnage-production, which the Americans publish from time to time, are quite accurate.

Lunched in the train, where we were joined by that foolish but rather pathetic man Londonderry[2] (Lord Lieutenant of Durham), and resumed operations at Durham. We finished up with half an hour in the cathedral, inside which I had never been before; it is most beautiful, and the choir sang delightfully (an anthem of Wesley's) while we were walking round. Prior to that, we were in the castle, which is well worth seeing, with a fine hall. The Mayor of Durham, when I asked him questions about it, could

---

1 This American comedy by Joseph Kesselring starred the very English actor Naunton Wayne as Mortimer Brewster.
2 Charles Stewart Henry Vane-Tempest-Stewart, 7th Marquess of Londonderry (1878–1949), was Secretary of State for Air 1931–5, but incurred much hostile criticism for accepting Nazi hospitality at the 1936 Winter Olympic Games in Garmisch Partenkirchen, and generally condoning Hitler's aggression.

tell me nothing save that the Bishop has a bathroom there which is built in the thickness of the wall. Perhaps he is a plumber, and took a professional interest in it. Finally to Aycliffe, where there is a vast filling-factory (explosives), a mushroom growth on what were playing fields in 1940, and where 16,000 people, mostly women, are now employed.

Friday 9 April

Back at Buckingham Palace for breakfast. Montgomery's victory has been a considerable one – prisoners now 9,000 – but there has been heavy fighting. Winston, to whom the Queen gave the draft of her broadcast on Tuesday, has sent it back with commendation, having only added some ten lines of his own. So I hope it is now nearing finality.

For the last few months the King has been urging that the Duchess of Kent's emoluments should be increased at the public expense; Alec Hardinge and I both felt that this would be a disastrous move, and that it would be most unwise, at this juncture, to provoke a parliamentary, and public, discussion on the general subject of the royal finances. Winston, whose head is often ruled by his heart in such matters, has hitherto inclined to the opposite view, but I am glad to say that Kingsley Wood,[1] who came in today to communicate his Budget secrets to the King, reported to Alec that Winston was now converted, and sees that anything of the sort would be folly.

Apart from any political implications, it has always seemed to me an iniquitous proposal; the Duke of Kent was left the best part of a million by his father, and, granted that she has three children to bring up, and that taxation no doubt leans as heavily on his widow as it does on the rest of us, she surely ought to be able to jog along on what she's got; and if she can't, she has a number of very rich in-laws who could quite well help her without any embarrassment to themselves.

Saturday 10 April   Windsor

All the shrubs just coming to their best and making a wonderful show; the berberis is especially good this year.

Sunday 11 April

I am fifty-six today. G. Kelly and I, after luncheon, listened to the St Matthew

---

1   Rt. Hon. Sir Kingsley Wood (1881–1943), solicitor and politician, Secretary of State for Air 1938–40, Chancellor of the Exchequer 1940–43.

Passion on my wireless; we both thought it an extremely good performance (conducted by Jacques), and later Harris, the organist, told G.K. that he thought it the best he had ever heard. G.K. asked Harris what he thought Bach's own reaction would be, if he could hear a modern presentation of his work. H. said he didn't suppose Bach would recognise it – the volume of sound was far greater today, the conducting and singing more expert, and the actual instruments, with the possible exception of the fiddles, incomparably better.

At 9 p.m. the Queen delivered her broadcast, and did so very well. In its final form it was the joint work of Winston Churchill, the Bishop of Lichfield and myself – a curious trio of collaborationists, who are unlikely ever to be in literary partnership again.

Hughe Hugessen telegraphs that the Netherlands minister in Ankara has been secretly approached by an emissary from the Hungarian Government who wants to be put in touch with him. The assumption is that the Hungarians are trying to reinsure, if not to ascertain on what terms they can buy themselves out of the war. From the undoubted activity of the rats all over Europe, it really is beginning to look as if the Axis ship is getting pretty leaky. We sent 502 bombers to Frankfurt last night, 21 missing. The wisteria is out on the Gothic ruin at Frogmore – surely a record for earliness.

The multiplicity of questions on which one is called upon to pronounce judgement in my profession is unlimited; today Clive Wigram brought me a letter from an old gentleman called James who wants to embody in his forthcoming reminiscences details of long conversations which he claims to have had with the spirits of King George V, Queen Alexandra, Princess Louise, the Kaiser and other lesser royalties. I've no idea if the law gives one any protection against spiritualists publishing the alleged utterances of the ghosts of one's departed relatives, but I know I should resent it fiercely if anything of the sort happened to me – and I am quite sure the King would feel the same, especially as many of the *obiter dicta* attributed to his father, grandmother and great-aunt are damned nonsense. However, the author was for many years steward to Princess Louise and the Duke of Connaught, so he may be amenable to gentle discipline without our having to invoke the aid of the law.

Wednesday 14 April

Back to London from Cloud's Hill, where I spent the last two nights and saw first swallow. Joan is now able to sit in a chair by the window, and is to be allowed to try and stand on her leg next Sunday. The recent gale blew down a beech tree in the field in front of the house, and I spent much of yesterday – as lovely an April day as I ever remember – trimming it up.

Dined at the Travellers with C. Meade and Conrad Russell.[1] Old Jimmy Meade[2] joined us after dinner; after commanding convoys for the first two years of the war, he has now, a full admiral aged sixty-eight, gone to sea again as mate in a small merchantman – and looks very well on it. I believe it was the continued presence at Uppark of his mother-in-law, Lady Mary Glyn, that finally decided him to take to salt water again.

The Queen's broadcast had a very good press, and I'm told that she had a flood of congratulatory letters about it. On Sunday night she sent me a charming note of thanks for my own share in it.

Thursday 15 April

Went to a Government luncheon for Mr Jones, the New Zealand Minister of Defence, a bootmaker who dropped more aitches in a five-minute speech than I've ever heard a man drop before. Sat next to the First Sea Lord, Dudley Pound,[3] whom I should have liked to ask various naval questions, but he was determined to talk about duck-shooting.

Friday 16 April

To Windsor, which is in great beauty. Heard garden-warbler in Frogmore. So warm that I was able to walk about after dinner without a coat. Winston has decreed that the ridiculous ban on ringing the church bells shall be lifted.

Alec Hardinge told me that Leo Amery had been round to see him in rather a stew, because Linlithgow had cabled that Moslem opinion in India would be much upset by the Queen saying in her broadcast that Christianity is the only sound basis for a healthy home life, etc. I think this is nonsense. One might as well argue that the Queen ought never to announce the fact (as she does each Sunday) that she has been worshipping in a Christian

1   1878–1947. Gentleman-farmer, first cousin to Bertrand Russell and the Duke of Bedford; devoted friend of Diana Cooper. After his death Tommy wrote to his sister Flora: 'I got more pleasure, and more value, from my thirty years of friendship with him than I have had from almost any other human association in my life. He invariably left one with the feeling that he was an even wiser and more amusing companion than one had ever realised before.'

2   Adm. the Hon. Sir Herbert Meade-Fetherstonhaugh (1875–1964), Extra Equerry to King George V, King George VI and Queen Elizabeth II. Commanded the Royal Yacht 1931–4.

3   Adm. of the Fleet Sir Dudley Pound, OM (1877–1943), First Sea Lord and Chief of Naval Staff, 1939–43.

church, and not a mosque or a synagogue or a Hindu temple, if one is always to consider the susceptibilities of the King's non-Christian subjects; and, if one pushes the argument to its logical conclusion, she ought not, from the Moslem point of view, ever to talk at all, being a woman.

On the other hand, Cardinal Villeneuve[1] has sent an ecstatic telegram saying what an admirable effect the speech had on Roman Catholics in Canada; so perhaps what we lose on the swings of the Infidels we gain on the roundabouts of the Faithful. The longer I stay at this job, the more clearly I realise that it is impossible to please all the people all the time. But, as I told A.H., Leo Amery has a perfectly good answer – namely, that all the Queen advocated was the observance of the *ethical* principles of Christianity (with which no right-thinking Moslem need quarrel), and that there is no evidence in the speech of dogma, nor of any attempt to proselytise. Anyway, the woman happens to be a devout Christian and the wedded wife of the Defender of the Faith; and if she mayn't admit it without disrupting the Empire, then God (whether Jahweh, Allah or Buddha) help the Empire.

Saturday 17 April

Another perfect day; I never remember such an April, and, indeed, we now need rain sorely if we are to have any vegetables. Last night we sent 602 bombers to the Skoda works, and to Mannheim. Fifty-seven fell by the wayside – it sounds a lot; but it means that, out of each 200, 181 returned safely; and if we damaged Skoda even half as much as we did Krupps, it is a relatively small price to pay, and the result might be the shortening of the war by six months. The moon is nearly full; that means that the target's visibility, and the risk to those attacking it, are greater.

Sunday 18 April

I have been able to be out in the sun most of the day. Tonight in Frogmore heard (and saw) a blackcap and a willow wren.

Monday 19 April

Harold Butler,[2] just back from USA on a month's leave, told me that

---

1   Son Eminence le Cardinal J. M. Rodrigue Villeneuve (1883–1947), Archbishop of Quebec 1931–47, Cardinal from 1933.
2   Sir Harold Butler (1883–1951), Minister at HM Embassy, Washington, 1942–6.

Madame Chiang Kai-shck's[1] visit had been disastrous from the Chinese point of view. By her capriciousness and exigencies she offended all the big-wigs, beginning with the Roosevelts (who were deeply insulted by her insisting on using her own sheets at the White House), spent a great deal of money on luxuries, and generally contrived to depreciate Chinese stock.

Ours, on the other hand, has risen from the trough in which it was sunk six months ago, and is now high, largely owing to the feats of the 8th Army. Isolationism is dead. America at large is highly critical of the lack of success achieved by their forces overseas – except in the air. In that element they have gained a notable victory this very day, destroying a large proportion of a fleet of Junkers transport planes and their escort off Cape Bon.

After luncheon I went to 10 Downing Street to see John Martin.[2] Winston has sent a flamboyant message to the Viceroy, congratulating the 4th Indian Division on its achievements, buttering up the Nepalese, etc., couched in terms distinctly suggestive of a royal message. The King read this in the newspapers yesterday, and was not unnaturally rather aggrieved. The object of my mission was to convey to the PM, via Martin, that there ought to be some general ruling arrived at as to when the King, and when the PM, should send such messages, and to suggest that the PM should broach the subject at the weekly luncheon tomorrow.

Martin said they had not yet found a new Viceroy; Attlee's name is being put forward, and the PM, rather surprisingly, favours the idea; so is Eden's, but it would surely be madness to send him to India now. I believe they will ultimately fall back on Sam Hoare.

Wednesday 21 April   Appleton

Heard cuckoo for first time this year, and a nightingale, singing hard in Clover's Wood, close to the high road, in the middle of the afternoon.

Saturday 24 April

The Foreign Office recently sent out a paper on the future of Germany, the conclusions of which were broadly that the following steps would be necessary: 1. Restoration of territories seized by Germany since 1937. 2. Cession to Poland of East Prussia, Danzig and the Oppeln district of Silesia. 3. Control of Kiel canal by United Nations. 4. International control of

---

1 1898–2003. Wife of Chiang Kai-shek (1887–1975), head of the Nationalist Government in China 1928–49. She lived to the age of 105.
2 John Martin (1904–91), PPS to Winston Churchill 1941–5. Knighted 1952. His book *Action this Day: Working with Churchill* was published in 1968.

industry, especially Rhineland. 5. Encouragement of spontaneous separatist movements with a view to the possible development of a Federal Germany; in other words, to ensure the dismemberment of Imperial and Hitlerite Germany. All of which depends, of course, on the victorious Powers retaining over a sufficiently long period a preponderance of armed strength, and the will to use it in case of need.

Top Selborne[1] has supplemented this paper with another very able one for the Ministry of Economic Warfare. He points out the major dilemma in the whole problem – viz., that a lasting peace is only possible with a prosperous Germany; economic distress and unemployment could only reproduce the situation which brought Hitler into power; while, on the other hand, if you permit the full development of industry, you are thereby making possible the manufacture of war potential, since practically all the great industries of peace play their part in total war. After examining, and rejecting, various alternatives, he plumps for dismemberment as the only solution.

Monday 26 April

The Germans, a few days ago, published a story of the discovery of the bodies of some 8,000 Polish officers whom, they say, the Russians did to death in 1939–40.[2] Whether true or not, it has had the effect of finally embroiling the Russians and the Poles, who have hardly been on speaking terms for months past; Stalin, in spite of appeals from Winston and F.D.R. to go slow, has announced that USSR has 'suspended' relations with Sikorski's government. This is a situation full of ugly possibilities, and engendering it is a triumph for Goebbels.

Tuesday 27 April

John and Charles Rutland[3] came over to luncheon. C.R. looks slightly more robust than he did; when he first joined the Grenadiers, they called him 'the ghost on toast'. Princess Margaret remarked with a sigh, 'I wish I had his eyelashes.'

At their last luncheon the PM told the King that Lampson would prob-

---

1 Roundell Palmer, 3rd Earl of Selborne (1887–1971), Minister of Economic Warfare 1942–5.
2 In May 1940, over 4,400 Polish officers were murdered by members of the Soviet Army in a wood at Katyn, near Smolensk – a massacre that had widespread political repercussions.
3 Charles Manners (1919–99) had succeeded his father as 10th Duke of Rutland in 1940.

ably be the choice for Viceroy in India. He has now changed his mind, and sent the King a long note saying that Eden ought to go. The King is replying with a letter, drafted by Alec Hardinge, setting out the various reasons why A.E. should *not* go.

Sunday 2 May

With C. Liddell to Albert Hall; a Beethoven concert – Egmont overture. G major piano concerto (Solomon), and the Eroica. Just the right length, and well played throughout. The second movement of the Eroica is intriguing; it seems to me to have little relation to the rest of the symphony, and to be much more in the vein of the posthumous quartets, though he wrote it in 1804. And I'd forgotten how good the scherzo is, though of course Beethoven's scherzos never fail. Probably they convey the atmosphere of what Heaven ought to be like more successfully than any other human attempt in any medium; the Sons of the Morning laughing together.

C. Liddell told me that examination of the prisoners taken in Tunisia has shown the Germans, though they realise that they are marooned and cannot escape, still less win, to be in a robot-like, fight-till-we-die frame of mind. This is confirmed by a story in Alexander's telegram to the PM of how some thirty Germans surrendered, and were being marched off when one of them snatched a rifle and incited the others to start fighting again; which they did, with the result that they all had to be exterminated.

The strain of that North African campaign must be terrible. Arthur Penn tells me that two Guards officers have asked to be sent away because they no longer find themselves capable of commanding men in the field. This does them credit. Loss of nerve doesn't show, as does the loss of an arm or a leg (obviously a compelling reason for honourable retirement from a battlefield), but it is just as much the physical consequence of too much war, and even more incapacitating from the military point of view. I think both these two have been fighting out there from the beginning of the campaign, and nobody should blame them in the slightest degree for confessing to nervous exhaustion. A month of that kind of warfare would finish me completely, even if I were ten years younger.

Friday 7 May

In today's newspapers it is stated that Lord Grantley,[1] aged 87, is being cited in the divorce court as a co-respondent; boys will be boys.

---

1   5th Baron Grantley (1855–1943) died in August that year.

Saturday 8 May

On the midnight news the capture of Tunis and Bizerta was announced. There are no details yet as to what has become of the German forces.

Sunday 9 May

There can be no doubt but that we have won a great and resounding victory in North Africa. The Afrika Korps has ceased to exist as a fighting force; the last bulletin spoke of 50,000 prisoners, and that figure may well be doubled in the next few days;[1] the enemy dead must be as many more. And it seems only yesterday that we were wondering if we could save Egypt.

I was determined that a projected message from the King to Eisenhower should not come too late, as such things so often do, and succeeded in getting it off in time for it to be read out on the 1 p.m. wireless news. Ed Murrow,[2] speaking at 9 p.m. (he has just come back from North Africa), gave an encouraging account of the happy relations between our men and the Yanks. That is almost as important as driving the Germans into the sea.

Wednesday 12 May

Bevir, from 10 Downing Street, came in this morning to talk over one or two things. He told me that often the PM would exchange no spoken word with any of his entourage for days at a time, communicating with them – including Mrs Churchill – by chits; rather like Queen Victoria and Sir Henry Ponsonby.

Winston, by the way, arrived safely in New York last night. He took with him, in the *Queen Mary*, the three chiefs of staff, Cherwell,[3] all the planners, the three Commanders-in-Chief in the East (Wavell, Peirse[4] and Somerville[5]), Leathers,[6] Ismay[7] and Jacob, the secretaries to the War

---

1   In fact it was more than trebled.
2   Celebrated American broadcaster.
3   Frederick Lindemann (1886–1957), known as 'The Prof.', experimental pilot and Director of the Physical Laboratory of RAF Farnborough, was PA to the PM, 1940, and Pay-master-General 1942–5. He was created 1st Viscount Cherwell 1956.
4   Air Chief Marshal Sir Richard Peirse (1892–1970), AOC-in-C India 1942–3, Allied Air C-in-C, SE Asia Command, 1943–4.
5   Adm. of the Fleet Sir James Somerville (1882–1949), C-in-C Eastern Fleet 1942–4, Head of the British Admiralty Delegation to Washington, 1944–5.
6   Frederick James Leathers (1883–1965), shipping magnate, Minister of War Transport 1941–5. Created 1st Viscount Leathers 1954.
7   Gen. Hastings Lionel Ismay (1887–1965), always known as 'Pug', CoS to Minister of Defence (Winston Churchill) 1940–45; throughout the war the main channel of com-munication between the PM and the Chiefs of Staff. Created 1st Baron Ismay of Wor-mington, 1947.

Cabinet, and Beaverbrook. *Was für Plunder,* as any young Blücher[1] in an Atlantic U-boat might exclaim.

Lennox, of MI5, told me yesterday that the rumour going round West Scotland was that the *Queen Mary* contained the Duke and Duchess of Gloucester, on their way to replace the Athlones in Ottawa! That part of the ship which was not occupied by the PM and his circus was, it seems, filled with German prisoners of war en route for Canada.

We wondered, at Grillions, if in the whole history of the British Army any victory had ever been won of such imposing dimensions, speaking quantitatively, as the present one, with its toll of 100,000 prisoners at least. I can't think of one. And how curious to think that only forty-three years ago all England went wild over a tinpot affair like the relief of Mafeking; and today, not a single voice is raised, not one flag waved, in exultation. It is, on the whole, a sign of progress.

Thursday 13 May

The King sent off congratulatory messages to Winston, Alexander and Tedder. Winston is so essentially the father of the North African baby that he deserves any recognition, royal or otherwise, that can be given him. It was his imagination (stimulated, perhaps, by Smuts to some extent) that first saw the prime importance of this theatre of war; and it was his unflinching courage that built up the 8th Army into the wonderful fighting machine that it has become. He has himself publicly given the credit for 'Torch' to Roosevelt, but I have little doubt that W. was really its only begetter.

Friday 14 May

To Windsor p.m. The swifts have arrived and are screaming round the quadrangle. A perfect evening, after a hot day, and I sadly missed not having John to play bowls with me.

Saturday 15 May

The King's message to Winston is front-page stuff in all the newspapers. The *Daily Telegraph* says it is 'a most unusual mark of honour from the Sovereign to the PM'. No doubt; but we live in most unusual times. Winston's reply came in tonight. It might have been written by the elder

---

1 Gebhard Leberecht von Blücher (1742–1819), Prussian commander in the Napoleonic wars.

Pitt; he has evidently given much thought to it. Also the first batch of minutes of the opening session of the White House meetings. V. interesting; Winston spoke admirably about future plans. He is going nap on Italy being knocked out of the war before the end of the summer, and I daresay it is quite a good bet.

Lovely day. They all went to Ascot races, but I stayed at home and sat in the sun, walking round Frogmore before dinner. I'm reading Guedalla's *Palmerston*,[1] I think the most continuously irritating and ill-written book that I've ever opened. Some seven or eight captured German generals have arrived in this country by air.

Monday 17 May

Back to London early. I wrote last night to Robin Barrington-Ward, suggesting to him that the exchange of telegrams between the King and the PM would be a good peg from which to hang a leading article on the general relationship of the Sovereign to his Ministers, especially in wartime, pointing out that the publication of these mutual testimonials (a proceeding unique in English history, to the best of my knowledge) brings home that aspect of a constitutional monarch's work more vividly to the average citizen than would innumerable books, or articles, on 'The King and the Constitution'.

I also wrote a long note to the King, telling him what I had done, and that I regarded the episode as infinitely better 'publicity' for himself and his office than a dozen artificially-inspired articles in the Press, which is what certain people are constantly clamouring for. Also (though I didn't say this) it will do much to scotch the silly talk about Winston trying to steal the King's thunder, or (to use a more homely metaphor) to push the Crown under the bed.

The thanksgiving service [for the victory in North Africa] had been fixed, after a lot of secret telephonic labour, for 12 noon on Wednesday; this evening, just before dinner, the Home Office rang me up to say that the security people had reported that somebody at Londonderry House had telephoned on an open line all particulars as to time, date and place, to that foolish Marquess in Northern Ireland, and that in consequence the Cabinet, though the risk of the Germans getting the information and acting on it is slight, recommended postponement of the time from 12 to 6 p.m. To this the King agreed, and now, owing to Londonderry's butler being as stupid as his master, the unfortunate Lord Chamberlain's office, and Home Office,

---

1   Philip Guedalla (1889–1944), biographer and historian, had published *Palmerston* in 1926.

must sit down and issue fresh notices to everybody all round.

Finally, I was interrupted in my dinner at the Lit. Soc. by an intimation that the Archbishop of Canterbury had come to the conclusion that the occasion was not suitable for an address by himself, so I had to go home and get the King to agree to this omission from the approved Order of Service; which, I am bound to say, he has done promptly and without demur.

Tuesday 18 May

The RAF attack on the three big dams in the Ruhr appears to be one of the most cleverly-planned and best-executed enterprises of the war. If its results are anything like as substantial as they say, it may have very important effects. Dam-busting has a cumulative effect on the enemy. For the first week he has too much water, and for many subsequent weeks, too little.[1]

Wednesday 19 May

The service at St Paul's was not very inspiring, though attended by a great concourse of swells. We had all done our thanksgiving already, and the atmosphere was more that of a fashionable wedding. Archbishop Temple officiated with dignity, and, as Princess Elizabeth remarked to me afterwards, read his share of the service beautifully. I was impressed by the majesty with which Joseph,[2] the Lord Mayor, carried the Pearl Sword up the aisle in front of the King and Queen.

Monday 24 May

Back to London after three days of complete and satisfying idleness at Holton. Joan and I spent much of it sitting on the island, or by the pond, watching birds and doing some desultory shikar for their nests.

Tuesday 25 May

For the second night running I dined with the Devonshires, this time to meet Harold Macmillan, who is home from Algiers[3] for a few days: a family

---

1 The dam-buster raid, carried out by Lancasters of 617 Squadron, was led by Wing-Cdr. Guy Gibson, who was awarded the VC for his courage and leadership that night.
2 Sir Samuel Joseph (1888–1944), Lord Mayor of London 1942–3.
3 Where he was Minister Resident at Allied Headquarters, NW Africa, 1942–5.

party, the Salisburys, Cranbornes, Dorothy Macmillan and Maud Baillie.[1] HM, who is the colour of a coffee-berry and has suffered no loss of weight, gave us a moving account of the review of the Allied troops in Tunis a few days ago. The 51st Division, Scots and Irish Guards, apparently had all their pipers in full dress – a considerable feat, after months of desert warfare. As they marched by, Eisenhower said to him, 'Here am I – a wild boy from Kansas. Am I fit to command troops like these?' The most inspiring sight of all, he said, was that of a large convoy (I think he said 120 ships) steaming eastwards past Bizerta.

Winston, a few days ago, sent a remarkable telegram from Washington, saying that the time had now come for us to drop de Gaulle, and have no more truck with him; in this the Cabinet refused to acquiesce – a rare instance of their not bowing to his will. I was on duty as a firewatcher at Buckingham Palace, a duty which I have undertaken to do every Tuesday night; but, as there was no enemy activity, I had no occasion to leave my bed. We, on the other hand, sent 750 machines to bomb Düsseldorf. It is becoming debatable how much more of this sort of thing the Ruhr can stand.

Last night I finished the seventh and final volume of old Charles Greville, who has been a good friend to me, on and off, for many months. I have become quite attached to the old boy, and shall miss him.[2]

Wednesday 26 May

Godfrey Thomas told me that some interesting 'overheard' conversations among the captured German generals had been reported. They are complaining bitterly (as generals habitually do) of the bungling of the administrative people at home – e.g., von Arnim had said that, when he most needed a further supply of land-mines, a shipload of 10,000 had arrived; but, unluckily for him, their 10,000 fuses had been sent in a separate ship, which we had sunk, 'and they were no more use to me than dinner-plates'. I asked Godfrey why they didn't put Hess in with the generals, and he said that they had only that day received a medical report saying that Hess was in need of company, and were contemplating doing this. But of course H. is quite cracky, as he has been ever since he left Germany, and the generals know this and probably wouldn't say a word in his presence.

---

1 Lady Maud Baillie (1896–1975), elder daughter of the 9th Duke of Devonshire, served in the Auxiliary Territorial Service (forerunner of the Women's Royal Army Corps) 1941–5.
2 Tommy had bought the seven volumes of Greville in 1939, committing what he regarded as a great extravagance to secure a fine edition of one of his favourite authors.

Thursday 27 May

Lunched at *The Times*, on John Astor's[1] invitation. Montgomery (still in battledress) was the principal guest, and of the others, besides John Walter[2] and R. Barrington-Ward, the only ones I knew were the egregious Campbell Stuart[3] and W. R. Matthews, the Dean of St Paul's. The latter walked with me to my bus, and suggested that the proper laying-out of the bombed area round the Cathedral would be a suitable national war-memorial; an excellent idea. There is a great chance to make the top of Ludgate Hill into something really beautiful, and I only hope we don't miss it.

Friday 28 May   **Windsor**

The Lord Chamberlain is off to the upper reaches of the Wye, and the Queen's Treasurer to the Dee, while I, *qualis artifex pereo*,[4] as another summer goes by without my putting a fishing rod together. However, when I am turned sixty, I too may go salmon fishing in May; anyhow, I have no right to complain, for there are few men in England who have spent, as I have, four consecutive midsummers on that noble, shining river the Bonaventure,[5] averaging five fish a day.

Saturday 29 May

The King this morning confronted me with a medal for Peninsular veterans, struck by Queen Victoria thirty years after the campaign had ended, and asked me if I could explain it. By an extraordinary coincidence, I could; for I had read in *Palmerston* (Guedalla) the night before a passing allusion to Q.V.'s preoccupation with the matter in the winter of 1846. In the excitement of Waterloo, the claims of the Peninsular army had, it seems, been entirely forgotten. He also showed me a Waterloo medal, which I had never handled before, and I was astonished to see that it bore the effigy of the Prince Regent, and not that of George III.

Tuesday 1 June

Tomorrow I start a fortnight's leave, taking Joan to the Penmayne House

1 Col. John Jacob Astor (1886–1971), chief proprietor of *The Times* 1922–66. Created 1st Baron Astor of Hever Castle, 1956.
2 1878–1968. Great-great-great-grandson of John Walter, founder of *The Times*.
3 Sir Campbell Stuart (1885–1972), Director of Propaganda in Enemy Countries 1940.
4 'What an artist dies with me!' Suetonius, *Life of Nero*.
5 His salmon-fishing Mecca in Canada.

Hotel at Rock, in Cornwall; new ground for us, but it sounds a pleasant place, and we are lucky in that John will be able to join us there next week.

The author was delighted with Penmayne House, which he pronounced 'the most peaceful and best-run hotel in which I've ever stayed'. The family read, walked, botanised, and one day saw 'a gigantic cheese, flotsam from some torpedoed ship, being pecked to bits by a flock of gulls'.

Wednesday 18 June   **Windsor**

On the twelfth the King, with A. Hardinge, P. Legh and D. Kavanagh, flew to Algiers, where he still is, to the great satisfaction of the Allied world. This trip, which began to take shape many weeks ago, has been one of the best-kept secrets of the war, and has had a remarkably good press, both here and in USA.

In general, things seem to be going well enough, with Pantelleria and Lampedusa falling without much trouble for us, and the toll of sunken U-boats mounting steadily. On the other hand, the rapprochement between Giraud and de Gaulle looks like being a sterile and short-lived union, and Stalin is again shouting for a 'second front'. Wavell is to succeed Linlithgow as Viceroy, Auchinleck becoming C-in-C again, *vice* Wavell. The only thing against Wavell is that he is a soldier, which will alarm and excite the Indians; but he will make a better Viceroy than would either of the two runners-up, Oliver Lyttelton and Lampson.

Sunday 20 June

The King arrived safely in Malta this morning. Coal-strikes in USA have flared up again. Our Government and the American Government are deeply dissatisfied with de Gaulle's conduct since he got to Algiers. The Duke of Gloucester is here this weekend, which simplifies my job; the Queen and he, as the two senior members of the Council of State, have to sign every submission that would normally be signed by the King, and it makes things much easier having them both under one roof. He told me this evening that he would like to go to Australia as Governor-General for two or three years when the war is over; this would be quite a good plan, I think, when Princess Elizabeth is old enough to take part in public affairs.

Monday 21 June

The King went to Malta yesterday, in *Aurora*, and has now returned to Tunis.

Tuesday 22 June

The PM came to luncheon with the Queen, who had held her first investiture in the morning. Joan came to St James's Palace from Evershot, looking very well. Winston has sent a masterpiece of a telegram to Joe Stalin, who has again been bleating for a 'second front'.

Wednesday 23 June

We went to a promenade concert in the Albert Hall – a good Bach/Handel programme, with Harriet Cohen at the piano, and L. Goossens[1] playing the Bach oboe concerto superlatively well. The Queen brought Princess Elizabeth into the box, in which, besides ourselves, was a remarkably representative cross-section of the Empire sent by the Overseas League – two New Zealand soldiers, three Canadian airmen, some English WAAFs, and a bluejacket from Kenya. The audience, when they spotted the Queen, gave her a good welcome, and then concentrated exclusively on the music, taking no further notice of her till the end of the programme, when they gave her an equally good send-off. Basil Cameron,[2] who conducted throughout, came to the box in the interval; poor old Henry Wood,[3] to whom we owe the Proms, which have been a delight to me for over thirty years, has broken down, I fear finally.

We went back to Buckingham Palace for an excellent supper, without which we should probably have gone hungry to bed, as it is difficult to get an adequate meal in any restaurant after 9.30 nowadays. Princess Elizabeth obviously enjoyed the concert, and I think may be really fond of music.

Friday 25 June

Rose at 5, and in the middle of a light breakfast got a message from the Cabinet Office to say that the King's aeroplane [returning from Morocco] was an hour ahead of schedule, and would reach Northolt at six instead of seven. E. Miéville and I dashed off as soon as possible, and arrived there, simultaneously with Winston, to find the aeroplane had already landed, and the King and the others drinking coffee in the mess. They all looked

---

1 Leon Goossens (1897–1988), solo oboist, for whom several leading composers wrote concertos.
2 Basil Cameron (1884–1975), conductor of numerous leading orchestras, including London Symphony, London Philharmonic, Berlin Philharmonic and Concertgebouw (Amsterdam).
3 Sir Henry Wood (1869–1944), conductor, inaugurated annual Promenade Concerts at the Queen's Hall in 1895.

well, though several of them, including HM, have had mild attacks of 'Gippy tummy'. The whole trip has been a great success. The PM drove back to Buckingham Palace with the King, and later brought the War Cabinet down to see him.

A short account of the Stalingrad sword, which I had previously vetted, appeared in the Press today. The King, when I was with him, made my blood run cold by pointing to the description of the leopards' heads at the end of the quillons, saying, 'I've had a brainwave. This sword is for Russia. Change the leopards into bears.'

I was inspired to say, I hope with some truth, that the bear was not, to the Russian, his national totem, but one invented by foreign cartoonists; and that to give him a sword with bears on it would be like giving the French one ornamented with frogs.

This went down all right; motion withdrawn. Please God he don't think of sturgeons in the watches of the night. I don't know what I say then.[1]

Saturday 26 June

The King told me today that he had lost a stone during his trip. I am bound to say he looks none the worse for it. The Queen sent me a charming note thanking me for helping her to administer the affairs of the nation as a Councillor of State; neither her duties nor mine, however, have been very arduous.

Sunday 27 June   Windsor

An agreeably quiet day; lovely weather, and I sat for some hours in my basket chair outside the George IV gateway. Dined with the P. Leghs in their rooms in the Henry VIII ditto, and heard Joey's inside story of the African trip.

Friday 2 July

I read today a paper recording Winston's exposition, at a small luncheon

---

1   The ceremonial sword was presented to Stalin by Churchill during the Tehran Conference in Nov. 1943. Its blade was engraved with the dedication, 'To the steel-hearted citizens of Stalingrad, a gift from King George VI as a token of the homage of the British people'. As Antony Beevor recorded in his book *Stalingrad* (p. 418), 'Churchill made the ceremony memorable by his oratory. Stalin, who accepted the sword with both hands, lifted it to his lips to kiss the scabbard. He then passed it to Marshal Voroshilov, who clumsily let the sword slide out of the scabbard. It clattered noisily to the floor.'

party in Washington five weeks ago, of his views for the machinery that should be set up to order the world after the war – the new League of Nations, in fact; I thought it brilliant. Of the old League, he said that its failure was not the fault of the League itself, but of the constituent states, and I should say this was true.

The Americans present seem to have agreed wholeheartedly with all that he said; Stimson[1] emphasised that it was essential to get the machinery set up, and USA irrevocably pledged to its operation, *before* the end of the war. Winston's idea for policing the world, internationally, is that each of the members of his new league should maintain, in addition to its own national armed forces, an international contingent which would be automatically at the disposal of the league in the event of trouble; and that Prussia, in addition to being 'disarmed' root and branch, should not be allowed to possess a single aircraft of any description, or to train a single man as an aviator.

Walking in the garden of Buckingham Palace at dusk this evening, I flushed a heron on the pond. I've never before seen one in the heart of London.

Saturday 3 July

John and Lavinia organised a party for us in the evening. It began with the theatre – a revue called *Sweet and Low*.[2] We then dined fourteen-strong at the Lansdowne Restaurant, our party being reinforced by various brother officers of John's and some young women. When we left, at 11.30, they were all going on to some other haunt. It was a pleasant evening for young and old, though I gather that the guests of honour will have to foot the bill. John has written an admirable Bellocian poem – a prayer to Dionysus on being forced to shelter from the rain in a milk bar.

Saturday 10 July

Operation 'Husky', the invasion of Sicily, began early this morning, and seems to have got well under weigh, with little loss to us so far. We have definitely accounted for fifty submarines in the past seventy days, which probably means that at least half as many more were also sunk or crippled. A very fierce Russo-German battle is raging on the Kursk salient.

E. Maclagan gave me a good *mot* of Winston's the other day: as one of

---

1 Henry Stimson (1867–1950), US Secretary of State 1929–33, US Secretary of War 1940–45.
2 Starring Hermione Gingold at the Ambassadors Theatre.

the trustees of Chequers, he had to go down there recently and stayed to luncheon. The PM was at the top of his form, and in the course of the meal remarked, apropos the de Gaulle–Giraud squabbles, 'I, of course, am exceedingly pro-French; unfortunately the French are exceedingly pro-voking.'

Saturday 17 July

Since June 25th I have been in the throes of a crisis, which has now ended in A. Hardinge tendering his resignation to the King, who instantly accepted it and asked me to fill his place.

For the last twenty years I have said, in jest and in earnest, that the one thing I wished to be spared was being called on to act as the King's private secretary, and, as far as my personal inclinations go, this was never more true than now; tired out by four years of my second world war, and with no real flair for public life, I wanted nothing better than to maintain the status quo, as *assistant* private secretary, till 1947 (when I reach sixty, our statutory retiring age), and then to go back to the supremely happy life that, for a brief interval, I led at Sutton after I had left the Prince of Wales.

For some years past I have been the unwilling target of a 'Hardinge must go' barrage inside this house (i.e. Buckingham Palace) from almost everybody, from the King and Queen downwards, and outside it from a variety of people whose opinion could not be altogether ignored; to all such criticism I have, I can honestly say, turned a rigidly deaf ear; partly because I believed that Alec Hardinge's great administrative and executive talents as a King's secretary compensated, on balance, for his complete inability to establish friendly, or even civil, relations with the great majority of his fellow-men; partly from natural loyalty to a departmental chief, whose ability I much admired; and partly, I fear, from indolence, in that I knew that, if he went, the lot would almost certainly fall on me.[1]

Lately, however, it was borne in on me that I could no longer maintain that attitude; a variety of circumstances contributed to that result, of which the most important were that he and the King were so temperamentally incompatible that they were rapidly driving each other crazy – the relationship had become like that of Queen Anne and Sarah Marlborough in the later period of the latter's ascendancy; that Alec's health was becoming seriously impaired – he is a man with no sense of flippancy, and no power to relax; and that, in our own office, his policy of splendid isolation had

---

1 Tommy was by no means the only contemporary who found Hardinge difficult. Harold Macmillan described him as 'idle, supercilious, without a spark of imagination or vitality'.

made him quite 'impossible' to colleagues like E. Miéville and myself, both men of some experience, the one his contemporary, the other eight years older than himself.

Of these factors, the first was easily the most weighty; the situation had become so bad that something had to be done about it. The Royal Family themselves are notoriously incapable of cutting that kind of Gordian knot; our present Lord Chamberlain (Bertie Clarendon), who should properly have wielded the scissors, could not be trusted with negotiating a change of scullery maids, let alone of private secretaries; so there was nobody to do it save my unfortunate self, labouring under the double disadvantage of appearing to conspire for the reversion of a job which, as a matter of fact, I would have given much to avoid.

The spark that fired the train was a departmental discourtesy – indeed a piece of departmental inefficiency – which forced me, for the first time in our association, to protest vigorously to A.H. He met this with his usual flat refusal to admit that he is ever anything but 100 per cent right, and, in the course of the episode, sent me a note so impertinent that I had no alternative but to write out my resignation to the King. As A.H. had himself declared to me a few days before that he had practically made up his own mind to resign, I warned him of what I had done – I felt that the poor King, just back from his exhausting African trip, could not fairly be given a right-and-left of resignations in the same week.[1] But, with my letter to the King in my pocket, I felt free, and obliged, in the King's interests, to take the opportunity in our final interview of telling A.H. that, if I went, he ought to go too, for the reasons which I frankly gave him.

Alec, who has a great deal in common with Sir Willoughby Patterne,[2] listened to my indictment with blank incredulity; realising this, I suggested to him that we should refer the whole matter to Bobbety Cranborne, one of the few friends we have in common, and one whose good judgement neither of us would question; if Bobbety should decide that I was talking nonsense, I was quite ready, I said, to believe him, to tear up my letter of resignation, and, for the present at any rate, to continue to do my job as best I could.

At first he favoured this idea, but later rejected it, and said he wanted to talk the whole thing over with his wife. On this we parted, quite amicably. That evening, just before dinner, I was rung up by the King (to whom I had said no word of all this, nor had anybody else), who, to my aston-

---

1   It was said that on the trip to Africa, Hardinge – always reluctant to delegate – had taken the keys of the royal dispatch boxes with him, so that his colleagues were unable to deal with their contents until he returned.
2   In *The Egoist*, George Meredith's best-known novel (1879).

ishment, told me that he had just had a letter from A.H. tendering his resignation, and that he had decided at once to accept it. The rapidity with which he came, unaided, to this decision was a remarkable proof that my diagnosis of the intolerable relationship between him and Alec was even more accurate than I had suspected.

When, after dinner, I went round to see HM, it was quite clear that there had never been the slightest hesitation in his mind as to what was the answer he wanted to send, and did send, later in the evening. When I suggested to him that it might be best to give Alec six months' leave, and then come to a final decision, he said emphatically, 'Certainly not – he might come back.' Neither then nor later did he consult me about his own share in the somewhat protracted correspondence which developed between him and A. during the days that followed, though he subsequently read out to me bits of the letters that he had sent and received – and very curious some of the latter were. A.H. was so clearly in an abnormal condition of mind and body that I am not going to quote them.

On the following night [7 July] the King dined with the PM at No. 10, and told him of the change which he proposed to make. So far as I know, Winston did not offer any objection; nor, indeed, have I heard of anybody who did not think that A.'s departure was timely, though I don't flatter myself that opinion is so unanimous about my own advent. Still, I have had some very kind letters from people whose opinions I value; and the welcome given to the change by all in the Household has been almost indecent. We had become, as the sailors say, a very unhappy ship; and A.'s conscious policy of '*oderint dum metuant*'[1] had resulted in his colleagues feeling the first emotion intensely and the second not at all.

There were some unpleasant phases in the subsequent developments, but they have now, I am glad to say, faded away, and there is general recognition on both sides of the fence that all is for the best, and that everybody has behaved with the best intentions. For this, Helen Hardinge, with whom I had a long talk, at her own request, one evening, and who behaved with more sense than might have been expected, is to a considerable extent responsible.

I have refrained throughout from mentioning the affair, at any of its stages, to anybody (save of course Joan) but Jasper Ridley, who gave me wise advice on it; yesterday, however, Stanley Baldwin, on one of his occasional visits to London, telephoned to me that he had just seen A.H. and would like to see me also. The old man has known both of us for many years, and I was only too glad to lay the whole story before his wise and

---

1   'Let them hate, so long as they fear', Cicero *Philippic,* I, 14.

impartial judgement. After hearing what I had to say, and asking some pertinent questions, he made it quite clear that he thought A.'s resignation was the best thing for all parties, and told me what I was glad to hear, that A.'s account of it all had been free from any bitterness. Today, a formal announcement was made in the Court Circular; A.H. has gone to Crichel, to begin the four or five months' complete rest that the doctors rightly order him; and I sit rather wearily in his chair, only too conscious of the heavy burden of responsibility and business that I have shouldered. Still, I have reached the top of my profession at the age of fifty-six, and I suppose that is something.

Later note: In my interview with Alec, I said I didn't know if I should be able to stand up to the job very long. 'You won't last six months,' said A., characteristically; but I lasted nine years.

After a long day at Buckingham Palace went out to get some dinner about 8.20 p.m. Found Pratt's shut, Wilton's ditto and the coffee room at the Travellers just closing down; however, I managed to get some bully beef and a slice of a nondescript fruit tart. Walked home with Cecil Liddell, who said that the MI contacts in Moscow report great exultation among the high-ups there, who consider that the abortive German attack on the Kursk salient has been something very near a major disaster for them.

The *Evening Standard*, in a particularly ill-informed paragraph, describes me as having 'a thick thatch of black hair', as if I were an Italian organ-grinder.

Tommy was bombarded with congratulations on his appointment. Enthusiastic letters came from Lord Mountbatten, Geoffrey Dawson (former editor of The Times*), Archbishop Lang and many other public figures. 'Hurrah, hurrah, ten thousand times hurrah!' wrote Delia Peel. 'I think you will go down to history as a* **super** *Ponsonby-Stamfordham, because you have so many more human and knowledgeable points of contact with every sort of person than they ever could have had, besides a sure hand with Royalty.' Cynthia Colville (for thirty years a lady-in-waiting to Queen Mary) was equally enthusiastic: 'It is simply grand when the right person and the right place come together; and I am so pleased, and don't know whom to congratulate more – you or the King!' Even the Duke of Beaufort, signing himself 'Master', was moved to send a tribute from Badminton in the depths of Gloucestershire: 'I understand the grouse are very bad this year, but hope you will be able to enjoy a few days "on the hill".' But none of Tommy's friends was more delighted than Conrad Russell:*

So now you sit in the chair of General Grey and Henry Ponsonby, of Knollys and Stamfordham, and I'll say you are a very handsome addition to the party. When I first knew you, you were a jobber's cad. You swept out the

*office and you swept the floor, and you polished up the handle of the big
front door. Now you are at the top of the tree, and I think the King is a lucky
boy to get you.*

Sunday 18 July

Arthur Penn, in a very nice letter to me a few days ago, wrote such an
admirable summing-up of A.H. that I transcribe it: 'Alec's is a tragic figure.
He is an old friend of both of us, and it is truer of him than of anybody else
that he is his own worst enemy. The highest principles, long experience,
great capacity and infinite devotion to duty – such a make-up should
combine to produce the ideal occupant of his position; but, alas, the Gods
have withheld too much. A contempt for *ser*vility had left barely standing-
room for *civ*ility; and what profiteth it a man in his position to be irre-
proachable if he is even more unapproachable? I am truly sorry for him,
for he is a most lonely figure.'

Later note: Alec died of cancer in 1960. He never really recovered his
health, and never took on another job of any importance. I saw him rarely,
but was on friendly terms with both him and his wife. He spent much time
and energy on the Moral Rearmament movement.

Yesterday I 'took over' formally, and spent an exhausting day moving my
accumulated papers and possessions from my own little room to the more
dignified apartment near the foot of the King's staircase that is traditionally
occupied by the Private Secretary. The King sent me a kind letter from
Windsor, with the PM's submission that I be sworn a member of HM's
most honourable Privy Council, and has instructed Privy Purse to raise my
screw from £1,500 p.a. to £2,500 p.a. as from August 1st.

Monday 19 July

Colonel Stimson, the American War Secretary, to see the King. One of the
amenities of my elevation is that I now get a chance of meeting the notabilities who call on HM. Stimson is now 73, and looks it; but he has been
a very good friend to us throughout.

I was bidden to luncheon at No. 10 by Winston, who arrived late from
Chequers, in his famous siren suit. The others were Leo Amery, Ramaswami
Mudaliar[1] and John Martin. Mudaliar is a strict Hindu, and the only dish
offered him was *beef*, which he, of course, rejected, almost with horror.
Winston, after a moment's embarrassment, ordered 'something else' to be

---

1   Diwan Bahadur Sir Arcot Ramaswami Mudaliar (1887–1976), representative of India at
the War Cabinet and Pacific War Council in London, 1942–3.

produced, and after an interval an omelette appeared. It is all wrong that such a gaffe should occur in the very heart of the British Empire.

The conversation consisted largely of a monologue, as W. was in his most loquacious mood. He began by 'thinking aloud' on the very real problem of maintaining a sufficiency of our armed forces to continue the war against Japan after it has ended in Europe. Then much serious talk, interlarded with lighter conversational excursions into more or less irrelevant by-paths. He was indignant at India having increased her population by fifty million souls in the past ten years. 'This vast and improvident efflorescence of humanity must stop,' he said to Mudaliar. 'Your people must practise birth-control.' But he did not forget to point the moral – that it was only thanks to the beneficence and wisdom of British rule that India, free from any hint of war for a longer period than almost any other country in the world, had been able to increase and multiply to this astonishing extent.

Mudaliar rebutted his accusation that Indians were ungrateful to us, and said that the great majority of his fellow-countrymen had no wish to contract out of the Empire. Winston said that the old idea that the Indian was in any way inferior to the white man must go. 'We must all be pals together. I want to see a great shining India, of which we can be as proud as we are of a great Canada or a great Australia.' In general, he was sound, and very liberal; but, though nobody mentioned it, he seemed to forget the main cleavage in Anglo-Indian social unity – that no white man can endure the thought of mixed marriages; and nature herself condemns such marriages by the almost invariably inferior quality of their fruits.

At one point somebody came in to say that our bombers had launched their long-discussed attack on the marshalling yards of Rome. 'Good,' said Winston. 'And have we hit the Pope? Have we made a hole in his tiara?' We sat long while he sipped brandy. The arrival of P. J. Grigg and B. Bracken[1] upstairs was announced. 'The Secretary of State for War and the Minister of Information are engaged in a bloody row because the former wishes to enrol many of the latter's personnel in the army. Let them come down here and compose their differences over the bottle.' So down they came, and B.B. counter-attacked roundly when Winston started inveighing against 'your pansies in the BBC who talk about "Syr-a-cusa"' – and this provoked an animated discussion as to how far it was legitimate for an Englishman, speaking English, to give foreign names a foreign pronunciation.

We didn't leave the table till 3.15 p.m., when I had a short talk with

---

1   Brendan Bracken (1901–58), red-headed newspaper magnate, was Minister of Infor-
    mation 1941–5 and First Lord of the Admiralty 1945. Created 1st Viscount Bracken of
    Christchurch 1952. His publishing interests included Eyre & Spottiswoode, the *Financial
    News* and *The Economist*.

Winston, who was very friendly. I told him that the King had changed his mind about giving Dudley Pound the OM, which he had previously been unwilling to do, and this pleased him. He then declared his determination, in the face of all opposition, to resuscitate the Order of St Patrick, dormant since the defection of Eire. I got away about 3.30, having been due at the Foreign Office to see Alec Cadogan[1] at 3 p.m.

Tuesday 20 July

E. Miéville went away for a week's leave, which means I am single-handed. Investiture. PM luncheon with the King. Joan came over to tea, to inspect my installation in this room. Afterwards, went with Their Majesties to the County Hall to see the exhibition of the 'London County Plan' – a scheme for reorganising London over a period of fifty years, at a cost of £250 million. It is difficult to digest a series of such designs; they seem sensible and imaginative on the whole, but obviously the whole thing must be extremely elastic and designed to conform easily to changes in Londoners' habits of life that none of us can foresee today. A lot of thought is devoted e.g. to the disposal of the railway termini. What guarantee is there that, in a few decades, there will be any railways at all? Fifty years ago, any building plan in residential London would have had to provide stabling on a grand scale; yet before long horses had vanished from the streets.

Talking of European capitals, our heavy raid on Rome yesterday seems to have accomplished its objects of smashing the marshalling yards completely, while doing practically no damage outside of them. But it is bound to excite a lot of protest among Roman Catholics all over the world.

I have had a vast quantity of letters congratulating me on my new job – many from friends whose good wishes I value, many from bores whose handwriting I never want to see, and quite a few from men whose very existence I had forgotten.

Wednesday 21 July

Lunching at the Beefsteak, Harold Nicolson quoted advice once given him by Edward Grey:[2] 'Never be afraid of being gullible; better be that than suspicious.'

---

1   Rt. Hon. Sir Alexander Cadogan (1884–1968), Permanent Under-Secretary of State for Foreign Affairs 1938–46.
2   1862–1933. Foreign Secretary 1905–16. Created 1st Viscount Grey of Fallodon 1916. Passionate politician and diplomat, ornithologist, remembered for his book *The Charm of Birds* (1927).

General Giraud came to see the King. I had not met him before: a fine figure of a man, with a pleasant, open countenance, and straight as a ramrod in his carriage. His ADC told me that he had managed his escape initially by making a rope out of many lengths of wire, which his wife sent him, concealed in cakes, etc.; and confirmed the story of his bluffing the German police when they were searching the railway train for him.

Thursday 22 July

Crinks Johnstone (Parliamentary Secretary, Department of Overseas Trade) and I were sworn members of the Privy Council this morning, and, after a brief rehearsal in the 44 Room with Leadbitter[1] (the Charles Greville of today) went through the ritual without putting a foot wrong. Our fellow members who watched us make the necessary obeisances to our Sovereign were the Lord President (John Anderson[2]), Norfolk,[3] Andrew Duncan[4] and Geddes.[5] We were allowed to keep the slim red testaments with which we took the oath, and they, so far as I know, are the only perquisites of the office. [*Note:* We are allowed to sit on the steps of the throne during a debate in the House of Lords – a very uncomfortable privilege.]

Lunched in the Goldsmiths' Hall, off Cheapside, one of the few halls of the great Livery Companies that came through the Blitz comparatively scatheless. Outside, on the ruins of a block of buildings, the Civil Defence people have planted, and cultivated, a neat little flower garden, now gay with hollyhocks. We lunched, not at all badly, off hot-pot of rabbit and a blancmange, and it was pleasant to see once more a display of good silver, well cleaned. I was next Sir G. Courthorpe,[6] the Prime Warden, who is also a director of the Southern Railway; apropos the place of railways in any plan for the London of the future, he agreed with me they might need no place at all in a few decades. He told me that in a single night the Blitz had deprived the Goldsmiths of rents to the value of £63,000 per annum. After

---

1 Eric Leadbitter (1891–1971), civil servant and author, Clerk of the Privy Council 1942–51. Knighted 1946.
2 John Anderson (1882–1958), Governor of Bengal 1932–7, Lord President of the Council 1940–43, Chancellor of the Exchequer 1943–5. Created 1st Viscount Waverley 1952.
3 Bernard Marmaduke Fitzalan-Howard, 16th Duke of Norfolk (1908–75), Joint Parliamentary Secretary to Minister of Agriculture 1941–5.
4 Rt. Hon. Sir Andrew Duncan (1884–1952), Minister of Supply 1941 and 1942–5.
5 Auckland Campbell Geddes (1879–1954), professor of anatomy at various universities, British Ambassador to the USA 1920–24. Created 1st Baron Geddes 1942.
6 George Loyd Courthorpe (1877–1955), barrister, forester and farmer, Forestry Commissioner 1923–48, Prime Warden of the Goldsmiths' Company 1943–5. Created 1st Baron Courthorpe 1945.

luncheon we went into committee on the design for the Stalingrad sword, which Gleadowe, who is responsible for it, unwisely wants to alter radically. They put me in the chair, and, stoutly supported by Eric Maclagan, I was able at last to get things settled – but not before 3.20, which wrecked my afternoon.

Brendan Bracken drew my attention to an advertisement of poor Madame Sikorski in the Agony Column of today's *Times*, and wondered if anything could be found for her at Hampton Court, the advert being an SOS for a small flat in or near London. We got four more submarines yesterday. That makes about eighty since May 1st, and a lot more 'probables', and more crippled.

Friday 23 July

To Windsor, p.m. Reading (when I have time, which isn't often nowadays) Helen Waddell's delightful novel *Peter Abelard*, which is not far off a masterpiece. Americans entered Palermo; two-thirds of Sicily is in our hands now, and the Russians are all round Orel.

Saturday 24 July

I had a very nice letter, on my elevation, from Lady Salisbury, which I value. My collection of such letters is now a formidable one, from a great variety of people, and all most generous. It is perhaps significant that gradually my colleagues in the present Household, and many in the last, have expressed delight, more or less veiled by discretion – sometimes not veiled at all – at the change.

Piers Legh and I went down to Eton to watch the final of the house matches, Butterwick's versus Tatham's. Slow cricket, from which I walked away with the Head Master, Claude Elliott,[1] whose company is always pleasant. He agreed that Geo Muff's[2] letter in *The Times* was an epoch-making document; he is the first of the Labourites to have courage to say openly what most of them have long admitted in secret, that the system of education among our 'upper classes' has certain solid virtues, and produces a type not wholly useless to the community at large.

---

1   Sir Claude Aurelius Elliott (1888–1973), Head Master of Eton College 1933–49, Provost of Eton College 1949–64. Knighted 1958.
2   George Muff (1877–1955), Labour MP and Army Welfare Officer. Created 1st Baron Calverley 1945.

Sunday 25 July

This evening, Rome radio announced that Mussolini has resigned, and Badoglio[1] has taken over all his offices. As the popular song has it, 'Oh, what a surprise for the Duce.'

Monday 26 July

Field-Marshal Sir John Dill[2] came in to see the King. He spoke highly of Michael Adeane, who has been working in his circus at Washington, and clearly thinks that the sudden collapse of 1918 might well repeat itself all over Europe this year. But what a hideous mess it will be if they all throw their hands in more or less simultaneously. Though one can't want the war to last a single day longer than necessary, the world might have a better chance of recovery if the armistices came at well-spaced intervals rather than one on top of the other.

Tuesday 27 July

Louis Greig, recently back from Cairo, gave me today a much more encouraging picture of King Farouk[3] than that drawn in Miles Lampson's telegrams. Little news from Italy, though many rumours via Berne, etc. Winston spoke on the situation to the Commons, to the text of 'No remission of our offensive until we have complete surrender from them'. The text of the 'Instrument of Surrender' was brought out of cold storage yesterday and circulated to the Cabinet.

Ismay came in to see me after luncheon, and told me some of the difficulties we have had in trying to get the Americans to see eye-to-eye with us on various points of major strategy. Most of them have never got over their distaste for campaigning in the Mediterranean, and are really only interested in the war in the Pacific.

Their Majesties went off to Scotland, where I have been busy arranging a two-day tour for them. After dinner Joan and I sat by the lake at Buckingham Palace.

---

1 Marshal Pietro Badoglio (1871–1956), former Viceroy of Abyssinia and Chief of the Italian General Staff. On the fall of Mussolini, he became PM of Italy, and later signed an armistice with the Allies.
2 Field-Marshal Sir John Dill (1881–1944), CIGS 1940–41. After the British Chiefs of Staffs' visit to Washington with the PM in 1941, he remained in the USA as head of British Joint Staff Mission.
3 King Farouk of Egypt (1921–65) ruled from 1937 until 1952, when a revolution forced him to abdicate, and he fled to Italy.

Wednesday 28 July

Yesterday our Air-Rescue people picked up seventy-three airmen floating about in the North Sea in their dinghies, all well and apparently quite happy. Mouse Fielden, who has just been to see me, says that his circus, who were asked to join in the rescue work, claim ten more.

There can be little left of Hamburg now, which had yet another terrible pounding last night – our losses only 2.4 per cent.

Lady Newall, wife of the Governor-General of New Zealand, called on me this afternoon, gushing as high as any of that country's far-famed geysers. Still, she sent me a 2lb pot of marmalade for Xmas, so much may be forgiven her.

Thursday 29 July

Dawson of Penn told me this morning that, at the request of the Government, he had just been to Holloway Gaol to see Oswald Mosley,[1] who has now been in prison for nearly four years. Dawson found him well, and showing no bitterness; he said he had no interest in politics now, and was quite absorbed by the study of philosophy, which he reads incessantly – Kant, Hegel, etc. Dawson has a high opinion of his intellect. His wife is with him, and they see their children from time to time. Incarceration, for a man of his age and vigour, is a terrible fate, and I don't believe he could do much harm now if they let him out. He wants to be allowed to retire, on parole, to a farm.

Talking of those grim days in July 1940, Harold Nicolson said that he recollected a conversation between the Argentine Ambassador and Rob Hudson.[2] The Ambassador, trying to prove that it was hopeless our trying to continue the war, enumerated the long list of items that were then incontrovertibly and overwhelmingly on the debit side. 'I agree with every word you say,' said Rob, 'but you have forgotten one thing – namely that God is an Englishman.' (I could not help interjecting that I had, nonetheless, often suspected at that time that the Deity might be contemplating taking out naturalisation papers.) Harold also said that when he was once deploring our forlorn situation three years ago to old Cartier de Marchienne,[3] the

---

1   Sir Oswald Mosley, 6th Bt., 1896–1980, British Fascist leader, married (2nd) the Hon. Diana Mitford, 1936. Both were interned under Regulation 18B at the start of the war.
2   Robert Hudson (1886–1957), farmer and MP, Minister of Agriculture and Fisheries 1940–45.
3   Baron de Cartier de Marchienne (1871–1946), Belgian Ambassador to the Court of St James 1927–46.

lattcr had said, 'Never forget, my boy, that you belong to the greatest people the world has ever seen.' Not bad, for a Belgian.

Tuesday 3 August

Yesterday 'Zip', the new and I hope final battle in Sicily, began and seems to be going on all right. American bombers have raided the Ploesti oilfields – expensive, but if they have put a proportion of the refineries out of action, it may shorten the war by six months.

PM to luncheon; the King gave him a letter, expressing to him, as Minister of Defence, HM's appreciation of the good work done by those who planned and organised 'Husky', as the invasion of Sicily was styled.

Wednesday 4 August

Got off a telegram from the King to F.D.R. congratulating him on Ploesti. The Prime Minister, in one of his amendments to the draft, wrote, 'Attack from a *low height*.' I pointed out that this was an Irishism, and got him to substitute 'low level'. He, by the way, left for Quebec to meet F.D.R. A few days ago I suddenly saw in one of his telegrams to the latter, about Italy, 'discarding etiquette, I have telegraphed direct to the King of Italy'. What would Queen Victoria have said, had Pam [Palmerston, her Foreign Secretary] telegraphed to a crowned head without first consulting her? However, as the King was in Scotland, and the matter a really urgent one, I was able to make out a case, which HM accepted, particularly after seeing the text of the message, which ran, 'Expect no mercy if you deliver our and Allied prisoners now in your hands to Germany.'

Thursday 5 August

Joan and I dined with Leonard Brockington[1] to meet Leonard Woolley,[2] the excavator of Ur, and his wife. He is a charming and most interesting man; he showed us many photographs of the numerous lovely things he found at Ur, and kept us enthralled for an hour.

Friday 6 August

I went p.m. to see Anthony Bevir, the Secretary at 10 Downing Street, who

---

1 Leonard Walter Brockington (1888–1966), Canadian adviser to the British Govt.
2 Sir Leonard Woolley (1880–1966), archaeologist, excavated at Ur 1922–34 and many other Middle Eastern sites.

is laid up in the London Clinic, and lent him the first two volumes of Greville. Hoping to pick up a taxi, I walked the whole way there (Marylebone Road) from Buckingham Palace without encountering one that wasn't already bespoke.

Tuesday 10 August

I had a very nice letter from Queen Mary, and, by the same post, one from her brother, Athlone, in Canada. Winston, who sailed for Canada in the *Queen Mary* last Thursday, has arrived safely at Halifax.

Wednesday 11 August

The King left for Scotland tonight, and, as always on the last day before he goes north, there was a string of people whom he had to see: Billy Harlech, who returns to South Africa in a few days: Attlee,[1] acting Prime Minister in Winston's absence – I found that he, as I have done, has been thinking [about] the Athenian expedition to Sicily all this last fortnight:[2] Philip Swinton, who came to get his recently-awarded CH; he has no news of his missing RAF son;[3] but has not quite given up hope: and Anthony Eden, debonair and cocksure, who shows no outward signs of feeling the strain of office.

Friday 13 August

Burghley,[4] who is about to be appointed Governor of Bermuda, came to see me, ostensibly to tell me of his recent successful trip to Australasia on behalf of the Ministry of Aircraft Production. His arrival in Australia was well-timed: the Australians were just emerging from their somewhat crapulous honeymoon with the Americans, and were feeling disillusioned, and, realising how foolishly they had alienated British sentiment, lonely. The appearance of one of our most modern Lancasters, bearing in its maw so thoroughly suitable an Ambassador of Antipodean Empire – a lord, an

---

1 Rt. Hon. Clement Attlee (1883–1967), barrister and politician, Deputy PM 1942–5, PM 1945–51. Created 1st Earl Attlee 1955.
2 The Athenian attempt to subdue Sicily in 415–413 BC ended in disastrous failure.
3 Philip Cunliffe-Lister (1884–1972), created 1st Earl of Swinton 1935. Cabinet Minister Resident in W. Africa 1942–4, Minister for Civil Aviation 1944–5. His son died of wounds.
4 David Cecil, Baron Burghley (1905–81), succeeded his father as 6th Marquess of Exeter in 1956. Winner of the 400-m. hurdles at the 1928 Olympics, and of many other international races. Governor and C-in-C Bermuda 1943–6.

MP, an MFH [Master of Foxhounds] and an Olympic hurdler – worked wonders.

He was rather reluctant to take on Bermuda, feeling that he could be more useful just now in MAP and the House of Commons, but I urged him to do so; Bermuda is of great importance now, being from its very adjacency, the one colony of the British Empire by which the Americans appraise our colonial system as a whole, and it is vital that its governor should be not only a capable administrator, but a man who can handle the Yanks. Moreover, it is no less important that our future pro-consuls, who are in lamentably short supply, should be reinforced by men of B.'s generation and potentialities.

Dined with Cecil Liddell, who is alarmed at the possibility of a Russo-German-Japanese coalition against ourselves and the Americans in the years to come. But the future is so entirely inscrutable that it is fruitless to speculate on possible permutations and combinations among the peoples of the world. The only thing of which I feel fairly certain, negatively, is that Winston's ideal of a restored and regenerated France is not likely to be realised in either his lifetime or mine. He, by the way, is quoted in today's *Times* as making the perfect retort, courteous but annihilating, to some bloody fool who asked him whether the falls of Niagara looked the same as when he first visited them in 1900. 'Well,' said W., 'the principle remains the same. The water still keeps falling.'

Saturday 14 August

Ned Grigg[1] came to see me this afternoon, bringing me a copy of his new book, *The British Commonwealth*. We sat and talked in the garden for an hour. He said the King and Queen ought to go to Canada, Australia and New Zealand, *now* – i.e., before the end of the war; that the effect of their appearing in these dominions while the war was still going on would outweigh the obvious risks inherent in such an enterprise. I doubt if it is feasible, though there is much to be said for the idea on paper. I'll talk to Bobbety about it when I see him at Balmoral. I doubt if the King would consent to fly all the way, especially if she went with him.

Discussing possible substitutes for Winston, N. agreed that, as things are at present, the King could only send for Eden. His next choice was Bobbety, and he would get round the difficulty of his being a peer by legislation putting all peers on the same footing, as Irish peers used to be, so that they

---

1 Edward Grigg (1879–1955), journalist, author, soldier and politician, Under-Secretary of State for War 1940–42, Minister Resident in the Middle East 1944–5. Created 1st Baron Altrincham 1945.

could, if they chose, sit in the lower house (and this may well come about). I don't believe it would be difficult to arrange things so that he could at any rate go down to the House of Commons and address it if the occasion demanded. Freddie Dalrymple-Hamilton dined with me, and I beat him at billiards on the Buckingham Palace table.

Sunday 15 August

Looking through P. Legh's notes on the King's African trip, I see that, in Malta, Gort[1] told him that it was the threat of starvation, rather than aerial attack, that had been most serious last year. When Gort took over in June 1942, he was told that the island only had food supplies for another six weeks; his predecessor had never instituted any proper system of rationing. In August the situation became critical – morale low, and everybody was on a starvation diet. Gort made all preparations for the surrender of the island; he, with a party of volunteers, planned to land in Sicily and sell their lives as dearly as possible. The arrival of the famous convoy eased the situation, and the capture of Tripoli by the Eighth Army saved it. Probably the island would have fallen, had not Gort been there.

Monday 16 August

Sam Hoare sent a series of telegrams last night telling of approaches made to him by an Italian general, Castellano,[2] who said he was empowered by Badoglio to say that, provided we would land on the mainland of Italy, they were prepared to join us and fight the Germans. He had no written credentials, but he succeeded in impressing Sam as 'a man of weight and sincerity'. He has been passed on to Lisbon, and may be flown to London. Military experts throw doubt on his assertion that there are thirteen German divisions in Italy.

Tuesday 17 August

I lunched with Daisy Bigge, whom I had not seen for a long time, and who entertained me with many recollections of the days when her father, Lord Stamfordham, sat at this table where I write. Dined with the Halifaxes, who

---

1 John Vereker, 6th Viscount Gort (Ireland) (1886–1946). In the First World War he won the VC, the DSO and two Bars, and was Mentioned in Despatches nine times. As Governor and C-in-C Malta 1942–4, he was widely credited for having saved the island from being overrun by Axis forces.
2 General Giuseppe Castellano, CoS to the Chief of the Italian General Staff.

got back from Washington a week ago, where were Mima Harlech, Lady Baba Metcalfe,[1] and their boy, R. Wood, who has lost both his legs from wounds in North Africa, and is very gallant and cheerful in his wheelchair. After dinner I had a talk with Edward in another room. He had propounded at dinner the same idea that N. Grigg put to me on Saturday about Their Majesties going to Australia, etc., before the end of the war. When we were alone, I told him how much it appealed to me as an idea, but had he considered the practical details of transportation? The sane and logical mind soon grasped the difficulties, and eventually he summed up by saying that going by air must be ruled out, on account of the risks, and that going by sea (entailing a strong escort in both Atlantic and Pacific) would be an unjustified diversion of naval strength; hence he reached the same conclusion as I did – that the trip ought to wait till the first possible moment after the armistice, when the Navy would have ships to spare, which they would be glad to use for such a purpose.

Wednesday 18 August

Winston and F.D.R. have decided to take General Castellano seriously, perhaps stimulated by a telegram from D'Arcy Osborne[2] in the Vatican, saying he had now got a signed letter from Badoglio guaranteeing General Castellano's *bona fides*. Eisenhower's Chief of Staff, Smith, and a British brigadier, Strong, are being sent to Lisbon to negotiate.

Both ourselves and the Yanks were very busy in the air yesterday. We made a heavy attack on Peenemünde, in the Baltic, losing about forty machines. This is the Baltic island on which all the German experts engaged in producing their secret 'rocket' gun are supposed to be collected.

Thursday 19 August

Before the Prime Minister went to Quebec, the King wrote him a letter asking him, as Minister of Defence, to congratulate all concerned on 'Husky', especially those responsible for its planning and organisation; the Prime Minister replied, and, by agreement, the two letters were put into cold storage against the final conquest of Sicily, when they were to be given to the world. The time having come, Hollis[3] and I made all arrangements

---

1 Lady Alexandra Metcalfe (1904–95), youngest daughter of Lord Curzon, married to Edward ('Fruity') Metcalfe (d. 1957), ADC and close friend of Edward, Prince of Wales.
2 D'Arcy Godolphin Osborne (1884–1964) British Minister to the Vatican 1936–47. Succeeded his cousin as 12th Duke of Leeds 1963.
3 Brig. Leslie Hollis, known as 'Joe', secretary to the Chiefs of Staff Committee, and Ismay's deputy.

for their publication tomorrow. I understood that this was to be the measure of the King's recognition of the achievement, and that it would not be incumbent on him to send any other congratulatory messages on what is, after all, only a single phase of our Italian campaign.

Friday 20 August

Lunch with Louis Greig, to meet Ernest Bevin. I had never had any sustained conversation with E.B. before, and liked him. He is an untidy feeder and a gross-looking chap, but impresses one as being sincere. He told us that he would dearly have liked to go to India as Viceroy, and propounded a scheme, that I confess I couldn't altogether follow, under which we would concentrate on the defence and economic betterment of India, and side-track the small, politically-minded minority by just paying no heed to them; his theory being that if we could guarantee security from external attack to, and raise the standard of living of, the Indian peoples as a whole, the vast majority of them would not trouble their heads about political development.

All the problems of caste, too, he claims are an anachronism, kept alive by vested interests; at one of the technical training establishments that he runs as Minister of Labour, he has succeeded for some years now in inducing the Indian students to forget all about class distinctions, and to live fraternally and communally with their fellow-Indians, even if they are 'Untouchables'. They are, of course, only a handful – there are, I think, never more than forty or fifty of them at one time; but it is an interesting experiment, which I believe has been entirely successful.

We talked of the Stalingrad sword, and he said that it certainly ought to be exhibited in some of the provincial cities, as well as in London. It struck me later that the ideal solution for its presentation would be for Winston to give it to Stalin personally, if and when they arrange to meet in the reasonably near future, as seems likely.

One thing about Bevin which struck me was that he obviously feels, rather sadly, that everybody thinks of him as a Trades Union boss, who had 'got on' in politics, whereas he would like to be considered a statesman with large imperial ideas; and I am quite prepared to believe that the latter is a truer estimate of him.

Monday 23 August

To see Hollis, who seems quite content with the result of the staff talks at Quebec. He thinks the Peenemünde attack was a good show. We are shortly going to plaster Wathen (near Hazebrouck), where for some time past the Germans have been feverishly digging an immense hole in the ground, which is thought to be for the installation of the rocket gun, or some other sinister purpose. As Wathen is within range of 'fighter cover', this should be a relatively simple job.

Tuesday 24 August

Joey Legh and I left for Scotland by the night train and reached Balmoral about noon. Cranbornes, Eldons, A. Penn, Delia Peel and H. Campbell here. After luncheon, fished the Boat and Rock pools, but moved nothing; there were plenty of fish showing.

We sent 710 bombers and seventeen Mosquitoes to bomb Berlin last night. We lost fifty-eight, but results are considered highly satisfactory. After dinner I took down a long telegram from Winston, asking the King's approval for Dickie Mountbatten's appointment to be C-in-C of the new South-East Asian command, and its immediate announcement. This HM gave. I hope D.M. is big enough for this job, but am not entirely confident about it. I am in a 'Minister's' room, and sleep surrounded by photographs of dead and whiskered Moderators of the Scottish Presbyterian Church.

Friday 27 August

Lovely morning, but a few showers p.m. Fished the Boat Pool before luncheon (Clachantarn after). Pricked a fish in the latter. A new emissary from Badoglio has arrived in Lisbon – General Zanussi, Chief of the General Staff, who brought with him old Carton de Wiart, VC, whom the Italians have held prisoner since his aeroplane fell into the sea a long time ago.[1] Winston and F.D.R. have now agreed the full terms for an Italian surrender, which have been cabled to Lisbon, and to Algiers, where Eisenhower and H. Macmillan, who had not yet heard about General Z., had arranged to meet General C. in Palermo tomorrow or Sunday. There are now so many doves flying over the face of the waters from the Italian ark that it is getting rather confusing. Anyhow, one or other of them ought to make contact with the olive tree.

The Quebec conference is now finally over, and Winston is retiring to a 'fishing camp' for a few days' rest prior to going to Washington, where,

---

1 Lieut.-Gen. Sir Adrian Carton de Wiart (1880–1963), VC, DSO, was wounded eight times in WWI. The author Peter Fleming described him as 'that legendary, admirable character', who had 'only one eye, only one arm, and – rather more surprisingly – only one Victoria Cross'.

inter alia, he will receive an honorary degree from Harvard. The conference has achieved the settlement of the question of the 'recognition' of the French Committee of National Liberation, after a bit of obstruction by Cordell Hull,[1] who has insisted on a slightly divergent form of recognition by USA. So I think it can fairly be called an 'outstanding success', as I have just suggested in a draft telegram of congratulation for the King to Winston.

Stalin sent a rude telegram to Winston and F.D.R. two days ago, complaining that he hadn't been kept informed about Italian negotiations, but has now followed it up with a much more civil one; he reiterates his wish to have a three-party meeting, but he won't go outside Russia, and I can't see how the President is to be got inside it.

Sunday 29 August

The Gloucesters, with Prince William,[2] have arrived. Jack Eldon and I have told A. Penn that his business is not to make the D. of G. laugh, but to make the D. of G. *not* laugh, and that we shall fine him 2s 6d every time the latter bursts out into that strange and irritating whinny for which he is justly celebrated.

Monday 30 August

The Moderator, Dr John Baillie,[3] Professor of Divinity at Edinburgh University, on saying goodbye to me, said he was greatly impressed (or words to that effect) by the sterling merits of the ladies and gents of Their Majesties' Household. Delia and I lunched alone in the Castle. Fished at intervals during the day, without moving anything. The Russians have recaptured Taganrog, which must be the final blow to Hitler's hopes of getting any oil out of the Caucasus. Boris of Bulgaria has died in mysterious circumstances; the official announcement says that he had angina pectoris (unusual in a man of forty-nine), and a newspaper reports that he was shot in the stomach. I rather liked him, on the only occasion that I saw him, when he boarded Edward VIII's train on its way through Bulgaria in September 1936. He was cultured and agreeable, and, though his eyes were too close together, did not give one the impression of that capacity for double-

---

1   Cordell Hull (1871–1955), Secretary of State of the US 1933–44.
2   Elder son of the Duke and Duchess of Gloucester (1941–72). Killed piloting his own aircraft in a race.
3   Very Rev. John Baillie (1886–1960), professor of divinity at the University of Edinburgh 1934–56, Moderator of the General Assembly of the Church of Scotland 1943–4, Chaplain to King George VI in Scotland 1947–52.

dealing and double-crossing with which he has always been credited.

The Danes are in revolt; the Germans have proclaimed martial law. Meanwhile, the Swedes are getting very bellicose, because the Germans have sunk some of their fishing boats.

After dinner last night they [members of the Royal Family] acted an indifferent charade, in the first scene of which A. Penn was wheeled about in Prince William's perambulator. This was not at all well received by the anxious parents, who have had great difficulty in finding a pram anywhere, and certainly would not be able to replace the springs of this one. Luckily, they stood the strain.

Wednesday 1 September

I took my luncheon up the river to MacLaren's pool, near the Braemar road, and ate it under a tree in heavy rain. The Duke of Gloucester came to consult me, before dinner, about filling in his time more usefully; since he left the army, he has been conspicuously out of a job, and is always agitating, rather aimlessly, for greater scope for his energies (though the latter are not supercharged). Queen Mary wrote to me at some length on the subject recently. I advised him to concentrate on the land, and all its kindred problems – agriculture, livestock, forestry etc. Workers on the land generally get very little recognition compared to people in the services and munition-makers, and it would be an excellent thing for the King's brother to constitute himself their especial patron, so to speak.

Moreover, if the Duke eventually goes to Australia as Governor-General, he will find a knowledge of such things, even if it is only superficial, of great value; and, as a by-product, he could also concern himself with the kindred problem of land settlement overseas. Now is a good moment for him to strike out on such a line, and it will be a great help to him having [the Duke of] Norfolk at the Ministry of Agriculture to advise him. He seemed to take kindly to these suggestions, though I daresay he will take no action at all on them.

At dinner May Elphinstone[1] told me a tale of her brother-in-law, returning from stalking in some remote forest in the north-west, having seen a ghostly procession of stags, with the magnificent heads the stags had in bygone days, crossing a burn near his path. He was told that this vision was commonly seen by shepherds and stalkers in that particular glen, but nobody could offer any explanation of it.

---

1   Lady Mary Bowes-Lyon, sister of the Queen, married the 16th Baron Elphinstone (1869–1955) in 1910.

Friday 3 September

11.40 p.m. Hollis just telephoned to me that Bedell Smith (on behalf of Eisenhower) and General Castellano (on behalf of Badoglio) signed the short armistice terms in Sicily this afternoon. Military talks as to how Italian troops can best help the Allies are now in progress. In fact, Italy is now in the war on the side of the Allies. We landed on the mainland of Italy (Calabria) at 4.30 a.m. today.

Saturday 4 September

Perhaps the most important thing that has happened in Europe during the last ten days is the appointment of Himmler[1] as Minister of the Interior in Germany, *vice* Frick. On the Harley Street analogy, the calling-in of so great a specialist in the elimination of civic malaise can only denote a grave condition in the patient.

Sunday 5 September

Winston, who is determined not to be caught in mid-ocean when what he calls the 'Italian climax' occurs, has postponed his departure from USA; as a result, the King's plans for going to London to meet him a week hence have all been scrapped. Little news from Italy, but a great spate of telegrams as to the setting-up of the proposed Anglo–American–Soviet commission to determine the fate of enemy countries who may wish to surrender.

Monday 6 September

Many telegrams are being exchanged between the PM and Cabinet as to the rendezvous best suited to the tripartite Foreign Secretaries' conference. In one of Winston's I saw that Windsor was contemplated as a suitable place for it to meet. As no word has been said to the King of this proposed use for his house, I rang up Eden to find out how the matter stood. He was very apologetic, and explained that all that had happened was that among various other houses which he had suggested to Winston in a private telegram, he had included Windsor as a possibility, but had never intended the idea to be followed up until he had had a chance of asking the King's permission. As the other parties now want to hold the conference in North

---

1   Heinrich Himmler (1900–45), possibly the most evil of Hitler's henchmen, was head of the Gestapo. Committed suicide after capture by the British in Apr. 1945.

Africa, and not in England at all, no harm has been done; but I thought it wiser to suppress the telegram in question.

This afternoon I killed a 15lb fish in the Boat Pool on a No. 3 Black Goldfinch, fished deep. I had him out in twelve minutes, and he did not give me much anxiety, though he jumped once or twice. The river, though still big, was falling steadily.

Tuesday 7 September

King Peter of Yugoslavia arrived, with Dunlop-Mackenzie, his English ADC. He was sent out stalking in a pair of the King's knickerbockers, all his own clothes having already gone to Cairo, whither he is due to follow them in a few days. He seems reconciled to postponing his marriage; the only person in favour of its taking place immediately seems to be his mother-in-law to be, Princess Aspasia.[1]

The Queen and half the people in the house, including Princess Elizabeth, are laid up with a mysterious gastric disturbance. Caroline telephoned after dinner to say that she had got four distinctions and three credits in her exam for School Certificate, which is a fine performance.

Wednesday 8 September

At 6 p.m. the Italian surrender was announced on the wireless; with Eisen-hower's pronouncement was one from Badoglio informing the Italians that hostilities with the Allies had ceased, and that aggression 'from any other quarter' must be resisted. At first, there was some doubt whether B. had or had not actually given this out on the Rome radio; but during dinner the FO telephoned me to say that he had done so, and Hollis's office have just (10 p.m.) confirmed to me that his announcement was definitely 'mon-itored' from Rome by the BBC.

The Queen is still in bed, though better and no temperature; so is Princess Margaret, and now Magdalen Eldon has succumbed to the same mysterious plague. Possibly it is due to a surfeit of grouse, which appears at every meal, so that I never want to eat another.

Thursday 9 September

Sam Hoare, dapper and urbane, arrived this morning. I had a talk with him before he, with the ladies, went out to join the King shooting at

---

1 Princess Aspasia (1896–1972), a Greek commoner, originally Aspasia Manos, had married King Alexander I of Greece in 1919.

Corndavon. He was quite interesting about Peninsular politics generally, and in particular about his first interview with General Castellano, which was really the *fons et origo* of the armistice.

Little authentic news; Operation 'Avalanche' started, and we have got four brigades safely landed at Salerno, and the Navy expect to occupy Taranto this evening. Germans said to be marching on Rome, but in what strength, we don't know. They have announced the establishment of a Quisling government, but who is the Quisling, and where he quizzles, they don't specify.

Saturday 11 September

Back in London, hot and thundery; but the plumbers (at my instigation) have rigged up a magnificent urinal in the Private Secretary's wash-place outside my room, which will be a great boon to me. The Italian battle-fleet has arrived safely at Malta (less the battleship *Roma*, which the Germans bombed en route), and other units have turned up in various Allied or neutral ports. Cunningham sent to the Admiralty a proud signal, quite in the Nelson tradition, 'Be pleased to inform Their Lordships that the Italian battle fleet now lies at anchor under the guns of the fortress of Malta.'

Monday 13 September

Old Carton de Wiart, VC, came to see me, looking very well and as jaunty as be damned, with his one eye, one arm, and bullet-riddled torso. He was interesting about his final departure from Italy; he was in so-called 'solitary confinement' (which he described as 'rather a pleasant change'), after trying to escape, when he was haled to Rome in a motor-car. He thought he was going to be shot, but, after being feasted on lobster and champagne, was, as I have already described, flown to Lisbon as a surety for General Zanussi; a Benjamin, so to speak, for Joseph's brethren. He told me that the hatred of the average Italian for the Boche now surpassed any hatred of which he had had experience in his stormy life, 'except perhaps that of an Ulsterman for a Sinn Feiner'. *Experto crede.*

I also saw Eastwood[1], Comptroller to Athlone, who gave me a lot of Canadian gossip. At Quebec, he said that Winston went out of his way to put the Governor-General in the foreground on every occasion. The latter sounds as if he were getting a bit senile and might have had a stroke; Princess Alice is one of those indefatigable women who cannot sit still, and

---

1   Sir Geoffrey Eastwood (1895–1983), Comptroller to Governor-General of Canada 1941–6, Comptroller to the Princess Royal 1959-65.

never allows her husband to do so either. Like Lady Willingdon,[1] her slogan is 'Keep His Excellency moving'.

Called on Bridges[2] in the War Cabinet Office, which is always a refreshing experience, though I make a point of not taking up more than ten minutes of his busy day. I wanted his advice on a letter I had recently from William Cantuar. He is disturbed at the amount of indiscriminate 'treating' – i.e., standing each other round after round of drinks – that goes on among the young men and maidens, which, he declares, leads to a vast deal of fornication. That may be something of a '*post hoc, propter hoc*' argument; I doubt if the love-making would appreciably diminish even if the whole country was teetotal. War, not beer, is the prime cause of that particular phenomenon. Anyhow, William suggests that the King – on Ministerial advice, of course – should make it known that he disapproves of treating, and urge that it should cease; he claims that his father, King George V, did this in the last war with excellent results, but I can find no record of this, nor can Wigram recollect anything about it.

I have always thought the habit of 'standing drinks' a most boring one, and have never been able to see why a man should insist on my drinking at his expense any more than buy me a ham sandwich. But I don't see how the King can do what William proposes. Bridges agreed, and said that the present Prime Minister would never advise in that sense – there is no tinge of Puritanism in Winston; but, like all wise counsellors, he had a counter-proposal to make – that the problem be treated not on a moral basis but on a strictly utilitarian one: that Woolton (or whoever controls our liquor main ration) should make it known that supplies are strictly limited, and appeal to all who wish to be festive to make such liquor as they can get go as far as possible, and not waste the precious fluid on rounds of drinks which probably half the party would prefer not to consume. That seems to be a much more commonsensical approach than William's; but, though a response to such an appeal may limit the power of Bacchus, it don't follow that it will have a like effect on that of Venus. To ration her, William will have to go back to the Garden of Eden, or further. As Lord Athlone exclaims when his fellow men act contrary to his wishes, 'They will do it – can't stop 'em, can't stop 'em.'

---

1   Marie, Marchioness of Willingdon (1875–1960), widow of 1st Marquis of Willingdon (1866–1941), Viceroy of India 1931–6. Tommy had first met her in 1920, in India, when her husband was Governor of Madras; he described her then as 'a bad, bossing woman, who makes herself a nuisance wherever she goes. She has now become a joke to All India.'
2   Sir Edward Bridges (1892–1969), son of the Poet Laureate Robert Bridges, Secretary to the Cabinet 1938–46. Created 1st Baron Bridges 1957.

Wednesday 15 September

Sat next to P. Guedalla, the writer, at the Beefsteak. The Air Ministry have commissioned him to write the story of the RAF's activities in Africa and the Middle East, and he was most amusing about a comprehensive tour that he has just finished in those parts. He has a great admiration for Tedder, who was on the point of becoming a don at Magdalene, Cambridge, but, feeling the urge to adventure, went into the RAF. There he rose steadily, but without any particular *éclat*, and in this war was stuck for a long time in some routine job under Beaverbrook at the Ministry of Aircraft Production. Eventually, Boyd[1] was chosen to be AOC Middle East, but fell into the sea, and into Italian hands, on his way out to his command. Tedder saw his chance, put in for the job, got it, and is now famous. I was very much struck by him the only time that I have met him, when he came here to see the King.

Thursday 16 September

Smuts telegraphs that he may arrive in this country on October 5th, which is in the middle of the week that the King has consecrated to shooting his partridges at Sandringham. John, telephoning from Balmoral, tells me he got a stag on Lochnagar today.

Monday 20 September

At Aberdeen station the other day I bought, in a slim volume, Charles Darwin's *Autobiography*, which has delighted me. It, with Francis Darwin's reminiscences tacked on at the end, gives a charmingly simple yet elevating picture of that great man (and his religious views, briefly recorded in an appendix, coincide almost exactly with my own). I never realised to what extent his whole life was a constant struggle against ill health; as I never realised, till yesterday, from J. Fortescue's *English Statesmen of the Great War* (i.e., the Napoleonic war), that the Duke of Wellington was a violinist, and only gave up his fiddle at the age of thirty because he thought it an unsuitable pastime for a soldier of high rank.

Tuesday 21 September

Kingsley Wood, Chancellor of the Exchequer, who had attended yesterday's

---

1   Air Vice-Marshal Owen Tudor Boyd (1889–1944).

meeting of the Cabinet, apparently in good health and spirits, died suddenly this morning.[1]

To the House of Commons, where Winston made his statement on recent events. He spoke from 12.15 p.m. to 1.25, when we adjourned for luncheon, and again from 2.30 to 3.30 p.m.; a sober, well set-out exposition, with no fireworks and a few mild jokes, which got their laugh all right; no heckling to speak of – those who tried it were either silenced adroitly by W., or shouted down by the House.

[After dinner with the Devonshires] Attlee volunteered to drive us home, but no sooner had we clambered into his car than his lady-chauffeur announced that somebody had been monkeying with the switch, and had wrecked it completely. So we got out and walked.

Old George Colville,[2] who died this week aged seventy-six, met his end in a curious way. He was having a bath, and, finding it too hot, turned on what he believed to be the cold tap. Actually, it was the hot tap, and when Cynthia, his wife, came in a little later to find out what had happened to him, he was unconscious and par-boiled. He never recovered from the shock, and died forty-eight hours afterwards.

Wednesday 22 September

Clive Wigram's boy Francis (6th Grenadiers) has been killed in action. He was a charming lad, for whom I had a great liking. Dined Grillions, sitting with old Lord Maugham,[3] Alf Mason[4] and Cromer,[5] with Camrose[6] next to him. Talking of the feasibility of trying 'war-criminals', Maugham said there was no court of law in England before which Hitler could be indicted; nor, under English law, can one try a foreigner for a crime against a British subject on alien soil.

---

1 Born 1881 – therefore only sixty-one or sixty-two.
2 Hon. George Colville (1867–1943), barrister. His wife, Lady Cynthia Colville, was Lady-in-Waiting to Queen Mary, and mother of Jock Colville.
3 Frederic, 1st Viscount Maugham (1866–1958), judge, Lord Chancellor of Great Britain 1938–9. Brother of Somerset Maugham, he also was an author (*The Tichborne Case, Lies as Allies or Hitler at War*, etc.)
4 A. E. W. Mason (1865–1948), author and playwright (*The Four Feathers, At the Villa Rose*, etc.).
5 Rowland Baring, 2nd Earl of Cromer (1877–1953), diplomat, Permanent Lord-in-Waiting to King George VI 1938–52.
6 William Ewert Berry (1879–1954), editor-in-chief and joint proprietor of the *Daily Telegraph* 1928–54. Confidant of Churchill. Created 1st Viscount Camrose 1941. When Churchill reluctantly decided to sell Chartwell after losing the 1945 general election, he combined with others to buy the house and present it to the National Trust, on condition that Churchill would have the use of it during his lifetime.

John, who got a fourth stag on Monday, was yesterday flown from Balmoral to York by Prince Bernhard[1] of the Netherlands.

Thursday 23 September

The King and Queen arrived back from Scotland today. The completed Stalingrad sword was handed over to me yesterday by Hughes, the Clerk of the Goldsmiths, and Gleadowe and Durbin, the designer and craftsman respectively. I took it in to the King and left it with him to show Winston after luncheon. I think it is a beautiful thing, and a fine achievement of British craftsmanship. The King's only comments on it were to ask how much it cost (which I don't know) and to remark that it had no date on it.

Sunday 26 September

Battle of Britain and Civil Defence Day. A thanksgiving service in St Paul's at 10.30 a.m., which I attended with Their Majesties. Very well done, and good hymns, beginning with the best of all, 'O Worship the King', which is one of the most sonorous poems in the English tongue. But William Cantuar preached a grey, rather lifeless sermon, beginning with a first-class gaffe – the reading of a letter which he had had from an American in July 1940, in which the writer assumed that this country must be over-run by the Germans in a few weeks, and that the Royal Family and Government would, as a matter of course, shortly be leaving for Canada. This will not go well among the Americans, all the more because it is an accurate enough specimen of what the great majority thought of our immediate prospects just before the Battle of Britain. And how few of us realised at the time the immense importance of that battle and the miracle of our deliverance; though I do remember writing to John Gore, just after 15 September 1940, and saying – I think with conviction – that we had seen Trafalgar fought and won in the skies of England.

William's lack of tact is curious in a man with such an ample sense of humour. Not long ago he wrote me a letter lamenting the tendency of Government departments to spring these 'Days' on the Church, regardless of whether the chosen Sunday has any special religious significance or not. 'They have not yet asked me,' he said, 'to ear-mark Easter Sunday for the anniversary of the founding of the NAAFI, but no doubt they will.'

After luncheon the King took the salute, on a dais outside Buckingham Palace, from a march-past of various units concerned in the defence of

---

1   1911–2004. German-born consort of Queen Juliana of the Netherlands, father of Queen Beatrix. During the war he flew with the RAF. Founded the World Wildlife Fund 1961.

these islands. But the whole lot of them did not contribute a hundredth part of the work done for our salvation by the man next to whom I found myself standing – Sir Robert Watson-Watt,[1] the Air Ministry's Scientific Adviser, to whose genius we owe radio-location and a dozen other black magical war-winning devices. He told me that it would not be long before we found the answer to this new German glider-bomb, whose antidote, he said, was relatively simple.

After the parade the King inspected, in the Quadrangle, the contingent of the famous 4th Indian Division now over here, and gave his VC to the Gurkha Subedar Thapa, four-and-a-half square feet of ferocity incarnate.[2]

Monday 27 September

Dined with Robin Barrington-Ward, whom I found remarkably optimistic about the internal state of Germany; all his information goes to show that it is very rocky, though of course he will give no hint of this in *The Times* as yet. We discussed what line he should take if ever there should be a serious demand for making Princess Elizabeth Princess of Wales. I told him he would be safe in reminding his readers that she is, after all, only Heiress *Presumptive*, not Apparent, and letting them draw their own conclusions – viz. that a Prince of Wales might yet be born to the King and Queen; or to the King and a second Queen, if this one should die and he should re-marry; remote contingencies, no doubt, but, constitutionally, they can't be rejected as negligible. Personally, I hope that delightful child will remain Princess Elizabeth for several years yet.[3]

Talking of our relations with Italy during the past decade, he said he thought that Simon[4] was probably the worst Foreign Secretary England had ever had. We agreed that the present one had appreciably gained in stature since the outbreak of war. I walked him as far as Temple Bar, on his way to put *The Times* to bed; and then, going to St James's Palace, found Dinah Colquhoun talking to Joan, and had to walk her to bed at the other end of the town.

For the first time since 1938 I've ordered a new suit, but, to my dismay,

---

1 Sir Robert Watson-Watt (1892–1973), expert in meteorology, radio and radar, Deputy Chairman, Radio Board of War Office 1943–6.
2 Subedar Lalbahadur Thapa (1907–68) won his VC leading a night assault against German forces in Libya during Apr. 1943. He killed at least four men with his kukri and shot several others with a pistol. His citation commended his 'unsurpassed bravery, outstanding leadership and gallantry'.
3 She was then seventeen.
4 1st Viscount Simon (1873–1954), barrister and KC, Foreign Secretary 1931–5, Chancellor of the Exchequer 1937–40, Lord Chancellor since 1940.

find it devoid of half the pockets which are indispensable to my well-being. This is one of the economies enjoined by the Board of Trade; so, on the advice of Poole's, my tailors, I've written to the Parliamentary Private Secretary, C. Waterhouse, telling him he must provide me with the necessary Board of Trade permit to have a Christian complement of pockets inserted. I don't the least mind going short of turn-ups to my trousers; but pockets in my coat and waistcoat I must have. [*Later note:* Mr Poole has now sent me the bill – £19-1-0 – roughly three and a half times what I should have paid for a similar suit before the last war.]

Tuesday 28 September

Godfrey Thomas sent round to see me one Brigadier E. C. W. Myers,[1] who was dropped from an aeroplane somewhere in the heart of Greece about a year ago, and has since led a precarious life there, blowing up bridges and organising the 'Partisans' (Greek patriots), which he seems to have done most successfully. He talked most interestingly for an hour – an impressive chap: a sapper, not more than thirty-five, I should say. He don't think much of George of Greece's[2] chances of recovering his throne.

Wednesday 29 September

Ismay tells me that the PM, who has always been a 'Western Front' man, has suddenly become obsessed by the idea of speeding up the war against Japan, and wants to divert much of our present, or prospective, forces in Europe, to Asia. Ismay said that Winston seemed to feel more strongly about this than about any strategic issue that has hitherto arisen, though the Chiefs of Staff were vehemently opposed to him. I said the only explanation I could offer was that the PM had become convinced that Germany couldn't last out the winter, and that he wanted to be in a position to exert maximum pressure on the Japs in the early spring.

We recently sent some submarines into the Altenfjord, where the major units of the German fleet are; the *Lützow* bolted, and has reached the Baltic; the others remained, and, though we have no direct news from the submarines, it is deduced from the immobility of *Tirpitz*, and from the

---

1 Brig. Edmund Myers (1906–97), Commander of British Military Mission to Greek Resistance forces 1942–3.
2 After the Nazi invasion in 1941, King George II of the Hellenes (1890–1947) escaped to Crete, then moved to Cairo, to London, back to Cairo and finally to Caserta, before returning to Greece in Oct. 1944. The country was then virtually in a state of civil war, and Archbishop Damaskinos was appointed Regent. In 1946, after a plebiscite, the King was restored to his throne but died suddenly in 1947.

variety of what appear to be repair ships that have been rushed up there, that she may be badly damaged.

I got the King to give a sitting to Mr Karsh,[1] the Ottawa photographer – a curious little Armenian, who was just rising to fame when I was there, and has now firmly established it all over the American continent.

Thursday 30 September

Bishop David Mathew[2] came to tea with me. He started life as a midshipman in the last war, when he was a shipmate with Dan Lascelles; then went up to Balliol, and, under Sligger Urquhart's[3] influence, became a priest. At first I was put off by his outward appearance and falsetto giggle, but eventually took rather a liking to him, and we talked for over an hour. He has kept up his connection with the Navy, and has spent his last two holidays on board destroyers, chasing E-boats in the North Sea.

C. Meade dined with me and Joan at Wilton's. He said that what really made the English into good fighting men, in the long run, was their inextinguishable love of games, and war was fundamentally a game. So the Duke was right after all, when he said that the battle of Waterloo was won on the playing-fields of Eton.

Ismay said today that we were wrong not to fight in 1938. The Germans made far better use of the intervening twelve months than we did, and were relatively weaker in '38, though, in his view, they did not really want war until 1941. Equally, the French would have been twelve months further away from collapse in '38, and would probably have fought better then. [*In 1968 the author added a note:* But of one thing I am certain. We should not, in 1938, have had the support of the majority of the Dominions, who, in the next twelve months, awoke to the realisation of what Nazism meant.]

Saturday 2 October

Cloud's Hill, for the last time as a resident. Blanche in bed after several days of high temperature due to some streptococcal infection; I wrote to Princess Mary[4] saying she would be quite unfit to do her next spell of waiting.

---

1 Yusuf Karsh (1908–2002) was taken to Canada by his uncle in 1924. His portrait of Churchill (1941) established his international reputation.
2 Most Rev. David Mathew (1902–75), Bishop Auxiliary of Westminster 1938–46.
3 Francis Fortescue Urquhart, known as 'Sligger' (1868–1934), Fellow and Tutor of Balliol College, Oxford, 1896–1934.
4 Princess Mary (1897–1965), only daughter of King George V and Queen Mary, had married Tommy's cousin Viscount Lascelles (later 6th Earl of Harewood) in 1922. Their son George Lascelles succeeded as 7th Earl in 1947.

Sunday 3 October

Picked many apples, of which there is a heavy crop this year. Said goodbye to the garden, which has been a great solace during the past two years, with much regret. I have put a number of shrubs and roses into it, and tending them was an interest. My *Tricuspidaria lanceolata*, defying seasonal laws, has lately produced a solitary flower.[1]

Ivor Plymouth[2] is dead, at the age of fifty-four. This is a blow to me, but no surprise; whenever I saw him in recent years, I felt that the finger of death was on him. He collapsed, after his chairmanship of that infernal Non-Intervention committee during the Spanish Civil War, and has been prematurely old and invalid ever since. A most unselfish and self-unsparing man, with a great sense of public duty, and a charming host.

Wednesday 6 October

Bobbety Cranborne is disturbed by Winston's persistent refusal to let the Dominions know our plans for future foreign policy etc. Winston is incurably colonial-minded.[3] After luncheon I went, on the King's instructions, to the Royal Masonic Hospital, to give poor old Dudley Pound his OM. He has reached the stage when, with a malignant tumour on his brain, he may live for weeks or die tomorrow. This was a heart-rending business, for, though he appeared to understand all that I said, he was incapable of speech, beyond saying, 'Well . . .', after which a struggle for words would follow, but no words came. His two sons were there, and later Freddie Dalrymple-Hamilton, who kindly came down with me, telephoned to say that one of them had told him that the old man had taken it all in, and had been greatly pleased by my halting, but perfectly sincere, compliments.[4]

Then went to see Harold Macmillan, back from Algiers on a short visit. I got little from him of interest; but he told me that on the famous day when Badoglio had threatened to run out of playing his prearranged part in the announcement of Italy's surrender, his statement, which he had

---

1 The Lascelles family's next home was Winchester Tower, at Windsor Castle.

2 Ivor Windsor-Clive, 2nd Earl of Plymouth (1889–1943), Parliamentary Under-Secretary of State, FO 1936–9.

3 *Note added in 1967:* 'By this I meant that Winston tended to think of the self-governing Dominions as Victorian colonies. I don't think he had ever absorbed the 1931 Statute of Westminster. At the time of the Coronation in 1953, when it was suggested to him that he should participate in the Naval Review on board the ship allotted to the other Commonwealth Prime Ministers, he was reported to have protested indignantly, 'What – am I to go round the British Navy with all that poor white trash?' But this story, if *ben trovato*, is very likely untrue.

4 Pound died two weeks later, on 21 Oct.

originally undertaken to make at 6.30 p.m. on the radio, was actually spoken by an American soldier, with a fluent knowledge of Italian, from Allied Headquarters. It was only after hearing his own speech thus delivered that B., a few hours later, delivered it himself on the Italian radio.

Friday 8 October

Dawson of Penn to see me; long talk about Nashville, the name used by Joey Legh and me to describe the King's sudden outbursts of temper, accompanied by gnashing of his teeth and raising his clenched fists to heaven – *cf.* King Lear.

Saturday 9 October

Yesterday we sent a small convoy to occupy (with the consent of the Portuguese, our ancient allies) the Azores, for the purposes of, and duration of, the war. This long-planned and voluminously be-telegraphed affair (Operation 'Alacrity') has passed off well. The Germans have not as yet reacted to it, so far as I know.

Down to Windsor. We spent much time at Winchester Tower, where the workmen are still busy with their paint-pots, though Joan and Caroline hope to sleep there Tuesday. I was delighted with it. Looking out over the tree-tops to Eton chapel on one side, and to St George's Chapel and the King's beasts on the other, it has an outlook which few houses in England can rival. Within, it is remarkably warm and dry, and every room feels snug. Though we have imported a certain amount of our own stuff, it is almost completely furnished, so the business of moving in is relatively light.[1] The Office of Works people are being very good about repainting it where necessary – especially those rooms in which Helen Hardinge's somewhat morbid taste in mural decoration found expression. But even if the whole house were monstrous, it would still be a blessing, in providing us once more with an anchored home after four years of Ishmaelitish vagrancy. Henry II began it, William of Wykeham completed it, and Geoffrey Chaucer lived in it – an honourable lineage for any house.

Sunday 10 October

Another perfect autumn day, when Windsor looks its best. I lunched and dined with the poor Wigrams, who are shattered by the death, at Salerno,

---

1 The flat had been fitted out as an alternative home for the King and Queen, should Buckingham Palace be put out of commission by bombs.

of their charming son Francis. We went to the organ loft in St George's, p.m., when Harris played us Bach's Toccata and Fugue in C.

Monday 11 October

London. Alec Hardinge came to see me, and we talked, in great amity, for nearly an hour. He is not well yet, but better. I went on to see the Duke of Gloucester, in the Curzon Street flat that he now occupies, and discussed with him his proposed succession to Gowrie as Governor-General of Australia.

Wednesday 13 October

Saw the new Portuguese Ambassador, the Duke of Palmella,[1] whose great-great-grandfather, when Ambassador here, was a great friend of my ditto, George Canning, which formed a useful link between us. He is premier duke of Portugal, was educated at Beaumont and Cambridge, is very rich and very agreeable, has eleven children, and looks as if he were quite ready to have eleven more. Then Smuts came to luncheon, looking younger and more alert than ever. He is outwardly very optimistic about things in general, but revealed to the King that he is very uneasy about Operation 'Overlord' – a feeling which I for one share. With him came his youngest son, J.C. junior, a charming lad, very much on the spot, like his father.

I had to buy a new sponge, and Pope Roach (the chemist at the bottom of St James's Street) charged me 35s for a thing which a few years ago one would have bought for 3s 6d to wash the dog with. But I have got the pockets put in my suit, thank God. Dined at Grillions among the old and the wise.

The King sent for me when I got in from dinner (11 p.m.). I found him wrestling with the draft of a letter to Winston, embodying his anxieties after his talk with Smuts about the rival claims of 'Overlord' and 'the soft under-belly of the Axis' – a phrase which will pass into history, as will Winston's *obiter dictum* about the minor parties to the Axis being given consideration 'if they work their passage'.

I thought it was a devilish good draft, and a devilish good idea, and said so. It is an obvious function of the Sovereign head of this Empire to bring his various prime ministers together in this way, with himself acting, so to speak, as an unofficial chairman. He told me to take the draft to bed, and sleep on it.

---

1   5th Duke of Palmella (1897–1969), Portuguese Ambassador to the Court of St James 1943–9.

Thursday 14 October

The night did not suggest to me any emendation to the draft, save the beginning of the last sentence, which I couldn't construe. When I told HM this, later, he was obviously much pleased and said, 'That's what I like about working with you – you are encouraging. Alec Hardinge would have told me that I couldn't possibly do this' – a remark which revealed the bruise of years of restraint, amounting almost to repression, that I have always suspected. My 'encouragement' was in no way sycophantic; and that both PMs thought the dinner idea a good one was shown by the alacrity with which they accepted when I got busy on the telephone.

At Pratt's P. Loxley[1] told me that every despatch sent to Madrid by Alba was read by the Japanese, and the contents reported to Berlin via Tokyo. I warned the King never to say anything to Alba that he did not want to reach the enemy. Apparently there is in the Spanish Embassy here a lady-clerk who favours the Japs.

Friday 15 October

Edward Halifax told me that Smuts had said that he had gathered the impression from members of the governments of some of the smaller Allies (Norway, Holland, Belgium) that they would like to be formally admitted to the British Empire after the war. A bloc of the North Atlantic seaboard powers, in fact. Very suitable, geographically, but there would be some hard constitutional nuts to crack. What, e.g., would become of their various royalties? Or would it be a sort of Holy Roman Empire, with our King taking the place of Emperor? A very interesting idea, anyhow.

Sholto Douglas,[2] Air Chief Marshal, came to see the King. Last time I met him, he was beginning to look dangerously like Goering;[3] but a spell in the Levant, where he has been Air Commander-in-Chief for about eighteen months, has reduced his waist-line and refined his features. At one time he was a candidate for the South-East Asian command since given to Dickie Mountbatten; but the Americans jibbed, as apparently he can't get on with them.

Windsor p.m., driving down with Joan and Caroline. They are now

---

1   FO official, killed in an air crash January 1945.
2   Marshal of the RAF Sir William Sholto Douglas (1893–1969), AOC-in-C Fighter Command 1940–42, Middle East Command 1943–4, Coastal Command 1944–5. Created 1st Baron Douglas of Kirtleside 1948.
3   Reichsmarschall Hermann Goering (1893–1946), loyal supporter of Hitler. Head of the Luftwaffe, much given to wearing make-up and fancy uniforms. Committed suicide by poison while in custody at Nuremberg, 1946.

dug-in in Winchester Tower, but I am still sleeping in the Castle.

Sunday 17 October

Stalin sent a most offensive telegram about convoys on Friday, to which Winston has replied firmly. The current theory is that these occasional bursts of ill-manners from Moscow are not sent by Stalin himself, but are the work of what Winston calls 'the machine' – i.e., their Chiefs of Staff committee – concocted over the vodka-beakers. They certainly have a quite different style from the telegrams which Stalin has obviously written himself.

Wednesday 20 October

The King took me to dine at No. 10. An amusing evening; the War Cabinet – Winston, E. Bevin, Attlee, O. Lyttelton, Herbert Morrison, John Anderson, plus Smuts and B. Bridges. We had a good dinner, in the underground dining-room constructed during the Blitz, with a Rehoboam of champagne; the talk, as is usual in male English gatherings, alternating between light badinage and intense seriousness. In the latter periods old Smuts, sitting like an owl on its perch, would hop down and play an always predominant part. At one moment he set out, with his blue eyes flashing and his beard all a-twitch, to expound to us his favourite philosophy of holism, based, I understand, on the paradox that the whole is *not* the sum of, but is greater than, its component parts. It is certainly true enough of the British Empire.

After dinner he told me with great earnestness and sincerity that he had observed 'a marked increase of stature' in the King in the last few years; and said that Their Majesties could visit South Africa as soon as they liked after the war – the sooner, the better. Winston was in robust form; I wish I could remember some of his more forceful *obiter dicta*. He said that the past twelve months had been the happiest year of his life, because it had been such a satisfaction to see things going the way he wanted them to. Apropos the ridiculous newspaper agitation against the Hereford magistrates for giving a well-deserved whipping to a juvenile delinquent, he said, 'Birch! What that boy wants is a good taste of the sjambok – eh, General?' With which Smuts cordially agreed.

Saturday 23 October

Came down to Windsor yesterday afternoon. The Claude Elliotts came to tea with us in Winchester Tower, and we took them to the showing of two

American-made films designed to instruct the average American citizen as to what, and why, he is fighting. They were excellently selected, and the commentary good, and never unfair. After the show was over I found old Quickswood[1] wandering in the dark, lost and forlorn, so escorted him down to the Henry VIII gateway; even his critical mind had nothing but praise for them.

Sunday 24 October

We had a bad day at sea yesterday, losing a cruiser (*Charybdis*) and a destroyer, off Brittany, and two of our destroyers and a Greek one in the Mediterranean.

Tuesday 26 October

The Government are taking the threat of bombardment of this country by outsize rocket-projectiles quite seriously, though we successfully bombed Wathen into inactivity some little time ago. There may be other Wathens which we have not discovered, and Winston today sent a long telegram to F.D.R. mentioning the thing for the first time, and saying that we couldn't discount the possibility of this kind of attack during November. Perhaps it was this that led him to advise the King against going to the British Legion's Festival of Remembrance in the Albert Hall on the evening of November 11, though the Minister of Home Security, when I consulted him, saw no objection. Winston intends to tell the House of Commons about these rockets at a secret session shortly. Incidentally, 'The Prof.' (Lord Cherwell) is said to have staked his scientific reputation that they are not a practical possibility.

I have been taking soundings as to the suitability of giving Max Beerbohm the OM, which I should dearly like to do. David Cecil[2] is wholeheartedly in favour, Eric Maclagan and Owen Morshead,[3] very reluctantly, advise against it. E. says, 'The OM is no place for the exquisite.' I am afraid they are right.

Wednesday 27 October

Beaverbrook to see HM. He was very genial while he was with me. He said

---

1   1st Baron Quickswood (1869–1956), Provost of Eton College 1936–44.
2   Lord David Cecil (1902–1986), younger son of 4th Marquess of Salisbury, author and don, professor of English Literature, Oxford University 1948–69.
3   Sir Owen Morshead (1893–1977), Librarian, Windsor Castle, 1926–58.

'The Prof.' was prepared to bet 5–1 against the German rockets being a serious weapon, and that if he could take charge of our anti-rocket measures, he would increase it to 100–1.

Walking home in a thick fog, I was accosted in an absolutely deserted South Audley Street by a little man who said, 'Can you tell me the way to the main high road?' – an unusual question to be asked in the heart of London. It transpired that he wanted to get to Kensington High Street.

Thursday 28 October

Visitors: Brendan Bracken, whom I like – he is a friendly man, of engaging frankness about himself; Bishop of Gibraltar (Harold Buxton[1]), who has, I suppose, as wide a diocese as any prelate of the Church of England, ranging from the Atlantic to the Caspian; Dorman-Smith,[2] Governor of Burma, an alert, boyish chap.

Lunched Ritz with Blanche Lloyd and Doreen Brabourne;[3] and then to the Foreign Office, where I had a long talk with P. Loxley and 'C'.[4] The latter optimistic about the internal state of Germany and the imminence of major political upheavals there, but takes a serious view of the rockets, as, from a report that I read today, do all the scientists except the Prof. It seems highly probable that they will loose off some of these things at us sooner or later, unless we can find some effective means of nipping them in the bud.

Telegram from the Duke of Windsor, asking the King to see Allen,[5] his solicitor, as soon as possible. When the Duke acquired the E.P. ranch, the Alberta Government put a clause in the agreement that neither the land nor the mineral rights should pass into the possession of anyone who was not a member of the Royal Family. Now, the Duke wants to bore for oil, but he has left the property to his Duchess, and the Albertans say she isn't a member of the Royal Family. The Duke thinks the King can put this right; but I doubt very much if it is anything whatever to do with the King. He can confer titles, courtesy or otherwise, on the Duchess – e.g. make her an HRH (which he will never do), but I don't see how he can change her *legal* status. Charles II made his bastards into dukes – but they were nonetheless illegitimate in the eyes of the law.

---

1 Rt. Rev. Harold Buxton (1880–1976), Bishop of Gibraltar 1933–47.
2 Col. Rt. Hon. Sir Reginald Dorman-Smith (1899–1977), Conservative MP, Governor of Burma 1941–6.
3 Widow of 5th Baron Brabourne (1895–1939), Governor of Bombay 1933–7 and of Bengal 1937–9.
4 Maj.-Gen. Sir Stewart Menzies (1890–1968), always known as 'C'. Chief of MI6, the Military Intelligence Directorate, 1939–45.
5 George Allen (1888–1956), Private Solicitor to King Edward VIII 1936 and thereafter. Knighted 1952.

It looks to me as though they would have to fight it out in the Albertan courts. What is 'a member of the Royal Family'? I can't find any attempt to define it in any of the constitutional textbooks. Ulick Alexander says it is somebody who is related to the Sovereign on both sides; if so, the Queen is not a member of the Royal Family, which is surely absurd. And what degree of kinship is necessary to be 'related'? I am myself descended from various Kings of England, yet nobody could say I was a member of the Royal Family.

Friday 29 October

The King saw Allen, who seems to me a very decent and sensible chap. He agrees that, whatever may be the Duke of Windsor's legal position *vis-à-vis* the Alberta Government, it is no concern of the King's. I slept for the first time in Winchester Tower, very comfortably.

Sunday 31 October

We went down to the P. Leghs' house over the Henry VIII gateway to meet Miss Cynthia Elliott, recently repatriated from Germany, where she has been a prisoner since June 1940. She was very encouraging about their internal condition, saying that since the collapse of Italy there had been a most marked improvement in their manners, and constant expressions of the hope that our armies would invade Germany before the Russians do. Her last place of confinement was a camp near Friedrichshafen (Swiss frontier), which, she said, had been filled to overflowing with German government officials, hurriedly evacuated there to avoid the bombing of Berlin. In this country we should certainly think ourselves in a bad way if half Whitehall fled for refuge to camps in the Isle of Man.

We got back to Winchester Tower to find a dim figure groping at our front door in the darkness; this proved to be Princess Mary, who stayed till dinner time.

Tuesday 2 November

Moscow conference is ending in a blaze of glory, which I hope may not prove a false dawn. Drafted a congratulatory telegram for HM to send to Eden, who has certainly handled the Muscovites with commendable tact and patience. Whatever the permanent effects of the meeting may be, the immediate one must be a facer for the Germans, who have been clutching frantically at the straw of dissension among the Allies.

Wednesday 3 November

Went with the King to dine at No. 10 – the Chiefs of Staff (Cunningham, Portal, Brooke[1]), Hollis and Bob Laycock,[2] who has succeeded Mountbatten as Chief of Combined Operations. There was one superb addition to my collection of Churchilliana. Apropos the burning question of whether Turkey should be coerced into active participation in the war or not, Winston said, 'The Foreign Secretary asks me, "What shall I say to Turkey?" I say to him, "Tell Turkey that Christmas is coming."'[3] It was an agreeable evening, though nothing sensational transpired.

Their great problem at the moment is to teach the Americans that you cannot run a war by making rigid 'lawyers' agreements' to carry out preconceived strategic operations at a given date (e.g. 'Overlord'), but that you must plan your campaign elastically and be prepared to adapt it to the tactical exigencies of the moment. They don't seem able to grasp that a paper-undertaking made in autumn to invade Europe (or any other continent) in the following spring may have to be modified in accordance with what the enemy does or does not do during the intervening winter. All present, however, agreed in high praise of the personal qualities of the various USA commanders with whom they have to deal.

Thursday 4 November

Went to a lengthy and boring luncheon-party given by the Belgian Ambassador, old Cartier, for the Grand Duchess of Luxembourg and husband. Cartier is all over me just now because I've induced the King to give sittings to James Gunn[4] for the portrait which the latter has been commissioned to paint for the Institut Belge. Lady George Cholmondeley,[5] who was next me, declared in the course of conversation that Max Beerbohm was dead. I said I knew very well that he wasn't, to which she rejoined calmly, 'Oh well, it may be that he is going to die shortly. I constantly get psychic forewarnings of people's deaths, and am never quite sure if they have actually taken place or not.'[6]

---

1   Gen. Sir Alan Brooke (1883–1963), CIGS 1941–6, ADC Gen. to the King 1942–6. Created 1st Viscount Alanbrooke 1946.
2   Maj.-Gen. Sir Robert Laycock (1907–68), Chief of Combined Operations 1943–7. Knighted 1954.
3   Eden, on a fruitless mission to Ankara, telegraphed back, 'Bird most reluctant to face table.'
4   Sir James Gunn (1893–1964), portrait painter. He also painted the Queen, in 1946.
5   Second wife of Lord George Cholmondeley.
6   The premonition was premature: Beerbohm did not die until 1956.

I have just opened Eden's reply to the King's message, wirelessed from Air HQ, Iraq. It seems to have given satisfaction, and A.E. concludes: 'At a banquet at the British Embassy in Moscow, M. Molotov[1] proposed Your Majesty's health in most cordial terms.'

Dined again at 10 Downing Street, this time on my own; a big Government dinner for Linlithgow. I was well placed, between P. J. Grigg and E. Bridges. Winston, proposing the ex-Viceroy's health, let himself go on India, and was more visibly moved than I have ever seen him. He feels very acutely the criticisms which the world at large has levelled at the British raj. Linlithgow, much aged, and with the over-tired man's tendency to facial contortions, spoke well and earnestly on the paramount need of building up the Indian Civil Service. Even P.J., who is no admirer of Linlithgow, had to admit the force of his eloquence.

After dinner, with Lord Chancellor Simon on a sofa, while he gave me his considered opinion on the Duke of Windsor's appeal to the King about his duchess's status as a 'member of the Royal Family' – which coincided surprisingly with my own ill-considered one. As I anticipated, there is no statutory or legal definition of the term, and the matter is one for the lawyers to decide, and nothing to do with the King. I also got from Simon a promise to send me a copy of the masterly operation-orders which he dictated to a midnight meeting that I attended in Downing Street on the eve of the Abdication, and which I have never been able to extract from him hitherto. They should certainly be in the archives at Windsor for the guidance of any who may be so unfortunate as to conduct another abdication in the future.

Friday 5 November

Somebody asked Linlithgow what was the most striking change that he noticed in England since he left in 1936. He said, 'The change in the King'; and of course, the difference between the Duke of York of 1936 and King George VI of 1943 must seem profound to anybody who has not seen him during the interval.

Saturday 6 November   Windsor

The Russians are in Kiev. In daylight yesterday we had over 2,500 aircraft, of all types, operating over the continent. Stalin, in his speech on the anniversary of the foundation of USSR, made far more complimentary

---

1   Vyacheslav Mikhailovich Molotov (1890–1986), Soviet Commissar (later Minister) for Foreign Affairs 1939–49 and 1953–6. Responsible for the Molotov–Ribbentrop pact of August 1939, allying Nazi Germany to the Soviet Union.

references to his allies, and their war-effort, than he has ever done before.

Delia Peel and two Eton boys (Michael Holland-Hibbert[1] and Nicky Ridley[2]) to tea at Winchester Tower. Michael H.-H. amazed me by producing a packet of butter out of his coat-tail pocket, a remarkable proof of how ration-conscious the young have become.

Monday 8 November

Joan drove me to London, and after luncheon we went to Kew to pay a long-projected visit to old Archbishop Cosmo Lang, in the little house on Kew Green that the King gave him when he left Lambeth. We walked through the gardens, beautiful even in November, till rain drove us in to tea, whereafter Joan returned to Windsor and I to Buckingham Palace.

Saw Allen, who entirely agrees with Simon's minute about membership of the Royal Family, and got the King's approval for a brief reply to the Duke of Windsor, saying in effect that it's not a matter in which HM could intervene, even if he wished to do so.

Stalin, in his speech, said: 'Together with our allies we have first to liberate the peoples of Europe from the German invaders, and then cooperate with them in the creation of their national states. The peoples of France, Belgium, Yugoslavia and other states now under the German yoke must again become free and independent.' Nothing could be more definite; will the smaller nations believe it?

Thursday 11 November

A. Eden, who got back yesterday from Moscow, to see the King. He looks well, and was in good spirits, but paced my room with the restlessness of a man who has lived long on his nerves. He is, with good reason, well pleased with the result of his pilgrimage, which I believe will prove to be one of the most important in history. *C'est le premier pas*, etc., and this is the first step that the Russians and ourselves have ever taken down the road of cooperation. Both he and Ismay (to whom I talked on the telephone) have come home feeling that the Russians are convinced that they can never rehabilitate their appallingly devastated country without our help. With the Turks, he has not been so successful; in fact, all our representations to them have met with a flat refusal.

---

1 B. 1926, succeeded his father as Viscount Knutsford 1986.
2 Nicholas Ridley (1929–93), Tory MP, in Margaret Thatcher's Cabinet 1983–90. Created Baron Ridley (Life Peer) 1992.

Monday 15 November

De Labilliere, the Dean of Westminster, to see me, and told me a curious story. Some time in the 18th century the tomb of Richard II and his Queen, Anne of Bohemia, partially collapsed, and from the resulting hole choir-boys and others purloined the royal bones as trophies. Some fifty years ago a jaw-bone was returned to the then Dean, which proved to be almost certainly that of Richard II, to whom it was appropriately restored. Now, a humerus, which purports to be that of Queen Anne, has been given to de Labilliere; he has had it vetted by some osteological expert, whose diagnosis confirms the claim. At present the tomb is heavily sand-bagged, but as soon as he can get at it, he proposes to open it and give poor Anne her missing shoulder-blade.[1] Richard II was passionately fond of Anne; and when, in the middle of her obsequies, the Lord Arundell of the day asked to be excused, pleading another engagement, the King drew his sword and felled him to the ground.

Thursday 18 November

One of 'C's' papers, based on the observations of some well-tried source, claims that Bormann[2] is now the virtual director of Germany's destinies. He, in close alliance with Himmler, and in opposition to Ribbentrop[3] and Goering, now has Hitler's ear, has converted him to the wisdom of abandoning the Ukraine, and is concentrating on infusing what he calls the *Frontstimmung* [fighting morale] into the admittedly dispirited German people. He believes firmly that, if they can only sit tight in the 'European fortress', the Allies' will to fight will peter out reasonably soon, though he pays us the compliment of excepting us. All of which may well have some truth in it; though, as F.D.R. grimly said the other day, 'Hitler forgets that his European fortress has no lid to it.'

The Government have released Oswald Mosley, on vague grounds of ill-health. Why not say frankly that he is suffering from acute thrombo-phlebitis, which has already been attested by a responsible panel of doctors? As it is, Labour is intensely suspicious, and is sending deputations to protest to the Home Secretary.

---

1 Strictly speaking, the humerus is the bone in the upper arm.
2 Martin Bormann (1900–?73), Hitler's secretary and Nazi Party treasurer, who disappeared at the end of the war. He was frequently rumoured to have escaped to South America but never traced. A court in Frankfurt officially declared him dead in 1973.
3 Joachim von Ribbentrop (1893–1946), former champagne salesman, was German Ambassador in London 1936–8, then Hitler's Foreign Minister. Convicted of war crimes at the Nuremberg Trials and hanged, 1946.

Friday 19 November

My life is being made a burden by the problem of King Peter's marriage; he is safe in Cairo, where he is apparently doing well, but his future bride, Princess Alexandra, and her mother, are moving heaven and earth to get him here, and get him married, before the Greek Orthodox Church's Advent season begins, which is next week. Yesterday they called at No. 10, with a long telegram, purporting to come from Peter, urging that he be allowed to return at once. This they left, for the PM, with the unfortunate Peck,[1] who couldn't, of course, reveal that his master was not in the country, and who had to get rid of them as best he could.

The situation is further complicated in that the King, who takes his responsibilities as 'Koum' [godfather] very seriously, has already sent a long telegram to Winston, asking him to see Peter when he gets to Cairo, and do his best to get him to postpone his marriage *sine die*; but no such meeting can take place for several days, and how poor Peck will hold the fort against the Maenads of Greece, I have no idea. Better he than I. The King himself is very doubtful whether the marriage should ever take place at all; I gather that Peter's mother, Queen Marie, recently gave him to understand that she would gladly see it all knocked on the head.

The crisis has not been made any smoother by a telegram from Winston (who obviously knows he has been naughty) saying that he has not only pinned his bit of ribbon on Alex's chest, but has done ditto to Eisenhower. As it was a fundamental principle of the creation of the Star that it should not be worn by any foreigner (a principle strongly insisted on by Winston himself), he is, like Pompey, *suarum legum idem auctor et subversor* [at the same time the creator and subverter of his own laws]; and I only narrowly dissuaded his Sovereign (who feels about the incident almost as strongly as Queen Victoria did about Palmerston's more flagrant peccadilloes) from sending him a very sharp telegram.

Stanley Baldwin to see HM, bringing a curious trophy – the pencilled message that King Edward VIII sent him just before he (Baldwin) made his Abdication speech in the House of Commons, saying his (E. VIII's) relations with his brother, the Duke of York, had always been the best possible, and that he (E. VIII) would now be the first to sing 'God save the King'. S.B. thinks, rightly, that the proper place for this document is in the Archives at Windsor.

I thought the old man had got perceptibly more nervy since I saw him in July. He said apprehensively that he hoped the King wouldn't keep him

---

1   John Peck (1913–95), Assistant Private Secretary to the PM 1940–46; later transferred to the Diplomatic Service. Knighted 1971.

too long, as he hated driving home in the black-out. I asked where he had to get to, and he said, 'The Dorchester Hotel' – which can't be much more than six furlongs from where we were sitting.

Monday 22 November

Anthony Eden, straight from the Cabinet, and almost on his way to the aerodrome (whence he leaves for Cairo tonight) to see the King at 7 p.m., about the Yugoslav marriage. He paced up and down my room like a caged beast – sure sign of a man overstrained in his nerves – but was otherwise in good form and very agreeable. His chief anxiety was leaving the House of Commons to be handled by Attlee during the next fortnight; I told him not to worry – that his presence in Cairo etc. was much more important than the temper of the House of Commons, and that the majority of them would be so pleased when they knew that Winston and F.D.R. were foregathering with Uncle Joe that they would forget all about the Aegean, and Oswald Mosley's release, and the Hereford birching, and all the other little things that now harry their little souls.

Wednesday 24 November

Opening of Parliament, the first in England that I have attended in an official capacity. In wartime it is of course a much simplified ceremony, taking place in the temporary House of Lords (formerly the Robing Room), with everybody in service-dress uniform or plain clothes. While we were waiting to go in, I overheard Simon saying to the Queen that it was wrong of *The Times* not to have reported the Prorogation speech (delivered yesterday) this morning. This is astonishing, in that one of the most stringent regulations of the Government (of which Simon is a member) is that no newspaper may make any mention of the Prorogation until the opening is safely over, because, since the latter invariably takes place the day after the former, any allusion to it would inevitably reveal to everybody, including the Germans, the exact date of the latter, which we are all at such pains to conceal, lest the Germans take the opportunity to bomb Westminster. As I said in a note to the Queen this evening, it is a case of Simple Simon.

This afternoon, a Thanksgiving Day party at Buckingham Palace for a number of Americans, of all services. Joan came up from Windsor for it, and it was highly successful. Went to Grillions, where I was much annoyed at the end of the evening by Londonderry saying to me, *coram publico*, 'Why was I passed over for the Chancellorship of the Garter?' – a monstrous question to ask the King's Private Secretary in front of other people. I was obliged to fence as best I could.

We again bombed Berlin heavily last night. The destruction on Sunday night seems to have been appalling. Our temporary RAF equerry, Pelly-Fry, went recently to see his former chief, Harris, head of Bomber Command. H. said to him, 'People are worrying because the Russian army may get to Berlin before ours does. They needn't do that, because by that time there won't be any Berlin to get to.'

Saturday 27 November   **Windsor**

Eton decided to celebrate St Andrew's Day,[1] but the saint was not to be caught by that sort of chaff, and produced his traditional weather – rain and fog. Colin and Irene Forbes-Adam[2] came to stay [in Winchester Tower], our first visitors; and the Manners and Cory-Wright families to tea. We sent some 700 bombers to Germany last night, Berlin and Stuttgart. Thirty-two missing and eight crashed – a higher percentage, but not surprising considering the weather, and under six per cent.

Read *The Taming of the Shrew* with immense pleasure, following *Measure for Measure* and *Love's Labour's Lost* in recent weekends. Why did Shakespeare never set the scene of any of his comedies in *England*? I've never seen that point explained in any of the commentaries. Was it because there were always Princes and Dukes on his stage, and he was afraid of offending their English counterparts, unless he gave them a foreign background? *The Merry Wives of Windsor* is the only exception, and that was written by direct royal command.

All this brouhaha about Mosley's release is curiously like the 'No Popery' outcry, which the British public has always been ready to raise on the slightest excuse. I don't believe there is any great animosity against Mosley personally; but he is the symbol of Fascism, and his ill-staged release is just the crevice needed to release the pent-up lava of anti-Fascism throughout the country. Similarly, the allegedly unjust birching of that miserable boy at Hereford touched off the 'anti-Gestapo' volcano, which is equally potent. Tiresome though such eruptions are, they are a healthy sign.

Monday 29 November   **London**

Harold Nicolson came to see me this afternoon, to tell me about his recent trip to Sweden. All the Swedes believe that Germany will disintegrate before

---

1 The proper date being 30 Nov.
2 Irene (formerly Lawley) was a cousin, daughter of Tommy's favourite Aunt Constance, Lady Wenlock.

long into complete chaos – except old King Gustav,[1] who still tries to work on us to make a negotiated peace with Germany, or the Russians will do so, which will mean the complete bolshevisation of Europe.

Tuesday 30 November

E. Bridges came this afternoon to tell me that there was a considerable row at yesterday's Cabinet between Bevin and Morrison, over this Mosley business. Bevin has always been opposed to Mosley's release, which is a red rag to his Trades Union people; and he don't love Herbert Morrison. The Cabinet support the latter, and Bevin is very sulky and threatening resignation. Unluckily, there is bound to be a division on the matter in the House of Commons tomorrow, and if Bevin votes against the Government, and a majority of the Labour members follow him, the position of Attlee and Morrison will be shaky.

The point about Mosley, which seems to have eluded all these politicians, is that he wasn't incarcerated as a punishment, but for preventive reasons; he has never been convicted of any crime, but was locked up because he would have been a danger and a nuisance if he had been left at large.

Horace Seymour,[2] on leave from Chungking, to see the King, who complained that he couldn't understand a word that H.S. says. I told him that everybody who knows Horace had had the same grievance for thirty years. To a Government dinner at Claridge's, to bid farewell to the Regent of Iraq. I sat next to McGowan of ICI who was not quite certain whether the chief guest came from Persia or Arabia, and was much puzzled when I said, 'Neither.' The Regent left commendably early, but the Duke of Gloucester, as usual, wouldn't go to bed, but stood about whinnying and drinking whiskies-and-sodas, till at last Clarendon and I went off on our own.

Wednesday 1 December

Yesterday's political crisis seems to have fizzled out, and the Mosley amendment was beaten by 327 to 62.

Linlithgow came to see the King. He finds the transition from the Viceroy's House at Delhi to a small manor near Hopetoun, with only 'dailies' to help his zenana in their domestic duties, very hard to bear. He told me that Gandhi's death would completely alter the political situation in India, though he saw no reason why G. should not last another seven or eight

---

1 Gustav V (1858–1950), King of Sweden 1907–50, held pro-German sympathies, but kept his country neutral throughout both world wars.
2 Sir Horace Seymour (1885–1978), Tommy's cousin, Ambassador to China 1942–6.

years; and that S. Cripps had definitely deceived him during his famous mission. I said that S.C. was probably one of those who are morally straight enough, but intellectually crooked – a not uncommon species. He looked better for his spell of rest, but still suffers from nervous contortions.

Monday 6 December   **Windsor**

John Weir has decreed that the King, though convalescent [from a chill] must keep his room for some days, so I stay here, which suits me well enough; there is nothing much I can do in London till the travellers come home from their several conferences, which won't be till the end of the week. They are being very uncommunicative about results, though the general indications are that they are satisfactory. The Turks are giving trouble, by the look of it, for Eden telegraphed tonight, 'Christmas dinner is proving tough.' Winston has an attack of 'gippy tummy', but sounds quite cheerful. He says they were all astonished at Tehran to find how bitter Stalin was against the French, saying that two-thirds of Frenchmen wanted the Germans to win.

The Tehran communiqué, over the signatures of the Big Three, was issued tonight; a notable document, with some palpable Winstonian touches in it.

Tuesday 7 December

The Tehran pronouncement has been well received. I think it cannot fail to strike cold on German hearts. Light, Foreign Office, sent me the report on the tour of the Stalingrad sword (which Winston presented to Stalin at Tehran) round the UK. Nearly half a million people went to see it at the various centres where it was exhibited.

Sunday 12 December

Have been here (Windsor) all the week, the King keeping his room. They had a dance for the Princesses on Friday night – young men and maidens, to which Joan and I took Caroline. They danced in the Red drawing-room, sitting out in the Green, two very beautiful rooms by night; and kept it up till 4 a.m. – but not me, for I left at 1.30, after supping excellently, for wartime, with Lady Joan Philipps.

Monday 13 December   **London**

The PM is laid up at Carthage, where he has apparently taken refuge in a very comfortable villa. He has had a temperature and what he calls a 'neuralgic sore throat', and is evidently thoroughly over-tired, so I hope he will stay there for a bit. Meanwhile, Randolph has gone to Yugoslavia with our SOE[1] man, Fitzroy Maclean,[2] which is all to the good. I'm told that he and his father bicker all day long, and far into the night.

Tuesday 14 December

The King, who is still at Windsor, is forty-eight today. I went to the House of Commons to hear Eden report on his recent Odyssey. He spoke well, and told his story clearly enough; but it was all flat, without any highlights, and the House, though attentive, was never stirred. The fact is, he is a dull speaker (and ditto writer), and his constant gestures, reminiscent of someone dandling a baby, distract and irritate one. He was unduly complacent, I thought, about the talks with the Turks. It don't look to me as if much of a dividend would be forthcoming there. The Turks, probably quite sincerely, say that the Germans are still quite strong enough to over-run them, in their present state of dis-equipment; and that, if that happened, they would only be another liability to the Allies – so what's the use? It is an understandable attitude, cleverly fostered, no doubt, by the astute von Papen.[3]

Wednesday 15 December

News of the PM is disquieting. Moran, in his report today, speaks definitely of pneumonia, and says his temperature is up to 102°. He is uneasy about the state of the heart, and has called in, from Cairo, Bedford and Scadding, two very good men (Middlesex Hospital) who are fortunately out there. Mrs Churchill is clamouring to go out there, but the Cabinet dissuaded her from starting today.

Thursday 16 December

Better news of Winston this afternoon. Moran says that unless the heart-disturbance, which has abated, gives further trouble, 'all will be well'. Mrs

---

1   Special Operations Executive.
2   Fitzroy Maclean (1911–96), diplomat, soldier, MP and author (*Eastern Approaches*, 1949). Brigadier commanding Military Mission to Tito and the Yugoslav Partisans 1943–5. Created Sir Fitzroy Maclean of Dunconnel, Bt., 1957.
3   Franz von Papen (1879–1969), a close associate of Hitler, was German Ambassador to Turkey 1939–44, and did his best to keep Turkey out of the war. Arrested by the Allies in 1945, he was tried at Nuremberg, but found not guilty of conspiracy to prepare aggressive war, and was sentenced to eight years' imprisonment by a German court.

C. has flown out to him. Meanwhile, Billy King has ordered prayers for his recovery to be offered up in all the churches in Canada; this seems a bit premature.

Saturday 18 December

Got draft of New Year honours from Bevir – a dullish list. The King rather favoured a knighthood being given to Noël Coward; but I pointed out that if N.C. had held the King's commission in any Service, he would indubitably have lost it after being found guilty in the proceedings that the Treasury instituted against him, over non-payment of income tax, not long ago. So it hardly seemed consistent to honour him at present – particularly as officers are continually being dismissed from the Service with ignominy for far less serious financial misdemeanours. He saw the point and has, I am glad to say, dropped the idea.

The Princesses gave the last performance of their pantomime, in St George's Hall, which Joan, Caroline and I attended. It was admirably done, and the principals and chorus alike would not have disgraced Drury Lane. Princess Elizabeth was a charming Aladdin, and Princess Margaret a finished and competent Princess Roxana. The Widow Twankey was magnificently played by the boy, Cyril Woods, who impressed me so last year. They netted £200 by their three performances.

Lavinia, who has come through her term of probation at Greenwich with flying colours and is now a half-, if not fully-fledged Wren officer, came for two nights. Read *Comedy of Errors* and *Timon of Athens*, which Raleigh says was the original sketch for *King Lear*.

Tuesday 21 December

Young Wilfred Thesiger[1] and his mother, K. Astley, lunched with me. Wilfred is a most impressive chap. Born in Abyssinia, he is one of the few Englishmen who really understand that unhappy country; Haile Selassie,[2] who has known him from birth, has now asked for him as bear-leader to his son and heir, Asfa Wosan.

Wednesday 22 December

An 'intercept' telegram from the Japanese Ambassador in Berlin to Tokyo

---

1 Wilfred Thesiger (1910–2003), explorer and writer, author of *Arabian Sands* (1959). Knighted 1995. After his father's death in 1920, his mother Kathleen married Reginald Astley.
2 1892–1975. Emperor of Ethiopia 1930–74.

reports an interview with Ribbentrop, at which the latter said that 'England, beginning with London, will shortly be completely destroyed'. Similar telegrams have indicated that the Jap is pretty gullible, but it is difficult to believe that he swallowed this. The Germans are making great play with this 'secret weapon' stunt all over Europe, declaring that it is now perfected and that they are only awaiting the psychological moment to bring it into action. Meanwhile, they have made, via Sweden, what appears to be the first genuine attempt to get in touch with us about peace-terms; which we are ignoring, merely replying that 'unconditional surrender' means just what it says.

One cannot altogether dismiss the possibility that they have got some secret device which they genuinely believe to be capable of changing the whole military situation; and it is unlikely that they have dug all these catacombs in the Pas de Calais (which we are bombing so sedulously) just for fun. But it seems highly improbable that, if they really have some such war-winning instrument, they would have talked about it as assiduously as they have during the past few months; and I feel quite certain that, if it were ready, they would use it instantly and not, in their present plight, wait for psychological or any other moments.

Another explanation is that they know the game is up, and that this sinister threat is a desperate attempt to bluff us into a negotiated peace. Two years ago, I remember, they flooded Europe with equally hair-raising stories of the devastating effects that their new U-boat campaign was going to have.

Dined at Buckingham Palace with the King and young Pelly-Fry. We heard a quantity of aeroplanes flying over London, but the Air Ministry told us it was only 'Eric', which is their name for some kind of exercise which they indulge in periodically. Sent the text of the King's broadcast to the Ministry of Information, who have to translate it into, I think, twenty-seven different languages.

Friday 24 December

Berlin bombed again last night, losses barely four per cent. We have been plastering the Pas de Calais excavations almost continuously. Bright, sunny day. Joan, Caroline and I heard the carols in St George's from the organ-loft. Very beautiful, though poor Harris complained bitterly that the 'flu had left him only one alto.

Saturday 25 December

The King delivered his broadcast well, in nine minutes. Hughe Knatchbull-Hugessen telegraphed yesterday from Ankara that Numan (Turkish Foreign

Minister) had told him – as 'news': he refused to communicate it officially – that the German Minister in Bucharest had called (in uniform) on the Romanian Foreign Minister, and told him Germany would accept peace on the following terms: they would surrender fleet, submarines, merchant fleet, air force, disarm completely, evacuate all occupied territory, undertake never to ask for colonies, and leave Europe to be organised according to the wishes of the Allies. The only condition they asked for is economic freedom for Germany, but this to be arranged as found suitable by the Allies.

On top of the Stockholm overture, this is not without significance; it is probably only an attempt to make trouble between us and Moscow, in the desperate hope that we should nibble privily at the bait without telling the Russians. Contrariwise, it may possibly be quite genuine.

Sunday 26 December

During the morning Freddie Dalrymple-Hamilton telephoned from Admiralty to say that a large enemy ship, believed to be *Scharnhorst*, was threatening our Russia-bound convoy in the neighbourhood of Bear Island. Our escorting cruisers, under Burnett, were engaging her, and the C-in-C Home Fleet (Fraser[1]) in *Duke of York*, with *Jamaica* (six-inch cruiser), was racing across the North Sea to try and cut her off from her base, the Altenfjord.

After luncheon he told me that one of our cruisers, *Norfolk*, had been hit aft; *Scharnhorst* was retreating south-eastwards, having done no damage to the convoy. At 7 p.m. his report was that *Duke of York* had found touch with *Scharnhorst*, and engaged her, apparently without result. *Scharnhorst*, steaming twenty-eight knots, had turned north and then due east, making for the direction of Nova Zemlya; *Duke of York*, steaming only twenty-six, was following her and still in touch by radar. This was more hopeful, as there seemed little prospect of S. being able to get home from those unfriendly waters. But at 8.10 p.m., while I was shaving, Freddie rang up again to say that S. was stopped and on fire. Finally, while we were finishing dinner at the Castle (where Joan, Caroline and I had been bidden), I was called to the telephone again to hear that *Scharnhorst* had sunk. We picked up a few survivors. It seems that our destroyers, *Saumarez, Scorpion, Savage* and the Norwegian *Stord*, made a very gallant attack and succeeded in

---

1 Adm. Sir Bruce Fraser (1888–1981), C-in-C Home Fleet 1943–4, in charge of Russian convoys, and of the action in which the German battle-cruiser *Scharnhorst* was sunk on 26 Dec. First Sea Lord and Chief of Naval Staff 1948–51. Created 1st Baron Fraser of North Cape 1946.

crippling *Scharnhorst*. The *Duke of York* then came up, and in an action lasting three and a half hours (in which *Duke of York* fired forty-five rounds per gun) sent her to the bottom. *Norfolk* was hit in one of her after-turrets, *Saumarez* also hit, but able to make for home at eight knots; otherwise, no casualties reported.

This is a piece of great good fortune for Fraser, who has only recently taken over Home Fleet, and for Guy Russell,[1] whose command of *Duke of York* is but a few weeks old. Apart from its naval importance, I believe that the sinking of *Scharnhorst* will have a shattering moral effect in Germany; it has some bearing, too, on all this 'secret weapon' stuff. If you have really got up your sleeve something capable of radically changing the whole military situation in your favour, you surely do not risk the principal unit of your remaining fleet on a subsidiary and desperate adventure.

A secondary benefit of the destruction of the S. should be the immobility of *Tirpitz*; they will hardly dare to move the latter from the Altenfjord to the docks, which are apparently essential for her repair, save under the cover of the *Scharnhorst*'s guns; and these guns will now shoot no more.

Carols in St George's. They did some of the old familiars – 'Wenceslas' and 'The First Nowell', as well as the incomparable '*In dulci jubilo*' and 'The Holly and the Ivy' – which last is the most beautiful of the lot. Dinner at the Castle; Caroline on one side of the King, with whom she seemed to hit it off well enough. Philip of Greece[2] and young Milford Haven also there. After dinner and some charades, they rolled back the carpet in the crimson drawing-room, turned on the gramophone and frisked and capered away till near 1 a.m. The King was wearing his tuxedo made of Inverness tartan, which is a source of much pleasure to him.

Monday 27 December

Young Andy Cavendish, the Devonshires' younger boy, went off to the Mediterranean recently. The first intimation that his father had of his having arrived in Italy was a telegram of two words: 'Pope trembling' – which was a sufficient indication to that black Protestant, Eddy, that a member of the Cavendish family was within striking distance of the Bishop of Rome; though I fear that Andy will not get much nearer to the Vatican for some time yet. When I came back from luncheon, I found old Cosmo Cantuar sitting in my room talking to Joan. Afterwards, she and I walked

---

1   Adm. the Hon. Sir Guy Russell (1898–1977). In 1943 he was a captain, commanding the 35,000-ton battleship *Duke of York*, which sank the *Scharnhorst*.
2   Prince Philip of Greece (b. 1921), son of TRH Prince and Princess Andrew of Greece, married HRH Princess Elizabeth in Nov. 1947.

up the tow-path for quite a way, past the racecourse; very still and mild – a perfect hunting day.

Wednesday 29 December

From the last report of the 'Crossbow' committee, it looks as if the Germans have more or less abandoned the rocket-gun idea in favour of the 'Queen Bee' – the radio-directed, pilotless bomber. The so-called ski-sites, all up and down the French coast, are being continually bombed by us.

1944

Friday 7 January

Pug Ismay came down to dinner, which was good of him, as he is up to his eyes in work, under a trilateral bombardment from Winston in Morocco, the Chiefs of Staff in Whitehall, and the American ditto in Washington; they seem to find it difficult to agree on future plans. I had not seen him since his expedition to Moscow with Eden, followed immediately by the even more strenuous one to 'Sextant' (Cairo and Tehran) with Winston, which nearly killed him. However, he seemed to have recovered, and was most amusingly reminiscent – and encouraging about the Russians, whose fundamentally changed attitude he confirms, as did Beneš ('Beans', as Winston calls him in his telegrams to Eden). The majority of the experts collected for 'Sextant' believe that Germany will collapse before the beginning of May; Ismay himself thinks not before the autumn, and believes that 'Overlord' will be the August 8th battle of this war.

Saturday 8 January

Sent the King an interesting letter from Garter, commenting on Sir H. Morris-Jones's[1] recent article on the matter of making Princess Elizabeth Princess of Wales. There will be a lot of talk about this in the next four months, and I expect the House of Commons will bring it up. The Commons have, I think, an immemorial right to approach the Sovereign on the subject – e.g., Edward III was formally petitioned by them at Eltham (1376) to make Richard of Bordeaux Prince of Wales.

Wednesday 12 January

George Sartoris, writing to me about Whittle's[2] jet-propelled aircraft which has been the sensation of the week, says the actual principle of the thing was discovered by Hero of Alexandria in 100 BC; and that as it operates in a vacuum, we shall now be able to fly through interstellar space. And perhaps to Mars?

---

1   Sir Henry Morris-Jones (1884–1972), doctor and MP.
2   Frank Whittle (1907–96), RAF fighter and test pilot, inventor of the jet engine. Knighted 1948.

Thursday 13 January

I got Their Majesties' consent to write to Simon [the Lord Chancellor] and ask him to draft a suitable Press announcement, to the effect that the King did not propose to change Princess Elizabeth's style and title for the present. This will check the spate of Press comment and general chatter on the question of creating her Princess of Wales. It is so much easier to do this before the waters have started to rise than to bury your head in the sand, and trust that the flood won't incommode you, which is the usual technique of the Royal Family in the face of such threatened agitations.

Tuesday 18 January

London, with the King. Winston, who arrived in this country last night, and made a dramatic entry into the House of Commons at Question Time this morning, came to luncheon. I met him at the Grand Entrance, and complimented him on his appearance after his illness – he looked plump and mellow. He said, 'I'm all right, except that I'm a little unsteady on my pins.' He then broke into a shambling trot and charged up the steps into the corridor like a tank, turning round on the top one to exclaim, with a broad grin, 'But I can manage these well enough, you see.'

The Russians, after a churlish answer to the Poles, have published in *Pravda* a mischievous story purporting to come from 'Greek and Yugoslavian sources in Cairo', to the effect that we had been having secret peace negotiations with Ribbentrop (of all men!) in Spain. This, of course, has gone round the world like a flame, and may do much harm, though the Foreign Office issued a very prompt *dementi.*

Thursday 20 January

Eisenhower, lately arrived to take over the command of 'Overlord', to see the King. I had not had any talk with him before, and was charmed by his frank and open manner; and manners, too, for after his audience with HM he took the trouble to come back to my room to say goodbye to me – a quite unnecessary courtesy (but nonetheless a courtesy) which few of our distinguished visitors pay me.

Saturday 22 January

Operation 'Shingle' – the landing by 6th Corps at Nettuno – started at 4.45 a.m. today, in perfect weather, which promises to hold for a bit. It appears to have taken the Germans by surprise, for the leading division has landed without opposition and advanced four miles inland. Last night we made a heavy raid on Magdeburg, following an equally heavy one (about 700 aircraft) on Berlin the night before. The Germans were more active over here than they have been for a long time, sending over ninety-nine, of which we destroyed about a dozen. They dropped some incendiaries in Westminster, but don't appear to have done much damage anywhere.

Monday 24 January

I wrote, and left for Eric Miéville to make what use he pleases of, a long memorandum on the idea of having a professional, whole-time 'public relations officer' at Buckingham Palace.

Thursday 27 January

The Cabinet came to the conclusion that, if anybody was to make an announcement about Princess Elizabeth's 'style and title' not being changed, it should be the Home Office, and not Buckingham Palace; that is all one to me – my motive throughout is to get somebody to make some decision before an undignified controversy erupts in Parliament and Press. But I suspect that some of the Cabinet rather favour her being made Princess of Wales – possibly the PM himself, whose pictorial imagination is no doubt fired by a vision of Princess Elizabeth looking charming on the steps of Carnarvon Castle, and blushingly acknowledging the loyal acclamations of a pan-Welsh Eisteddfod. That, of course, is all very nice; but I doubt if any of them have really thought out the full implications of such a step – particularly what I described in a letter to John Martin as the physiological contingencies.

Lunched with Godfrey Thomas at Boodle's, and then to Windsor. The workmen are now out of the Rampart room, the roof of which had threatened to collapse under the weight of Helen Hardinge's ridiculous 'garden' on the leads, and it should be habitable in a few weeks, which will be a great relief.

Friday 28 January

The Argentines, as a result of the revelations consequent on our exposure of Hellmuth[1] (a good bit of work by MI), and also on the brandishing of

---

1 The Argentine Consul. Elsewhere the author wrote: 'He was definitely on a secret mission to Himmler, and his capture seems to have been an adroit bit of work by MI, who picked him up, despite his diplomatic visa, at Trinidad.'

the big stick by Cordell Hull, have at last broken off relations with the Axis. Hull is getting very bellicose all round; he has also insisted on publicly denouncing the abominable treatment of our prisoners by the Japanese, and has cut off American supplies of oil to Spain. His precipitancy has somewhat shocked the Foreign Office, but the British public will not quarrel with it, for they have long been restless about the prisoners question, and are furious with Franco for putting bombs in a precious cargo of oranges.

Sunday 30 January

The Americans, after their heavy attack on Frankfurt yesterday, sent 820 bombers to Brunswick this morning, only losing twenty-one, and their fighters claim to have downed forty-six Germans, with a loss of five to themselves. Eric Miéville, telephoning from Appleton, tells me that Princess Elizabeth counted 284 Flying Fortresses going over the house, and then gave it up! Our Typhoons, looking for trouble over Paris today, had a remarkable sortie; attacking some airfield, they destroyed two Messerschmitts on the ground, and two in the air; coming home, they fell in with another covey of them, of which they shot down eight – all without loss to themselves. But on the other side of the ledger we have lost two good ships – the destroyer *Hardy*, escorting one of the convoys to Russia, was torpedoed by a U-boat; and the light cruiser *Spartan*, participating in 'Shingle', sunk by glider-bomb. The escort to the Russian convoy claim, however, to have sunk two or three U-boats.

Edward Halifax's Toronto speech on the possible future of the Empire has excited varied passions in Canada, and thrown Mackenzie King into one of his more temperamental frenzies; but he was much mollified, says Malcolm MacDonald,[1] when the latter drew his attention to certain passages in the speech containing flattering personal references to himself which had been omitted from the Press report. A little flattery always acts on him like cream on a cat.

Tuesday 1 February

Monty came this afternoon, to get his KCB [Knight Commander of the Bath]. I had ten minutes' talk with him before he went in to the King. He told me his recipes for winning (a) battles, (b) the affections of his men, with an egotism which is so naïve that it is disarming. Of his famous beret, he said, 'My hat is worth three divisions. The men see it in the distance.

---

1   1901–81. Son of Ramsay MacDonald, Labour and National Govt MP, High Commissioner to Canada 1941–6.

They say, "There's Monty" – and then they will fight anybody.' I advised him to make this point to his Sovereign, who has been very critical of Monty's flagrant departures from the orthodox uniform of a general – not knowing, perhaps, that Picton fought Waterloo in a pot-hat and a plain frock-coat. Monty is now setting about the task of whipping his 21st Army Group into the same dervish-enthusiasm that he produced in 8th Army in Africa; and I have no doubt that he will do it; the man has great faith.

Wednesday 2 February

At luncheon yesterday the PM seems to have dissuaded the King from making any definite pronouncement to the effect that he don't propose to change Princess Elizabeth's title: he will leave it to Brendan Bracken to 'damp down' any Press publicity about it. This I think a poor compromise – a reversion to 'ostrich' tactics, which won't stop the Welsh going on being troublesome, nor private individuals from writing foolish letters.

However, Winston himself does not, apparently, advocate any change, and has told John Martin to rebuke the Home Secretary for saying in a memorandum that making Her Royal Highness Princess of Wales 'would be an effective answer to any suggestion that the Government are unsympathetic towards Welsh sentiment'! In other words, that the title of the Heiress Presumptive should be a bait to catch the Welsh votes. I wonder if Henry Ponsonby would have shown such a paper to Queen Victoria? I certainly have not done so to her great-grandson.

With the King to dine at No. 10: the PM, three Chiefs of Staff, Eisenhower, Bedell Smith,[1] Omar Bradley[2] and Montgomery. I was between Bedell Smith and Andrew Cunningham, with Eisenhower on his other side. We dined in the underground rooms, with a Rehoboam of champagne and some admirable South African brandy sent to Winston by Smuts. It was all very agreeable, but I can't recollect that anything of great import was said.

Eisenhower told with gusto of the finding, in Tunis, of a 15th-century sword of German manufacture, with *Eisenhauer* inscribed after the maker's name; I suppose it meant 'Armourer' in those days. E. is a great talker, full of strange oaths, but his simple directness has all the marks of greatness. Andrew Cunningham said to me, 'Don't let the King under-rate Eisenhower on any account'; he evidently thinks most highly of him, as does every one of our people who know him well.

---

1 Gen. Walter Bedell Smith (1895–1961), US Army CoS 1942–5, negotiated surrender of Italy (1943) and Germany (1945). US Ambassador to the USSR 1946–9, CIA director 1950–53 and Under-Secretary of State 1953–4.
2 Gen. of the US Army Omar Nelson Bradley (1893–1981) commanded American troops in the invasion of Normandy (1944), and 12th Army Group 1944–5.

Bedell Smith, his Chief of Staff, is clearly the brains of the partnership – a relationship not dissimilar from that of Louis Botha and Smuts twenty years ago. Bedell said, and Cunningham agreed, that Darlan's murder was really a bad blow for us. C. said that he was a great sailor, and that the cornerstone of his war creed was never to let a single French ship fall into German hands. Oran was a shocking blunder on our part – but with Winston sitting on Bedell's right, this had to be said *sotto voce*.

Bedell is the well-read, intellectual type of soldier; he said S. Benét's *John Brown's Body* [1928] was his favourite book. We remarked on the dearth of poetry in this war, and I undertook to send him a copy of McRae's 'High Flight', almost the only really good poem it has produced. (The reason, I believe, is that this generation of fighting-men has lost any feeling for the traditional romance of war – which we still had in 1914 – through continually hearing from us, their fathers and uncles, what an irredeemably beastly thing it is.)

After dinner I sat with Winston and the First Sea Lord. W. is sore with Stalin for the latest of his churlish telegrams – a very ill-mannered one, about the transfer of the Italian men-of-war. 'If my shirt were taken off now,' he said, 'it would be seen that my belly is sore from crawling to that man. I do it for the good of the country, and for no other reason.' True enough, for his worst enemy could not say that W. is a crawler by nature. We did not get back to Buckingham Palace till 1 a.m.

Thursday 3 February

The Germans are now lying fantastically in their communiqués – e.g., their recent raids, with sixty to eighty aeroplanes, are reported as having been carried out by *900* – which left London in flaming ruins; in fact they have practically reproduced our communiqués, substituting London for Berlin. Then again they claim that U-boats sank ten of the escort, and a number of the merchantmen, in the recent convoy to Russia; the facts are that they sank the destroyer *Hardy*, and that the entire convoy reached port intact, our people claiming to have sunk two U-boats certain, three probable. This artificial boosting of an obviously failing morale is a good sign.

Friday 4 February

Sholto Douglas, who has taken over Coastal Command, to see the King; and Doolittle,[1] the hero of the American raid on Tokyo and now com-

---

1   Lieut.-Gen. James H. Doolittle (1896–1993), US Army Air Force 1917–30, 1940–45. On 18 Apr. 1942 he commanded a flight of sixteen B-25s that took off from the deck of the

manding the American bombers over here. I congratulated him on the 800 aircraft that bombed Wilhelmshaven yesterday having got back with a loss of only four; but he said, No, it wasn't a matter for congratulation, as an important object in these daylight raids was to destroy a quantity of German fighters, who, on this occasion, hadn't shown up at all. Then, looking at his watch, he added: 'Right now we have a similar number bombing Frankfurt.'

To the King, he said that Leipzig is now the target which they most want to knock out, as the bulk of German fighters are produced there; he would not mind losing 100 bombers if he could deal with it to his satisfaction. Doolittle, having won the Schneider Cup, retired from the American airforce some years before the war, and went into Standard Oil. He was interesting about the world's oil supplies, and is convinced that an international aerial police-force is essential if peace is to be preserved in the future.

Saturday 5 February

The King gave me Wavell's first letter to him since he became Viceroy – a masterly survey of the whole Indian field, which I must try to answer tomorrow.

That foolish fellow Sidney Herbert[1] wrote to *The Times* last week gibing at Acland[2] about his recent gift of his Devon property to the National Trust; he has now, of course, got involved in a heated political controversy, in which he has already been severely trounced, having got his facts all wrong. But even if he had emerged triumphant, he has no sort of business to write to *The Times* on such matters over his own signature while he is private secretary and comptroller to the Duchess of Kent, and I got the King's approval to my writing and telling him so. Lord Stamfordham would turn in his grave if he thought that a member of any royal household had done this; and rightly, for the labourer should be worthy of his hire, and, as Dick Molyneux said to me when I took on my present job, 'it entails the renunciation of the world, the flesh and the devil' – in one of which three categories is included writing to the newspapers or speaking on a public platform.

aircraft carrier *Hornet* and bombed Tokyo, Yokohama and other Japanese cities. Most of the planes landed behind friendly lines in China – a raid that gave an enormous boost to American morale. In 1925 he had won the Schneider Trophy by flying a Curtiss Navy racer seaplane at 232 mph, the fastest it had ever flown.

1 Sidney Herbert (1906–69,) Comptroller and Private Secretary to the Duchess of Kent 1942–8, succeeded his father as 16th Earl of Pembroke 1960.

2 Sir Richard Acland (1906–90), variously Liberal and Labour MP, had given his house, Killerton, near Exeter, to the National Trust.

Monday 7 February

En route for London, went to Bomber Command HQ with Their Majesties at West Wycombe; a very successfully camouflaged group of buildings, in a beech wood, and put up in 1938 or 1939. It has never, so far as is known, been detected by any German aeroplane. We were shown an astonishing development of radar, a kind of *camera obscura* in which the observer in a bomber can see, through the thickest cloud, the burst of the bomb and its immediate surroundings 20,000 feet below. The Germans have not got this apparatus, nor anything like it. I asked if, in peace-time, it would reveal to the aeronaut passing over a house all that was going on in the first-floor bedrooms, and they seemed to think it would. Also a book of photographs and diagrams of bombed German cities, with ditto of Coventry for purposes of comparison; Coventry, which we were wont to think of as a devastated town, appears relatively untouched alongside Rostock, Hanover, Cologne, Mannheim, Hamburg and others. It is a terrible record of devastation; but, qualitatively, no worse than shooting fine young men in the stomach or sending fine ships to the bottom of the sea with all hands on board. We had tea with Bert Harris, a quiet, determined man, with obvious powers of explosion, and with his staff.

Wednesday 9 February

The Cabinet tonight again discussed the question of the announcement about Princess Elizabeth, and Bridges has just told me (10.30 p.m.) that they agreed to its being made from here, in the form originally drafted by Simon. I had come to the conclusion that it would be wrong to announce it from No. 10, as the PM wanted to do, for the Dominions would at once say, and quite justifiably, that any question affecting the style and title of the heir to the throne was as much the concern of their governments as of that of the United Kingdom; and that if the PM of UK tendered advice on the subject, their PMs had an equal right to do ditto.

Thursday 10 February

Lunched alone with R. A. Butler,[1] in his house in Smith Square. In the throes of steering his Education Bill through Parliament, Winston has now made him take on the India Office, as locum to Leo Amery, who is laid up

---

1 1902–82. Conservative MP, Minister of Education 1941–5, gave his name to the far-reaching reforms of the 1944 Education Act. Served in the governments of Churchill, Macmillan, Eden and Home. Created Baron Butler of Saffron Walden (Life Peer) 1965.

with inflamed kidneys. I like Rab; he has plenty of ego in his cosmos, and not a vast deal of humour, but he is very able, and sincere. The Viceroyalty is clearly his ultimate goal.

The Cabinet made no bones about the Princess Elizabeth announcement, and, having cabled it to the four Governors-General, I hope to get the wretched thing published here on Saturday. [*Later note:* It appeared in the morning newspapers of 12 February, and went off well enough. But even *The Times* referred to her 'coming of age' on 21 April.[1] Simon got busy about this, and on 14 February *The Times* published a correction – though not, I fear, prominently enough to kill the widespread idea that she *does* come of age this year.]

Friday 11 February

The King, Grant and I left Victoria 7.15 p.m. for Ringwood, where we spent a quiet night. Philip Vian,[2] of the *Cossack*, came with us, and after dinner explained exercise 'Savoy', to see which was the object of the journey.

Saturday 12 February

We detrained at Swanage, in bright moonlight, at 6.43 a.m. Monty, Ramsay, Leigh-Mallory[3] met us on the platform, and we drove to Fort Henry, a concrete dug-out on the bluff overlooking the southern shore of Studland Bay. The exercise consisted in a landing operation on a hostile beach, supported by a heavy bombardment from destroyers, rocket-craft and the new amphibious D.D. tanks, which between them made a noise reminiscent of a Somme barrage – they were, of course, using live shells.

It began in what is known as 'nautical twilight', and was completed, with fair success, about 8.30. It was spectacular, and most interesting; one or two of the destroyers shot lamentably short, and the timing of the various waves of assault was not very accurate. But it was a formidable and impressive display, and I gathered that the pundits of the High Command found it instructive. At times I was intensely cold, and was not sorry for breakfast provided in a tent by the Canadian brigadier. Thereafter we walked along the shore to inspect one of the D.D.s, and left by train from Swanage at 10.45, reaching Windsor just after luncheon. It was remarkable how Monty, though theoretically on the same level as Ramsay and Leigh-Mallory, entirely dominated the show.

1 The Queen was born on 21 Apr. 1926.
2 Adm. of the Fleet Sir Philip Vian (1894–1968).
3 Air Chief Marshal Sir Trafford Leigh-Mallory (1892–1944), Air C-in-C Allied Exped-

Tuesday 15 February

Investiture, and PM to luncheon. Arthur Smith[1] to see the King, on exchanging command of London District for that of Mesopotamia; and Moyne,[2] on his way to become Resident Minister in Cairo, where he will have to cope with the increasingly complex affairs of Peter of Yugoslavia. It looks as if Tito,[3] whom I suspect of being a big man, will discard him pretty quickly if he for his part don't discard his present government and throw in his lot with Tito; it is a terribly difficult decision for the poor boy, and we don't seem able to do much to help him make up his mind.

Friday 18 February

John sent an amusing account of 'Monty Day' – i.e., Monty's inspection of the Guards Armoured Division. The great man's spell-binding tactics make no impression on the sophisticated Grenadiers. He is not liked by Guardsmen generally, as he is supposed to deny them their fair quota of medals, while placing them always in the forefront of the battle.

Saturday 19 February

There was a heavier air-raid on London between 1 and 2 this morning than there has been since the Blitz ended; the reverberations of it woke us up here in Windsor. In Avenue Road the Tim Nugents had a narrow squeak, the house next theirs being demolished by a bomb. Their Majesties, with Princess Elizabeth, went to the England v. Scotland football match; practically their first public appearance since the summer.

Tuesday 22 February

I dined with the Jack Egertons,[4] to meet Nye,[5] the VCIGS, and his wife, a daughter of old General H. Knox. They are a pleasant couple; Nye, who was in the same regiment as Monty (Royal Warwickshire) gave some amusing

---

itionary Air Force 1943–4. Killed when his aircraft crashed in the Alps.
1 Lieut.-Gen. Arthur Smith (1890–1977), GOC London District and Maj.-Gen. Commanding the Brigade of Guards 1942–4, GOC Persia and Iraq command 1944–5.
2 1st Baron Moyne (1880–1944), Deputy Minister of State, Cairo, 1942–4, Resident Minister in Cairo 1944, until he was assassinated (see p. 268).
3 Josip Broz Tito (1892–1980), Partisan leader, Marshal of Yugoslavia 1943–80, PM 1945–80, President 1953–80. During the war, as Supreme Commander of the Yugoslav National Resistance Army, he led resistance to the Axis powers.
4 Vice-Adm. Jack Egerton (1892–1972) and his wife Marion.
5 Lieut.-Gen. Sir Archibald Nye (1895–1967), Vice-CIGS 1941–6, High Commissioner for India 1948–52, and for Canada 1952–6.

sidelights on M.; he was, apparently, a complete failure as a commanding officer. J.E. said that the disintegration of the atom might be achieved in eight or ten years, and that a complete transformation of our methods of motive power would result.

Another raid, about midnight, when our guns were so noisy that I got out of bed and went upstairs to join P. Legh and E. Miéville, who were fire-watching – an occupation which would seem to have lost its point now, in that the phosphorus bombs now used by the Germans are inextinguishable by any domestic appliance such as the stirrup pump. The current type of raid has the merit of only lasting about an hour, though that hour is a very noisy one; however, it is preferable to the interminable dusk-to-dawn affairs of 1940–41.

Wednesday 23 February

I spent the day in bed, with a severe cold in my chest. Sad news from Holton, Melville Balfour writing to say that Anthony [his eldest son], who was given an MC recently, had been killed on the Anzio beach-head.

About 11 p.m. the Germans dropped a bomb in Pall Mall, just in front of Hardy's shop. All the north-east corner of St James's Palace was severely blasted, and the Legh family, Godfrey Thomas and Winifred Murray (née Hardinge) had to come over to Buckingham Palace, where beds were found for them. Joey Legh, who was doing *The Times* crossword in the window of their sitting-room, was badly cut all over his head, and arrived streaming with blood, his face looking like a jam tart. However, nobody was seriously hurt, though they were all a good deal shaken.

Thursday 24 February

Went over to St James's Palace before breakfast, to assess the damage. A sad sight, but the actual structure of the building don't seem to have suffered much damage. All the north-east corner will be uninhabitable for some time, and I fear the Leghs and Hardinges will recover little of the furniture etc. which they had still got there. My house is not much the worse, though those windows which face east have been blown in. Marlborough House has also lost many windows.

The actual crater in Pall Mall is not very big, and was half full of water, as a water-main had burst. Will Goodenough,[1] walking home soon after the bomb fell, tumbled into the crater, and, like Alice in the pool of tears,

---

1   Sir William Goodenough (1899–1951), Chairman of Barclays Bank 1947–51.

swam about in it for some time till he was pulled out by a policeman.

Another bomb from the same stick fell in King Street, demolishing Spink's and Partridge's shops. I went back and telephoned a report to the King, who had spent the night in his train near Newmarket between two days of inspecting troops; and to the Hardinges at Crichel; and to Queen Mary at Badminton.

Thursday 2 March

Had a bad night, as, having lain awake coughing till about 2 a.m., was woken at 2.45 by the arrival of the Germans, the moon being then set; and, as it was my night for fire-watching, had to get out of bed and prowl ineffectively about the first floor of Buckingham Palace with Arthur Penn for three-quarters of an hour. The Germans then went home, having, I heard later, been diverted from their original target some forty miles by one of our new devices.

I was to have gone to a dinner of industrial magnates, but I felt too sleepy and bronchial to face them in the murky and draughty wilderness of the Reform Club, so I stayed at home and had a bowl of bread and milk by my own fireside.

Friday 3 March

Two MI men called on me yesterday and explained how the King's visits in the next few months could assist the elaborate cover scheme whereby we are endeavouring to bamboozle the German Intelligence regarding the time and place for 'Overlord'.

Saturday 4 March

William Temple, who wants to have a day of prayer in connection with 'Overlord', keeps writing letters to me and others in which he implies that the military really must fix the date for the invasion of Europe soon, or we shall find it clashing with Palm Sunday or Easter. He is, in some ways, most curiously out of touch with realities.

Sunday 5 March

John came for the day. I had a useful hour with the King and Queen before luncheon, when I got decisions about various future plans and about the answers to be given to the multifarious questions about Princess Elizabeth with which the Press constantly bombard Eric Miéville.

Roosevelt's Press conferences are really more deadly to the Allied cause than any of Hitler's secret weapons. He calmly announced yesterday – or was reported as announcing – that the Italian fleet was to be distributed in equal thirds to us, USA and USSR; Winston telegraphed to him the text of this disastrous pronouncement, as it appears in our Press, commenting, more in sorrow than in anger, 'Can this be true?' F.D.R.'s reply is singularly lame. Meanwhile, Moscow has of course reproduced the report with banner headlines; and Badoglio, not unnaturally, has threatened to resign. It would be hard to imagine a more effective monkey-wrench to throw into delicate machinery.

Monday 6 March

In the Travellers Jock Colville told me what a shattering disappointment 'Shingle' has been to the PM. He says, 'We meant to put a wild cat ashore; instead, we have only left a stranded whale on the beach.' I think this is an unnecessarily gloomy epitome of the situation. J.C. said the PM was meditating flying out there; I hope wiser counsels will prevail.

Wednesday 8 March

Went with HM to luncheon at the Royal College of Surgeons in Lincoln's Inn Fields, when the Duke of Gloucester was inducted as an honorary fellow. I had an extremely boring meal, next to a garrulous old surgeon called Walton; but there was good turtle soup. Later, walked to the Fifty Shilling Tailor in the Strand and bespoke a black coat and waistcoat – eighteen coupons, price 78/–. I had ascertained that Poole would have charged me 15 guineas. The Americans gave Berlin another hammering, in daylight.

Thursday 9 March

Arthur Penn and I went to the Churchill Club, to hear H. Agar[1] address a packed house on 'Why We Are Fighting', with Eden in the chair. I had some talk with Agar before, and at, dinner; a handsome, attractive chap, and a superb artist at lecturing. Listening to him was like watching Jack Hobbs on a good wicket. He was very trenchant, with fine sarcasm and well-tempered indignation, about the American attitude to world problems in the period between the two wars, and his audience – eighty per cent

---

1 Herbert Agar (1897–1980), American author and editor, Special Assistant to the US Ambassador in London 1942–6.

American – took his castigation of their fatherland in very good part.

He told an effective story of President Coolidge telling a reporter that he attributed his equanimity to the fact that he 'avoided the major problems', and said it was to the eternal shame of Americans of that age that they had applauded this wisecrack, and made it the keystone of their attitude to life. Altogether it was a very fine performance, and as near first-class oratory as anything I have ever heard.

Got back to Buckingham Palace to find the King waving a note from Peter of Yugoslavia (who is due to arrive here any day) and demanding to see Eden at luncheon tomorrow. It was midnight before, in the jargon of today, I succeeded in 'contacting' the latter.

Friday 10 March

Joey Legh drove me to Windsor after luncheon. Joan has given me, as a memento of the approaching anniversary of our wedding day, a first edition of Trollope's *Bullhampton*, with delightful contemporary illustrations.

Sunday 12 March

King Peter arrived on Friday, and rang me up in the evening to know when he could see the King; the latter firmly refuses to do this till Wednesday, when some of the political fog may have cleared off. Meanwhile the King has had a letter from 'Mignon' (Peter's mother), saying roundly that she won't allow the marriage. But can she stop it?

Monday 13 March

Moran came to see me, saying that Winston is set on going on the *Bummel* [spree] again (this time to some Atlantic rendezvous with F.D.R.), and can the King stop him? I doubt if he can, but he told me he would try. Moran said that, apart from his various proclaimed illnesses on these adventures, Winston had a sort of heart-attack in Washington, which I didn't know before.[1]

Tuesday 14 March

With the King to dinner at No. 10. Here were the War Cabinet, plus E.

---

1   This had occurred when Churchill visited Roosevelt in Washington over Christmas and the New Year 1941–2, to plan the Atlantic alliance, after America, goaded by the Japanese attack on Pearl Harbor, had decided enter the war against the Axis.

Bridges. I sat between Oliver Lyttelton and Ernie Bevin, two as gross men as you would find anywhere in a long summer's day, but both agreeable. I don't find the War Cabinet, unbuttoned and in an after-dinner mood, a very impressive company. Winston said he didn't anticipate that the Japs would last very long – 'They are wearing very thin.' The King, Winston and Eden went into a huddle over King Peter's affairs after dinner. At about 10.45 the sirens went, and we trooped into the shelter, a sort of double bathing-machine, in one half of which was our company, talking affairs of state not *sotto voce*, and in the other, all the housemaids of No. 10, who must have been much edified. The raid, which was a sharp one, in the Paddington–Marylebone neighbourhood, lasted the customary three-quarters of an hour, and we then sat about till ten past one.

Thursday 16 March

My wedding-day; and, appropriately, I called on King Peter after breakfast and told him (by direction of the King, who left London to visit 1st Airborne Division overnight) that if he would arrange to be married at the Yugoslav Embassy on Monday afternoon, Their Majesties would both be present and give him their blessing. (I had taken the precaution the night before of ascertaining that the Foreign Office had no political obstacles to put in the way, and that Eden would undertake to attend the ceremony himself.) King George of Greece had tried to induce our King to have the wedding at Buckingham Palace, but I firmly resisted this, and the Queen, who was in the room, supported me. The British public would not be pleased at a Balkan wedding, with all its (to them) pagan ritual, being celebrated in so sacred a shrine of the Church of England; and, if the marriage should prove unfortunate, the blame therefore might well be saddled on HM, who would seem to have been far more responsible for it than he actually is, if it began in his own house.

Peter blushed with pleasure when I broke the news to him, and gave me the impression of being in love with his Alexandra.

Friday 17 March

This morning there came to see me a young woman straight out of one of Peter Cheyney's books, Princess Natasha Bagration – a tall and slender Russian émigré, with legs like pillars of ivory and fine eyes set in a very level head. She is secretary to Puritch, the Yugoslav Prime Minister, and I should say a highly efficient one.

When I got back from luncheon, I found a message asking me to go and see King Peter at Claridge's as soon as possible. This I refused to do, saying, relatively truthfully, that the King was shortly returning here – so Puritch came down to see me. He made a strong plea for holding the wedding at Buckingham Palace, but I said NO.

Saturday 18 March   **Windsor**

With John Gore to Eton after luncheon, he to interview his son's future housemaster, and I to the Vice-Provost, Henry Marten,[1] who wanted to consult me as to how he should instruct Princess Elizabeth in the constitutional position of the Crown. I advised him to hide nothing, not even Dunning's[2] famous resolution of 1780 – 'That the influence of the Crown has increased, is increasing, and ought to be diminished' – carried by 233 votes to 215.

Monday 20 March

Back to London a.m.; and at 4 p.m. King Peter was duly married in the presence of Their Majesties – but not of myself. The King seems to have performed the various duties required of a *koum* with sang-froid, and not without relish; anyhow, he returned home in good feather. The bridegroom's mother, Queen Marie, who don't like the bride, sulked in her tent and refused to come, but this don't seem to have marred the general harmony of the proceedings. As the Yugoslav Embassy in Washington had told the Press all about it yesterday, Upper Grosvenor Street and its immediate neighbourhood were packed with people all day.

Tuesday 21 March

Winston told the King today that his projected journey was off. F.D.R. says he can't come and meet him, as he has got to have a course of medical treatment. I wonder if somebody has put F.D.R. up to that, in order to keep Winston at home – perhaps that cunning old fox Moran.

Wednesday 22 March

A broken night, as there was a raid from 1 a.m. to 2 a.m., for which I had to leave my bed and fire-watch. Noisy, but nothing fell nearer this house than Vauxhall.

---

1   Henry Marten (1872–1948), Assistant Master, House Master, Lower Master, Vice-Provost and finally Provost of Eton (1945–8), tutor to Princess Elizabeth. Knighted 1945.
2   John Dunning, 1st Baron Ashburton (1731–93), barrister, MP for Calne.

Saturday 25 March   Windsor

We went down to Eton to watch the school sports, in blazing sunshine. A fine pipe band from the Camerons was performing at intervals, and there were many officers from the 51st Division, which is now in these parts – magnificent specimens they were, too.

Sunday 26 March

Stalin has sent Winston two really outrageous telegrams (Poland), ill-mannered and overbearing beyond belief. Hence, W.'s very complimentary allusions to Russia in his long broadcast this evening showed praiseworthy forbearance; perhaps too much so – some think he would do better to give up turning the other cheek to Stalin. It was not a good speech – obviously dictated by the exigencies of home politics, and showing little of the accustomed fire and fantasy. In fact, it was the speech of an old man.

It was almost a summer's day, and we sat for a long time by the lake at Frogmore after tea. I wonder if the passage of hordes of aeroplanes through the sky, plus the disturbances that radio-location must cause, is robbing us of our normal rainfall.

Friday 31 March

Returned to Windsor last night with Their Majesties and Princess Elizabeth, after a two-days' tour of South Wales – Newport, Cardiff, Merthyr Tydfil, Barry and Swansea. The Welsh turned out in great numbers, and showed commendable enthusiasm everywhere. My appearance in the second car continually evoked cries of 'There's Monty', though the resemblance between us can only be very slight. In Cardiff docks they told us that they now had so much shipping coming in that they didn't know where to put it.

On Tuesday night, soon after our train had tied up at Portskewett, Eric Miéville telephoned to me from London to say that the Government had been beaten by one vote (117 to 116) in the House of Commons on Thelma Cazalet's[1] amendment to Clause 82 (equality of pay for men and women teachers) to R. A. Butler's Education Bill. From this arose a two-day crisis, which the PM insisted on resolving by making the matter the subject of a vote of confidence on Thursday, when, of course, the Government got a huge majority – 425 to 23. The Cabinet, who discussed their course of action

---

1 Thelma Cazalet-Keir (1899–1989), MP, campaigner for women's rights, particularly in education; much feared on the lawn-tennis court for her diabolical under-arm service.

at a special meeting, were unanimous in supporting these tactics; but I can't help feeling they were wrong.

The whole transaction suggests taking a Nasmyth steam-hammer to crush a walnut, and there is a suggestion of petulance and ill-temper about it all which has left an unpleasant impression both here and abroad. I feel they would have done better to have treated it with a lighter touch, and not to have forced the rebels – Hinchingbrooke,[1] Hogg[2] & co. – to eat their words publicly and to stultify their own votes only forty-eight hours after they had given them. Parliament's reputation, and that of the PM; have undoubtedly suffered from the episode. The root of the trouble is that Winston is tired, anxious and in a devilish bad temper; his tendency to use dictatorial methods, long familiar to his Cabinet and his immediate advisers, has been brought sharply to the notice of the world, which is rather shocked at the discovery. I suspect that the malign influence of the Beaver was largely responsible for those Rehoboam tactics. The net result of it all is to make the PM of England appear slightly ridiculous, which is a bad thing at any time, and especially now.

Tuesday 4 April

Edward Bridges dined with me at the Travellers. He said Winston was much better in himself (the King got the same impression at luncheon), but definitely thought (and spoke) of himself as an old man now; at Cabinet meetings he talks, or rather rambles, incessantly, often with a rather hazy background of fact. Talking of the Beaver, Bridges agreed with me that he was wholly evil, and said he had rarely in his life been so shocked as he was by the final interview between the B. and Winston when they parted company two years ago; they abused each other like a pair of fishwives.

MacGeagh,[3] the Judge Advocate-General, telephoned today to ask if he could discuss a somewhat delicate court martial case with us. So I asked Eric Miéville to go and see him; we both surmised that some member of

---

1 Victor Montagu, Viscount Hinchingbrooke (1906–95), MP, son of the 9th Earl of Sand-wich, disclaimed his peerages for life after the death of his father in 1962. Chairman of the Tory Reform Committee 1943–4.
2 Quintin Hogg (1907–2001), barrister and politician, succeeded father as 2nd Viscount Hailsham 1950 but disclaimed peerages for life 1963. Joint Parliamentary Under-Secretary of State for Air 1945. Many other public appointments, including First Lord of the Admiralty 1956–7, Lord Privy Seal 1959–60, Minister for Science and Technology 1959–64, Secretary of State for Education and Science 1964. Created Baron Hailsham of St Marylebone (Life Peer) 1970.
3 Col. Sir Henry MacGeagh (1883–1962), Judge Advocate-General (Army and RAF) 1934–54.

the Royal Family was in trouble, but, had we discussed it till kingdom come, we should never have guessed the right one – for it proved to be Queen Mary! She has apparently been buying sausages, contrary to the food-regulations, from some RAF depot, and there is a great shindy about it.

Wednesday 5 April

The King told me this morning that he would never appoint Eric Miéville as my successor, and that I should have to find, and train, another. I have always had it in mind that Michael Adeane should do that some day, and do not intend to abandon the idea, though I did not allude to it on this occasion. Anyhow, it is quite useless to search for suitable young men till the war is over, when there ought to be a wide choice. But I foresee a difficult and painful situation *vis-à-vis* poor E.M., who will some day have to be told that he can expect no promotion; and I suppose I shall have to be the man to do it.

Went to, and round, the Admiralty with the King and Queen, after which we had tea with the Alexanders in Admiralty House – in a room which I had last seen as my own bedroom when I used to stay there during Chelmsford's brief reign in 1924. A. Cunningham gave me a bad account of Winston, who has become impossibly prolix and obstructive.

The Greek fleet and army in Egypt seems to be in a state of revolution – republican rather than Communist, perhaps. King George, by his procrastination and refusal to accept advice, is largely to blame for this situation; my impression is that he would rather prefer to lose his throne than keep it. His spiritual home is Brown's Hotel.

Thursday 6 April

Their Majesties and the Princesses to Appleton, with Eric Miéville and Townsend.[1] I retired to Winchester Tower. Heard first chiffchaff in Frogmore. Wind has got round to NE. I fear it may be the beginning of the blackthorn winter, though the Admiralty meteorological experts assured us yesterday that several deep depressions were on the way.

---

1   Group Capt. Peter Townsend, DSO, DFC and Bar (1914–95), Equerry to King George VI 1944–52, and Comptroller to Queen Elizabeth the Queen Mother 1952–3, had been a gallant Battle of Britain pilot. Tommy got on well with him, and was fond of his wife, Rosemary, but described him in a letter to his friend John Gore as 'a devilish bad equerry: one could not depend on him to order the motor-car at the right time of day, but we always made allowances for his having been three times shot down into the drink in our defence'.

Friday 7 April Good Friday   **Windsor**

Foreign Office telephoned to say that Eden had gone away for a fortnight's complete rest; if he comes back restored to health, he may remain at the FO. Meanwhile, Winston is to take charge of it, which won't do him any good.

Tuesday 11 April

Fifty-seven today. Joan gave me a second-hand copy of Trollope's *Is He Popenjoy?*, of which I've long been trying to get hold.

Friday 14 April

London, for the day. Dentist. Lunched with Harry Harewood at the Turf. He told me Princess Mary was quite ready to surrender the title of 'Princess Royal' to Princess Elizabeth, if the King wants it; but I don't think that he does.

At the War Office saw P. J. Grigg, who has received from Monty a project for an elaborate service to be held in St Paul's on the anniversary of the Coronation, for the 'hallowing' of the fighting men who will be engaged in 'Overlord'. The proposed form of service was adapted from that of the Coronation (one could not help feeling that it was not far from being the Coronation of Monty), the Coronation regalia to be paraded, etc.

I then saw Puritch, the Yugoslav Prime Minister (for the moment – he is going to get the sack any day, though he don't know it), whom I rather like. He wanted a date for King Peter to see the King, which he won't get before Monday. Then on to Kew, where Joan and I walked round the gardens with Archbishop Cosmo, and had tea with him. With P.J.'s consent, I showed him the papers about Monty's idea. He was horrified at [the idea of] the Coronation service being re-hashed in this way, and justly remarked that it, and the regalia, were consecrated to a unique purpose. Altogether, he didn't like the proposal any more than P.J. and I had; on security grounds, it is surely risky to concentrate so many swells in one place at that particular moment; moreover, the whole thing has a bogus flavour. The 'hallowing' of the troops would be done in the presence of a congregation of 'representatives', ninety per cent of whom would not be fighting men; the latter would know nothing of it until they read about it in the *Daily Mirror*, *Daily Sketch* and *Daily Express* (their three favourite news-sheets) on the following day; and the countless other troops, who have long been serving in different theatres of war, might well ask why they too hadn't been hallowed before they set out. I have been to a number of such services;

however well they may be done, their atmosphere invariably approximates to that of a society wedding; in this case, there wouldn't even be a bride and bridegroom.

This evening we finished Fisher's *History of Europe*, which we have been reading aloud, on and off, for the past two years.

Saturday 15 April

We had tea with Marten, Vice-Provost of Eton, and his twin sister. Quickswood, the Provost, being away, they took us round his beautiful house, full of charming Romneys, Hoppners, etc. of 18th-century Etonians. In a telegram to F.D.R. Winston says he is becoming 'very hardset about "Overlord",' which I suppose means enthusiastic.

We started reading C. Whilley's *William Pitt* aloud. In 1782 W.P. said in the House of Commons, 'This is neither a fit time nor a proper subject for the exhibition of a gaudy fancy or the wanton blandishments of theatrical enchantment.' This seemed to me so appropriate to Monty's Coronation service that I copied it out and sent it to P.J. and to Cosmo.

Sunday 16 April

Went over to Royal Lodge p.m. and walked round the garden. Heard first cuckoo – and saw it.

Monday 17 April

To London by car, picking up Delia Peel at Englefield Green. Their Majesties back from Sandringham before luncheon. Stettinius,[1] US Under-Secretary of State, to see the King. He made a very favourable impression on me; I hope he may some day be President. Also Harold Alexander, whom I had never met before. Stettinius is said to have asked Winston which part of the British Empire he thought ought to be rehabilitated first, and Winston to have replied 'Grosvenor Square'.[2]

Dined with the Devonshires – only William Temple and Miss Kathleen Kennedy,[3] the pretty daughter of ex-Ambassador Joe (a bad man) whom I escorted to her home in Hill Street.

---

1 Edward R. Stettinius Jr (1900–49), US Under-Secretary of State.
2 Tommy described the square in wartime as 'a sort of American enclave'.
3 The second daughter of Joseph P. Kennedy, US Ambassador to the Court of St James. Known as 'Kick', she married William Cavendish, Marquess of Hartington (heir to the Duke of Devonshire), in 1944, but he was killed in action a few months later. She died in a plane crash in May 1948.

Tuesday 18 April

Lunched with the Industrial Welfare Society, as guest of Hyde, the secretary, and sat between him and First Lord Alexander (the world seems full of Alexanders today), who made a good, stereotyped speech. He was thanked by Mr Ojo, the Nigerian delegate; he did it very prettily, and was roundly applauded by his 150 co-members. Thence I went to the Fifty-Shilling Tailors in the Strand, to try on my black coat and waistcoat.

Pug Ismay came to tea with me. He is happier about the PM's health, but they are all hot and bothered about the future conduct of the SE Asian campaign. 'Overlord' preparations going well. Johnny Bevan,[1] just back from Moscow, has done a good job with the elaborate 'cover' scheme, intended to bamboozle the Germans, and seems to have succeeded. They are again anxious about 'Crossbow' – the Germans have been doing a lot more work on the 'ski-sites', despite our persistent bombing, and have surrounded them with heavier flak, which they can ill spare, so it looks as if they set great store by them.

Dined at Claridge's, with Letty Benson,[2] to meet her daughter-in-law Lady Wemyss,[3] just arrived from South Africa, where David wooed and wed her three years ago. I thought her charming, with looks reminiscent of her aunt-by-marriage, Marjorie Anglesey, thirty years ago; and that is high praise.

John's division is evidently moving south; he writes that they are all being entertained by 'Charlie the Duke' – i.e. Rutland – which indicates the neighbourhood of Belvoir. He says that a letter one of his men recently wrote to his wife, which J. had to censor, ended, 'I'm sorry you've had such a bad cold. It must have been a very bad one to leave you with a black eye and a swollen jaw.'

Wednesday 19 April

Harold Macmillan, in one of his telegrams to the Foreign Office, speaks of George III having the delusion that he had been present at the battle of Waterloo; I wrote and told him that he was a reign out. Dined Grillions, between Lords Maugham and Camrose. E. Devonshire revealed to me that the inwardness of our dinner last Monday was to initiate a friendship

---

1   Col. John Henry Bevan (1894–1978), strategic deception specialist, architect of the cover-plan which misled the Germans about Operation 'Overlord', the invasion of Normandy.
2   Originally Lady Violet Manners, sister of Lady Diana Manners who married Duff Cooper. Letty was the wife of Guy Benson, and one of Tommy's oldest friends.
3   David Charteris, 12th Earl of Wemyss, had married Mavis Gordon, of Cape Province, in 1940.

between W. Cantuar and Miss Kennedy, so that the former might convert the latter from her Papistry, and thus fit her to marry Billy Hartington, who loves her dearly. She is, it seems, ready to contemplate, if not to embrace, conversion; Chatsworth, in fact, *vaut bien* whatever is the opposite of a Mass.

Firoz Khan Noon, now one of the Indian representatives to the War Cabinet, came to see the King. Urging the advisability of sending the King's private secretary out to govern an Indian presidency instead of remaining indefinitely at Buckingham Palace, he said, not very felicitously, to Eric Miéville and me, 'How much more useful Sir Alexander Hardinge might have been as Governor of Bengal, rather than rotting away here!'

Friday 21 April

Princess Elizabeth's eighteenth birthday. There was an elaborate changing of the guard ceremony by the Grenadiers, in the Quadrangle, at 11 a.m., and Queen Mary, the Gloucesters, Princess Mary and Harry [Harewood] came to luncheon; otherwise, no special festivities, though a mass of telegrams and letters came in during the day.

Thursday 27 April

Went to one of the periodical luncheons given by the Lobby journalists at the Savoy. Eden spoke, amusingly and well – these luncheons are always rigorously 'off the record'. He emphasised the need for real cooperation between us, USA and USSR, as the absolute *sine qua non* if the world is not to relapse into chaos.

Friday 28 April

I called on Mackenzie King (who arrived by air last night) at the Dorchester. He was most amiable, and seemed genuinely glad to be here again. I warned him that he would find most people very tired, and possibly rather cross. Smuts has also arrived, and I had a few words on the telephone with young Jamie [Smuts].

Monday 1 May

Dinner at Buckingham Palace for the Dominions Prime Ministers etc., who had arrived during the weekend. Their Majesties and Princess Elizabeth (her first official dinner); Gloucester, Princess Mary and Harry, Duchess of Kent, Winston and Mrs Churchill, Smuts, Mackenzie King, Curtin[1] (Australia), Fraser[2] (New Zealand) and Mrs, G. Huggins[3] of Southern Rhodesia, Kashmir and F. K. Noon; the Cranbornes, Cynthia Spencer, Joey and I. I was next to Kashmir, who is easy enough. As usual, it lasted just twenty minutes too long, but was, I think, quite successful. Winston was rather querulous because we hadn't asked Attlee, for which I saw no reason whatever, and said so; it was an Empire, not a domestic, party.

Tuesday 2 May

On my way to see Bridges after luncheon, fell in with Alan Brooke, CIGS, observing the young ducks in St James's Park. He has had a week off, fishing with Ivan Cobbold[4] on the Dee, where he enjoyed himself. Asked Hollis if the experts had any explanation of the mysterious explosions from the Calais coast which have lately been shaking the denizens of Dover out of their beds; nothing definitely known, but one theory is that they are due to mines on the French coast exploding as a result of our air-raids.

Wednesday 3 May

To Grillions, hoping to find Ilchester[5] there; and did. I told him that I wanted to buy the Headlam plot (14½ acres, in Evershot) to which I took a great fancy when we were there last June. F. Nixon[6] had told me that Ilchester might be a formidable rival in the forthcoming auction, but, as I suspected, he is only interested in it from a defensive point of view – i.e., to keep out any undesirable neighbours, and readily undertook not to compete with me.[7]

Thursday 4 May

The minutes of the Prime Ministers' meetings are now coming in from the Cabinet Office, and very illuminating they are. Winston has given a masterly survey of the war situation, and all of them have made worthy contributions

---

1 Rt. Hon. John Curtin (1885–1945), PM of Australia 1941–5.
2 Rt. Hon. Peter Fraser (1884–1950), PM of New Zealand 1940–49.
3 Godfrey Huggins (1883–1971), Minister of Native Affairs in Southern Rhodesia 1933–49, Prime Minister, Federation of Rhodesia and Nyasaland 1953–6. Created 1st Viscount Malvern 1955.
4 Killed when a bomb fell on the Guards' Chapel on 18 June 1944.
5 Giles Fox-Strangways, 6th Earl of Ilchester (1874–1959), editor, author and historian, President of the London Library 1940–52.
6 Tommy's brother-in-law, Fergus Nixon.
7 A couple of weeks later Tommy decided not to make a bid, as the property seemed too expensive and faced due north.

to the ensuing discussions – save, perhaps, Fraser of New Zealand, whose remarks seem to me facetious and ill-informed. Smuts is clearly not convinced that an attack on North-West Europe is the best policy; he would have preferred a campaign in the Balkans, etc. But of course the answer is that the Americans would never play in that theatre.

Mackenzie King has not said much yet, but his brief speeches show a commendable appreciation of past achievements and present difficulties; he paid a generous, and deserved, tribute to Winston's wisdom in refusing to be induced by USA to launch a European venture in 1942 or 1943.

Fitzroy Maclean, head of our mission to Tito, was here to see the King this morning – a most impressive young man, of whom we shall hear more. He thinks Tito is a great man, and that Peter has lost any chance of holding his throne by not going out to Yugoslavia twelve months ago; by advertising the fact that he invited a representative of Mihailović[1] to attend his wedding; and by the two disastrous speeches that he has made since. There is a chance that he might save his bacon even now if he would go out and serve in Tito's air force, but I doubt if he will take it.

Party at 10 Downing Street, to which Joan and Caroline accompanied me. A great collection of notables and demi-notables, among whom we found many friends, and stayed till 7 p.m. 'C' told me hair-raising stories about the effects of the bombs of the future – and maybe not a distant future either. He don't consider that we have scotched the 'Crossbow' menace yet, by any means.

The Devonshires have taken the plunge. Billy Hartington's engagement to Miss Kennedy is announced today. Eddy Devonshire wrote to the King about it yesterday; the children are to be Church of England, and the young couple are to be married in a registry office, publicly, and with a Church of England service subsequently at Compton Place, very hush-hush. But if they think they are going to keep the latter dark from the Papists, they flatter themselves. In an article on Princess Elizabeth, Rebecca West says, 'Man has up till now found monarchy intolerable, except when constantly revised by assassination.'

Saturday 6 May

Bishop of Shrewsbury,[2] first favourite for the Deanery Stakes, arrived. We

---

1 Draža Mihailović (1893–1946), leader of the wartime Chetnik resistance movement. At first this was recognised by King Peter and the British, but later Mihailović collaborated with the Germans, and was executed for treason.

2 Rt. Rev. Eric Hamilton (1890–1962), Suffragan Bishop of Shrewsbury 1940–44, Domestic Chaplain to King George VI 1944–52 and to Queen Elizabeth II 1952–62, Dean of Windsor 1944–62.

gave him tea at Winchester Tower, after which I walked him to Frogmore and back. I think he'll do – a very nice man, good looking, with an agreeable voice and manners.

Sunday 7 May

Shrewsbury preached a good sermon, and has, I'm told, made a good first impression on Their Majesties. Norman Robertson,[1] now head of External Affairs in Ottawa, came down with Charles Ritchie.[2] I gave them my now-familiar personally-conducted tour of the Castle, and we took them to Frogmore after tea, in a brilliant evening, though it is still cold after the recent storms. Caroline went back to Oxford.

Monday 8 May

The King told me that I could write to Shrewsbury and find out if he would accept the Deanery if a formal offer were made to him.

Sunday 14 May

On Tuesday night the King, with H. Campbell, Ritchie and myself, left by train to visit the Home Fleet at Scapa. Reached Thurso 2 p.m. on 10th, whence we were driven by Harwood,[3] now Admiral of the Orkneys and Shetlands, to Scrabster. There we embarked in a destroyer (*Milne*) which took us to the flagship, *Duke of York* (captain Guy Russell, whom I hadn't met since *Enterprise* brought the Prince of Wales, Joey Legh and me back from Dar-es-Salaam in December 1928), which was our home for the next three days.

Bruce Fraser, the C-in-C, was a genial host, who is evidently much beloved by the whole fleet, and is said to be a very competent sailor, though I'm bound to say he don't look it. We visited many ships, great and small, and after being so long on one plane, I found the constant running up and down ladders rather exhausting by the end of a long day. The most interesting episodes were a trip to sea in the aircraft-carrier *Victorious*; the landing on her deck of some forty or fifty Barracudas and Corsairs was a remarkable sight; and the inspection of *Bonaventure*, the parent-ship of the X-craft, where we saw Shean, the young Australian, who recently did sensational things in Bergen harbour.

---

1 Norman Robertson (1904–68), Canadian Under-Secretary of State for External Affairs 1941–6.
2 Charles Ritchie (1906–95), Canadian First Secretary in London, 1943–4, Canadian High Commissioner in London 1967–71.
3 Adm. Sir Henry Harwood (1888–1950), Flag Officer Commanding Orkney and Shetlands 1944–5.

There were dinner parties each night on board the flagship, one of them followed by an admirable entertainment in the wardroom. We saw Scapa at its best, with no wind to speak of, and only an occasional light drizzle; there were even rare glimpses of the sun, to relieve the stark severity of those grim and treeless hills. On the last evening, before we went to bed, I got Guy Russell to tell me, on his quarter-deck, the whole story of the sinking of the *Scharnhorst*. The great moment in it was when, with one of his star-shells, he illuminated the *S.* and saw that not one of her guns was trained in his direction – proof that she had no suspicion that a British battleship was approaching from that quarter.

We were taken back to Scrabster yesterday by Freddie Dalrymple-Hamilton, who gave us luncheon in *Belfast*, his flagship, and then came on to London with us in the train. Reached Buckingham Palace after breakfast, and I have had a very busy day catching up arrears.

Monday 15 May

Went with the King after breakfast to Eisenhower's headquarters in St Paul's School, where the whole 'lay-out' of 'Overlord' was expounded to us by Eisenhower, Monty, Ramsay, Leigh-Mallory, Spaatz[1] and Sholto Douglas – and very interesting it was. The audience was a select one, headed by Winston and Smuts, and going no lower than the Army Commander level. Just before we left, the King, to my astonishment, stepped on to the platform and delivered an admirable impromptu speech, in which he said exactly the right things, and said them very well.

I could not help reflecting, as I looked round the room, that there has probably been no single assembly in the last four years the annihilation of which by a single well-directed bomb would affect more profoundly the issue of the war. However, no bomb came, and we went home to luncheon, I, at any rate, a good deal overwhelmed by this portentous shadow of the shape of things to come. But my mind was much relieved when I noticed, in one of the military charts, that John's lot are not cast for any role before the second, or even third, act.

Tuesday 16 May

Went with Their Majesties to see London House,[2] where Will Goodenough

---

1 General Carl Spaatz (1891–1974), US Commander of the General Strategic Bombing Force operating against Germany 1944.
2 Neo-Georgian building in Mecklenburgh Square, designed by Sir Herbert Baker, part of Goodenough College, founded in 1931 by Frederick Crawford Goodenough (1866–1934) to provide postgraduate students with a collegiate home in London. During the

had assembled a mixed bag of folk to meet them. I had some talk with Nuffield[1] (who has just given £225,000 to L.H.) and reminded him of Oxford days, thirty-five years ago, when, in his shirtsleeves, he used to mend my bicycle for me in his little shop in Holywell after its periodical disablements at bicycle polo. He was delighted, and declared that he remembered me well – which I beg leave to doubt.

Wednesday 17 May

The Imperial Conference wound up yesterday, all members throwing substantial bouquets at each other, and more especially at Winston. It has certainly been a remarkable testimony to the unity of the Empire, well expressed in the communiqué which they are issuing tomorrow over the signatures of the several Prime Ministers.[2]

Anthony Bevir came to see me about Bishops and Lords Lieutenant. The latter are misbehaving like chorus-girls, right and left. Old Trevelyan[3] is suspected of putting his secretary in the family way (who would have thought the old man had so much blood in him?); Sutherland[4] has been cited as a co-respondent and made to pay damages, and Argyll[5] has been found guilty of an assault on the Town Clerk of Inveraray.

Thursday 18 May

When we got back [from the theatre] to St James's Palace, I found a note from John saying he hoped he wouldn't spoil my dinner, but he and Elspeth Stirling want 'to get engaged before the Second Front'. I'm not quite sure what 'getting engaged' involves, but he has promised to write fuller details from Hove, where he rejoined his battalion this evening.

Sunday 21 May   Windsor

'Diadem', the Italian attack, goes well, geographically, but we have not yet

---

war, London House became a rest and recreation centre for overseas officers.
1 William Morris (1877–1963), motor manufacturer and millionaire philanthropist. Created 1st Viscount Nuffield 1938.
2 In 1968 Tommy appended a footnote: '*Mais ou sont les neiges d'antan?*'
3 Sir Charles Trevelyan, 3rd Bt (1870–1958), Labour MP for Central Newcastle 1922–31, Lord Lieutenant of Northumberland 1930–49.
4 George Leveson-Gower, 5th Duke of Sutherland (1888–1963). Through his appearance in court he had incurred much hostility in his own county. Eventually he bowed to pressure from the Government (and indirectly from the King) and resigned his Lord Lieutenancy.
5 10th Duke of Argyll (1872–1949).

secured any considerable quantity of prisoners. The main purpose of the operation is not to acquire Italian territory, but to destroy the German armies there.

We started, yesterday, reading Trevelyan's *England* out loud: 700 pages. I wonder when we shall finish it. Leonard Brockington repeated to us his *mot* about Bessborough, when the latter began his Governor-Generalship of Canada: 'If he had a little more animation, he would make a damned good cod-fish.' Cruel, but not far from the truth.

Wednesday 24 May

Saw Ismay after luncheon; he is well satisfied with our progress in Italy, including the attack from the Anzio beach-head, which started yesterday. He told me that an actor, who has been trained to look, act and talk like Monty, is to be taken to Gibraltar and thence to Algiers, a day or two before 'Overlord'. Care will be taken that the news reaches the Germans, who will then assume that nothing is likely to happen for a week or two. Also that a certain American naval captain, named Wright, was under arrest for having disclosed the date and direction of 'Overlord' to his fellow-guests at a dinner-party. He stands a good chance of being shot.

Joan came to London, and Mrs Stirling, mother of Elspeth [John's fiancée], came to see us in St James's Palace. A nice woman; he is a colonel or brigadier, doing some kind of administrative job in Syria; he is an expert on the Middle East, and was a friend of George Lloyd. But they haven't a bean.

Thursday 25 May

Mrs Stirling, Elspeth, John and Joan lunched with me at the Ritz. It was agreed that, if the Colonel cabled his approval, the engagement should be announced next week. Prior to that they had been to Wellby's and bought a ring, which will cost me £25.

Very cheerful telegram from Alex to Winston; he has got 10,000 prisoners and 100 guns, and seems to have destroyed a considerable moiety of the German forces opposed to him [in Northern Italy]. But Alan Brooke, whom I consulted, agrees that the moment has not yet come for a congratulatory telegram from the King.

Friday 26 May

Told the King of John's engagement.

ay 27 May

Brooke telephoned that he thought HM could now telegraph to Alex, via Maitland Wilson. I sent it off, being careful to avoid any assumption of final victory in the wording.

Perfect summer day; I trust we are not using up all the fine weather which is so vital for 'Overlord'.

Tuesday 30 May

Some days ago John Martin sent me a note covering a memorandum from Oliver Stanley to the PM, which raises the whole question of the Duke of Windsor's future; the PM invited my comments. I have long known that, sooner or later, the time would come when I should have to have this out with Winston, so I took great pains with my answer, tore up several drafts during the weekend, and sent off the final version this morning as soon as I reached London.

The answer was as follows:

Buckingham Palace

Personal and Secret   30 May 1944
My Dear Martin,

I will do my best to answer your letter briefly, but it is a big subject.

As you know, I was once closely associated with the Prince of Wales, and, since that association began, nearly twenty-five years ago, I don't think any problems in my life have given me so much anxiety as those arising from this. I have continually found, as John Churchill did in 1688, that the equation of 'personal indebtedness to the Prince and the interests of his native land' is a terribly hard one to resolve.

So you will believe that, for sentimental no less than professional reasons, I have very often given thought to the question of the Prince's future. I wish to God I knew the answer.

There are, it has always seemed to me, only four possibilities. The Prince could:

(1) Undertake Ambassadorial or Pro-consular jobs abroad.
(2) Live in this country as a quasi younger brother of the King.
(3) Live in this country as a private individual, and devote his great
     wealth to some useful object in which he is interested.
(4) Do ditto in the USA.

These are my comments, under these four heads:

(1) I cannot get away from the stark fact that there is in the British

Happier times: Tommy with Edward, Prince of Wales, aboard the RMS *Berengaria* sailing for the royal tour of America and Canada, September 1924.

The Duke and Duchess of Windsor, after their wedding at the Château de Condé in Touraine, on 3 June 1937.

'Tommy was every inch the Private Secretary.'

John in his Grenadier Guards uniform.

John and Lavinia with their mother, Joan, on holiday in Canada.

'The appearance, as from the skies, of the King and Queen naturally had an immense effect': their Majesties inspect bomb damage.

With the King on board HMS
Arethusa, en route to the Normandy
beaches, June 1944.

At the King's shoulder on a visit to
General Montgomery (left) at his
battle headquarters in France, June
1944.

'A great pride of Royals' on the steps of St George's Chapel, Windsor Castle, after Lavinia Lascelles's wedding to Edward Renton, 30 March 1945. Left to right: Queen Mary, Queen Elizabeth, Joan and Tommy, the Earl of Harewood, King George VI, Peter Townsend (in background), Princess Elizabeth, and the Rt. Rev. Eric Hamilton, Dean of Windsor.

Tommy escorts his daughter Caroline at her wedding to Antony Lyttelton, May 1949, also at St George's.

Lavinia and Edward Renton after their wedding.

Partners in victory:
Winston Churchill with
King George VI.

Peter Townsend (in
Tommy's view 'a devilish
bad equerry') and Princess
Margaret.

'He grew a luxuriant grey beard': Tommy at the age of 88, drawn by his son-in-law, David Hankinson.

'In fact I am just a hermit.' Tommy photographed by Derry Moore in his sitting-room at the Old Stables, Kensington Palace.

cosmos no official place for an ex-King. How can a man who has renounced the British Crown personally represent the Sovereign, or even impersonally HM Government? Many of my friends in the Dominions have made this point to me; the Prince himself understood it, when he abdicated. He said in his farewell broadcast, 'I shall take no further part in public life' – or words to that effect. Moreover (I am writing, of course, quite frankly), I doubt if he would be safe in any ambassadorial or pro-consular post of importance. I will instance only two of the grounds on which I base this – one, his constitutional inability to see the wood of the public weal apart from the trees of private inclination; two, his Rehoboam-like tendency to take up with undesirable, and dangerous, associates. The latter may have diminished; but, from the episodes of the scoundrel Bedaux[1] and the egregious Gren,[2] it doesn't look like it.

(2) and (3) I cannot see, in practice, how this would ever work. What-ever camouflage were used, there is no room for two Kings of England. He would never be happy here; she would be bored to distraction – the kind of life that meant anything to her is, for at least a generation, as dead as Queen Anne; and their proximity would be a constant agony (I use the word advisedly) to the present King, which might have really serious consequences. However, I understand that the Prince has no wish to return permanently to this country; those who are intimate with his financial affairs tell me, incidentally, that to do so would cost him something like £20,000 per annum in taxation.

(4) When Stettinius was in my room the other day, he talked very kindly of the Prince and asked me what his future was likely to be. I told him of some of the difficulties. He said, 'Of course what he ought to do is to buy a nice place in Virginia and use his money to develop, for the benefit of the world at large, some of the ideas on which he is so keen.' I said I had for a long time thought that was the only possible solution, in the interests of himself, his wife and everybody else.

The Prince, I understand, is one of the richest men in the world, without encumbrances of any kind. He could make himself a charming home – a thing he has never yet had; he could make wonderful use of his money by furthering some of the many schemes that have successively caught his interest. Stettinius told me that he is at present absorbed in

1 Charles Bedaux, American millionaire and Nazi sympathiser, who lent the Duke of Windsor his home, the Château de Condé in the South of France, for his wedding in May 1937.
2 Axel Wenner-Gren (1881–1961), millionaire Swedish entrepreneur, owner of an estate in the Bahamas, friend of both Hermann Goering and the Duke of Windsor, aroused suspicion through his efforts to reconcile the two sides during the 1930s.

the dehydration of vegetables. That sounds a somewhat dreary hobby for a man's middle-age, but it is just as useful, and maybe as amusing, as agriculture, stock-raising and so on. There are a dozen ways in which a man of his imagination could use his wealth to interest himself and benefit his fellow-men. There was a Prince of Monaco, I believe, who, with a yacht and a fortune, did wonders in the world of hydrogaphy; and we can all think of millionaires whose private activities have been as beneficial as their public ones were deleterious.

My conclusion, then, is that the best chance for the Prince's happiness and for the peace of the world at large, is that he should adopt course (4).

If the Prime Minister should at any time wish to talk to me about all this, I am, as always, at his service.

Yours sincerely,

A. Lascelles.

In June, thanking Tommy for this advice, Churchill pointed out that the Prince still possessed all his rights as a British subject and as a Peer of the Realm. 'Nothing that I am aware of,' wrote the Prime Minister, 'can stop him returning to this country.' Anxiety about the Duke of Windsor's future ran high in the Royal Family throughout that fraught summer and autumn.

Tuesday 30 May (continued)

Winston, lunching with the King today, revealed that he proposed to watch the opening of 'Overlord' from one of the bombarding cruisers, and when the King said he would do ditto, did not (according to the King) discourage him. This will never do; but I think I shook the King by asking him whether he thought the project would be quite fair to the Queen; and whether he was prepared to face the possibility of having to advise Princess Elizabeth on the choice of her first Prime Minister, in the event of her father and Winston being sent to the bottom of the English Channel. Another point, of course, is the paralysing effect which the presence on board of either the Sovereign or the PM, or both, would inevitably have on the unfortunate captain trying to fight his ship in the middle of what can only be an inferno.

However, I deliberately took the plan more casually than seriously, for I can't believe that the King's common sense will let him proceed with it.

Wednesday 31 May

I persuaded the King, without much difficulty, that it would be wrong, from many points of view, for either him or Winston to carry out their projected 'Overlord' jaunt. He bade me take a letter from himself to Winston, written in his own hand, to 10 Downing Street – which I did after dinner, and handed it over to John Martin. I found that Winston, who is just like a naughty child when he starts planning an escapade, has said nothing about this one to Martin, who was much relieved to hear that the King was trying to deter him.

I had a visit from Marcus Haywood of MI, who is just back from carrying out the project of the bogus Monty, which seems to have been entirely successful. The Rudolf Rassendyll,[1] so to speak, was a sergeant in the Pay Corps called James,[2] an actor by profession, who has a remarkable facial resemblance to Monty. He was attached to Monty's staff for a short time, and then flown to Gib. a few days ago with Haywood. H. says that James was quite perfect, in word and gesture, and that Eastwood,[3] Governor of Gibraltar (the only other person in the know) revealed himself as actor of parts, doing his share admirably. Arrangements were made for some Spaniard, who is known to be a German agent, to be at Government House that morning, and to get a good view of the pseudo-Monty. It all worked, and within a few hours a telegram to Berlin was intercepted by our people, reporting that General M. and an unknown French general (this must have been Haywood himself) were in Gib. on their way to Algiers. The object of the whole manoeuvre is to encourage the Germans in their belief that a large-scale invasion of the French Riviera is imminent, to make them keep certain divisions in their present station near Marseilles. It was originally conceived by Johnny Bevan, who has done remarkably well as a manipulator of 'cover' of this kind.

Thursday 1 June

After luncheon, the King and I went to the Downing Street annexe in Storey's Gate. There, in the map room, Admiral Ramsay[4] expounded to the King and myself exactly what would be involved in Winston's scheme in sailing on D-Day in *Belfast*, the flagship from which Freddie Dalrymple-Hamilton will conduct the bombardment. It was soon obvious to me that

---

1   The hero of Anthony Hope's novel *The Prisoner of Zenda*, particularly prized by Tommy because the author (whose real name was Anthony Hope Hawkins) was an old Marlburian.
2   The actor was Clifton James (1893–1963). His book *I Was Monty's Double* was filmed in 1958, with him and Montgomery both playing themselves.
3   Lieut.-Gen. Sir Ralph Eastwood (1890–1959), Governor and C-in-C of Gibraltar 1944–7.
4   Adm. Sir Bertram Home Ramsay (1883–1945), Naval C-in-C of the Expeditionary Force, 1944. Killed in an air crash in Jan. 1945.

any passenger would run considerable risks from mines, torpedoes and bombardment from land and air, and would see devilish little. The ship will at no time be nearer the French coast than 14,000 yards, and those on board will have less information about the general progress of the battle than we shall in London.

After a bit, Ramsay was told to withdraw, and, after a few minutes, was recalled and told that 'Operation W.C.' (the name he has given to the scheme) might include his Sovereign as well as the Prime Minister. To this the unfortunate man, naturally enough, reacted violently.[1] After a short discussion, Winston, in his most oracular manner, opined that he would feel bound to get the Cabinet's approval to the King going, and that he would not be able to recommend them to give it. This the King accepted with good grace; but it soon became clear that Winston had no intention of applying this wise decision to himself. As he unfolded his determination (quite regardless of the King's letter) to persevere in the project, the King made some half-hearted protests.

All I could do was to register strong disapproval; eventually this induced HM to say, 'Tommy's face is getting longer and longer.'

I said, 'I was thinking, Sir, that it is not going to make things easier for you if you have to find a new Prime Minister in the middle of "Overlord".'

'Oh,' said Winston, 'that's all arranged for. Anyhow, I don't think the risk is 100–1.'

Later on, when he said something to the effect that no constitutional issues were involved, I got my oar in again (not easy in such loquacious company), and said that I had always understood that no Minister of the Crown could leave the country without the Sovereign's consent. This gave Winston pause for a few moments; but he countered it by saying that it didn't count as going abroad, because he would be in a British man-of-war. I pointed out that, even so, he would be a long way outside territorial waters. However, nothing was any good; but, as we left the room, I managed to whisper to Ramsay, 'For God's sake, stop him going,' and he said, 'I think I can.'

Winston knows perfectly well that he oughtn't to do this, but when he gets these puckish notions, he is just like a naughty child. In this instance, his naughtiness is sheer selfishness, plus vanity. Just to gratify his love of theatre, and adventure, he is ready to jettison all considerations of what is

---

1   In a memorandum to Churchill on 18 May Admiral Ramsay had written: 'You told me not to mention this plan to the First Sea Lord, and I have not done so, but you will appreciate that, as Supreme Commander, it was essential that General Eisenhower should know of what was in the air, and I must tell you that he is very averse to your going.'

due to his Sovereign, his colleagues and the State. Moreover, he might, by his foolishness, defeat his own ends. He is passionately anxious for 'Overlord' to succeed; if he should be killed in its early stages, the news of his death might easily have such an effect on the troops as to turn victory into defeat. Another point that he would not see is that his presence on board *Belfast* cannot but cramp the style of those engaged in fighting her, and might impair her value as a fighting unit.

At one point in the discussion, the King said to me, 'What do you think Freddie [Dalrymple-Hamilton] will feel about all this?' My answer was that I thought he would have a fit.

Pug Ismay, who had been waiting in the anteroom all this time, came to Buckingham Palace to see me shortly afterwards. Like everybody else who knows of the scheme, he is dead against it, and from the professional point of view emphasised how wrong it was for the Prime Minister and Minister of Defence to be inaccessible (if not dead) on a day when vital decisions might have to be taken in a hurry.[1] But the trouble is that none of those who have access to Winston can influence him once he is set on a course, not even Mrs Churchill; nor, apparently, his anointed King.

The King decided to go to Windsor, where we arrived just before dinner; after which I sat down to prepare the draft of a final appeal from him to Winston.

Friday 2 June

Ismay said this morning that he thought the PM was wobbling. We agreed that a second barrel from the King might push him over, and at the same time give him a graceful excuse for changing his mind; so the King wrote his letter, and I sent it off to Downing Street by despatch rider at 11.45 a.m.

Later John Martin telephoned to say that the PM, 'though not yet actually showing the white flag', had been impressed by it, saying at the beginning, 'That is certainly a strong argument' – this being the plea: that it was very unjust that the PM, having advised the King against going, should then go himself and steal the King's thunder.

Saturday 3 June

At 11 p.m. last night the King telephoned to me to ask if I had had any reply from Winston. I explained that Winston could hardly have written one yet, as the King's letter had only reached him just before he left Downing Street

---

1 Churchill had tried to secure Ismay's support for his scheme by promising that, if he went on HMS *Belfast*, he would take the general with him.

for his train, which is parked somewhere in Hants. However, the King seemed so disturbed by the whole episode, threatening to go off by car at dawn next day, and personally ensure that Winston should not go to sea on D-Day, that I rang up Peck, who is in charge at No. 10, and asked him to tell Rowan,[1] on the train, that it was highly desirable that some intimation of what Winston's probable answer would be should reach the King that night. Shortly after, Rowan rang me up, and Winston spoke to me himself. He was not always entirely audible, but was clear on the only point in which I was interested – namely that, in deference to the King's wishes, he would abandon his plan of going to sea; for the rest, he was concerned at the idea that he was not entirely free, as Minister of Defence, to watch any battle he thought fit: and that he was under any obligation to consult his colleagues in the Cabinet about his own movements – academic points that I did not attempt to argue.

They are not relevant, either; the King's only contention is that it is foolish for an indispensable Prime Minister to take a wholly unnecessary risk to his own life on a wild goose chase that can have no military value whatever; and, as to his colleagues, even if he is under no constitutional obligation to reveal such a project to them, it is surely an act of common courtesy, the omission of which must infuriate them, if they are men of any spirit at all, and weaken their confidence in him as their leader.

The King, in fact, was only trying to save Winston from himself, for the real motives inspiring him to go to sea in *Belfast* are his irrepressible, and now most untimely, love of adventure, and, I fear, his vain, though perhaps subconscious, predilection for making himself 'front page stuff'.

Our conversation was quite friendly; at one point he said, with his chuckle, 'And I suppose that if that poor ship should go to the bottom, you will all say, "I told you so."' I replied that as the admiral on board was one of my oldest friends, I sincerely hoped no such fate would overtake her. I then reported, on the telephone, to the King, who, I hope, slept all the better for it. But let nothing I may say of Winston's minor failures ever seem to imply an apostasy from my firm faith that he is the greatest war leader we have ever had (not forgetting John Churchill or Chatham), an orator of a quality that has seldom been equalled, and one to whom we owe a debt we cannot even estimate, let alone repay, for his superb courage in 1940.

This morning, just before breakfast, Winston's letter was delivered to me by a young officer on a motor-bicycle. I sent it up to the King, who gave it to me to copy later in the morning. It reiterates the arguments which Winston rehearsed to me last night, and gives one the impression of a man

---

1   Leslie Rowan (1908–72), Assistant and later PPS to the PM 1941–5. Knighted 1949.

fighting a rearguard action for a cause that he knows is a bad one; but it is quite a nice letter. Anyhow, we have bested him, which not many people have succeeded in doing in the last four years!

We all went down this afternoon to see the usual Eton Ramblers' match. I could not stay long, and, as always happens, met, one after another, all the bores to avoid whose company I habitually cross the street; and, John and Elspeth's engagement having appeared in yesterday's *Times*, they were even more boring than usual. With one eye on the weather all the time, and most of my mind on 'Overlord', I felt throughout the afternoon as though I were dancing at the Duchess of Richmond's ball before Quatre Bras.[1] The Queen sent me a nice letter about John and Elspeth.

Sunday 4 June

Blowing hard from the west still. At 10 a.m. Hollis told me that Eisenhower had decided to postpone D-Day from tomorrow, for 24 hours. All day I have been cricking my neck at the flag on the Round Tower; and just now (11.30 p.m.) it had, for the first time, started to droop instead of flying stiffly and uncompromisingly eastward; moreover, it has started to rain, and the sky seems to me to have taken on the complexion which generally denotes the passing of a summer gale. Eric Miéville has just told me that Eisenhower & co. are meeting tonight and again at 4 a.m. tomorrow to decide whether there is to be a further postponement. Apparently the critical factor is the airborne division, for whose function anything more than a moderate wind would be fatal.

At 7.30 p.m. War Cabinet Office reported the arrival of a telegram from Jumbo Wilson saying that the Allies had entered Rome. This will sound all right; but strategically, and politically, the occupation of the Eternal City may prove more of a liability than an asset.

Monday 5 June

Eric Miéville telephoned at 9 a.m. to say that Eisenhower had decided that there should be no further postponement of 'Overlord'. Wrote out, this morning, a note covering the recent exchange of letters between the King and Prime Minister; this evening after dinner took them to the Cabinet Office, and got E. Bridges to read them through. He had no criticisms, thought the King's letters excellent, and that HM was entirely right to stop Winston going; also that Winston was wrong, in his letter, in trying to lift

---

1 The battle fought in Belgium on 16 June 1815, when Wellington repulsed the French under Marshal Ney: the first phase of the battle of Waterloo.

the matter from a personal to a constitutional plane. Thompson (Winston's naval ADC),[1] whom I met on the stairs, made exactly the same point. Smuts had said to Thompson, 'The danger might not be very great, but the King was absolutely right not to let Winston go; and it is sometimes good for him to be prevented from doing exactly what he likes.' Which reminded me that if Winston had refused to respond to the King's second appeal, Smuts would of course have been the man for me to go to.

The wind is sensibly less this evening, and the glass, though lowish, has not fallen at all for twenty-four hours. The great armada must be well on its way by now; what I cannot understand is why the Germans have made no serious attempt to damage it while it lay, for miles and miles, along the south coast. There can be only two explanations: 1, that they hadn't got any aeroplanes to do the job; 2, that they have a device or devices with which they believe they can destroy as many of our ships as they like before they reach the French coast, and prefer to deal with them in this way than to attack them piecemeal from the air.

Eric Miéville told me that James Stuart[2] (who knew nothing of Winston's project) had said to him in White's the other night that he couldn't make out what was in Winston's mind – he kept on talking as if he were about to die, and had asked James to take charge of a lot of his private papers. Curious.

Tuesday 6 June D-Day

Back at Buckingham Palace. I was awoken at 5 a.m. by streams of aircraft passing across London, the harbingers of 'Overlord'. The weather, though not ideal, has been very much better than it looked like being, and, so far as one can judge, the first stage of the great adventure has gone well, and surprisingly cheaply. Naval and air casualties are practically negligible, and of the four main landings, only one (the second American force from the west) seems to have met any serious opposition. The three airborne divisions achieved very successful landings, and have all, apparently, carried out the tasks allotted to them. It is too early to feel anything in the nature of jubilation; but the relief of feeling that the thing is at least under way, and that all the immense and complicated preparations for it have been well and truly laid, is very great; in fact, all those who have been entrusted with the very well kept secret, look ten years younger.

---

1 Commander C. R. (Tommy) Thompson (1894–1966), personal assistant to the Minister of Defence 1940–45.
2 James Stuart (1897–1971), Govt Chief Whip 1941–5, Secretary of State for Scotland 1951–7. Created 1st Viscount Stuart of Findhorn 1957.

After luncheon, went with the King and Winston (who had been lunching at Buckingham Palace) first to Leigh-Mallory's headquarters at Stanmore, and then to Eisenhower's at Bushey, where, on outsize maps, we were shown the progress of the battle, so far as it is yet known. Winston, when he first saw me, *tauredon eblepsen* (glared like a bull), I thought; but this was probably my imagination, for he said goodbye very genially. Though they had lunched together, and driven a number of miles in the same car, neither of them, apparently, made any allusion to their recent exchange of letters!

I have just seen a telegram from Monty in which he says (12 noon), 'I could not wish the situation of this army to be better.'

Wednesday 7 June

Went again with the King to SHAEF [Supreme HQ, Allied Expeditionary Forces] at Bushey, but they had no news of any interest, so it was rather a fruitless expedition. Dined at Grillions, where that normally unemotional assembly, at the suggestion of Simon, drank the health of the King, and then that of the Allied troops, after dinner. Wind still strongish, but dropping, and forecasts optimistic. We have not yet got to Caen, though we are in Bayeux.

Thursday 8 June

Duff Cooper, who is over here with de Gaulle, to see the King. Went to tea, with the King and Queen, in the Downing Street annexe; only the Churchills there. Winston very bitter against de Gaulle, who is being very troublesome; he has definitely made up his mind that de Gaulle is a danger to the peace of Europe, a view that F.D.R has long held. In the map room after tea, where we were shown, with models, the whole layout of a 'Mulberry', the amazing artificial harbours which we are rapidly building on the Normandy beaches; I should think it is the greatest feat of human ingenuity and resource ever applied to warfare, and it is a factor in the whole battle which may well prove the Germans' undoing, for they have assumed that we should be dependent for the build-up of our forces on the harbours of Cherbourg and Havre, which, of course, we have not got, and can for the present do without. Winston said he had fully expected that we should lose 10,000 men in the initial landing.

Mention of de Gaulle reminded me of Winston's memorable remark to him at the end of one of their stormier interviews eighteen months ago. '*Et, marquez mes mots, mon ami – si vous me double-crosserez, je vous liquiderai.*'

Meanwhile, Alex [Field-Marshal Alexander] has not paused in Rome, and is making spectacular progress northwards. In a confident telegram to Brooke, he says that of the twenty German divisions opposed to him, there are now only six in fighting shape, and that the morale of our men is such that they will cheerfully tackle 'the Apennines, and even the Alps'. He expects to have cleared practically the whole of Italy by mid-August. The King this morning (his official birthday) gave me my KCB, and I thoughtlessly and tactlessly left it on his table when I went out of the room.

Saturday 10 June

The PM rang me up after tea to say that, if the naval authorities raised no objection, he proposed to cross the Channel on Monday in a destroyer, and see how the Mulberries were getting on, returning the same evening. The King made no demur to this, provided that Ramsay did not advise against it, a stipulation to which Winston readily agreed.

Stalin telegraphed that he had launched his offensive; so now the Germans, who were always frightened of fighting on two fronts, are deeply engaged on three. We bombed Ploesti again last night, and other oil installations. Canon and Mrs Fellowes[1] to tea; we have now done our duty to all the clergy in the Cloisters. Fellowes, who has the most beautiful reading voice that I ever heard in a church, is a world-wide authority on ecclesiastical music, especially that of the Tudor age. He practically re-discovered Purcell and Byrd.

Tuesday 13 June

PM, and later the Cabinet, approved the idea that the King, on Friday, should visit the beaches in Normandy. I arranged details with the First Sea Lord. Air-raid at 4 a.m. this morning, due to presence of some twenty-seven 'pilotless aircraft', which did little damage. This is presumably the first fruits of 'Crossbow'.

Wednesday 14 June

Generals Marshall[2] and Arnold,[3] USA, to see the King. Joan came up for

---

1 Rev. Edmund Fellowes (1870–1951), author and editor in musical subjects; Minor Canon of St George's Chapel, Windsor, 1900–51.
2 Gen. George C. Marshall (1880–1959), US Army CoS 1939–45, Secretary of State 1947–9. The programme for the restoration of Europe which he proposed in 1947 became known as the Marshall Plan.
3 Gen. of the Army Henry H. Arnold (1886–1950), Commander US Army Air Forces 1942.

dinner with the Devonshires, which I had to chuck, as I had to go with HM to No. 10: Smuts, Marshall, Arnold, King,[1] three Chiefs of Staff, Pug Ismay and C. Attlee – the last on one side of me at dinner, with Andrew Cunningham on the other. After dinner, the King and Winston, having waylaid 'C' in the passage, brought him in, and he read us a sheaf of Intelligence telegrams, all decidedly encouraging. Winston then started a long argument with the CIGS on the extent to which 'Q' stuff should be transported in the build-up of an invasion force, Winston maintaining in his rhetorical fashion that the progress of an army could only be delayed by the importation of dental chairs and units of the YMCA, while Brooke stubbornly rejoined that no army could fight, let alone progress, unless it had adequate supplies of ammunition etc. This lasted till 2 a.m. Winston talking without a break for long periods, while Smuts and Attlee, on either side of me, slept unashamedly. About 1 a.m., the King said tentatively to Winston, 'Well, aren't you going to bed tonight?', but Winston's only answer was. 'No, Sir' – after which he resumed the flow of his eloquence.

Thursday 15 June

De Gaulle went over to Normandy, and concerned everybody by losing himself, somewhere in the neighbourhood of Bayeux, for two hours, during which nobody knew what had become of him. When he turned up, it was too late to send him back in the destroyer that brought him over, and he had to sleep offshore in some other ship.

Friday 16 June

The King, with Harold Campbell[2] and me, left Victoria 7.45 p.m. yesterday. In the train were Pug Ismay, Grantham (the Admiralty representative on the planning board), C. Portal and Bob Laycock (Combined Ops). Eden had been of the party, with Pierson Dixon[3] (his secretary), but, late in the afternoon, he rang me up to say that he had come to the conclusion that he had better stop at home – partly because he thought he would be wanted in the House of Commons for the debate, and partly because he felt he would be in the way. With the latter reason, I entirely agree, and told him so; there was no question of his being officially in attendance on the King,

---

1   Adm. Ernest J. King (1878–1956), US Chief of Naval Operations 1942–5.
2   1902–80. Civil engineer, Belfast Harbour Commissioner 1955–77.
3   Sir Pierson Dixon (1904–65), archaeologist and diplomat, PPS to the Foreign Secretary 1943–8, UK Permanent Representative to the UN 1954–60, British Ambassador in Paris 1960–64.

who don't take Ministers-in-attendance on that kind of trip, and he would have been nothing but a sightseer among people who are all going over on military duty of one kind or another. I feel strongly, as do many other parents with sons on the beaches, about peripatetic parliamentarians going to battle just to see the show; moreover, their presence is only an added responsibility to those on the spot, who have plenty to do without bothering about the safety of stray visitors.

We spent the night at Horsley, in Surrey, and reached Portsmouth 8 a.m., when we went on board the cruiser *Arethusa* (Captain Dalrymple-Smith[1]), finding the First Sea Lord and Ramsay already there. Weather gusty and cold, with a choppy sea, and we took nearly four and a half hours getting over, instead of three and a half, which Andrew Cunningham had promised me. The whole way across to Normandy, the sea was congested with shipping – strings of landing-craft coming and going, huge Phoenixes (the component parts of Mulberry, the synthetic harbour) being towed, and a host of small craft of every description. There was no untoward incident on the voyage, which was, indeed, tedious and chilly, but one realised forcibly how impossible 'Overlord' would have been had we not had complete command of both air and sea.

As we approached the coast, we heard, as the first sign of battle, some of our cruisers intermittently bombarding targets on shore. Arrived off Cousseulles, we took to a landing-craft, from which we later transferred to one of the amphibious 'Dukqs', which duly waddled up the beach and deposited us at the feet of the expectant Monty. We then drove, in a string of jeeps, to his headquarters in the garden of a small château at Creully. Here, after a visit to his famous caravan, we lunched – the King, Monty, Dempsey (GOC Second Army),[2] Kit Dawnay,[3] Ramsay, two ADCs and myself; a good luncheon, with genuine Camembert cheeses – a thing we've not seen in London since 1940.

The King then held a small investiture, elaborately staged by Monty, who made a speech about each investee (whose decorations, by the way, I had been carting about in a pouch ever since we had left London). This done, he took us to his map room, where he and Dempsey explained their plans for the next stage in the battle. They are both very confident of the issue, and believe that our air attacks on his communications have seriously disrupted the Boche's flow of supplies. Moreover, whether by luck or

---

1 Capt. Hugh Dalrymple-Smith (1901–87) commanded HMS *Arethusa* during the Normandy landings.
2 Gen. Sir Miles Dempsey (1896–1969), Commander of 2nd Army for the invasion of Normandy.
3 Lieut.-Col. Christopher Dawnay (1909–89), staff officer.

cunning, they have manoeuvred him into using up his reserves, intended for attack, in defensive action – stopping the holes which we constantly threaten to make in various parts of the line.

On the other hand, they have induced him to believe that the Guards' Armoured Division (of which only a few elements have arrived) is already *in situ*, ready to be thrown in at any one of two or three vital points. Meanwhile, the Americans are doing well on our right, and should have possession of the Cotentin peninsula in a few days. The Germans are busy demolishing the harbour-works at Cherbourg, not knowing that our several Mulberries will soon give us harbours just as good, or better.

At luncheon, Monty's mess waiter was made to produce one of the currency notes, made in America, the issue of which has so sorely ruffled de Gaulle. This the King put in his pocket, while I had to give the waiter sixpence, to compensate him for the loss of his five francs. Monty would not hear of the King going nearer the line (some six miles ahead of us), as the intervening country is still full of stray snipers. In the gardens of the château itself they had only just discovered a German soldier who had been there four or five days, and could have easily shot Monty or anybody else, had he wanted to; he was, as it happened, a mere boy who was hiding there only for self-protection, and, when found, burst into tears, thinking that he would be shot out of hand.

The Canadians, on the other hand, had a number of casualties at the hands of female snipers, some of whom they had, quite justifiably, shot. The French, as a whole, are not enthusiastic over our arrival; for four years they have been selling their farm produce to the Germans, who appear to have treated them well enough: they do not all relish being 'liberated' by an invading army, whose passage must inevitably disturb the even tempo of their lives, even if it don't actually knock their buildings flat. Dempsey told me that when de Gaulle arrived in Normandy the other day, he was given a by-no-means-unanimous welcome; only about three-fifths of the people showed signs of being glad to see him.

From Monty's château we drove to Dempsey's headquarters, and then to one which John Grant[1] is busy making habitable for his admiral (Rivett-Carnac),[2] and then to the beaches again, where, at 4 p.m., we re-embarked. There had been some idea of our cruising along the shore to see the Mulberries now being constructed; but the Germans had dropped a lot of mines there the night before, and Cunningham, to the King's disappointment, ruled it out as unsafe. We reached Portsmouth again just

---

1   John Grant, RN (1908–96) had won a DSO in 1942, and in 1959 was promoted Rear-Admiral.
2   Vice-Adm. James Rivett-Carnac (1891–1970), Flag Officer British Assault Area 1944.

before 9 p.m. I had asked the Admiralty to parade Lavinia, and found her at the railway station; as she had been engaged in enciphering many of our telegrams to Monty, the expedition was no secret to her.

We left the train at Staines and reached Windsor about 11.30 p.m. On this drive the King inveighed, with some bitterness, against the governmental interference to which he was constitutionally liable. Suddenly, he threw his arm out of the window and exclaimed, 'And that's where it all started!' We were passing Runnymede.[1]

Saturday 17 June

The 'Crossbow' air-raids have increased in intensity during the last few nights – and days – and, as H. Morrison made a statement about them in the House of Commons yesterday, the public now know all about them, and the newspapers are full of them. So far, they have done no very serious damage, though they have caused quite a few casualties, here and there. Bob Laycock told me last night that they are not radio-controlled, and are of very simple design – a glorified kite directed by some form of gyroscopic compass and driven by a petrol engine. Their supply of petrol is regulated in accordance with the desired range, and, when the thing is over its target, the petrol runs dry, the engine stops, and the whole outfit falls to the ground and explodes. Charles Portal said he knew of no way of dealing with them, save shooting them down in mid-air (which we have apparently done with some success), bombing the sites from which they are launched (as, of course, we have been doing all through the winter), and destroying the factories that produce their component parts.

Sunday 18 June

Gerry Wellington[2] (who has just been appointed Lieutenant of the County of London in the teeth of some opposition – the Prime Minister toyed with the idea of recommending Camrose) came over to present the Waterloo flag to the King – a custom that has been in abeyance since the old Duke elected to die on this very date. But it was an inauspicious Waterloo Day, for at 11.10 a.m. one of these Crossbow aircraft hit the Guards' Chapel in Wellington Barracks while a service was going on. There seems to have been a congregation of about 200, the majority of whom were killed,

---

1   Where King John signed the Magna Carta in 1215.
2   Lieut.-Col. Gerald Wellesley (1885–1972) had succeeded his nephew as 7th Duke of Wellington 1943. Lord Lieutenant of the County of London 1944–9.

including E. Hay[1] and Ivan Cobbold, whom I saw at Eton only yesterday. Arthur Penn's sister Olive was also among the dead.

Apart from that, the day has been fairly quiet, though Joan and I, walking in Frogmore Gardens after dinner, heard gunfire and an explosion, and, when we reached the top of the hill, saw a mushroom of black smoke rising from the neighbourhood of Staines. Winston called a staff meeting at 6 p.m., at which SHAEF agreed to release from operational duties a considerable number of aircraft to bomb the suspected sites very heavily – including one or two which, it is thought, may house rocket guns. They have forbidden the London anti-aircraft guns to shoot, which is wise, for they make an infernal noise, bad for everybody's nerves, and banishing sleep, and probably wing a number of the Crossbows which might otherwise carry on into open country and do relatively little damage.

Monday 19 June   Windsor

The King rightly cancelled the investiture due to be held at Buckingham Palace tomorrow, and remained at Windsor. Last night was much disturbed, with constant sirens and flying bombs, as we are now told to call them, exploding at intervals in the Staines area.

Wednesday 21 June   Buckingham Palace

About 1 a.m. this morning a flying bomb, which I had heard passing over the house, came to earth near the arch at the top of Constitution Hill. The flash of it illumined my bedroom so vividly that I retired to the shelter, where I slept peacefully till 7.30. This bomb has left a remarkably small crater, but has blown away about fifty yards of our garden wall. A policeman is constantly on duty there to stop opportunist American dough-boys from wandering into the garden. Henry Dale[2] came to get his OM and old Henry Wood, with whom I had a pleasant talk, his CH.

Smuts, who leaves for South Africa tonight, was full of the burning question of the day – how best to utilise Alex and his victorious army when they have cleaned up Italy. Alex himself wants to march on Vienna via Trieste, liquidate the Balkans and join hands with Russia; alternative schemes are to launch him at Marseilles or Bordeaux. Smuts strongly favours the Pas de Calais, which would have the additional advantage of

---

1   Lord Edward Hay (1888–1944), soldier.
2   Sir Henry Dale (1875–1968), surgeon and medical researcher, winner of Nobel Prize for Medicine 1936, President of the Royal Society 1940–45, member of the Scientific Advisory Committee to the War Cabinet 1940–47.

cleaning up the Crossbow sites. He attended a Chiefs of Staff meeting on the subject this afternoon. It is a very difficult decision. There is much to be said for Smuts's alternative, but it would surely take months to implement. The old man looked well, and said goodbye to me most affectionately.

At luncheon P. Loxley told me that, a few days ago, Catroux[1] had asked Duff Cooper to see a certain French officer, urgently. This man, who is a big noise in the French Intelligence service, told Duff that he had very reliable information that Hitler had fled from Berlin to a villa near Perpignan, where he is now hiding and waiting a favourable opportunity to slip across the Spanish frontier. 'C' has been asked to check the story, and meanwhile we are considering the advisability of dropping a few bombs on Perpignan to speed the parting guest. It is a fantastic story, perhaps; but so would the flight of the Kaiser have seemed, and so did seem the arrival of Hess in Scotland.

The day before yesterday I got a letter from de Guingand,[2] Monty's Chief of Staff, to say that, owing to the incredible folly of the Censor, the *Daily Telegraph* had published a story by Louis Wulff (the Pressman who normally covers the King's activities) which revealed, by implication, the whereabouts of Monty's headquarters in Normandy; that Monty was greatly upset, and had been obliged to shift to another place. This is most unfortunate, but, as I pointed out to de Guingand, the SHAEF Censor had Wulff's stuff in his hands for at least an hour before it was released; and what is a censor for if not to cut out such palpable indiscretions on the part of Pressmen, who, quite naturally, try to put as much local colour into their stories as they can?

Saturday 24 June

Midsummer Day, and perfect weather, for the first time this year. Stalin has started his big offensive, with 130 divisions. Slight increase in Crossbows last night, but none came over during the day. We took tea down to Eton and watched the match on Upper Club, against Sandhurst. After dinner, Harris came in and accompanied May Harrison[3] – Brahms sonata, César Franck, Delius's *Legende*, and Sibelius's *Einsame Lied*. CIGS's office tele-

1 Gen. Georges Catroux (1877–1969), C-in-C Free French in Levant 1941, Gov.-Gen. Algeria 1943–4, Minister for N. Africa, French Provisional Govt 1944, French Ambassador in Moscow 1945–8. Duff Cooper had recently been appointed British Ambassador to France.
2 Maj.-Gen. Sir Francis de Guingand (1900–79), CoS 8th Army 1942–4.
3 May Harrison (d. 1959), violinist, one of four musical sisters, including the celebrated cellist Beatrice (d. 1965).

phoned to me that George Lascelles was missing (Italy), and I had to ring up poor Harry [his father] at Harewood and tell him.

Sunday 25 June

The King, before church this morning, sent the Dean a message asking him to omit, from our usual service in St George's Hall, the prayer for our enemies. The Dean complied, but preached a sermon on the obligation of all Christians to forgive their enemies, and on the general duty of being a little blind to the faults of our neighbours at large, and of trying to see the good in them. Opinions are divided as to whether or not he was justified in making this somewhat personal attack, in the manner of John Knox. It won't do any harm.

Monday 26 June

War Office telephoned that G. Lascelles, though wounded, is almost certainly alive and a prisoner of war.

Tuesday 27 June   London

Constant air-raid warnings all day. The Crossbow menace has not abated. Otherwise, all news pretty good.

Wednesday 28 June

We all slept, peacefully enough, in the shelter here which was built in 1942. Eden has circulated a paper to the effect that all the current stories about French snipers, male and female, having fired on our troops have proved to be without any foundation at all; the French population have, in most cases, received us very well. The PM has replied to my 'interesting' letter of May 30; he doesn't agree with my conclusions, and thinks that we should now send out to the Duke of Windsor somebody who can accurately assess what he really wants. The only man who could do this with any hope of success is Walter Monckton.[1]

Early this morning the German-controlled 'European' radio broadcast an announcement that George Lascelles, though seriously wounded, was

---

1 Sir Walter Monckton (1891–1965). As Attorney-General to the Prince of Wales 1932–6, and an intimate friend and adviser, he witnessed the events of the Abdication from close quarters. Solicitor-General 1945. He went on to serve in the Churchill and Eden govts. Created 1st Viscount Monckton of Brenchley 1957.

in a condition satisfactory to himself and his doctors; they asked that this message from him might be duly delivered to his father, whose name and address was then given. I rang up Harry and told him. This was a gentlemanly act on the part of the Germans, though there may be some ulterior motive behind it. In the last war, Winston, when First Lord, did much the same thing for Tirpitz's son, who had fallen into our hands. Lavinia came of age yesterday, and Joan gave a party for her at Windsor today.

Saturday 1 July

Eton and Winchester match. Just at the end of the Winchester innings, a flying bomb hit the dust-destructor at Deadworth, with a great bang. It blew off the top of the chimney, but did not kill anybody.

Sunday 2 July

In the kitchen garden this afternoon saw a great spotted woodpecker among the apple trees.

Monday 3 July

Steady rain all day, but no wind. Russians have taken Minsk. Monty telegraphed yesterday to PM that he was 'entirely satisfied' with the situation on his front. Edward and Dorothy Halifax arrived to stay at the Castle; I took him for a short walk before he went up to see the King. He is inclined to agree with me that there is something to be said on the American side in the great 'Anvil' controversy – in which we appear to have given in. Winston is very bitter about it, and not so sure as he was that he really likes F.D.R.[1]

Tuesday 4 July   London

Constant alerts. The King held a small investiture in the basement, near the air-raid shelter – a new development evolved by him and the Lord Chamberlain. Winston, who had observed the preparations as he left, telephoned to me later that he thought it all wrong – a bad example, when the Government were urging people to go about their business as usual during working hours, no matter how many sirens sounded. I passed this on to the King, who at once agreed to hold the next of these functions above ground.

---

1   'Anvil', later renamed 'Dragoon', was an amphibious landing in the South of France.

Wednesday 5 July

Went to see Pug Ismay, and found him busy trying to tone down a decidedly petulant telegram which the PM wishes to send to F.D.R. He said that he believed the war would be over before the end of October. Incessant air-raid alerts all day.

Thursday 6 July

The first fine day we have had for weeks. There was a marked diminution of Crossbows – perhaps due to the weather, or to one of its consequences – viz., that we were able to bomb the suspected sites heavily and accurately.

J. J. Mallon,[1] Warden of Toynbee, came to see me; the conversation turned on Oswald Mosley, of whom he has seen a good deal over a period of years. I asked him if O.M. were really evil, or merely deluded; Mallon said, with great emphasis, that he was essentially and fundamentally evil.

Friday 7 July

Winston's pronouncement about Crossbow in the House of Commons yesterday has had a uniformly good press. It has particularly stirred the Americans, who do not seem to have grasped that London was the principal target for flying bombs, which they thought were falling relatively harmlessly in coastal areas in Kent and Sussex.

Von Rundstedt[2] has been superseded by Kluge[3] in the command of the German armies in France. Possibly he resigned from the knowledge that he had a hopeless task in front of him. Anyhow, it is a bull point, for he was undoubtedly a very able general. While we were having dinner at Winchester Tower, there was a very loud bang, which proved to be from a flying bomb that came down about half-way up the Long Walk.

Monday 10 July

Bernard Norfolk came to luncheon, and we went with the King and Queen

---

1 James Joseph Mallon (1875–1961) had been Warden of Toynbee Hall, Whitechapel, since 1919.
2 Field-Marshal Gerd von Rundstedt (1875–1953), one of Hitler's most successful generals, was Supreme Commander of the German forces in W. Europe until July 1944. He was captured by American troops in May 1945, but released by the British in 1948.
3 Günther von Kluge (1882–1944) succeeded Rundstedt as C-in-C German forces in the west on 3 July 1944, but he committed suicide on 18 Aug. under suspicion of involvement in the Stauffenberg plot against Hitler on 20 July.

to visit volunteer agricultural workers at Maidenhead Thicket and else-where, finally having tea with them in their camp at Shurlock Row. A successful afternoon, admirably supervised by Tommy Loyd,[1] the Lord Lieutenant of Berkshire and chairman of its agricultural committee. Bernard, on Saturday, had tried to get to Peterborough to address a meeting; he sent a minion to Liverpool Street to keep him a seat in the train, but when he got there, the crowd in and near the train was so dense that not only could Bernard not get within fifty yards of it, but his unlucky *locum tenens* had the greatest difficulty in getting *out* of it, and was all-but carried off to Peterborough. This is typical of railway travel in current conditions; what a shining example of the democratic principle, when even dukes are left struggling on platforms.

Tuesday 11 July

At luncheon the King told the Prime Minister that he wanted to go to Italy and see the troops, in ten days' time. The Prime Minister approved the plan, and said, 'And before you come back, I will go out and meet you in Rome,' adding, I believe, that they would present themselves to the Romans hand-in-hand on Mussolini's famous balcony – a typical instance of how instant he is to dramatise any situation which catches his imagination. In this, he showed himself '*suarum legum idem auctor et subversor*,'[2] for hith-erto it has been a sacred canon with him that the Sovereign and his First Minister should never be out of the country at one and the same time; nor must he be allowed to depart from it now.

All this sent me round to Whitehall, where I got Pug Ismay to send off a telegram to Alex (through 'C', whereby we ensure that it has no domestic circulation at all): Bridges, to initiate the institution of the necessary Council of State during the King's absence; and C. Portal, to find out if one of the York aeroplanes will be available. I was rather torn as to whether I had better go on this trip, or stop at home and mind the shop – and the Council of State; so I was relieved when the King himself suggested that E. Miéville should go this time, and that I should reserve myself for the next visit to France. This fits in on the whole with my own inclinations, for, on general as well as personal grounds, I am more interested in the French than the Italian campaign; moreover, I don't much want to be away from this country for any length of time just now.

---

1 Arthur Thomas Loyd (1882–1944), Lord Lieutenant of Berkshire 1935–44.
2 'At the same time the author and subverter of his own laws.' The canon was not all that sacred. Churchill had tried to subvert it before D-Day (see pp. 224–9).

At the Beefsteak, Ned Grigg, speaking of Shakes Morrison,[1] said he had once heard him, in a Foreign Office debate, say, 'The great difficulty about Foreign Affairs is the existence of foreigners,' the gallery at the time being packed with members of the Diplomatic Corps: an extraordinary gaffe to be made by any man with his experience of public affairs. Yet not so extraordinary, perhaps, for Shakes, a most charming and lovable creature, is a half-fey child of the Hebrides who will never grow up in worldly matters. He is quite unsuited to parliamentary life. [*Later note:* Yet he makes a very good Speaker.]

Wednesday 12 July

Left Buckingham Palace 10 a.m. with the King and Queen and motored into the heart of Sussex to see something of the aircraft batteries which are trying, not conspicuously well, to protect us from the flying bombs. As we were leaving the first site, at Maresfield (where I spent a miserable ten days during the last war), Pile,[2] Commander-in-Chief, Anti-Aircraft Command, mentioned that one of the things had pitched in East Grinstead that morning. Their Majesties at once agreed to make a small detour to visit the scene, and we found a very nasty mess in the main street of the town. As the thing had exploded at 7.20 a.m., few people had been about, and there were only three fatal casualties; but the devastation was considerable. The appearance, as from the skies, of the King and Queen naturally had an immense effect; they spent some time, every minute of which, from every point of view, was worth its weight in gold, talking to all and sundry.

We then went to a second site on the outskirts of the town, where all was quiet; and as it was the first fine day for weeks, the chances of our seeing any of the guns in action seemed small. But, at our final port of call, Lingfield, the klaxon sounded the alarm just as we were emerging from the luncheon tent, and in a few seconds every gun in the battery had opened up at a target about 7,000 yards' distance. Soon we could see the flying bomb approaching, at fantastic speed – the experts said not less than 450 mph – and it passed almost over our heads at an altitude of, I suppose, about 2,000 feet, looking incredibly sinister, like a cur-dog with its ears back and teeth showing.

The guns made beautiful and concentrated patterns of shell-bursts right

---

1 William Shepherd Morrison (1893–1961), lawyer and politician, Minister of Town and Country Planning 1943–5, Speaker of the House of Commons 1951–9, Gov.-Gen. Australia 1960–61). Created 1st Viscount Dunrossil 1959.
2 Gen. Sir Frederick Pile (1884–1976), GOC Anti-Aircraft Command 1939–45.

in its path, but always just fifty yards behind its tail. It went on to London unscathed, flying with uncanny accuracy through the intervals between the balloons echeloned some three miles behind us. This happened four or five times during the afternoon, though eventually one of the things did crash in the middle distance, possibly a victim of the guns, but more probably of a roving Mustang that had been chasing it. I found this rather discouraging, for these guns, heavies, were static, and operated by all the latest radar gadgets, which are reputed to eliminate any possibility of human error.

I could see, too, that Pile and his pundits were even more depressed than I was myself. Pile said that this battery had shot down three out of five birds the previous day, and that he thought that the young ladies of the ATS who operate the radar were over-excited by the presence of Their Majesties, but I did not find this very convincing. With practice, I suppose, they will be able to adjust their apparatus so that the shells shall burst in front of, instead of behind, the target; but it took me many years to achieve much the same art of adjustment when confronted with driven partridges.

Meanwhile, it gave one a feeling of physical sickness to see the devilish things flashing over the English countryside, to plunge into the bowels of poor, defenceless London. The sun came out, and we sat about in the camp till long past our scheduled hour for leaving, and did not reach Buckingham Palace till 6.30 p.m.

The King told me before dinner that, on reflection, he was not at all disposed to go to Rome in his coming trip, and still less to see the Pope. So at 10 p.m. I went round to Eden's flat in the Foreign Office to find out what he thought. To my relief he was strongly of the King's opinion, saying that on political grounds, as well as those of security, it was most inadvisable that HM should go nearer Rome than he could help, or see the Pope or any of those now prominent in Italian politics – including members of the House of Savoy. Winston, he told me, had come round to the same point of view. He [Eden] has great personal charm, and is always extremely agreeable when one has to do business with him.

Thursday 13 July

Edward Bridges told me that in one of the few flying bombs which have come down intact they found that the gyro compass bore the date July 1944, which looks as if the Germans were making them from day to day, and had no reserve stock. There were none of them over England last night, and only a few alerts today. I was pleased to see in the *Daily Telegraph*'s version of the Court Circular yesterday that Delia Peel featured as 'the Lady

Elia Peel'; so I sent it to her, with the hope that it would stimulate her to produce another of her well-known Essays.[1]

Julian Cory-Wright,[2] Felicity's eldest, and the most charming of boys, has been killed in France; another of the little band that grew up at Brancaster each summer. Heard from C. Portal that the York would be available for HM's journey.

Saturday 15 July

St Swithin, and several heavy showers. Leigh-Mallory told the Queen yesterday that more than half of our vast air force had been immobilised and useless ever since D-Day owing to this consistently damnable weather. An air fleet is, in fact, much like a sea fleet in Nelson's day – if the weather is against it, it has got to stop at home.

John Kennedy[3] is convinced that the Germans can't keep it up much longer. He said that perhaps the most important factor in their defeat was the breaking of their naval and military cipher two years ago, which they still don't suspect. Without it, we should never have beaten the U-boats; and it enabled Monty, in his African campaign, to have on his breakfast table every morning a series of messages between Rommel and the German GHQ which our people had intercepted.

Sunday 16 July

Harold Macmillan was recently asked by the Foreign Office for his view on the advisability of Peter of Yugoslavia going to Naples; he telegraphed back laconically, 'No kings in Naples at present, please.' This arrived on the very day that the King himself decided to go to Naples; to set H. Macmillan's mind at rest, I wrote to him today to say that his own Sovereign had not seen the telegram in question – thanks to our forethought in removing it from his box. Michael Adeane, in a letter to his mother, says he thanks God he ain't a German when he sees what both the RAF and Royal Artillery are doing to them day and night. John says ditto about the effect of our rocket-firing Typhoons, which sound terrible weapons.

---

1 A reference to Charles Lamb's *Essays of Elia*, which first appeared in the *London Magazine* between 1820 and 1823.
2 Eldest son of Sir Geoffrey and Felicity Cory-Wright. Another of their three sons was killed in 1945.
3 Maj.-Gen. John Kennedy (1893–1970), Assistant CIGS (Ops and Intelligence) 1943–5. Knighted 1945.

Tuesday 18 July

The King and Queen, Cynthia Spencer (whose son Althorp is now in Normandy with the Greys), P. Townsend and I left Paddington 7.30 p.m. halting for the night at Kingham, on the head waters of the Evenlode, between Oxford and Honeybourne.

Wednesday 19 July

We visited 'TRE' [the Telecommunications Research Establishment], now housed in Malvern School, a most interesting morning; we were shown many ocular demonstrations of the achievements of radar in its various manifestations. Without these astonishing inventions, we should certainly have never overcome the U-boats, nor the German bombers; our own bombing would have been relatively negligible in its effects; we could not have invaded Normandy; and the *Bismarck* and the *Scharnhorst* would still have been afloat. In fact, had a few well-placed German bombs exterminated TRE, when it was precariously housed at Durnford, my old private school on the Purbeck coast, we should almost certainly have lost the war. This small and devoted band of scientists, originally led by Watson-Watt,[1] has built up a truly wonderful organisation, the spirit of which greatly impressed me. Stafford Cripps,[2] as Minister of Aircraft Production, and his lady (looking very proletarian, in a curious white beret) came with us.

After lunching in the TRE canteen, we drove to Cheltenham, and went round Smith's works, where they make watches and various instruments of precision for the RAF. I noticed that the watches were enclosed in neat little round boxes made of talc, or some such transparent material, which struck me as admirable receptacles for dry flies; I asked for one, and was generously given half a dozen.

Thursday 20 July

The German wireless put out a story tonight that Hitler and a number of his entourage had been damaged by a bomb – whether dropped from an aeroplane or planted by hand, they don't say.

---

1   Sir Robert Watson-Watt (1892–1973), scientific adviser, author and lecturer, radio and radar specialist.
2   He had taken charge of aircraft production on his return from India in 1942.

Friday 21 July

This morning's wireless told extraordinary tales from Berlin, with pro-nouncements by Hitler, Goering and Dönitz,[1] of an attempt by military 'usurpers' to seize the reins of government, and exhortations to all German troops to pay no attention to any orders that they might issue. Since then Stockholm and Berne have been bubbling with rumours of 'civil war' in Berlin, but there is no authentic news. The Foreign Office take a cautious view of the whole business; but even if it were all a fake, it is surely a pretty desperate form of propaganda, and not calculated to make the German fight with increased confidence.[2]

As I said to the King, our men would be, to say the least, uneasy if they were suddenly told that Alan Brooke and a posse of generals had tried to assassinate Winston and take charge of affairs. We must wait developments; but I have a feeling that this might well be the proverbial pebble that starts the avalanche.

Saturday 22 July

The King, with Eric Miéville and Mouse Fielden, left Northolt aerodrome 11.15 p.m. The Queen, Princess Elizabeth and I went to see him off. The York aeroplane, which I had never seen before, looked as big as Noah's ark, and a deal more comfortable.[3] While we were inspecting it, a flying bomb, brilliantly illuminated by the local searchlights, approached from the dir-ection of London. The assembled air marshals audibly held their breaths; but it sailed on, to explode a long way off, in the neighbourhood of High Wycombe.

'C' gave me his views on the Berlin 'revolt'; his agents have been fore-casting something of the sort for some time, even predicting a dénouement for the latter part of this month. But, as he said, if *he* knew that there was

---

1 Adm. Karl Dönitz (1891–1980), architect of the U-boat campaign, C-in-C of the German Navy from 1943, was named by Hitler as his successor in Apr. 1945. He negotiated the surrender to the Allies, was tried at Nuremberg and sentenced to ten years' impris-onment.

2 These were the first reports of the attempt on Hitler's life organised by Count Claus Schenk von Stauffenberg (1907–44), who planted a briefcase containing a bomb under the table at a staff conference on 20 July. The bomb exploded, but failed to kill the Führer. Stauffenberg was executed by firing squad that same day.

3 The Avro York, based on the Lancaster bomber, had gone into production in 1943 as a long-range transport aircraft. Tommy was evidently much impressed by its dimensions: 78 ft 6 in long, with a wingspan of 102 ft. He would have been astounded by the size of a double-decker A 380 Airbus – 239 ft long, with a span of 261 ft, and the capacity to carry up to 800 passengers.

a plot afoot, it is very certain that Himmler knew too, and took his own precautions.

Wednesday 26 July

John wrote the other day that all his spare kit had been 'brewed up' (which presumably means destroyed by a shell), including the admirable .450 revolver that I used to carry. In another letter, which I got tonight, he says he has suffered far more inconvenience from mosquitoes than from any enemy projectiles. He described their beating of hedges and copses for lurking Germans, left over by our advance, who were, at first, 'as difficult to flush as old cock pheasants'.

Thursday 27 July

A flying bomb fell close to the tennis court at Buckingham Palace on Tuesday, and another pitched in one of the paddocks at Hampton Court today, all among the carriage horses, not one of which was injured.

Friday 28 July

Joan and I went to the Deanery, where Albert Baillie[1] had induced A. Lunt[2] and Lynn Fontanne to give a performance of Sherwood's play *There Shall Be No Night* in his drawing-room to an audience of some twenty-five denizens of Windsor. It was superbly done, by the whole company, with no scenery, props or make-up, and in such intimate circumstances the emotional strain which it set up was almost intolerable. The play is far too near the bone for such times as these, and I for one (and Owen Morshead) was greatly relieved, not disappointed, when Lunt announced that they would omit the penultimate scene altogether.

The Queen nearly broke her nose this morning, by pulling down a heavy curtain rod on to its bridge. A letter arrived from John, written only three days ago.

Monday 31 July

The Americans have reached Avranches, which is very good news. I can't

---

1   Rev. Albert Baillie (1864–1955), Dean of Windsor 1917–44, Chaplain to King George VI 1944–52.
2   Alfred Lunt (1892–1977), successful American actor, husband of Lynn Fontanne (1887–1983). He played numerous roles in England and America, and held honorary degrees

see how the Germans can hold their line in front of our 2nd Army, with their left flank thus threatened; and if they have to fall back, where are they to go to? Monty considers the situation 'very highly satisfactory'; and there are persistent rumours that Rommel has died from a bullet in the lung from one of our Spitfires.[1]

Tuesday 1 August

Joan's birthday. We went to see *The Way Ahead* in the Windsor cinema, a remarkably well-constructed story of the conscripted man's life in the Army, and well acted too.[2] It is better than the naval counterpart, *In Which We Serve*, in that it avoids the pitfalls of theatricality into which Noël Coward occasionally tumbled in producing the latter. But I came away with a melancholy reflection: all the men who figured in the film were indisputably better, and nicer, human beings after their period of war training and warfare than they were in civil life, in which most of them had been pretty nasty; from which it would seem to follow that war, or at any rate the conditions of war service, are still necessary for man's improvement.

Thursday 3 August

The King arrived [from Naples] at Northolt shortly after seven a.m., very well and cheerful, having evidently enjoyed himself. H. Campbell and I went over to meet him, which meant leaving our beds at 5.15. While we were waiting for the York to arrive, a flying bomb again passed over, this time shutting off its engine while directly above us; fortunately it was one of the gliding type, and passed on.

London at 12. The PM came to luncheon, and the members of the War Cabinet came later to say howdyedo to HM; the whole party were photographed outside the Bow Room, in brilliant sunshine. I found them all very optimistic. Letter from John dated July 30.

Monday 14 August

Arthur Penn telephoned to say that he had a letter from Goulburn,[3] com-

---

from twelve universities and colleges.
1 In fact Rommel had been suspected of complicity in the Stauffenberg plot to assassinate Hitler, and on 14 Oct. rather than face trial, committed suicide by taking poison.
2 Originally planned to be a short documentary film, this was directed by Carol Reed from a script by Eric Ambler and Peter Ustinov.
3 Brig. (later Maj.-Gen.) Edward Goulburn (1903–80), Grenadier Guards, was then commanding 8th British Infantry Brigade in Holland and Germany 1944–5.

manding 1st Battalion Grenadiers, in which he mentioned that John had been wounded, not gravely, in the behind.

Tuesday 15 August

Postcard from John to say that he had been evacuated to England. Tried unsuccessfully to find out from the War Office to which hospital he has been sent; all they know is that he has reached the neighbourhood of Wolverhampton.

Wednesday 16 August

Heard from the Adjutant General's office that John is in the Burntwood Hospital, near Lichfield. I rang up the matron, who gave a good account of him, saying they had extracted a 'foreign body' from his wound. This may mean anything. Victoria Adeane[1] writes that they found a lot of grass in Michael's stomach.

Moscow is behaving badly in refusing to cooperate with us and the Americans in helping the unfortunate Poles in Warsaw, who undoubtedly started their rising prematurely, and unwisely. The Cabinet met on this today.

Thursday 17 August

Ismay cannot see how the Germans can get their army, in any shape as a fighting force, out of the jam in which it now is. He did not seem disturbed about Anglo-American relations – there have been stories of Eisenhower and Bedell Smith having fallen out with Monty. Ismay takes a sane and broad-minded view of the Americans – they have won their spurs, and the days are past when we could treat them as green and untried soldiers; in fact, he went so far as to say that we might well have something to learn from them, and that maybe we have been a bit too 'staff collegey' in our conduct of the war.

Sunday 20 August

Joan and I, with Caroline, left Winchester Tower 8 a.m. and motored to Burntwood to see John; it rained in sheets all day – about the only wet day we've had this year. However, we did the 125 miles in under four hours, and

---

1 Mother of Michael Adeane, daughter of Lord Stamfordham.

found John looking better than I have ever seen him, and able to lie right-side-up. The surgeon, a young man called Jones, told me they had taken a large fragment of some German projectile out of him, and found an abscess, which had to be drained. Thanks to penicillin, the wound is now healing well, though a few fragments of bone, which was chipped, are still coming out of it. He will probably have to keep his bed for two or three weeks, but, though the muscles have been torn, they don't anticipate any lasting ill-effects, and the sciatic nerve is not affected.

Wednesday 23 August

Went to a dinner at the Dorchester given by Anthony Eden in honour of Massigli,[1] the French National Commissioner for Foreign Affairs. Brendan Bracken, who talked to me unceasingly through practically the whole meal, is good company. He told me of the first meeting between Winston and Harry Hopkins[2] in the autumn of 1940, when the latter was sent over by Roosevelt to find out if we really could go on fighting. Winston had never met Harry Hopkins before (they are now, of course, as thick as thieves) and was not inclined to be expansive. At the first dinner, at No. 10, Harry Hopkins asked if there was anything USA could do for us; Winston said, 'I should like a million rifles. I don't like telling the British Army to fight the Germans with dummy rifles made of wood.'

H.H. said, 'I'm not sure if we've got a million rifles. Perhaps we could find 500,000.' He then made some excuse for leaving the room, and returned ten minutes later to say that he had been telephoning to Roosevelt, who had undertaken to ship the first consignment of a million rifles on the following day. Winston burst into a flood of tears.

Friday 25 August

I got off a congratulatory telegram from the King to the Allied Expeditionary Force, through Eisenhower, yesterday; and a personal one to Monty, whose plan for the campaign, as he expounded it to us on 15 May, and again in his caravan on 16 June, has been followed by the march of events with the exactitude of a game of chess. There have, of course, been chronological variations, partly due to the execrable weather in the early stages; but in outline and in detail he has made the Germans do just what he intended them to do – and this, I suppose, is the very essence of high strategy. Having imposed his will on them, he has given them a sounder

---

1   René Massigli (1888–1988), French Ambassador to London 1944–55.
2   Harry L. Hopkins (1890–1946), close friend, adviser and representative of Roosevelt.

thrashing than any army has had, perhaps, since Waterloo, or at any rate Sedan.

It has been, in every way, an overwhelming fortnight – too big to write about. Meanwhile, there is still much uncertainty as to the true state of things in Paris. Premature reports of its 'liberation' led the Lord Mayor of London to fire off a telegram of congratulation and ring the bells of St Paul's on Wednesday. That evening, before dinner, I asked Eden and Orme Sargent[1] if they thought that the moment was approaching for the King to send something to de Gaulle. In the morning they opined that it had, and I got a draft approved. Later, in the evening, SHAEF advised that there were still Germans in parts of Paris; however, as both Roosevelt and Stimson had already hailed its liberation, and Eden was about to do so on the 9 p.m. wireless, I thought HM had better be in the same *galère*, so got the FO to send the message off.

The Russians have been behaving badly in refusing to help, or to help us and the Americans to help, the Polish rising in Warsaw, where they are desperately in need of arms, etc. Both Winston and F.D.R. have sent several forcible telegrams to Stalin, but so far he won't budge. The Russians claim that the rising was engineered by Sosnkowski,[2] for political ends, and was premature and ill-advised. The fact is, they had a pretty heavy reverse in their advance on Warsaw, when several German Panzer divisions appeared unexpectedly, and are smarting under it; they blame the Poles, with what justice I don't know, for not having warned them about the German reinforcements.

Michael of Romania,[3] and M. Mavric, with whom we have for so long been negotiating, have suddenly announced their country's defection from the Axis.

Later: 1 p.m. wireless announced that Leclerc's[4] divisions are now in the centre of Paris, with the bells of Notre Dame ringing, etc., so it looks as if the *libération* was accomplished, though there are still Germans fighting in the outskirts. Eisenhower and Monty are rightly refusing to modify their

---

1 Sir Orme Sargent (1884–1962), FO official, Permanent Under-Secretary of State for Foreign Affairs 1946–9.
2 Gen. Kazimierz Sosnkowski (1885–1969), C-in-C of the Polish Army 1943–4.
3 King Michael I of Romania (1921–). During the war Romania had become a satellite of Nazi Germany, but then embraced Communism. King Michael abdicated in 1947 and lived for a while in England, before settling in Switzerland.
4 Jacques-Philippe Leclerc (1902–47) was wounded and captured by the Germans as a French infantry captain in 1939, but escaped to England, where he joined Charles de Gaulle and the Free French. He commanded a French armoured division during the Normandy landings, and on 26 Aug. 1944 entered Paris in triumph, along with de Gaulle, and took the German surrender.

plans by diverting Allied troops to clean up Paris, which they never intended
to occupy till the far more urgent business on the Seine is concluded.

Saturday 26 August

De Gaulle has now entered Paris, amid acclamations.

Sunday 27 August

On the wireless this evening we heard the most remarkable account, broadcast from the spot, of the scene in Notre Dame, when snipers concealed in
the galleries opened fire on de Gaulle as he was walking up the aisle. He
seems to have behaved with the utmost sang-froid, and the episode will
probably be worth several million votes to him. But I cannot understand
how the snipers came to be there at all, unless they passed themselves off
as Maquis. They appear to have been in plain clothes, and those that were
captured will, I hope, be hanged.

Later note, added on 15 September:

In a recent conversation with Holman,[1] our Chargé d'Affaires in Paris, de
Gaulle said that nobody had tried to shoot him. 'It was simply a case of
one man letting off his rifle, possibly accidentally, and everybody firing in
the direction of the first shot.' He added that the English and Americans
loved beautiful stories!

Another note, dated 27 September:

Desmond Morton,[2] who was recently in Paris, was quite entertaining about
his experiences there. According to him, the famous shooting affray in
Notre Dame started with someone dropping a Sten gun, which went off;
thereupon every Frenchman who had a lethal weapon started discharging
it in the direction whence the shot came.

Monday 28 August

I represented the King at a thanksgiving service for the liberation of Paris,
held in the crypt of St Paul's; a congregation of about 500, Cabinet, *Corps
Diplomatique*, etc., through which I was escorted by the Dean to a solitary

---

1   Sir Adrian Holman (1895–1974), Minister at HM Embassy, Paris, 1944.
2   Maj. Desmond Morton (1891–1971), PA and Chief Security Adviser to the PM, 1940–46.
    Knighted 1945.

seat in the chancel. Good lesson, from Ecclesiasticus. Back to Windsor for luncheon.

Tuesday 29 August

Winston flew back from Italy, and, having been very well all through his trip, arrived with a temperature of 103°. However, it is down to 101.5° tonight, and the doctors say they can find no trace of pneumonic infection. This is a nuisance, with the King coming down tomorrow [from Balmoral] on purpose to see W. on Thursday. Heavy, dull day, with many air-alarms p.m.; so I suppose there is a recrudescence of flying bombs, which have been relatively few lately. Our troops are now well across the Seine, and the Americans across the Marne, so let us hope it is the flying bombs' swan-song – though I fear the Germans now have a number of sites operating in Belgium, and possibly Holland, too. I have begun Evelyn's diaries, which I never read before.[1]

Wednesday 30 August

To London early. Winston better – temperature down, and X-ray shows only a faint suggestion of pneumonic infection. Some days ago I wrote to Alec Hardinge, telling him that while it fell to me to send congratulatory telegrams in these days of victory, I never forgot his courage during the bad years, when all looked black; I have had a nice letter from him in reply, in which he says he is still a sick man.

   We are now well across the Seine, and driving fast for the Somme country, and the Guards Armoured Division are at the top of the hunt, which will be mortifying for John.

Thursday 31 August

The King came down from Balmoral for the day. At 12.30 p.m. after he had knighted Willoughby Norrie, the Governor Designate of South Australia, he and I drove to the Downing Street annexe, where Winston is lying up. I had a long talk with Mrs Churchill, and at the end was summonsed to the PM's bedside, where I found him, in a sumptuous pale-blue dressing gown of oriental design, looking surprisingly well and in good spirits. He proposes to hold to his plan of going to Quebec to meet F.D.R., but will go by sea in the *Queen Mary*, whose sailing has been postponed forty-eight

---

1   John Evelyn (1620–1706), eccentric scholar, for most of his life kept a diary, which was discovered in an old clothes basket in 1817, and first published a year later.

hours. On his pillow lay a submission appointing Monty a field-marshal, which he had asked the King to sign, as I had warned him would happen, having been myself warned of the project overnight by Bevir. I don't think a general has ever before been thus promoted in the middle of a battle, and certainly none has ever had his appointment signed by his Sovereign on the Prime Minister's pillow.

This puts Monty ahead of Alex, which is rough on the latter, though he is too big a man to resent it, as Rawlinson[1] did when they put Birdwood[2] over his head in the last war. But I think it is well timed, and certainly deserved – and will put the changes in command in their right perspective. The latter have had quite a good press, and Eisenhower helped by making a frank and generous statement, in which he praised the British share in the battle, and eulogised Monty.

At 7 p.m. the King and I left Euston for Balmoral. The train was stopped at Blisworth for the Duke of Gloucester and Prince William; accommodation for the latter and one nurse had been asked for, and provided, but he turned up with two nursery-maids as well – a typical Royal Family muddle. As the train was already full – we took up Betty Cranborne[3] and her maid – I've no idea where the women slept in the end.[4] The Duchess of Gloucester had another son a few days ago – a Caesarian operation – and there is much discussion as to what name the child shall be given. The King favours Charles, which I think would be a good idea, but the Gloucesters apparently fancy Richard.

Tuesday 5 September

Killed a fish in the stretch below Invergelder Farm, on a 1/0 Wilkinson. Only 7lbs, but it was satisfactory in that the river was still in moderate spate (after heavy rain all yesterday) and not really fishable. He missed it first time, but imprudently showed his back fin, so, after waiting the statutory five minutes, I gave it him again, and hooked him.

Winston left Glasgow in *Queen Mary* for his meeting with F.D.R. in Quebec.

---

1 Gen. Sir Henry Rawlinson (1864–1925), KCB, GCB, KCVO, GCVO, GCMG, commanded 4th Corps and 4th Army in WWI, during which he was Mentioned in Despatches eight times. Created 1st Baron Rawlinson of Trent 1919.
2 Field-Marshal William Birdwood (1865–1951), commanded 5th Army in France 1918–19. Created 1st Baron Birdwood 1938.
3 Elizabeth, wife of Bobbety Cranborne (later 5th Marquess of Salisbury).
4 Accommodation on the royal train was strictly segregated, men at the front, women at the rear.

Wednesday 6 September

The President of Poland has written to the King about Warsaw; but what can the King do? Warsaw is a tragedy, but the Polish cause has not been helped by Sosnkowski's astounding outburst two days ago. Stalin is not far wrong when he says, 'These are an impossible people.' People are inclined to say that we have let Poland down over this; they might just as well argue that we have let down our prisoners now in Japanese hands by not rescuing them. Of course we would rescue them, if we could; but, as a military operation, it is simply 'not on'; nor is supplying Warsaw from the air, as both Portal and Evill[1] (not men to be turned aside by difficulties which can be overcome) have testified to the Cabinet.

Friday 8 September

Monty writes to me ('private and personal') on the 4th: 'We are now approaching a very critical time in the war; if we take the right decision *now*, we could win the German war in a few weeks; if we take the wrong decision, the war will be prolonged. Our great allies are very "nationally minded", and it is election year in the States; the Supreme Commander is an American. I fear we may take the wrong decision. I am throwing all my weight's influence into the contest; but fear of American public opinion may cause us to take the wrong decision.' This is all a bit Delphic, for he gives no clue as to what *is* the right decision, and what the wrong.

Saturday 9 September

Two explosive missiles fell in Epping and Chiswick respectively yesterday evening. The experts are sure that they were some form of rocket projectile. They only made craters eighteen feet wide, and didn't do nearly as much damage as the flying bombs. But the latter began in this relatively innocuous way, and this may easily be the beginning of a disagreeable attack, which will be a sad blow to Londoners, who have just been told by Duncan Sandys[2] that their Blitz troubles may be considered over.

---

1   Air Chief Marshal Sir Douglas Evill (1892–1971), Vice-Chief of the Air Staff 1943–6.
2   Duncan Edwin Duncan-Sandys (1908–87), MP and diplomat, Chairman of War Cabinet Committee for Defence against Flying Bombs and Rockets 1943–5, Minister of Works 1944–5, Minister of Defence 1957–9. In 1935 he had married Winston Churchill's daughter Diana. Created Baron Duncan-Sandys (Life Peer) 1974.

Thursday 14 September

About half a dozen more of the 'rockets' have fallen in the London area in the last few days, fired, they think, from a single site somewhere in the Rotterdam area. The King of Greece has been here for the past two days; he was very agreeable, and I felt sorry for the poor man, who is in an acute dilemma over his return to his country and the proposed plebiscite on the future of the monarchy. I had several talks with him, one in the presence of the King, and have just sent Eden (who has gone over to Quebec) a note about them. Both the Americans and ourselves are getting very impatient with the generally-obstructive attitude of Moscow on a variety of questions, and what Winston calls 'a showdown with the bear' seems imminent.

Cartier has sent the Queen a cheque for £10,000, as a parting thank-offering from the Belgian Government, who have now returned to Brussels, where nobody seems to be particularly glad to see them. Princess Elizabeth caught her first salmon yesterday, an eight-pounder, in the Birkhall water, on a Green Charm. John has heard that his platoon was actually the first British unit to enter Brussels, which is hard on him.

Tuesday 19 September

Two bad bits of news today – the deaths of Billy Hartington and of David Peel, Delia's nephew and adopted son. The latter is perhaps the greater tragedy of the two. I lunched at the Manse, with the Lambs, and later, with bright sun shining down the river, killed an eight-pound fish in the Boat Pool. He was a reasonably fresh fish, and took a small and battered Dark Fairy (two hooks) in the rough water, with an *élan* that suggested March rather than September.

The landing of 3 Airborne Division at Arnhem, and in the area south of it, on Sunday, has gone off well, and has inspired Monty to make one of his more optimistic speeches. The plan was his, so evidently he prevailed over the Americans. Eden is back from Quebec; from Winston's telegrams, the results of the conference appear to be satisfactory.

Thursday 21 September

The King held an investiture in Holyrood, where we lunched, and thereafter toured Edinburgh.

Friday 22 September

Investiture, and visits to service clubs after luncheon, to which the Elphinstone family came. Their Majesties and I returned to London.

Saturday 23 September

Windsor p.m., finding Joan and Caroline there. Our airborne division is having a rough time at Arnhem, one brigade having been captured. The weather, as usual, has gone back on us.

Tuesday 26 September   London

I went to a luncheon at the Mansion House, where the appeal for the extension of London House was launched. Vincent Massey spoke well and elegantly as usual. Other speakers were Bruce of Australia and R. B. Bennett, who told us (the English) that we were the finest people on earth, with every appearance of conviction. He buttonholed me in the hall about Anglo-American relations, about which he is very pessimistic, saying that the Americans had made up their minds that we were finished as a first-class power, etc. I don't believe this.

   Went on to see Alan Brooke, about a projected visit to France by the King, and on to Pug Ismay, who sent off a telegram to Monty for me. Both of them were well satisfied with the Quebec talks, from which they have just returned, but agreed that Winston had been very troublesome behind the scenes. Met Mrs Churchill in Whitehall, who told me that W. was much better for the trip. The Arnhem situation is bad; but the general opinion seems to be that the operation as a whole has achieved its object, and this could not have been done without taking heavy risks.

Thursday 28 September

HM with Eric Miéville and P. Legh, went to Sandringham to shoot his partridges, and I to Windsor. John looks pretty well, but a bit tired, as is only natural after six weeks in bed.

Friday 29 September

Kit Dawnay came to see me, sent by Monty to discuss plans, which we concerted satisfactorily. Monty is well pleased with the gross result of his airborne adventure, but thinks that had he been allowed to put it on a fortnight earlier, when the weather would have been better, he would have pushed the Germans right across the Rhine. He will now have to fight what he calls a 'killing battle', which will start next week, and may be protracted.

Saturday 30 September

P. J. Grigg has blotted his copybook badly by announcing that private soldiers can now wear collars and ties in uniform, without saying a word to the King. He has sent a letter of apology, but it may well be that he has acted *ultra vires* as well as discourteously, for I believe it is unconstitutional to make any change in the uniform of HM forces without a submission to the Sovereign. I cannot find printed authority for this belief, but I do know that one of the things that Councillors of State are expressly forbidden to do is to approve any such change, which looks as if it must be a matter of some constitutional importance. I am consulting the Pundits of Whitehall.

Joan, John, Caroline and I went blackberrying in Windsor Forest, getting $7\frac{1}{2}$ lbs. Lovely day.

Sunday 1 October

Bevir rang up about 11 p.m. to say that the PM had made up his mind to go to Moscow, with Eden, next week, and was on the point of sending a telegram to Stalin to that effect. I said he (the PM) certainly ought to telephone the King personally, and tell him all about it, before despatching his telegram. This he did. They are arranging a route whereby he will not have to fly over the Caucasus, and two doctors, Moran and Whitby[1] will accompany him – and Mrs C; I suggested that they had better take a hospital nurse with him, too. It is a hazardous enterprise, so soon after his recent illness, and it annoys me that he should have to go to Russia, just because Uncle Joe says *his* doctors won't allow him to travel. However, U.J. has been sending some very friendly telegrams lately.

Tuesday 3 October

London, for the day, John and Elspeth accompanying me. Lunched with the Churchills at No. 10, to meet the King of Greece, who was the only other guest. General conversation, and I gathered little of how the King's affairs were progressing. He and Winston went off for a heart-to-heart after luncheon. Before it, W. took me into the Cabinet Room and said, in effect, that the Cabinet didn't like the idea of the King sleeping at TAC [Tactical Air Command] HQ next week, unless the salient were considerably broader and more solid than it is now. With this I entirely agree. Winston looked quite robust again, and was in good spirits, though a bit distrait – but who isn't, after five years of this war?

Have written to the King, suggesting that he and the Queen should go at the earliest opportunity to 'Hellfire Corner' (Dover, Folkestone etc.),

---

1 Brig. Lionel Whitby (1895–1956), bacteriologist to the Middlesex Hospital, Consulting Physician in Blood Transfusion to the Army. Knighted 1945.

where they are celebrating their relief at last from the cross-Channel guns of the Germans.

Wednesday 4 October

Air Commodore Geddes,[1] from Tactical Air Force Headquarters, came to see me about next week's trip, and told me that the RAF could not, in present circs, take airborne passengers beyond Brussels; further, the new German Messerschmitt 262s, which go upwards of 500 mph, are becoming something of a menace, and, until we have plenty of our own jet-propelled machines (Meteors), are difficult to deal with. They have not yet started shooting up the roads in the Nijmegen salient (which, with their very limited range, is about as far as they can reach), but if they do, it would make motor travel for the King rather problematical.

As we have no cook, and Joan is doing all the cooking, we all dined at the Old House Hotel, to give her a night off.

Thursday 5 October

Yesterday I saw for the first time the stained-glass picture of George II, after Reynolds, which was revealed in a recess behind the picture of Catherine of Braganza in the Charles II dining-room, when they took C. of B. down to store her. Owen Morshead has lit up George II very effectively: it's an interesting discovery, and there is no record of how it got there.

Friday 6 October

Went to London and saw C. Dawnay in Ismay's room. He gave me a letter from Monty, dated this morning, in which he says that Coningham's[2] contention that it is in any way unsafe for the King to arrive by air at Eindhoven, and stay there, is 'complete and utter nonsense'. We then went to the Chiefs of Staff meeting, down the passage. With C.D.'s consent, I gave Monty's letter to Alan Brooke, who read it aloud. He said that, from the land point of view, he saw no reason why the King should not carry out the proposed programme. C. Portal said that there was certainly an element of risk from the air, but he was not prepared to advise postponement. I

---

1 Air Commodore Andrew Geddes (1906–88), Royal Artillery officer seconded to the RAF. Air Commodore, Operations and Plans, HQ 2nd Tactical Air Force, for the invasion of Normandy.
2 Air Marshal Sir Arthur Coningham (1895–1948), AOC-in-C 2nd Tactical Air Force 1944–5.

pointed out that, in no war, could you guarantee immunity from a chance shell or bomb to any distinguished visitor to a battle area. I asked him, if he were an insurance broker, what premium he would quote for the King's safety. He said, 'In the neighbourhood of the hundreds' – i.e., it was at least 100–1 against any untoward happening. Dawnay said that Monty, and his visitors, regularly used Eindhoven airfield, as did hospital planes.

Saturday 7 October

Martin told me on the telephone that Monty's principal anxiety seems to be that the King will catch a cold, and he reiterates his instructions about bringing plenty of warm clothing, which he has already given me, and which I knew already, having had some experience of autumn and winter campaigning in Flanders.

Went to London, and saw the PM in his siren suit in the Cabinet Room, at 6 p.m. He began by showing me a letter he had written to the King on the fifth, but held up, and asked me what I thought of it. It was tantamount to advice to the King not to go, and I said I hoped he would not send it. Winston was obviously anxious about the Eindhoven part, but the Cabinet, on Thursday, had given general approval to the project in principle; eventually he rang for his stenographer, and in my presence dictated another letter, the effect of which was to give the thing his blessing, though he put in a general caveat against staying too long in the same place, etc. I was grateful to him for listening to me so patiently, and for taking the various points which I made.

He told me that if, as seems probable, his Liberal and Labour colleagues leave the Cabinet for party reasons, he would then consider that the task for which the King had originally appointed him – namely, to lead a Coalition Government – would have come to an end, and he would resign. The King would then be free to ask him, as the leader of the largest party in the House of Commons, to form a new administration; this he could, and would, do – and it would be quite a strong government, too. He did not think that, at such a juncture, he would ask for a dissolution immediately (he disliked the idea of a 'khaki' election), but he would probably have to do so after an interval of a few months.

Winston himself looks well. He leaves for Moscow this evening, but is not, I am sorry to say, taking either Mrs C. or a second doctor. Winston said that he would not have undertaken this trip to Moscow but for his conviction that it was essential to prove to the world that Stalin is as much a partner in the Triumvirate as is Roosevelt. 'Next time,' he said, 'we must get Joe Stalin to meet *us* somewhere – perhaps at the Hague – though he is always miaowing about his health, and pretending that he is too sick to travel.'

Monday 9 October

Winston and Eden arrived Moscow safely this morning.

Tuesday 10 October

Our departure from Northolt, timed for 3 p.m., had to be cancelled, after much telephoning, owing to bad weather over the Continent. Monty will be furious; but Charles Portal told me that he would certainly not undertake the trip today himself, so *a fortiori* it is not to be undertaken by the Sovereign. It is a great nuisance, as I was all packed up, and had got myself, for the first time, into my new 'battle-dress', which the King insisted on my getting. The King, with Joey Legh and myself, went to see Lonsdale's play *The Last of Mrs Cheyney*[1] at the Savoy.

Wednesday 11 October

Though it was a lowering morning, the air people said we could safely fly to Brussels, and probably to Eindhoven. So we (the King, P. Legh and myself) left Northolt a few minutes before 11 a.m. in Harris's Dakota, with an escort of Spitfires. The weather improved as we got eastwards, crossing the south coast at Dungeness, and thence via Boulogne to Brussels, and so without misadventure to Eindhoven, which we reached just before 1 p.m. This was the first time I had flown; I did not enjoy it much, and should think a long journey must be intolerably monotonous. Just beyond the French coast, we passed over several flying bomb sites, pocked with craters like a lunar land-scape, but otherwise saw little of interest.

At Eindhoven we were met by Monty and Coningham, and drove through the town to TAC HQ, 21st Army Group, a cluster of caravans and tents laid out among the shrubs of a public garden. The King was accommodated in a couple of caravans, with a bath tent, and Joey and I had a caravan apiece. They are most comfortable, with electric light, a good bed, and writing table.

Luncheon in the mess-tent – ourselves, Monty, Kit Dawnay and four ADCs, including Michael Chavasse,[2] son of the Bishop of Rochester, who was at Trinity with me; also Hitler and Rommel, the dogs, and a couple of tame rabbits. Then to visit the RAF at Erp, where we saw a demonstration of rocket-carrying Typhoons bombing a selected target given them by wireless

---

1   Starring Jack Buchanan, and the young Coral Browne as Mrs Cheyney, the play was directed by Tyrone Guthrie.
2   His father, Rt. Rev. Christopher Chavasse (1884–1962), was Bishop of Rochester 1940–60. Christopher's twin brother Noel (1884–1917), an army doctor, won a VC and Bar during WWI, one of only three men ever to win the supreme award twice.

telephony, and tea at the Mess, which is established in the club house of the Eindhoven golf links.

On our return to TAC HQ Monty gave the King and me a résumé of the past campaign in his map-caravan, and of how he would have liked it to develop, had he been able to bring off his Arnhem thrust, and dash for the Ruhr and Berlin. He evidently feels that he was frustrated in this by the Americans insisting on making a simultaneous thrust for the Saar, and on dividing the command between himself and Omar Bradley.

As it is, the whole campaign is at a standstill till the port of Antwerp is functioning, which they do not anticipate can happen till about the middle of November. The Germans knew what they were about when they decided to deny us all the Atlantic and Channel ports at all costs; it is a policy which has undoubtedly prolonged the war by several months, suicidal though it seemed at the time. When he claims that the conduct of the campaign in the field must be in the hands of a single commander (that man, of course, to be himself), Monty is on sounder ground.

After dinner we again adjourned to the map-caravan, and heard the four or five most intelligent young officers, whom he sends as liaison officers to the different sectors of the front, making their daily reports; when they had done, Monty dictated to Dawnay a potted version of them, to be telegraphed to CIGS. This séance took place every evening, and I found it most interesting, though, as it happened, the LOs never had anything of much importance to tell us while we were there.

I wore my new battledress for the first time; it is quite a comfortable rig for this sort of trip, but the pockets, in unfamiliar places, take some getting used to.[1]

Thursday 12 October

Started at 9.15 a.m., by car, for Dempsey's 2nd Army HQ at Langebrun, whence to HQ 12th Corps (Ritchie[2]) and 30th Corps (Horrocks[3]). On leaving the latter we saw some of the Guards Armoured Division at Grave. Lunched with Dempsey, and then on to 8th Corps (O'Connor[4]) at Mill; they had that

1 In 1968 Tommy added a footnote: 'When the war was over, I used the trousers regularly for salmon fishing, and found them invaluable. I still wear them when gardening in cold weather.'
2 Gen. Sir Neil Ritchie (1897–1983), Commander 12 Corps British Liberation Army 1944–5, GOC-in-C Scottish Command 1945–7.
3 Lieut.-Gen. Sir Brian Horrocks (1895–1985), Commander 30 Corps 1944–6.
4 Gen. Sir Richard O'Connor (1889–1981), Corps Commander, had been taken prisoner in the N. African campaign, in which he commanded the Western Desert Corps, and had escaped in December 1943.

morning launched an attack on the east flank of the salient, towards Veuvray, but there was not much news of its progress.

The Dutch people were very friendly in the various villages through which we passed, displaying much bunting – the Dutch flag and that of the House of Orange. They appeared to me well-fed and well-clad, but it is, of course, the corner of Holland which has suffered least from the German occupation. A few bombs were dropped in the outskirts of Eindhoven during the afternoon, but we heard, and saw, few signs of battle during the day, even when we were in the northern end of the salient.

Friday 13 October

Left TAC HQ and flew to the airfield at Melsbroek, outside Brussels, where Coningham met us, and Simonds,[1] now commanding the Canadian Army in the absence of Harry Crerar,[2] who has gone home sick. Motored to Canadian Army HQ, in a château at Mortiel (outskirts of Antwerp), where the King held an investiture in the garden. Prince Charles, now Regent of Belgium, came to luncheon.[3] I had not seen him since he was a midshipman in the British navy 20 years ago; he has grown into a fine-looking chap, but shows signs of the hard time he has had during the German occupation – he grew a beard and went into hiding somewhere in Flanders, and the Boches never succeeded in finding him.

Rommel had used the Mortiel château as his HQ, and we saw an elaborate catacomb of dug-outs which he had built. The Germans left all the telephone-apparatus intact, which was a great boon to our signallers. Our drive back to the airfield was thronged with the citizens of Brussels, who gave the King a very cordial welcome.

Saturday 14 October

Left TAC HQ 9.10 a.m. and drove, for the best part of three hours, through Hasselt and Maastricht to HQ 1st US Army in a château outside Verviers, owned by a Belgian industrialist called Pinto. We were welcomed by Ike Eisenhower and Omar Bradley (to whom the King gave the KCB), and after a staff lecture on the present and future aspects of the campaign, went into luncheon. I was next to Bradley, but was chiefly monopolised by my other

---

1 Lieut.-Gen. Guy Simonds (1903–74), Commander 2 Canadian Corps 1944.
2 Gen. Henry Crerar (1888–1965), Commander 1st Canadian Army 1944–5.
3 Brother of King Leopold, who had been held prisoner by the Germans since 1940. Prince Charles had become Regent of Belgium when the Govt returned to Brussels in September 1944.

neighbour, the celebrated George Patton,[1] a Virginian MFH, with whom I talked fox-hunting at length. He looked like Raeburn's 'The Macnab' – a perfect reproduction of an 18th-century English fox-hunting squire. He was excited at my telling him that opposite to him, in the person of Joey Legh, sat the grandson of the author of 'The Dream of an Old Meltonian' [William Bromley-Davenport]. Thereafter he couldn't take his eyes off Joey, who became acutely embarrassed. At the end of the meal, Ike proposed the King's health in a nice little speech. It was, incidentally, Ike's 54th birthday. He and the King had a talk after luncheon, and we then drove home to Eindhoven.

Sunday 15 October

Church parade in an Eindhoven church, Hughes taking the service. The King held an investiture at TAC HQ, knighting Dempsey, de Guingand and Crocker.[2] We were to have left by air immediately after luncheon, but the weather over the Channel was too bad. The King, with Rhys (formerly Welsh champion and now a corporal in the RAF) played nine holes of golf against Joey and J. Henderson (ADC) on the Eindhoven links, which is rather a pleasant course.

Monday 16 October

Weather still unfit for flying. It is a most chancy means of transport. So, at 8.30 a.m. we left by car for Ostend, via Malines and Brussels, and at 1.30 p.m. embarked in destroyer *Garth*, which took over five hours to get us to Dover, over a damnably rough sea. Reached London 8.30 p.m. I like Monty, and there is much in him to admire; but I could not spend more than five days in his company without a feeling of considerable strain; such canalised egotism, though maybe necessary to a successful general – who must keep his mind on a single track – makes a man an exacting companion. But he is a good and thoughtful host, and sent us each away with a large case of excellent Dutch apples. Both he and Ike think the war cannot end before the spring, and I notice in the Moscow telegrams that Stalin is of the same mind.

---

1 Lieut.-Gen. George S. Patton (1885–1945), ruthless and aggressive commander, led US armies in N. Africa, Sicily and Normandy with conspicuous success, but after the war was removed from command of the US Third Army because of his outspoken criticism of Allied policy.
2 Gen. Sir John Crocker (1896–1963), Commander 1st Corps in France and Germany 1944–5.

Monday 23 October   London

Dined at No. 10 with John Martin and company, off caviar and vodka fresh from Moscow. Their verdict on 'Tolstoy' (the code-name for the conference) was that it was 100 per cent successful, except for the Polish end of it, and even that was sixty per cent successful. The PM is none the worse, and was paid unprecedented compliments by Stalin, who dined at the Embassy, saw him off at the airport, pushed him into the front of the box at the opera, and gave him, for Sarah Churchill,[1] a box on which were enamelled the Russian flag and Union Jack intertwined, with 'Victory' underneath. Today is the anniversary of Alamein; Monty sent the King a telegram from the dinner which they are holding to commemorate it in Brussels.

Thursday 26 October

While I was with Ismay this p.m., Eric Miéville telephoned to say that William Cantuar died suddenly this morning. The last Archbishop of Canterbury to die in harness was his father. I am sorry about this. I liked W., though I am not sure that he was going to be a great archbishop. I hope they will appoint Geoffrey Fisher[2] to succeed him. The King gave a first sitting to Oswald Birley[3] for the picture which the latter is to paint for the naval Mess at Greenwich.

Friday 27 October

The long-drawn-out Sutherland affair looks like being settled at last. The PM, after an inquiry made by the Lord Chancellor, has written to him to tell him to resign his Lord Lieutenancy; and I have written to him telling him that the King is not disposed to receive him, which he has been demanding.

Monday 30 October

The King and Queen, with both Princesses, spent yesterday saying goodbye to HMS *King George V* at Greenock, whence she left for the Far East today. Jasper Ridley told me this evening that he was being pressed to take the vacant Provost-ship of Eton. I urged him to accept.[4]

---

1 Winston's third daughter, who accompanied him to the Yalta Conference in February 1945.
2 Most Rev. and Rt. Hon. Geoffrey Fisher (1887–1972), Archbishop of Canterbury 1945–61. Created Baron Fisher of Lambeth (Life Peer) 1961.
3 Capt. Oswald Birley (1880–1952), New Zealand artist who painted portraits of King George V, Queen Mary, King George VI, Queen Elizabeth, etc. Knighted 1949.
4 Ridley declined the offer a week later.

Sutherland has refused to resign his Lord Lieutenancy; the PM, on hearing this, said (in the manner of the Duchess in *Alice* crying 'Off with his head!'), 'Prepare the Letters Patent.' So I hope we may soon be rid of S.

Tuesday 31 October

Went to memorial service for William Temple in the Abbey – in a purely private capacity, HM being represented by the Duke of Gloucester. The funeral took place simultaneously at Canterbury. Sutherland has sent the PM five pages of apologia, as lamentable a document as ever I saw. Most of it is *qui s'excuse s'accuse*; but none of his various accusations against others hold more water than a sieve.

Quite a few rockets have been exploding within earshot during the last day or two, though none very near. The Germans are supposed to be firing them from the neighbourhood of the Hague; if so, they should not be able to do so much longer, for we have made considerable advances into Holland this week.

Wednesday 1 November

With the King to dine at No. 10. War Cabinet. Sat between Woolton and Oliver Lyttelton, and we did not break up till 1.45 a.m. Rather dull – much talk of housing, and, at 1.15, the PM and Anderson began a heated argument about Indian monetary problems. Before that, the PM took the King into the Cabinet Room and showed him a long letter from the Duke of Windsor about his future plans. On rejoining the general company, Winston thrust the letter into my hand, saying in a hoarse whisper, '*Pretend you want to leave the room, and read this in the passage*' – which I did, and I'm bound to say it was an uncommonly good letter. Winston asked me if it would be a good thing for him to go and talk it all over with Queen Mary, which I warmly recommended. Ernie Bevin told us innumerable stories, none of them very funny. What a way to spend the First of November![1]

Friday 3 November

They buried Princess Beatrice [Queen Victoria's youngest daughter] at Windsor. I kept away till it was all over, and took Joan, John and Lavinia (who is shortly to be posted to Naples) to the movies. Beachcomber[2] has been in

---

1 The opening day of the fox-hunting season.
2 The pen-name of J. B. Morton, poet, author and journalist, who contributed a satirical (and often farcical) column to the *Daily Express* for almost fifty years, 1924–75.

good vein lately; I walked all the way from Buckingham Palace to the Ritz repeating to myself, 'Enter the fairies Grogblossom and Quartbottle, trundling a prefabricated egg', which is his highlight today.

The King tells me that Cosmo Lang, who came to the funeral [of Archbishop Temple] this morning, has written to Winston to the effect that Geoffrey Fisher ought to be the new Archbishop. Winston rang me up to say that he would very likely be in Paris on 11 November, and, if so, would the King mind his taking the front of the stage (as this country's representative) in the Armistice Day celebrations which the French are planning. The King raised no objection, though he is a bit anxious about the security aspect.

Tuesday 7 November

Lord Strathmore[1] died this morning; the Queen left for Glamis 7 p.m. Monty, who is over here in strict incog., came to get his Field-Marshal's baton. He told me that he now thought there was no possibility of finishing the war this year.

Moyne[2] was assassinated in Cairo yesterday, apparently by members of the same secret Jewish organisation which tried to murder MacMichael[3] in Jerusalem. His death, hard on that of John Dill in Washington a few days ago, makes another vacancy which it will be hard to fill. Maybe the best plan would be not to fill it at all; I don't see why we should have a Minister Resident in Cairo any longer, now that the Middle East has virtually ceased to be a theatre of war.

Wednesday 8 November

Roosevelt has been re-elected, pretty comfortably. At present, this is a good thing, provided there is not a hostile Congress. I have a feeling that he may not last another term; they tell me that, at Quebec, he had sadly aged. He never ventures to wear his 'braces' now – i.e., never walks at all; and, in a long sitting, his jaw would drop, and his thoughts obviously wander.

On getting back to Buckingham Palace after dinner, joined the King and Anthony Eden, who had been dining with HM. A.E. was in good form, and looked little the worse for the gruelling time he has been having in Moscow,

---

1 Claud Bowes-Lyon, 14th Earl of Strathmore and Kinghorne (1855–1944), father of Queen Elizabeth.
2 He was shot at point-blank range by two Palestinian assassins who turned out to be members of the Stern gang. Both were captured and hanged.
3 Sir Harold MacMichael (1882–1969), High Commissioner and C-in-C for Palestine, where he survived an assassination attempt, 1938–44.

Cairo and Athens successively. He was amusing about Moscow, and said that Stalin had promised Winston and himself that he had no intention of trying to 'communise' any country outside USSR. He favours the idea of HM going to India in the early spring, to see the troops in Burma, on which Winston had tended to pour cold water on Tuesday.

I told the King that W. had come to luncheon immediately after pronouncing a funeral oration in the House on one of his oldest friends, Moyne, and so was probably not in a responsive mood. A.E. agreed, and added that W. had also had a crashing row in Cabinet with Leo Amery, who had got very angry with W.'s continual jeremiads about the Indian debt, and had described them (*ipsissima verba*) as 'damned nonsense'. He promised to send the King some of the spoils from Moscow – a tin of caviar and a bottle of vodka.

Thursday 9 November

Winston has lately been urging on the King that, when the Duke of Windsor passes through this country early next year, on the expiry of his Bahamas governorship, the Royal Family should bury the hatchet and 'receive' the Duchess. This they are all very loath to do; but W., who has got to answer a letter from the Duke on the subject, is very persistent. The King, apart from his recollection that the D. of W. has, on more than one occasion, been extremely rude to, and about, the Queen, Queen Mary and other royal ladies, thinks that such a gesture is wrong in principle, and would imply that the Abdication had been all a mistake; and I have no doubt that a number of people all over the Empire might so interpret it, and ask themselves, 'If the Duchess of Windsor goes to luncheon at Buckingham Palace, what was all the row about in 1936?'

I suggested that he might take this line with Winston: 'On personal and family grounds, we are all averse from meeting the Duchess of Windsor; but if you and your colleagues advise me that it is to the interests of the Monarchy and the Empire at large that we should do so, that is, of course, another matter.'

My impression is that the PM has no right to advise the Sovereign on a purely private matter; if it is one of *public* import, then it should be discussed in Cabinet; and I doubt if the majority of W.'s colleagues would support him on this particular issue, for they know well (as we do) that he only takes this line for purely sentimental reasons.

I think this reasoning is sound constitutionally, but am not positive, so I have asked the wise Bridges to give me an opinion. This evening I went to see John Anderson; W., the last time he saw the King, had suggested the governorship of Madras as a possible sphere of activity for the Duke of Windsor.

This seems to me unthinkable, for (1) no Indian could ever understand how an ex-King-Emperor could come to represent the regnant one. (2) The Viceroy's position would be impossible. (3) As we are continually kicking Indian princes off the *gaddi* [throne] because they make unwise marriages, the Windsors' position would be, to say the least, equivocal. (4) The Abdication was a great strain on the loyalty to, and belief in, the British raj. How then could we send the *fons et origo* of the Abdication to govern an Indian province?

John Anderson did not hesitate to endorse these arguments, and further said that it would be out of the question to make the D. of W. either a governor-general, or an ambassador, *anywhere*. I told him – our talk was strictly off the record – that Winston's sentimental loyalty to the D. of W. was based on a tragic false premise – viz. that he (W.) really *knew* the Duke – which he never did. I also warned him – as I have warned Winston – that constant harping on this problem might have a really serious effect on the present King's health.

Sunday 12 November

The King had a secret pow-wow with Queen Mary, somewhere in the wilds of Wiltshire, re. the Windsors. Heard in the evening that the *Tirpitz*, after an attack by our Lancasters, had turned turtle and sunk in the Tromsø fjord – a fitting end to her ignoble career.

Wednesday 15 November

Lentaigne[1] to see the King. He now commands the famous Chindits, or long-range penetration groups, in Burma, having succeeded the famous Wingate,[2] who caught the public imagination to a degree that nobody since T. E. Lawrence[3] has done. Lentaigne, who impressed me favourably, is evidently not a blind admirer of Wingate. He admitted that the latter was a remarkable man in many ways, but clearly found him very difficult to work with, or under, in the field. Like many visionaries, he had no imagination for details, and could

---

1 Maj.-Gen. Walter Lentaigne (1899–1955) commanded Allied Special Forces in Burma 1944–5.
2 Maj.-Gen. Orde Wingate (1903–44), DSO and two Bars, commanded Allied Special Forces, India Command, establishing a legendary reputation for toughness, courage and bloody-mindedness, not least towards senior officers.
3 T. E. Lawrence (1888–1935), known as 'Lawrence of Arabia' and later T. E. Shaw, soldier, author and adviser on Arab affairs. Publications included *Revolt in the Desert* (1927) and *The Seven Pillars of Wisdom* (1935).

not grasp the fact that complex preparations had to be made before his visions could be put in action.

Friday 17 November

K. Feiling[1] came to see the King regarding the publication of certain letters to and from Neville Chamberlain, whose life he is writing. He lunched with me at the Travellers and told me there was no justification for the theory that, at Munich, N.C. bought us a year's respite knowing that war was inevitable. According to K.F., he came back from Munich still believing in the possibility of peace, though not at all convinced of its probability.

Saturday 18 November   Windsor

The King shooting at St Paul's Walden. I had a long talk with the Queen, primarily to ask her opinion on Henry Moore's[2] 'Madonna' at Northampton, of which Eric Maclagan has sent me some photographs. She agrees with me – and with Owen Morshead – that Moore, who is only forty-six, can well be put in cold storage for a bit. When I showed these photographs to the King, his only comment was: 'The child is hydrocephalic, and the mother has got housemaid's knee.'

Apropos the Windsors, the Queen told me that Queen Mary and she had signed a brief statement to the effect that they were *not* prepared to receive the Duchess, now or at any time, for the same reasons that they would not do so in 1936. She agreed with me that the King would have to make it clear to Winston that either this is a purely family matter, in which case the family should be left to settle it; or it is a state one, on which the Cabinet should tender advice.

The King was moved to suggest to me last night that the *Vanguard*,[3] the new battleship which Princess Elizabeth is to launch in a fortnight's time, should be named the *Home Guard*, as a compliment to the HG. Andrew Cunningham nearly had a fit when this was put to him, and said, 'I suppose we shall be asked to call the next one *Bomber Command*.'

This afternoon I went to see Marten, the Vice-Provost of Eton, and told him that the King proposed to give him a KCVO [Knight Commander of the

---

1 Sir Keith Feiling (1884–1977), political author and university lecturer in history. His *Life of Neville Chamberlain* came out in 1946.
2 Henry Moore (1898–1986), leading modernist sculptor, became a Companion of Honour in 1955 and was awarded the Order of Merit in 1963.
3 The 54,000-ton battleship, with eight 15-inch guns, was not completed until 1946. Later that year she was fitted with special accommodation for the royal tour of South Africa.

Royal Victorian Order] in recognition of his tuition of Princess Elizabeth in history. He made no demur. Leigh-Mallory, who left this country by air for Ceylon a day or two ago, has disappeared, and no trace can be found of his aeroplane. His wife was with him.

Sunday 19 November

Cadogan sent in a recommendation for an MBE for a secret agent whose trade name is 'Immortal'. His story is a most remarkable one, and shows him to have been largely instrumental in the wonderfully successful 'cover' that we built up before D-Day, as a result of which the Germans, long after we had landed in Normandy, continued to believe that our main attack would be on the Pas de Calais, to which they diverted divisions that might have turned the scale against us in those first critical days.

Tuesday 21 November

Other private secretaries have their troubles, too, thank God. They rang me up from No. 10 to say that Winston couldn't find the letter from the Duke of Windsor, and had we got it? I assured them that we hadn't, and advised them to look in the breast-pocket of the dinner jacket that he was wearing on 1 November, which is where I last saw it.

Wavell is at loggerheads with the Government, and may resign. If he does, the PM says he will recommend Sam Hoare as Viceroy. P.m. went with the King to look at the new Islamic Centre, now in Regent's Lodge, Regent's Park, once Lady Ribblesdale's home.

Wednesday 22 November

This afternoon I had – exceptionally – an interview every moment of which I enjoyed, the offering to Lord Gowrie[1] the use of Norman Tower, with the Deputy Constableship of Windsor. The old man was clearly delighted with the idea, bringing to him, as it would, relief from a weary period of house-hunting, apart from its financial amenities. Wavell's son, Archie John,[2] came to see the King, and had quarter of an hour with me first; he is here to get an artificial hand to replace that which the Japs blew off with an explosive bullet in the Chindit campaign, and when he has got it, will rejoin his regiment, the

---

1 Alexander Hore-Ruthven, 1st Earl of Gowrie (1872–1955), DSO and Bar, soldier, Gov.-Gen. of Commonwealth of Australia 1936–44, Deputy Constable and Lieut.-Gov. of Windsor Castle 1945–53.
2 Archibald John Wavell (1916–53), soldier, succeeded his father as 2nd Earl Wavell 1950.

Black Watch, in India. I liked him – he has a square, well-carved face, and is a great student of Shakespeare.

Thursday 23 November

The *Daily Express*, by an ingenious exposition of the difference in the ears of Hitler in his recent photographs and those of former years, proves fairly conclusively that the man in the former cannot be the real Hitler.

William Jowitt[1] came to kiss hands on his appointment as Minister of National Insurance. The first time I ever saw him was in September 1900, when, a new boy at Marlborough, I found him, a hulking lout, in Lower V, 2(a), the form in which I was placed. He stayed in it indefinitely, and would certainly have been superannuated had he not got into the cricket XI as a medium right-hand bowler of some merit. He became notorious for wearing a white *silk* shirt at cricket – a piece of athletic foppery sacred, in those days, to the immortal Ranjitsinhji.[2] Later on, he nearly killed me one evening at Oxford when, in the interval of a smoking-concert at Univ., I was admiring the Shelley memorial and he, two storeys up, dropped a full siphon of soda-water at my feet, missing my head by inches. Had he hit me, it is doubtful, I suppose, if he would ever have gone on to earn £15,000 per annum at the Bar and to become one of HM's Ministers.

Saturday 25 November

John told me this evening that Elspeth had asked for an amicable termination of their engagement. I am sorry, but not altogether surprised; he is too nearly of her age. The old formula, that a woman's age should be half the man's plus seven, generally holds good in nine cases out of ten.

Tuesday 28 November

Quite apart from the war, the world is a melancholy place just now: civil war threatening in Greece, Italy, Belgium, possibly Spain, not improbably France, and not impossibly USA; relations with USA very strained over civil aviation and Argentine meat; Russia, however friendly she may be in Moscow, con-

---

1 William Allen Jowitt (1885–1957), First Minister of National Insurance 1944–5, Lord Chancellor 1945–51. Created 1st Earl Jowitt 1951.
2 Kumar Shri Ranjitsinhji, HH Maharaja Jam Saheb of Nawanagar (1872–1933), incomparably elegant batsman for Sussex and England. In 1896 he headed the English batting averages with a record aggregate of 2,739 runs, and twice scored over 3,000 runs in a season.

stantly flouting us in the Balkans; Palestine and the Middle East all ripe for a flare-up; China disintegrating; and now, all the makings of a first-class row between the Viceroy and the India Office over the political programme. Sometimes one cannot help but feel that we are rushing towards a state of things dreadfully like Wells's forecast in *The Shape of Things to Come*. And, with all the men capable of taking charge dog-tired after five years of war, one does not know where to look for direction.

Wednesday 29 November

At 12.30 last night my bedside telephone rang just as I was finishing a chapter of Trollope's *The Prime Minister*, and there, appropriately enough, was Winston. He said he was too tired to start work on his speech on the Address, and that the only chance he saw of finishing it was to stop in bed this morning. Could the King excuse his non-attendance at the opening of Parliament? I said I was sure that the last thing the King would do on the eve of his (W.'s) seventieth birthday would be to refuse him such a request. W. said, 'It's hell being seventy.' I rejoined that it wasn't nearly such hell as being eighty, which made him laugh, and then I told him (in so many words) to go to bed and stop there – a vicarious decision which, I am glad to say, the King confirmed after breakfast this morning.

   Dined at Grillions – only Ilchester, J. Ridley and E. Devonshire; an agreeably small and congenial party. E.D. told us that the recent explosion of the ammunition-dump at Hunbury, Staffs, had broken all the windows at Hardwicke, over fifty miles away; and his sister Blanche Cobbold, whose house in Suffolk had 300 windows, now has none at all, owing to a flying bomb having hit in the park.

Friday 1 December

Princess Elizabeth yesterday launched *Vanguard* in John Brown's yard at Clydebank. It seems to have gone off very well, and tonight I got an ecstatic letter from the First Lord, praising her general deportment and the way in which she delivered her little speeches.

Saturday 2 December

The Times and the *Daily Telegraph* both announce today that 'The King *has appointed* the Duke of Sutherland to be his Lieutenant for the County of Sutherland'. This idiotic and very tiresome mistake is no doubt due to a misinterpretation of the word 'determining', which the Scottish Office ought to have explained to the Press before publishing the announcement in the *Edinburgh Gazette*. It is a good example of how misleading can be the legalistic use of words which have quite a different meaning in common speech.

Monday 4 December

The situation in Athens is bad. ELAS[1] are out to seize control, and something very like civil war is imminent. The number of rocket bombs arriving in this country (mostly in Essex and the Thames Estuary) is increasing slightly; hitherto the average has been about six or seven a day, but recently it has been about ten. Some of them burst in the air, and some fall in the river, but the others do considerable damage, though the casualties, as a rule, are not heavy.

Tuesday 5 December

The King authorised me to offer the OM to Professor Whitehead,[2] who, from the testimonials about him that have accumulated in my file, must be the brightest star in the British philosophical firmament since Darwin. He is eighty-three, but Edward Halifax, whom I consulted (Whitehead now lives at Harvard, where he used to be Emeritus Professor of Philosophy), says he is extremely vigorous, both in mind and body. I wish I could find somebody younger, but cannot; and, as somebody remarked the other day, posterity might think it a lasting disgrace to the OM if Whitehead should be allowed to die without it.

A remarkable telegram from Winston to F.D.R. gives a brilliant analysis of the Saragossan Sea of frustration into which the war has entered on all fronts. Pug Ismay, who came tea with me, said that W. had dictated this straight out of his head to his stenographer as he drove to London from Chequers, and that the Chiefs of Staff had only altered a very few words in the original draft.

The general situation of the war now is that we are, in the terminology of the last war, in for a prolonged period of trench-warfare until the spring. The promised Russian offensive in January, on top of continual pressure from us on land and in the air, might bring about a German collapse, but there seems little chance of any other decision before next summer. As Roosevelt seems disinclined to come over here, we are now trying to induce the American Chiefs of Staff to come. I am beginning to wonder if anything would be achieved if F.D.R. *did* come; Pug, today, for the first time, used that ominous word 'gaga'.

---

1 The National Popular Liberation Army, a Communist organisation formed to fight the occupying Germans.
2 Alfred North Whitehead, OM (1861–1947) mathematician and philosopher, professor

Balfour of Burleigh[1] came to see me with a scheme for getting disabled ex-servicemen to make a modern Bayeux tapestry of our Normandy campaign; quite a good idea.

Thursday 7 December

The first West End rocket arrived about 11 p.m. last night, falling in Duke Street, just behind Selfridge's.

Friday 8 December

Prince Charles of Belgium lunched with Their Majesties, and his two equerries, Barons de Macre and Goffinet, with us, the Household; nice men, whose hatred of the Germans blazed from their eyes. They both looked pretty hungry, and ate all they could get.

Robin Barrington-Ward dined with me at the Travellers. He said there were two essential measures for dealing with Germany after the war. (1) The *permanent* occupation of the country by Allied forces, in the same way that we permanently occupy India. (2) The integration of German heavy industry with that of Belgium, Holland etc. – a non-national cartel. Only by these means could the world be secured against the development of the new forms of warfare (flying bombs, rockets etc.) of which we have only seen, so far, the first embryonic stage.

The 'pastoralisation' of the Ruhr and Saar (Harry Hopkins's scheme) he dismissed as uneconomic; the loss of these industrial centres would impoverish all Europe. The political nostrums – the dismemberment of the Reich, revival of the ancient kingdoms, etc. – he thought quite futile, as I do myself.

Tuesday 12 December

The PM suggested today that the King should give the Garter to Eden, Alex and Monty. The King said No. As to Eden, it seemed to him all wrong to give it to the PM's lieutenant when the PM himself would not take it. At this, Winston (in the words of the King, reporting the interview to me later) 'became all blubby', and they seem to have fallen on each other's necks in an ecstasy of fraternal emotion. As to the two soldiers, the King wisely insisted that they should wait till the end of the war, for various reasons. It was quite on the cards that Alex might be unwilling to accept it now; Monty would

---

of philosophy Harvard University 1924–37.
1   George Bruce, 7th Lord Balfour of Burleigh (1883–1967), Representative Peer for Scotland 1923–63.

certainly not refuse it – and then where should we be? Winston eventually withdrew all his recommendations, leaving the King considerably elated at this unusual triumph.

Wednesday 13 December

Started out to walk to Grillions, but the fog was so thick that, after wandering for some time in the Green Park and Mall, with a foreign gentleman (I suspect he was a Polish officer, but never got a clear view of him), I put into Pratt's.

Thursday 14 December

The King's forty-ninth birthday. Two kings called on him, *et dona ferentes*:[1] Greece and Yugoslavia. There was a dance at Buckingham Palace, some forty couples, which John attended, but I did not. They danced in the Bow Room, and kept at it till past 3 a.m. Instead, I went to see Laurence Olivier's[2] film of *Henry V*. There are some beautiful scenes in it, and on the whole the colour photography, and the production, succeed; but in places it smells strong of Hollywood – though filmed, I believe, in Ireland; especially in the battle of Agincourt, where troops of knights on fleet hacks gallop about as if they were playing polo. I am sure that no charger of that day could raise more than a lumbering canter – the bowmen would certainly not have hit them otherwise. Also the French charge in the film took place over hard ground, whereas one of their chief handicaps in the actual battle was that they were bogged to the hocks. But I enjoyed it, and did not feel that any violence had been done to Shakespeare. George Robey[3] gave an admirable *tableau mourant* of Falstaff on his death-bed – his last interview with Hal, lifted from *Henry IV Part 2*, being spoken off, while he lay playing with the bed-clothes. Pistol was not good – a posturing baritone, instead of the roaring, bull-mouthed bass that he ought to be.[4]

Friday 15 December

Lehmann, Director-General of UNRRA,[5] came to see the King. I doubt if

---

1 '*Quidquid id est, timeo Danaos et dona ferentes.*' Of the wooden horse at Troy: 'Whatever it is, I fear the Greeks, even when they are bringing gifts.' Virgil, *Aeneid*, II, 48.
2 Laurence Olivier (1907–89), noted actor, especially in Shakespeare's plays. Knighted 1947, created Baron Olivier of Brighton (Life Peer) 1970.
3 George Robey (1869–54), actor and entertainer. Knighted 1954.
4 Pistol was played by Robert Newton, an actor with a bibulous reputation.
5 United Nations Relief and Rehabilitation Administration, formed 1943.

HM, who is always hypnotised by any eccentricity in dress, took his eyes off L.'s tie, which was a turquoise blue confection, covered with bronze lozenges, and embellished by a pearl as big as a sparrow's egg.

The King of Greece, who has not yielded an inch to the representations of Winston and Eden, sent W. a letter yesterday which, though eloquent and dignified, don't convince me that he is right in his refusal to nominate the Archbishop Regent. As I said to the King today, it's no use staking everything on a throne if you haven't got a country to put it in. The King of G. yesterday told the King that, at the stormy height of his last interview with the PM and Foreign Secretary (who, after the manner of Englishmen arguing with a foreigner, seem to have said it very loud and clear), Winston rose from his seat with a smile and, putting his hand on K. George's shoulder, said, 'I know, Sir, we ought not to be talking to you like this. Have some more brandy.'

Went to the Duke of Gloucester's flat in Curzon Street, to take informal leave of him and his Duchess [before he left to take up his position as Governor-General of Australia]. Her brother, Buccleuch, proposed their health which we drank in indifferent sherry. Two people told me today that when John [Lascelles] and Iris Peake were dancing together at the party last night, they were the handsomest couple in the room.

Sunday 17 December

Winston dropped one of his typical bombshells into the weekend by asking if the King would approve an earldom for old Lloyd George; and, in the same list, recommended L.G.'s private secretary (Sylvester[1]), who has had no part in public life for twenty-five years, for a knighthood. This seemed to me overdoing it, and both Bobbety and Bridges, whom I consulted on the telephone, agreed. So, I'm bound to say, did Winston himself, who rang me up later; he readily consented to withdraw Sylvester's name, and the King has now authorised me to tell him (W.) that he can sound L.G. I rather doubt whether the old man will take it. He could, of course, have had it for the asking in 1919, but preferred to violate the statutes of the OM, and got that instead. Telegram from Whitehead to say that he will be glad and proud to accept OM.

Monday 18 December

The German break-through has achieved considerable success; one of their two thrusts is within twenty miles of Liège, and two pockets of American

---

1   Albert James Sylvester (1889–1989), Principal Secretary to Lloyd George 1923–45.

troops, each about the strength of a brigade, are isolated, though still fighting. Our Intelligence seems to have been badly at fault, for the Germans have thrown in four or five divisions of whose presence we had no knowledge. But on the whole, and even if they do a certain amount of damage, it is not a bad thing that they should feel constrained to attack now.

Mackenzie King has sent Winston a telegram which filled me with rage, asking that no Canadian troops may be deployed in Greece, and that he may be allowed to announce the fact publicly. Winston sent him a strongly-worded rebuke for his poltroonery. Contrast Smuts, who sends telegrams full of wise counsel and is always helpful.

The Cabinet have agreed to take over Apsley House¹ on Gerry Wellington's terms; my impression is that His Grace has done pretty well out of the transaction.

Tuesday 19 December

Mackenzie King telegraphs that he has been misunderstood, and that he never meant to imply that he was going to make a public announcement. Lloyd George has accepted the earldom, rather to my surprise.

Chiefs of Staff's appreciation of Rundstedt's attack is that he has been ordered to delay our campaign at all costs, and has undertaken this undoubtedly hazardous – and even desperate – gamble feeling that, if it comes off, it will certainly interrupt our plans and our communications, while, if it don't, it will only hasten the inevitable end for the German Army, whose plight (in the opinion of the Cs of S) is already hopeless from the administrative angle. Thick fog, which can only benefit the Huns; it was considered bad enough to stop us going down to Windsor.

Saturday 23 December

The fog cleared on Thursday, and we got down to Windsor in time for luncheon, John driving me in our car. We all went to the Princesses' pantomime. It was too long, and the funny parts were not funny, but it was redeemed by a really charming and amusing ballet, a seaside scene in the nineties – rather like a Boudin picture. Princess Elizabeth, in clothes of the period, was, as the King remarked, extraordinarily like the photographs of Queen Mary at the same age.

The Greek skein (on the political side) is more tangled than ever; the Greeks are all sending each other contradictory telegrams verging on false-

---

1   Known as 'No. 1, London', on Hyde Park Corner.

hood, and it is not altogether apparent that King George himself is being entirely truthful.

The Government announced that they intend to produce another 250,000 men for the armed forces; and that the headlights of our motor-cars need no longer be masked. Reading Bryant's *The Years of Victory* with relish, and have begun Brett Young's *The Island*.

Sunday 24 December

After church this morning I pressed ten shillings into the hand of Griffith Philipps, aged ten; he thanked me elegantly, and then added, 'But are you quite sure, Sir, that you can spare it?' I assured him that if ever I were in great need, I would not fail to come to him, and ask for its return. Bright sun, after many days' fog, which should enable us to make things ugly for the German columns in Belgium and Luxembourg.

John Martin told me, for my ear alone, that the Prime Minister is plotting to fly out to Athens – and worse, that he might take Eden with him. They certainly should not both go; and for Winston to go may be magnificent, but it certainly ain't war – nor would his arrival necessarily bring peace to that distracted country. They would all promise to do what he told them, and then, as soon as he had left for home, do something entirely different.

Later. Winston telephoned to me at 5.35 p.m., saying that he proposed starting for Athens, with A.E., this evening, Charles Portal having guaranteed them a spell of exceptionally good flying weather. He had obviously made up his mind, and, equally obviously, nothing that I or even the King could say was going to shake him (it is rare that one gets a chance of saying anything when Winston has the telephone, plus the bit, between his teeth). So there was little I could do save to promise to put the proposition, for his approval, before the King. This I did at once; he took it with sang-froid, and at once rang up Winston himself.

Monday 25 December

The King delivered the [Christmas] broadcast excellently, with only one bad pause, on the hard G in 'God'; time, $7\frac{1}{2}$ minutes. Joan, John, Caroline and I dined at the Castle; 15 couples, and they danced to the gramophone till 1 a.m.

Wednesday 27 December

Kit Dawnay came to see me, bringing Part Six of Monty's story of the campaign, a highly inflammable document. He told me that for three days after

Rundstedt's attack started, SHAEF made no sort of communication at all to Monty. The latter, on his own initiative, moved our 30th Corps down to the area behind Liège–Dinant, and took charge of the Meuse bridges, all of which, save two, we have now blown up. Eisenhower, shortly afterwards, put M. in charge of the whole sector up to and including the northern flank of the German corridor, which flank is now stable. Eisenhower, according to Bedell Smith, finds great difficulty in giving a decision about anything. The fact is, he is quite incapable of directing armies in the field.

Winston is so exalted by the gallantry shown during the siege of Athens by the ladies employed in the Embassy, and at Scobie's[1] headquarters, that he has telegraphed home proposing that all fifteen of them be given immediate awards of BEM [British Empire Medal] and OBE. He asks my opinion, so I gave it to John Martin, who duly transmitted it; it is that, without questioning the bravery and devotion of these females in what has obviously been an unpleasant three weeks, such a mass-award is over-spectacular, and inequitable, in that it would actually be only possible through the accident of a visit to the scene of action by the Prime Minister, and that scores of their opposite numbers in London have, for over five years, gone faithfully to their work, undeterred by bomb, doodlebug and siren (which is just as testing of morale as are stray rifle bullets), knowing that only a fraction of them will ever be mentioned in any honours list. I pointed out, too, that the King and Queen had often visited towns heavily and continuously bombed, in which the local women have done devoted service; yet have always resisted the temptation to interfere with the normal stream of honours. The curious thing is that when, a little while ago, there was a foolish and semi-hysterical agitation for a shower of immediate honours, medals etc., for the 'men of Arnhem', it was Winston himself who killed it with a commonsense pronouncement in the House of Commons.

Friday 29 December

The Athens party reached London safely about 5 p.m. Winston rang me up about 7.30, after the Cabinet. He sounded well and tolerably cheerful, but was clearly dreading his interview with the King of Greece after dinner. He had to tell the latter, he said, that he had come back convinced that the only hope for Greece was for Archbishop Damaskinos[2] to be appointed Regent, and the only hope for the Monarchy was for the King of Greece to appoint

---

1 Lieut.-Gen. Sir Ronald Scobie (1893–1969), GOC Greece 1944–6.
2 Archbishop Damaskinos – originally Dimitrios Papandreou – (1891–1949), Archbishop of Athens 1938–49, Regent of Greece during the civil war of 1944–6. He resigned his office when Greece voted for the return of the Monarchy.

him; if the King refuses to do so, then he will be appointed by other means – and that will be the end of the King.[1] I was much relieved that Winston made no mention of the Fifteen Brave Ladies.

Saturday 30 December

The King of Greece agreed last night to appoint the Archbishop Regent; better late than never. It is now settled that Fisher be asked to be Cantuar. German U-boats are becoming more active; two American transports were torpedoed yesterday off Portland Bill, though both got to port. Winston tackled the King about the fifteen ladies, but HM would have none of them. Conrad Russell came to stay.

---

1   Writing to his friend John Gore after his retirement, Tommy recalled 'the best of all Winston's *obiter dicta* – his famous assessment, at Athens, of General Plastiras's value as an ally: "Well, gentlemen, it seems to me that we can't do better than put our money on General Plaster-arse, and hope that his feet are not made of clay." I would rather have said that than written Gray's elegy.'

1945

Monday 1 January

Heard from Lavinia that she reached Naples safely, Xmas eve. Joan and Caroline skated at Frogmore, p.m. Last night I finished *Years of Victory* [by Arthur Bryant, 1944], with great regret. However, I have now started to read it aloud to Joan.

Tuesday 2 January

Bertie Ramsay has been killed in an air crash, leaving Paris. A great loss to the Navy, and to the world. I liked him particularly.

Wednesday 3 January

Winston to F.D.R., apropos the recently-chosen rendezvous for the meeting of the Big Three: 'Everything can be arranged to your convenience. No more let us *falter*! From *Malta* to *Yalta*! Let nobody *alter*!'

The King sent me a copy of a letter from George Lascelles[1] to Princess Mary, saying that he has suddenly been transferred to Oflag IV C, where are also assembled John Elphinstone (the Queen's nephew), Romilly (Mrs Churchill's nephew), Haig (son of the late Field-Marshal) and Hopetoun (son of the ex-Viceroy). There is something rather sinister about this herding-together of all these boys with eminent relations, suggesting that they might be used as hostages. It is clear from George's letter that the same idea has occurred to him. Howard-Vyse[2] tells me that, as a matter of fact, Hopetoun and Romilly have been in this Oflag for a long time, owing to their bolshie attitude to their captors, and that a number of other young men, who have no claim to be 'well-connected', have also been moved there lately. Nonetheless, I am sending a copy of George's letter to the PM – who, at the moment, is visiting Eisenhower for a few days.

Thursday 4 January

---

1 B. 1923. Son of Tommy's cousin Harry, 6th Earl of Harewood and Princess Mary, the Princess Royal. He succeeded his father as 7th Earl in 1947.
2 Maj.-Gen. Sir Richard Howard-Vyse (1883–1962), Chairman Prisoner of War Dept of Red Cross and St John 1941–5.

As I hoped, Geoffrey Fisher, Bishop of London, has been appointed Arch-bishop of Canterbury. He was the only possible choice; but Winston, who declared he had been rushed over W. Temple's appointment, would not be satisfied until he had seen, and vetted, a number of other episcopal candidates. He has, of course, concerned himself little with church matters (like me), and hardly knows the difference between a dean and a deacon.

Geoffrey Fisher came to Marlborough on the same day as I did, forty-four years ago, and we went up the school together. At one time we were close friends, but in my somewhat bolshevik adolescence I found his muscular Christianity uncongenial, and though we were always on good terms, I saw little of him in my last year there, and still less when he came up to Oxford. In fact, I hadn't set eyes on him for a very long time till he came to Windsor to preach in 1941. Then, I liked him very much, and he delighted me when we went for a walk and came to a locked gate by vaulting over it, in all his episcopal caparison of top hat, apron and gaiters. He will be a quite different sort of archbishop from W. Temple – competent rather than inspiring – but I believe he will be a good one.

Friday 5 January

Walked this afternoon some way down the Long Walk, where for months past they have been cutting down Charles II's elm trees, which are con-demned as unsafe through elm disease. Most of their butts look pretty rotten to me, so they are probably well away. The further half of the Long Walk has now been re-planted with double avenues of chestnuts and planes alternately, which are already about seven feet high. In her middle years Princess Elizabeth will have to decide which of the two are to remain. I hope she plumps for the chestnuts; there are far too many planes about this place already.

The King of Greece has behaved in the most unaccountable manner. When they got back from Athens, Winston and Eden saw him, and, at his urgent request, gave him for his private and confidential record a note of their impressions of the attitude of the Regent-Archbishop on various points. Having promised, 'on his kingly honour', as Winston said in Tues-day's Cabinet, not to pass this on to anybody, he went home and telegraphed it to Papandreou, the late Prime Minister, who communicated it to the Press in Athens; and didn't even telegraph it correctly, for he made out that the Archbishop had said that he did not intend to have any representatives of EAM[1] in the new government; and that the Archbishop would, as Regent,

---

1   One of the Greek factions manoeuvring for power.

remain in close touch with the King, and be guided by him – both of which statements, in fact and by implication, are false. Unless King George can produce a really convincing explanation of this curious breach of confidence, it will be hard to feel any sympathy for him, whatever his fate may be.

There has been a considerable increase in the number of rockets and flying bombs in the last few days; one of the former landed on Chelsea Hospital on Wednesday, killing the doctor and his daughter, but not apparently doing much damage to the buildings.

Tuesday 9 January

Heavy snow showers – about two inches. Heard from Michael Adeane,[1] to whom I wrote recently suggesting that the time had come for him to return to us, that he would have no objection to this in two or three months' time.

Wednesday 10 January

Of the forthcoming meeting of the Big Three, Winston says in a telegram to F.D.R., 'This may well be a fateful conference, coming at a moment when the great Allies are so divided, and the shadow of the war lengthens out before us. At the present time, I think the end of this war may well prove to be more disappointing than was the last.' This is, for him, an uncharacteristically gloomy note; he may have sent it in one of his temporary depressions; or it may be calculated ground-bait, put out with the idea of warning the Americans that they have lately been dangerously self-centred.

As I anticipated, Peter of Yugoslavia has started asking if he can see the King; I have told him that HM is away for some time, and tried to convey that no good can come of such an interview. Peter has been told by the PM and Foreign Secretary, with the approval of the War Cabinet, that he ought to accept the arrangement proposed by Tito and Subasic,[2] and temporarily delegate his powers to a regency. He may not like this, though I'm convinced that only under some such arrangement can he have any hope of saving his crown. But, whether he likes it or no, he can do no good by trying to draw the King into it. It is not a personal matter, but an affair of State, involving high policy; consequently, the King can only endorse the advice already given by his own Ministers.

---

1 Who had been serving with the Coldstream Guards in NW Europe, where he was wounded and earned a Mention in Despatches.
2 Dr Ivan Subasic, former Governor of Croatia and leader of the Yugoslav government-in-exile.

About a week ago, Peter sent an ill-spelled but rather pathetic letter to the King, enclosing six sheets of typescript that he had already sent the PM, and asking the King to persuade Winston 'to see my point of view'. With the King's consent, I sent a copy of this missive to Winston, who, of course, only replied that he was doing what he thought right, in the best interests of both Yugoslavia and Peter, and that he could do no more. I urged the King to answer Peter only by a non-committal telegram, and not to attempt a letter. This, I understand, he has done. I gather that Peter himself is not unreasonable; but that as soon as he gets back to his mother-in-law[1], and the intransigent, die-hard Serbian politicians who advise her, she prevails on him to harden his heart and play the twopenny pharaoh.

Friday 12 January

King Peter yesterday announced his intention of making a statement to the Press, the gist of which was the contents of a further letter he has recently written to Winston, who has not yet had time to digest, still less answer, it. He was dissuaded from his first attempt, but loosed the thing off later in the day, and there it is, in all the newspapers this morning. This is not only a flagrant discourtesy to Winston and Eden, who have been doing their best for him, but is an unconstitutional act, since his own Ministers disapproved of what he wanted to say, and advised against his making any statement at all. He ends his statement with some crude flattery of Russia; this is very naïve – he won't get much encouragement from Stalin.

Sunday 14 January

Old Willy Desborough[2] is dead; after the evening service in St George's tonight, a memorial march was played, as always when a Knight of the Garter dies. Harris, the organist, chose the Nimrod march, from Elgar's *Enigma Variations*, which was appropriate to the old man, who was a mighty hunter if ever there was one. It was impressive, as is everything in that lovely place, with the banners above to remind one that chivalry never dies in England.

---

1 Princess Aspasia (1896–1972), Aspasia Manos, widow of King Alexander I of Greece.
2 William Henry Grenfell (1855–1945), created 1st Baron Desborough 1905. MP, acclaimed athlete and game shot. Among his achievements he listed 'swam twice across Niagara; stroked eight across Channel'. His elder son, Julian, author of 'Into Battle' and other poems, was Tommy's closest friend at Oxford. Both Julian and his brother Billy were killed in WWI.

Monday 15 January   London

Saw Budget Loyd,[1] GOC London District, about getting Michael Adeane
back here in April.

Tuesday 16 January

A little Dane called Muus came to see me, bringing a letter from King
Christian[2] to the King. He makes periodic trips here from Copenhagen,
and returns by parachute; next time, he is taking his wife back with him –
she, poor woman, has never yet jumped out of an aeroplane, for which she
is now having a course of instruction. He told me that the food situation
in Denmark is better than it is in England, and that a four-paged letter
could now be reduced photographically to the size of a pin's head.

Wednesday 17 January   Appleton

Queen Wilhelmina[3] has sent the King a copy of a memorial [sic] she has
addressed to the PM, pleading for immediate action to save the Dutch
nation from extinction, through famine and deportation. It is a heart-
rending document, and her fears are probably only too well founded. But
what can we do to help the poor Dutch – probably the most decent people
in Europe – save to go on trying to end the war as soon as possible? The
prospects of this happening look brighter since the spectacular advances
made by the Russians in the last few days. They have covered an amazing
amount of ground, so quickly that one wonders if there were any Germans
on it.

Saturday 20 January

The Bishop of Norwich,[4] who arrived last night, enlivened the evening by
going off into a dead faint in the drawing-room after dinner, while the King
was telling golf stories. I had just time to steer him into an armchair
before he became unconscious; we then laid him out on the floor, and H.

---

1 Gen. Sir Charles Loyd (1891–1973), GOC London District 1944–7.
2 King Christian X of Denmark (1912–47) retained his throne throughout the war, and
   did his best to maintain a show of independence from the occupying Germans.
3 Queen Wilhelmina of the Netherlands (1880–1960) acceded to the throne at the age of
   ten. In 1940 she fled to England, whence she sought to keep up the morale of her people
   by weekly broadcasts. After the end of the war she returned to Holland, and ruled until
   1948, when she abdicated in favour of her daughter Juliana.
4 Rt. Rev. Percy Herbert (1885–1968), Bishop of Norwich 1942–59.

Campbell, acting on medical lore picked up in some naval cockpit, vig-orously massaged his legs and stomach. Whether as a result of this treat-ment, or in spite of it, he eventually came to after about twenty minutes, and we got him to bed and summoned the doctor from Dersingham[1] to have a look at him.

Sunday 21 January

The Bishop, apparently none the worse for his syncope, preached a good sermon about death, in Sandringham church, and took a brisk walk with me after luncheon. He is a good, broad-minded man.

Monday 22 January

Princess Margaret has got mumps. Nobody else in the house has had it, so we are very vulnerable.

Tuesday 23 January

Harry Hopkins arrived from USA. I had not seen him since the summer of 1940. He said, rather gloomily, that the Russian advance across Poland was going to provide them with many political problems. Maybe, but a Russian advance across Silesia – should it happen – will solve several more.

Peter of Yugoslavia yesterday dismissed his Cabinet, without any warning. This will probably finish him. Yesterday, Ralph Stevenson,[2] our Ambassador, went to see him. Though Peter knew that R.S. was the bearer of a personal letter from Winston, he refused to receive him; just damned impudence.

Friday 2 February

The only news of the past ten days has been the spectacular advance of the Russians to the line of the Oder, and arctic weather all over England, with constant snow-storms and sharp frost, until Wednesday, when a rapid thaw set in.

Monty came to luncheon. He was in high spirits, as Eisenhower has come round to his way of thinking, and is giving him most of what he wants for the conduct of his forthcoming operations, due to start on the eighth.

---

1 Sir Frederic Willans (d. 1949), Surgeon-Apothecary to HM Household at Sandringham since 1924.
2 Sir Ralph Stevenson (1895–1977), Ambassador to Yugoslavia 1943–6.

Saturday 3 February

One of the aeroplanes on its way to the pre-'Argonaut'[1] meetings at Malta got out of its course and crashed in the sea somewhere near Lampedusa; there is, as yet, no explanation. The only survivor is an Air Commodore Sanderson; among the dead are Barney Charlesworth, the CIGS's ADC, and Peter Loxley. The latter is a great loss to me personally, and to the public service; he was quite the most promising of the younger men at the Foreign Office, and certainly had a distinguished future before him. I have seen a good deal of him in the last few years, both in the way of business – he was Alec Cadogan's secretary – and at the Travellers and Pratt's; he had a delightful and distinguished mind, was well-read, and fond of fishing. I like to think that it was with my gaff, which I had lent him, that he killed his last salmon, in the Don last spring. He married Guy Dawnay's daughter, who had a still-born child only a few days ago. So his life had a sad and anxious close. His father also died at sea, for he was in command of HMS *Audacious*, which sank in Lough Swilly early in the last war.

Sunday 4 February

I represented the King at the installation of Henry Marten as Provost, in Eton chapel. Joan came with me, under Miss Marten's wing. After the service, which was short and impressive, we adjourned to the Head Master's house and drank coffee.

Both the RAF and the Americans have given Berlin a drastic bombing in the last twenty-four hours. The chaos there, with refugees pouring in and troops trying to pour out, must be indescribable. Thrushes singing in Frogmore – the first time this year.

Monday 5 February

Cartier told me at luncheon that the Belgians still have no idea where King Leopold is incarcerated by the Germans, and have no means of communicating with him.

Tuesday 6 February

Saw Oliver Stanley in the Colonial Office, p.m. He has just returned from a tour in West Indies etc., in the course of which he spent some time in the

---

1 Code-name for the conference at Yalta, in the Crimea.

Bahamas. He said the Duke of Windsor looked remarkably young and well, and was still obviously in love with his wife; moreover, he was a competent Governor, and knew all there was to know about his islands. The Duke evinced no desire to come back to this country, at any rate for any length of time; he wants to avoid any tropical, or sub-tropical, climate, as his wife can't stand heat. O.S. thought that what he would really like is the Embassy at Washington, but agreed with me that this was not on, and that the best solution was the one which I have always advocated – that he make himself a home in USA.

Geoffrey Fisher came to do homage as Archbishop. The Home Secretary, who was in attendance, told me that he doubted if he could hang Mrs Jones, the villainess of the 'Cleft Chin' murder[1] – not because she didn't deserve hanging, but because public opinion in this country would not stand for the execution of a girl of nineteen.

I had to write today a letter of sympathy from the King and Queen to a poor woman, a Mrs Lane, who has just lost her *fourth* son in the RAF. This was made all the more difficult because she had already been sent all the usual clichés of condolence in a letter from here when the second boy was killed, and in another from A. Sinclair after the third's death.

Algernon Cecil has sent me a copy of his book *A House in Bryanston Square*. It is a fanciful life of Guendolen, who, from what I've seen of it, would probably have thought it rather dreadful.[2]

Wednesday 7 February

The Russians yesterday established themselves on the west bank of the Oder, on a stretch of fifty miles. This should make Berlin untenable before long. I have in cold storage a telegram from the King to send to Kalinin, as soon as the Russians get there; and another for Dickie Mountbatten, when he takes Mandalay.

---

1 On 7 Oct. 1944 a London taxi driver, George Edward Heath, who had a cleft chin, was shot dead at Staines. Private Gustav Hulten, a 23-year-old American serviceman who had gone absent without leave, was arrested, along with his accomplice, Elizabeth Jones. After a trial at the Old Bailey in Jan. 1945 both were convicted. Hulten was hanged at Pentonville on 8 Mar. but Jones was reprieved and released two days before the date set for her execution.

2 Algernon Cecil (1879–1953), author and historian, had married Lady Guendolen Osborne (1885–1933) in 1923. Daughter of the 10th Duke of Leeds, famous among contemporaries for her beauty and wit, she was Tommy's most devoted correspondent in their youth, particularly during WWI. After her death Cecil returned Tommy's letters to her: he had them typed, and edited them for possible publication, but never carried the project through.

Thursday 8 February

Sir Edward Appleton, FRS,[1] who runs the Government's Scientific Research department, came to see me, to advise about 'hush-hush' places which the King wants to visit; a genial little man, who looks like a fox-hunter, and is an ardent Trollopian. I asked him about the progress of the harnessing of the atom: apparently you can't do this without about ten acres of laboratories etc., and had the Germans got such a layout, we should certainly know about it. Our own outfit has been transported to USA, since it was considered too vulnerable for this country during the Blitz; there, with help readily-given by American scientists, there has been rapid development.

Appleton did not think that there would be time to use any sort of atom-filled bomb against the Germans, but there might be an opportunity of doing so in Japan. I asked what would be the result. 'Oh,' he answered, 'a couple of them would end the war overnight – there is no doubt about that.' I said that it might be a good thing if humanity were given proof of the effects of these fearful engines, as it might convince it that any further indulgence in war would inevitably end in its own annihilation. He said that the deterrent aspect was an important one, and had not been overlooked; but, apart from its military side, the atom had immense commercial possibilities, and was destined to replace the world's already-dwindling resources of coal and oil. I wish I understood these things better.

He also told me that he had himself discovered the existence of the Ionoform Ceiling, which enables us to wireless direct to Australia and New Zealand; without it, our messages would fly off at a tangent into space. This ceiling is very susceptible to atmospheric influences, particularly sunspots; but Appleton has evolved some system of predicting these vagaries, and can advise the BBC exactly what wavelength must be used to counteract them, on any given day.

Friday 9 February

William Haley,[2] the new Director of the BBC, who was for years on the staff of the *Manchester Guardian*, to see the King. He looks capable enough, but was afflicted by that tongue-tiedness which attacks many people when they first come to Buckingham Palace, and I was only beginning to thaw him out when he was summoned to his audience.

---

1 Sir Edward Appleton (1892–1965), physicist and specialist in wireless telegraphy. Secretary, Dept of Scientific and Industrial Research 1939–49, winner of Nobel Prize for Physics 1947.
2 William Haley (1901–87), Director-General of the BBC 1944–6, editor of *The Times* 1952–66. Knighted 1946.

Sunday 11 February

Spent much of the day wrestling with innumerable telegrams to and from the Yalta Conference ('Argonaut').[1] They bear the appropriate code-names, of 'Jason' (incoming) and 'Fleece' (out). It is going well, and Uncle Joe seems pretty tame, but he wants his pound of flesh over Poland, dismemberment of Germany, and reparations. I should have thought that, after our experiences in the last post-war period, the idea of *cash* reparations was dead and buried; but Uncle Joe thinks different. He is very cheerful about the military situation; says that Rundstedt's Christmas offensive was foolish and wasteful, and that the Germans now have no generals left save Guderian,[2] 'and he is an adventurer'. If the Germans leave Berlin, he means to pursue them to Dresden, and beyond if necessary.

Monday 12 February

An advance copy of the official pronouncement on the Crimea Conference reached me this afternoon; it was made public at 9.30 p.m. It is, I suppose, one of the most important documents in the history of the world, which may have deeper effects on the human race than such relatively local landmarks as Magna Carta, the Edict of Nantes, or the Declaration of Independence. It seemed to me highly satisfactory, both in its general terms, and in particular because it indicates that we, broadly speaking, have got our way in most of the matters on which we set store – e.g., Poland, the future participation of the French, the dismemberment of Germany question, etc. Reparations 'in kind' are mentioned, but nothing said about cash, though the Russians may well return to the charge about this at the next conference, which, it is boldly announced, will meet at San Francisco on 25 April.

My general impression, after reading all the conference telegrams, is that the Americans have supported us loyally, and the Russians have been far more accommodating than one might have expected. This is perhaps partly due to the realisation by the Russians that in the post-war period they will be greatly dependent on us and USA for their financial and industrial rehabilitation. But I suspect that Joe Stalin has a real personal regard, and admiration, for Winston, and this no doubt has helped too. What we should have done at these conferences without Winston, one cannot imagine;

---

1   The Yalta Conference between 'the Big Three' – Roosevelt, Churchill and Stalin – took place in the Crimea between 4 and 11 Feb.
2   Gen. Heinz Guderian (1888–1954), tank warfare specialist, resigned Mar. 1945 when Hitler refused to accept his advice.

nobody else but he could have carried our flag so resolutely and so wisely, for he has always shown himself a reasonable and sympathetic negotiator.[1]

Before sending the report in to the King, I rang up Attlee and asked him if the general feeling of the Cabinet towards it was one of satisfaction, and he assured me that it was. It will catch the German propagandists out. They have been forecasting some sort of peace offer, after the manner of Wilson's Fourteen Points. But there is not the faintest hint of any such thing – only a stern reiteration of the Casablanca 'No Surrender' formula.

Tuesday 13 February

Dined with the Devonshires, to meet, for the first time, Peter Cheyney,[2] who has long been one of my favourite authors. Though rather gross in appearance, he is good fun, and talks with engaging freedom about his books and their making. Despite the mastery of the American idiom which he shows in all of them, he has never been in USA in his life. A fabulous number of his works have been printed for sending out to the troops, on all fronts – I think he said five million. A lady once wrote to him to say that Lemmy Caution, his most famous creation, drank more in a day than was humanly possible – her husband was a drunkard, so she ought to know. Cheyney replied that, in the year 1938, he had habitually drunk more *per diem* than he had ever poured down the throat of Lemmy, and he was at the time a member of the English fencing team.

Thursday 15 February

Caroline's seventeenth birthday. Joan and I gave her a set of Racine, which she coveted.

Leathers to see the King on his return from Yalta. He told me that the 'give and take' atmosphere of the conference had been excellent, and that after some initial difficulty he had got practically all he wanted out of USA in the matter of shipping and oil. Winston, in a telegram to Attlee, says that it was a different Russia from any he had known hitherto. He and Eden had a great welcome in Athens yesterday, where he was given the Freedom of Athens – still something on which a man may plume himself, though Pericles be dead twenty-four centuries.

---

1 In fact Stalin had a higher regard for Roosevelt than for Churchill; but by the time of the conference the American President was seriously ill, and visibly deteriorating.
2 Peter Cheyney (Maj. Reginald Evelyn Peter Southouse-Cheyney), 1896–1951, journalist, editor and prolific author of thrillers.

Sunday 18 February

John Martin writes to me from the PM's aeroplane, approaching Alexandria, on the 15th: 'It would not be unfair, I think, to say that the Americans' contribution to the conference was the lightest, and there is no doubt that the President is now much below his best form. Uncle Joe gets on excellently with the PM, and sees the funny side of everything.'

Living conditions at Yalta do not seem to have been as bad as they had anticipated, though he speaks of 'sixteen American colonels in one bedroom'. Sebastopol, he says, is 'a complete and utter ruin – one can understand the Russian demand for reparations.' He obviously considers the conference to have been, in sum, a great success; and the day in Athens was a triumph.

John Gore and family came over to luncheon. He left with me a Shakespeare-Bacon book by a man called Roderick Eagle. I have, in a general way, little use for Baconians, but once I had started this book, I could not put it down. The evidence he adduces for Bacon is more convincing than any I have yet read, though I daresay it has all been published elsewhere. The parallels between passages from Bacon, and passages dealing with the same thought in Shakespeare, are very striking, as is the cover of the file found in Northumberland House eighty years ago, with its strange, inconsequent contemporary doodlings of the names of S. and B.

Why should any sensible scribbler, whoever he may have been, have conjoined the two names, not once but many times, all over a sheet of foolscap, if there was not some significant link between them? I don't much care who did or who did not write 'Shakespeare', any more than I care who built Westminster Abbey. But, if Bacon's claim is ever proved, he will emerge, with all his other attainments, as the greatest of all Englishmen.

Monday 19 February

The PM and fellow-Argonauts returned safely this afternoon. Alan Herbert, who knows Monty well, tells me that M. is quite serious in his wish to be considered for the headship of an Oxford college after the war.

Tuesday 20 February

Saw Bridges p.m.; he is generally satisfied with the results of 'Argonaut'; its highlight is the definite undertaking by USA to do their share of helping to put Europe on its feet; its low light, the failure to reach a final conclusion as to the voting rights on the World-Reconstruction Council.

I got John Martin to dine with me at the Travellers. He told me much the same tale as Bridges. The initial dinner-party at Yalta was a very sticky affair; Stalin was out of humour, and refused to drink the toast of the King, saying he was a republican. But next day the atmosphere cleared, and all was merry and bright; nor did Uncle Joe demur to drinking any toast that was proposed at the subsequent dinner-parties. (Incidentally, at the first dinner, Roosevelt made a somewhat elephantine effort to make the party go, by saying cheerily, 'You know, we always refer to you as "Uncle Joe".' This well-intentioned sally had exactly the opposite effect to what was intended, and Stalin's brow, from being merely overcast, became thunder-black.)

J.M. showed me the bill of fare of one of these Belshazzars – a list of dainties about a foot long, which makes the mouth of any strictly-rationed Londoner water; also the roll of those in attendance on Ibn Saud[1] for his weekend in Cairo, about forty souls, including an astrologer and a brace of 'coffee-tasters'. Ibn Saud sounds as if he were a worthy successor to Solomon – a magnificent figure of a man who keeps not less than 400 concubines. He embarrassed Winston by giving him an Arabian Nights chest of rare gifts, at the bottom of which was a diamond ring worth £750, not to mention ropes of Red Sea pearls, etc. Winston formed a low opinion of Haile Selassie, but did not think so badly of Farouk. He, Mrs Churchill and Eden dined with the King and Queen this evening, and kept it up till 1 a.m.

Wednesday 21 February

On my way home from luncheon I found an excellent pair of secateurs, which we badly need for the roses at Winchester Tower, in Hill's shop, 1 Haymarket; this is great luck, as such things are practically extinct – and these only cost 4s 6d.

Friday 23 February

Ismay told me that his impression of F.D.R. at Yalta was that he was more than half gaga, and might not last many months. Like everybody else, he was impressed by the change for the better in the Russian attitude; they were far more forthcoming and far less suspicious than ever before.

Tuesday 27 February

Lunched with Archbishop Cosmo Lang, whose mind is as good as ever,

---

1   Ibn Saud Abd al-Aziz (1880–1953), King of Saudi Arabia.

despite his evident physical frailty (he is eighty-one). He gave me good, and welcome, advice on sundry matters. I asked him if, in his long life, he had noticed any tendency among Ministers, and government minions generally, to encroach on the privileges of the Crown, or in any way to circumscribe its dignity. He said, almost indignantly, that no such tendency existed – rather the contrary.

Thursday 1 March

Went p.m. with Their Majesties to see Top Selborne's secret exhibition of SOE appliances in the South Kensington Natural History Museum; this was so interesting that the visit, estimated at forty-five minutes, lasted one and a half hours. We saw a great diversity of death-dealing devices, as used by the Maquis, paratroops, commandos etc., and some very ingenious methods of communication. I had a special interest in it all, as I saw the birth of SOE from MI (R), the department of the War Office in which I was a voluntary worker during the summer of 1940.[1]

The Russians are behaving in a sinister way in Bucharest, where Vyshinsky[2] is bullying King Michael into forming a minority Communist government, with tactics redolent of Hitler. Winston has not yet intervened, pending further news from Moscow. It may be that Vyshinsky is acting on his own, and will be called to order by Stalin when the latter realises how he is behaving; but I don't accept this theory with any great confidence.

Sunday 4 March

The King and Queen attended the morning service in Eton chapel, and afterwards, in the presence of the whole school, HM knighted Henry Marten on the steps in School Yard. Marten had said to me that, as soon as he knelt down on the 'fold-stool', the thoughts of every boy present would inevitably turn to the whipping-block; if so, they suppressed any outward indication of it, for the solemn hush was not broken by even a titter. On the other hand, when, as we were sitting in chapel, waiting for the royal arrival, the air-raid warning sounded above our heads, I was pleased to notice a broad grin on the face of every boy opposite me. I wish Hitler could have seen that, after five years of war, the morale of our youth is still so high that they can only see the humorous side of such an incident. The

---

1   Special Operations Executive, the undercover sabotage and espionage organisation, developed out of the earlier MI (R).

2   Andrei Vyshinsky (1883–1954), aggressive courtroom lawyer, prosecutor in many Soviet show trials during the 1930s. Stalin's Deputy Commissioner for Foreign Affairs 1940–9, Foreign Minister 1949–53. Always a vitriolic opponent of the US.

all-clear went as we started the first hymn. After the accolade had been given, we repaired to the Fellows' Library, that very beautiful room, where coffee and cakes were distributed by a party of hand-picked young sprigs of the aristocracy. The boys sang excellently in chapel, and the descant of the two hymns was a delight to hear.

Meanwhile, the Battle of the Rhine is nearing its end – or rather the end of the cis-rhenane[1] phase; we still have to get across the river. With an insolence that one can but admire, the Germans have renewed attacks with flying bombs and aircraft on this country (not v. successfully), and have made a sally to a depth of two and a half miles from their beleaguerment in the Gironde. But they have withdrawn permission to the Swedish Red Cross to send a party into North Germany to arrange the evacuation of certain Danish and Norwegian internees, and Stockholm infers that this is because they daren't let the Swedes see how bad things are with them internally.

Tuesday 6 March

Lunched with Lady Willingdon, where we were all astounded by the appearance of a female air commodore in a red wig; on closer examination, it proved to be Mrs Corrigan, a well-known American hostess between the wars.

Wednesday 7 March

Before he left yesterday, the King signed a conditional pardon for Mrs Jones [the murderer]. There is a heavy correspondence going on about the case in *The Times*, stimulated by a long letter on capital punishment from George Bernard Shaw.[2] Joan Bright dined with me, and gave me an amusing account of the domestic arrangements at Yalta (of which she was in charge), and news of Lavinia, whom she saw in Italy on her way back.

Oliver Stanley has forwarded the Duke of Windsor's formal application to be relieved of his governorship, together with a note for the Press, drafted by HRH himself; it contains two bad grammatical errors.

Dawson of Penn died this morning. I shall miss him; he was a good friend to me, and gave me valuable advice on many occasions. I always enjoyed talking to him. He never allowed his age to appear in any book of reference, but his secretary told me he was nearer eighty than seventy-five.

---

1   On this side of the Rhine.
2   Irish playwright (1856–1950), (*Man and Superman, Androcles and the Lion, Pygmalion* etc.), winner of the Nobel Prize for Literature (1925). Latterly gave recreation as 'Being past ninety'.

The Americans occupied Cologne yesterday; the Russians have made a spectacular stride to the shores of the Baltic.

Thursday 8 March

Arthur Penn and I went to the Churchill Club this evening, to hear A. L. Rowse[1] lecture on 'Shakespeare and His Age', with R. A. Butler in the chair. Rowse is a discursive lecturer, continually darting up side-alleys, but they are usually amusing ones; he talks of the Elizabethans with the enthusiasm of a true prophet. He hopes for an intellectual burgeoning in this country after we have emerged from our present troubles, similar to that which occurred in Elizabethan England when they had rid themselves of the Spanish menace; but one thing we must do is to become less sophisticated and pay more attention to art and less to art critics.

He only touched lightly on the question of the authorship of the plays, and confined himself to telling us the known facts (such as they are) about Shakespeare of Stratford. A. Penn asked me why, when the Elizabethans had so recently triumphed over Spain, there is no allusion to the Armada, and hardly any to Spaniards generally, in the whole of Shakespeare. I don't know the answer; perhaps it was too recent, or perhaps it was politically too delicate a subject to play with. Maybe the omission is due to a sort of subconscious escapism – as Jane Austen never alluded to the Napoleonic war.

The PM is justifiably disturbed at Molotov's attitude, so inconsistent with the Yalta agreements, over Poland and Romania.

Friday 9 March

Radescu,[2] the late Prime Minister of Romania, has sought sanctuary in the British Legation, fearing for his life. Winston, with true Palmerstonian spirit, has told our people they may open fire on anybody who may try to remove him by force. I believe the total strength of our garrison is a sergeant and twelve men, with one sub-machine gun. Meanwhile, Winston has sent a long telegram to Roosevelt, saying that the Russian handling of both Romania and Poland constitutes a test case, and that we ought to make it clear to them now that we do not think they are correctly interpreting the Yalta agreement. It will be a terrible thing if, after declaring in the House of Commons that they had implicit confidence

---

1   Alfred Leslie Rowse (1903–96), prolific, combative author and historian, specialising in studies of Shakespeare and the Elizabethans.

2   Nicolae Radescu (1874–1953) had been interned in a concentration camp by the Germans during the war, but regained power during the anti-Fascist coup of Aug. 1944, only to be forced out of office, and of the country, by Soviet pressure.

in Stalin's good faith, Winston and Eden have to eat their words.

Went to a small party given by the Harold Nicolsons in their rooms in King's Bench Walk, where I saw for the first time the devastation suffered by the Temple in the Blitz. I had not met Vita Nicolson since we both stayed with the Wellingtons at Ewhurst in 1911. Julian Huxley[1] was there, looking very ill after malaria and what he called 'an old-fashioned nervous breakdown'; Desmond MacCarthy,[2] the ineffable sophist C. E. M. Joad;[3] and some long-haired young men. That done, we drove down to Windsor. The King and Queen spent the day at Rosyth, saying goodbye to *Implacable*, who is just off to the Pacific.

Saturday 10 March

The American capture of the Remagen bridge seems to have been a very dashing feat of arms – an unexpected windfall, of which the troops on the spot took prompt and praiseworthy advantage.

Ran into Princess Elizabeth, wearing her new ATS uniform, in which she looks a duck. I consulted Findlater Stewart[4] yesterday about the advisability of Their Majesties visiting one or another of those districts in which rocket bombs have been falling regularly for the past two months, knowing that he was in charge of the organisation which is engaged in misleading the Germans – I believe most successfully – as to the targets reached by these beastly missiles. As I anticipated, he said that any such visit would inevitably prejudice his plans, and he begged urgently that we would resist suggestions in that sense. Such visits by Their Majesties would inevitably reveal to the Germans that their rockets are not falling in the heart of London, as they believe, but in districts wide of the target, and would consequently lead them to adjust their sights, so to speak.

Monday 12 March

Wolff,[5] the chief SS man in Italy, and other Germans have made

---

1 Sir Julian Huxley (1887–1975), zoologist, biologist and author.
2 Sir Desmond MacCarthy (1877–1952), author and literary critic.
3 Cyril Edwin Mitchinson Joad (1891–1953), notoriously mendacious author, broadcaster, university lecturer in philosophy.
4 Sir Samuel Findlater Stewart (1879–1960), temporary Director-General of the Ministry of Information 1939, on special duty 1940–45.
5 SS General Karl Wolff (1900–84), Himmler's CoS, in Feb. 1945 made secret peace overtures to the Allies. Later Hitler gave him permission to continue negotiations, in the hope of stalling for time. After the war Wolff was sentenced by a German court to four years' imprisonment, but was released after a week. In 1962 he was arrested, charged with the murder of Jews and sentenced to fifteen years in prison, but released in 1971 for good behaviour.

overtures to Alex, suggesting that they are prepared to discuss the 'capitulation' of the German armies in Northern Italy. It is admitted that this move has been made without the authority of Kesselring.[1] Our Chiefs of Staff are very suspicious, but, with Washington's concurrence, Alex has been authorised to send two of his people to Switzerland, where Wolff & co. have already arrived; but it has been enjoined on him that no meeting is to take place until Moscow has been brought into the picture.

Walked home [after dinner] in a perfect night with Vincent Massey and Jasper Ridley, who have plunged themselves into a proper hornets' nest by intimating to Lindsay,[2] Master of Balliol, that they and other old Balliol men are dissatisfied with his conduct of the college. He has demanded, not unnaturally, to be confronted with his critics, so they have jointly invited him to dinner. It will not be a very convivial evening.

Wednesday 14 March

Alan Brooke told me that Rundstedt had now been superseded by Kesselring; the former has been drinking heavily – and God knows, he has had enough to drive him to it. Kesselring's Italian army is now in a bad way as regards supplies, especially petrol. It takes them fourteen days to move one division back across the Alps, so that a mass evacuation, in face of our bombers, would hardly be practicable. Perhaps Alex may yet be able to round them up.

Walter Elliot[3] came, just back from his tour of Russia with the Parliamentary delegation, which was a well-chosen one, in that it embraced all shades of political opinion. Walter had been in Merv and Tashkent, etc., places where they had scarcely seen an Englishman for fifty years, and found them charming and cultivated people. In Tashkent *Othello* is given at the theatre about three times a month.

---

1 Field-Marshal Albert Kesselring (1885–1960), one of Hitler's most able strategists, took over command of German armies in the west in 1944. It was he who surrendered the southern half of German forces on 7 May 1945. In 1947 he was sentenced to death for war crimes, but reprieved in 1952.
2 A. D. Lindsay (1879–1952), Master of Balliol 1924–49. Created 1st Baron Lindsay of Birker of Low Ground 1945.
3 Rt. Hon. Walter Elliot (1888–1959), MP, Director of Public Relations, War Office, 1941–2.

Admiral Land,[1] US Navy, came after luncheon – an engaging, friendly little man, who told me he had started life as a cow-puncher in Wyoming. He is now head of the War Shipping administration in USA, the counterpart of Lord Leathers. He has been a consistently good friend to this country, and we owe him much. He gave me a better account of Roosevelt, and said that the Yalta photographs had given a false impression of him; he was 'having trouble with his dentures', which had affected his speech and caused his face to fall in unduly.

Friday 16 March

Our silver wedding day. My sisters gave us a fine Crown Derby tureen, Lavinia a pair of silver wine coasters, and Lady Chelmsford a silver mustard pot. Joan, John and I had for dinner (at Windsor) one of the three bottles of champagne left in my cellar at St James's. When our golden wedding comes, I shall be all-but eighty-three; but sufficient for the day is the evil thereof. Patton is making another of his spectacular dashes in the direction of Mannheim.

Tuesday 20 March

He has dashed to some purpose. The 3rd and 7th US Armies have practically overrun the Koblenz-Saarbrücken-Mannheim triangle, where they must be doing immense damage to whatever German forces remain in it. Mandalay has at last fallen to us, and I've got off the King's telegram to Dickie Mountbatten, which I have been nursing uneasily for the last fortnight.

Wednesday 21 March

Cunningham,[2] C-in-C Mediterranean, came today; he gave a good account of Lavinia, to whom he has been most hospitable. The Admiralty are still anxious about the new German U-boats, to which we have not yet found the answer. C. said that one of them lay up alongside a wreck off Gibraltar recently, and sat on the bottom of the sea for seven days and seven nights without surfacing. That sort of life must be an almost unbearable strain on any crew.

---

1   Adm. Emory S. Land (1879–1971), Chairman US Maritime Commission 1938–45.
2   Adm. of the Fleet Sir John Cunningham (1885–1962), C-in-C Mediterranean 1943–6. First Sea Lord and Chief of Naval Staff 1946–8.

Friday 23 March

This morning, I had a letter from M. Nixon[1] to say that Guy has been seriously wounded in Burma. I got Mayne, Military Secretary at the India Office, to telegraph about him, and heard tonight that the boy had died on 21 March – the third of my nephews to go in this war. Rang up Fergus Nixon, and the Balfours.[2]

Joan came with me to a matinée of *Richard III* at the New Theatre: Laurence Olivier as Richard, N. Hannen[3] as Buckingham, and some indifferent women. It was a one-man show, as indeed it must be, for it is not a play, but a psycho-analytic exposition of the development of a sadistic megalomaniac; whether Richard was really that, I doubt. Olivier was good, though somewhat shrill and hysterical in the later acts. The play began at two and ended at five, and at 6.15 the unfortunate actors were due to do it all over again.

Saturday 24 March   **Windsor**

'Plunder' started a.m. today, and we have now got four bridgeheads across the Rhine between Emmerich and Hamborn. All apparently going well, and Patton has further enlarged his bridgehead at Oppenheim. The PM has gone over to see the battle, taking the CIGS with him. Another lovely spring day – about the tenth in succession; this weather has been a godsend for all the preliminaries of 'Plunder'; and I pray that it may hold for a bit, though the glass is falling. Heard first chiffchaff, on the slopes.

Sunday 25 March

News very good; all bridgeheads held and enlarged, and Patton has taken Darmstadt and reached Aschaffenburg, thirty-five miles on. Winston has been rowing about on the Rhine; he telegraphed to John Martin that our casualties had been remarkably light. There were no rockets in this country in the past twenty-four hours.

Monday 26 March

Saw Ismay, and arranged for despatch of congratulatory telegrams from

---

1 Tommy's sister Maud had married Lieut.-Col. Fergus Nixon in 1912.
2 Tommy's sister Daisy and her husband Melville Balfour.
3 Nicholas Hannen (1881–1972), actor, lived for many years with the actress Athene Seyler, having to wait for the death of his own wife in 1960 before he could marry her.

the King to Eisenhower and to Montgomery. I'm a little nervous about using the phrase 'great and glorious victory', but I believe that the passage of the Rhine will rank as such, and there is very little risk of a setback now. One of 'C's' reports describes how the Nazis have been pouring stores of food, and their wives, into the 'Nazi redoubt' in the Bregenzerwald. Winston returned from the Rhine. Their Majesties, with Mima Harlech, H. Campbell and me, left Euston for Liverpool 7 p.m.

Tuesday 27 March

A naval day in Liverpool. Spent a.m. on board the *Duke of York*, which leaves shortly for the Far East. Lunched with Max Horton at Western Approaches HQ. I sat next Mrs Laughton Bell, a high-up Wren, who is a sister of Mrs Laughton Matthews, the Queen Wren, but no relation, she told me, of Charles Laughton the actor, who is commonly said to be their brother. After luncheon drove through the Mersey tunnel, which I had never done before, and visited some of the small ships and their establishments. Returned to London, dining in the train.

Wednesday 28 March

Winston telegraphs to F.D.R. that he is gravely disturbed by the Russian behaviour since Yalta. I don't wonder – everything they have said and done in the last few weeks suggests that they are trying to wipe Yalta off the slate.

Wavell, who got back last Friday, came to see the King, I had about ten minutes with him first. A great letter-writer, he is, in conversation, about as communicative as a clam. The King complained bitterly of this.

Norfolk also came, with schemes for a State opening of a post-war Parliament. This don't seem feasible to me, unless they can induce the House of Commons to vacate, for the day, the Lords' chamber, which they now occupy. I doubt if their stiff-necked pride will allow them to do this.

Friday 30 March Good Friday

Michael Adeane rang up to say that he was safe home; this is a relief. He only left the Guards Armoured Division on Tuesday. He is convinced that the Germans are finished.

Lloyd George was buried today. I knew him little, but several times felt the power of his oratory – intoxicating, but like all intoxicants, its effects were usually transitory.

Yesterday Winston cabled to F.D.R. his grave anxiety about the post-

Yalta attitude of Russia – no, he did this on Wednesday; anyhow, F.D.R. has replied in the same vein, and sent the draft of a firm message to Uncle Joe.

Note of 4 April: Winston, a day or two later, sent F.D.R. the draft of his own message to Uncle Joe. F.D.R. cabled his approval. Winston, in reply, said, 'Thank you for endorsing my message. I shall now bung it off to the Bear.' On second thoughts, he judged this to be a bit too colloquial, and his secretaries were ordered to call in all copies of this cable.

Saturday 31 March

Michael Adeane, looking very well, came down and distinguished himself by going up to see the King with no rank-badges in his shoulder straps, having forgotten to put them back after cleaning them this morning. Needless to say, the defect was noticed before he had been in the room ten seconds. The King supplied him with another pair of crowns out of his private store.

Sunday 1 April

Winston brought Barney Baruch[1] over to see the King this evening. The Press, who are inclined to be hysterical from so much good news, got wind of his being here, and inferred that he could only have come to see the King on a Sunday afternoon if he had received an offer of surrender from Hitler, or something equally momentous. The 1st and 9th US Armies have now joined hands, thus completely encircling the Ruhr, which is still full of German troops. Monty is being rather secretive about his movements, but his armoured divisions are still obviously making rapid progress. There have now been no V-2 rockets on this country for four days. We have probably seen the last of them.

Monday 2 April

Eisenhower, a few days ago, telegraphed to Stalin informing him that he proposed to modify his plan of campaign, and to thrust not straight on Berlin, but on to the Leipzig–Dresden axis; for this purpose, 9th US Army would be taken away from Monty, and revert to Omar Bradley. This has caused a pretty fluttering of the wires not only because Eisenhower's procedure in telegraphing straight to Stalin before he had consulted the Chiefs

---

1 Bernard Baruch (1870–1965), Jewish financier who saved Churchill's finances after the Wall Street crash of 1929. American representative on the Atomic Energy Commission.

of Staff is considered very strange, but also because the new plan has serious disadvantages: it relegates the northern thrust (to Berlin), with its attendant aims of freeing the Dutch and of cleaning up the U-boat coast, to a secondary place; and, politically, it might be a grave mistake to leave the occupation of Berlin entirely to the Russians, whose impression that it is they, and they alone, who have beaten the Germans, would be proportionately strengthened. Moreover, the new alignment appears to leave the British Army in the air.

All these arguments have been set out by Winston with his usual marvellous blend of firmness, tact and disarming courtesy, in a series of telegrams to Eisenhower and the President. There is, as in every human controversy, something to be said on both sides; but the balance of argument seems to me to be against Eisenhower, who should certainly have referred the matter to higher authority before dashing off a message to Moscow on his own.

In Washington, it is refreshing to find that Admiral King,[1] probably for the first time in his career, supports our point of view, agreeing that Ike has evidently overlooked the naval implications of the question. I don't know how much Monty has been told of this; his rage would be pretty to watch. I fear that his having contrived to make himself *persona ingrata* to various individuals at SHAEF is a ponderable factor in the situation; though it is, of course, utterly wrong that personalities should enter into so vital a matter of high policy as this.

I have warned P. Legh to be ready with floodlighting apparatus in Buckingham Palace, in case the King has, at short notice, to show himself to cheering crowds from the balcony.

Tuesday 3 April

Vincent Massey came to see me; we both lamented that we found it impossible to feel any lightness of heart from news which, only two years ago, would have made us rejoice and be merry. The truth is that, after a certain period, the winning of a war is nearly as tedious and exhausting a business as the losing of it.

The storm over Eisenhower's telegram seems to be subsiding to approximately teacup dimensions.

Wednesday 4 April

PM to luncheon, whereafter the King and he, with Tim Nugent and me,

---

1 The US admiral Ernest J. King was renowned for his anti-British views.

foregathered in the House of Lords with Norfolk, Algar Howard,[1] Duncan Sandys, Esme Lennox[2] etc., to discuss ways and means for a possible State opening of Parliament when the German war is over. The crux of the problem is to find temporary accommodation for the House of Commons while the ceremony is going on; this can only take place in the House of Lords proper, now occupied by the House of Commons since their own chamber got blitzed. Winston's solution is to decant them into St Stephen's Chapel (their pristine home, under the floor of which Guy Fawkes operated) for the day. But James Stuart clearly thought that the faithful Commons wouldn't relish this – how sensitive they are to their rights and privileges is shown by the refusal of Mr Speaker to be in any way associated with our party this afternoon.

I'm inclined to think that it is much too early to worry about such things. After the last war, they didn't attempt a State opening till February 1920, and to stage a heavily over-dressed procession now, when every citizen and his wife are clamouring for more clothing coupons (which they won't get) is asking for trouble.

Thursday 5 April

The Cranbornes gave a cocktail party at Claridge's for the Delegates. Smuts was there, looking young and rosy, and none the worse for the flight from South Africa, in the course of which his aeroplane was struck by lightning. I complimented him on the remarkably good speech which he made at the opening session of the conference.

Having successfully steered a middle course between the Scylla of Lady Willingdon and the Charybdis of Lady Anderson, I went home to dress for the dinner at No. 10 for much the same set of people, but no ladies. I was well placed between Alan Brooke, with whom I talked birds for the greater part of the meal, and John Martin; a good dinner, and Roederer champagne. We stayed talking till late, and I did not get back to Buckingham Palace till past midnight. Herbert Morrison drove me part of the way home.

The sensation of the day has been a telegram from F.D.R. embodying a quite incredibly insulting message to him from Stalin, which, in effect, accuses us and USA of having made a secret compact with the Germans at Berne, whereby the Germans, in return for a promise of easier peace-terms,

---

1 Sir Algar Howard (1880–1970), barrister and genealogist, Garter Principal King of Arms 1944–50.
2 Lord Esme Gordon-Lennox (1875–1949), Yeoman Usher of the Black Rod and Secretary to the Lord Great Chamberlain 1929–46.

are not seriously opposing us in the west. F.D.R. sent an excellent answer, a strong and dignified rebuke. The War Cabinet met this afternoon to consider our action. The general view is that the approach by Wolff was a plant from the outset, staged by the Huns to make trouble between us and Russia, and sedulously reinforced by adroit propaganda; if so, it has succeeded in its object. Another theory is that Stalin is not quite as all-powerful as he seems to be, and is continually under pressure from a group who are jealous of, and suspicious of, his relations with us and USA, and always trying to drive him into a more isolationist policy; telegrams such as this are the voice of this group.

A third possibility, which instantly occurred to me when I read the thing, is that Russia is definitely resolved to break with us; certainly a telegram such as this would, not so long ago, have been held to be practically a *casus belli* by any friendly power to whom it was addressed. Eden and Cadogan think that good may come of it, on the view that this is the final eruption of suppressed discontent with her allies on the part of Russia – manifested hitherto by a series of obstructions and intransigences in every point at issue during the past few weeks – and that if it is surgically treated now, Russia may revert to normal. Anyway, it is distressing that there should be such symptoms, whatever the causative disease, so short a time after Yalta.

Saturday 7 April

Their Majesties went to the cup-tie final at Wembley – an admirable opportunity for showing themselves to 90,000 loyal subjects. Gerry Wellington to tea, bringing a coffer full of the Iron Duke's swords of honour, which the King wanted to examine. Two were very fine specimens – one, the gift of the Tsar after Waterloo, the other, from the people of Bengal, after Assaye, etc. But what excited me was the original sword worn by him at Waterloo – a plain enough affair, with a curious square hilt; it gave me real pleasure to handle it, and to feel that Wellington's hand, perhaps, rested where mine was, at the very moment when he said, 'By God, so you have!' to Lord Uxbridge.[1] Gerry fussed over these things like a hen with chicks, and refused to eat his tea till I had brought them in out of the hall, though I reminded him that we were in a fortress, ringed by policemen and soldiers.

Caroline last night made her first visit to a London nightclub, going to a party at 'The 400' organised by various young cornets of horse in the Blues.

---

1   In reply to His Lordship's 'By God, I've lost my leg'.

Sunday 8 April

Clark Kerr has been discussing with Maisky[1] and Madame Kollontay[2] (two of the few Muscovites who also know the Anglo-Saxons) the attitude which the Russians have adopted since Yalta. Maisky said that it all meant very little – 'ripples on the surface' etc.; the Russians have 'a sense of infirmity' about which they are always very touchy, and we must have patience, and remember that 'the world would quickly become normal again, and that our real interests clashed in no part of the world'.

Madame Kollontay said that the Russians are at about the same stage of development as we were at the time of Cromwell. 'They are bad psychologists – they have no idea of when or why they give offence. In their turn, they take it, whenever any proposal they make is not accepted with eagerness. At present, they are deeply conscious of their success and their strength, and they want the world to pat them on the back. They are children, and must be treated as such. Their present unruliness will pass. We need have no anxiety for the future. There is a very real and widespread feeling that they must cooperate with us.' Clark Kerr sums up: 'The truth is that the Russians are in a hurry to be great, and that is uncomfortable.'

The Dean (Hamilton) preached on the Resurrection this morning. He is, at times, irritatingly insistent on dogma. It is a mistake to lay down, axiomatically, that you can't be a good Christian unless you are convinced of the truth of all the physical facts in the New Testament story; that takes one no further than the Athanasian creed. Hamilton quoted the story of *When It Was Dark*, Guy Thorne's shilling shocker which created such a stir during my first year at Oxford. Its burden was that a papyrus was discovered in Palestine, in which Joseph of Arimathea confessed that he had secretly removed Christ's body from the tomb, and that consequently there had been no resurrection. The effect of this revelation on mankind, its belief in a future life shattered, was to make half of it commit suicide, and the other half to indulge in every form of riotous living; morals and manners vanished from the Christian world. Eventually the parchment was proved to be a fraud, and everybody turned over a new leaf, and went to church far more regularly than before.

Even at the age of nineteen, I thought this great nonsense, and a very poor tribute to the solidity of Christian ethics. A faith that is based on the

---

1 Ivan Mikhailovich Maisky was now Deputy Commissar for Foreign Affairs.
2 Alexandra Kollontay (d. 1952), Soviet Minister of Welfare before the war, became Soviet Ambassador to Sweden and then to Norway. She was said to speak thirteen languages fluently.

physical truth of alleged supernatural phenomena – miracles, whether of healing or of bodily return from death – is only one degree better than magic. The physical facts don't *matter*. R. L. Nettleship[1] puts this well in one of his letters. The physical authorship of Shakespeare (interesting enough academically) has no relation to one's attitude to the value of Shakespeare's contribution to human welfare. Similarly, I have a deep-seated belief in the Englishman's fundamental rights to liberty of thought and action; one of the chief historical sources of those rights is Magna Carta; but the discovery that King John had never physically signed it, or indeed that the charter itself was a fake, would have no effect whatever on my belief. Anyhow, I don't like being told what I ought to believe by any other man. I am always ready to be told how I ought to *behave*; but a man's faith is his own.

Queen Mary lunched at the Castle, and Cynthia Colville, in waiting on her, came to tea with us.

Monday 9 April

Monty periodically sends the King, as they are ready, the successive sections of his very private record of the campaign in north-west Europe, in all its bearings. Today he writes to me to ask whether he should not withhold Part 9 from HM, because 'it contains the full story of the intrigue to get Alexander to SHAEF, as Deputy to Eisenhower *vice* Tedder. It is not possible to get the full story without giving the views of various people (including myself) on the *military* ability of Alexander. The only person who considers that Alexander is a high-class soldier is the Prime Minister; no one else does. I have merely written the factual account of the matter. I do not want to upset or annoy the King, nor do I want him to feel that I am jealous, unkind and so on. Alexander is one of my greatest friends; but I am under no delusions as to his military ability.'

I had no hesitation in advising him *not* to send Part 9 to the King, whose reaction to it would, I am confident, be exactly what Monty says he don't wish to produce; moreover, having read it might be a grave embarrassment to the King later on. Sometimes I wonder whether Monty's undoubted genius does not occasionally bring him to the verge of mental unstability. The newspapers are full of a story of the discovery in a salt-mine at Merkers (near Eisenach) of the Reichsbank gold reserves,

---

1   Richard Lewis Nettleship (1846–92), tutor in philosophy at Balliol, died of exposure attempting to climb Mont Blanc.

amounting to 100 million sterling, together with a great number of paintings.[1]

Wednesday 11 April

I am fifty-eight today. With HM to one of the War Cabinet dinners at No. 10: dullish, but good dinner – caviar and vodka, and Pol Roger. E. Bevin, next to me, fell stertorously asleep at the table, gurgitating like a buffalo. He did it twice more during the evening. They are all very tired, yet we sat there till 1.45 a.m. Winston and Bevin seemed to be on the best of terms, despite the latter's outbursts on the electioneering platform at the weekend. W. is pleased with the effect of F.D.R.'s telegram to Stalin – he said it was the strongest thing, short of an ultimatum, that he had ever read from one Head of State to another.

Thursday 12 April

Their Majesties gave a party at Buckingham Palace for the delegates to the San Francisco Conference. With HM's approval, I put to Smuts an idea which occurred to me yesterday – that the four Dominions' Prime Ministers should unite in sending the King a joint submission that he give the Garter to Winston. This would get round the difficulty (though it has, of course, been surmounted by previous sovereigns) of the PM having, theoretically, to recommend himself for such an award; it would also be a striking example of the unity of the Empire, and symbolise, through their Prime Ministers, the recognition of Winston's outstanding services, by the citizens of the Dominions. After a moment's reflection, Smuts seemed taken with the idea; he said he would 'chew on it', and if this masticatory process revealed no obstacle, would, as I suggested, tackle Mackenzie King about it at 'Frisco.

The party was a success, though, as always, it lasted quarter of an hour too long, so that everybody, except the King and Queen, was late for his dinner. I ate mine with Kathleen Rutland,[2] at the Dorchester; her boy, Charles, has just got home from the 1st Grenadiers, having shot himself in the foot.

---

1 Early in 1944 the Nazis had transferred the German State currency reserves and over 100 tons of gold bullion to the extensive potassium mine at Merkers. In March, dismayed by the speed of the American advance, officials of the Reichsbank tried to recover the hoard, but they were too late: all the gold, and 550 out of 1,000 sacks of paper Reichsmarks, were captured by the Americans.
2 Widow of the 9th Duke of Rutland, known as Kakoo.

Friday 13 April

It was announced on the midnight news that F.D.R. died suddenly yesterday afternoon – cerebral haemorrhage. It was no great surprise to me, as many of those who saw him recently at Yalta have told me that his days were numbered. Truman,[1] under their constitution, automatically becomes President, as Teddy Roosevelt[2] did forty-odd years ago. He is an unknown quantity, relatively.

This has kept me busy, not only with the preparation of the King's various messages, etc., but also with the postponement of a visit to Glasgow (for the international football match) on which we were due to start tonight. Winston toyed with the idea – and came back to it in the evening – of flying over to the funeral. I opposed this firmly on the King's behalf, and I'm glad to say that it has now been decided that Eden should go.

Saturday 14 April

The tributes to Roosevelt are remarkable; I cannot recollect a greater volume of regret and eulogy for any notability who has died in my lifetime. He was certainly a great man – if only for the superb courage with which, in the early days of the war, he risked everything to give all the help he could to this country in its lone and seemingly desperate struggle; with the skill of a psychologist with a sure knowledge of his own countrymen, he led, cajoled and ordered them into giving that help, almost against their will, until the folly of the Japanese made them our allies. Yet all the time he held his grip on all but a small section of them, steadily educating them to the realisation that this was no war in the old-fashioned sense, but a fundamental struggle to the death between good and evil. I knew him only slightly, but am glad I knew him at all. Winston will miss him sadly. The King wrote Winston a letter of sympathy in his own hand yesterday – a good letter, which he read out to me before sending it. He has also sent a letter to Winant.[3]

Joan and Caroline went to London for a small and secret party given by Grace Selborne.[4] Princess Elizabeth was there, her father sensibly ruling that it would be an unnecessary deprivation for her to stay at home on

1 Harry S. Truman (1884–1972), Democratic President of the US 1945–53, had volunteered for active service in France during WWI. In 1935 he was elected junior senator for Missouri, and in the 1944 election he ran as Roosevelt's Vice-President, taking up that office in Jan. 1945.
2 Theodore Roosevelt (1858–1919), President of the US 1901–8.
3 Hon. John G. Winant (1889–1947), US Ambassador to the Court of St James 1941–6.
4 Wife of 3rd Earl of Selborne, sister of Jasper Ridley.

account of Court mourning. I am very sure that *his* father and grandfather would unhesitatingly have decided in the opposite sense!

Sunday 15 April

Edward Halifax telegraphs an encouraging character-sketch of President Truman, who sounds an honest and sensible man; a staunch friend of this country, with the right ideas on international affairs.

Eisenhower reports his plan for the next stage of the fighting – roughly, to clean up both his flanks before attempting a major thrust on Berlin; in the north, we are to get Lübeck and Hamburg, liberating Denmark and possibly Norway, thus scotching the U-boat threat; in the centre, he will hold the Elbe, taking Berlin if a good opportunity offers, but not concentrating on it; in the south, he will join up with the Russians and endeavour to clean up the 'Nazi redoubt' before they can make it too formidable a stronghold. Our Chiefs of Staff seem to be in general agreement with this scheme.

Bernadotte,[1] the Swede, has recently seen Himmler; he reports (via Stockholm) that Hitler is indubitably mad, spending most of his time on architectural plans for rebuilding German cities; but such is his prestige that his orders are still obeyed; Goering has taken to cocaine again, dresses in Turkish pyjamas, and paints his nails red: the man they all fear – even Himmler, who is nominally his boss – is Kaltenbrunner.[2] Himmler does not hide his conviction that the game is up. Murrow,[3] on the wireless this evening, gave a terrible account of a concentration camp at Buchenwald, near Weimar, which he went over on Thursday last.

Heard the cuckoo for the first time this year, in Frogmore; and, I think, a willow warbler. The shrubs are wonderfully beautiful this early spring; this evening it was like June, and John and I played chess on the roof garden before dinner.

The really striking bit of news today is that, at the eleventh hour, Molotov has decided to go to 'Frisco. This change of plan is said, in Moscow, to be a generous gesture to the memory of F.D.R. I suspect that it is a convenient face-saving excuse, for there are various indications that the Muscovites are ashamed of their recent behaviour, and anxious to be friends again.

---

1 Count Folke Bernadotte (1895–1948), leader of Swedish delegation to Germany for recovery of concentration camp prisoners 1945, President Swedish Red Cross 1946.
2 Ernst Kaltenbrunner (1903–46). As head of the Nazi Sicherheitsdienst (Secret Service) from 1942, he controlled the Gestapo and the concentration camp system. He was captured in 1945, tried at Nuremberg, and executed for war crimes in Oct. 1946.
3 Edward R. Murrow (1908–65), well-known American reporter, broadcasting from London and Europe during the war.

Monday 16 April

At the Beefsteak today Eddie Winterton,[1] who is usually silly and often choleric, had a slanging match with our admirable steward, Pegram. Both were entirely in the wrong; but the steward's service is far more valuable to us than Eddie's company, so we prevailed upon the latter (when his blood had cooled) to make the *amende honorable* as he went out.

Saw Ismay, who said that the Eisenhower plan was likely to be accepted, though the PM is inclined to fight for the immediate capture of Berlin, which tickles his political and histrionic sense.

James Stuart came to tea with me. An interval of forty-nine days must elapse between the end of the European war and a general election; if the former don't come by 24 May, the latter (according to James) must wait till October. Even in these days, it seems, we can't go to the polls in August and September, months sacred no longer to grouse, but still to harvest and holidays.

At 12.30 a.m., just as I had gone to sleep, Winston telephoned to me to say that he wanted to be excused lunching with the King. The next hour was made hideous by hundreds of aeroplanes flying low over London – very unnecessary.

Tuesday 17 April

With Their Majesties to St Paul's, for the memorial service to F.D.R. It was very well done, and the trumpeters sounded the Last Post and Reveille beautifully. The cathedral was full to overflowing. John Winant read the lesson with dignity and distinction, but he has not a good voice. Fisher, functioning as Archbishop for the first time on an occasion of this kind, pronounced the blessing admirably.

I had a curious experience [before dinner with the Jack Egertons] for, on rising from my chair to go into dinner, found myself unable to move my legs. I was wearing an ancient pair of drawers, the last of the underwear that I inherited from Doll Liddell[2] in 1920, and the tapes through which one's breeches go had apparently broken during my walk through the park; the drawers had slipped down to the level of my knees, completely hobbling me. I had to call the party to a halt while I made the damage good.

Felicity Cory-Wright's[3] boy John has been killed. Since the war broke

---

1   Edward Turnour, 6th Earl Winterton (1883–1962).
2   A. G. C. Liddell (1846–1920), Tommy's uncle, his mother's elder brother.
3   1892–1969. Daughter of the actor-manager Sir Herbert Tree, and wife of Sir Geoffrey Cory-Wright.

out, Felicity has had two sons killed; one, a prisoner at Singapore, has not been heard of for two years; her husband, after killing two people in his motor, has spent eighteen months in gaol; and her youngest boy was expelled from Eton a few weeks ago. Job himself was not more hardly treated by Fate; but Felicity will bear her burdens with far more courage and dignity than Job did.

Wednesday 18 April

Lunched with Louis Greig at the Dorchester to meet Charles Portal, Slessor[1] and Quintin Hogg, newly appointed Under-Secretary of Air. Hogg said that Faringdon,[2] a notorious pansy, had recently thrown the House of Lords into consternation by addressing their Lordships as 'My Dears'. Portal told me that the inquiry into the Lampedusa crash (when Peter Loxley lost his life) had shown up the pilot in the worst possible light. The story that, on finally coming down to the sea, he had the bad luck to hit a partially-submerged wreck is untrue; what he did do, was to make the most unskilful descent possible, with the terrible result that we know.

Thursday 19 April

Joan and I started off 10 a.m. in the car and drove to Sutton Waldron, my birthplace and home for fifty years, through an England of incomparable beauty, on a perfect spring day: Ascot, Basingstoke, Stockbridge, Salisbury, Tarrant Gunville, as of old. It is eight years since I went down that road, and we were pleased to see how little changed it and its surroundings are. Considering the enormous volume of war traffic that has poured over it, its surface is astonishingly good.

Sutton is now a girls' school, but the young ladies were away on their Easter holidays. The proprietress, Mrs Cole, made us welcome and took us round the house, which she keeps in marvellous good order, and with taste. We ate our luncheon under the apple trees, now in full blossom. The garden has got v. jungly, inevitable in wartime, and some of the shrubs which I planted so devotedly ten years ago (many of them in most unsuitable places) have died; so have the bay trees and escallonias. The great frost last winter killed them; the thermometer went down to zero, which has never happened before in Dorset that I can remember.

---

1 Air Marshal Sir John Slessor (1897–1979), C-in-C RAF Mediterranean and Middle East 1944–5, Air Chief Marshal 1946, Marshal of the RAF 1950, Principal ADC to the King 1948–50.
2 Alexander Gavin Henderson, 2nd Baron Faringdon (1902–77).

John left Windsor to rejoin his battalion.

Friday 20 April

Joan and I drove up to the top of the hill, Dairy Lodge, where the Chase was looking its primeval best – primroses, bluebells and anemones all out together, and an occasional nightingale rehearsing tentatively. Then on to Fontmell golf course, where we ate our luncheon, and back via Penn Hill and Sutton, where we called on William Green, once my tenant and now bed-ridden and failing fast.

Saturday 21 April

Weather fresher, with wind NW – rather a relief after the almost unnatural midsummer perfection of the last few days. We lunched at Stapleton with Ronald Lindsay,[1] who walked us home through the woods above Everley. Selina Baker came home for a weekend rest from her labours on some farm near Blandford. She is a magnificent young woman, six feet high, with a flaxen head which Botticelli would have been glad to put in a picture.[2]

Russians all round Berlin. A party delegation has been flown out to see the horrors of Buchenwald and Belsen camps, which the Americans have publicised widely. I am glad that it was they, and not we, who came face to face with these unanswerable proofs of German wickedness; an American sergeant is reported in the *Daily Telegraph* as having said, after going round Buchenwald, 'Now I know what I am fighting for; up till now, I have thought it was all propaganda.' The revelations from these camps will do more to kill Isolationism in USA than would years of inspired instruction.

Wednesday 25 April

The author was still on holiday touring in Dorset.

A code telegram from Eric Miéville reached me after dinner, telling me that Himmler has asked, via Bernadotte, for an opportunity to surrender to Eisenhower. Hitler is desperately ill, and not likely to live for more than a few days.

---

1   Rt. Hon. Sir Ronald Lindsay (1877–1945), diplomat, British Ambassador at Washington
    1930–39.
2   Daughter of Sir Randolph Baker of Ranston Park, in the village next to Tommy's former
    home.

Thursday 26 April

I thought it prudent to get back to Windsor as soon as possible, so we left Evershot after breakfast and reached here 3.30. Rang up E. Miéville at Sandringham; he says Himmler's offer applied only to the western front – he is under the illusion that he can still go on fighting the Russians – with what object, God knows. Our Cabinet, having discussed the matter yesterday, at once telegraphed full particulars to Stalin; what else could they do? Perhaps this evidence of our loyalty as allies may induce the Russians to be a bit less intransigent over Poland; Molotov is being unbelievably stubborn in USA, in spite of joint representations by Stettinius and Eden, and of a stiff talking-to from Truman.

Friday 27 April   London

The King and Queen came back from Sandringham 6 p.m. Stalin is pleased at our having referred Himmler's offer to him, and has sent quite a gracious telegram to Winston – 'Knowing you, I should not have expected you to act otherwise', or words to that effect. Meanwhile Alex, who has completely routed the German armies in North Italy, has again been approached by their emissaries with a view to surrender. The newspapers are crackling with rumours; but the actual events of each day now are striking enough without any fictional embroidery. As I went to bed at Buckingham Palace, it struck me that, maybe, we have heard the air-raid warnings for the last time in our lives – a solemn thought. Had we, in April '41, been vouchsafed even a five-minutes' glimpse of a newspaper of April '45, what a difference it would have made; though the realisation that the thing was to last another four years would have been a shock to most of us. I recollect that when, in early September 1939, I went to say goodbye to Andy McNaughton,[1] packing up for his return to Canada, he said, 'As I see it, the first seven years of this war will be the worst.' It seemed, at the time, a fantastic prophecy; but he was not far wrong.

Sunday 29 April

Himmler's approach to Bernadotte 'leaked' all over the world last night; they got very excited in New York, and Truman had to go on the air to tell them that the war was not over yet. As a result, when I rang up Chequers at 10 a.m. I was told they were all still in bed, having only

---

1   Gen. the Hon. Andrew McNaughton (1887–1966), GOC-in-C First Canadian Army 1942–3, Minister of National Defence, Canada, 1944–5.

reached it in the small hours of the morning. Got off a telegram to Alex from the King; it could not wait, as that campaign may well be all over tomorrow.

Monday 30 April

Just before midnight the War Cabinet office telephoned that the Germans had accepted Alex's terms. Mussolini has been done to death by Italian partisans near Lake Como, his body, and those of his mistress and his minions, being subsequently taken to Milan and publicly exposed in the main plaza. Italian methods of dealing with discredited politicians have changed very little since the days of the Gracchi.[1] But the partisans have unwittingly done the Allies a great service.

Tuesday 1 May

Michael Adeane reported for duty after five and a half years on active service. Dined with the Godfrey Thomases, and on my return was rung up by No. 10, who told me the German wireless have announced that Hitler 'was killed' in Berlin at 12 noon today; Admiral Dönitz succeeds him as Führer. What, I wonder, has become of Himmler? Hit. and Muss. in forty-eight hours – not a bad right-and-left. I never thought we should get many of them alive.

Wednesday 2 May

Hostilities in North Italy ceased. Ribbentrop dismissed by Dönitz, in favour of von Krosigk;[2] Laval reported to be in Barcelona. We have reached Lübeck and Wissar on the Baltic, and the Americans are in Schwerin.

I dined at Grillions; a full house, and my candidate, Alan Brooke, was comfortably elected a new member. Woolton was chosen to fill the other vacancy. We are now quite bankrupt, and a special committee was set up to investigate our financial affairs.

E. Devonshire has broken his arm, jumping out of his bath to answer the telephone in a hurry – always a mistake.

---

1 The brothers Gaius and Tiberius Gracchus, aristocratic politicians in Rome in the second century BC, were both murdered by enemies.
2 Count Lutz Schwerin von Krosigk (1877–1977) was appointed Chancellor of Germany in May 1945 and presided over the surrender with Dönitz.

Thursday 3 May

The Russians have now occupied all Berlin. De Valera, according to *The Times*, called yesterday on the German Minister in Dublin, to offer his condolences on Hitler's death; this will not easily be forgiven him. Dined with Hughe Knatchbull-Hugessen, home from Brussels for a few days; he confirms that the majority of Belgians have no wish to see Leopold restored to the throne. Meanwhile, L.'s whereabouts remain a mystery.

One of Monty's young men brought me his Part Ten, with a note explaining why he hasn't sent Part Nine, on the lines that I suggested to him. He told me that when he left 21st Army yesterday morning, Monty was hourly expecting an approach from Dönitz or some other German plenipotentiary, with a white flag.

Friday 4 May

Down to Windsor, and just before dinner the PM telephoned to the King that Monty had received the surrender (apparently through Keitel[1]) of all the German forces now operating in North Germany, Denmark and Holland; Keitel is to be sent on to Eisenhower to discuss the position of Norway, the Channel Islands and the pockets still holding out on the French coast. Until that position is finally cleared up, the war is obviously not over; but Winston anticipates that 'VE Day' can be celebrated on Monday.

Saturday 5 May

About 2.45 p.m. Martin telephoned that Eisenhower had reported that he expected the Germans about 4 p.m. and that by 6 p.m. he hoped to have negotiated the final surrender of all German land-forces. He anticipates that it may take another twenty-four hours to tie up all the loose ends, and that by tomorrow (Sunday) evening, he will be in a position to report to the three Allied governments that all is really over; in which case, Winston could announce our VE Day early Monday, and the King make his broadcast that evening. The King sent a telegram (personal only) to Monty.

Sunday 6 May

Service in St George's in honour of the patron saint. Anthony Deane[2]

---

1 Wilhelm Keitel (1882–1946), chief of Hitler's personal military staff, was convicted of war crimes at the Nuremberg Trials and hanged in 1946.
2 Rev. Anthony Deane (1870–1946), Canon of St George's, Windsor, 1929–46, Chaplain to the King 1934–46.

preached a good sermon. The special psalm selected was 'Lord, remember David and all his troubles' – not a happy choice, with the King sitting there, almost under the Duke of Windsor's banner.

George Lascelles, John Elphinstone and young Winant have been safely picked up by US 7th Army, and have reached Paris. I am now negotiating with SHAEF to get them flown over tomorrow. The Germans have been trying to induce Eisenhower to suspend the surrender for several days, in order that as many as possible of their refugees may escape from the Russians and come under the charge of us and the Americans; but Ike won't have this, and has only given them forty-eight hours. If they agree, VE Day will be on Tuesday. As I said to the King yesterday, it is just like waiting for one's wife to have a baby.

If I told the world that I had had a letter from a gentleman signing himself 'C. Cherry Chumple', the world (with the possible exception of Beachcomber) would not believe me. Yet it is true. He lives at Budleigh Salterton.

Monday 7 May

Jodl[1] and the other German plenipotentiaries signed Eisenhower's terms at 3 a.m. this morning; hostilities cease officially at midnight tomorrow, but, in effect the war is now over. Winston was anxious to proclaim the fact at 6 p.m. tonight, but both Truman and Stalin were opposed to this. So after a Cabinet meeting, it was decided to issue a statement proclaiming both tomorrow and Wednesday to be VE Day holidays, with an official pro-nouncement by the PM at 3 p.m. and the King's broadcast at 9 p.m. This was really the best they could do, in face of the fact that all the world now knows the news – it was broadcast by von Krosigk, the new German Foreign Minister, early this afternoon – and would probably treat itself to a holiday tomorrow anyhow. A fair-sized crowd came and shouted in front of Buck-ingham Palace after dinner, but the King did not make an appearance on the balcony, not wishing to shoot his grouse before the Twelfth, so to speak. George Lascelles and John Elphinstone turned up this afternoon, both looking remarkably well after their imprisonment.

Tuesday 8 May VE Day

Fine and warm, after heavy thunderstorms during the night. Investiture. Lunched hurriedly at the Travellers; streets beflagged, but empty, save in

---

1 General Alfred Jodl (1882–1946), chief of Hitler's operations staff, convicted and hanged at Nuremberg.

front of Buckingham Palace and other popular foci, where growing crowds have mustered all day. At 3 p.m. the PM broadcast the official pronouncement of the end of the war. Short and good – but he 'gagged' a bit, interpolating an extempore sentence about Russia – an obvious dollop of honey for the Bear and alluding to Bedell Smith as 'Chief of Staff to the US Army', which he isn't.

Immediately after this, Their Majesties and the Princesses made the first of a series of appearances on the balcony. At 4.30 p.m. the War Cabinet, with the Chiefs of Staff, Bridges and Pug Ismay, came to wait on the King, who gave them a short address of thanks. While this was going on in the 'Forty-four' Room, I took the opportunity of putting on Winston's hat, which he had left in the Bow Room, as a gesture of which to tell my grandchildren, should they ever ask me how I spent VE Day. I similarly crowned Joey Legh and Peter Townsend. Thereafter, the whole party were photographed outside the Bow Room. It was remarkable that the only members of it who were holding their present jobs at the outbreak of war were the King, Ismay and Bridges.

At 9 the King delivered his broadcast – a trifle slow, but otherwise excellent. I listened to it in my own room; it was relayed to the immense crowd outside Buckingham Palace, after which Their Majesties went again to the balcony, repeating these appearances till past midnight. The Princesses, under escort, went out and walked unrecognised about St James's Street and Piccadilly.

Wednesday 9 May

A public holiday. After luncheon Their Majesties drove through various boroughs in north-east London. Buckingham Palace and its approaches were blocked with throngs of people all day, and it took me twenty minutes to get into the place this afternoon, having gone over to St James's to have tea with Joan and Caroline, up for the night. After dining at Grillions, I took Joan and Caroline round the town to see the floodlighting, which was admirably done, especially in Trafalgar Square. Crowds very happy and good-humoured. Very few police in evidence, and in the course of a two hours' walk we met hardly anybody the worse for drink.

Thursday 10 May

Drove with Their Majesties through south-east London – New Cross, Greenwich, Streatham. Large crowds, all very enthusiastic.

Friday 11 May

The swifts have arrived at Windsor. This evening, after dinner, a brown owl sat and hooted for a long time on one of the chimney-pots to the west of Henry III Tower. I've never seen an owl do this before.

Saturday 12 May

Joan and I drove to lunch with Gerry Wellesley at Stratfield Saye ('Strat' = 'street', i.e., the Roman road from Silchester, which runs through the village: 'field' = an open clearing in the primeval forest: 'Saye' = the name of the family in occupation in Norman times). I hadn't been there since November 1911, when, staying at Ewhurst, we shot the Stratfield Saye pheasants. It is a good, plain house, temp. Charles II, originally in the possession of the Pitts. Full of relics of the Great Duke, and some good pictures of various Wellesleys of that period, especially four Hoppners, and some Hogarths. I was interested to see that the Iron Duke had installed a modern-looking bath in the closet adjoining his bedroom – this must have been a very rare luxury in a country house in the 1820s. There is practically no flower-garden, but attractive pleasure-grounds, though too full of Wellingtonias (the importation of the 2nd Duke) and other conifers. The park is still dotted with Nissen huts, full of shells and other explosives, stored there for use after D-Day last year. Gerry is an admirable showman, and enjoys every minute of it.

I find it impossible to allude to world-happenings, which are too big just now for this small canvas. Germany being beaten, the dominating problem is, of course, the future relations between Russia, on the one hand, and USA and ourselves on the other. The realisation of its very thorny nature has certainly brought us and the Americans together, more closely than did any issue in the war itself.

Sunday 13 May

Drove to London, taking Michael Adeane with us. We – the Household, plus a sprinkling of wives and ADCs of the foreign royals, who were lunching with Their Majesties – had luncheon at Buckingham Palace. At 2.30 drove in procession to St Paul's; Their Majesties and the Princesses in one open landau, and Cynthia Spencer, Mary Herbert[1], Peter Townsend and I in another. Queen Mary and the foreigners had gone on ahead in their motors.

---

1   Formerly Lady Mary Hope (1903–95), wife of Lord Herbert, later 16th Earl of Pembroke. Lady-in-waiting to Princess Marina, Duchess of Kent.

It is a long time since I travelled in a horse-drawn vehicle, and it was something of an adventure, in that the royal horses have spent the war carting hay rather than facing crowds. However, D. Kavanagh had schooled them well, and there was no mishap. He told me that he had installed the wireless in the stables, and had made the unfortunate animals listen regularly to the Forces' Programme for some weeks past. This, no doubt, inured them to any combination of cacophony. Mary Herbert, normally a sensible woman, had elected to put on a large, floppy hat without any means of attaching it to her head. As it was blowing half a gale, she spent the drive clutching it with both hands. Streets well lined, and decorously applausive; it was, save in Fleet Street, an essentially Sunday crowd.

At Temple Bar the Lord Mayor performed the sword ceremony, and we reached St Paul's exactly on time, greeted by an impressive fanfare from the trumpeters of the Household Troops, in all their pre-war panoply. Geoffrey Cantuar preached; rather good, but he delivered it too rapidly, and has not learned how to *speak* a written sermon, as distinct from reading it. I found it difficult to assume a mood of thanksgiving, knowing what formidable clouds are hanging over the eastern horizon. Winston, who was across the aisle from me, looked pretty sombre, too. But perhaps he was only thinking of his broadcast tonight. This he delivered well. It was a fine speech, the warning to Russia and Yugoslavia very cleverly worded, the trouncing of de Valera scathing but not immoderate.

Monday 14 May

Queen Mary, who spent the weekend at Windsor, sent for me at 10 a.m. ostensibly to discuss the possibility of guarding against the heirs of the Duke of Cambridge making undesirable use of two boxes of his letters deposited in their names in Coutts' bank. They are probably abysmally dull, and as they have lain there for God knows how many years, there seems little likelihood of their being disturbed. I pointed out to Queen Mary that there was no means that I knew of whereby the legal owners could be prevented from making what use they please of their own property, but undertook to write to Jasper Ridley, which I have done. I hadn't seen Queen Mary for some time; she had aged considerably, but was gracious as ever.

A collection of royal letters which might well be more interesting is that which the Duke of Connaught wrote to his old friend Léonie Leslie, to whom he was long attached. The King is exercised about the fate of these, and I have commissioned Owen Morshead to sound Shane Leslie,[1] whom

---

1   Sir Shane Leslie (1885–1971), 3rd Bt., Irish author and poet, son of Léonie and Sir John Leslie, 2nd Bt.

he knows better than I do, about them. Lady P. Ramsay[1] has destroyed all the letters from Shane's mother to the Duke, so perhaps he will gallantly retaliate in kind, and set royal minds at rest.

In the library met for the first time Anthony Blunt,[2] director of the Courtauld Institute, who has just been made Keeper of the King's pictures, *vice* Kenneth Clark.

Tuesday 15 May

Their Majesties left for Scotland 7.15, having previously charged me with getting Joey Legh to organise a garden party for upwards of 1,000 returned prisoners, etc., on the 24th. Jordan,[3] the New Zealand High Commissioner, had just got back from Germany, bringing the now-familiar tale of horrors seen in one or another of the concentration camps. I think it is partly the realisation of the extent of these abominations which has made it impossible to feel any exultation in our period of thanksgiving.

Wednesday 16 May

The *New York Times* suggests that the kingdom of Hanover should be reconstituted under the Duke of Windsor. So says the *Daily Mail*; and in the next column is an announcement that a Mr E. S. Solomon has invented a machine which will wash up plates, knives, kitchen utensils, etc. in a few seconds, and costs only 15 gns. If this is true, it marks an epoch in domestic economy.

Thursday 17 May

The King had a great triumph at Westminster this afternoon, delivering his reply to the addresses from the two Houses with a dignity and eloquence surpassing anything that I have yet heard from him. He had one bad stammer, on the word 'imperishable', but otherwise it was all good; and a

---

1 Lady Patricia Ramsay (1886–1974), younger daughter of the Duke and Duchess of Connaught, wife of Adm. Hon. Sir Alexander Ramsay (1885–1972).
2 Anthony Frederick Blunt (1907–83), did wartime service with MI5. Keeper of the King's Pictures 1945–52, and of the Queen's Pictures 1952–72. Director of the Courtauld Institute 1947–74. The fact that he had spied for the Soviet Union from his time at Cambridge in the 1930s until the early 1950s was discovered in 1964, when his former associate Kim Philby defected to Moscow; but his career in espionage was not made public until 1979, when he was stripped of the knighthood awarded in 1956.
3 Rt. Hon. Sir William Jordan (d. 1959), High Commissioner for New Zealand in London 1936–51.

wholly spontaneous touch gave the speech a really dramatic and moving quality, when, in alluding to the Duke of Kent's death, his voice faltered and broke.

The Royal Gallery was packed with members of both Houses – save for the Dominions' High Commissioners and the permanent officials, there was room for hardly anybody else, which probably enraged a number of peeresses. Simon read the Lords' address well, with that smooth orotundity which delights him even more than his audience; the Speaker, Clifton Brown,[1] was very nervous and not very audible. But it was a perfect example of British ceremonial at its best, ordered and impressive, with a vent for suppressed emotion at the end, when Winston, flourishing that rare object, a silk hat, leapt on to the dais and called for three cheers. I feel that the events of the past ten days, and the wonderful demonstrations of enthusiasm for the Royal Family that they have evoked, have given the King fresh confidence, and removed in great part the feeling of frustration that I have so often tried to argue out of him.

There has been considerable, and not unjustified, protest in this country and in USA against the seemingly generous treatment which it is thought was being given to Goering, Dönitz, etc.; the broadcasts which the Germans were allowed to make from Flensburg have especially exasperated people, and their annoyance has been increased by some injudicious and probably exaggerated newspaper articles, depicting captured German notabilities living comfortably in luxurious quarters. A timely stern pronouncement by Eisenhower, and the incarceration of Dönitz, have done a good deal to allay these feelings here. But no doubt such stories do much mischief in Russia; much of the Russian high-handedness and independence of action is, I am sure, due to their belief that if the sentimental and easy-going western democracies are allowed to run things in their own way, they will fritter away the results of the victory over the Germans and allow the latter to prepare for a third war, just as they did in the years after 1918. For which one cannot altogether blame them.

A very lovely evening. On my way to dine at the Beefsteak I sat in St James's Park and thought of those equally lovely evenings in June 1940, when one used to sit there and try to be convinced by the gallant blackbirds (who were singing their victory-songs with gusto tonight) that there was no cause for despair, and that England was unconquerable. The blackbirds are seldom wrong.

---

1 Douglas Clifton Brown (1879–1958). Created 1st Viscount Ruffside 1951. Speaker 1943–1951.

Monday 21 May Whit Monday

Monty came to luncheon, having been summoned to see the King this afternoon. He was in good form, looked very well, and talked without drawing breath. The crowd of holiday tourists, to whom the castle has now, alas, been re-opened, spotted him on arrival and made egress from Winchester Tower difficult. However, we took him round to the Deanery after luncheon, and got Eric Hamilton to take us into St George's through the cloisters. Later, I took him for a walk round the castle, out of reach of the pursuing crowds, and duly delivered him to the King.

Monty has now been definitely appointed our representative on the Allied military control commission, but is having trouble in getting a deputy. He said he found Winston obsessed with the general election, and unable to take decisions. He likes the Russians generally, for their light-hearted childishness, though he admits that they are barbarian children. His view is that they have no stomach for any further wars at present. This is much what Archie Clark Kerr thinks also – he came down here for the night, on his way from 'Frisco to Moscow. He says the Russians have no idea of promoting a world revolution, and are entirely concerned with their own future security, for which they consider a cordon of subservient buffer-states is essential.

Both he and Monty referred to Winston's sudden and temperamental change of attitude since Yalta – from a convinced philo-Russianism he has swung, momentarily, to regarding her as Public Enemy No. 1, and talks quite seriously of the possibility of having to fight her.

Tuesday 22 May

The exchange of letters between Winston and Attlee now makes the break-up of the Coalition government inevitable. Attlee was guilty of a great breach of taste (and of tactics) in suggesting in his reply that Winston's suggestion of a referendum savoured of Hitlerite methods. Winston, on the telephone, asked if the King would receive him at 12 noon tomorrow so that he might tender his resignation; and again at 4 p.m. when the King could inform him of his wishes. Winston is strong on there being this interval, in order to emphasise the Sovereign's right to have a period of reflection. I got the King's agreement to this; Winston, later in the day, put it all on paper in a formal letter to HM. Discussing it with the King, I pointed out that the arrangement involved his being without a Prime Minister between twelve and four. 'Then,' said the King, 'I shall send for Winston and give him the Garter – he won't be able to refuse!'

I had a hurried dinner at Pratt's, and then back to the office. The King propounded to me an idea (his own) for giving Winchester Tower a garden, by walling-off the last twenty yards of the North Terrace, removing the gun in the embrasure under the windows of my room, and earthing-over the terrace on our side of the near wall – which, I stipulated, must be six feet high, with a solid door to protect us from the tourists – who, by the way, stole Caroline's mackintosh from our front hall yesterday.

The reconstruction of the Government is complicated by the fact that I am determined to get it all over by Tuesday night, so that Their Majesties (and myself) can get up to Deeside for five days' holiday; they badly need it – and so do I. Winston gave me a guarantee that this would be possible. I spent much time looking through our own records, and the textbooks (Anson, etc.) to get authoritative information about the granting of a Dissolution of Parliament by the Sovereign. It is curious how little mention there is of it – I suppose because it is not a request that any Sovereign has not granted, as a matter of course, since I don't know when.

Wednesday 23 May

Auchinleck to see the King, but I only had a few minutes with him; he is a very good-looking man, with great charm. Then Winston, at noon. He was in jaunty spirits; a violent thunderstorm was raging. 'I hope the omens are favourable,' he said. I said that unless the sheeted dead squeaked and gibbered in the streets, thunderstorms were traditionally an augury of victory.[1]

Then he to the King, where he tendered his resignation; and I to the Queen, whom I convinced that it would be a good thing if Princess Elizabeth accepted an honorary Bachelor's Degree of Music from the London University at the same time as Winston is given an hon. doctorate. I also told her of the King's idea for Winchester Tower, thinking it advisable to get it registered, so to speak. Winston came back again at 4 p.m., when the King, having (in theory) reflected on the matter since noon, accepted his resignation and then invited him to form a new administration. W. asked for a dissolution as soon as he had been re-appointed, and the King granted it. Later in the evening he telephoned to get the King's approval to it being fixed for 15 June, which will make the polling-day 5 July. From what Winston said, he has already got his Ministry – at any rate the major posts – pretty well fixed up. He proposes to have about eighteen to twenty in the Cabinet.

---

1 'A little ere the mightiest Julius fell,
    The graves stood tenantless and the sheeted dead
    Did squeak and gibber in the Roman streets.'
                                        Hamlet, Act 1, Sc. 1

Wording the Court Circular to give a correct constitutional picture of all these doings cost me some labour.

Thursday 24 May

An Empire Day garden-party at Buckingham Palace for about 1,750 repatriated prisoners of war from all parts of the Empire, and some of the devoted Red Cross ladies who packed the parcels, which, as they all admitted, saved their lives. They looked, on the whole, remarkably fit and well-nourished. Those who had been in contact with the Russians spoke of them as completely uncivilised; they took from them, if necessary at pistol-point, their wrist-watches and anything else of value they had with them; apart from that, they were kindly but utterly inefficient. This was a very successful party, at which Their Majesties and the Princesses did their stuff admirably.

Friday 25 May

Himmler's suicide was announced on the midnight news last night, dramatically told by a sergeant-major who was an eye-witness. He as near got away as don't matter, and the fact that he was held up, and his faked papers suspected, does great credit to the vigilance of our Intelligence people. This was much the best end for him; the fewer of them that fall into our hands alive, the better. Only Ribbentrop is at large now; I suspect he may have reached the Argentine, for he had a long start.[1]

Greased my salmon lines before dinner, and wrote to M. Balfour to borrow some Thunders and Blue Charms, of which I am short. One cannot buy fishing-tackle anywhere in London now, though I got one of the new 'nylon' casts at Ogden Smith's. Looking through the large stock of flies left me by my father, I was struck by the complete absence of the smaller sizes of any pattern. The modern theory is that one must never fish with anything bigger than a No. 6, and more often than not with things like large trout flies. Yet those old boys rarely used flies smaller than size 1/0, and they killed just as many salmon as we did.

Saturday 26 May

Justin McKeurtan, one of Lavinia's beaux in Italy, came to tea. Alex has written to me suggesting that the King go out to Italy this summer. From a recent letter of Lavinia's, this seems to have been the result of a plot made

---

1 For once Tommy was wrong. Ribbentrop was soon captured. He was tried at Nuremberg and executed.

by her and the Field-Marshal in a box at the opera. Queen Mary is seventy-five today.

Monday 28 May

A busy day. The seven outgoing Ministers came to take leave of the King before and after luncheon. I was touched by the kind things that Attlee, Bevin and Morrison said about the good relations that prevail between their offices and mine. I got the impression from all of them in turn that the Government would not have broken up now but for the machinations of Beaverbrook.

At 4.30 I was bidden to No. 10 for a tea-party which Winston gave for the ex-Ministers and the new ones. As I said to Jimmy Rothschild[1] (one of the former), it was a gathering that could have happened in no other country but ours – and not even in England not so many years ago. It was all very merry, and I'm not sure that Winston (who was obviously feeling emotional about it all) was best pleased when I said to him later in the evening that it was more like a wedding than a funeral.

He made a capital speech towards the close of the proceedings, saying that the coming election, like all English elections, would not be mealy-mouthed, but whatever they might say about each other during its course, the fact remained that as a united team the late Government had steered the country through the five most dangerous, and glorious, years of its history. Attlee replied, monochromatically as usual, and then, as nobody had mentioned the Liberal Party, Archie Sinclair said something on its behalf. Then I hurried back to Buckingham Palace, for the Council, at which the new men were sworn in. And so the 'Caretaker Government' is legally established.

Tuesday 29 May

The King and Queen and I left Euston 7 p.m. for Balmoral.

Sunday 3 June

Left Balmoral in the evening. The river was too heavy to fish most of the time; which was a disguised blessing. On Wednesday afternoon I fished for a few hours, which completely exhausted me, and revealed to me how tired I was. Thereafter I did no more wading, and contented myself with

---

1   James de Rothschild (d. 1957), MP, Joint Parliamentary Secretary, Ministry of Supply 1945.

desultory fishing of the Boat Pool. Thus I got some good out of the visit, which I certainly should not have, had I kept hard at it all the time.

Monday 4 June

Listened to Winston's election speech on my little wireless. It gave me the impression of a tired man unwillingly reading something that had been written for him and that he didn't much like.

Wednesday 6 June

In the Travellers today Jock Colville told me that the PM had written every word of his speech on Monday evening. The only share that the Beaver had in it was the deletion of a tribute to Ernie Bevin. Jock said the PM was now greatly apprehensive of the Russians, and that his mind was largely dominated by this.

Their Majesties were to have flown to the Channel Islands, but the weather was hopeless, so we had to call on the Admiralty to produce naval transport at short notice. They responded nobly, and the whole party got off tonight. It will be years before air travel will be really reliable for these royal visits, which cannot be postponed indefinitely, as other folks' can.

Dined Grillions, between Oswald Birley and Billy Harlech. Billy has much the same views about the House of Lords as I have, and would like to see the hereditary principle lapse.

Thursday 7 June

Old Fabian Ware,[1] head of the Imperial War Graves Commission, told me this morning that, since they obviously can't bury another Unknown Soldier in Westminster Abbey, they were considering the idea of burying one British and one American in a shrine at Runnymede, the home of both British and American liberties. I wondered why they need bury an Unknown Soldier anywhere at all. It was a brilliant idea in 1919, but such inspired *coups de théâtre* don't bear repetition a generation later.

Dined Travellers, next to that engaging creature Dunglass.[2] His crazy

---

1   Maj.-Gen. Sir Fabian Ware (1869–1949). Adviser to the War Office on Graves Registration 1944–9, Vice-Chairman War Graves Commission 1917–48.

2   Alexander Dunglass (1903–95), elder son of the 13th Earl of Home, disclaimed his peerages for life in 1963, but was created Baron Home of the Hirsel (Life Peer) in 1974. In June 1945 he was Joint Parliamentary Under-Secretary at the FO; PM and First Lord of the Treasury 1963–4. When his political opponent Harold Wilson sought to ridicule him by dismissing him as 'the fourteenth Lord Home', he retaliated by dubbing the

brother, lately released from a term of imprisonment to which he was sentenced by court martial (for refusing to obey orders in the field), is about to stand for Windsor as an Independent. D. spoke of him with a detached humour, which is the only attitude towards such domestic liabilities.

The weather having improved, Their Majesties flew back from the Channel Islands, reaching Buckingham Palace soon after 8 p.m. They had a tumultuous welcome. Eric Miéville said the islanders did not look as if they had suffered severe privations, and their cattle are intact and sleek, the Germans not having molested them. Nor did the Germans, though on very short commons themselves, ever interfere with the Red Cross parcels which we have been sending since February; they are a most curious people. The islanders have no conception of our own straitened circumstances in this country. They complained bitterly of the quality of the 'utility' clothing that we have sent them.

Friday 8 June

The wreckage of Leigh-Mallory's aeroplane has been found on a mountainside near Grenoble. Evidently, they flew into an Alp.

Saturday 9 June

The King and Queen went to the Derby at Newmarket, won by Dante. Astor, whose ill-luck in the race is extraordinary, ran third for the nth time. Joan and I went down to Eton to watch cricket, and sat with the Claude Elliotts.

Sunday 10 June

With Their Majesties to the farewell parade of the Civil Defence forces, in Hyde Park. Speech by the King, march-past, etc. It was a moving affair – this motley army, in an infinite variety of semi-uniform clothing, of the middle-aged of both sexes, most of them obviously feeling their corns, who have worked devotedly all through the war. Yet the Press next day, almost without exception, missed the chance of paying them the tribute they deserve and devoted the bulk of their space to a description of two infernal police dogs that figured in the procession. I was glad to see that Herbert Morrison, who deserves much credit for the creation and organisation of

---

Labour leader 'the fourteenth Mr Wilson'. His 'crazy brother' was the Hon. William Douglas-Home (1912–92), author of many successful plays.

Civil Defence, was put in the front row of the privileged spectators and given his chance of being complimented by the King.

Tuesday 12 June

Went to the Guildhall to see Eisenhower get the Freedom of the City; big crowds all the way east from the Strand. I was on the dais, among the swells, which involves a walk up half the length of the Guildhall, to shake hands with the Lord Mayor, after one's name has been bawled out to the assembled guests in the body of the hall, who greet one's arrival with applause that varies in intensity with his, or her, degree of notoriety; rather an ordeal.

After the ceremony, very well conducted with all the time-honoured civic ritual, went on to luncheon at the Mansion House. Eisenhower had to make three speeches – one in the Guildhall; one to the crowd, from the balcony of the Mansion House; and one in reply to his toast after luncheon. All three were first-rate, delivered with a simplicity and sincerity that were most impressive. I was between old Courtauld-Thomson,[1] a moderate bore, and Bomber-Command Harris, who drove me home. Harris told me that his Command had suffered about 40,000 casualties (dead) during the war – more than those sustained by the joint British and Canadian Armies between D-Day and the capitulation. This is remarkable, seeing that Bomber Command's strength was never more than 110,000.

Later, Eisenhower came to Buckingham Palace and was given the OM by the King. So it was a great day for Ike, who was clearly deeply moved by it all; and he got nothing that he did not deserve, for he is a great man. I should like to see him President of USA some day, but those who know him best say that nothing but a national crisis of the first water would induce him to run.[2] He told me he had written most of his Guildhall speech in an aeroplane.

Wednesday 13 June

Shuldham Redfern[3] lunched with me at the Travellers and propounded a scheme for the closer association of the Sovereign with Canada by making periodic flights to Ottawa, opening Parliament and conducting other governmental and social business. That is all very fine in theory; but in practice,

---

1   Col. Courtauld Courtauld-Thomson (1865–1954). In 1942 he presented his house Dorney Wood and its contents to the nation for the use of the Prime Minister or, at his nomination, a Secretary of State. Created 1st Baron Courtauld-Thomson 1944.
2   Eisenhower did become President, for two terms, 1953–61.
3   Sir Shuldham Redfern (1895–1985), Secretary to Gov.-Gen. of Canada 1939–45.

I reminded him, any such activities must be quadrupled, for what the Sovereign does for one Dominion, he must do for all (apart from India – and the larger Colonies would eventually stake a claim, too). You then get a considerable accretion of work, and travel, in the life of the only functionary in the world (save the Pope, and he don't become Pope till late in life) who can never look forward to retirement, and can never really take a holiday which is wholly free from business. Consequently, though the idea is sound enough in principle, the personal and physical limitations imposed by it make it almost unworkable.

Redfern said that flying made it all so much simpler; true, but even flying to and from Canada is a physical strain, and for many years to come there will be an element of danger in long-distance flights which could not be ignored.

Thursday 14 June

The King today offered me the use of Craigowan, traditionally the Private Secretary's house at Balmoral. This would be a very great boon, solving several acute family problems. I doubt if it will be ready for us this year, as the Grand Duchess Xenia is still in possession; and even if she can be shifted, the house will need painting etc.

Lunched Beefsteak, next to Osbert Sitwell[1] and opposite Evelyn Waugh.[2] On to Holbrow's, in Duke Street, where by great luck I have found a spinning-rod and reel for John, who is anxious to attack the German pike. Fishing-tackle is hard to come by now, but with an assortment of my old spoon-baits (to which L. Ritchie contributed a magnificent plug-minnow) I can now equip him fully.

Friday 15 June

General Slim,[3] who has commanded 14th Army all through the Burma campaign, was in today; he impressed me very favourably – a fine type of soldier, physically reminiscent of Alan Brooke. The Japs, he says, should not be likened to humans or to animals, but to insects; they are an army of fighting ants, with all the defects and the qualities of the termite. Dickie

---

1 Sir Osbert Sitwell, 5th Bt. (1892–1969), writer, who, in his own words, conducted 'a series of skirmishes and hand-to-hand battles against the Philistines'.
2 Evelyn Waugh (1903–66), novelist and biographer. His novel *Brideshead Revisited* came out in 1945.
3 Field-Marshal Sir William Slim (1891–1970) held many commands in the Far East. C-in-C Allied Land Forces SE Asia 1945–6, CIGS 1948–52, Gov.-Gen. of Australia 1958–60. Created 1st Viscount Slim 1960.

Mountbatten, who knew nothing whatever about soldiering when he took over SEAC and had nobody there to teach him, is now beginning to learn.

News has just come in of Ribbentrop having been at last run to earth; he was found in bed in a Hamburg lodging, where he had been living under an assumed name for many weeks. He had with him a phial of the usual Nazi poison, which was impounded before he could take it, and letters addressed to Winston, Eden and Monty. R. was the only man I have ever met to shake hands with (which I only did once, in 1937 or '38) who gave one all the physical sensations of touching a snake. I cordially disliked him from the moment I set eyes on him, and have always regarded him as the most evil of his evil gang.

Wednesday 20 June

Spaatz came for his honorary GBE [Knight Grand Cross of the British Empire], and talked, in the Eisenhower vein, of the wonderful spirit of cooperation that prevailed between the US forces and ours. It is encouraging to hear one after another of these American generals say the same thing, with undoubted sincerity. He was followed by James Somerville, admiral, whom I'd never met before; he, too, is doing his bit for cooperation by keeping Ernie King sweet in Washington. He told me that King's habitual intransigence throughout the war was not due to any fundamental anti-British feeling, but to a flaring jealousy of our navy *vis-à-vis* that of USA. Finally that good man Ernest Gowers[1] (GBE), who did sterling work as regional commissioner in London. (Immediately after the severe Blitz of 10 May 1941 Gowers told me that if the Germans put on a similar raid in the next few days, London would have to be evacuated, for, after the raid of 10 May, all the principal services – light, water, drains, telephones etc. – were, so to speak, hanging by a thread. Another raid would have put them out of action.)

After luncheon, the King, flanked by his Archbishops of Cantuar and Ebor (in their cassocks) received His Beatitude the Metropolitan Nikolai Krutitsky and his delegates from the Russian Orthodox Church. None of the three of them has any English, but a person called Sergeant interpreted fluently. The King made them a short address, of which he gave His B. a signed copy.

Winston lunched with the King, and discussed with him the various political combinations that may result from the general election. W. has now convinced himself that all the young men and women in the Services

---

1 Sir Ernest Gowers (1880–1966), Regional Commissioner for Civil Defence London Region 1939–45.

will vote against him, I don't know on what evidence. There is a dance at Buckingham Palace tonight, the echoes of which will probably give me a restless night. Caroline, looking very pretty in one of Joan's frocks, is attending it, under the wing of Delia Peel and the Adeanes. I have, mercifully, not been invited, and feel that there are after all some compensations for being nearly three score years.

Thursday 21 June

Saw Ismay and Bridges p.m. As I anticipated, everybody in Whitehall has become like an unstrung bow since the end of the war with Germany. They are all exhausted, from the PM downwards. Ismay told me that he had not set eyes on the latter for a month, so absorbed is he in the election.

Friday 22 June

Joan and I entertained old Charles Kavanagh,[1] *ci-devant* GOC Cavalry Corps, and his wife at tea. He makes no sense now, and I doubt if she ever did at any time. She told me that the best cure for a cold was to gargle Friar's Balsam; no doubt she meant inhale, but she *said* gargle, and I suppose if anybody was fool enough to take her advice, he would be dead by morning.

Monday 25 June

The King suggested to Winston some time ago that while the Big Three are conferring in Berlin, he (HM) should visit Monty in Germany, spend three or four days seeing the troops, and go to Berlin for a few hours, when he would entertain Truman and Stalin at luncheon. Winston telegraphed to Truman and Stalin to get their reactions to this; T. acquiesces cordially, S. very grudgingly, saying that he had arranged to go to Berlin to see Truman and Winston, and hadn't contemplated being asked to meet the King; but if W. thinks this plan is essential, he will fall in with it.

    Winston (who is away on an election-tour) told L. Rowan that he would advise the King that no answer be sent to this for some time, and that then Stalin should be told that HM's programme with his troops did not permit of his visiting Berlin. Meanwhile, I wrote privately to Monty to find out what he thinks about it. I got his reply tonight; he is all for the King going to the British zone, 'but the project of going to the Russian zone is, I

---

1   Lieut.-Gen. Sir Charles Kavanagh (1864–1950), Governor of the Military Knights of Windsor. He had married May Woodrooff, from Co. Tipperary, in 1895.

consider, not a good one. I cannot think it is wise. The Russians are curious people; their ways are not our ways; some awkward situation might well arise. My advice is that the King should NOT go there.' With all of which, I agree.

Saturday 30 June

After talking it over with Winston yesterday, the King has decided not to go to Germany at all next month, but to go instead to Northern Ireland, which has been clamouring for a royal visit ever since VE Day. This is perhaps the wiser course, though personally I should have enjoyed the German expedition.

Yesterday Cartier came to see me, on the vexed question whether, if Princess Elizabeth goes to Brussels next month, she should be allowed to assist at one of the traditional ceremonies at the Manneken Pis statue.[1] Cartier was shocked at the idea, and I don't think it a good one, for apart from any embarrassment that might be caused to HRH herself, the subsequent publication of the inevitable Press photograph would be sure to excite many sections of the still-prudish British public, who would avow that the ill-mannered Belgians had affronted our Heiress Presumptive, whence might spring a well-developed international incident. However, Hughe Hugessen telephoned to me later in the day that he was confident he could so arrange matters that the Princess would be elsewhere when the statue function took place.

Sunday 1 July

I had a long talk this evening with Gray Phillips, who has been Comptroller to the Duke of Windsor in the Bahamas. He told me that the Duke's ultimate aim was to make his home in the south of France, as soon as things have settled down there. He apparently has no wish to return to this country, nor to hold any official post once the war is over. G.P. said he had aged little, though he had got very thin; he has not been unhappy in his post-abdication life, and we agreed that he would certainly have been very much so had he attempted to be a king. He is still as devoted as ever to his Duchess, whose chief hobby is running a house at perfection level.

Eric Miéville yesterday broke to the King, who took it calmly and kindly, that he wished to leave us at the end of the year. Curiously, I heard the same day from Edward Ford, in Haifa, saying (in answer to a letter that I wrote

---

1   The bronze fountain, dating from 1619, cast in the form of a small boy urinating.

him some weeks ago) that he would like to be considered as a candidate for E.M.'s chair. I have had an idle weekend, staying in bed till 11 a.m.; and I have re-read *The Big House at Inver*,[1] which is one of the best novels in the English language.

Friday 6 July

Returned to Windsor after a three-day visit to the Isle of Man, with Their Majesties. We had intended to fly over on Tuesday afternoon; but as usual the weather was pronounced unfit for flying, so we had to fall back on the alternative route – train to Liverpool, and then crossed to Douglas in the cruiser *Dido*. We reached Douglas after breakfast on Wednesday, in a thick fog, in which that corner of the island remained shrouded throughout our stay, with an infernal fog-horn moaning day and night. Consequently, we saw little of the island's scenery, though we drove assiduously round and about it; some of the inland bits seemed attractive.

The Granvilles,[2] our hosts [at Government House], are on the verge of leaving the island to succeed the Abercorns in Belfast; they have done a good job in the I. of M. Granville, born when his father was sixty-five, is the most robust of Benjamins, and his rugged commonsense is just what is wanted in that kind of microcosm – supplemented as it is by her sympathetic charm and light-heartedness.

The highlight of the tour was the ceremony on Tynwald Hill, dating back to the Norse occupation. This went off well, though a great many of us had to group ourselves, chamois-like, on the top of the hill, which is not much bigger than a dining-room table.[3]

Wednesday 11 July

The Regent of Iraq[4] lunched with Their Majesties, and later Anthony Eden (now acting PM)[5] came to see the King. A.E. looks outwardly well but is

---

1   By Edith Somerville, first published in 1925.
2   William Leveson-Gower, 4th Earl Granville (1880–1953), Lieut.-Gov. Isle of Man 1937–45, had married Lady Rose Bowes-Lyon, younger sister of the future Queen Elizabeth, in 1916.
3   Probably because he was away, Tommy did not record the fact that polling in the general election had taken place on 5 July. A three-week moratorium was declared, so that the votes of military personnel serving overseas could be counted before the result of the election was announced.
4   In May 1944 the British Army had occupied Baghdad, having driven out Raschid Ali and his supporters, who had carried out a *coup d'état* in 1941.
5   Churchill was on his way to the conference with Truman and Stalin at Potsdam.

still far from strong; his boy was reported missing in Burma a few days ago. Lord Salisbury[1] to see me about Their Majesties' visit to Hatfield tomorrow; he is very frail now; and then Joe Airlie, with whom I afterwards called on Bobbety Cranborne in the Dominions Office.

After dinner went to see Edward Bridges, busy packing up for 'Terminal' (the Berlin conference). Young William Armstrong[2] has just come back from Berlin, where he was sent, with Joan Bright, to make the billeting arrangements. He showed me a large-scale map on which were marked the enclaves allotted to Truman and Winston, in a suburb close to Wilmersdorf, where he said they would all be comfortable enough, as that district had escaped the bombs. I asked him where Stalin and his people would be, and he told me that the Russians, though most accommodating in all other respects, had refused to tell them this.

Thursday 12 July

Ismay came to see me after tea, and said that an invasion of Japan would cost us and the Americans half a million men, and he didn't think it was worth it.

Joan gave me a good letter from John, his first from Berlin. He says the Russians have been obstructive and uncooperative, and that in the house which the Grenadiers took over from them was a German eight weeks dead, whom nobody had troubled to bury. Flies very bad, and a lot of the men down with tummy trouble.

Sunday 15 July

Last night there was a thunderstorm of a length and violence such as I have seldom seen in England. Before going to bed, we went to the top of Winchester Tower and watched its progress all round the horizon till driven in by torrential rain. It went on till nearly sunrise, yet the air is little cooler this morning.

Monday 16 July

Colin Forbes Adam and I lunched at the Travellers, and then watched the third Test Match from the top of the pavilion at Lord's. It was very pleasant,

---

1 James Cecil, 4th Marquess of Salisbury (1861–1947) had been an MP, and was Lord Privy Seal 1924–9 and Leader of the House of Lords 1925–9. Hatfield House was his home in Hertfordshire.
2 1915–80. Civil servant and banker, Private Secretary to the Secretary of the War Cabinet 1943–6. Knighted 1963, created Baron Armstrong of Sanderstead (Life Peer) 1975.

and like old times; every seat in the ground was full, and the cricket interesting.

Tuesday 17 July

Their Majesties went to Belfast, with Princess Elizabeth, by air. To Lord's, with P. Legh and Tim Nugent, where we spent another agreeable and restful afternoon, seeing Australia win the match by four wickets.

Friday 20 July

In White's Randolph Churchill[1] has recorded a bet with Stokes (MP for Ipswich),[2] whereby Stokes is to pay R.C. £5 for every seat below 300 held by the Labour Party, and R.C. to pay £1 for every seat over 300.[3]

Sunday 22 July

Joan and Caroline gave a very successful dance at Winchester Tower, attended by the Princesses and about fifty couples of young men and maidens. It was luckily a lovely night, so that the roof-garden was available for sitting-out – otherwise the congestion would have been dreadful. I stayed till 12.30, and thought that, on the whole, Selina Baker was the best of a good-looking bunch. I slept at the Castle throughout the weekend, Winchester Tower being uninhabitable.

Monday 23 July

PM telegraphed from Berlin that Truman could not come here on his way back from Potsdam – this, on the whole, is a relief – and that the conference will probably last till the end of the first week in August.

Tuesday 24 July

Harry Crerar,[4] looking better than I have seen him for a long time, came to get his CH; he has now handed over his Army to Simonds, and is on his

---

1 Hon. Randolph Churchill, son of Winston, had been MP for Preston since 1940, but lost his seat in 1945.
2 Rt. Hon. Richard Rapier Stokes (1897–1951), MP for Ipswich 1938–51, Cabinet Minister in Attlee's 1950–51 government.
3 In the event, Labour held 396 seats.
4 Gen. Henry Crerar became ADC General to King George VI 1948–52.

way back to Canada where he proposes to have a long rest. He has earned it; he has had a good war, and comes out with an unblemished reputation. I should like him to come to London as Canadian High Commissioner some day.

Monty has sent the King Part One of his latest literary effort, 'Notes on the Occupation of Germany'. Leslie Rowan writes tolerably cheerfully of the progress of 'Terminal', though the Russians are demanding a full pound of flesh on every point that comes up for discussion. He says that John had lunched with them, 'full of information about the Germans'. John wrote the other day complaining indignantly that Winston was flying the Royal Standard on his car, but this proves to be only the standard of the Lord Warden of the Cinque Ports.

Wednesday 25 July

I have just (10.30 p.m.) got a note from Alex, back at his home in Windsor Forest from Berlin for forty-eight hours, saying that he 'accepts with alacrity' Mackenzie King's proposal to recommend him to the King as the next Governor-General of Canada. This is a great relief. I am delighted.[1]

Winston is also back from Berlin, for the announcement of election results tomorrow. He came to see the King at 6 p.m., and greeted me with a eulogy of John, who had dined in his Potsdam Mess last night, and evidently had made a good impression on him. He looked well, and Leslie Rowan, who came and talked to me while W. was with the King, said he was quite in his old form at the conference. Truman is a good chairman, but a bit inelastic – inclined to say, 'This is the policy of the USA', and refuse to modify it; but this is largely due to inexperience of public affairs, and he is learning fast.

The PM told the King that the Americans would probably drop on Japan towards the end of next week one or two of the bombs of which Appleton told me. They have tried them out in the Mexican desert with spectacular results.[2]

Thursday 26 July General Election

The results of the general election started coming in about 10 a.m. By luncheon-time, it was clear that Winston was out, and something very like a landslide in favour of Labour had taken place. This evening, Labour's

---

1 Tommy had lobbied hard and long to have less suitable candidates excluded, and for the choice to fall on Alexander.
2 See entry for 8 Feb. 1945.

majority is about 200. Many Ministers beaten; even Winston himself, though in by a big majority, had 10,000 votes against him in his constituency.

Eddy Devonshire was right in his forecast; though I hadn't anticipated as big a swing as this, it don't surprise me; nor, as I told the King, do I look on it as an unrelieved disaster; in five years' time we may look back on it as the best thing that could have happened, on balance. Anything is better than an uncertain situation, with one party or the other kept in power by the day-to-day support of the Liberals (not that they have much support to offer, as it turns out – there are only a dozen of them returned, and Archie Sinclair himself was beat in a three-cornered fight in Caithness, as were Violet Bonham-Carter[1] and her son Mark in their respective West Country constituencies).

Winston asked me to go and see him at the No. 10 Annexe at 4 p.m. In the office, Edward Bridges and Rowan told me that his intention was to do nothing until after Sunday, have a Cabinet on Monday and then resign. This we all felt was wrong, for obviously Truman and Stalin won't wait at Potsdam indefinitely, and, as Winston says nothing will induce him to go back there himself, somebody from this country must take his place.

Then I was called into his room, where he was sitting in his siren suit, with the usual banana-sized cigar, taking counsel of David Margesson.[2] He did not look depressed, nor did he talk so. He attributed his defeat to the people's reaction from their sufferings of the past five years – they have endured all the horrors and discomforts of war, and, automatically, they have vented it on the government that has been in power throughout the period of their discontent. The only time when he became at all emotional was when I gave him a personal message from the King, and told him how much HM would miss him. He had changed his mind about his course of action – perhaps David and I helped him to make it up afresh. Anyhow, he decided to resign tonight, and in our presence dictated a new letter to Attlee, tearing up the draft of a previous one. This was the final version:

My Dear Attlee,
 In consequence of the electoral decision recorded today, I propose

---

1 Violet Bonham-Carter (1887–1969), known as 'Lady Vi', eldest daughter of H. H. Asquith. President of the Women's Liberal Federation 1939–45 and of the Liberal Party Organisation 1945–7. Created Baroness (Life Peeress) Asquith of Yarnbury 1960. Her son Mark (1922–94) was Liberal MP for Torrington 1958–9, became first Chairman of the Race Relations Board in 1966, and was created Baron Bonham-Carter (Life Peer) of Yarnbury in 1986.
2 David Margesson (1890–1965), Secretary of State for War 1940–42. Created 1st Viscount Margesson of Rugby 1942.

to tender my resignation to the King at seven o'clock this evening on personal grounds. I wish you all success in the heavy burden you are about to assume.

    Yours v. sincerely,
      W.S.C.

The last sentence is not grammar – he meant 'success *in the bearing of the heavy burden*'.] This letter was sent off. We then discussed future possibilities. Winston said that, with the Opposition so weak, the House of Lords would be the only watch-dog left, but he hoped that they would not bark too loud, or they would find themselves in trouble. David forecast that the House of Commons would sit till about August 17th, and then adjourn for four to six weeks; both he and Winston agreed that the King ought not to leave London till the House rose, but that it was not necessary for him to return immediately it met again in September. I asked whether he thought the King could contemplate taking any overseas trips – e.g. India – this winter; Winston was emphatic in saying that he could not, but must remain in this country. As to Potsdam, Winston felt that Attlee ought to get the name of his Foreign Secretary approved at once, and take him to Berlin tomorrow.

When I got back to Buckingham Palace, it occurred to me that this could not be done until Eden surrenders his seals, and the new Foreign Secretary receives them and is sworn in before the Council – otherwise he is impotent. Leadbitter, Secretary to the Privy Council, confirmed this, and we made tentative arrangements for a Council to be held for this purpose before luncheon tomorrow. However, when Attlee arrived to see the King, he said it would be quite impossible for him to form even a skeleton Cabinet before tomorrow night – his colleagues are scattered over their constituencies – or to leave for Potsdam before Saturday.

About 5.30, I said I must go back and report to the King, and left after further talk with Bridges, Rowan and Ismay. In the passage I saw Oliver Lyttelton, whom I congratulated on his recent miraculous escape, when the aeroplane in which he had just taken off stalled in both engines and eventually belly-crashed in a field. Nobody was seriously hurt, but Oliver said he was quite sure for several minutes that death was inevitable. He said the cause was just lack of petrol – the tanks had not been filled, which seems an incredible piece of carelessness.

I told the King the substance of our talk; he has taken all today's happenings with great calm and reasonableness. Winston came at seven, and left 7.25. He told me on leaving that the King had again offered him the Garter, and that he had refused – which fact he would like made public. But the King agreed with me afterwards that we must make another effort to get him to accept it.[1] Rowan told me that Winston felt it would be wrong for him to do so after 'the rebuff that the electorate have given him as a leader'. I suggested to the King that the Queen might see what Mrs Churchill can do.

Attlee came 7.30, obviously in a state of some bewilderment – the poor little man had only heard a couple of hours before that he was to be called upon immediately to fill Winston's place; it struck me that he may not be sure whether his followers are prepared to follow him, or may prefer another leader – he has had no chance of consulting them. Anyway, he kissed hands all right, so is now committed to forming a Government – or trying to.

He told the King that he was thinking of making Dalton Foreign Secretary; HM begged him to substitute Bevin. HM asked him if, in view of the hurry with which it had been necessary to change the Government, owing to the exigencies of Potsdam, he would have any objection to Winston taking some little time in the preparation of his Dissolution honours list; he said he would not. I had previously asked him the same question, and had the same answer. He was in with the King till about 7.50 p.m., when HM sent for me again.

Friday 27 July

It was not until 7.20 that Rowan was able to tell me the names of those whom Attlee is submitting to the King for Cabinet posts. They are: Lord Chancellor, Bill Jowitt; Lord President and Leader of the House of Commons, Herbert Morrison; Chancellor of the Exchequer, Hugh Dalton; Lord Privy Seal, Greenwood;[2] President of the Board of Trade, Stafford Cripps; Foreign Secretary, Ernest Bevin. That is as far as he can get at present. I warned their opposite numbers to come and hand over their seals tomorrow – all except Oliver Lyttelton, who had already left for the country, and has no seal to deliver, so I left him in peace. The King seemed quite pleased with these appointments, which he accepted without demur.

The Japs have rejected the joint ultimatum, so I suppose they will shortly get what is coming to them.

---

1   *Later note:* Which he did in 1953. It fell to me to make the final assault, in the Bow Room at Buckingham Palace, while he was waiting to go in and see the Queen. He capitulated without much resistance, and, wiping his eyes, said with his schoolboy's grin, 'Now Clemmie will have to be a lady at last.'
2   Rt. Hon. Arthur Greenwood (1880–1954), Lord Privy Seal 1945–7.

Saturday 28 July

The King, H. Campbell and I left Windsor 9.15 a.m., reaching Buckingham Palace shortly before 10. Simon, Anderson, Eden and Beaverbrook handed in their seals in a series of five-minute audiences, and Woolton took leave as Lord President. Council at 10.30, which I attended. The King and his new Prime Minister were photographed, and, after I had disposed of the Great, and other, seals, we went back to Windsor. Attlee and Bevin flew to Potsdam, arriving there about 5 p.m. I don't think 'Terminal' will achieve much more, and they will probably all come home in a few days, leaving the many loose ends to be tied up at the Peace Conference.

Old Margot Asquith is dead; a great figure in her day, and she was always very kind to me. The younger generation owe her a good deal, for she was a vigorous breaker-down of the Victorian conventions.

Sunday 29 July

We lunched with Lady Gowrie,[1] to meet Lady Willingdon, whose volubility is now completely destructive of all conversation. Much telephoning and telegraphing about the King's projected meeting with Truman, and Alex's appointment. The *Observer*, in its biographical notice of Margot Asquith, speaks of her having been the reputed heroine of Anthony Hope's *Dolly Dialogues*; this is nonsense, for she had no resemblance to Dolly; what they mean is E. F. Benson's *Dodo* – as bad a best-seller as ever was, incidentally.

Monday 30 July

Winston asked me to go and see him at No. 10 after luncheon, to talk about his dissolution honours list, though it is still in embryo. He wants to give peerages to five or six safe-seated old gentlemen in the House of Commons, to make room for some of his younger and more vigorous colleagues who have fallen by the wayside. He emphasised the importance of maintaining a proper balance in the H. of C. by building up a reasonably strong opposition front bench. The Conservative Party (which he said might be re-christened 'The National Union Party') was now at its nadir, and before long the pendulum would begin to swing, very slowly at first but with increasing velocity, back to normal. He again said how important it was that the Lords should restrain themselves at first, and reserve their opposition for any measure that was fundamentally subversive of the Constitution.

[In the honours list] Pug Ismay is down for a CH, John Martin for a CB,

---

1 Zara Gowrie, wife of the 1st Earl of Gowrie (1872–1955).

and poor little Leo Amery, who can hardly be made a peer when his eldest son is on the steps of the gallows, for a GCB. I was relieved that the list was free from any enormities, and said that I saw nothing in it to which the King would be likely to object. In the middle of our conversation Winston again eulogised John, saying that he was 'a fine chap'. I said that was because he was descended from John Churchill. Winston, who never remembers that my wife is his cousin, did not take the point at first; when I elucidated it, he was delighted, and spontaneously held out his hand to me. We then reminisced for a bit about Cornelia, Lady Wimborne, and the Guest family generally. Finally he thanked me very kindly for having helped him during the past two years, which, God knows, I have been glad enough to do, for he is one of the handful of great Englishmen who have kept England inviolate through the centuries.

Anthony Bevir told me that he had mentioned to Attlee one or two appointments which are outstanding, among them the Regius Professorship of English Literature at Cambridge. Attlee said at once that there was only one man for that – David Cecil. So, if he pursues the idea, his first piece of patronage as Prime Minister will be preferment for a Lord, grandson of a Tory Prime Minister. This will bewilder more than ever those foreign students of politics who seek to understand our curious system.[2]

Tuesday 31 July

This evening I at last got definite news of the President of USA's movements. He is due to leave Potsdam Thursday morning, so I pressed all the necessary buttons for the King's journey to Plymouth to meet him.

Wednesday 1 August

Joan's 50th birthday.

General Freddy Morgan[3] came to receive a long-overdue KCB. This was given him last year for being the *fons et origo* of 'Overlord', which was in its early stages known as 'Morgan's plan'. Monty, who will never admit military ability in anybody at all except Monty, once told me that F. Morgan was perfectly useless, and that the Order of the Bath had been prostituted by his having been given a K.

---

1 Winston's aunt, and Joan's grandmother Lady Cornelia Spencer-Churchill, daughter of 7th Duke of Marlborough, married Ivor Guest, later 1st Baron Wimborne, 1868.
2 Lord David Cecil (1902–86), author and lecturer in English, was not appointed.
3 Lieut.-Gen. Sir Frederick Morgan (1894–1967), Deputy CoS to Supreme Commander, Allied Expeditionary Force 1944–5. He became Controller of Atomic Energy 1951.

At 10 p.m. the King, Edward Halifax (who got back from Washington on leave yesterday), H. Campbell and I left Paddington.

Thursday 2 August

We reached Millbay station, Plymouth, at 10.30 a.m. and went at once by barge to *Renown*, lying in the Sound. A perfect summer's day, and the old ship, though still in the process of refitting, looked clean enough to my landsman's eye. The King took the opportunity of being photographed on her fo'c'sle for a 'trailer', for which the film world have been plaguing poor L. Ritchie for weeks, while I talked to Edward Halifax in the cabin.

Soon after 12.30 President Truman came on board, being met by the King at the head of the gangway with all due naval ceremonial. He brought with him Admiral Leahy,[1] and Byrnes,[2] now Secretary of State; those three, plus our lot and Sir R. Leatham[3] (Commander-in-Chief, Plymouth), were the luncheon party.

The King, who had had twenty minutes' talk with Truman before luncheon, had him on his right, Byrnes on the left, with Edward Halifax on the other side of Truman, and myself the other side of Byrnes. It was a cheerful meal, but Byrnes, who rarely draws breath, made me and Edward gasp by talking freely about the 'T.A.', or 'heavy water', atomic bombs, with the stewards still in the room. As this is so secret a matter in this country that only about six people have ever heard of it, this seemed somewhat indiscreet, even for an American.

I suppose Byrnes's excuse would be that the thing is to be loosed on Japan in a few days' time, after which its existence will be public property. E. and I discussed the effect that the invention of the thing may have on the whole future of civilisation. So long as its secret is in the hands of the Americans and ourselves, there is reasonable security against its misuse – in fact, the mere knowledge of its existence might be an instrument for peace, in that trouble-making nations would think twice before risking its employment against themselves. But if the Russians got hold of it, it would be a terrible danger.

At present, the expense of producing it is fantastic – Byrnes mentioned an astronomical figure of dollars already spent by US Government – and a

---

1 Adm. William D. Leahy (1875–1959) had seen service in the Boxer Rebellion in China in 1900. He retired from the US Navy in 1939, but in 1941 was brought back into service as CoS to the President.
2 James F. Byrnes (1879–1972), US Director of War Mobilisation (1943–5) and Secretary of State 1945–7.
3 Adm. Sir Ralph Leatham (1886–1954), C-in-C Plymouth 1943–5.

vast plant is necessary; so it can hardly be manufactured in secret, and certainly not by the smaller nations. But the processes, and the cost, may be simplified as time goes on, and, if so, civilisation might be at the mercy of any unscrupulous group of scientists. However, if its effects are demonstrated on the Japanese, it may help to bring home to everybody that war doesn't pay – the only real way of preventing war – and attention may be diverted to its potentialities for good, as a source of heat, power, etc. But, on the whole, I would rather that it had never been invented at all.

I have no idea what the King said to Truman, but they seemed to get on very well. I formed a favourable impression of T. He has a good, resolute face, with a firm chin, and a quick mind to take a point, whether grave or humorous. He, Byrnes and Leahy chaffed each other pleasantly. Leahy evidently has the reputation of a cynic, with a propensity for looking on the dark side of everything. He only speaks once in a while, but when he does, it is worth hearing and often witty. Byrnes is very voluble – a Southerner, I should say[1] – and clever as a wagon-load of monkeys. I believe he is a remarkably good lawyer. But in the matter of character, I should say he came third of the three.

Shortly after luncheon the Americans went back to *Augusta*, lying quarter of a mile away from us; we then repaid their call. Then we went back to *Renown* and watched *Augusta* steam away on her homeward journey; the King and the President interchanged farewell signals, and so back to the train, reaching Paddington 10 p.m. all pretty tired. I expect it was a memorable and historic meeting, and have no doubt it did a lot of good. Our visitors were obviously well pleased by the encounter, and could not have been more friendly.

Friday 3 August

Late last night Attlee sent round the submission for the majority of his remaining Government appointments, and at 12 today he came to get the King's final approval of them. Immediately after luncheon we started a procession of ex-Ministers handing over their several seals This done, a Council at which the new men received their seals, and the necessary admissions to the Privy Council were made – Shinwell[2] (a Jew) and Aneurin Bevan (Agnostic) 'making affirmation' in lieu of the customary oath. I was

---

1 Quite right: he came from South Carolina.
2 Emanuel ('Manny') Shinwell (1884–1986), Minister of Fuel and Power 1945–7, Secretary of State for War 1947–50. Created Baron Shinwell of Easington (Durham), Life Peer, 1970.

not present at the Council, but apart from some difficulty over Barnes's[1] wooden leg when he kissed hands, it all seems to have gone off in orderly fashion.

Saturday 4 August

Attlee's administration is now practically complete; the Cabinet is a large one, and the average age of the Ministry is high. But, from what A. said to me the other day, I gather that he will promote some of his young hands as soon as they have got the necessary Parliamentary experience. He said that there was a lot of good stuff among the recruits. Hartley Shawcross, of whom I saw a certain amount when he was regional commissioner in Lancashire, has been made Attorney-General straight away, which I should think is unprecedented for a man newly elected to his first Parliament.[2]

Their Majesties went to Ascot races, where the King's colt Rising Light won his race.

Tuesday 7 August

Yesterday the Americans dropped the first atomic bomb on the Japanese town of Hiroshima; it has not yet been possible to observe the results. Attlee has published the admirable statement on it written by Winston which I read at No. 10 the other day; Truman has also issued a statement from the *Augusta*. The newspapers today scarcely mention any other subject; and no wonder, for the introduction into human history of this particular form of energy may be the most important event since Noah's ark. Its implications, for good and for evil, are unpredictable and alarming.

Pug Ismay was pleased with the net results of Potsdam; said it had improved our personal relations with the Russians, as to whom he shares Leslie Rowan's opinion; he is convinced that they are feverishly anxious to keep in well with us, and that they knew nothing at all about the atomic bomb.

Now that the shock of the election-result is blunted, I find that most people are of the opinion that the continuance in power of Winston's Government, exhausted as most of its members were, would have been disastrous. Wrote to Edward Ford, in Haifa, asking him to come here as assistant private secretary at the end of the year – subject, of course, to his being approved after an interview with the King.

---

1 Rt. Hon. Alfred Barnes (1887–1974), Minister of Transport 1946–51.
2 In a later note the author added: 'His allegiance to the Labour party was not very firm, and in the House of Commons they talked of him as Sir Shortly Floor-cross.'

Wednesday 8 August

It struck me that it would be all wrong for the King to make no mention, in the speech from the throne next week, of the atomic bomb and its immense potentialities for good and evil. As most people, all over the world, are talking and thinking of little else, the omission would surely seem strange.

Thursday 9 August

The Cabinet adopted my suggestion that some allusion should be made. Another bomb was dropped, on Nagasaki, this morning.

Friday 10 August

As I was leaving the Travellers after luncheon, Jock Colville told me that a radio announcement from the Japanese 'Domei' had been picked up, saying that they were prepared to accept the Potsdam terms – i.e., surrender to the Allies. This was assumed by many to mean that the war was over, and there was a certain amount of indiscriminate junketing in London, mostly of the 'boat-race night' order, by the young and exuberant. This was premature, as a lot of telegraphing remained to be done, especially as to the regularisation of the Emperor's position.

I stayed in London and dined with Robin Barrington-Ward, talking mostly of the immediate and long-distance effects on civilisation of the sudden opening of the door on to a new world of atomic energy. A great deal of nonsense has been spoken, and written, on the subject during the past fortnight, and my old friend Cuthbert Thicknesse,[1] now Dean of St Albans, has made an ass of himself by refusing to allow any thanksgiving for victory in his cathedral, on the ground that it was won by devilish means. This is a wholly illogical position; it recalls the Chevalier Bayard,[2] who, *sans peur et sans reproche*, treated all his prisoners with knightly humanity save those whom he caught with arquebuses in their hands. These he hanged instantly, in that they had profaned Christian warfare by the use of the diabolical weapon of gunpowder. The plain fact is, of course, that it is war itself which is evil; the evilness of its various weapons, progressively more destructive as human ingenuity develops, is only a matter of degree.

---

1 Very Rev. Cuthbert Thicknesse (1887–1971), Dean of St Albans and Rector of the Abbey Church, St Albans 1936–55, had been a contemporary of Tommy's at Marlborough.
2 Pierre Terrail, Seigneur de Bayard (*c.* 1473–1524), French soldier celebrated for his many heroic deeds in battle, and for his chivalry.

Sunday 12 August

The King, wonderful to relate, had a letter from the Duke of Windsor ('Dear Bertie ... Yours, David' – the first so begun and ended for many a long day), in which he announced his intention of taking his Duchess to Antibes next month, and subsequently paying a short visit to this country, *en garçon.* This was actually stale news, for the Duke, with his usual propensity for doing everything in the order exactly opposite to that which normal people would follow, had already communicated his plans, first to Duff Cooper in Paris, and next to Attlee (who showed me the letter, which he was not at all pleased to get). Finally he has written to his mother, with whom he proposes to stay while in England.

The whole Windsor problem has recently been complicated by the discovery among the German Foreign Office archives at Marburg of a set of top-secret telegrams between Ribbentrop and Stohrer (German Ambassador in Madrid), regarding certain alleged overtures made to the Windsors by German agents when they were marooned in Portugal in May 1940. If the Windsors' reactions were as implied in this correspondence (which both Godfrey Thomas, to whom I showed them, and I agree cannot be wholly discounted; internal evidence indicates that there is at any rate a substratum of truth in it), the result is, to say the least, highly damaging to themselves.

Only one other copy of this set of telegrams is said to be in existence, and that is in American hands; the Foreign Office are taking steps to recover it. Meanwhile, I advised the King to discuss the whole thing with Bevin, and to urge him to let both Winston and Walter Monckton read the telegrams.

Wednesday 15 August

VJ Day, happily coincident with the opening of Parliament, restored to something of its pristine splendour by the revival of a carriage procession so the holiday crowds got their money's worth, and Their Majesties much kudos by refusing to have the carriage shut up, in spite of intermittent showers. Probably for the first time in our history, two alternative speeches from the Throne had been prepared and signed by the Sovereign – one for use if the news of the Japanese surrender had not arrived, the other for use if it had. I had a nervous moment lest Bill Jowitt, now Lord Chancellor, should produce the wrong speech out of his embroidered bag. It was a dull speech, only interesting in that it foreshadowed no legislation beyond what everybody had already anticipated. The King read it well, but surpassed himself in the evening when he delivered his broadcast. Everybody has commended it, and agrees that he has never yet spoken so fluently and forcefully.

I listened to it in the forecourt at Buckingham Palace, with a vast crowd, in what Winston has called a 'pin-drop silence', stretching out behind us half-way down the Mall. Immediately after, Their Majesties and the Princesses appeared on the balcony – flood-lit, of course – and were tumultuously received. When we went in, I lured Edward Halifax into my room and made him read the Marburg telegrams. I had actually received them from the Foreign Office the day before, but had deliberately withheld them from the King, thinking that they would certainly upset him and that he should not be troubled with them on the eve of making two major speeches. Indeed, I was not entirely convinced in my own mind – though nearly so – that it was necessary for him to see them at all, and it was on that point that I sought E.'s advice. He confirmed my opinion that I must show them to HM, which I did the following day.

During the afternoon Attlee brought Bevin, Morrison, Greenwood, Alexander (A.V.),[1] three chiefs of staff (now peers of the realm), Edward Bridges and Ismay to congratulate HM on the end of the war. L. Rowan and I had plotted to include Winston in this party; Attlee was all for it, but Winston said he wouldn't come unless he could bring with him those of his former colleagues who had served in the War Cabinet; so he came alone, half an hour after the others had gone. He was gleefully anticipating the speech which he was going to make in the House of Commons the following day, and evidently looking forward to the delights of front-bench opposition warfare.

Friday 17 August

Michiels, the Dutch Ambassador, brought an immense basket of flowers to give Their Majesties as a token of gratitude from the Dutch, whom we have harboured in this country throughout the war; with it, a very nicely-worded letter of thanks, which he read on the wireless on the following Sunday evening.

Sunday 19 August

Buckingham Palace before luncheon, and then processed (carriages) to St

---

1   Albert Victor Alexander (1885–1965), First Lord of the Admiralty 1940–45 and 1945–6, Minister of Defence 1947–50. Created 1st Viscount Alexander of Hillsborough 1950, 1st Earl 1963.

Paul's for the national thanksgiving service. Helen Northumberland,[1] Mary Nunburnholme[2] (two of the handsomest, but stupidest, women in England – when we got into the cathedral, they wandered about like a couple of lost ewes, despite careful previous coaching), Harold Campbell and self in second carriage, and the three chiefs of staff in the third. Large but decorous Sunday crowds.

Monday 20 August

The five Saudi Arabian princes to see Their Majesties, and Leo Amery and Ismay to get CH – two of Winston's resignation honours. Amery would normally have got a peerage, but as his eldest son is in imminent danger of hanging, this could not be.

Tuesday 21 August

The King received, and replied to, addresses from both Houses of Parliament in the Royal Gallery. Good attendance by the faithful Commons, but there were many empty chairs among the Lords; one of the absentees was the Lord Chamberlain, which I thought disgraceful.

Thursday 23 August

E. Bevin, very spruce in a new suit, had a long talk with the King a.m.; they discussed the Marburg papers etc. The new Bishop of London, Wand,[3] came to do Homage. He is suspected of Popish practice, and was roughly handled by Protestant demonstrators at his Confirmation yesterday.

Friday 24 August

The King dubbed nine new knights; received the new Egyptian Ambassador; held a Council, to which I was summoned; had half an hour with his Prime Minister; and then entertained him and Mrs Attlee to luncheon – a typical morning of the day of departure for Balmoral. They got off safely, with Princesses, dogs, Delia Peel, Piers Legh and Arthur Penn, at 7 p.m.

1 Lady Helen Gordon-Lennox, Dowager Duchess of Northumberland (d. 1965), widow of 8th Duke, Mistress of the Robes to Queen Elizabeth 1937–64.
2 Lady Mary Nunburnholme, wife of the 3rd Baron Nunburnholme, who divorced her in 1947. She then married Tommy's colleague Ulick Alexander.
3 Rt. Rev. and Rt. Hon. William Wand (1885–1977), Bishop of London 1945–55, prolific author on religious topics.

from Euston. I went down to Windsor, quite ready for a few days' quiet.

Tuesday 28 August

John, now a captain and appointed Intelligence Officer to E. Goulburn's brigade [8th British Infantry] has been with us since Friday. On Saturday, to celebrate his promotion, we broached the bottle of Veuve Clicquot which Monty gave me on Whit Monday.

Wednesday 29 August

Joan, the cook and I left Windsor 1 p.m. and, plus John, caught the 7 p.m. train from King's Cross. London seemed fuller of people than ever, and all forms of transport full to overflowing.

Thursday 30 August

Reached Aberdeen in good time, and after a welcome breakfast – we had dined off sandwiches in our sleepers – reached Ballater 11.43. Went straight to Craigowan, and spent the rest of the day unpacking and getting settled in. Walked up to the Castle after tea and saw the King. The grouse situation is not quite so bad as expected – they have been getting about eighty brace a day.

Thursday 4 October   Craigowan

We have had a very pleasant, peaceful time here, with wonderful weather on the whole. John, having returned to Hawick to report to 1st Guards Brigade, came back for another week's leave. The King sent him out stalking three days, and he got two stags; but all my efforts failed to get him a salmon. There are very few fish in the river, and what there are, more dour than ever. Still, it was pleasant enough: fishing is like playing the piano: an audience is not necessary for the satisfaction of the performer. We have made various expeditions – Corndavon, the Glasalt, Inveraray, etc.; having a car of my own for the first time has made it possible to explore this lovely country as I have never been able to before.

On 26 September Attlee came up for the night. I went to Aberdeen, and drove out with him. We had a good talk; I find him excellent company when he thaws out; like most men with no natural presence, he seems to be fighting a continual rearguard action against his physical insignificance, though his mental stature is good enough. His visit was a success, and the

King got on very well with him. The Queen was laid up with a chill. Joan and I dined at the Castle the night he was there.

The only other visitors have been Ritchie, GOC Scottish Command, and the King of Greece. The latter had previously been staying with the Duchess of Kent at Birkhall, where I went to see him and had to listen to a prolonged exposition of Balkan politics, as I did yesterday at Balmoral. His principal grievance at the moment is that Bevin has not seen him since he took over the Foreign Office. I wrote to A. Cadogan about this, but, as I anticipated, his answer was that, with the Regent Damaskinos in London, it would be embarrassing for Bevin to see the King. The latter thinks Damaskinos is a slimy intriguer, only out for his own glorification; I cannot say whether he is right or not, but the fact remains that Winston, Anthony Eden, etc. came to the conclusion that D. was the only man to take charge of Greece in its present state – and who am I to gainsay them?

Friday 5 October   **Buckingham Palace**

We left Ballater 7 p.m. last night. The King kindly gave Joan and Caroline a lift in the royal train, also the King of Greece. Several of the train staff were killed or injured in the railway accident at Bourne End a few days ago,[1] including Plummer, the excellent cook, so we were surrounded by strange faces. Euston 10 a.m.

E. Bevin came 11.30, looking little the worse for the gruelling month he has had at the Foreign Secretaries' conference, which broke up in confusion and sterility yesterday. He has no doubt that Molotov was under orders to sabotage it, though what the Russian motive was for doing so is obscure. Bevin had some very straight talks with Molotov, which may do some good. But the failure of the first serious attempt at constructive peace-making is discouraging, even if it may prove, in the long run, more fruitful than glib and hasty settlements which are subsequently disowned. There is a danger, too, that these lovers' quarrels may divert attention from the three priority problems – de-militarising the German people; feeding the world; and controlling the development of atomic energy.

Attlee also came to see the King after luncheon. I told him of the wish of the Duke of Windsor (who arrived in London this afternoon, to stay with Queen Mary at Marlborough House) to be made our ambassador at Buenos Aires, and said – as I had already told the King – that I saw three major objections to this. 1. The present Foreign Secretary would certainly not

---

1   On 30 Sept. 1945 the Perth to Euston express came off the rails at about 60 mph, killing 39 people and injuring 94.

recommend such an appointment. 2. The Duke has certain disagreeable personal skeletons in his cupboard – e.g. Axel Gren, Bedaux and Ricardo Espirito Santo Silva,[1] all proven German agents. No professional diplomat with such associations would ever be given an important embassy – or indeed employed anywhere. 3. The Argentine Government, when approached for the *agrément*, could legitimately ask, 'Is his wife received at the Court of St James?' To this, the only answer could be, 'No.' The Argentinos would then be quite within their rights in refusing the *agrément* – an intolerable insult to our Royal Family, and to our national prestige.

Attlee agreed. I also sounded him about Winston being given the OM for his literary achievements, which he cordially approved. Before luncheon, I had half an hour with George Allen, the Duke of Windsor's solicitor – a good chap, who fights a loyal rearguard action in his client's interest, but I don't fancy his heart is in it. He has already discovered the deplorable streak of meanness over money matters which has always been one of the Duke's worst failings. Queen Mary came to luncheon with the King, who dined *à trois* with her and the Duke at Marlborough House.

I had Leslie Rowan to dinner at the Travellers. He seems quite satisfied with Attlee's form as PM; and said it was an immense relief that the foul shadow of Beaverbrook no longer brooded over No. 10.

Saturday 6 October

The newspapers, even the *Daily Express*, give remarkably little publicity to the Duke of Windsor's arrival, with no editorial comment. He came to see the King at 5 p.m. and stayed two hours. I did not see him; Joey Legh reports him as looking well, with an even stronger American accent than ever. Joey and I dined with the King, who is now back in his rooms on the first floor; the last time I was in the dining-room was one day late in August 1939, when I had to interrupt him at luncheon with Tim Fortescue,[2] to get him to sign the order mobilising the Army.

The King (who won two races at Ascot today, with Hyperion and Fair Glint) was in excellent form; his interviews with the Duke of Windsor, which he had obviously been dreading for days past – and small wonder – seem to have gone off far better than he expected. There was no row, and they seem to have parted on amicable terms. I gather that the King has at last convinced him that there is no possibility of his Duchess ever being 'received' or getting the title HRH. Ulick Alexander, who went down to Windsor with the Duke this morning, says he told him that he could never

---

1   Ricardo do Espirito Santo Silva (1900–55), Portuguese banker.
2   5th Earl of Fortescue (1888–1958), Lord-in-Waiting 1937–45.

come back to live permanently in this country. The Athlones, recently back from Ottawa, and Queen Mary lunched with the King, doubtless for an intensive family post-mortem.

Ralph Verney,[1] who has just been on a ten-days' tour of Germany with the Speaker, told me that among other entertainments provided for them was a morning at the Belsen trial. Kramer was a horrible creature, he said, but nothing like as horrible as the woman, Irma Grese.[2] He also told me that nobody, of high rank or low, ever ventured into the Russian zone after dark; to do so courted being beaten up and robbed of all one's possessions. Russian soldiers frequently wore a string of wrist-watches, looted from unfortunate civilians, from their wrists to their elbows – some even from their ankles to their knees.

Sunday 7 October

The King, with Eric Miéville and Joey, went to Sandringham to shoot his partridges. I went down to Windsor a.m.; golden autumn weather, and we picked a fair dish of mushrooms in the Home Park.

Monday 8 October

Joan and I saw the play *First Gentleman*[3] at the Savoy, in which Morley does a first-class performance as the Prince Regent. It has some capital scenes, and I should say the dialogue is pretty accurate. I got back to Buckingham Palace, after we had supped at the Savoy, to find that the Duke of Windsor had been ringing me up, but took no action and went to bed.

Tuesday 9 October

Saw Edward Bridges after luncheon, consulting him about an OM for Winston, and the wording of any citation, if he accepts it; also about a list of ten men whom Attlee wishes to make peers – a curious collection, comprising Lindsay, the Master of Balliol; Wyndham Deedes,[4] and several of whom neither E.B. nor I had ever heard. Attlee's object, I think, is sound;

1 Lieut.-Col. Ralph Verney (1879–1959), Secretary to the Speaker of the House of Commons 1921–55. Created 1st Bt. 1946.
2 The Nazi extermination camp at Bergen-Belsen was liberated by the British Army on 15 Apr. 1945. Forty-eight members of the camp staff were tried, and eleven of them, including the commandant Josef Kramer (1906–45) and his accomplice Irma Grese (1923–45), were condemned to death and hanged on 13 Dec. 1945.
3 By Norman Ginsbury. Wendy Hiller played Princess Charlotte.
4 Brig.-Gen. Sir Wyndham Deedes (1883–1956).

)use of Lords is to continue to be a genuine second chamber and ltain its high debating level, the Labour Party must be adequately ented in it – which, at present, it is not. Moreover, creation of this – on a general principle, and not to meet some particular political emergency – is much sounder, and meets the common charge that the House of Lords is purely a Tory preserve. So I had not much hesitation about sending Attlee's letter to the King, with advice that he give the proposal his informal approval.

At 3.30 p.m. went to see the Duke of Windsor (who had telephoned in the morning asking me to come) at Marlborough House. I had not seen him since November 1936. The first thing that struck me about him was his voice, which seems to have got shriller, and is now more pronouncedly American than that of many Americans. When he spoke of the 'Bahammers', I had some difficulty in realising that he meant the islands which he has lately been governing. He is noticeably, almost painfully, thin, and his face is much lined, though not unhappy. Altogether, he has changed little.

We talked for one and a half hours, mostly confronting each other from armchairs on either side of the fireplace, and with periodic interruptions from the telephone; he dealt with these himself, with a strictly transatlantic technique. I had had a hint from Allen that he looked on me as having been 'obstructionist' towards his plans, but there was no suggestion of any hostility in his manner, which was courteous, and even friendly, through-out, even when I spoke most frankly.

After saying how grim life in Europe now is, particularly in Paris, he declared that he had come to the conclusion that America is the only place in which one can live in tolerable comfort at present, and that the Duchess and he would shortly 'return to that great country, at any rate for a time'. He then tackled the question of the Duchess being received by the King and Queen Mary, and advanced all the familiar arguments. I said that I was convinced that both his mother and his brother had definitely and finally made up their minds *not* to receive her, and that no expression of opinion by myself or anybody else would cause them to change their minds; anyway, it was primarily a family matter. He took this up, saying that Attlee had also told him it was a family matter, but it was really more than that; he knew that they (the King and Queen Mary) did not look at the problem purely from the family point of view; they were thinking also of public opinion – they had told him that they got anonymous letters.

Here I interpolated that the King certainly got a number of letters on the subject, but to my knowledge the majority of them were signed. He then asked me what my own opinion would be if the King asked for it. I said that I had always told him the truth, and would do so now, though it was not a pleasant thing to say to any man about his own wife; my considered opinion was that, if the Duchess were to be formally 'received', it would have a very damaging, if not dangerous, effect on public opinion both here and all over the Empire. He then mentioned various people who had been involved in divorces yet were received at Court. I said that did not affect the issue – they were private individuals; he, though an ex-King, was still a King; the Abdication had been a conflict of *principle* – otherwise there would have been no need for any Abdication at all – and that principle held good now just as much as it did then. It was one of the curses of kingship that there is in this world one law for Kings and another for commoners.

The other main topic was whether a job could be found for him under the Crown. I said that I, and others wiser than myself, had spent many hours in the course of the last few years trying to think of some post which he could fill consistently with his position. We had all wished to find something that would make for his happiness, and give him an opportunity of doing useful work. But we had not succeeded. The British Empire was like the clock on the mantelpiece; it had to be kept ticking away, but its machinery was delicate and was getting more and more so with the passage of time. We had, so to speak, taken that clock to pieces a hundred times and tried to fit it together again with the inclusion of an extra wheel – the wheel of an ex-King. We had never found a way of doing this without damaging the works.

The Duke said that the wheel had fitted in all right in the Bahamas. I said that might be, so far as his actual running of the Governorship went; nobody denied that he had been a good Governor, and done remarkably well there. But his appointment to the Bahamas had been an emergency solution of the problem of what to do with him during the war (and, incidentally – though I did not say this – of how to keep him and the Duchess out of this country); the experiment had worked once, but it couldn't be safely repeated.

So far, I then went on, I have been talking quite *im*personally, and in general terms; I have said to you exactly what I should say to the present King if he suddenly told me that he proposed to hand over the throne to Princess Elizabeth, and asked me if there was any other job he could do elsewhere in the Empire; but now I am going to make a *personal* appeal to you. In 1936 you made a tremendous sacrifice on behalf of your wife, who, you have told me, has made you far happier than you have ever been before; could you not now make another sacrifice, on behalf of your brother, who, in order that you might lead your own life, took on, in your place, the most difficult job in the world, and saddled himself for life with cares and responsibilities which he had never expected to assume, but for which you had always been prepared; could you not now, to save him embarrassment, accept the two decisions once and for all, and not continually go on arguing against them, which could only make things difficult for him?

The Duke said, 'But I want to do something useful; if I do go and live in America, what am I going to do?'

I said, 'What do you want to do?'

He said, 'Improve Anglo-American relations.'

'Well,' I said, 'there is nobody who could have a better opportunity for doing this than yourself. As you said just now, you are past fifty-one, and behind you you have thirty years of full and varied experience; with your name, and your resources, you could do a great deal of good in that particular direction. In your home in USA you could do just what I was advising Alex to do in Ottawa, by constantly getting his war-friends – Eisenhower, Marshall, H. Hopkins, King, etc. – to come and stay with him and keep alive their British associations. You could make your house what the great houses in England used to be – a common meeting-ground for all the most interesting people, native or foreign, of your generation. Besides that, you could take up any one of the more special activities in which you've always been interested.'

'You mean something like Anglo-American educational schemes?' he said.

'Yes,' I said, 'that's just what I do mean. Or you could develop some particular branch of science – or agriculture – or architecture. There are a dozen forms of activity that you could take up.'

He seemed to think there was something in all this; anyhow, he did not contest it. Eventually five o'clock struck; he went up to tea with his mother, and I went down the passage to do the same with Claud Hamilton, and that very nice woman Cynthia Colville (with whom I had already had a talk that morning). I believe I did some good. It was a very interesting interview. The old charm is still there, no doubt, but I am quite impervious to it. Indeed, I found myself thinking several times during his long soliloquies that I might almost be listening to the Prince Regent of Monday night.

I had G. M. Young[1] to dine with me at the Travellers, after three-quarters of an hour with the Bishop of Norwich and half an hour with M. Balfour, and then went home to write a full account of my afternoon for the King, which kept me out of bed till 2 a.m.

Wednesday 10 October

Hughe Knatchbull-Hugessen confided to me that the Prince Regent of Belgium has commissioned him to find him an English wife, and how was he to set about it? Not so easy, for Prince Charles, though not unattractive, is

---

1   1882–1959. Trustee of National Portrait Gallery from 1938 and British Museum 1947–57. Member of Standing Commission for Museums and Galleries from 1938.

forty-three, a Roman Catholic, a Belgian (out of a Wittelsbach, the maddest blood in Europe) and a prince – none of them attributes which make much appeal to a right-minded English girl. I told him the best thing he could do was to consult M. Devonshire,[1] but we could not get hold of her.

I had a scrambler installed in Marlborough House so that the Duke of Windsor could talk to the King at Sandringham.

Thursday 11 October

The Duke of Windsor telephoned to me just before his departure for Paris, in a friendly mood. He said to me that he had talked to the King for forty minutes on the scrambler last night. I should like to see Claud Hamilton's face when he gets the bill! He has evidently taken to heart my suggestion about his developing Anglo-American relations in an American home, and talked about it with some enthusiasm; but, characteristically, he has now got the idea that, to do this, he must be given some sort of diplomatic immunity from taxation. I can't see how that could be done if he ain't a diplomat.

He was evidently satisfied with his visit; I told him it had done good, and promised to help him so far as in my power lies. Anyhow, he has come, and gone, without a breach of the peace. I feel rather as one did on hearing the all clear after a prolonged air-raid.

I had a letter from Lavinia's Edward Renton, and quite a good letter, too. I liked the style of it, and answered it. I hope he will be in England soon, when I can have a look at him. At present, I have not the remotest idea whether he is in a position to support a wife.[2]

Heard from Conrad Russell, who says Diana Cooper reports meeting the Windsors in Paris recently, 'both looking as thin as if just out of Belsen. She grown a little more common, and he more pointless, dull and insipid.' Hard words from an old friend.

Saturday 13 October   Windsor

Went to Denman & Goddard, the Eton tailors, to try on a suit (the second

---

1   Mary Cecil, wife of the 10th Duke of Devonshire.
2   In a later note the author added: 'He wasn't.' When Tommy asked Lavinia if Edward had any money, she replied proudly, 'Oh yes – he's got £1,000.' Tommy said, 'D'you mean £1,000 a year?' and was dismayed by the answer, 'No – that's his capital.' Edward was a highly talented musician. He came from Edinburgh, studied music under Sir Donald Tovey, and won scholarships to go to Salzburg and Vienna. When he returned to England, he worked as personal assistant to Fritz Busch, a close friend of John Christie, who was then preparing to open his opera house at Glyndebourne.

in which I have indulged since 1939), ordered last February; even so, after eight months, the trousers have not yet been begun, and only the coat and waistcoat were ready. After luncheon Joan and I picked 5 lbs of blackberries on High Standing Hill. It is pleasantly peaceful here (apart from the sightseers) now that the wartime denizens of the Castle have disappeared. Am re-reading Soapy Sponge.[1] The Lord Chamberlain has fallen over his suitcase in his own hall and fractured two ribs, one of which has penetrated his lung.

Monday 15 October

Monty came to get his GCB, looking none the worse for his recent aeroplane crash. I asked him if he would like to be Lord Warden of the Cinque Ports, if Winston gives it up, and if they make Walmer habitable; he said it would suit him admirably. He told me he was going to give a lecture on 'The Secret of Leadership' at St Andrew's University. I asked how he would approach the subject; he said, 'I shall take three great leaders of men – Moses, Cromwell and Napoleon – and analyse their qualities of leadership. Then I shall turn to modern times, and tell them how I did it.'

Laval was shot today, after a last-minute effort to poison himself. His recent trial was a hurly-burly, reminiscent of one of Mr Justice Cocklecarrot's cases, as reported by Beachcomber. The French have never been able to conduct a *cause célèbre* with any approach to judicial decorum. But nobody will question the justice of the sentence, however ludicrous the proceedings in court.

Tuesday 16 October

Attlee came 6 p.m. I asked him (unofficially) if he saw any objection to the revival next year of the Ascot summer meeting, with the Royal Enclosure as in pre-war days (but no top hats), and he had none. But I suppose I shall have to ask the Home Secretary for his official opinion.

Wednesday 17 October

Darnley initiated a debate on the atomic bomb in the House of Lords yesterday. Cherwell, replying, alluded to 'the noble Earl's hereditary dislike of explosions', which was a happy historical touch.[2]

---

1   Central character in R. S. Surtees' *Mr Sponge's Sporting Tour*, first published in 1853.
2   Peter Stuart Bligh, 10th Earl of Darnley (1915–80). His ancestor Lord Darnley married Mary Queen of Scots, but was murdered in a bomb attack in 1571.

Tuesday 23 October

Dalton brought his Budget to show the King last night. This morning I asked HM how the Chancellor of the Exchequer impressed him. The King looked out of the window for a space, then said, 'The Chancellor of the Exchequer stinks like the main drain.' And that was the only secret of the Budget revealed to me.[1]

Thursday 25 October

With Their Majesties to the centenary celebrations of the Imperial College of Science and Technology, one of the many institutions in this country which owe their existence to the wisdom and drive of the Prince Consort. The Albert Hall was packed, and gaudy with the gowns of male and female doctors (the Queen wore her robes as a Doctor of London University). The King delivered his speech remarkably well, with all the students assembled in the arena below him. We always used to say that the safety of ourselves and our children was in the hands of the Army and Navy; nowadays, it is in the hands of these young scientists in their back rooms. After cakes and ale in the College, behind the Albert Hall, we went back to the hall, and Their Majesties joined the students in a dance – an unrehearsed incident which was, of course, wildly popular, but I think rather shocked Algy Athlone, who will always remain a rigid Edwardian.

Friday 26 October

The King said to me rather bitterly this morning that Winston had come back from his Italian holiday looking a new man, and that while Ministers out of office always got such opportunities for recuperation, he never did. To that, I am afraid, the only possible answer is on the lines of *il faut souffrir pour être belle.* It is a melancholy but inescapable fact that the Pope of Rome and the King of England are almost the only two human beings who can never expect a complete holiday until they reach the grave. Even the King's private secretary can count on being allowed to go into honourable retirement some day.

Saturday 27 October

E. Bevin made a notable speech on the state of Europe in the House of

---

1 Elsewhere Tommy wrote of Dalton: 'I cannot like that man – as *faux* a *bonhomme* as God ever made.'

Commons yesterday. He is gaining in stature every week. The whole world is now growing alarmed by what I have always said was a quite inescapable aftermath of the war – that the first winter of peace would be marked by famine and pestilence in most parts of the continent on a scale that we have never yet known.

Diana Legh was this afternoon married to young Kimberley[1] in St George's. A great to-do; the service was perfect, but the reception, held by the King's permission in the Crimson Drawing-room, was a sad scrimmage, made worse by the Royal Family planting itself (as it always does) at the one point where traffic can be most overwhelmingly dislocated. The King of Greece was there; he, by the way, came to see me at Buckingham Palace yesterday afternoon (delaying my departure for Windsor) with, I suspect, the sole object of pumping me as to the Foreign Office's ideas about Greece. As I do not profess to understand the bewildering complexities of the Greek situation, and am not at all interested in them, I found it easy to play the role of the village idiot.

Wednesday 31 October

Just before tea Lavinia rang up from St James's, saying she had just arrived from Naples, which she left at 7.15 this morning. I gave her dinner at Prunier's, and thought her remarkably well, after her pneumonia. I saved myself a fiver today, having resisted the temptation to back a horse called Joan's Star in the Cambridgeshire. I was restrained by my lifelong prejudice against three-year-olds in that particular race, which was narrowly justified, the animal running second, beaten only by half a length.

Aneurin Bevan to see HM. I rather like him, and his ideas on housing. He has a respect for the countryside and the amenities generally. He advocates sky-scrapers (ten or twelve storeys) on the outskirts of country towns, rather than sprawling settlements; the former, he says, need not be a blot on the landscape any more than a church steeple, and they would save acres of green fields covered by the latter.

Thursday 1 November

Went to see Dale, President of the Royal Society, about giving OM to Fleming[2] and Florey.[3] He is against it – said they had already had their

---

1 John Wodehouse, 4th Earl of Kimberley (1924–2002).
2 Sir Alexander Fleming (1881–1955), bacteriologist, discoverer of penicillin, winner of Nobel Prize 1945.
3 Howard Walter Florey (1898–1968), Australian-born pathologist, main creator of penicillin therapy. Awarded OM and created Baron Florey (Life Peer) 1965.

deserts, and that, by the standards of pure medicine, they were not of OM calibre. If any scientist got the OM as a war-winner, it ought to be Tizard.[1] Now, all in Whitehall who have worked with T. say that he certainly does *not* deserve the OM.

Friday 2 November

Monty's Intelligence people have published a convincing summary of the cumulative evidence of Hitler's death.

Saturday 3 November   Windsor

Six years ago, almost to a week, I played my last game of golf, at Brancaster [in Norfolk], with Lavinia. Today I braced myself to take out two clubs – and, again, Lavinia – on to the little course here, to see if I could hit the ball at all. To my surprise, I did so with reasonable accuracy, and, on a perfect autumn afternoon, we played a pleasant nine holes, finding a ball, too, which is worth diamonds in these days. What a lot of trouble it would have saved me on that October afternoon in 1939 if some angel could have assured me that six years hence I should be playing a peaceful round at Windsor, still a free Englishman, and with all of us alive and well.

Tuesday 6 November

Alex [who had been appointed Governor-General of Canada] came to see me this morning; he lunched with Mackenzie King on Saturday, and thought him 'a charming old gentleman'. Maybe, I said, but don't forget for one moment that he is a spin bowler, whose balls break both ways. He (Alex) is determined to have a Canadian secretary, which I applaud. I cautioned him about being too much the soldier when he gets there, and quoted the example of wise old Byng,[2] who used to say, 'Once I land in Canada, I cease to be a general and become merely a governor-general.'

Wednesday 7 November

King and Queen in Birmingham. Casals,[3] who had asked through Myra

---

1 Sir Henry Tizard (1885–1959), scientist, much involved with development of radar and air defence.
2 Field-Marshal Julian Byng (1862–1935), Gov.-Gen. of Canada 1921–6. Created 1st Viscount Byng of Vimy 1926.
3 Pablo Casals (1876–1973), Spanish cellist and composer.

Hess[1] if he could see me, on Spanish affairs, came this morning. I got the Foreign Office to send a *rapporteur*, versed in the politics of the Peninsula, to come and help me. Casals hadn't much to say, beyond urging that we should break off relations with Franco; what he couldn't guarantee, however, was that anybody in Spain would be prepared to give us active support if we did. He is a nice little man, a fervid patriot, and naïvely conscious of the fact that he is the most famous living Spaniard. He told me that he had played to Queen Victoria here, and also at Osborne, in 1898.

To the House of Commons after luncheon, to hear Winston open the debate on foreign affairs, which he did very forcibly, in a speech of thirty-five minutes; he said roundly that we, USA and Canada should disclose no secrets of the atomic bomb to anybody at all (including Russia); and warned the scientists that these matters of high policy were for governments to decide, and not for them, who are only servants of the State like anybody else. He was in good voice, and confident, holding a full house, in which there were few interruptions.

Thursday 8 November

Pug Ismay, who has had two months' holiday in USA, came to tea. He says the apprehension of Russia's intentions is almost universal there.

At Winston's request, I went before dinner to see him in his new house, 28 Hyde Park Gate. After a short lamentation about the state of the world at large, and of British politics (though he admitted that he probably would have been a dead man by now had he remained in office), he fell into his most jovial mood. He wanted to know if it would be all right for him to accept a high Czech decoration ('which my old friend President Beans is most anxious to give me') and a ditto from the Belgians. I had already asked the King about this, and though the rule is that British statesmen do not ordinarily accept these foreign dingle-berries, HM agreed with me that no rule is worth anything if it can't be broken, and that Winston's case was certainly exceptional and non-recurring.

So I reported accordingly, but seized the opportunity to add that, if he accepted these things from foreign Heads of States, his own Sovereign expected him to accept the OM at the New Year. At this he wept a little, as he so easily does when deeply moved, and paced the room in silence for a while. Then he said, with obvious sincerity, that this was only one more instance of the many kindnesses which the King had consistently shown him, and he would of course be honoured to take it. He then asked if it

---

1   Dame Myra Hess (1890–1965), pianist and music teacher, declared herself to be of 'British parentage'.

would be given him for his literary achievements. I said that I didn't think the King intended to specify why he got it, and that it would be very good for posterity to keep on guessing whether he had earned it as an author or as a statesman.

Then Walter Monckton came in, and we fell to discussing the Duke of Windsor's future, Winston propounding an ingenious expedient whereby the Duke can be settled in USA on some quasi-diplomatic basis.

Friday 9 November   Windsor p.m.

The King rang me up after tea and read to me (on the scrambler) a letter which he is sending over to the Duke of Windsor in Paris tomorrow morning; quite a good letter, but he still advises against any outward and visible link with the Embassy in Washington, however slender; but I got him to put in an offer to send a letter to Truman on the Duke's behalf, if the latter would like this done.

I got last night a letter from Duff Cooper, reporting the Duke's activities in Paris; he seems to be making himself a bit of a nuisance, 'talking big' to various French officials whom he meets at dinner, and telling them how to run their own country, which naturally they don't like. He was always given to holding forth, and indeed, as long ago as 1926, showed increasing signs of becoming a hearth-rug bore; with increasing years, he may be developing George IV's tendency to arrogate to himself capabilities, and performances, which are actually beyond him – e.g. George IV's claims to have fought at Waterloo, and to have ridden Fleur de Lys to victory at Goodwood races.

We went after dinner to St George's, where, in complete darkness save for the lights in the organ loft, Harris, Mrs Hare and a viola-player made music for an hour and a half. Mrs H. sang some of Vaughan Williams's hymns, and 'How beautiful are the feet'. She had a throstle-like voice which is perfectly suited to that environment; and Harris played César Franck's *Pièce Héroique* – a magnificent thing, which I should like to have at my, or anybody else's, funeral. Finished *Tom Jones* and began *Lord Jim* again.

Sunday 11 November

Remembrance Day service in St George's. Very well done, and A. Deane preached an excellent sermon. Speaking in Manchester on Friday, Tizard said (of the atomic bomb): 'Just as the fear of eternal damnation after death has for centuries served to subdue the evil passions of individuals, so it may be that the immediate threat of a hell upon earth may be even more effective in removing the worst features of nationalism until the affairs of nations are guided by nobler motives.'

Monday 12 November

The Convocations of Canterbury and York, headed by their respective Archbishops, and all in full panoply, came to present addresses to, and receive replies from, the King. This took place in the Bow Room, and was a picturesque little show; the first time it has been done since 1932 – and the first time I have donned a tail-coat since 1939. It felt quite odd.

Tuesday 13 November

To the House of Lords to see Addison,[1] I told him my idea for solving the problem of a Council of State, should the King and Queen and Princess Elizabeth ever go [on a visit] to one of the Dominions. As things are at present, the government of the Empire would be left in the hands of Princess Mary, George and Gerald Lascelles, and Princess Arthur of Connaught[2] and Lady Southesk[3] – which is absurd.

My suggestion is that the Dominions should be told that the King himself can carry on the affairs of the Empire from his capital of Cape Town (or Ottawa) as he can from his capital of London, and that for this purpose no Council of State is necessary – this is sound Statute of Westminster doctrine. In this country, an old-fashioned Council should be set up, composed of Princess Mary, the Archbishop of Canterbury, the Lord Chancellor and the Speaker, etc. – as it always used to be, until the Dominions protested that they could not have any UK officials on the Council, which must consist of the five adults next in succession to the Throne, and the present arrangement was adopted. I propounded this to Attlee at Balmoral, and he thought it a good idea, as did Addison.

Wednesday 14 November

Bad news about poor Gort. The doctors have now decided that he has got cancer of the liver, and has but a few months to live. Spoke to Garter at the Colonial Office, and Edward Bridges, about getting him some honour; I

1 Christopher Addison, 1st Viscount Addison (1869–1951), Secretary of State for Commonwealth Relations 1945–7.
2 Princess Arthur of Connaught (1891–1959), elder daughter of the 1st Duke of Fife and of HRH Princess Louise, the Princess Royal (daughter of Edward VII), married Prince Arthur of Connaught in 1913. She succeeded her father in the dukedom in 1912, and acted as a Counsellor of State during King George VI's absences abroad.
3 1893–1945. Wife of the 11th Earl of Southesk, whom she married in 1923, she was HH Princess Maud, younger sister of Princess Arthur. She died a few weeks later (see page 374).

believe he has set his heart on having his Irish peerage converted into a UK one, which should not present much difficulty.

Thursday 15 November

At the Beefsteak today Geoffrey Dawson[1] said to Nicholas Hannen that he was looking forward to seeing him in *Henry IV* today. N.H. said he was afraid D. would be disappointed, as they were playing *Oedipus*. D. quoted *The Times*, and the box office; N.H., unconvinced, said he was sure he was right, for the last thing he had seen before leaving the theatre was his Oedipus beard laid out ready for him to don for the matinée. However, he was sufficiently shaken to curtail his luncheon and hurry back to the theatre. Ten minutes later – and about the same time before the curtain was due to rise – he telephoned to say that G.D. was quite right, and it *was Henry IV*. I daresay the sudden transformation from the Choregus in *Oedipus* to Bolingbroke in no way affected his performance of the latter part; but actors must be remarkably adaptable.

Friday 16 November

Having got Attlee's concurrence by telegram, I was authorised by the King to send Gort a letter offering him a UK peerage, which I've heard is what he wants most. There was no time to lose, for his doctor tells me that he might die any time.

Monday 19 November

Lit. Soc. dinner, noteworthy for the reappearance of Peter Fleming,[2] who has been out east most of the war; and of Granville-Barker,[3] an old member but hasn't dined with us within my recollection; he's a wonderfully well-preserved sixty-eight.

Tuesday 20 November

Luncheon, organised by the King George V Jubilee Trust, in St James's Palace, to launch the book *The Royal Family in Wartime*, which they are

---

1 1874–1944. Editor of *The Times* 1912–19 and 1923–41.
2 1907–71. Author and traveller. During the war he had been working in strategic deception of the Japanese.
3 Harley Granville-Barker (1877–1946), playwright and lecturer, author of two classic plays, *Waste* and *The Voysey Inheritance*.

publishing, and for which Morrah[1] of *The Times* wrote an admirable fore-word on that threadbare theme, the duties of a monarch. The principal speech was by Christie,[2] headmaster of Westminster, and very good he was – on the needs of 'Youth', to satisfy which is the main object of the fund.

Much of what he said was an elaboration of the theme that I had just been trying to express in a letter to Robin Barrington-Ward – the idea that HM might tell the younger generation *not* that they must buckle-to and work like blacks (which they have already been told *ad nauseam* and might be spared at Xmas), but that they must rid themselves of the sombre attitude towards life which six years of the danger, discomfort and beastliness of war must have created for them; that they must recover some of the 'mer-riment' (in the best sense) which is one of the features of Xmas; not falter in 'their great task of happiness'; and realise that life can be a joyous and creative adventure instead of the grim, destructive one which they have had to embark upon hitherto.

He also said, what I have always felt strongly myself, that it is fatal to talk incessantly of 'Youth' movements, organisations etc. with a capital 'Y'. It can but make young people self-conscious, and distrustful of their elders, if they are thus herded, patronisingly, into a pen by themselves. If the boot were on the other leg, which of us would have anything to do with an organisation for the Middle-Aged?

Old Jack Mottistone has given me one of the new 'Biro' stylographic pens, reputed to write thirty miles without a re-fill; it is quite an agreeable instrument to handle, and, having many letters to sign in the course of the day, I hope to be saved much labour by it.

Attlee returned from Quebec, and came to see the King as soon as he reached London. He seemed the better for the trip, and had found Truman congenial. He said he did not know that the Americans had as yet developed any post-atom-bomb weapons; was fairly well satisfied with the financial negotiations, and did not know when the Big Three meeting was likely to take place, as it depended on the Russians, who had given no sign of life for some time. So far as he knows, there is nothing amiss with Joe Stalin, despite all the rumours about his state of health.

Friday 23 November

Poor Mrs Leo Amery came to get her CI [Imperial Order of the Crown of India] from the King. The trial of her son John opens next week, and he

1   Dermot Morrah (1896–1974), journalist and author.
2   John Traill Christie (1899–1980), headmaster of Westminster School 1937–49.

will most probably be hanged. She brought Leo, with whom I had some talk. I am immensely sorry for both of them. Also Lady Paget (wife of Bernard Paget), to get the DSO [Distinguished Service Order] of their son, who was killed in Germany shortly after winning it.

Saturday 24 November

Bevin made another excellent speech in the House of Commons, developing the idea which Eden put forward on Thursday, that the state of the world demands from the nations an all-round modification of their notions of national sovereignty.

Sunday 25 November

Joan and I went over to lunch with the Peter Flemings at Merrimoles, the house they have built themselves in the Chilterns. She (Celia Johnson[1]) has just finished a magnum opus as the heroine of the new Noël Coward film *Brief Encounter*, just produced and favourably reviewed. Tim Nugent was there too, and Bernard Fergusson.[2]

Wednesday 28 November

John Amery today pleaded guilty to high treason, and was sentenced to death. I was impressed at dinner last night by the way in which Bevin spoke of Eden, calling him 'a great gentleman' and 'a great statesman'. There is nothing small about E.B., who may well be both those things himself.

Friday 30 November

To see Bevin at the Foreign Office about the Duke of Windsor's relationship with our Embassy in Washington. He don't think that Winston's 'silken thread' is practicable, if only because no ambassador – not even Edward Halifax, let alone his successor, whoever he may be – would take it on. What would be his personal relationship with an ex-King, either on the same plane as himself or under his orders? Bevin, without any prompting from me, at once laid bare the obvious nigger in the woodpile – that if any sort of diplomatic status, however carefully camouflaged, were given to the

---

1 Dame Celia Johnson (1908–82), actress.
2 Brig. Bernard Fergusson (1911–80), soldier and author. Director of Combined Operations (Military) 1945–6, Gov.-Gen. New Zealand 1967. Created 1st Baron Ballantrae (Life Peer) 1972.

D. of W., the Americans would immediately say that the chief reason for it was to get the Windsors immunity from taxation (and the Americans would not be far wrong).

In the Travellers on Thursday Jack Maffey told me that Shane Leslie had mentioned to his son, a few days before, that he had had a letter from the Duke of Windsor asking if he could come and stay with S.L. at Castle Leslie 'to study the Irish background of Anglo-American relations'. This is a good instance of the D. of W.'s irresponsibility and lack of political (and personal) judgement, for it is a crazy idea, the execution of which would certainly do him harm, besides infuriating the Ulstermen – and, if he had any contact with de Valera, many people in this country.

As Shane Leslie is Winston's first cousin, it is a little tricky; so I wrote a note to W., asking if he knew anything of it, and suggesting the obvious arguments against it. W. has replied that neither S.L. nor the Duke has said a word to him about it, and that he considers it a most dangerous plan, which ought to be stopped at all costs. It is not easy to take any further steps, as, so far as I am concerned, it is still in the stage of a bazaar rumour; however, I have warned Walter Monckton, and Machtig[1] at the Dominions Office has undertaken to find out from Maffey, who has gone back to Dublin, if there are any further developments.

Saturday 1 December

Hess has startled the world by telling the court at Nuremberg that he is quite sane, and has only been pretending to be *non compos mentis*. Well, all the people who had to deal with him during his captivity here were convinced that he was wrong in the head, so if the whole thing has been an elaborate pretence, he must be a superb actor.

Thursday 6 December

Another Winstonism. S. Cripps and Cherwell, two rabid vegetarians, arrived ten minutes late for a Cabinet meeting during the war. Winston, who had got very impatient, greeted them with, 'Well, gentlemen, if you have finished toying with your beetroot, we will get on with more important matters.'

Burrows,[2] Governor designate of Bengal, came to luncheon and got a

---

1 Sir Eric Machtig (1889–1973), Permanent Under-Secretary of State for Commonwealth Relations 1940.
2 Sir Frederick Burrows (1887–1973), Governor of Bengal 1946–7. He once made a speech at a club in Calcutta in which he said that, while most of his colleagues were hunting and shooting, he was busy shunting and hooting.

GCIE [Knight Grand Commander of the Order of the Indian Empire]. He started life as a railway porter at Ross-on-Wye, and has been head of the National Union of Railwaymen. A nice, square-shouldered, straight-eyed man, who may do the job very well. Mrs B. is a nice old cup of tea, with the figure of a cottage loaf. She will not bring much glamour to Government House, Calcutta; but she will certainly do less mischief than Lady Ronaldshay[1] did.

After luncheon, E. Bevin, who reluctantly, and having been rushed into it by Byrnes, has agreed to go to Moscow next week, and try and coax Molotov back from the tent in which he has been sulking since September. Then W. Monckton. Between us, we have contrived a rational solution of the Windsors' move to USA.

Before dinner, met Edward Renton for the first time – he arrived home on leave today. I liked him.

Sunday 9 December

Madge Boyne is here for the weekend. So is Edward Renton, who has confirmed good impressions. He is a fine pianist; I made him play me the Waldstein sonata, a test which he came through well enough.

Wednesday 12 December

Went with Their Majesties to Twickenham to see the Oxford v. Cambridge rugby match – a thing I've not done for about twenty years, and I was glad to find it stirred me as of old. Cambridge won, 11–8, entirely owing to the refusal of the Oxford centre three-quarters to pass; they starved the two wings continually. Still, it was a good, fast game, with some exciting moments.

Thursday 13 December

Brief Encounter is a great triumph for Celia Johnson, who carries the whole thing on her competent shoulders. As a film, it suffers from the defect endemic in every film which tries to portray an emotional situation – that it cannot create 'atmosphere', as a book or play can, save by artificial devices which are apt to be tedious, and even ridiculous, to the audience. A stock instance is the film of *Rebecca*;[2] the atmosphere to be created is the familiar

---

1   Cicely Archdale, wife of Lord Ronaldshay (later 2nd Marquess of Zetland), Governor of Bengal 1917–22.
2   The novel by Daphne du Maurier, first published 1938. The film was directed by Alfred Hitchcock.

one of the young wife, newly married to a widower, who finds herself overwhelmed by the personality of the dead wife brooding over the home that she has to make her own. In the book, or the play, this is conveyed without difficulty or strain; in the film it is generated by such mechanical devices as the old housekeeper taking the young bride into the first wife's bedroom, opening a chest of drawers and holding up various articles of lingerie so that the audience can clearly see that they are marked with the dead lady's name.

So too, in *Brief Encounter*, the fact that the lovers' meetings take place, for the most part, in the squalid discomfort of a railway refreshment-room has to be continually underlined by the noisy passage of express trains, and by flirtatious passages between the barmaid and a porter. However, apart from this essential and I suppose inevitable shortcoming, it is a very interesting bit of work, and Celia Johnson's interpretation of her part is superb. She is probably the most gifted actress that the English stage has produced in my life-time.

Friday 14 December

The King's fiftieth birthday. Maudie Southesk, after much indecision, died in the afternoon, which raised a formidable problem, in that a dance had been arranged at Buckingham Palace in the evening. However, after consultation with Queen Mary, they decided to let the dead bury their dead, so to speak, and the dance was held. Fortunately, the demise was too late for the evening newspapers, and, by luck or cunning, was not mentioned on the wireless.

Monday 17 December

Dickie Mountbatten is giving trouble by adopting a somewhat film-starrish attitude towards his proposed barony – saying that SEAC [South-East Asia Command] will not understand his accepting it while they are still fighting the Indonesians. This strikes me – and the King – as great nonsense; the really fatal blunder would be to omit the name of SACSEA [Supreme Allied Commander, South-East Asia] from a victory honours' list, when the men of SEAC already feel themselves neglected, and that all the credit for victory is being given to 8th Army, etc. But his protestations have revived the King's wish that he should have a viscountcy, and I had to go and see Attlee again this afternoon. But Attlee was adamant, basing his view, I am certain, on the advice of the Services, in the persons of Andrew Cunningham and Pug Ismay, who, I discovered, had been with him immediately before I went in.

The King took this reverse very well (his duck-shoot in Kent this morning was very successful), and allowed me to send off another telegram to Dickie telling him that he must, on public grounds, accept the barony. As, according to the King, he was also worried about losing his precedence as second son of a Marquess (a baron being an inferior animal), I sent him another telegram from myself telling him that his precedence would not be affected.

Wednesday 19 December

Long cipher telegram from Dickie Mountbatten, who persists in declining a peerage of any kind. After a hurried dinner at the Travellers, I had to go round to No. 10 to consult L. Rowan as to the next step in this tedious correspondence.

I got the King to see Edward Ford, and to approve his appointment as assistant private secretary from 1 January. HM seems to have been favourably impressed by him.

Vincent Massey asked me if I could do anything to stop Monty carrying out his projected tour of Canada next spring, just after Alex's arrival as Governor-General. This obviously won't do, and I have written to Alanbrooke suggesting that he tell Monty privately that he must at any rate wait till the autumn before poaching on his brother Field-Marshal's preserves.

Thursday 20 December

Duff Cooper, who came in this evening, thinks, as does every diplomat of experience, that any form of outward liaison between the Duke of Windsor and our Embassy in Washington would be impracticable; but he is very anxious to get the Duke out of his own bishopric, Paris.

Farewell party in my room for Miss Milsom, who had been chief clerk in my office for many years, and is now about to leave us. We presented her with a corner cupboard, and then drank her health (jointly with that of Eric Miéville), proposed by me.

Joan and I lunched with the John Andersons in Lord North Street. After luncheon our host, usually a man of meticulous accuracy in speech and thought, had a curious lapse, saying to me, 'Won't you come and sit here, Hardinge?' If he must address me by a generic name in that way, I would prefer him to call me Bigge.

John Amery was hanged yesterday.

D. Mountbatten is being allowed to refuse his peerage, and SEAC is to have an independent honours list later on. Cartier, to whom I confided yesterday that my sock-suspenders were almost worn out, and irreplaceable, sent me a new pair as a Christmas gift.

Friday 21 December

Christmas dispersal: Their Majesties to Sandringham (first Xmas there since 1939), and I to Windsor. Edward Renton came down later.

Monday 24 December

Guy[1] and Cecil Liddell came, the former bringing his cello. Carols in St George's, and much music at home.

Thursday 27 December

Liddells, and Caroline, went away. A peaceful and cheerful Xmas, the first I've had for years which has not been punctuated by telephone calls and telegrams. The King spoke well on Xmas day – eleven minutes, and no serious hitch.

The first official summaries of the Moscow talks are coming in. Bevin has kept his end up well – his contributions are Palmerstonically firm, and full of commonsense. At the final banquet, when Molotov made a facetious reference to the atomic bomb in toasting Conant,[2] Stalin rebuked him, saying that the subject was not one for joking, and seems to have spent the rest of the evening in close talk with Conant.

Sunday 30 December

Drove over to Egham before luncheon to see Pierson Dixon, who got back from Moscow with Bevin yesterday. His summing-up of the conference was that the Americans had conceded a good deal, we had conceded nothing that mattered, and the Russians had conceded nothing at all. Stalin is in good health, showing no sign of decay, and has designed himself a new uniform; but there is renewed evidence of his not being master in his own

---

1 Guy Liddell (1892–1958), Tommy's first cousin, described as a 'Civil Assistant, War Office', but in fact the MI5's Director of Counter-Espionage, and his brother.
2 James Conant (1893–1978), American scientist and author, who, as chairman of the National Defense Research Committee, played a key role in the project to develop the first nuclear weapons.

house. More than once his overnight decisions were reversed next day for no apparent reason (especially in the case of his talk with Bevin on Persia) – presumably because the mysterious clique in the background did not approve of them. Nobody seems to know the exact composition of this little group, but all are agreed as to its sinister character. Molotov, too, is only an instrument. Dixon was full of praise for Bevin, his restraint, commonsense and quickness.

After tea Joan and I went to see Alex and Lady Margaret in their house near Ascot. Alex in capital form, and increasingly full of zest for Canada. He has now got most of his staff, but not a secretary. I suggested young Tweedsmuir,[1] which he thought a good idea. I told him that I had asked Alanbrooke to squash Monty's plan to tour Canada in the spring. He said it had probably never entered Monty's head that this might be an embarrassment to him, 'for Monty has never in his life considered anybody's plans except his own'.

Monday 31 December

Thick fog all day. So ends 1945, which, as I wrote to the King today, may prove to have been the most exacting year of his whole reign. It has been a tough year for me too. But we beat the Boche.

---

1 John Buchan (1911–96) had succeeded his father John Buchan, the novelist, as 2nd Baron Tweedsmuir in 1940 and had served with distinction in the Canadian Army during the war. His father had been Gov.-Gen. Canada 1935–40.

1946

Tuesday 1 January

Nice letter from the King, which crossed mine of yesterday, so I had to write him another. The old year's fog cleared at midnight, and this morning was fine and bright. *Prosit omen.*

Tuesday 8 January

The King came back from Sandringham. He saw Bevin after luncheon. He (Bevin) told me he was going to see the Duke of Windsor (who flew over from Paris last night) immediately after leaving the King, and intended to tell the Duke plainly that he couldn't recommend any form of attachment to the Embassy in Washington. After Bevin came Winston, to get his OM. He was in a fighting mood, indignant (a) at Bevin opposing the Duke of Windsor scheme; (b) at Bomber Harris having been given no honour at New Year, but only promotion to Marshal of the Air Force; the latter will be far more use to him than any other honour, and W. had quite forgotten, till I reminded him, that Harris was given a GCB in the Birthday List, at his recommendation; (c) at Monty taking the title 'Alamein', which belonged more rightly to Alex. I talked subsequently to Pug Ismay about this, and he took the opposite view, saying that the *battle* of Alamein, as distinct from the whole campaign, was rightly Monty's battle; he instanced 'Byng of Vimy', which was not thought to be a reflection on Haig.

When I saw Bridges the other day, he mentioned to me that Eden was anxious to be considered as a candidate for the Secretary Generalship of UNO. Winston favours the idea. Attlee, and everybody else, are against it. I think it is a bad one. On general grounds, the ex-Foreign Secretary of this country is too big a figure to become the handy-billy of the Tower of Babel – imagine E. Grey or Lansdowne[1] doing it. Moreover, A.E., with all his qualities, is not fitted for it – he is notoriously a bad organiser; his political background is too sharply defined to make it possible for him to be all things to all men, and he don't suffer fools gladly. I can see him being the reverse of patient with an importunate Ecuadorean. Further, he is needed in the House of Commons, especially if Winston, as rumour has it, means to take a less active part in future as leader of the Opposition.

---

1   Henry Petty-Fitzmaurice, 5th Marquess of Lansdowne (1845–1927), Foreign Secretary 1900–5.

Lavinia's engagement appeared in today's *Times*; though I had drafted the announcement carefully in my own hand, they gave our address as 'St James's *Place*' – an error which I immediately pointed out to Robin Barrington-Ward. The King this evening gave permission for the wedding to be held in St George's, and the reception in the Waterloo Chamber.

Wednesday 9 January

8.15. The State banquet [to mark the inauguration of the United Nations Organisation] in the William IV room in St James's Palace. It looked very well, with much gold plate, etc., clothes agreeably comfortable for such a function – dinner jacket and black tie, service-uniform, or plain clothes for such as had neither. Of the last concession, hardly any availed themselves, save Jack Lawson,[1] who was in a neat blue suit, and Aneurin Bevan, who, characteristically, wore an ugly tweed and contrived to get himself photographed in it.

At dinner, food very moderate, wine good. I was between the Ethiop delegate and the Lebanese; I could get little out of the former, but the latter, though he only spoke French, was quite agreeable. Eighty-six was the limit that the table would hold, so the party was limited to the fifty number-one delegates, the Cabinet (twenty), a sprinkling of the Opposition – Eden, Anderson, Law, R. A. Butler (Winston had sailed for USA, and Bobbety was burying his father-in-law), plus about eight Household, etc.

The King spoke excellently. I think about two-thirds of the company understood what he was saying. I had refused to allow the circulation of translations of his speech, as HM would certainly have been put off by the sight of people conning in advance what he was about to say; but I had translations – French, Spanish, Russian – waiting for all who wanted them as soon as they left the dining-room.

After dinner, in the Queen Anne room, the King talked to various selected guests, beginning with Byrnes, and going on to a prolonged *tête-à-tête* with Gromyko,[2] the head Russian in Vyshinsky's absence. We got away by 11.20 p.m.

Before dinner the King brought the Duke of Windsor into my room. He had been seeing Attlee and Bevin. He thought he had made some progress in converting the latter to his Washington plan; but from what E.B. said to me later, at the dinner, I suspect this to be wishful thinking.

---

1   John Lawson (1893–1977), Principal Assistant Secretary at the Admiralty.
2   Andrei Gromyko (1909–89), Soviet Ambassador to the US 1943–6, representative at the UN Security Council 1946, Foreign Minister 1957–85.

Thursday 10 January

The King's speech has a very good press; most newspapers make it the subject of a leading article. He seems pleased with it himself, and I have heard nothing but praise of it. The only untoward incident last night was the behaviour of Eden; he arrived in one of his temperamental paroxysms, probably stimulated by alcohol, the effects of which were certainly evident after dinner. When shown his place at the table by Joey Legh and Tim Nugent, he complained loudly at being put next to the Nicaraguan, and in the near neighbourhood of the Prime Minister. Later, he was most offensive to L. Ritchie because, at the beginning of the King's talks with the various delegates, photographs were taken, and the lights annoyed him.

I did not hear the episode myself, but he must have behaved very badly, for both Edward Bridges and R. A. Butler, who were standing near, thought it necessary to apologise for him – one of them (I think R.A.B.) saying that he had certainly had too much to drink. This morning, having heard exactly what he said to L.R. – most abusive language, of the Billingsgate order – I thought I ought to take some notice of it. So, after taking counsel of Bridges, who agreed, I have drafted a letter to him in my own hand, quoting the words he used, and pointing out not merely the un-courtliness of that sort of behaviour (from a prominent Tory, of all people), and the injustice of it, not merely to L.R., who was doing exactly what the King, in his own house, had ordered him to do, but to all of us who spend our lives trying to prevent any tinge of political feeling manifesting itself at any of the King's public functions.

Friday 11 January

Sent off my letter to Eden, having pruned it of all adjectives save those used by A.E. himself. I think it is a restrained and moderate document, though it don't mince its words. I can't think of a precedent for such an episode save Palmerston's famous assault on Lady Dacre in her bedroom at Windsor; even that had the excuse that it was inspired by Venus – a more sympathetic deity – rather than by Bacchus.

Monday 14 January

Got Eden's reply, which, to my great relief, is exactly the one I hoped for – the answer of an honest gentleman who knows he has made an ass of himself, and is not afraid to say so; it contains a generous apology to all concerned. I have thanked him for it, and told him that, as far as I am concerned, the incident will never be mentioned again.

Wednesday 16 January

I got another letter from Eden, from which it appears that his previous one was a spontaneous apologia written before he had got mine. However, no harm is done, and it is no bad thing that he should realise that we were not prepared to let his behaviour go by default. This second letter is in the same strain as the first; he is evidently deeply perturbed by the whole affair – not without reason.[1]

Sunday 27 January

Jones, of South Africa House, and Andrews, South African Minister in Washington, came to luncheon at Winchester Tower. Jones came to see me about a month ago with a verbal message from Smuts, asking if it would be any good his suggesting to the King that he should visit South Africa either next autumn or in the spring of '47. I put this to HM and today told Jones that autumn was not practicable, but that there would be a good chance of Their Majesties and Princess Elizabeth coming in '47.

Monday 28 January

Went 3 p.m. to the session of the UNO Security Council in Church House, hoping to see a lively exchange between Bevin and Vyshinsky over Persia, Greece or Indonesia, but was disappointed. The ventilation not good, and with the body of the hall full of spectators, all smoking, the atmosphere during most of the session was suffocating.

They spent the first hour discussing whether Albania should or should not be considered for membership of UNO. Then they got on to Persia. The Persian Ambassador, who is their principal delegate, read an interminable statement, in clipped, bazaar English, which I only understood with difficulty; it seemed to me to be a pretty strong recital of Persia's grievances against Russian interference. When he had done, an interpreter repeated it all in French. Then Vyshinsky spoke for twenty-five minutes in Russian, which had to be repeated in English and then in French. I had a nice nap while V. was talking, but woke up in time for the translations. From watching V. throughout the session, I got the impression that he was not comfortable; Bevin, on the other hand, looked fairly happy. At one moment, before the Persian debate began, he and Vyshinsky seemed to be exchanging quips, with all the outward manifestations of friendliness. How

---

1 In a later note Tommy added: 'When I retired from Buckingham Palace, I burnt this correspondence.

people like Gladwyn Jebb[1] (who is still the acting executive secretary), A. Cadogan, etc., can sit through that sort of thing day after day, I can't imagine.

Tuesday 29 January

Michael Adeane writes from Sandringham that Edward Ford, who went down there with him for his first spell of duty, has caught on well with both old and young. This is a relief, for I pledged my reputation that both the King and Queen (who don't know him) would like him, and it would have been a bore if they had not done so.

Sunday 3 February   **Windsor**

In the adjourned Security Council meeting on Friday, Bevin let the Muscovites have it good and proper, denouncing their insidious methods of propaganda very frankly. 'We play chess, Mr Bevin plays darts,' one delegate is reported to have said. What a good thing that the King persuaded Attlee to put Bevin, and not Greasy Dalton, into the Foreign Office; and what a good thing that Bevin is our spokesman at this juncture rather than Eden, or any other Tory. If Eden, or even Winston, had made this slashing attack on Communism, the foreigners would only have shrugged their shoulders and said, 'What else can one expect from a British capitalist and aristocrat?' They can't say that of Ernie.

Whatever the immediate consequences of the speech, it is perfectly clear that nowadays it is foolish, and dangerous, to veil these international differences under the cloak of diplomacy – people won't stand for being told indefinitely that everything in the garden is lovely; and when they suddenly discover that it isn't true, then comes war.

Saturday 9 February

Went last night to the City's dinner for UNO delegates. Guildhall, still only half recovered from its blitz, but with all the traditional ritual, trumpeter etc. I was well-placed between Philip Noel-Baker,[2] whom I like, and

---

1 Hubert Gladwyn Jebb (1900–96), diplomat, UN adviser 1946–7. Created 1st Baron Gladwyn of Bramfield 1960.
2 Philip Noel-Baker (1889–1982), MP for Derby 1936–50 and for Derby South 1950–70, Minister of State, FO 1945–6, Nobel Peace Prize 1959. Created Baron Noel-Baker (Life Peer) 1977.

Humphrey Gale,[1] of UNRRA. Spaak,[2] who is a real orator, made a fine, resounding speech, and Attlee quite a good reply; in the latter's diction, I noticed several obvious Winstonian inflections.

Public dinners are made easier for me by the presence of G. Cantuar, who invariably smokes a pipe, and, following the archiepiscopal example, I have no shame in doing likewise. Bevin, at the reception prior to dinner, got easily the best welcome of anybody; he was in good heart, though obviously somewhat worn. It struck me that, now that the world has woken up to the imminence of famine, large-scale entertaining, either at Buckingham Palace or by the Government, had better be avoided, once UNO has dispersed. I have written to Rowan to this effect.

The Russians, *en bloc*, refused their invites to the Guildhall (except Miss Vyshinsky, who didn't answer); the theory is that Moscow forbade them to enter this shrine of capitalism, toryism and reaction.

Sunday 10 February

Successful party at Buckingham Palace last night for UNO delegates – 9.30 p.m. to 11.30. About 950 people all told, including the Muscovites. The King had a long, and apparently cordial, talk with Vyshinsky – and with Miss Vyshinsky, who HM declares is not his daughter, but his mistress. I had ditto with Bevin, on a sofa in the '44 room (which was empty); he is pleased with his week's work, but has no illusions about the Russians – says they are out to dominate the world, Hitler all over again. He told me that the man who gave him most support in Cabinet over foreign affairs was Aneurin Bevan. Queen Mary talked indefatigably to a long string of delegates, and at the very end, when the King was obviously fretting for bed, insisted on my bringing Mudaliar up to her. A meagre buffet, appropriate to the food situation, but there was champagne for all.

Monday 11 February

I got Lavinia's wedding invitations (700) from Harrison, the printers.

---

1 Lieut.-Gen. Sir Humphrey Gale (1890–1971), personal representative in Europe of the Director of UNRRA.
2 Paul-Henri Spaak (1899–1972), lawyer and politician, Belgian Minister of Foreign Affairs 1939–46, PM of Belgium 1947–9, President UN Assembly 1949, Chairman of the Council of Europe 1950–55, Secretary-General NATO 1957–61.

Tuesday 12 February

Queen Mary has sent Lavinia two very pretty silver dishes. Took Edward Ford to see E. Bridges, Ismay and No. 10.

Wednesday 13 February

Joan and I lunched with Cartier, to meet Mlle de Jongh, the Belgian heroine who performed prodigies of valour rescuing our airmen etc. from German hands, and was given the George Medal this morning by the King.[1] A remarkable, and attractive, young woman, with a glow in her eyes like Jeanne d'Arc. Ben Smith,[2] Minister of Food, the anathema of all good housewives, whom he has robbed of their dried eggs, came to see the King. He did not seem at all dismayed by the gruelling he has had in the Press lately.

Saturday 16 February   **Windsor**

Thrushes singing, and heard first chaffinch of the year. Caroline was eighteen yesterday. Joan and I busy writing wedding invitations. Row in Ottawa, because certain officials, as present un-named, have been selling secrets to Russia. Reading *Ralph the Heir*, one of Trollope's best.

Wednesday 20 February

Went with Joan to the opening night at Covent Garden, for which they chose Tchaikovsky's ballet *Sleeping Princess*. It was adequately, though not flawlessly, done by the Sadler's Wells company, but décor (Messel[3]) and music (Constant Lambert[4]) good. The King and Queen, the Princesses and Queen Mary were there, and the house was full to capacity. I had not been to Covent Garden since the gala performance in the summer of 1939, when Winston strode up and down the foyer exclaiming prophetically, '*Götterdämmerung, Götterdämmerung*, we shall never see the like of this again.' He was right, for though it was a cheerful and enthusiastic audience, it was a drab one, and, with memories of those great Wagnerian nights of thirty-five years ago, the place was full of ghosts for me, and others of my generation. Lady Ripon's box, the Delphic shrine of opera, was full of

---

1 Andrée de Jongh's award of the George Medal had been announced on 29 Oct. 1945.
2 Rt. Hon. Sir Ben Smith (1879–1964), Minister of Food 1945–6.
3 Oliver Messel (1904–78), artist, designer and theatrical producer.
4 Constant Lambert (1905–51), composer, conductor and critic.

cameras. But it was a gallant effort to open a new chapter, and in that sense it was a great success – largely due to the initiative of Keynes,[1] who was there to welcome Their Majesties, but at the last moment got palpitations of the heart and had to remain in his box.

We saw many old friends; but I, at any rate, was conscious all the time of many absent ones. An engaging spectacle was that of Bevin floundering like a great bluebottle in the web of that old harridan Maud Cunard,[2] whom accident or design had placed in the next seat to his. I shouldn't be surprised if she paid the management handsomely to put her adjacent to the lion of the hour.

We went back to an excellent supper with the Clarendons, now our neighbours in St James's Palace. He has some very interesting pictures, which look well enough in that house.

Thursday 21 February

Mutiny of ratings in certain Royal Indian Navy ships in Bombay has taken a serious turn and seems to be spreading. The India Office, in spite of repeated telegrams to the Viceroy and others, have no official report of it yet. With India in its present explosive state, these might well be bad developments. Maurice Hallett,[3] retiring Governor of the United Provinces, to see the King; he agrees with me that the time has come for Pakistan, in some form, to be granted to the Muslims.

Friday 22 February

Dined last night with Munnings[4] at Burlington House – a stag party of about thirty, to meet the PM. Munnings, who always gives the idea of being slightly tight, even when strictly sober, as he was on this occasion, made a series of ejaculatory speeches inveighing against Picasso, etc., and there was a general debate, to which the only contribution of any value was that of

---

1   John Maynard Keynes (1883–1946), economist, banker and author, leader of the British delegation which negotiated the American loan in Washington, 1945. He was married to the Russian ballerina Lydia Lopokova, and it was he who encouraged a reluctant Treasury to give financial aid to the arts – hence the reopening of the Royal Opera House. Sadly, he died in Apr. 1946.
2   Lady Cunard (1872–1948), American widow of Sir Bache Cunard (1851–1925). Relentless London hostess, friend of King Edward VIII and long-time mistress of Sir Thomas Beecham, she was christened Maud, but preferred to be called Emerald.
3   Sir Maurice Hallett (1883–1969), Governor of the United Provinces 1939–45.
4   Sir Alfred Munnings (1878–1959), celebrated, irascible painter of horses. President of the Royal Academy 1944–9.

Professor Bodkin,[1] an amusing old Celt with a strong Irish accent and a Shavian appearance. The sense of the meeting was that the Picasso technique was, at best, nonsense, and possibly harmful nonsense.

Tuesday 26 February

Attlee at 6 p.m. The King's complaint that he can never get anything out of A. is well-founded. He is agreeable and friendly, but closes every subject with a snap of his jaws, and if you don't try to launch a new one yourself, the rest is silence.

Wednesday 13 March

E. Bevin after luncheon. I told him that he had one of the most difficult jobs in the country, trying to make both ends of the King's Civil List meet. He said, 'I suppose you've got so much money to spend that you don't know what to do with it.' I came back at him strongly, and told him, in effect, not to talk nonsense, quoting the fact that HM has to pay some £15,000 a year in war bonuses. This set him off on a long exposition of how hardly he himself was used by the income-tax people – Satan rebuking sin, with a vengeance. I could not get him off the topic till the King sent for him, which was a bore, as I wanted to find out how much truth there is in the American report that the Russians, so far from withdrawing their troops in Persia, are reinforcing them.

Sent off a long cipher telegram from the King to the Duke of Gloucester, telling him he ought to come home next January so as to head the Council of State while HM is in Africa.

Thursday 14 March

Their Majesties entertained the Amir Abdullah of Transjordan[2] to luncheon. He gave the King a small portrait of King George V, etched on a gold plate, surmounted by a circlet of diamonds; in return, HM gave him a large oil painting of KG V steaming through the fleet for the Coronation review in 1911, and a pair of photos. The choice of this present has been a bit of a problem, as it always is with these gifts for oriental potentates. We were told that the Amir was particularly interested in souvenirs of KG V, and in

---

1 Thomas Bodkin (1887–1961), Irish barrister and professor of the history of art.
2 Abdullah al Hussein (1882–1951), first King of Jordan (formerly Transjordan, a British mandate), which became an independent kingdom on 22 Mar. 1946.

ships, so this picture, in a very gaudy gilt frame, seemed to fill the bill; anyhow, he was delighted with it.

Friday 15 March

The South African visit was formally announced, here and in the Union, and has had a good press.

Saturday 16 March

Our wedding day. There was a good Indian debate in the House of Commons yesterday, especially Attlee, who took what is really the only line with the Indians now – 'If you want to go, go, but let us part friends.'

Monday 18 March

Went to the Guildhall, Pug Ismay driving me there, to see Alex receive the freedom of the City. I was well placed on the dais, between Oliver Lyttelton and Tedder, and at the Mansion House luncheon, between that good man Auchinleck and young de L'Isle & Dudley, formerly Sidney,[1] VC. He was one of a party of about ten officers and other ranks who won the VC under Alex's command. He is a striking example of the iniquity of our law of primogeniture: he had just got elected to the House of Commons, where he could have been a most useful member, when his uncle died suddenly, and he finds himself banished to the House of Lords for life.

Thursday 21 March

I had a long talk yesterday with Billy Harlech about South Africa. He strongly advises that Their Majesties should do all their travelling within the Union and Rhodesia by air – except for the Durban–Pretoria trip, which is tricky, as one has to fly over the Drakensberg mountains, where eighty per cent of the air crashes in South Africa have occurred. The King agrees with me that we must use aeroplanes, but I gather that the Queen feels otherwise. I have now definitely fixed with Admiralty that we make the voyage there and back in *Vanguard*, which I hope can do the journey without having to call at any intermediate port for refuelling.

---

1   William Sidney (1909–91), only son of 5th Baron de L'Isle and Dudley, was awarded a
    VC for his exceptional gallantry in attacking German positions behind the Anzio beach-
    head in February 1944. Secretary of State for Air 1951–5. Created 1st Viscount De L'Isle
    1956.

Saturday 23 March

The Foreign Office rang up last night to ask if the King would have any objection to Averell Harriman[1] succeeding Winant as American Ambassador. HM thought it a good idea, especially in view of Harriman's recent experience of Russia while in Moscow.

The indefatigable Mr Iwi, who spends his life writing to *The Times* about technical anomalies in the British constitution, claims that the Regency Bill of '37 was faultily drafted (by John Simon), and that as a result our subsequent Councils of State may have been acting *ultra vires*. The Lord Chancellor's people, to whom I sent on Iwi's letter, are considerably fluttered – Iwi is nearly always right – and I am to see Jowitt about it on Monday.

[At a cocktail party] I asked Alex [Field-Marshal Alexander] how he would view the proposed abolition in the Army of compulsory attendance at church services. His view was that, though actual church-parades might perhaps be done away with, the men should still be under orders to go to church on a certain number of Sundays much as undergraduates are (or were) required to attend so many chapels per term. Edward Renton returned from Austria, and he and Lavinia came down to Winchester Tower, where a stack of wedding-presents awaited them.

Tuesday 26 March

Saw Arthur Street[2] about a letter from Prince Adalbert (Hohenzollern) to Queen Mary. I've little sympathy with these German princelings, who are now so busy explaining how much they disliked the Nazis – for whose existence they are as much responsible as anybody.

Wednesday 27 March

Lawson came to see the King about the proposed abolition of compulsory attendance at church in the Army. On balance, I am against the abolition, strongly as I believe in the individual's right to resist any interference by any human being in his own mental or spiritual exercises. But, when a man puts on a uniform (actually or metaphorically) he must be ready to surrender some of his individual liberties. I go to church far more

---

1 Averell Harriman (1891–1986), successful banker, USA Ambassador to Soviet Union 1943–6, and to Great Britain 1946.
2 Sir Arthur Street (1892–1951), Permanent Secretary, Control Office for Germany and Austria 1945–6.

often than I want to, because I am the King's private secretary.

Saturday 30 March

Lavinia's wedding, which was a roaring success, thanks to perfect organisation by Joan, and perfect cooperation by the weather. It was a lovely
spring day, and St George's, whose full beauty is very much dependent on
the light, looked its best; as did also the bride and bridegroom, who won
all hearts by their brave bearing and obvious happiness. Though I had not
looked forward to the long walk up the aisle (in my wedding patent leather
boots, which had not been out of their stable for seven years), I enjoyed the
service. The choir sang 'Ye Watchers and Ye Holy Ones' superbly.

A great pride of Royals attended – King and Queen, two Princesses,
Queen Mary, Princess Mary and Harry Harewood; the majority of them
insisted on coming into the vestry, which entailed a lot of chattering and
waiting about – especially as the Dean contrived to get entangled with
Lavinia's train, which is exactly the kind of unrehearsed effect that always
gives the Royal Family exuberant pleasure.

Reception in the Waterloo Chamber, which looked noble and comfortably held our 600 guests. Among them were some twenty people from
Sutton who had come all the way in hired motors at 30/– a head – this
touched me very much, and I wish I had had time to do more than shake
them by the hand. The King proposed the health of bride and bridegroom,
in a moiety of the three bottles of champagne I had procured, and Edward
replied gallantly (my draft). Then photographs, which as usual was a protracted business, and they finally got away about 5.30, to Cloud's Hill, where
they honeymoon. They have done well in the way of presents, considering
the austerity of the times, and got over £600 in cheques. Now I must settle
down to pay the bills; I reckon I shall have small change left out of a monkey,
but don't grudge it – and have no right to do so, having sold my Canadian
Brewery shares, about which I had entirely forgotten, at about 100 per cent
profit. I also find that considerable holding in Canadian and American
Celanese has appreciated to about the same extent.[1]

Wednesday 3 April

At Grillions R. A. Butler told me that a rift is imminent between A. Eden
and Winston, whose ideas as to the running of the Conservative Party do
not square with those of A.E. I thought R.A.B. very overstrained; he kept

---

1   During the 1930s Tommy had been very well advised on investments by his brother-in-
law Melville Balfour.

saying how badly he needed a rest – true enough, but it's a bad sign when men start reiterating that.

Thursday 4 April

Went with Joan, Doreen Brabourne etc. to the Victoria League concert in the Albert Hall – Malcolm Sargent[1] conducting the Philharmonic, Moiseiwitsch[2] at the piano. He played the 1st Beethoven concerto, which is too delicate and intimate a thing for the Albert Hall.

Monday 8 April

Dalton came, to expound the Budget to the King. He seemed very bobbish, and confident that the next financial year would be an easier one. He told me he was going to restore some of the earned income allowance, and reduce excess profits tax, and purchase tax, but said nothing about income or surtax. The deficit will be £700 millions, instead of £1,000, as was expected. Also said that the American loan had gone through; the Pope had helped in this, by telling the Irish Catholics in USA to stop opposing it. Whatever the reason, they have certainly changed their tune lately.

Dalton is a very unlikeable man. When he was Minister of Economic Warfare, he was so unpopular with all his subordinates that they formed an 'Apple Club', each member being obliged to buy an apple in rotation, and place it on the doorstep, 'to keep the Doctor away'.

There the journal comes to an abrupt halt. Twenty years later, the author appended a two-line explanation on the final page: 'I gave up keeping a diary, not for any particular reason, but because I just hadn't the energy left to go on with it.'

---

1 Sir Malcolm Sargent (1895–1967), conductor, professor at the Royal College of Music from 1923.
2 Benno Moiseiwitsch (1890–1963), celebrated Russian-born pianist.

APPENDIX:
1947 – SOUTH AFRICAN LETTERS

The royal tour of South Africa, which Tommy had suggested and planned, took place in the spring of 1947. He was not keeping a diary at the time, but described the journey in letters to Joan.

7 February 1947   *H.M.S. Vanguard,* off Gambia

My Darling,

We had a bad dusting for the first two days, with a full gale all across the Bay of Biscay – so full, that our poor escort ships had great difficulty in keeping up with us in the mountainous seas. I went to bed on the Saturday night and stayed there firmly till Tuesday, for which I felt all the better. I am very lucky in my cabin, which, besides being very commodious and cool, is on the same deck as the Royals, and so out of sound of the ship's traffic. Usually, on a man-of-war, one is woken up at 5 a.m. by endless processions of sailors dropping chains, buckets and whatnot in the passage, and shouting loudly to each other; all this I am spared, and sleep peacefully till 7.45 a.m., when I hear the London news from a neat wireless fixed above my bed.

We are now running through the Tropics, with calm seas, and the usual slightly sticky, somnolent atmosphere, though it is not unpleasantly hot. Life has settled into a smooth routine – deck chairs, deck games after tea, three or four officers to dinner, a film or dancing afterwards. I have little work to do, save to read and pass on the intermittent telegrams from the Cabinet Office, giving us the lowdown, which are deciphered and typed for me by our admirable cipher-officer, with no trouble at all to me.

I have finished *Mr Scarborough's Family,* which is one of Trollope's more ingenious plots, though lacking the humour of the earlier books; but Mr S. himself is one of his best character-studies, and the lawyer's daughter, Dorothy Grey, is a good figure, reminding me occasionally of Helen.

Our Captain, Agnew[1] (of the picture-dealing and *Punch*-producing family) is a very nice man, and has a good lot of officers. Last night, the Princesses and Household were entertained by the midshipmen at a cocktail party in the Gun-Room, which was like a Turkish bath but otherwise agreeable.

---

1   Vice-Admiral Sir William Agnew (1898–1960), knighted 1947.

Goodbye, my Darling. The older I get, the less I like being away from you, and though I am reasonably content, my chief feeling is happiness that one week of the fifteen that I must be away has already gone.

12 February 1947   *Vanguard*

Since the Biscay storm our voyage has been uneventful, and pleasant enough from my point of view, in that I have days of comparative idleness, with long siestas every afternoon, and reasonably early bed. But this is not what one can call an ideal pleasure-cruise, for, as soon as it stopped being cold and rough, it got hot and sticky, and has stayed so ever since. Personally, I have never come through the Tropics feeling so well, but other members of the party, especially the females, have been rather overpowered by the heat. I am thankful that I brought my silk suits, which have been a godsend. It is not unpleasant on deck, provided one can get out of the sun and into some place where these restless sailors are not scrubbing or cleaning or shouting; but in these great steel ships the cabins get very hot, and stay so until the metal has cooled off, which it hasn't had a chance to do yet.

The ceremony of 'crossing the line' was observed with most elaborate ritual. It began with a lovely discharge of fireworks on the night that we actually crossed the equator. This was very enjoyable. The whole of the next forenoon was devoted to the mummery of 'Neptune's Court', with scores of people dressed up, more or less humorously, shavings, duckings in the bath, etc. The Princesses went through a token ceremony, and were given elaborate and artistically got-up certificates. As we are a very young ship's company, there were about a thousand 'initiates'. I don't know whether they got through them all or not, as we withdrew after about an hour, when it seemed to have degenerated into a free fight, with everybody ducking everybody else.

I am now going along to the quartermaster's store, as I am told that he has quite a good line in underwear, which he can sell me cheaply and without coupons. [Later.] My visit to the store was most rewarding. I came away with six pairs of winter drawers, six ditto vests, two pairs pyjamas, ten semi-stiff collars, four pairs socks, two nail brushes, one shaving ditto, all in a beautiful zip bag with a padlock. The whole lot cost me £7, and no coupons. In London, the bag alone would have cost very nearly as much. The underclothes are excellent, but I didn't greatly fancy the pyjamas, though they will do well enough for hot weather.

Our party seemed to be enjoying themselves, especially the Princesses. Yesterday a treasure hunt was organised for them and the midshipmen, which appeared to be most successful.

15 February 1947

This morning I at last got from the Cape the final copies of the official programme, which they had promised me by Jan. 1st! I had to make them send them in an aeroplane, which dropped them into the sea this morning, in a canister, which was hauled on board with a grappling iron.

The royal party landed at Cape Town in a temperature of 105° F, on what Tommy called 'a real Bombay day'.

18 February 1947   **Government House, Cape Town**

Outwardly, however, everything was most successful, with unexpectedly large and enthusiastic crowds and vociferous cheering throughout the day. In the evening there was a State banquet: 504 people, in a hall as hot as Hades, and a terribly slow and dreary dinner, through which we had to sit on very hard little chairs. In thirty years of public dinners, I can't recall one that caused me greater misery. However, the King spoke well, and made a deep impression, and, to my great surprise, I found when we got home that the Royals had enjoyed it, and thought it great fun – especially the young ones.

Princess Elizabeth is delightfully enthusiastic and interested; she has her grandmother's passion for punctuality, and, to my delight, goes bounding furiously up the stairs to bolt her parents when they are more than usually late. This is one of those incredibly uncomfortable Government Houses, with good rooms, but lacking all the essentials like writing tables, tooth glasses, etc., and staffed by a scratch lot of servants, who don't know if it is Christmas or Easter.

22 February 1947   **On the White Train, *Die Wittrein,* near Swellendam**

Cape Town was unquestionably a roaring success, in outline and in detail. The climate was unpleasantly like Bombay at times, and the crickets and turtle-doves were noisy at night and in the small hours; but the populace, British, Afrikaans and coloured, could not have behaved better or more enthusiastically. They are just as demonstrative as Canadians, but much more self-controlled and orderly – they never try to overwhelm the police in waves of mass-hysteria, as Canadians so often do; and the crowds are as patient as London crowds, waiting hours in good-tempered expectation.

The set-pieces went very well, especially the Opening, where the King, after repeated spasms of stage fright, which gave me much trouble, got out his few sentences of Afrikaans to his own satisfaction and that of all who heard him. The Queen looked lovely, despite a too-massive tiara of Queen Mary's, which she felt obliged to wear because it is made of the chippings of the Cullinan diamond.[1]

The last night, I went with Their Majesties and the Princesses (who left early to go to a dance) to dine with Smuts at Groote Schuur. The old man was a bit tired, and not as amusing as usual, but seeing the house excited me. Every room is redolent of Cecil Rhodes,[2] and I was not at all surprised when a woman staying there, a Lady Moore, told me that he still haunts it, and that Mrs Smuts (who hated Cecil Rhodes and all his works) never will stay there, for that reason.

Before dinner, the Queen handed back to Smuts the Kruger Bible.[3] I forget if I told you the history of this, a vast family Bible which I could hardly carry: Horace Smith-Dorrien[4] looted it during the Boer War, and took it home to England. He then went out to India, and while he was there, I suppose about 1904, an appeal was made for all such Boer family relics to be returned to South Africa. He wrote home asking that this Bible might be sent back to the Kruger family, but it could not be found. A few months ago, his widow, Lady Smith-Dorrien, discovered it locked away in an old box, and wrote to the Queen, asking her to give it to Smuts, to dispose of as he thinks fit. So, at Groote Schuur, the home of Kruger's bitterest enemy, it was given back to the Prime Minister of a united South Africa by Queen Victoria's great granddaughter-in-law. This struck me as a remarkable picture in the kaleidoscope of history.

2 March 1947   On the White Train, approaching Aliwal North C.P.

Today we have met our first rain – and real cloud-burst rain it is. At the last wayside station at which we stopped, the whole place was ankle-deep in water in about two minutes, and the Royal Family were unable to get out to do their usual perambulation up and down the platform. They have been crying out for rain for weeks past – the customary native greeting in these parts is 'Pula pula' (which means 'May the rain come'), and it is pleasant to see the parched earth soaking it up. The King will get the credit for it, and be hailed as a Rain-Maker.

---

1 At 3,106 carats the largest diamond ever found. Discovered in 1905 at the Premier Mines, east of Pretoria, belonging to Sir Thomas Cullinan, and presented to King Edward VII on his 66th birthday in 1907 by the government of the Transvaal.
2 Rt Hon. Cecil Rhodes (1853–1902), pioneer South African statesman.
3 Stephen J. Paul Kruger (1825–1904), South African settler, soldier and politician. Commandant General of the South African Republic 1863.
4 General Sir Horace Smith-Dorrien (1858–1930), commanded a brigade and a division during the Boer War 1899–1901.

It has been fine, rolling country, always with a spectacular sky-line of mountains, for the past few days, but there is not much to look at save sheep and cows and kaffirs, who dance themselves into ecstasies of delight as the train goes by. They all look extremely plump and well, and no representative of UNO could detect any signs of malnutrition or oppression.

We have had several native shows, not very impressive except when they sing, which they do marvellously, generally in five of six parts (which apparently comes quite naturally to them), with very deep basses.

To his son John

10 March 1947   **On the White Train, approaching Bethlehem,**
                                  Orange Free State

Mr Dear Wool,

Many of the older men are most amusing about their adventures in the Boer War, and have no diffidence about recounting them, whichever side they took. The O.F.S. is overwhelmingly national in politics, and largely Afrikaans-speaking; none the less, they are rolling up in their thousands to give Their Majesties an amazingly good welcome. Our Minister in Attendance, Colin Steyn (his father[1] was President of the O.F.S. all through the Boer War, and on one occasion escaped from one of our cavalry patrols in nothing but his nightshirt and beard) told me just now that he is astounded by his fellow-countrymen. He anticipated they would be polite, for they are a naturally courteous people, but he never imagined that they would show anything like the enthusiasm that is evident everywhere, even from the back-veldt farmers, who drive miles to meet the Royals at some wayside station at which the train probably stops for only a few minutes.

This morning, at a little place called Kroonstad, the day was made for us by the happy chance that when one of the local worthies took off his hat, it was observed that his hat was full of bees. Knowing the Family, you can imagine the instantaneous success this had with them. I was able to get off, in a whisper, a quick one about bees in the bonnet being better than ants in the pants, which the King used as his own, to the unbridled delight of the rest of the assembly. It sounds, I admit, a curious bit of natural history, but it is factually true. There were a lot of bees about, and this chap had anointed himself with a particularly greasy form of Honey & Flowers, which proved irresistible to them. From that moment, the proceedings at Kroonstad were a wow.

---

1   Martinus Steyn (1857–1915), barrister, President Orange Free State 1896–1900.

14 March 1947   Natal National Park

We drove in last night from Ladysmith, sixty-five miles away, through fine country and a lurid sunset, with a cyclopean thunderstorm going on miles away behind the Drakensberg mountains. I was in a car with Smuts and Mima. The old man was in his most boyish mood, repeating at intervals, 'We are going to the mountains, we are going to the mountains,' like a child on its way to its first pantomime. On the way we passed Spion Kop, and I was thrilled to hear his account of the battle, told with complete detachment, so that one could not have said whether he had fought as a Boer or a Briton.[1]

In Harrismith, where we were in the morning, there was a memorial on one side of the square to the men of the Grenadiers and Scots Guards who died in Natal fighting; on the other, 100 yards away, was a memorial to the Boers. In almost any other country in the world, one or both of them would inevitably have been destroyed or defaced in the years after the war; but there has never been any such attempt by either side. This morning I got up at 6.45, and rode with the Princesses and the boys. It was only an amble, on the local ponies, so I hope I shan't be stiff tomorrow. I don't think I've been on a horse since 1934.

21 March 1947   King's House, Durban

I had a great morning among the Durban shops, and spent money like water. For myself, I bought twelve pairs of slap-up English socks, some more vests, and drawers, two shirts (moderate), and two pairs of pyjamas, very Hollywood in design but not bad stuff – all this was £16. I have also bought a trout-line which is unprocurable in England.

All Fools 1947   Johannesburg

[Having praised the country he had been through as 'some of the loveliest in South Africa'] I should be quite glad to live here – if only it wasn't for the blacks. Everywhere we go, they swarm like ants; there are seven million of them to two and a half million whites, and they are increasing prodigally. The colour problem hangs like a grim cloud over the whole Union; it is a terrifying one, and I should be very sorry to try to live here permanently now. The only solution is to import several million more whites, and they, of course, could not be absorbed, economically, unless spread over a period of about fifty years. Yet, if one could live an 'isolationist' life, there are many

---

1   The hill-top site of the battle fought on 23–24 January 1900 in which the Boers defeated the British forces. At that stage Smuts was fighting with the Boers.

places where one could be happy enough gardening, farming, etc., in country of supreme beauty.

Johannesburg has been a remarkable popular success – I've never seen larger and noisier crowds save perhaps in Montreal in 1939, but I don't like the 'city of gold', which is a modern Babylon, if ever there was one. I prefer the simple Free Staters of Bloemfontein and its neighbourhood, who are as different from the Jo'burgers as a West Country yeoman is from a Birmingham stockbroker.

They originally wanted us to motor back to Pretoria – one hour's drive – after our 'banquet' here tonight, but I struck at that, and made them bring the train to the quiet siding in the outskirts of Jo'burg, where we are now lying up before dressing for dinner (white tie and stars), and whither we shall return to sleep at, I hope, about 10.30 p.m. The King's Pretoria speech has gone over very well here, and so far as I can judge has made a good impression in England. I heard it on the wireless from my bed, for when we reached Pretoria at midday, I realised I had a chill on my stomach. So I went to bed, starved, and have slept for the best part of twenty-four hours, waking up the next morning feeling all the better for it.

Later. At this point I was told that Edward Ford was going to ring me up shortly from Buckingham Palace. This warning always throws me into a frenzy of apprehension, and sets me imagining every sort of disaster. However, in this case the news was nothing worse than poor George of Greece's death, which we have disposed of pretty easily, with a week's Court mourning in London, and no notice at all to be taken by anybody out here, because we haven't any becoming mourning with us – a typical Royal Family compromise.

Edward said he died of heart failure, but I should not be at all surprised if he was bumped, poor chap. There are plenty of people who would be glad enough to see him out of the way. I suppose his brother Paul will succeed him. I've always understood that Paul was the one they really wanted to be king, so perhaps they will now settle down under him.

P.S. In twenty-five years of royal 'stunting', I've never yet seen a dog killed by our motors. Today I saw *five*, at intervals, laid out in the middle of the road.

7 April 1947   Government House, Salisbury, Southern Rhodesia

This place – I mean Southern Rhodesia as a whole – strikes me as every bit as agreeable to live in as any part of the Union, so far as climate and scenery go; and much more so, in that it is wholly English in habit and outlook –

the atmosphere of this place is that of a pleasant English country town, with better shops than most of them. The servant problem doesn't exist; the housewife has no worries; the air is like wine; the gardens bloom; and though it can rain and freeze (at night only), they think the end of the world is coming if there are three consecutive days without a cloudless sky.

All this, of course, is a very superficial impression; but, if I were a lonely bachelor, I should be very strongly tempted to come and live here when, in a few years' time, I can quit this job; and this though, as you know, I have a passionate devotion to England, and Scotland in my bones. But, with things as they are now and are going to be, the England and Scotland of the rest of my life are not, I am afraid, going to be places where we can hope to find either peace or happiness.

The Minister of Agriculture (on whom I am billeted) tells me that, for £5,000 or thereabouts, a couple of middle-aged immigrants could make themselves a charming home in one or another of the country districts round this town, or Bulawayo, or further afield if necessary. The Prime Minister, Huggins,[1] flew here from London in *forty-eight hours* last month; but, at present, a single air passage costs a private individual £160.

All this is airy speculation; but I want you to take it reasonably seriously. I spend most of my time thinking about you, and the greatest anxiety that I have for the future is the thought of you going on toiling indefinitely at the dreary business of keeping a present-day English house going, away from flowers and sunshine, which, apart from the children, are two of the few things left which we can both enjoy. The children are, of course, the main problem. But it is not beyond the bounds of probability that John might like to come and lead an active life out here on his own. If I were his age, and had his physique, I should be very strongly tempted to do so. It is certain that this part of Central Africa is going to have a very important future.

30 April 1947   On board *Vanguard*

We had a great send-off from Cape Town, with everyone crying. The South Africans are a generous, warm-hearted people, and there is no doubt they have thoroughly enjoyed having the Royal Family in their midst. The King spoke well at a farewell luncheon, the Queen adding her little piece at the end, and the proceedings ended with Smuts formally handing over their presents – a gold box full of enough little diamonds to make up a Garter

---

1 Sir Godfrey Huggins (1883–1971), Prime Minister of Southern Rhodesia 1933–53, created 1st Viscount Malvern 1955.

star for the King; a lovely single diamond, and a little gold tea-set for the Queen: and a diamond bracelet for Princess Margaret.

They had previously given Princess Elizabeth her present on her birthday – twenty-one most beautiful stones, to make up a necklace. To me fell the uneasy task of guarding them during the three days before our departure. I am not used to looking after £200,000 worth of diamonds, but fortunately there was an adequate strong-room with a safe inside it at Government House, so they were deposited there, and eventually sent down to the ship under a police escort. Now, I trust, they are lying safe in the Paymaster's safe; anyhow, I have his receipt for them.

The only incident in an uneventful voyage so far has been our call at St Helena yesterday afternoon. I enjoyed this; it is an interesting though slightly uncanny little island – a line of reddish cliffs, very precipitous, is all you see as you approach, until Jamestown, the capital, reveals itself in a narrow valley running up into the hills.

I don't wonder that Boney[1] was a bit depressed by his first sight of the island. Jamestown is little more than a village, but not unattractive, with a fine 'castle', which is really a group of Georgian offices, library, council room, etc., and some pleasant old houses of the same date. All the motors in the island had been mobilised, and in them we drove up a precipitous mountain road, full of hairpin bends, looking down the khud into the hinterland. There isn't much of it, for the whole island is only ten miles by six. Some of it consists of bare volcanic hills, but there are a number of steep valleys, very green, rather reminiscent of Wales, and when you get to the top, wonderful views of the sea on all sides.

Our objective was Longwood. I have never found a place so permeated with melancholy – it gave us all the heeby-jeebies, and I think that if one lived there, one would become quite fey in a week. Both the house and the garden could be made charming, and it stands beautifully. But the French, to whom it was handed over years ago, have allowed it to fall into the most deplorable state of disrepair, doing nothing to combat the ravages of white ants and the damp. If they don't do something about it soon, the house will tumble down.

But even if it were in good order, there hangs over it an almost tangible atmosphere of grey gloom; in the little rooms and in the garden you can still feel the black bitterness of Napoleon and that dreadful little party that made up his entourage, and it is only increased by the rather bogus collection of relics in the house. There is a gazebo in the garden, looking out

---

1 After his defeat at Waterloo in 1815, Napoleon was imprisoned at Longwood House, on St Helena, where he remained until his death in 1826.

to the sea, that gave me exactly the same sensation as that summerhouse in the Nishat Bagh in Kashmir.[1] It was a relief to drive on to Plantation House, the Government House of the island.

This is a charming, square, late Georgian building, like a smaller edition of Clovelly,[2] with some lovely rooms and a number of bits of quite good furniture. Here we had tea, and disported ourselves with a giant tortoise reputed to be 200 years old, so it must have known Napoleon intimately.

It was a well-spent afternoon, for of course no reigning Sovereign has ever before set foot on the island, and the population, some 4,000-odd, of all shades of colour, got a tremendous kick out of it all. That will be our last public appearance before Portsmouth, and is really the last little scene of the whole tour.

Looking back, I know that it has been an immense success, and amply achieved its only object (at least from my point of view) – to convince the South African people that the British Monarchy is an investment worth keeping, and that the present Royal Family in particular can mean a good deal to them.

From the inside, the most satisfactory feature of the whole visit is the remarkable development of Princess Elizabeth. She has come on in the most surprising way, and all in the right direction. She has got all Princess Mary's solid and enduring qualities, plus a perfectly natural power of enjoying herself without any trace of shyness, and a good, healthy sense of fun. Moreover, when necessary she can take on the old bores with much of her mother's skill, and never spares herself in that exhausting part of royal duty.

For a child of her years, she has got an astonishing solicitude for people's comfort; but what delights me especially is that she has become extremely businesslike, and understands what a burden it is to the Staff if some regard is not paid to the clock. She has developed an admirable technique of going up behind her mother and prodding her in the Achilles tendon with the point of her umbrella when time is being wasted in unnecessary conversation. And, when necessary – not infrequently – she tells her father off to rights.

My impression, by the way, is that we shall all be subscribing to a wedding present before the year is out. Her sister, too, has come on a lot, and is much more agreeable in character, besides being very good company. There must have been many moments in this tour which seemed intolerably dreary to both of them, but on the whole they have been as good as gold.

---

1 Where Tommy and Joan had spent part of their honeymoon.
2 Clovelly Court, home of the Manners family in Devon, one of Tommy's favourite houses.

APPENDIX:
LAST LAP

In 1951 Tommy suffered a grievous blow with the death of his son John, at the age of twenty-nine. John had enjoyed a varied and successful career in the Grenadier Guards. Wounded in Normandy in 1944, he rejoined his battalion before the war ended, and in 1947 was seconded to Mountbatten's staff in India as personal assistant to Lord Ismay. After Independence he returned to England, but soon left for Malaya, where he commanded a company and distinguished himself in operations against the insurgents. He also commanded his company on ceremonial duties in London.

In 1950 he fell ill with cancer, and was operated on by the leading surgeon, Julian Taylor. In June 1951 he was still able to command the Escort to the Colour at the King's Birthday Parade; but the disease spread, and he died on 11 September 1951.

The King and Queen, at Balmoral, both wrote warm personal letters of sympathy in their own hands, saluting the courage which Tommy and Joan had shown during their son's illness. Queen Mary did the same, recalling how she had suffered when her own son, the Duke of Kent, was killed in 1942. Many former colleagues praised John's excellence and efficiency as a soldier, his courtesy and charm as a host. He was buried in the graveyard of the church at Crathie, by Balmoral, and a memorial service was held in the rebuilt Guards' Chapel at Wellington Barracks, where the Last Post was sounded by a bugler of the Grenadiers.

***

King George VI died on 6 February 1952. It is a great pity that Tommy left no account of the funeral, for he had described the passing of George V most eloquently, and he would surely have written still more memorably about the obsequies of the monarch he had come to know so well. He continued to serve as Private Secretary to the Sovereign for the first year of the Queen's reign.

A serious constitutional crisis threatened early in the 1950s, when Princess Margaret wanted to marry the equerry Group Captain Peter Townsend, who was divorced from his first wife, Rosemary. Tommy knew the Townsends well: he had worked alongside Peter since 1944, and the couple had stayed with him and Joan at Winchester Tower. Soon after his retirement he set down his own part in the affair in a memorandum which is undated, but was probably written in 1955, and corrects several errors perpetrated by later writers.

Towards the end of the Queen's stay at Balmoral, in September 1952, Group Captain Peter Townsend, being then Equerry in Waiting, came to see me one morning in the Private Secretary's room. He wished to consult me on some routine matter. When that business was finished, I told him that it was being commonly, and widely, said that he was seeing too much of Princess Margaret. I reminded him that in our profession there was one cardinal and inviolable rule — that in no circumstances ought any member of a Royal Household to give cause for such talk, particularly if the member of the Royal Family concerned was the Sovereign's sister, and the member of the Household a married man. Townsend, who had often consulted my wife and myself about his private affairs during the past eight years, left the room without making any reply.

In the following November Townsend obtained a divorce from his wife, she being technically the guilty party.

Shortly before Christmas [1952], Townsend came to see me again at Buckingham Palace. He told me that Princess Margaret and he were deeply in love with each other and wished to get married. I had never until then envisaged the possibility of such a marriage. My only comment at the time was that, as Townsend must realise, there were obviously several formidable obstacles to be overcome before the marriage could take place.[1] I also asked him to whom, besides myself, the idea had been communicated. He told me that the Queen and the Duke of Edinburgh knew about it, and nobody else. I suggested that the Queen Mother ought to be told at once, and he agreed; but, as a matter of fact, the Queen Mother was not told until February.

The following day, the Queen discussed the matter with me, and I gave Her Majesty an outline of the provisions of the Royal Marriages Act [of 1772], and told her what I understood was the current attitude of the Church of England towards the re-marriage of divorced persons. A few days later, the Queen and other members of the royal family left for Sandringham. I went there myself at the end of January, and on various occasions discussed the problem with the Queen and the Duke of Edinburgh, and with Princess Margaret. No definite conclusions were reached.

The death of Queen Mary [on 25 March 1953], and the imminence of the Coronation, kept us all busy throughout the spring. There were, however, increasing signs that the association of Townsend's name with that of Princess Margaret would soon become a subject of comment in the trans-

---

1 The contemporary account differs markedly from the record of the meeting left by Townsend himself twenty-five years later in his memoir *Time and Chance* (1978), where he claimed that Tommy, 'visibly shaken', could say nothing but 'You must be either mad or bad'.

atlantic, and the British, Press. Eventually, on 12 June 1953, the Press Secretary at Buckingham Palace (Commander Richard Colville), showed me a copy of an article which he had been privately warned would appear in the *People* newspaper on the following Sunday. This article gave what purported to be a circumstantial and veracious account of the affair. Knowing that this article would inevitably come to the notice of the Prime Minister of the United Kingdom (Mr Winston Churchill, to whom no communication on the subject had so far been made), I sought, and obtained, the Queen's permission to tell him the whole story as I knew it.

On the afternoon of Saturday 13 June, I accordingly saw Mr Churchill at Chartwell; his private secretary, Mr J. R. Colville, was present throughout the interview. I had not said more than a few sentences when Mr Churchill, with his unerring power of seizing a point, interrupted me: 'This is most important,' he said. 'One motor accident, and this young lady might be our queen.'[1]

Subsequently he agreed with what seemed to me an equally important aspect of the affair – that the contracting of such a marriage by Princess Margaret was not in itself a matter of so much weight as was the possibility that, some day, the Sovereign's subjects all over the British Commonwealth and Empire might have to ask themselves whether or no they were prepared to accept a child of the marriage as their King or Queen. Indeed, this side of the problem – the Commonwealth's possible reaction to the marriage and its consequences – clearly disturbed Mr Churchill more than did the entirely certain reaction of the Church. He made it perfectly clear that if Princess Margaret should decide to marry Townsend, she must renounce her rights to the throne.

After a long talk Mr Churchill told me to thank the Queen for sending me to tell him about the matter; I was also to ask Her Majesty if she would approve his consulting two of his colleagues in the Cabinet (Lord Salisbury and Mr R. A. Butler – Mr Anthony Eden was then abroad) so that they might be in a position to give her informal advice, should she need it; this proposal, however, did not commend itself to the Queen, who felt that the matter was still in the stage of being a family affair.

Mr Churchill had concurred in my view that Townsend should be offered employment abroad as soon as possible, and with this the Queen agreed. I therefore told Townsend, Sir Michael Adeane being present, that in our opinion it was essential, in the interests of all concerned, that he should go abroad for a period. Townsend accepted this, and I so informed the Prime

---

1 Churchill was being uncharacteristically pessimistic: the Queen already had two children, Prince Charles and Princess Anne.

Minister, who then instructed the Secretary of State for Air (Lord de L'Isle and Dudley) to make the necessary arrangements. In due course the Secretary of State sought the Queen's approval to Townsend being posted to either Singapore, or South Africa, or Brussels. The Queen, after consulting Princess Margaret – and presumably Townsend himself – told me a few days later that she considered Brussels to be the most suitable post.

Instructions to proceed there were then issued to Townsend by the Air Ministry, and he left England to take up his new duties early in July. In November, the day before she left for her Australasian tour, the Queen told me to get from the Law Officers of the Crown a clear statement of the implications of the Royal Marriages Act in the case of a member of the Royal Family wishing to contract a marriage to which the Sovereign was not prepared to give approval in Council.

Accordingly, on the afternoon of 25 November 1953 I saw the Attorney-General, Sir Lionel Heald,[1] in my house in St James's Palace. Some days later Sir Lionel sent me a memorandum, prepared by himself. I sent this memorandum to Sir Michael Adeane, Acting Private Secretary to the Queen, who had left England on 23 November. With it I sent a covering letter in which I pointed out the danger of 'splitting the Empire' if an issue of this kind had to be referred to the several parliaments of the Commonwealth, some of which might take a diametrically opposite view to that held by others. I also sent a copy of the memorandum to Princess Margaret, who thanked me for it verbally when I met her at the house of her aunt, Lady Elphinstone, on 10 February the following year.

Even if, in later years, Princess Margaret bitterly criticised Tommy for frustrating her plans, and cursed him as the man who ruined her life, it is clear from a letter which she wrote in September 1953 that she did not blame him at the time.

Townsend served as Air Attaché in Brussels from 1953 to 1956. In the autumn of 1955 he began seeing Princess Margaret again; but at the end of October 1955, after frenzied speculation in the media, she announced that she would not marry him. In 1959 he married the Belgian Marie-Luce Jamagne, with whom he had two girls and a boy, and a year later the Princess married Antony Armstrong-Jones (created 1st Earl of Snowdon in 1961), with whom she had a son and a daughter.

In 1962, from his grace-and-favour house in the Old Stables of Kensington Palace, Tommy reported a meeting with Princess Margaret to Joan:

---

1 Rt. Hon. Sir Lionel Heald (1897–1981), MP, Attorney-General 1951–4.

18 May 1962

While I was digging the compost heap on Friday, Princess Margaret, pushing her pram, suddenly appeared and talked amicably for ten minutes. The baby, I must say, is a fine specimen, with beautiful blue eyes.[1]

The Princess's marriage was dissolved in 1978. She died in 2002, aged seventy-one. Townsend died in 1995.

---

1 Her son David Armstrong-Jones (Viscount Linley) was then seven months old.

APPENDIX:
RETIREMENT

After a total of twenty-seven years in royal service, Tommy retired on the last day of 1953, aged sixty-six. Churchill had asked him twice, and the Queen once, if he would like to go to the House of Lords, but he declined every time. Instead, he gratefully accepted a GCB which, he said, he 'rated much higher than a peerage'.

The Old Stables at Kensington Palace were built in 1760 for the Duke of Cumberland's eleven horses and sundry dogs. Tommy described it as 'one of the nicest houses in London', and there he spent most of the rest of his life. He took on various part-time jobs – as a director of the Midland Bank at a salary of £2,200 a year (reading Shakespeare as he travelled to and from the City on the Tube) as Chairman of the Historic Buildings Council and of the Pilgrim Trust. He derived much enjoyment from his involvement as a director of the Royal Academy of Music. He also kept up a spirited correspondence with many old friends.

As he was about to step down as Private Secretary, Harold Nicolson saluted him:

20 October 1953

My Dear Tommy,

You look back on a great period of service which you have steered through many early rocks and rapids without for one moment losing either your sense of humour or your dignity, and without creating a single enemy or at least a single critic who would dare to confess to disapproval of your policy or attitude.

Once you resign, I am going to let my hair grow in long curls like Lloyd George. It has only been your Jorrocks attitude to this subject, and my deference to your opinion, that has kept it short for all these years.

Yours ever,
Harold

Churchill's admiration came out in a letter written while he was still Prime Minister:

1 January 1954   10 Downing Street, Whitehall

My dear Tommy,

In the difficult and delicate and also highly important work you have done during so many years you have made your country your debtor. Your knowledge has enabled you to steer the best course through tangles which would have baffled others. It will always be a joy to you to have played the distinguished part which fell to your lot in the Coronation of our brilliant young Queen and to have advised and helped her during what must have been to her the anxious ordeal of the opening years of her reign.

For all your kindness to me and the help you have given me I am deeply grateful. I do hope that you will enjoy the years that are to come and find them full of interest and activity. Please keep in touch with me whether I am bearing the burden or following your example.

Give my cousinly love to Joan.

Yours ever, W

Tommy was fond of recording 'Winstoniana':

> At an all-Commonwealth party in Buckingham Palace, in 1952 or 1953, Winston beckoned to me to come and sit beside him on a sofa. Soon after, he summoned the Prime Minister of Pakistan, Nazimuddin,[1] to sit on his other side. A footman confronted us with a tray heavily laden with a variety of drinks. Winston took a strong whisky-and-soda and invited the Pakistani to help himself. The latter, a devout Mahommedan, shook his head.
>
> 'What?' said Winston. 'You don't drink? Chrisht! I mean God! I mean Allah!'
>
> In 1952 Winston gave a luncheon party at No. 10 for Ismay and Bridges. Ismay was about to go to Paris as Secretary-General of NATO, and, in an admirable speech, said how much he regretted leaving his home in Gloucestershire, and his beloved herd of Jersey cows. Winston ejaculated loudly from the chair, 'Quite easy. Milk the cows in the morning, fly to Paris and milk the Americans in the afternoon.' I don't think there were any Americans in the room.
>
> His private secretary warned him one morning that, in an hour's time, the tall and gaunt Lord Reith[2] was coming to see him. 'What?' said Winston, 'that Wuthering Heights?'

As Keeper of the Royal Archives from 1943 to 1953, Tommy encouraged a new and more open style of biography, and gave much help to Harold Nicolson, whose King George V: His Life and Reign, *came out in 1952, and to Sir John Wheeler-Bennett,*

---

1   Khawaja Nazimuddin (1894–1964), PM of Pakistan 1951–3.
2   John Reith (1889–1971), a dour Scot who hated Churchill; Director-General of the BBC 1927–38, Minister of Works 1940–42. Created 1st Baron Reith 1940.

for his King George VI: His Life and Reign, *published in 1958. Nevertheless, he remained extremely cautious about what he considered to be the premature revelation of sensitive matters.*

One of his principal contacts in retirement was Rupert Hart-Davis (1907–99), the publisher, editor and author, who left London to live in North Yorkshire in 1964. From his home in Swaledale he often sought help in identifying people Tommy might have known. Tommy replied on any old scrap of paper, typing on the back of circulars from the Midland Bank, writing 'Ken. Pal, W8', or, later, 'Ken. Pal. W8 4PY' in red at the top right-hand corner, and posting the letters in re-used envelopes with new labels stuck on.

He much enjoyed managing the affairs of the Literary Society, the dining club of which he was President from 1955 to 1970. Without actually breaking the club's rules, he manipulated them energetically in his efforts to repel bores, and lobbied for the election of friends like Siegfried Sassoon.[1] *'Three fine fish in the basket,' he wrote to Rupert in February 1967 after receiving acceptances from Lords Birkenhead and Antrim and the historian Robert Blake. 'It's gratifying to see how pleased – and flattered – people are by being asked to join our little circus. One would think they were being offered the OM.' There was a certain irony in the fact that, although not himself a published author, he tried to insist that all members should have demonstrated some literary ability.*

He corresponded with many old friends, and occasionally with new ones.

To Flora Russell
4 January 1955

After Flora had caused confusion by putting two letters in the wrong envelopes.

Forty-three years ago Lady Manners said she would write to the then Lord Rothermere and ask him to find me a job, I having just failed for the FO. She did the envelope trick good and proper, as the letter to myself, which she sent to Ld. Rothermere, began, 'My Dear Tommy, I have written to Lord R. emphasising that your sister is a Maid of Honour to the Queen, and as he is a fearful snob, he is bound to play up.' It was not surprising that Lord R. did *not* find me a job.

---

1 Siegfried Sassoon (1886–1967), poet and author, celebrated for his poems about the trench warfare of 1914–18, and for his *Memoirs of a Fox-Hunting Man* (1928). He and Tommy were contemporaries at Marlborough, but did not know each other then, becoming friends only when Dennis Silk, then a housemaster at Marlborough, brought them together.

To Rupert Hart-Davis
24 January 1958

We are a *literary* society: therefore [in revising the list of members, past and present] I've always put 'author' first. What is an author? For my purpose, it is chap who has had a *book* published. If he has done nothing better than articles, essays etc., then I call him 'writer'. If he's a poet who counts, then I give him 'poet' as well as 'author'. It's silly, e.g., to describe Hilaire Belloc simply as 'author' when (in my opinion) it is his poetry that will live. 'Writer of prose and verse' sounds horrid to me. If any pedant says that 'poet' is subsumed in 'author', tell him that the monkey subsumed the nuts.

In January 1959 Tommy put together a collection of his own clerihews, all concerning composers and their cats, and sent it to John Betjeman (later the Poet Laureate).

> 'My cat makes me uneasy,'
> Said little Georges Bizet.
> 'Her reaction's alarmin''
> When I play her some *Carmen*.'
>
> Richard Strauss
> Called his cat Pauss.
> But he didn't expect her
> To sit through *Elektra*.

And so on. Betjeman was enthusiastic, and suggested that, if embellished with amusing illustrations, the poems might be published as a paperback. But when Tommy showed them to Rupert, back came a dusty answer:

The dangerous thing about asking for a candid opinion is that you may get one, and I truly think your clerihews had better be left to your executors. It isn't that I don't find them amusing (for I do) but I don't think they are strong enough to stand up by themselves, even with a first-class illustrator.

To Rupert Hart-Davis
1 February 1959

You are an honest friend, and I'm grateful for your letter. To tell the truth – which I do from time to time, when convenient – I never thought my poetry was more than an agreeable drawing-room exercise. It was my family who gave me inflated ideas, now painlessly deflated by you.

To Rupert Hart-Davis
25 September 1961

S[iegfried] S[assoon] will be with us [at the Literary Society dinner] on 10 October. He says it's the Feast of St Francis Borgia, and 'I hope there won't be any monkeying with the wine'. So you must lock up your arsenic pills that night.

To Rupert Hart-Davis
15 June 1963

When my cousin George Sartoris and I were sitting with Siegfried on our lawn here on Wednesday evening, S.S. suddenly sat down on the grass and threw a series of back-somersaults 'to show how supple I am'. George and I were astounded – and apprehensive, for it is that sort of goings-on that gives an old man a rupture, or something worse. S, however, assured us that it was a routine procedure with him.[1]

To Joan
[no date]

It was a superb performance of *Otello* last night [at Covent Garden]. I've never heard two male singers get such a reception as Gobbi[2] (Iago) and McCracken[3] (Otello) at the end of their immense duet which finishes Act 2; and they well deserved it. Gobbi was a very interesting Iago, superficially charming in a sinister, feline way, but villainous enough when he was being his natural self. Desdemona rather colourless – but then she always is. McCracken a fine, robust Otello, looking rather like Mr Christopher Soames[4] in his jealous moments – but no doubt O. was very uninhibited, or he wouldn't have smothered his pretty wife.

To me it's the best of all tragic operas, though I always find Act 4 an anti-climax, perhaps because one is emotionally exhausted by the other three. Last night, not having missed a single note of them, I slept soundly through the Willow Song, and found Desdemona's 'last words' (after she's been soundly bumped off) more unconvincing than usual.

---

1 Sassoon was then seventy-six.
2 Tito Gobbi (1915–84), celebrated Italian operatic baritone.
3 James McCracken (1926–88), leading American tenor, for many years principal at the Metropolitan Opera, New York.
4 Christopher Soames (1920–87), politician and diplomat, married Winston Churchill's daughter Mary. He was Minister of Agriculture 1960–64 and Ambassador to France 1968–72. Created 1st Baron Soames of Fletching (Life Peer) 1978.

To Rupert Hart-Davis
20 April 1964

Sassoon had been to stay, on the latest of many visits. The joke was that he always forgot something when he left.

S.S. was in blooming form. As usual, I went all round the house just before he went, and thought I had established that he had left nothing behind. But no. Even as he was on his way to Waterloo, I found lurking in my pet armchair one of those vast, Isabella-coloured silk handkerchiefs which he habitually twists round his fingers, and which I had to post on to him. Another 3d stamp gone down the drain. I'm reminded of Denys Finch-Hatton saying to Bunt Goschen[1] (who was rather like S.S. in this way), 'Blast you, you cost me more than a bloody kept woman.'

To Rupert Hart-Davis
11 December 1964

Thanking Rupert for sending a volume of letters between Max Beerbohm and Reggie Turner, which he had edited:

The book has been my constant companion for the past forty-eight hours, and I never want a better one. It is my rod and staff, my comfort still. In the kirk at Balmoral we used to sing that hymn about every third Sunday, and I, being a fisherman, and with the Dee running almost through the churchyard, thought it much more appropriate to sing 'Thy rod and *gaff*' etc., until one day the King heard me and said I was blasphemous and mustn't do it any more.

Another regular correspondent was the author and playwright John Gore, whom Tommy had known since Oxford days. John described their friendship as 'a remarkably constant one, between two men of utterly different characters and tastes'. As young men they had shared lodgings in London; over the years they played numberless games of tennis, stump cricket, billiards and golf, and they exchanged many hundreds of letters.

To John Gore
2 July 1964

Here's a strange proof of how easy it is to falsify history, and of how

---

1   George Gerard Goschen (1887–1953), one of Tommy's oldest friends, a good pianist and the butt of innumerable jokes mainly for his academic incompetence.

scrupulously careful all we biographers ought to be. On page 224 of a book called *Behind the Throne* (Hodder, 1934), the author – one Paul Emden – says in his appreciation of Lord Stamfordham, 'One of the Liberal leaders replied to the doubter: "You can rule out that possibility. It is as unthinkable that Arthur Bigge should cheat at this game as that Arthur Balfour should cheat at cards."'

That saying is pure fiction; what Kipling calls 'flat, flagrant mechanism'. How do I know this? I know it because *I made it up.*

In the summer of 1929 the *Daily Telegraph* commissioned me to write cold-storage obituaries of some half-dozen of the eminent people I have met. Lord Stamfordham was one of them. I remember, as if it were yesterday, sitting in my library at Sutton, re-reading what I had written about Lord S., and thinking how drab it was; then, to give it some colour, I took up my pen and inserted this *wholly imaginary* quip about the two Arthurs. Of this I have often been ashamed, but, as I was in Canada when Lord S. died, I never knew whether or no the *DT* published my stuff *in toto*. Evidently they did, and my sin has found me out.

To Rupert Hart-Davis
19 January 1965

When I got KG VI to give T. S. Eliot[1] his OM, I wrote to tell the Secretary of the Order. He wrote back, 'Who is this man Eliot? All I can find about him is that he wrote a book about cats.'

To John Gore
30 January 1965

I've just written to Bernard Norfolk telling him that of all the ceremonies that I've had to attend, this morning's service in St Paul's [Winston's funeral] was the most perfectly organised; and deeply moving. I cried a good deal. I was very fond of the old man, who was, for many years, abundantly kind to me. And I am more sure than I am of future life that, but for him, I should not be sitting here a free man.

---

1 Thomas Stearns Eliot, OM (1888–1965), born in America, later a naturalised British subject. Major poet – *The Waste Land* (1922), *Four Quartets* (1935–42) – and playwright – *Murder in the Cathedral* (1935), *The Family Reunion* (1939). His *Possum's Book of Practical Cats* (1939) formed the basis of the immensely successful musical *Cats* by Andrew Lloyd Webber, first produced in 1981.

To John Gore
24 February 1965

All I *know* about Roger Casement[1] is this: 1. If High Treason has any meaning, he was incontestably a High Traitor to the country that he professed to serve when it was in deadly peril; that he was fanatically devoted to Ireland is true enough, and, in itself, laudable; but if he wanted to help Ireland by helping the Germans, he should in honesty have broken with Britain and *openly* joined the Germans. Lord Haw Haw[2] was, to that extent, far more honest than he. 2. Men who have worked with him in the Colonial Office have told me that he was the most devastating, egocentric bore that could be imagined. 3. When I was home, wounded, in the winter of 1917–18, I went to see Alan Parsons[3] in the Home Office, where he was doing Private Secretary to Reggie McKenna,[4] then Home Secretary; as we were leaving his room, being late for luncheon, he pointed to a safe and said, 'In there are the diaries of that man Casement, but they are so revolting I don't think I could show them even to you.'

Alan was completely a-moral – he had the make-up of a Greek faun – and I think he and I, at one time and another, had discussed every conceivable facet of human conduct; I had never before heard him suggest that anything in the world was too 'revolting' for our joint examination. So his use of the word in connection with Casement is significant. Within the last few years others who have seen these things have said much the same.

That is my mental picture of Roger Casement. It leaves in my mind the impression that to give the bones a State funeral is the most ridiculous manifestation of Statesmanship in all history. Yet, in so far as the transfer of the bones may help to heal the equally ridiculous rift between the English and the Irish, I should, if I had to vote on the matter, vote for it.

In 1965 Nigel Nicolson sent passages from the first volume of his forthcoming edition of his father's letters, Harold Nicolson: Diaries and Letters. *Tommy did not keep a copy of the amendments which he suggested, but, as usual, his first point was about timing:*

---

1   Sir Roger Casement (1864–1916), Irish republican, was executed for treason in August 1916.
2   William Joyce (1906–46), known as Lord Haw-Haw, broadcast anti-British progaganda from Germany during WW II, after which he was executed for treason.
3   1887–1933. A friend of Tommy's at Oxford and afterwards.
4   Rt. Hon. Reginald McKenna (1863–1943), financier and politician, Home Secretary 1911–15, Chancellor of the Exchequer 1915–16.

19 May 1965

Please understand that everything I may say refers only to *immediate* publication, in the lifetime of both Harold and the Duke of Windsor. As regards ultimate, posthumous publication, I hope that not one word in the present script will be omitted or altered. In, say, twenty years' time it will be a historical, and human, document of first-class importance.

I am not the Duke of Windsor, and I've no idea how thick or thin his hide now is. But I know for sure that were I the subject of the passages which I've enclosed in blue brackets, I should feel badly hurt by their publication in my life-time. I might just swallow the passages against which I've put a blue question-mark – but only just.

The trauma of the Abdication haunted Tommy for the rest of his life. Historians and biographers frequently sought to consult him about it. To most he denied help, but occasionally a serious inquirer drew him into further reminiscence. When Lord Birkenhead,[1] an old friend, wrote in September 1965 about his projected life of Halifax, Tommy replied:

Edward, and his colleagues in the '38 Government – or some of them – may have been convinced that, if we fought Germany at the time of Munich, we should inevitably be beat, and a defeated England would be no use to the Czechs or anybody else. To what extent such a conviction would have been justified, I've never been able to make up my mind. Pug Ismay has said to me emphatically that, from the military point of view, we ought to have fought, because we should then have had the support of the fine Czech army.

Of one thing I have always been certain, for at the time I saw all the relevant papers – letters from the governors-general to the King, etc. – and that is that, in 1938, we could only have counted on half-hearted support from the Dominions, or possibly no support at all. They had not, by then, realised what Hitler was or what a German victory would mean. In after years, Smuts, Mackenzie King and Mike Pearson – and possibly Bob Menzies[2] – all confirmed this point to me. The great majority of Americans, too, still thought that we were war-mongering imperialistically in our opposition to Hitler.

---

1 Frederick Smith, 2nd Earl of Birkenhead (1907–75), biographer of Kipling. His life of Halifax was published in 1965.
2 Robert Menzies (1894–1978), PM of Australia 1939–41 and 1949–66.

Also in 1965, he recorded:

Dining the other night with Eny Strutt, I was told the following by Jock Colville, who knew both Winston and Beaverbrook intimately.

A few years ago, when Winston was still *compos mentis*, Jock asked him what he really felt about the Abdication, looking back on it after quarter of a century. Winston replied with all his well-known emotional gambits about the gallant young prince and the lady of his heart's choice, etc., etc. But when he had done Jock said, 'Yes, but were you really prepared to accept Mrs Simpson as your queen?' – to which Winston, after a slight pause, replied, 'Never for one moment did I contemplate such a dreadful possibility.'

Jock went on to say that Winston and Max Beaverbrook decided quite early in the Abdication crisis that 'Cutie' (their private name for Mrs S.) must leave the country as soon as possible. 'It must have been fairly easy to persuade her,' said Jock, 'when people started throwing bricks through the windows of her flat, and threatening to throw vitriol at her.'

'Max,' said Winston with one of his deepest chuckles, 'Max arranged all that.'

A little later Jock found himself next to Beaverbrook after dinner. He put to him the same question that he had asked Winston. B., with his gargoyle smile, answered, 'I thought it was all great fun.'

The irony of this is that Edward VIII never forgave poor Alec Hardinge for suggesting exactly what his two principal supporters were secretly working for – namely, that Mrs S. should leave England at once. The reaction of the British people to the problem of the Abdication is often said to have been canting and hypocritical. Looking back, I am certain that this charge is unjust, though a great deal of canting stuff (both pro- and anti-Edward VIII) was published in the newspapers.

The attitude of the vast majority of the King's subjects was pragmatical; they did not regard the problem as a moral one; they did not condemn the King as a fornicator and an adulterer – they did not set up to judge him, or Mrs S., on these counts. What they *did* feel, overwhelmingly, was that, since they were called upon to support a monarchy, they would not tolerate their Monarch taking as his wife, and their Queen, a shop-soiled American, with two living husbands and a voice like a rusty saw.

The clergy, the Press and the Puritans undoubtedly overlaid this starkly simple and practical reaction with a veneer of cant; but that there was no hypocrisy in the attitude of nine-tenths of us, I can testify.

Although he never wrote about the Abdication for publication, he was prepared to help serious authors in their search for the truth. When Lord Birkenhead was working on a book about the Abdication, Tommy sent him the following memorandum:

The story of the Abdication has been invested with a complexity for which there is no warrant. Its basic problem was, in fact, ordinary and simple – only specifically different from the kind of problem that countless parents had had to face when dealing with a strong-minded, recalcitrant son. Edward VIII was a remarkably self-willed man, with exceptionally strong primitive passions. Once he had made up his mind that something was essential to his happiness, nothing would turn him from his course. He had no conception of general principles; his only test of conduct was whether or no he could 'get away with it'. His intellectual development never progressed after adolescence. He had, in fact, many of the traits of both his predecessor, Edward IV, and of his Hanoverian forebears.

About 1935, he became immutably resolved to marry Mrs Simpson. It is probable that, had King George V lived a little longer, the Prince of Wales would have told his father of this resolve, and of his readiness to renounce the succession to the throne if it could not be implemented. That King George V had an inkling of the situation is suggested by the terms of his will, in which he left his eldest son not a penny, and no realisable assets; also by the fact that, a few months before his last illness, he said to a friend of the Prince, 'My son will never succeed me. He will abdicate.' So 'abdication' was not an idea invented by intriguing Statesmen and Churchmen!

When it became necessary, in 1936, to tell his Ministers of his matrimonial intention, Edward VIII's attitude was perfectly simple. From the outset he declared clearly that he intended to marry Mrs S. and to make her his queen. When it was intimated to him that such a marriage would not be constitutionally possible, he replied that in that case he would renounce his kingship. From that position, he never moved an inch; nothing in the world would have averted the final abdication save his falling out of love with Mrs Simpson, and into love with somebody else. The task of Baldwin was to make it clear to his Sovereign that the latter's Government in the UK, and his several Governments in the Dominions, were unanimous in reporting that the marriage would be unacceptable to his constitutional advisers, and to his subjects generally throughout the British Commonwealth – the great majority of them would never tolerate Mrs Simpson as their queen and as the possible mother of their future sovereigns (Winston Churchill, late in life, admitted that he himself was one of that majority).

Baldwin, having convinced the King of this, and the King having convinced Baldwin that if he could not have the wife he wanted, he would abdicate (the word was first introduced into the discussions by the King himself), the subsequent discussions were really only concerned with ways and means. Various people (including Queen Mary) tried to induce the King to change his mind, without any success whatever. There is not a shred of evidence to support Lord Beaverbrook's contention that the subsequent discussions were influenced by a conspirationial tendency on the part of Baldwin or of anybody else who served the King. Baldwin, in particular, had been on friendly, even affectionate, terms with the King for some years, and there is no indication that this relationship was destroyed by the Abdication crisis; it was only after many months that the King got the idea that Baldwin, and others, had betrayed him – the truth being that nobody betrayed the King except the King himself, to whom his kingship meant nothing if it happened to be an obstacle to his personal wishes.

Beaverbrook has subjected Hardinge to fierce holier-than-thou criticism because he was in close touch with Dawson, editor of *The Times*. There has never, before or since, been any suggestion that the Sovereign's Private Secretary ought not to, if he thought fit to do so, take private counsel of the Elder Statesmen of Fleet Street. Would Beaverbrook have been equally indignant if Hardinge had sought the advice of the editor of the *Daily Express*?

In point of fact, Dawson rendered great service by his diplomatic handling of the British Press in the days of reticence, before the innocent and foolish Bishop of Bradford had nullified that restraint by his dropping of an unintended detonator.[1] Once the matter had become a subject of universal discussion, the attitude of *The Times* was equivocal, but not tendentious; it said firmly that the marriage wouldn't do, and, in saying it, reflected the opinion of the British people as a whole. Archbishop Lang is commonly accused of playing a reprehensible part in the discussions. He had, directly, nothing whatever to do with them, save that he declared, *ex cathedra*, that under the existing rules of the Church of England, its Sovereign head mustn't marry a lady with two husbands living – which, after all, is what archbishops are paid to declare.

In May 1966, when Birkenhead sent Tommy a copy of Beaverbrook's book on the Abdication, asking for his comments, he got a forthright reply:

Personal and Confidential

Sorry to go back on my word, but I cannot read this book. I've told too

---

1   The Bishop of Bradford, the Rt. Rev. A. W. F. Blunt (1879–1957), preached a sermon on the theme of the King's duties as head of the Church of England, thereby setting off a spate of speculative reports in the newspapers.

many people that I don't intend to read it, or to discuss its contents, and I want to go on saying so. This resolve is not due to cowardice, nor to idleness.

The personal factor is that the Abdication was a real tragedy in my life. From 1920 to 1928 – my best working years – I gave Edward P, as we always called him, everything that I could put into his service, and genuine personal affection. During that period, in the course of which I twice travelled with him through America and once through Africa, I knew him as well as any man could – far better than Beaverbrook or Churchill ever did.

The Abdication threw all this down the drain. It is therefore not a subject on which I want to brood, though in the years that followed it I have had to do all too much brooding on the constant problems that arose over his relationship to the family and the State. But, apart from any personal considerations, I'm too heavily biased to attempt any detailed comment on this book; I realise that I could not possibly do it calmly.

For fifty years I've been learning more about Max Aitken than I ever wanted to – and learnt it in both this country and Canada, where I lived for four years. So far as I know, he never did me any personal harm, but I've always been 100 per cent antipathetic to the man and all his works. He was, in my opinion, habitually ready to sacrifice truth to his personal likes or dislikes – the latter being always irrationally virulent. Consequently, I am not equipped for passing judgement on anything he said or wrote.

He was, throughout the crisis, actuated by only one motive – his fury that, after Bonar Law's death, he had been denied a private latch-key, so to speak, to No. 10 Downing Street, coupled with his knowledge that, if Edward VIII left Buckingham Palace, he, Beaverbrook, would not enjoy like facilities of entrée there.

Brian Inglis,[1] late editor of the *Spectator*, is writing a book about the Abdication – as a historical event, not as an emotional drama. At his request, I gave him, in conversation, a brief account of my own objective view of it. I cannot do less for you, so, at the risk of repeating what I may have said when we lunched together at Brooks's, and what I wrote to you, I enclose a written version of it on a separate sheet. Provided you don't mention my name, you can make use of any of this that you like. But I warn you that, without endless rummaging in papers to which I no longer have direct access, I cannot give chapter and verse for any statements I have made. I could only say that I am myself convinced of their truth – as surely convinced as I am that Churchill was not in the pay of Hitler – though I can't prove it.

---

1 1916–93. Journalist and author, editor of *The Spectator* 1959–62. His book *Abdication* came out in 1966.

Birkenhead replied:

10 May 66   **24 Wilton Street, SW1**

Many thanks for your letter of 6 May. I must say, I do not blame you for
being unwilling to face Beaverbrook's ghastly book. For once, Randolph
did a good service when, in reviewing the book, he recalled that when he
asked Beaverbrook why he had taken so much interest in the Abdication,
he replied 'To bugger Baldwin'. This, I feel sure, as you say, was the real
reason for his mischievous activity, which we cannot get away from, even
after his death.

To Rupert Hart-Davis
17 December 65

In the last war Eddie Marsh billeted himself at Chatsworth, and they
couldn't get rid of him nohow. At last they told him that he simply must
go, because Lady Hartington [the former Kick Kennedy] was going to have
a baby. Shortly afterwards I met him in St James's Street, and he said
ecstatically, 'Isn't it splendid – she's had a miscarriage, and I can stay.' I,
who didn't know the background, thought he had gone mad.

To Nigel Nicolson
February 1966

*Suggesting that the family should not go ahead with its proposal to hold an elaborate
eightieth birthday party for Harold Nicolson at the Banqueting Hall in Whitehall:*

I was devoted to Winston. He continued, far too long, to go to public
dinners etc. It was tragic to see him, and to hear the universal comment,
'Poor old man – they ought not to let him come out to dinner now' – they
being his family and his doctors.

On a small scale, the same thing happened at our Literary Society
dinners, to which Harold used to come every year. Gerry Wellesley and I –
the two survivors of his coeval friends – did, I think, everything possible to
make the evenings happy. They were the reverse, and I was under the
constant apprehension that pressure would be put on me, as President of
the Lit. Soc, to persuade H. not to come any more. I should have hated
that, and was thankful that the problem was solved by his giving up [his
flat in] the Albany.

I hate the idea of H. being butchered to make a social holiday for middle-aged ladies who like to display their intimacy with artistic and literary celebrities.

To Rupert Hart-Davis
23 August 1966

The great and good Lord Nugent gave me and my Lyttelton grandson the run of his box at the Oval for each day of the Test match. As I've just written to Siegfried, they were the reddest of all red letter-days in my cricket-watching life.

To Rupert Hart-Davis
12 October 1966

A young man from the BBC spent an hour here this evening, trying to induce me to appear in a television orgy on The Future of the British Monarchy. I told him I would as soon walk stark naked down Piccadilly. He was a Wykehamist, and rather shocked.

To Rupert Hart-Davis
22 December 1966

The man W. is what my dear Conrad Russell used to call 'a galloping, throttling bore'; he is also a copper-bottomed snob. I've suffered too often from him at the Beefstcak. Probably he wouldn't be elected [to the Lit. Soc.]. But we must run no risks, and I've always favoured taking bulls by the horns. Cows, too, for that matter. Respectability – to adapt Edith Cavell[1] – is not enough. Not for the Lit. Soc. A candidate might be a Cardinal and a Bishop and Chief Eunuch to the Sultan; but if he is a certified *Bore*, he is no good to us.

He then wrote to Jack Wheeler-Bennett and the Duke of Wellingon, asking them to withdraw their candidate Esmond Warner[2] from the forthcoming election.
    In January 1967 Nigel Nicolson sent Tommy pages from his father's diaries covering the period when Harold was writing his life of King George V.

---

1 Edith Cavell (1865–1915), nurse and matron, executed for harbouring refugees and allowing them to escape during WWI.
2 Son of the cricketer Sir Pelham Warner.

To Nigel Nicolson

I've never been a dedicated 'courtier'; my view of the institution of Monarchy is essentially pragmatical: I have never idealised any member of the House of Windsor, though I respect several of them. So if I advise you to cut out all the remaining references to KG V and his family, please believe that I do so primarily in Harold's own interest and only secondarily in that of his victims.

King George V: His Life and Reign is unquestionably Harold's magnum opus. As a biography and as a history, it will be widely read by many generations. Outside the inner circles of literature, H. will be known and admired as the author of this book. He will be identified with it as Boswell is with Johnson, or Lockhart with Scott.[1] It is a splendid, stately book, without any trace of sycophancy or whitewash; as dignified and realistic a painting of an important period as is a Velasquez portrait of an important individual.

But a premature revelation of H.'s inner distaste for the personality of the King (which, as distinct from the reign, did not come within H.'s terms of reference) might well give people the idea that the book was a false, put-up job – an elaborate pro-monarchical façade – which would be wholly unjust.

A reader of the diary in its present form, who has not read the Life, would characterise H. as a witty but rather malicious gossip. That would be a great pity. Now, H. can't have it both ways. He can't be both Tacitus and Suetonius; both Macaulay and Creevey.

In all human set-ups – such as families, regiments, ministries, business partnerships and royal households – individuals can legitimately, among themselves and in their private records, have their little jokes and spikes about their bosses and about each other; but, if civilised, they don't dine out on them, still less turn an honest penny by them. Such *jeux d'esprit* are kept in the family, so to speak. Curzon's staff in India, for example, used playfully to refer to him as 'the biggest cad in Asia'; but they never did so outside the privacy of the ADCs' room.

The observance of that unwritten law is specially necessary in royal households. In my time, the only breach of it was made by Miss Crawford; elsewhere, more recently, one has been made by Lord Moran.

Harold was chosen for the job not solely because Trevelyan, or any other literary pundit, vouched for him as a distinguished and competent biographer, but even more because he was a highly civilised chap, who could be trusted never to make unauthorised use of anything he might read in the Archives, or hear in conversation; because he was, in the obsolete jargon of that age, a gentleman. For that reason, he was shown *everything* – even the intimate letters

---

1   James Boswell (1740–95) published his *Life of Samuel Johnson* in 1791. *Memoirs of the Life of Sir Walter Scott* by John Gibson Lockhart (1794–1854) came out in 1838.

which I, though Keeper of the Archives, had never seen; and we all talked to him as if he was our Father Confessor.

In your letter of January 26 you ask, 'Has sufficient time elapsed for part of the truth to be publicly told?' My answer obviously is an unequivocal 'No'. (I'm talking about immediate publication. I don't advocate the *destruction* of anything.) Anyhow, what do you mean by 'part of the truth'? What particular facet of truth? KG V has never been canonised or idealised in any way; there is extant no gilded myth about him (such as that created about the Prince Consort by Theodore Martin).[1] When, on his accession, H. Belloc wrote his little poem beginning

> God save King George the fif'
> Wot bores his subjects stiff

nobody contradicted it, and it was universally accepted that, whatever virtues he might have, he *was* a bore – though most people welcomed his mediocrity as an agreeable change from the vulgar, Rothschildian opulence of Edward VII.

When we first discussed the writing of the book, I warned Harold that he wouldn't get any inspiration from the King. He *was* dull, beyond dispute – but my God, his *reign* (politically and internationally) never had a dull moment. I can't think why H. thought it worth while beating the dead dog of KG V's dullness and costiveness. He tells us nothing new. It is stale news that KG V couldn't spell, and wrote 'ect, ect, ect' when he meant et cetera; that if he'd been asked what he thought of Shakespeare, he would probably have said, with KG II, 'Sad stuff, sad stuff.'

But now let me tell you, if I may (in confidence), what *I* consider 'part of the truth'. I probably saw as much of KG V, in the flesh, as Harold did, and no more. From 1920 on I worked and lived in that Palace world, knowing all its denizens well – though my actual face-to-face encounters with the Sovereign were few, and I only became one of his secretaries a few weeks before he died. Moreover, I too had for a father a bearded ex-naval officer, who ran his house like a man-of-war, and treated his progeny like naval ratings – so I understood the domestic problems of KG V's family.

Harold obviously came to the conclusion that KG V was an unusual type, with unusual characteristics. I assure you that, in that late-Victorian/Edwardian country house world (which H. in his youth rarely entered, for he was so much abroad, but which I never left till I was past twenty) there were dozens of English gentlemen exactly like KG V. My own father left the Navy when thirty, settled in the country, and (though he

---

1 Sir Theodore Martin (1816–1909), biographer of Prince Albert.

could ill afford it) did nothing whatever for the next forty years save hunt four days a week and shoot all through the winter: go to Norway salmon-fishing in the summer; go to church, top-hatted, every Sunday, without fail; and read the *Morning Post* and an occasional book on travel from Day's library. Nobody, in those days, thought such a life in any way eccentric, and all his contemporaries accepted it as normal.

So, too, with KG V, in those seventeen years which shocked Harold so much. He, poor Heir Apparent, could do nothing else, and had to avoid like the plague anything that had a remote tinge of politics. He shot, admittedly, an extravagant number of game-birds, and we boys, who were glad enough to walk all day for a few partridges, used to feel some disgust (not perhaps without a shade of envy?) when we heard tell of the immense battues provided by his rich friends; but even so, he was known to be one of the three best shots in England, and it seemed as natural for him to shoot as it was for W. G. Grace[1] to play cricket, Harry Vardon[2] to play golf, or George Thursby[3] (you've never heard of him) to ride in the Derby.

On the credit side: if he 'quarter-decked' his sons (who deserved it often enough), he used to write to them 'My darling David' or 'My darling Bertie' – an exhibition of affection very rare in the parents of those days. He was not a *bad* man in any sense of the word – he wasn't, like so many of his predecessors, a glutton, a lecher, a seducer of other men's wives, or a spendthrift; he was scrupulously fair to his ministers, of all parties; even his stamp-collecting resulted in his leaving an heirloom worth God knows how many thousands. In fact, he did his dreary job as well as he could, and as long as he could.

If he didn't have many friends, he had the respect and affection of men like Stamfordham, Lord Derby, Edward Peacock,[4] Lord Salisbury and Charles Cust[5] (one of several naval cronies who stuck to him through life); and after his death the manifestations of public sorrow were quite extraordinary – I saw them all, for I was at Sandringham when he died. I shall never forget the groups of people standing bare-headed in the fields, all the way to London, as the train bearing his coffin passed.

I'm not trying to suggest that KG V ought to be 'written up'; but I do feel strongly that these is no need – at any rate at present – to write anything more at all about him, poor little man. 'R.I.P.' is the right motto for him.

---

1   William Gilbert Grace (1848–1915), surgeon and cricketer supreme.
2   Harry Vardon (1870–1937), six times Golf Open Champion between 1896 and 1914.
3   Sir George Thursby (1869–1941), leading amateur jockey, rode twice in the Derby.
4   Sir Edward Peacock (1871–1962), Canadian-born banker.
5   Sir Charles Cust (1864–1931), naval officer, Equerry to the King. Created 3rd Bt. 1886.

Tommy made many suggestions for reducing criticism of members of the Royal Family. On 16 May 1968 he was sent by the Queen as her representative to the memorial service for Harold Nicolson at St James's, Piccadilly.

To John Gore
Winter Equinox, 1967

Just 202 years ago Horry Walpole[1] wrote to Lady Hervey: 'It is scandalous at my age to be carried backwards and forwards to balls and suppers and parties by very young people.' Horry – though he was only forty-eight when he wrote that, the ridiculous old basket – generally gets the right cat by the tail; he would have applauded, I think, my resolution in *not* going to N. Renton's twenty-firster two nights ago, for which Lavinia collected over fifty people in her dolls' house. I gave them four bottles of pop – all there was in my cellar, and I never drink it nowadays – and by a miracle that challenged the loaves and fishes they were still drinking it when the party broke up to the crowing of such cocks as there are in Kensington. But fancy that child having reached years of discretion.

I follow Horry's line very firmly. As the Fifeshire lassie sings, in the song with which your concertina-playing children are familiar,

> No, no, no, Geordie Munro,
> No, no, no, my wee laddie.
> I don't want to go
> To Idaho.
> I'd rather stay here in Kircaldy.

For me, anything outside W.8 is Idaho.

From a speech at the Travellers Club, toasting Sir Arthur Norrington, the President of Trinity, Tommy's Oxford college:

19 February 1968

In an uncharacteristically sombre mood, Horace[2] wrote, *Post equitem sedet atra cura* – a line which, you will remember, that mythical hero Smith Minor translated as, '*Post equitem* – after riding, *sedet atra* – the black lady sits down, *cura* – carefully.'[3] But those of us who managed to climb out of

---

1 Sir Horace Walpole, 4th Earl of Orford (1717–97), author and letter-writer. He converted his house at Strawberry Hill, Twickenham, into a small Gothic castle, thereby creating a long-lived architectural fashion.
2 The Roman poet Quintus Horatius Flaccus (65–8 BC).
3 The line means, literally, 'Behind [every] knight, black care rides [postillion].

the Third Form know that in Rome an *eques* was a Knight, and that *cura* has a much wider connotation than common or garden anxiety over the cares of life. In English, *cura*, a cure, is a sphere of activity, a charge of responsibility. The *eques* whom we honour tonight has one *cura* that he will never wholly abandon, and that is the *cura* of Trinity, and of Trinity's well-being.

To John Gore
7 February 1969

I haven't read Helen Hardinge's book.[1] It deals, I understand, with matters of which I've long been sick; but those who have read it tell me it's quite harmless. I've not seen Helen since Alec died, but at long intervals we have corresponded amicably about this and that.

She is obsessed by the idea that she is the only person left who can speak with authority about the Abdication. For instance, when Birkenhead's life of Walter Monckton was serialised in some Sunday newspaper, H. wrote to ask me if I would advise her 'what she ought to do about this book'. Had she been a man, I should have replied, 'You ought to do nothing whatever save hold your tongue and mind your own business.' As it was, I wrote her a nice kind letter, telling her (quite truthfully) that I had read the proofs of the book, and that Birkenhead had impeccably done his duty, which, as a biographer, is to record faithfully the opinions held by his subject, without obtruding his own or anybody else's views.

This, I hope, contented her, for I've heard no more; but not long after, I saw in the agony column of *The Times* a curious little advertisement, to the effect that anyone who read the life of Lord Monckton should also read *Loyal to Three Kings*. This struck me as so odd that I sent it to Mima [Harlech], who characteristically said, 'She's as batty as an owl.'

To John Gore
17 February 1969

Here, the main interest in my life has been the Adventure of the Pantry Mouse. The pantry mouse appeared about a month ago, and night after night I set one of my Little Nipper traps with which I have had notable successes in the past. To my great annoyance the P.M. responded by removing my securely-pinned pieces of cheese without touching off the

---

1   *Loyal to Three Kings* (1967), an account of her husband's royal service, which did not mention that Tommy succeeded him as the King's PPS.

Little Nipper's hair trigger. I tried various dodges, such as tying the cheese on with a piece of fine pink silk used by Hon. Frdk. when he went prawning. But it was all in vain. However, I remembered Bruce's spider[1] and old Johnny Gore's ingenious tricks for defeating the larger fauna that attacked his poultry, and at last got the idea of putting a little blob of Rawlplug Durofix under the cheese and letting it dry hard. That brought me victory. The P.M. managed to remove half the bait, but the other half stood fast. Down came the Little Nipper. He was, unlike his forebear whom the great Duke found in the port bottle, not a damned big mouse, but a lightweight. I buried him yesterday morning, the sods with my bayonet turning, for the ground is frozen hard.

To John Gore
6 March 1969

I saw Alfred Douglas[2] several times in the mid-1920s. He was, at that time, making efforts to meet the Prince of Wales, and came several times to my room in York House. Although I admired several of his poems, I decided beyond peradventure that he was a very horrid man. The fact that he looked like Dorian Gray[3] – no trace remained of his unquestioned beauty – and had been 100 per cent sexually perverted, active and passive, had nothing to do with this decision. I was convinced, as I have been by very few other people, that he was essentially evil.

Incidentally, it is worth remembering that Douglas was no starry-eyed undergraduate when, in 1891, he first crossed Wilde's path. The acquaintanceship [was] started by Douglas's brother writing to Wilde and asking him to help Douglas, who was 'in terrible trouble with people who were blackmailing him'; and which of them was responsible for converting that fond acquaintance into so passionate a friendship, don't ask me. Fifty-fifty is probably a fair guess.

I hold no brief for Wilde, whom I've always considered a much over-rated figure, both as a writer and as a man (though I well remember hearing George Wyndham say, 'But you boys must not judge him by his plays, or any of his writings, which give only a faint idea of the brilliance of his conversation'). For me, he was never anything but a gross, vain, vulgar,

---

1 Robert Bruce (1274–1329), King of Scotland and national hero, was said to have watched a spider near his bed trying to attach its web to a beam. After six failures, it succeeded at the seventh attempt, inspiring him never to accept defeat.
2 Lord Alfred Douglas (1870–1945), son of the 9th Marquess of Queensberry, poet and notorious lover of Oscar Wilde.
3 In Wilde's only novel, *The Picture of Dorian Gray* (1890).

licentious poseur, whom I can never forgive for the legacy he left our generation by creating an image which led our seniors to look on the appreciation of any form of beauty as a certain road to Reading gaol, and imposed on ourselves daunting inhibitions in the making of natural and adolescent friendships. No: I never saw him; and very rarely heard any good of him from those who did.

To Rupert Hart-Davis
30 January 1970

I see in the current *Radio Times* that a man called Thomas Clarke, who had written a film purporting to portray Siegfried S. (in which he is played by some loutish fellow who looks no more like S.S. than does my arse), has said of him: 'Sassoon was a desperately conventional man *who wanted to be considered a Foxhunting Man.*' Did you ever read such balls? If there was one thing sticking out a mile, it was that S.S. was crudely *un*conventional; and he no more *wanted* to be thought a F-H man than he *wanted* to walk on two legs, to play cricket and the piano, or to write poetry. He was incapable of anything in the way of a *pose* – all his activities came naturally and even unconsciously to him.

To Rupert Hart-Davis
14 March 70

You ask, 'Are you a Trollope fan?' My dear boy, by the end of the late war I had read 95 per cent of what A.T. wrote, and had compiled, in the long, Blitz-ridden nights of my solitary occupation of Buckingham Palace, a Trollope *Who's Who*, which I only abandoned because the old man contradicts himself so often in one book what he wrote about some character in another that he made a nonsense of it. He is said never to have opened any of his books again once they were published. *Barchester Towers* is a great book, and Bertie Stanhope ('an apish-looking man in baggy trousers,' said Mrs Proudie) one of my favourite characters. I have got practically everything he wrote in pocket editions.

To Rupert Hart-Davis
27 August 1970

Discussing his wartime diaries, which he had sent to Rupert for his opinion:

Remember that I was a cautious secretary, always conscious of the possibility of my diaries falling into other hands. Any *direct* assessment of KG

VI, for instance, would have been foolish, and very bad taste. KG VI had to be shadowy. He was my boss, and one can't write objectively of the man who employs one. On the other hand, I think that Winston is vividly lit up – sometimes critically, but always affectionately, for I loved the old bastard.

In March 1970 Tommy and Joan had celebrated their golden wedding, but she then fell ill with cancer, and in April 1971 she died.

To John Gore
18 May 1971

You will never write a better letter than your last. Thank you for it. All that you say of Joan is true, and percipient. I've always thought that the most remarkable trait in her character was her complete inability to *pose*, in any way. I never heard her say, or do, anything in public or in private which had a trace of affectation. Her opinions, and her emotions, were wholly sincere. All of which is rare, in the world in which you and I have lived – a world in which so few coins rang completely true. Her body is being cremated at this moment. My daughters are there, but I could not face it. Indeed, my doctor forbade me to go. To me, rightly or wrongly, a burial or a cremation is nothing but a final *physical* operation – only different in its finality from one performed on the operating table.

Lavinia is staying here, and her son Nicholas replaces her tomorrow.

Thereafter Tommy lived alone in the Old Stables, buoyed up by frequent visits from Lavinia, Caroline and his six grandchildren, in whom he took great delight. Even in his eighties his memory was still crystal clear, and he retained much of his mental vigour, rarely lamenting the discomforts of old age. Having decided to stop shaving, he grew a luxuriant grey beard, and referred to himself in letters as 'a pot-bellied old beaver'.

In 1971 he contributed an introduction to one of his favourite books – a new edition of Siegfried Sassoon's Memoirs of a Fox-Hunting Man, *published by the Folio Society – and included a memorable evocation of the scene in which he had taken such delight:*

It is difficult to explain to anybody who was not growing up in those golden years before the Deluge of 1914 what the status of fox-hunting was at that time, and just how it came to be the natural background – even fore-ground – of Siegfried's memories of his youth, when the horse was still the only means of getting across country whether in pursuit of business or the fox. All through the century between Waterloo and Mons, fox-hunting was – to the constant bewilderment of foreigners – an essential thread in the tapestry of English life. It was a national institution – far more than a mere pastime for the well-to-do.

Anthony Trollope's Duke of Omnium, who had probably never been out hunting in his life, thought it was his bounden duty, even when he was Prime Minister of England, to give careful consideration to the problems of local fox-hunters on his property. Moreover, it was a national industry, providing employment for a multitude of people, in which money was sunk, directly or indirectly. It was a constant inspiration to writers and artists; and it was an inexhaustible interest to all those, of any degree, who lived and worked in the country. Participation in it was a top priority.

In the eighties my grandmother wrote in her diary: 'Today F. was summoned to serve on a Grand Jury, but as it was a hunting day, of course he could not go.' There is no suggestion in the rest of the diary that F. got into any sort of trouble as a result of his non-attendance, or that the summoning authority questioned the validity of his excuse. Indeed, hunting was almost a religion; and when a staid late-Victorian Member of Parliament wrote of it as 'the glory of Youth, consolation of Age', nobody thought him eccentric, or his language extravagant.

To Rupert Hart-Davis
20 August 1971

Commiserating on the sudden death of Peter Fleming, aged sixty-four:

There is no cure, no cure at all, for such blows. Time may give one, slowly, a tougher carapace, but it never heals the wound underneath. But for myself – I'm now well-nigh anaesthetised; when any one of the few remaining leaves on my tree of happiness falls to the ground, I just say, with Glaucus in the *Iliad*, ὅίη πέρ φύλλων,[1] and realise once more that Poe was dead right with his raven, in what I used to think was an unnecessarily morbid and unnatural poem.

But I never forget, I'm glad to say, to be deeply grateful for having been privileged to know people like Peter. The gods have been immeasurably

---

1 Homer, *The Iliad*, VI, 146–9:
   ὅίη πέρ φύλλων γενεή, τοίη δὲ καὶ ἀνδρῶν.
   φύλλα τὰ μὲν τ᾽ἄνεμος χαμάδις χέει, ἄλλα δέ θ᾽ὕλη
   τηλεθόωσα φύει, ἔαρος δ᾽ἐπιγίγνεται ὥρη.
   ὣς ἀνδρῶν γενεή, ἡ μὲν φύει, ἡ δ᾽ἀπολήγει.
   The generations of men are like those of leaves. The wind scatters some upon the ground, but the forest, bursting out, puts forth others when the season of spring is at hand. So are the generations of men: one springs up while another passes away.

good to me in the friends they have sent me, all my life long.

To Rupert Hart-Davis
28 August 1971

Time hangs heavily on my hands now, and will hang heavier when winter comes. I read, of course, and I listen to the wireless and all that. But I've no settled occupation, and though I'm always glad to see old friends and grandsons when they come here, I can't face going out to look for them. And they are very few.

How would it be if I let some author or publisher (e.g. Jock Murray) know that if ever the services of an *unpaid* proof-reader are needed, I would gladly cooperate? I've done quite a bit of proof-reading, and I'm rather good at it. Proof-reading pure and simple, of course – spotting technical errors, factual inaccuracies or obvious *lapsus calami* [slips of the pen]; no attempt to offer any criticism or even comment on style or sentiment. My only stipulation would be *no novels.*

To Rebecca West
28 October 1973

Dame Rebecca had reviewed Portrait of a Marriage, *Vita Nicolson's previously unpublished autobiography, with a biographical section by her son Nigel, in the* Sunday Telegraph. *Tommy repeated his earlier remark to Nigel that he was sorry 'all these intimate letters of his parent should be published'.*

Isn't *timing* the real point at issue when we try to assess the rights and wrongs of publication? If Marlborough's letters to Sarah had been published soon after his death, many people then alive would have been appalled. As it is, Posterity (that hideous clique to which we all belong, willy-nilly) has got a much kinder, and truer, picture of the Marlboroughs after reading the letters than it would have had if the 'Gladstone bag' had been popped into the fire at Blenheim.

If someone brought me a Gladstone bag full of love-letters written by my father and mother, to each other or to other people, I should beg that the bag be locked up for another 50 years. But if the letters had been written by my grandparents, I would gladly say 'Publish and be damned'.

At the end of his letter he asked if he might call on Rebecca West one day in her flat at Kingston House North – but she never answered.

To Rupert Hart-Davis
5 March 1974

Only yesterday I came on Dennis Silk's account of Freddie Truman[1] at some cricket luncheon; he was told he must take great care to be civil to the Indian High Commissioner, who was sitting next to him. The only remark that Freddie addressed to him was 'Pass mustard, Gunga Din'.

To Lady Delia Peel
8 September 1975

Like you, I have practically no outside contacts, and, frankly, it is nothing but a relief to be able to say to the two or three people who occasionally invite me to luncheon or dinner that I no longer 'go out' – even to the houses of the Pope, the Prime Minister or the Queen of England, were they to summon me. In fact, I am just a hermit. Puran Bhagat (*Second Jungle Book*) is my model.

P.S. I dreamed last night that when Harry Harewood died, they tried to make me marry the Princess Royal.

To John Gore
3 September 1976

When Winston had his weekly audience [of the Queen] in the Bow Room at Buckingham Palace, I, having shown him in, would sit next door till he came out, when we shared whiskies and sodas for half an hour. I could not hear what they talked about, but it was, more often than not, punctuated by peals of laughter, and Winston generally came out wiping his eyes. 'She's *en grande beauté ce soir*,' he said one evening in his schoolboy French.

I told Philip Ziegler that in his *William IV* he had omitted my favourite story of that eccentric monarch. See Greville on 25 July 1830. 'The other night the King had a party, and at eleven he dismissed them thus: "Now, Ladies and Gentlemen, I wish you a good night. I will not detain you any longer from your amusements, and shall go to my own, which is to go to bed; so come along, my Queen."' How often, in those interminable evenings at Buckingham Palace, Windsor or Balmoral used I to long for the courage to read that to my host and hostess.

I am re-reading Byron's letters for the nth time. There is no doubt that he was the Eclipse[2] of letter-writers – the rest nowhere, even H. Walpole

---

1   1931–2006. Yorkshire and England fast bowler.
2   The celebrated eighteenth-century racehorse, never beaten.

and John Keats. And no doubt, either, that he was fundamentally a cad, if a charming one; but eternally a paradox, for every now and then in his letters he reveals himself as a right-minded man and a warmly affectionate friend.

To John Gore
7 February 1977

I can recall several instances of the King using his veto [over the Honours List]; notoriously, the application for a knighthood for Noël Coward, put forward through the Foreign Office by Edwina Mountbatten, who was very partial to N.C. The King asked me what I thought about it. I pointed out to him that he was constantly approving court martial sentences on young officers in the RAF for issuing dud cheques and other financial peccadilloes; can you fairly, I asked, give a knighthood to a man who has just been fined several thousand pounds for diddling the income tax people over his tax return? N.C., as you may recall, pleaded that it had all been done by his agent, without his knowledge – but that, to my mind, was irrelevant, and didn't alter the fact that the young RAF officers were being punished for robbing the public, while N.C. was being honoured in spite of it.

The King, whose innate sense of fairness never failed him, saw the point at once, and N.C.'s ennoblement was postponed *sine die*.[1] There were several other such cases. Before my day, King George V and Lord Stamfordham had a stand-up fight with Lloyd George over the latter's recommendation of a peerage for a notoriously crooked South African politician.

To John Gore
11 April 1977

The Grand National gave me more pleasure than any race I've ever watched. The sight of that gallant little horse galloping up to the winning post with his ears cocked made me cry aloud. Incidentally, I'm surprised that none of his commentators has pointed out that Red Rum backwards is 'Murder', a coincidence that must have led countless punters of the Flying Ghost school back to him.[2]

---

1 Sir Noël Coward received his knighthood in 1970.
2 Red Rum also won the Grand National in 1973 and 1974, and came second in 1975 and 1976. The only horse to have won the race three times, he lived to the age of 30, and is buried beside the starting gate at Aintree.

To Lady Delia Peel
13 April 1977

Your letter reached me when I was ninety years and twenty-four hours old, so there was nothing wrong with your timing. Thank you very much for it. I had a quiet birthday. The Queen sent me not only a nice little letter in her own hand, but also a dozen of supremely good claret, which touched me deeply. The claret, according to my wine merchants' catalogue, is 'very elegant, with good body and well-defined flavour, showing charm and fruity fragrance'. Thus, every glass I drink will recall to me one or another of the long line of notable women whom I've been lucky to number among my friends – the Queen's ladies-in-waiting; a line that starts with beloved Mabel Airlie, fifty years ago, and has been very rarely broken.

To John Gore
St Grouse, 1977

I used to think that only three of my achievements in life could be recorded on my tombstone as differentiating me from my fellow man – One, I was the only undergraduate who ever tufted a live pig in the Senior Common Room at Balliol; two, I was the only citizen of London to be accosted by a whore when walking its streets with the Archbishop of Canterbury (W. Temple); three, I was the only stock-jobber's clerk who successfully defied a major-general on the field of battle and got away with it. But, as I'm not going to have a tombstone, that situation, as they say, does not arise.

To John Gore
8 September 1977

Since you ask for it, here is my timetable for every day of every week. No clock is more persistent.

7.50 a.m. Leave my bed and go down to the hall to collect the newspapers, and possibly a letter or two – they don't usually arrive before 8.30.

8.45 a.m. Leave my bed finally. Dress and bath. No shaving nowadays.

9.20 a.m. Breakfast, and *The Times* crossword. Clear breakfast table. Dispose of letters – if any; bills, etc. Desultory reading and perhaps a household job or two.

---

1   What Tommy did not mention was that he looked up the wine in the Berry Bros' catalogue to see how much the Queen had spent.

11.30 a.m. approx. Put on outdoor shoes, and take the air. Walk to pillar box (350 yards) and back. Gentle jobs in the garden maybe. If weather invites, a spell on the Ale-house Bench (by this I mean, of course, my own bench in my own garden, not a real one in some local public house, where old men sit in silence staring at the sky and chewing the cud of Memory). The spell may last for anything between five and fifty minutes.

12.50 p.m. Go indoors, listen to News.

1.15 p.m. Luncheon, with crossword, if not finished.

2 p.m. Horse-racing on TV, if there is any. Or cricket. Not football. Thereafter a short nap, followed by a repetition of the morning's programme, if weather permits. If it don't, read a book, possibly something not already read in *The Times* or *D.T.*
  More Ale-house Bench; or maybe an armchair on my little balcony with the French window wide open. No tea – I gave it up long ago. Books. I always keep three books going at once – a serious book – history, biography, etc; a lighter book – *not* a modern novel; and, for the last three-quarters of an hour before bed, the current volume of my 35-volume set of Horry Walpole. I have now got through nearly half of them. But I very often pull a stray volume of something else out of my shelves and spend an evening with it; and, of course, re-read a chosen few old friends. I think I've read *Kim* twenty-five times, and *Ravenshoe* and *Moonfleet* and the *Barsetshires* pretty often.

7.45 p.m. Dinner – soup, a light mess of fish or eggs, half a bottle of claret – my only alcohol throughout the day, with an occasional glass of Somerset cider or Watney's Pale Ale at luncheon.

After dinner, News, and anything on radio or TV that takes my fancy – lamentably little nowadays; there's hardly ever any music worth listening to.

Books, and maybe a doze. Bed at 11.30 p.m.: lights out about 12.15.

My daughters and grandchildren, one or another, take luncheon off me two or three times a week most of the year. I have no other living relatives, and only two surviving contemps – Mima, and K. Rutland, who are very good about coming to luncheon at intervals. Beyond them, I only see some of the young scribes, who, poor boys, think my opinion of their writing is worth getting, e.g., Philip Ziegler and C. Douglas-Home.

To John Gore
20 December 1977

When Noah evacuated the raven from the Ark, he probably said to himself
(or maybe Mrs Noah), 'God knows where this bird will finish up, but I
suppose he must have a go.' That is how I feel when I write a letter in what
they call Yuletide, when everybody goes mad.

To John Gore
19 January 1978

Rosemary Townsend, Peter T.'s ex-wife, asked me if I'd sit to her for a
portrait she would like to give me. Rosemary was always a friend of ours,
so I said Yes, and gave her about a dozen sittings. The final result seemed
to me not very flattering, a rather drab likeness of myself, but harmless.
But when it arrived here, Joan said very firmly that it was horrible, and
nothing would induce her to have it in this house. The two girls said much
the same, so I agreed, and for many years the wretched thing was parked
on the floor of my bedroom under the lee of a chest of drawers. Recently I
got Lavinia to remove it, and what she has done with it, I neither know nor
care.

To Lady Delia Peel
31 March 1978

The Queen wants to have portraits of her four private secretaries, which
means that I've got to sit to her chosen artist, one David Poole. But I've no
ground for complaint, for, besides being a very competent artist, he is a
most agreeable young man. So I shall sit as steadily as an old Buff Orpington
through the four or five sittings that he wants. He comes here, of course –
I am far too old to go trotting off to artists' studios. And, equally of course,
I am not going to cut off my beard, though I think Henry Ponsonby was
the only private secretary hitherto to have one.

To Rupert Hart-Davis
15 August 78

When I was a young subaltern in Flanders, some 60 years ago, our GSO3
at the divisional HQ (1st Cav. Div.) was a kind, sympathetic officer, always
ready to give good advice to us boys when we were in any difficulty. Such
advice generally began with the following preface: 'What you tell me is a
matter of supreme imbuggerance to me, but if I were you ... etc., etc.' Since

then I've never met anybody who used that form of words, but it has impressed me greatly.

To John Gore
23 August 1978

Rupert Hart-Davis has written a book about his mother (Duff Cooper's sister), of which I've promised to read the proofs. I knew her but little. She married that old rascal, Richard Hart-Davis, who was a partner of Antony Lyttelton in Panmure Gordon. Antony tells of him that he said one morning, 'I had a most curious dream last night. I was on a balcony, looking out on a lawn, on which were gathered all the women that I've ever slept with; and shouted out, "Brigade, *SHUN!*"'

To John Gore
19 September 1978

So Horace Seymour is dead. My second cousin, and a nice man, whom you probably knew better than I did. He was the most notorious Mumbler in the world. The Foreign Office were happily inspired when they sent him to be our Ambassador in Peking. Throughout the years he was there, the natives could never make up their minds whether he was speaking Chinese or English; and, being a generous people, they credited him with infinite wisdom. There has never been a more popular British Ambassador in Peking.

I recollect that immediately after his farewell audience of the King, the latter sent for me. I found him distraught. 'I must be going mad,' he said. 'Stark mad. I've been listening to that man Seymour for twenty minutes, and I've not understood one syllable of what he said to me.' So I told him about the Chinese, which reassured him. But finally he threw off one of those non-sequiturs for which his family is famous. 'But I'm not a China-man, you know,' he said. To which I made the only possible reply: 'No, Sir' – and we parted, as ever, good friends.

To Penelope Hughes-Hallett
1 October 1978

You could not have found me a more acceptable present than Birkenhead's *Rudyard Kipling*. Thank you very much indeed for it – it was good of you to think of it.

It's not Freddy Birkenhead's best biography, but probably the best life of

R.K. that anybody will ever write. I danced with Mrs Bambridge[1] at her coming-out ball at Batemans, and thought her a very dull little girl; I never saw her again, and have always thought her treatment of F.B. was monstrous. But, after reading extracts in the *Sunday Telegraph*, I can see why she, as a daughter, was disappointed. F.B. made R.K. slightly inhuman, and he was, of course, 100 per cent human.

To John Gore
[**No Date**]

The leaf-sweeping season is in full swing, but I can't rake for very long at a time nowadays. Winter draws on, as the curate said when he handed the vicar's daughter a cup of tea. To which she replied, if memory serves me right, 'Not yet. But why do you ask?' – and we've never been told what his answer was to that one.

To Sir Philip Moore[2]
27 November 1978

If Madame Suzanne Blum is correctly reported on Page 3 of *The Times* of 27.11.1978, her asseveration about the pre-marital relations of King Edward VIII and Mrs Simpson is, to me, just as credible as would be a statement that she had seen a herd of unicorns grazing in Hyde Park and a shoal of mermaids swimming in the Serpentine.[3]

To Rupert Hart-Davis
Michaelmas 1978

In roundabout fashion, Tommy tried to warn Rupert off publishing The Arms of Time, *a memoir of his mother Sybil (which he brought out, nevertheless, in the autumn of 1979).*

---

1 The younger daughter of Rudyard Kipling, Elsie (1896–1976) married George Bambridge. After the deaths of her father in 1936 and her mother in 1939, she bought Wimpole Hall, a large house and estate near Cambridge, and bequeathed the Kipling family home, Batemans, in Sussex, to the National Trust. Having commissioned Birkenhead to write the biography, she suppressed it, and the book could not be published until after her death.
2 1921–. Private Secretary to the Queen and Keeper of the Queen's Archives 1977–86. Created Baron Moore of Wolvercote (Life Peer) 1986.
3 In seeking to refute allegations made in the television series *Edward and Mrs Simpson*, the Duke's lawyer claimed that publication of his letters would prove that Mrs Simpson had not been his mistress before their marriage: 'This legend is an absolute negation of the truth.'

I know exactly what has made you write this book. Not the quest of money or fame – not the pressure of any *cacoethes scribendi:*[1] but for two very good and honourable reasons. One: your relationship with your mother was, as it were, a bright fire, making happier a rather bleak and sombre boyhood; and now you want to warm both your old hands before you die. Two, you want to make a memorial, worthy of her, with the only artistic tool you possess – your pen.

The mother–son relationship was denied to me. My own mother died on 17 March 1891, when I was almost four years old. Paradoxically, her absence was a continual presence of sadness all through my boyhood and adolescence; until I married, in fact.

To John Gore
19 December 1978

Our neighbour here has an immense white Persian cat. I have nothing against cats, as cats; but I can't have them in my garden, where they upset my birds. So whenever this one shows its nose on my premises, I give it my well-known imitation of a fox-terrier accosting a cat, and it goes half-way to Tehran before you can say miaow.

To Rupert Hart-Davis
8 January 1979

You will recollect that there was once a young clerk in the FO who differed sharply from one of Ld. Curzon's memoranda. He thought it was Balls. But he was afraid to say so out loud, so he just pencilled faintly in the margin 'Round objects', to which Ld. Curzon replied in a note, 'Who is Mr Round, and why does he object?'

To Rupert Hart-Davis
30 May 1979

At a London dinner in 1919, when the ladies withdrew, A. J. Balfour[2] found himself alone with three or four of my contemporaries who had served in France. He made them relate some of their more alarming experiences, and finally said, 'Well, you young men have certainly seen some dreadful sights. But you never saw Mr Gladstone's eyes when he was angry.'

---

1 Malign compulsion to write: a quotation from Juvenal.
2 Arthur James Balfour (1848–1930), politician, First Lord of the Admiralty 1915–16, Foreign Secretary 1916–19. Created 1st Earl of Balfour 1922.

To Lavinia
9 June 1979

The Derby was of special interest to me, because I was told, seventy years ago, never to back a horse with a monosyllabic name to win the race, and none such had since the Duke of Bedford's Sam won in 1819. This was sound advice, which had saved me money more than once, but this time Troy has broken a record that has held good for 160 years.

To Penelope Hughes-Hallett
[Postcard]
15 January 1980

It was *not* Emerald Cunard whom Cynthia called a spat-out bull's eye. It was her half-sister-in-law, Elizabeth Asquith (later Bibesco). And a very apt description, too. No answer.

To Penelope Hughes-Hallett
21 January 1980

Thank you for your letter. You say you don't know how the envelope ought to be addressed.

My father, a retired naval officer, who always called a spade a spade, used to say, when people asked him if he liked to be called Commander or plain Mister, that he didn't care what they called him so long as they didn't call him late for dinner.

I entirely agree with him. But if you want an official ruling, I should say that if you put 'Sir A. Lascelles, GCB' on the envelope, nobody will ever say you did wrong. After all, what matters is that it should reach me safely, and provided you don't absent-mindedly address it to the Pope or the Dalai Lama, it's pretty certain to do that sooner or later.

To Lady Delia Peel
19 February 1980

Last night I dreamed that King George VI was dead, and that Helen Hardinge had somehow or other got herself proclaimed Queen of England, and that I was detailed to go and tell her that it wouldn't do at all; and when I did this, all she said was, 'You see, I am really Queen Mary,' and I said, 'Oh very well' – or words to that effect, and woke up.

I get such dreams quite often, and can't explain them.

After another strange experience he wrote:

Last night I dreamed that Eisenhower came to stay with us, and he insisted on being put to sleep in the dog kennel, with a collar and chain about his neck.

To Rupert Hart-Davis
18 May 1980

Defending Queen Victoria's sense of humour, which he said was far greater than generally supposed:

Princess Helena Victoria used to tell me that when they were all just a family party at Windsor, the grandchildren would be told to do charades, dumb-crambo, etc. to amuse the Queen. 'But we often had to stop, because Grandmama laughed so much that she turned purple all over.'

To Rupert Hart-Davis
3 August 1980

Still hankering for publication in some form, he sent Rupert the typescript of two diaries, from 1914 and 1918.

I've re-read the script, and I find it quite good stuff and amusing; but that may be just vanity. I want your strictly objective verdict: is it *qua* diary, any good – is it gamma, beta or alpha? But, whatever your verdict, I do *not* want it published in my lifetime. If it were a flop, it would annoy me; if it were a success, it might lead to my present secure little hermitage being violated. I've always hated seeing my name in print, and at my age (rising 94, remember) I can't face talking about my private affairs to strangers.

What I *should* like is to get this script printed 'for private circulation only' in a slim little cheaply-bound book, of which I could distribute copies – say thirty or forty – to my descendants and my few surviving friends. A kind of valedictory Xmas card, so to speak.

My aim is to show how the unforeseen thunderbolt, war, struck us boys in 1914, and what a hell it plunged us all in. I've done some very necessary editing. For example, we always spoke of Germans as 'Huns' or 'Boches' – which is exactly how we thought of them in those days. I've amended that to 'Germans', for the others seem to me now unnecessary terms of abuse. In 1918 I *hated* all Germans; I don't think we could have gone on with that cursed war if we *hadn't* hated them. But I soon realised that it did no good to anybody to keep such post-war hatred alive, and vocal, and I've amended my diary accordingly. I don't think your generation, still less the later ones, ever realised what the end of the war meant to all of us.

I never contemplated showing these books to anybody, or had any idea of publishing them. The armistice was something so overwhelming as to be quite inexpressible.

When Rupert replied that he had a friend who might be able to produce what was required, Tommy asked:

6 August 1980

Do you think your friend will be able to let me have forty copies before Xmas? There is really no urgency about it – but *Der Tod ist ein rascher Gesell*,[1] and I should like to see it all concluded before I die.

To Penelope Hughes-Hallett
23 December 1980

In 1899 I was at Thomas Pellatt's famous prep-school [Durnford] in the Isle of Purbeck – Langton Matravers. Every Saturday night the whole school – about sixty of us – would pack into the little hall, and Mrs Pellatt would read aloud to us. She read beautifully, and chose a very good string of books, every one of which is a delight to me to this day.[2]

But no book made so deep and lasting an impression as *Moonfleet*.[3] I can still remember the agony of those Saturday evenings, when she would close the book after half an hour – never more – and leave us in torture as to the fate of John Trenchard and Elzevir Block for six days, which seemed like centuries. For the rest of my life those two have remained as close to me, and as devoted to by me, as any blood relations. I can think of no book that has been so real to me as *Moonfleet* has, and I suppose I've read it ten, or twenty, times.

So I was excited when Caroline told me that you might be embarking on a book, or essay, about Falkner. I hope this is true. It is high time that

---

1   Death is a nimble fellow.
2   In his memoir *The Precarious Crust* the artist and author Laurence Irving recalled how Nell Pellatt used to read, lying on a sofa while 'privileged pages stroked her neck and tickled her silk-stockinged feet'.
3   The novel about smugglers by John Meade Falkner, first published in 1898. Tommy's admiration was increased by the fact that, like Anthony Hope, author of *The Prisoner of Zenda*, Falkner was an Old Marlburian.

somebody put him in his proper place, which is at the top of writers of English fiction.

Tommy's final months were made miserable by an attack of shingles, and in the summer of 1981 he gradually sank.

Lavinia Hankinson to Rupert Hart-Davis
15 June 1981

I fear his time is running out. Over the last few months he indicated – no, said with perfect plainness – that he wouldn't be around for very much longer. He felt a great weariness which one could sense. The shingles coming on him like this is mean and unfortunate, as it gives him so much discomfort and pain. Kipling has been his chosen reading, and we have got through several short stories.

In the last weeks of his life he became fascinated by the preparations for the marriage of Prince Charles and Lady Diana Spencer: he watched the celebratory fireworks set off in Kensington Gardens on the night of 28 July 1981, and next day wanted to know, every few minutes, how the wedding was going.

He died on 10 August 1981, aged ninety-four. Edward Ford, whom he had recruited to the royal household, and who had by then retired, quickly rang the Queen and the Queen Mother in Scotland to tell them the sad news. Tommy had left instructions asking that there should be no elaborate funeral or memorial service – so he was cremated, at his wish, and the family scattered his ashes at Golders Green crematorium.

Letters of condolence poured in. From Balmoral, the Queen sent Lavinia a telegram saying, 'His work for my father and me will be long remembered and appreciated.' Also from Balmoral, Robert Fellowes, the Queen's Assistant Private Secretary (and son of Sir William Fellowes, formerly the agent at Sandringham), recalled how Tommy had seemed 'to a child, impressive, kind and gloriously unpompous ... He was truly a great man.'

His former colleague Sir Michael Adeane told Lavinia, 'Like most jobs, royal employment has its trying moments, but so long as he was in charge, it seldom had any dull ones, and, at the risk of being pompous [I must say] it has lacked a certain amount of distinction ever since he left it in 1953, nearly thirty years ago.' Jean Lloyd, his niece-in-law, declared that 'he was the best company of anyone I have ever met, and one never tired of being with him. I never heard him make a banal remark. He was one of those rare beings – a really contented old person.'

Trying to sum up his character, John Gore decided that 'he was stoical, unsentimental, wordly wise and usually cool in judgement, but at the end of it all the essentials of his inner life elude me.' From Rupert Hart-Davis came a final tribute:

'As you know, he meant a tremendous amount to me, and I relied absolutely on his wise advice, which was never sought in vain. From our first meeting he treated me as an equal in age and intellect, which did a great deal for my morale. I have never known anyone like him, and never shall again.'

Acknowledgements

Lavinia Hankinson and Caroline Erskine, daughters of the late Sir Alan Lascelles, wish to thank her Majesty the Queen for her gracious permission to publish their father's wartime journals. They are also grateful to Sir Edward Ford, formerly Assistant Private Secretary to the Queen, and Sir Alan's Literary Executor, for his help in arranging publication.

The Editor would like to thank Allen Packwood, Director of the Archives Centre at Churchill College, Cambridge, and his staff, for their prompt and friendly assistance.

Index